THE ULTIMATE EU TEST BOOK
Administrators 2020

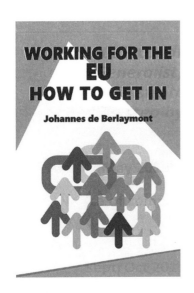

Working for the EU:
How to Get In

By Johannes de Berlaymont

This is *the* book for anyone wanting to know about the opportunities a career in the EU public administration can provide – and the many different ways to 'get in'. It is also highly relevant to those already with temporary positions or internships who want to move their careers forward. Among the many topics covered are:

- The wide range of positions in the EU institutions and agencies, in Brussels, Luxembourg and worldwide
- The types, advantages and disadvantages of permanent and temporary posts
- How temporary posts can become stepping stones to permanent or very long-term jobs
- The critical difference between being selected and being recruited – and how recruitment really works
- The little-known alternatives to passing an open competition
- The value of *stages* and other types of traineeships
- The crucial importance of building your networks
- Why and how you should think strategically, keeping as many options open as possible

Johannes de Berlaymont is the nom de plume of a widely experienced former EU insider.

€17
Local prices may vary

ISBN: 9781999959531

'I think you should stress one positive particularity of working in the institutions; nobody works here by accident. Given the whole competitive selectiveness of the system – no matter which way you get in – there are hardly any of the indifferent, random colleagues one encounters in other organisations. Most colleagues worked really hard to get in. That changes the dynamics. People want to be here.'

A quote from one of the many EU officials who contributed their insights to the book

For the latest information about all our books visit

www.johnharperpublishing.co.uk

For information specifically about The Ultimate EU Test Book visit its dedicated website:

www.eu-testbook.com

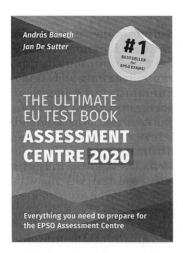

The Ultimate EU Test Book Assessment Centre 2020

By András Baneth and Jan De Sutter

This book has become the absolute must-have for candidates hoping to succeed at their EPSO Assessment Centre. The 2020 edition is up-to-date with all the latest developments including the motivational interview and with expanded coverage of the interview in the field and the talent screener.

- How the Assessment Centre works
- What the competencies are and how EPSO measures them
- The exercises in detail
- How to behave, what to do – and what not to do
- Comprehensive guide to competency anchors and indicators
- Competency passport and recruitment
- Packed with sample exercises and presentations
- Relevant for all EPSO competitions

€42
Local prices may vary

ISBN: 9781999959593

The Ultimate EU Career Development Book

By Jan De Sutter

This book shows you how to evaluate and improve your personal performance in the EU core competencies, for job satisfaction and career advancement.

It is designed for all EU staff at all levels, permanent, temporary or contract and is supported by a free online toolkit.

Author Jan De Sutter is a former EU official and now a professional coach and trainer working with EU staff and EPSO selection competition candidates..

€35
Local prices may vary

ISBN: 9780993454936

THE ULTIMATE EU TEST BOOK
ADMINISTRATORS 2020

András Baneth

JOHN HARPER
PUBLISHING

The Ultimate EU Test Book Administrators 2020
ISBN 978-1-9999595-7-9

Published by John Harper Publishing
27 Palace Gates Road
London N22 7BW, United Kingdom.
www.johnharperpublishing.co.uk

Sales and distribution: Turpin Distribution Services Ltd.

The Ultimate EU Test Book – edition history
First edition, November 2005
Second edition, May 2007
Third edition, March 2008
Fourth edition, April 2009
Fifth edition, March 2010
Assistant edition 2011, November 2010
Administrator edition 2011, February 2011
Assistant edition 2012, October 2011
Administrator edition 2012, October 2011
Assistant edition 2013, January 2013
Administrator edition 2013, January 2013
Administrator edition 2015, December 2014
Assistant edition 2015, December 2014
Assessment Centre edition, May 2015
Administrator edition 2016, February 2016
Assistant edition 2016, February 2016
Assessment Centre 2018, February 2018
Administrators 2018, March 2018
Assistants 2018, March 2018
Assessment Centre 2019, November 2018
Administrators 2019, March 2019
Assistants 2020, March 2020
Assessment Centre 2020, March 2020
Administrators 2020, March 2020

Typeset mainly in 9 & 10/11pt Palatino

Printed and Bound in the EU at the Gutenberg Press, Malta.

TABLE OF CONTENTS

INTRODUCTION

Purpose of the Book

The purpose of *The Ultimate EU Test Book* is to help candidates prepare and practise for the European Personnel Selection Office (EPSO) competitions, so as to be eligible for jobs in the EU institutions.

EPSO competitions (often called by their French name, *concours*) are divided into two main types: those for Administrator (AD) level positions and those for Assistants (AST), with a sub-category being Secretaries (AST-SC). The AD level includes Linguists and many Specialist roles.

While the structure of competitions shows some variability (in essence, the more specialised and specific the role, the greater the weight put on applied specialised and specific job-related knowledge), the core elements of competitions are the reasoning tests (psychometric tests) and as the final stage the assessment of a candidate's "competencies" at the Assessment Centre.

The resoning tests, which for the vast majority of candidates constitute the first phase of the exams, make up the "pre-selection" round. This comprises a range of psychometric tests, administered on a computer, which measure candidates' skills in numerical, verbal and abstract reasoning and (possibly) situational judgement tests. Nowadays almost everybody must take all of these tests.

For most candidates, it is the pre-selection round that proves the stumbling block, and in the big "generalist" competitions a large majority fall at this hurdle. For this reason, the focus of the *The Ultimate EU Test Book Administrators 2020* is on the pre-selection tests. Successive chapters explain what the various types of test involve, the skills needed to tackle them, and the errors to avoid – and in each case this methodology is followed by extensive practice questions with detailed explanations of the answers. All the questions have been specifically designed to mirror Administrator-level competitions.

Only a minority of candidates make it as far as the Assessment Centre phase, and they are in reach of becoming "laureates", eligible to take up permanent posts in the EU institutions. A more specialised book, with guidance and practice exercises specifically for those who reach the Assessment Centre, is also available: *The Ultimate EU Test Book Assessment Centre 2020*

Overview of the chapters

Chapter 1 provides an overview of EPSO selection procedures for Administrators, including what is tested, where and how, as well as issues such as the language rules and the relative chances of success in different competitions. **Chapter 2** then takes a step by step look at typical competitions, generalist, linguist and specialist. Topics include timelines for what tests are taken when, the importance of understanding the scoring rules, commonly made mistakes to avoid, and recruitment. Also covered are internal and CAST competitions, which can provide an alternative route to AD permanent official jobs and also AD-type contract roles.

Few candidates instinctively feel comfortable with the full range of pre-selection psychometric tests: everyone has their strengths and weaknesses, and there are also many hazards in tests which people think they are good at. **Chapter 3** offers a brief overview of what these tests are and why EPSO uses them, with a much fuller look at each test type in the following chapters. Candidates who do not reach the required level in these tests will not be offered the chance to proceed further in the competition. It is therefore vital to study carefully the methodology to learn the principles and shortcuts involved and then make sure to practise to increase your speed, accuracy and ratio of correct answers.

With **verbal reasoning tests**, a common problem is that candidates consider them relatively "easy", without being aware of the traps they contain. In an EPSO competition you are presented with a short text and have to say which one of a series of statements is correct, based on the information in the passage. The nub of the problem for many proves to be the requirement "based on information in the passage", because the statements always include superficially attractive answer options which "seem" right, but in fact cannot be properly based on what the passage actually says. Sometimes, too, the correct answer is a statement which seems rather bland or even immaterial but is in fact soundly based. **Chapter 4** explains the common errors candidates make, and then **Chapter 5** provides a full test exercise with questions designed to probe your ability to spot the hazards.

In the case of **numerical reasoning tests**, the questions are not designed to assess your high-level mathematical skills: nothing is required beyond the maths you will have learned at school. What is tested, however, is your ability to grasp the essence of a problem quickly – to work out what data in the jumble of information in the tables or charts is actually needed to solve the problem, and to calculate in the fastest and most direct way possible. Sometimes, indeed, no or scarcely any real calculations are needed at all, if you know how to see this. For this reason, **Chapter 6** focuses on the fundamental types of calculation needed and how to speed up your application of these.

Chapter 7 then provides a series of targeted warm -up exercises for specific types of numerical reasoning operations. In this chapter you are immediately given the answer explanations along with the questions so you can "walk through" the reasoning involved. **Chapter 8**, in contrast, follows with a full test where the answers are separated off from the questions, and the operation types are all mixed together, to simulate a real test.

You are not alone if your first reaction to **abstract reasoning tests** is one of anxiety or even dismay, as you try to work out which in a series of shapes is "next in the series". However, as **Chapter 9** shows, such tests involve in a systematic way the application of often quite simple rules – and the key thing is to learn to spot what those rules are. Chapter 9 explains the patterns and operations test designers use. **Chapter 10** is a new feature of the book. It consists of a comprehensive warm-up in which you can follow step by step how to systematically discover the rules and eliminate incorrect answer options in a variety of abstract reasoning questions. We then go on to **Chapter 11** where you can test yourself in applying these techniques. In each case, the answers explain the rules so if you get the answer wrong, you can work backwards to see where you made your mistake.

Chapter 12 explains the principles and methodology of **situational judgement tests** (SJTs), which are based on real-life workplace scenarios, where a complex interplay of factors is often involved. SJTs are used selectively by EPSO, most importantly in the annual AD5 graduate competition. Here you are being measured against the "competencies" EPSO uses more intensively at a later stage at the Assessment Centre. Unlike with the verbal, numerical and abstract reasoning tests, there is not a simple "right" or "wrong" answer with SJTs – rather there is a progression from a "most" to a "least" appropriate or effective response to a given situation. **Chapter 13** gives you the opportunity to see how your responses match those set as standards in a test exercise. While, unlike with the other psychometric tests, you cannot simply improve your SJT scores by learning and practising techniques, how you do in the test should help guide you as to what interpersonal or other skills you need to think about and work on.

The Assessment Centre exercises are very different from the reasoning tests and are covered in *The Ultimate EU Test Book Assessment Centre 2020*.

Keep up to date!

As is emphasised at many points in this book, you must always check carefully the exact rules for your competition (as announced in the Notice of Competition), because the shape of competitions, including such important matters as the weighting of marks between different tests, can vary. Make sure also that you keep up-to-date with the EPSO website and, for more informal but often useful news and tips, www.eu-testbook.com and *The Ultimate EU Test Book* Facebook page.

András Baneth
Brussels, February 2020.

A Brief History of The Ultimate EU Test Book

2003

EPSO becomes operational

2005

The Ultimate EU Test Book 1st Edition

2010

Total redesign to match new EPSO testing system

2011

Separate Administrator and Assistant Editions created

2015

1st Assessment Centre Edition

2016

Career Development Edition

About the authors

About András Baneth

András Baneth has been the guiding hand behind the development of The Ultimate EU Test Book since its first publication, then as a single volume, in 2005. A graduate from the College of Europe in Bruges, András worked for seven years at the European Court of Justice and European Commission. He is a co-founder of EU Training (formerly known as Online EU Training) with which he remains actively engaged, and the managing director of the US–based Public Affairs Council's European office. András is also a regular speaker on EU careers, strategic communication and public affairs. His personal website is available at www.baneth.eu and his direct e-mail is andras@baneth.eu

About the Test Book team

Many individuals have contributed over the years to The Ultimate EU Test Book. There are too many to list here individually, but they know who they are and András would like to thank them all.

András would particularly like to note, however, the contribution of Gábor Mikes, the former managing director of EU Training, who played an important role in the design of methodologies for psychometric tests to meet the needs of the new-style competitions introduced by EPSO in 2010. At that time Ben Williams, an occupational psychologist with experience of designing 300 Assessment Centres internationally, helped shape the framework for the book's coverage of the testing of competencies, paving the way for the eventual creation of the Assessment Centre edition in 2015. Much valuable work on coordinating the creation and editing of multiple choice questions was done by Zoltan Arany-Szabó, a role which more recently has been taken on by Veronika Koseluk of EU Training.

EU TRAINING
www.eutraining.eu

Wish to practice more tests? EU Training offers:

- *1600+ verbal reasoning questions in 19 languages*
- *1300+ numerical reasoning questions*
- *1600+ abstract reasoning questions*
- *25+ Situational judgement full tests*
- *250+ organising & prioritising full tests*
- *300+ basic IT literacy questions*
- *30+ language comprehension full tests*

Simulate the EPSO exam online with:

 Exam Mode with Realistic Time Limits

 Sophisticated Statistics of your Standing and Progress

 Detailed Explanations of the Correct Answer

1.   What Are Administrators and How Are They Selected?

Who are the Administrators?

The administration of the European Union offers a huge range of jobs under an at times bewildering variety of names. There are Administrators (AD), Assistants (AST) and Assistants-Secretaries (AST-SC). There are different staff categories such as contract agents and temporary agents (both of various types), local agents, seconded national experts, parliamentary assistants and different types of paid traineeships. There are "profiles" and "function groups" for particular types of jobs. To make it even more complex many of the titles are peculiar to the EU administration and not found in other walks of life. And of course all these job titles exist in a range of national languages.

All about EU careers

For a full picture of the careers available in the EU administration, read **Working for the EU: How to Get In** by Johannes de Berlaymont.

This explains the many types of jobs available, the routes in (including little known side routes), and the best strategies for building a career.

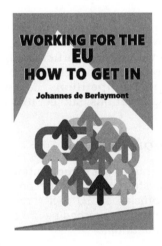

At the heart of the system, however, are the Administrators. About 36 per cent of the staff of the European Commission, by far the biggest of the institutions, are Administrators and it is the AD-level grades who are the engine room of EU policy making and delivery. The Administrators are at the core of the vision of a European administration of permanent civil servants serving the Union. **Administrator level jobs start at grade AD5** (there are no AD 1 to 4 grades) and go all the way up to AD 16 (Director-General). Most Administrators start at AD5, though for some more specialised roles, where candidates typically have to have had several years of relevant experience, first appointments may be made at AD6 or AD7.

While AD5 posts are described as "entry-level" it would be a mistake to imagine that most AD5s are fresh-faced young graduates straight out of a university first degree course. The average age of recruitment of AD5s in the Commission, for instance, is 34, so a majority have significant previous work experience, including many who have held traineeships or temporary posts in the institutions.

The greatest concentration of Administrator jobs is, not surprisingly, in the "EU capital", Brussels. This is where the European Commission and the Council of the European Union are based and it is also the key location of the European Parliament even though its official seat is Strasbourg. There are however Administrator-level jobs in many other locations: Luxembourg, especially, where many "back office" functions are located (as well as many translator jobs) but also in agencies around the Member States as well as representations of the Commission and Parliament in every Member State capital (and some other cities). Furthermore, there are jobs in the EU delegations all around the world.

The "classic" Administrator job is the civil service generalist moving through their career from one task to another as a permanent official. But many specialist roles also exist. For example, two of the biggest categories of AD-level jobs are highly-specialised – linguists and lawyer-linguists – and there are many other specialist AD jobs as will be seen below.

How are Administrators Selected?

A very important distinction in the EU administration is between "selection" and "recruitment". It is the various EU institutions and other bodies who actually recruit. However for permanent official Administrator jobs they recruit from lists of eligible candidates who have been "selected" by succeeding in competitions. Most recruitment is via so-called **open competitions**, i.e. competitions that are open to any EU citizen with the relevant qualifications, subject to a few criteria.

Key point

There are numerous career options in the EU administration. But to become a permanent official, an EU civil servant, now usually involves succeeding in an EPSO open competition.

Open competitions (and some closed internal ones) are run by the **European Personnel Selection Office (EPSO)**. EPSO became operational in 2003 in an effort to make the hitherto fragmented personnel selection procedures of the institutions more consistent, efficient and transparent. EPSO organises competitions for all the EU institutions with the notable exception of the European Central Bank.

There is a way to become a permanent official without taking an EPSO open competition, which is via an **internal competition**. However such internal competitions, open only to people already working in another capacity in the institution concerned, are unpredictable as to when they will occur. Traditionally they have been most frequent in the European Parliament, where they tend to occur a couple of times per mandate and may be organised without the involvement of EPSO. In late 2018, however, the European Commission launched a very large internal competition seeking candidates for a wide spectrum of positions. Despite these exceptions it is true to say that, broadly speaking, the usual direct route nowadays to secure a job as a permanent AD official is through succeeding in an EPSO open competition.

Selection of Contract Agents

The original conception of an EU administration of permanent officials has been eroded with the creation of the category of **Contract Agents for Specific Tasks (CAST)**. By 2018 some 22% of Commission staff were contract staff. These roles in effect have come to substitute for some permanent official posts, providing the institutions with greater flexibility as these roles are not "jobs for life" in the way of permanent officials. However, as contract agents have come to take on ever greater shares of the workload many of these positions have de facto become semi-permanent, with much of the job security and many of the benefits of the permanent officials.

> **Key point**
>
> EPSO organises selections for contract agents. However only a limited number of candidates with the right qualifications and experience are invited to the pre-selection tests.

There are two types of CAST posts. So-called **3(b) contract agents** are found in the larger institutions and have contracts of defined duration. They have the advantage of usually being eligible for internal competitions. Type **3(a) contract agents** are usually employed in the agencies and although they may get an indefinite contract after extension they are not able to compete in internal competitions.

EPSO is involved in the selection of contract agents, though its role is very different than in the case of the permanent officials. This is described more fully in chapter 2. Suffice it to say at this point that the CAST selections organised by EPSO will involve the types of verbal, numerical and abstract reasoning tests covered in this book.

A further category in the EU administration is that of **temporary agents**, of which there are multiple types. Unlike with contract agents, EPSO is not usually involved in their selection, although rare exceptions are possible. Temporary agents may, however, (depending on their category), have the opportunity to participate in internal competitions which can be organised by EPSO on behalf of the institutions, enabling them to become permanent officials.

The decentralised agencies, employing mainly contract and temporary agents and now found in nearly all Member States, sometimes select staff directly and sometimes make use of EPSO. Vacancies are usually posted on the EPSO website.

> **Key point**
>
> CAST candidates need to receive an invitation from an EU institution and not from EPSO. Many candidates are unaware of this.

EPSO Procedures

The EPSO system has evolved considerably over time, most notably with the establishment of a new system of assessment of reasoning skills and competencies in 2010. This opening chapter gives an outline of the EPSO selection system and what it tests: who can take part in competitions and the rules applying, the skills and competencies that are tested, how the competitions are administered, the language rules, and other practical matters.

Chapter 2 then explains the sequence of competitions step-by-step, looking in more detail at what is tested at each step and how.

The System in Outline

The EPSO system of testing has two primary components.

1. **Computer-based tests (CBTs) using multiple-choice questions (MCQs)**. These typically (though not always) occur as the first element of testing and include numerical, abstract and verbal reasoning questions as a general rule and sometimes situational judgement tests as well. Linguist tests will also include language comprehension tests. This is what is often referred to as the **"pre-selection"** stage.

2. The **Assessment Centre**, where candidates are evaluated by human assessors in a series of planned exercises. These exercises are a mix of "generic" tests of what are called "core competencies" with additional tests specific to the field of the competition.

While these are the two primary components the mix of tests between the two will vary from competition to competition and the annual graduate Administrator competition in 2019, for example, also included an intermediate test using an e-tray exercise.

Generally speaking, ALL eligible applicants for Administrator profiles, get the chance to take the computer-based MCQs as the first round of testing. There is an important exception: for specialists whose tests are quite often deferred to the Assessment Centre. In that case some candidates are eliminated before taking any tests. This is done on the basis of a **"Talent Screener"**, where the assessors look first at the candidates' relevant experience and qualifications in that specialised area.

Although ratios vary, typically about 3 times the number of successful candidates sought are invited to the Assessment Centre. This means that for the more popular competitions only a small minority will ever make it that far; for some specialised competitions, however, a significant proportion will reach the Assessment Centre.

The system is a complex one and there are variations which are discussed below.

Applications in General

Key point

EPSO does not *recruit*; it *selects* those who are available to be recruited but the actual recruitment is done by the various EU institutions and bodies.

EPSO will not consider any ad hoc applications or CVs that are submitted outside the framework of an official competition, not least because EPSO itself is not recruiting new staff: it "only" selects applicants who can later be hired by EU institutions and bodies. On the other hand, vacancies for non-permanent posts or a limited number of senior positions (Director level and above) that do not require the selection procedure described below are regularly posted on the EPSO website with links to the given agency or body where applications should be submitted directly.

Planning and Transparency

One of the key aims of EPSO is to make selection as transparent as possible by giving more information to candidates about the stages and methodology of the system, along with detailed and timely feedback about the applicants' very own performance in the tests.

It is in this framework that strategic human resource planning is now used in all institutions, meaning that each Directorate General, service or high-level administrative unit must signal a forecast of its staffing needs for the upcoming three or so years. This is to help EPSO to plan competitions and to try to reduce the number of situations, such as used to be common, when a successful laureate received no job offer for months or even years. Planning is further reinforced by analysing employee fluctuations, political developments (e.g. the creation of the European External Action Service) or other factors affecting staff turnover or intake.

Nowadays, while being selected by EPSO is certainly not a guarantee of being recruited, there is generally a better match between the numbers of successful candidates and the jobs actually available. The steps you need to take to maximise your chances of getting recruited are covered in our book *Working for the EU : How to Get In.*

Increasing transparency is an ongoing effort that includes disclosing the names of Selection Board members, communicating test results and Assessment Centre reports to candidates and helping candidates plan their preparation efforts by providing a relatively precise timeline of exam schedules.

Skills vs. Knowledge

The most significant element in the current selection system is the shift from the old pre-2010 system of testing knowledge about the EU institutions and policies to an emphasis on **reasoning skills (psychometric tests) and competencies ("soft skills")**. Broadly speaking, reasoning skills are tested in the first pre-selection phase of competitions and the competencies at the final Assessment Centre stage. The reasoning tests are of three types, verbal reasoning, numerical reasoning and abstract reasoning, which are described in full later in this book.

EPSO has created a **competency framework** against which candidates are evaluated. This is to assess the all round suitability of candidates to the EU working environment, alongside any specific skills they need for the particular job profile. The weight given to these general "core competencies" varies by competition and is greatest for generalist roles. The testing of competencies is mainly at the Assessment Centre but this may also be done to some degree at pre-selection in the form of situational judgement tests, although they have mainly been used in the AD5 generalist graduate competition..

Core Competencies

According to EPSO, the following are considered as core competencies (which are required for all profiles independent of the competition):

- **Analysis and Problem Solving** – Identifies the critical facts in complex issues and develops creative and practical solutions
- **Communicating** – Communicates clearly and precisely both orally and in writing
- **Delivering Quality and Results** – Takes personal responsibility and initiative for delivering work to a high standard of quality within set procedures
- **Learning and Development** – Develops and improves personal skills and knowledge of the organisation and its environment
- **Prioritising and Organising** – Prioritises the most important tasks, works flexibly and organises own workload efficiently
- **Resilience** – Remains effective under a heavy workload, handles organisational frustrations positively and adapts to a changing work environment
- **Working with Others** – Works co-operatively with others in teams and across

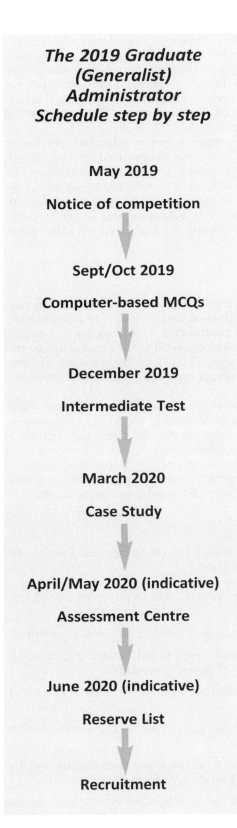

The 2019 Graduate (Generalist) Administrator Schedule step by step

May 2019

Notice of competition

Sept/Oct 2019

Computer-based MCQs

December 2019

Intermediate Test

March 2020

Case Study

April/May 2020 (indicative)

Assessment Centre

June 2020 (indicative)

Reserve List

Recruitment

organisational boundaries and respects differences between people

- **Leadership** – Manages, develops and motivates people to achieve results (only for Administrator grades)

For senior or management-level posts (usually AD9 and above), one or two further competencies may be identified for specific job profiles or competitions, depending on the analysis of the given position. The above general competencies are always tested by two different exercises to ensure their validity and reliability as organisational psychologists and human resource experts have created a specific method to ensure the above quality criteria. (For more details on what each competency means and how it is measured, see the latest edition of *The Ultimate EU Test Book Assessment*.)

Duration

EPSO has tried to streamline and professionalise the selection procedure as much as possible. When the new style testing regime began in 2010 the announced intention was to have a well-defined annual cycle, including the announcement of the major generalist (graduate) Administrator competition in March, followed by the publication of competitions for linguists (AD and AST) around July, and closing with the call for application for Assistants in November or December. Smaller, more specialized competitions would be fitted around these major fixed points.

However in practice, and for a number of reasons, there has been considerable variation. We won't go into these reasons here in much detail, other than to note that they mostly don't have anything to do with EPSO itself. It is essential, therefore, to check the EPSO website for the latest information on the schedule. Usefully, EPSO publishes details on its website showing upcoming competitions as well as those already announced.

Each cycle was also intended to be completed within a year from announcement until the publication of the reserve list. In practice the timescale is usually longer. In reality a typical AD competition lasts thirteen or fourteen months from beginning (Notice of Competition) to end (Reserve List). Of course, actual recruitment takes longer still. However, it is possible to plan ahead your preparation as it is fairly clear what type of competition is to be announced and when. The chart on page 6 shows the timings for the 2019 AD5 generalist competition, the biggest AD competition of the year.

On a related note, it is advisable to focus your efforts exclusively on preparing for the next upcoming competition phase (pre-selection reasoning tests or Assessment Centre competency tests) and not the entire procedure as such from the very beginning. This book accordingly concentrates on the pre-selection phase while the very different tests used at the Assessment Centre are covered in latest edition of *The Ultimate EU Test Book Assessment Centre*.

Soon-to-be Graduates Welcome

The "cut-off date", meaning the date by which a candidate must meet all eligibility criteria, especially that of possessing a degree or other qualification, is often moved to a later specified date instead of the application deadline for a given competition. This is true for most of the Administrator and AD linguist exams. However, always check this requirement in the Notice of Competition to ensure that you are eligible for the competition.

Take a practical example. Let's say EPSO announces a competition in March 2020. The way the system works means that if you are a graduating student and you expect to receive your degree in June 2020 but the EPSO exam, where a university degree is a pre-requisite, has its application deadline in April, you can still apply, as long as the degree is obtained by the time of the date specified. The rationale behind this is to offer soon-to-be graduates the opportunity to apply in their last year of studies, thus broadening the scope of the candidate pool.

Candidates with Special Needs

European Union institutions have always been keen to respect the principles of equal opportunities and non-discrimination given this policy's pivotal place in the EU Member States' legislation and obviously inside the institutions themselves. Therefore in the EU selection procedure candidates with special needs, such as seriously limited eyesight, physical disability or other issues that require adaptation in the test centres, should notify EPSO well in advance to make sure that both their access to the testing and the scoring of their exams are adapted to their condition. Supervised one-on-one tests or other measures may exceptionally also be made available to encourage such candidates to apply.

Chances of Succeeding

An obvious basic question for candidates is *"what are my chances of succeeding?"*

There are two factors of supply and demand involved in answering this question.

The first factor, the demand, is **the number of successful candidates EPSO is looking for**. The driver of this is the institutions. After a period of

> ### *Key point*
>
> In 2018, 25% of Commission officials and temporary staff were 55 or older. Because of the numbers coming up to retirement age, the institutions need to keep recruiting just to stand still.

buoyant growth, largely due to the accession of 12 new Member States in 2004/2007, staff numbers were subject to a theoretical 5% cut in the period 2013-17 as the EU came under pressure from the Member States to control its spending. In practice, however, total staff levels remained almost unchanged as recruitment for some specific tasks like Croatian accession added headcount. And of course even during that period competitions continued as new types of post were created, people retired or moved on and had to be replaced, etc. While recruitment of permanent AD officials has dropped significantly, an aging workforce means there is a strong underlying need to continue recruiting.

However, while aggregate demand is one thing, the detail at the level of specific job profiles is another. One year might have a large competition to select specialists in a par-

Competition	Reference	No. of successful candidates sought	No. of applications
AD5 Irish language translators	EPSO/AD/361/18	72	190
AD5 Italian language translators	EPSO/AD/345/17	14	2332
AD7 Irish language lawyer-linguists	EPSO/AD/350/17	8	26
AD6 Food Safety Policy and Legislation	EPSO/AD/341/18	35	799
AD5 Graduate 2019	EPSO/AD/373/19	147	22,644
AD7 Financial Economics	EPSO/AD/339/17-1	55	905
AD7 Spanish language lawyer-linguists	EPSO/AD/332/16	8	619
AD6 Building Management Engineers	EPSO/AD/342/17	24	1044
AD5 Administrators in the Field of Audit	EPSO/AD/357/18	80	4755
AD6 Administrators in the Field of Data Protection	EPSO/AD/360/18	30	970

ticular field, or translators for a particular language, and another none at all for those profiles. The numbers sought in such competitions can also vary widely, depending on the needs of the institutions.

The second factor is the **supply of candidates.** This is influenced by such considerations as the strength of the job market in the different Member States and the level of specialisation required. By definition, an AD5 competition open to graduates with no prior experience from any of the Member States is going to attract more applications than a competition for nuclear specialists, or for lawyer-linguists in the Finnish language.

The table on page 8 shows the relationship between the number of successful candidates sought by EPSO and the number of completed applications in some recent or ongoing Administrator competitions. As you can see, most competitions attract a large number of applicants relative to the number of successful candidates sought.

However while most EPSO competitions are intensely competitive, some are not, and a few can be categorised as distinctly uncompetitive because of the obscurity of the profile being selected. Look at the figures in the table for the 2018 competition for AD5 Irish-language translators. This competition sought 72 successful candidates but (despite the deadline being extended) attracted only 190 applications. Compare that to the 2017 AD5 for Italian-language translators where only 14 successful candidates were sought but there were 2332 applications!

Most likely few of the candidates for the Italian-language competition had an alternative option. But if you do have one, you should be aware of it. Imagine you are an Italian native speaker who also has a very good command of Maltese and there are competitions for both languages. In an EPSO competition your nationality is not relevant so you can apply for either. Your first instinct might be to choose the Italian-language competition, simply because it is your native language. However, the EU has a similar need for Italian and Maltese language translators but there are 127 Italians for every 1 Maltese. It is obviously the case, therefore, that there will be many more Italian candidates and you would be better off choosing the Maltese competition.

As a general rule, the more specialised the competition the better your chances of success. There is one main proviso to that statement, however. It is also the case that the more specialised the competition, the more likely it is that the other candidates will be highly qualified in that specific field and also highly motivated. In contrast, for example, you can be sure that for a big competition like the AD5 graduate, open to all-comers, a lot of the candidates will simply be "having a go" and poorly prepared. Indeed, a proportion will not even turn up to the pre-selection tests (which are usually held on a weekday, but occasionally on Saturdays) if they decide their chances are not good enough for it to be worth taking a day off from work or other pursuits.

> 5251 of the people who completed the first part of the application form for the 2019 AD5 graduate competition never finished the second part, meaning nearly 1 in 5 dropped out before taking any tests at all!

Beyond that, of course, comes the issue of preparation. Where there are two candidates of potentially equal ability, the one who is best prepared, who has practised for the tests and understands what the examiners are looking for, will be the one who wins out.

You must therefore always consider carefully which competition profile to apply for. For example, if you have a qualification in human resource management and relevant professional experience, you can sit both an Assistant exam and also an Administrator exam (if your qualification is a university degree), and may also be eligible for a specialist competition if that fits your profile.

Another aspect to consider is the **long-term repercussions of your choice**: not only will your competition profile determine the required professional knowledge but it will also affect your recruitment prospects once placed on the reserve list. It is for obvious reasons that EPSO creates sub-profiles and specialist profiles in the selection process: if an expert on environment law is sought, those on a lawyers' reserve list may have better chances of being offered a job than those on a Public Administration list (though this is not a formal rule and depends a lot on other external and individual factors as well). Important to note, however, is that de facto *anyone* can be recruited from ANY reserve list as long as their personal profile and the function group (Secretary,

Assistant or Administrator) matches the specific vacancy's requirements, though EU institutions try to respect an internal policy of not "poaching" candidates from other reserve lists than the one from which they are meant to recruit.

What is also important to bear in mind is that **the hierarchical division into Administrators and Assistants is quite rigid**. The EU administration is nothing like a private sector company where talented individuals can be fast tracked out of one type of job into another on a quickly moving escalator. Everything to do with promotions and career progress follows very defined rules. Although there is a procedure for moving from AST to AD, known as "certification", this is by no means straightforward. So if your goal is to get an Administrator job be cautious about taking an Assistant competition just because you think it will be easier. Note also that, for Assistant competitions, EPSO may require specific qualifications among the "essential selection criteria" and this may prove an obstacle to passing such a competition.

Deciding on which profile to sit is therefore a tough decision for many, given its repercussions on the chances to succeed. Nevertheless, *you can apply for an unlimited number of competitions* (provided the Notice of Competition does not specifically exclude this). **Candidates are often not aware that they can apply for multiple profiles** so do be alert to this possibility. As long as you are aware of these aspects, you can evaluate the position better for yourself – this will, in fact, be your first numerical reasoning practice exercise!

Feedback and Complaints

When discussing feedback and complaints, it must be borne in mind that given the significant number of candidates, both are handled in an automated way in the first place until human intervention is required.

Feedback (on test results) is only given in an automated format for the pre-selection phase while those who take part in an Assessment Centre are given more comprehensive feedback in the form of a written report called a **competency passport**, which is provided for everyone regardless of whether they passed or failed (see below for more on this). EPSO also often requests feedback online or immediately after the computer-based test on screen, so as to improve its procedures.

Only well founded and serious complaints can be taken into account by the Selection Board, for the above reasons. This also means that individual cases are always examined by the Selection Board or exceptionally by EPSO as a body. Moreover, complaints can only concern the lack of respect for the exam rules or other administrative procedures and they can hardly ever relate to "revision" of the scores or exam results. As an example, if you missed the pass mark by one point, you cannot argue in favour of leniency or flexibility unless there was an error in one of the exam questions and it must be "neutralised" for all candidates. Another scenario when your complaint may be substantiated is when an exam rule was not respected, e.g. your relevant qualification was not accepted by the Selection Board even though the issuing university is accredited and recognised by your Member State.

As mentioned above, the first place to lodge a complaint with is the Selection Board where strict deadlines apply (usually within 10 days from the communication of the results), but both the Ombudsman and ultimately, the Civil Service Tribunal may deal with the case. While the Ombudsman can only deal with "maladministration" (this term refers to a situation when an EU institution or body fails to respect the exam rules or procedures – as opposed to individual exam results or evaluations of the Selection Board), the EU Civil Service Tribunal does examine individual cases on their merits but acts only as a second level judicial review body after the Selection Board has refused your formal complaint. It must nevertheless be borne in mind that these are long and cumbersome procedures that are only worth the effort if you are truly and reasonably convinced that you have been discriminated against or that your application's treatment can be challenged on legal grounds.

Another important aspect is that regardless of any failed efforts to pass the exams you can, as mentioned above, apply for new competitions without any limitations. If you do not pass an exam, EPSO does not retain your scores or keep a file on your results, therefore *you can start with a "clean slate" if you decide to have another go at passing the exams*, and you may even apply in parallel for multiple competitions (provided you meet the eligibility criteria and there is no clause in the Notice of Competition forbidding this).

The Selection Boards

Selection Boards have traditionally been composed of EU officials who volunteer to take part in such tasks. Their background, motivation and interests vary greatly which ensures objective and fair treatment based on strict guidelines that each of them must follow. Selection Boards, including most assessors, are still chosen from among volunteering active and even retired personnel, though some expertise, especially in developing multiple choice tests and administering the exams in various locations around the world, is now provided by external contractors. EPSO has been trying to professionalise the Selection Boards by extending the scope of their members' assignments for several months or even years instead of using them on an ad hoc basis, thus ensuring the accumulation of more insight and knowledge on their part, and also by providing proper training before their assignment commences.

Members of the Selection Boards generally perform the entire administration of an exam while being independent from EPSO and, legally speaking, they are the ones who are solely responsible for the administration of a competition and not EPSO. Each competition has its own Selection Board, which takes on tasks such as preparing the tests, admitting candidates on the basis of their files or marking the exercises. In a case brought before the European Court of Justice, a candidate in the 2010 Administrator exam challenged the Selection Board's ability to control and supervise the computer-based tests created and run by an external company. He won the case, requiring a re-run of the 2010 Administrator exams in 2013. This case demonstrates the importance of the Selection Board and their duty to supervise all elements of the competition.

You, of course, may never approach a Selection Board member for any additional information other than that formally communicated to you, even though the board members' names are always made public on EPSO's website for reasons of transparency. Some candidates think that a quick online search to find the professional background of board members could help identify their favourite topics (e.g. if a member works in DG Competition of the European Commission, it may have some bearing on the questions they ask), though this is rarely the case especially since the Assessment Centres have a very different approach in testing candidates.

Venues and Costs

The **pre-selection** exams take place all over Europe and in several other locations around the world. Where citizens of all Member States are eligible for a competition (which is the normal situation), there will be exam centres in each country's capital, and in case of bigger countries, also in other large cities.

As almost all exams under the EPSO system are administered on computers, exams are generally held over a certain period of time at the designated centres.

Candidates are required to pick and book a date and venue online that suits them. You should chose carefully. Although EPSO does allow you to reschedule your MCQs appointment right up to the last day, you may find all the time slots that suit you are gone. Also some test types cannot be rescheduled other than in exceptional circumstances.

> ### Key point
>
> Pre-selection tests can be taken in your home country, at your own expense. Assessment Centre tests are usually in Brussels and your expenses are paid.

After you validate your application (i.e. submit it formally online), you then have to wait until EPSO closes the application period and opens the booking period. Both these phases have strict timescales. The minute the booking period is opened, be sure to sign up as soon as possible given that the most popular places and time slots tend to fill up fast, and to avoid any last minute internet blackout or server crash that may prevent you from securing your place in time.

No contribution is made by EPSO towards any travelling or subsistence expenses associated with the pre-selection phase of the exam. As these exams take place in your own country or at multiple venues elsewhere in the world, travelling from your home to these centres is always on your own budget.

For the assessment phase, you will be given a specific date some time in advance with limited or no option to amend it unless compelling events prevent you from attending and you can duly justify the reason.

Assessment Centres are located centrally in Brussels though exceptionally and only for lawyer-linguists, there is an Assessment Centre in Luxembourg too. Candidates who need to travel there are reimbursed for their travel costs and also given a daily subsistence allowance for hotel and food costs. The specific rules are always communicated in advance either as early as in the Notice of Competition or later to those who actually make it through to the assessment phase. The underlying principle is that nobody should suffer any disadvantage in attending the competitions due to budgetary issues. The same rule of equal opportunities applies for those flying in or travelling to a specific job interview unless a telephone or videoconference is a feasible alternative.

Motivation

Before applying, it is useful to reflect on what factors motivate you in wanting to work for an EU institution. Usually it is a mixture of various considerations – such as the desire to work on international affairs in a multicultural environment, belief in European integration, the opportunity to travel, getting an attractive salary and benefits, having an interesting and varied job, speaking and learning foreign languages, job security etc.

Being aware of which factors are the most important for you personally can help in identifying which profile to apply for – and it should also help in the structured interview, if you get to the Assessment Centre, when assessors try to find out more about your personality. "Being part of something larger than yourself" is a vital aspect that you may also emphasise in your application's motivation section. Also on this topic, for the 2018 AD5 generalist (graduate) competition EPSO introduced an "EU Motivational Interview" at the Assessment Centre, to assess candidates' commitment to the "European idea". This was repeated in 2019.

The Candidates

It is very hard, if not impossible, to outline a "typical" candidate profile given the large number and diverse backgrounds of applicants. However, I have formed the impression that most of the serious applicants have some key things in common. They:

- Are interested in EU affairs, committed to European integration and wish to work for a "good cause"

- Are flexible and willing to work abroad in a multi-cultural environment

- Have a strong motivation to study for and pass the exams to get into the EU institutions

- Understand and accept that EU institutions are different from the private sector inasmuch as they are a hybrid of a diplomatic corps, an international organisation and a government administration that is based on a hierarchic model

The above qualities will also be looked at by assessors if only on an indirect or informal level. EU institutions deal with such a wide variety of issues that you can certainly find the job that best suits your interests and personality if your motivation is right.

There is no minimum age as such for candidates, this in effect being determined by the requirement of a degree/diploma or work experience. Obviously the EU is keen on ensuring a level playing field in terms of candidates' backgrounds, ensuring equal opportunities for all based on merit, regardless of whether they belong to any particular religious, sexual, ethnic or other minority, social segment or age group.

Whatever your age, you will be required to pass a medical check that will serve as a benchmark for your social security and health insurance file before taking up an EU job. This also serves to ensure that you are physically capable of doing the job you are to be required to perform.

Quotas

It is frequently asked whether the EU institutions apply a quota system for allocating posts to a certain number of officials from each Member State. This is a somewhat delicate issue given that EU civil servants work for the EU not for their national governments so in theory their nationality should be irrelevant. In practice however the situation is rather different.

In fact, the Staff Regulations, the legal document that lays down the conditions of employment of staff in the EU institutions, provide that officials are to be "recruited on the broadest possible geographical basis from among nationals of Member States of the Union". This reference to "the broadest possible geographical basis" explains the special competitions in recent years e.g. to select candidates exclusively from Croatia based on their recent accession to the EU, but such targeted competitions are the exception, not the rule.

Apart from such special circumstances, where new Member States are starting from a base of zero, the "broadest possible geographical basis" provision in practice means there is an ongoing effort to maintain an allocation of posts that more-or-less reflects the proportion of each Member State's population in the EU as a whole. This is true for all grades, including

Key point

Eight countries were identified, because of their under-representation, as "focus countries" for EPSO communication efforts for the 2018 AD5 generalist (graduate) competition. These were the Czech Republic, Denmark, France, Germany, Ireland, Netherlands, Poland and Sweden.

senior management. Yet, despite this principle, there are no hard-coded quotas for Irish or Cypriot or any other citizens given the merit-based competition system. Natural imbalances therefore always exist and they could only be challenged by the introduction of specific staff allocations, which would then likely infringe upon the principle of non-discrimination based on nationality. This is certainly not an easy issue to handle politically as it touches on the very essence of the principles guiding European integration.

An issue that is likely to come to the fore in the coming years is the under-representation of the older (now EU-14) Member States among younger officials in the AD5-8 bracket. As older officials, where the EU-14 are over-represented retire, this imbalance will transfer itself up the ranks as time goes by.

Language Rules

Generally speaking, other than for linguist competitions, you will be asked for knowledge of two official languages: one at C1 level (thorough knowledge) and one at a minimum of B2 level (satisfactory knowledge). **These are your so-called language 1 and language 2**.

The levels are defined in the "Common European Framework of Reference for Languages".

One of the most common misunderstandings regarding EU competitions is the exact meaning of your first and second language. In practice the term "language 1" usually but not necessarily means your mother tongue, *as long as it is an official EU language*. The reason why this latter point needs to be emphasised is because a Lithuanian candidate, for example, may have Russian as their mother tongue but that cannot be offered as their language 1 choice since it is not an official EU language.

In some cases, especially for enlargement-related or linguist exams, the candidate's citizenship or the given competition's specific language profile automatically determines the required first language. Examples would be competitions for Croatian Administrators and Assistants requiring the first language to be Croatian; or having French as the compulsory first language for translator exams in the French language. In other instances you are free to choose your language 1 as long as the above rules on citizenship and the official EU language requirements are respected. Thus, for instance, if you have Luxembourgish citizenship, your "first language" may well be French or German as Luxembourgish is not an official EU language.

It is important to note that "mother tongue" can also mean that if you have a perfect command of a language that you "learned" – and if you are confident that your speaking and writing is close to perfect in that language, you can indicate it as your first language. For example, if your citizenship is Slovak but

Languages of the candidates for the 2019 Graduate Administrators competition	
Languages Declared at B2 level or above (percentages), in rank order	
English	98.02
French	51.37
Spanish	29.66
Italian	26.69
German	18.36
Greek	8.75
Dutch	8.30
Romanian	6.70
Portuguese	4.97
Polish	3.65
Bulgarian	2.80
Czech	2.56
Croatian	2.34
Hungarian	1.79
Swedish	1.73
Slovakian	1.60
Finnish	1.53
Lithuanian	1.13
Danish	0.92
Slovenian	0.80
Latvian	0.48
Estonian	0.43
Maltese	0.32
Gaelic (Irish)	0.30

Competition	Reference	2nd language requirement	Notes
Administrators (AD 7) in 1. Financial economics 2. Macroeconomics	EPSO/AD/339/17	English, French or German	
AD5 Graduate Administrators 2019	EPSO/AD/373/19	1 of the 5 languages selected (the 5 declared by most candidates, subject to the needs of the service)	See the first "Key point" on page 16! You must declare a minimum of 2 languages at stage 1 of the application. You can ONLY complete part 2 of the application if you have declared one of the 5 selected languages
AD5 Administrators in the Field of Audit	EPSO/AD/357/18	English or French	
AD7 in 1. Customs, 2. Taxation	EPSO/AD/363/18	English or French	
AD6 Building Management Engineers	EPSO/AD/342/17	English, French, German	
AD6 Food Safety Policy and Legislation	EPSO/AD/341/18	English, French, German, Italian	The European Food Standards Agency is in Italy and agencies will use local languages as well as the EU working languages.
AD6 Administrators in the Field of Data protection	EPSO/AD/360/18	English or French	

you speak Greek perfectly, and you wish to apply for an exam where one of the first language choices is Greek, feel free to do so. But bear in mind that your second language must also be at a high level.

Language 2 is in fact normally your first foreign language. Traditionally you have only been allowed to choose between English, French or German. However following a ruling by the European Court of Justice (which actually led to the cancellation of the AD5 generalist competition in 2016) EPSO is now offering in the generalist competition as language 2 the five languages most frequently declared by candidates at B2 level or higher in the first part of their application form for the competition in question (meaning it can vary from one competition to another).

The first time this new procedure was applied, for the 2017 AD5 generalist competition (EPSO/AD/338/17) the following 5 languages were declared by the most people: English, French, Spanish, Italian and German (in that order, from highest to lowest number), which was as might have been expected. Exactly the same happened in the 2018 competition and again in 2019 (see table on page 14).

However, it is worth pointing out that the Notice of Competition in such cases states that while EPSO intends to offer as language 2 "the 5 languages most frequently declared by candidates" this would be only *"while also taking into account the needs of the service"*. Therefore there is discretion in deciding which languages will be treated as language 2. Variations in language rules can also occur in other competitions. For

Key point

For the AD5 graduate competition (as of 2019) you have in the first stage of the application process to declare a minimum of 2 languages. These can be ANY of the official languages. EPSO then says what the 5 most-declared languages are (with a proviso that this must be subject to the needs of the service) and you can ONLY proceed further in the competition if your language 2 is among those 5. In other words, there is no point in declaring Estonian and Lithuanian, or Croatian and Portuguese, as your 2 languages in part 1 because none of those will ever qualify as a language 2.

example, for the 2019 competition (EPSO/AD/374) for Administrators in a variety of finance-related sub-profiles, the permitted second languages were English, French, German or Italian. Sometimes, in contrast (see table on page 15), only English or French might be offered as options.

For linguist exams the second language is usually the one for which candidates are sought. For example, if EPSO announces a linguist exam for Bulgarian translators, the first language is required to be Bulgarian, the second language would likely be English, French or German, with a third language (in fact, second foreign language) requirement as well. Note that there is no requirement of Bulgarian citizenship as the goal is perfect command of a language regardless of which EU citizenship you may have. This is a fundamental rule in the system: the citizenship requirement is almost always decoupled from the language requirements.

EPSO now provides for abstract reasoning, verbal reasoning and numerical reasoning tests to be done in your first language. This shows that the aim of such tests is not to test your linguistic knowledge but to assess your psychometric reasoning skills. Situational judgement tests and other tests (e.g. domain specific tests for specialists, Assessment Centre exercises and others), however, are in language 2 and as these are linguistically very demanding your language 2 has to be very good.

Once recruited, AD level officials will also need to demonstrate their ability to work in a second foreign language (their "third language") before their first promotion. The language 3 level required of existing officials is, however, in practice fairly unexacting compared to the language 2 requirements of candidates in EPSO competitions.

Key point

Your language 1 will most likely be your native language – but it doesn't have to be, and in some cases it might not be the best option. Imagine your native language is French but you have a good command of German and you are entering a competition where either can be chosen as language 2. You might decide to do the pre-selection tests in German and keep your native language for the Assessment Centre, where more sophisticated and interactive linguistic skills are required.

An important piece of advice to bear in mind is that once you know which language you will be assessed in (i.e. the choice for language 2; in case of linguists/interpreters, your first language will also be tested), read all preparation materials only in that/those language(s). Needless to say, French, German and all other names of EU institutions, abbreviations, programmes and concepts may differ significantly from each other, and you certainly do not wish to mix up the European Council with the Council of Europe because of a language issue.

	Administrators (AD)	Linguists (AD)	Assistants (AST) Secretaries (AST-SC)	Specialists (AD or AST)
Minimum Qualification	Degree (min. BA level or 3 years of studies, EPSO may require it to be related to the chosen sub-profile, e.g. Audit)	Degree (min. BA level or 3 years of studies)	Relevant high school diploma or post-secondary qualification (a minimum of 3 years study-related work might also be required)	Same as for ASTs and ADs
Work Experience	None (AD5); 3 years (AD6); 6 years (AD7); 12 years (AD9) (exception: see Specialists' column)	None (AD5); 6 years (AD7); 12 years (AD9)	None to 3 or 6 years, depending on the qualification (AST3 and above and SC1 and SC2 unless relevant diploma available)	Same as for ASTs and ADs (with possible exceptions, e.g. AD7 lawyer-linguists may need only 3 years of work experience instead of 6). Experience required may also depend on qualifications
Type of Qualification (in many cases, though not always, qualifications are eliminatory, so make sure to read EPSO's Notice of Competition carefully)	Arts, Law, Economics, Political Science, Statistics etc.	Language Studies, Interpreting	Clerical Studies, Arts, Finances, IT, Technical skills etc.	Lawyers, Linguists, Engineers, Scientists, Doctors, Veterinaries, etc.

Important note: the terminology relating to qualifications varies greatly from country to country – what is called a "degree" in one country is a "diploma" in another, and so forth. For a country-by-country list of what EPSO regards as examples of qualifications corresponding to those required by the Notices of Competition, see http://europa.eu/epso/doc/diplomes-fortheweb_en.pdf

Please note that the above table is for information purposes only and the actual requirements may differ; please always consult EPSO's official communications for up-to-date information

Formal Criteria

As a candidate applying for EU exams, you must meet certain formal (objective) criteria. These, as a general rule, say you must:

- Be a citizen of a Member State of the European Union (though exceptions might occur as in the case of enlargement-related competitions)

- Be entitled to full rights as such a citizen (e.g. no legal limitations as a result of criminal acts or other issues) and meet the character requirements for the duties involved

- Have fulfilled any obligations imposed by the laws on military service (only relevant for those Member States where such service is compulsory, and even there you may prove that you were exempted from the service)

Key point

The "minimum qualifications" in the table above can be a bit misleading. Most Assistants these days will have college degrees and the majority (but by no means all) of newly appointed AD5s will have post-graduate degrees.

- Have a thorough knowledge of one of the official languages of the European Union and a satisfactory knowledge of a second (this is the minimum requirement but further linguistic prerequisites may be set out in the given Notice of Competition as also mentioned above)

- Have the sufficient minimum education and/or work experience as set out in the Notice of Competition (see the table on page 17)

These formal criteria are required for ALL profiles, regardless of the specific provisions of the competition; if you do not meet the eligibility criteria and this is discovered later you will be disqualified however well you do in the tests.

Choosing a Profile

Choosing a profile is determined by both objective and subjective factors: depending on your qualifications and work experience (which are "objective" facts you cannot change overnight), you may be limited to only one "choice"; it may nevertheless happen that you are formally eligible for multiple profiles and it remains your individual choice which one to sit for. For example, a lawyer with three years' experience and fluent knowledge of three languages would potentially be eligible for a whole range of profiles. In that case the choice would be determined by career aspirations and perhaps the relative chances of success in different competitions.

Multiple Applications

A general approach taken by many candidates is to apply for all competitions they are eligible for, this way increasing their chances. This is also an excellent way to practice the tests you need to pass and it is a highly recommended strategy. There are certain circumstances where you cannot apply for two exams in parallel, where these are sub-profiles in a competition. You should not attempt to create two accounts (profiles) on EPSO's website, because this will lead to disqualification from the competition.

The rules regarding multiple applications will be given in the Notice of Competition. For example, in the 2019 competition for Administrators in various finance-related sub-profiles (financial law, EMU law, financial rules applicable to the EU budget, protection of euro coins against counterfeiting), you were not permitted to apply for more than one of these sub-profiles.

Another important aspect is that if you do not succeed in a competition you can apply for new competitions without any limitations. If you do not pass an exam, EPSO does not retain your scores or keep a file on your results, therefore you can start with a "clean slate" if you decide to have another go at passing the exams. This is an important aspect because many candidates improve their test scores with practice and succeed at a later attempt.

2.   Administrator Competitions Step by Step

Introduction

Having looked at the principles and procedures of EPSO competitions, we can now move on to the specific phases of the competitions in more detail.

For the AD5 generalist (graduate) competition (as of 2019) the phases were:

1. Notice of Competition, Self-Assessment, Registration

2. Pre-selection Phase (first round of exams)

3. Intermediate test

4. Assessment Centre (second full round of exams)

5. Reserve List, Recruitment

The various phases can look different depending on the competition. For linguists, for example, phase 3 would be translation tests, while the sequence for specialists can be different because of the use of the Talent Screener.

Below we provide an outline of each of the stages and tests, along with some practical advice. Later chapters in this book provide very detailed coverage and practice materials for the critical pre-selection phase.

On the next two pages you will find charts showing the tests used at each stage of competitions for some sample profiles. Bear in mind these are just samples and you will need to check the Notice of Competition for the exact tests used at each stage in your competition.

Phase 1: Notice of Competition, Self-Assessment, Registration, Talent Screener

The Notice of Competition

The Notice of Competition (NoC) is a special administrative notice addressed to all EU citizens and it is therefore published in the Official Journal of the EU (EUR-Lex) both in print and online. It is important to underline that the NoC is the only official source of information, therefore if you see any contradicting or different interpretation in the

2019 AD5 Graduate Administrator Competition

PRE-SELECTION

Verbal reasoning
Numerical reasoning
Abstract reasoning
Situational judgement

INTERMEDIATE TEST

E-tray exercise

ASSESSMENT CENTRE

Oral presentation
Case study
Group exercise
Competency based interview
Motivational interview

RESERVE LIST

Sample AD6/AD7 Specialist Competition

PRE-SELECTION

(a) if number of applications above threshold set by EPSO

Verbal reasoning
Numerical reasoning
Abstract reasoning

(b) If below threshold, these tests will be at the Assessment Centre

TALENT SCREENER

Comes first if (b) above applies

ASSESSMENT CENTRE

Case study
Group exercise
Competency based interview
Interview in the field

RESERVE LIST

Sample AD5 Translators Competition

PRE-SELECTION

Verbal reasoning
Numerical reasoning
Abstract reasoning
Language comprehension
(languages 2 and 3)
Main language skills (language 1)

TRANSLATION TEST

Language 2 to 1
Language 3 to 1

ASSESSMENT CENTRE

Oral presentation
Group exercise
Competency based interview

RESERVE LIST

Sample AD7 Lawyer-Linguist Competition

PRE-SELECTION

Verbal reasoning
Numerical reasoning
Abstract reasoning
Language comprehension (language 2)

TRANSLATION TEST

Legal text from language 2 to 1

ASSESSMENT CENTRE

Oral presentation
Group exercise
Competency based interview
Field specific competencies

RESERVE LIST

AD 5 is the grade at which graduates begin their careers as administrators in the European institutions. Administrators recruited at this grade can undertake, under supervision, three main types of work in the institutions: policy formulation, operational delivery, and resource management. We are particularly looking for candidates with a potential for career development.

The general role of administrators is to support decision-makers in fulfilling the mission of their institution or body.

Their main duties, which may vary from one institution to another, include:

– devising, implementing, monitoring and control of programmes and action plans,

– managing resources including staff, finances, and equipment,

– assisting decision-makers by means of written or oral contributions,

– drafting policy analysis briefings,

– external communication as well as internal reporting and communication,

– relations with external stakeholders and with the Member States,

– inter-service and inter-institutional coordination and consultation regarding policy,

– coordinating working groups set up by the Member States, the institutions and other external stakeholders,

– drafting contracts, preparing calls for proposals and invitations to tender, and participating in evaluation committees for monitoring selection procedures and the allocation of proposals.

press or on a website, make sure to check the original authentic source which is always referenced on EPSO's website.

The NoC is a rather extensive document that sets out all the formal eligibility criteria, language requirements, deadlines and other practical arrangements linked to the competition. Just as important, the NoC contains a wealth of information that you can use to your benefit by reading it attentively, such as the size of the reserve list (so you can estimate your chances and thus decide which sub-profile or domain to apply for).

The basic "job description", also detailed in the NoC, is particularly interesting as it is not only an indication of what sort of tasks you would need to carry out once employed; from it you can also deduce lots of hints about the topics to cover when preparing for the domain-specific parts of the assessment phase, especially the case study.

Above, by way of illustration, are extracts from a **Notice of Competition for a generalist Administrator competition**, where the main aspects of the role are described.

It is crucial to understand and analyse every detail provided in the NoC. This will also help you avoid seemingly evident pitfalls that might lead to disqualification (such as a requirement to submit a certain certificate or sign a submitted document) – you would be surprised to know how many people get rejected on formal grounds by accidentally overlooking a date, a provision or a prerequisite.

Self-Assessment

Self-assessment as a tool is widely used in international organisations and multinational private sector companies and EPSO makes use of it as well. The objective is to ensure candidates realise what EU jobs are really about and dispel misconceptions at the earliest stage. This is intended to reduce non-eligible applications and candidate frustration.

Self-assessment, which is not to be confused with the Talent Screener used for specialists, is non-eliminatory, meaning that you cannot pass or fail based on your answers.

Registration and Application

Registration is done exclusively online on the EPSO (EU Careers) website at the start

> ### *Key point*
>
> Competitions are often heavily over-subscribed. The incentive for EPSO is to reduce numbers to manageable proportions. Don't give grounds to be thrown out of a competition just because you made a careless mistake in your application form.

of the procedure. The first step is to create an **EPSO account or profile**, which is an online personal profile where your correspondence with EPSO will take place. If you change your postal or e-mail address during the procedure or any other contact information becomes obsolete, make sure to update your online account immediately.

If, after registration, the confirmation e-mail does not arrive in your inbox within a few hours, check your spam or bulk mail folder as it may have been misfiled by your e-mail application; should you still not receive anything, ask EPSO for technical assistance. Make sure, however, that you do not register twice as it may lead to potential disqualification if other signs show you had second thoughts when doing so.

What you need to do at the application stage will depend on your competition. Confirming your eligibility for the competition (e.g. your citizenship, level of education achieved) and declaring your language 1 and language 2 is standard, but other aspects do vary. As with everything to do with EPSO competitions, you have to carefully observe the rules laid down in the Notice of Competition.

If you are entering an **AD5 generalist competition** the application process is straightforward because every eligible candidate will be invited to the pre-selection computer-based testing. You only have to make sure that the information you provide is accurate because if it isn't you may end up being disqualified from the competition through sheer carelessness. You can also submit your application in your language 1.

For **linguist competitions** you will have to complete your application form in language 2 and may also have to provide additional information relevant to the competition but, assuming you are eligible, you can expect to be called to the pre-selection round of MCQ tests – i.e. there is no elimination by Talent Screener (see page 24).

Declarations in the application form are made "on your honour" and proof of what you claim is not required at the application stage. However there is absolutely no point in trying to "put a gloss" on what you claim (e.g. pretending to have a higher level of proficiency in language 2 than you really have, or claiming a period of work experience that was longer or with more responsibility than was really the case). The whole process of selection is a rigorous one and you will be found out – and might end up being disqualified from a competition where you could have succeeded on the basis of truthful statements and your own merits.

Finally, an obvious point but a necessary one. *Don't leave your application to the last minute.* You will end up panicking about finding a missing piece of information you need for the form or losing the internet connection at a crucial moment. If you rush the process and make a mistake you will not be able to correct it once you have validated your application. And if you miss the deadline, that's it; there is no provision for late applications.

Talent Screener

If you are entering a **specialist competition** you will have to provide additional information about your diplomas and work experience and answer questions specific to the field you are applying for. This is the **Talent Screener** and EPSO are now making much more use of this than previously. It is absolutely crucial that you not only provide correct information but also don't miss anything that could help your application (including relevant information you have provided in other parts of the application form). The reason for this is that you may not get a second chance to go further – the Selection Board may very likely make the "first cut" of candidates simply based on the Talent Screener. Even if it doesn't, and all candidates are called to a pre-selection round, the Talent Screener will be used as a basis for your assessment at the Assessment Centre. The Talent Screener must also be completed in your language 2 so that the Selection Board can make an objective comparison of all the candidates. Sometimes the entire application form for specialist competitions has to be done in language 2.

Phase 2: Pre-Selection

Key point

Pre-selection is the point where the majority of candidates fail. The core Administrator pre-selection tests are the main subject of this book.

Having taken the above steps and provided that you meet all formal eligibility criteria, you should receive an official invitation to the pre-selection phase, communicated to you in your online EPSO profile. Once this eagerly awaited message arrives, you should get on with your preparation immediately (if you haven't already started) as the booking period may open straightaway and the exam be imminent.

Once the booking is open, you can choose a venue and a time from the available exam centres and time slots. If you live outside Europe, you can choose an exam centre outside the Member States; EPSO has extended the reach of exam centres to other continents via international test centres in China, the USA and elsewhere, which is a welcome development (though it does not necessarily apply for all exams).

When choosing an exam centre, make sure you are fully aware of the logistical issues: print the map of its location, find out which public transport goes there on the exam day, make sure that no strike or service interruption is foreseen for that day, and have a fallback plan in case you are running late, such as the phone number of a reliable taxi company.

My general advice for test-takers is to start practising as early as you can; preferably straight after deciding to sit an EPSO exam. In the pre-selection phase, competition is usually fierce and you must achieve the highest possible score in demanding psychometric tests. (Remember, however, that for certain specialist competitions, the "pre-selection" phase is the Talent Screener, and the psychometric tests are part of the Assessment Centre.)

Key point

Pre-selection tests of the type described in this book may be given at the Assessment Centre in some competitions for specialists. It depends on the number of candidates.

I strongly advise creating a concrete study

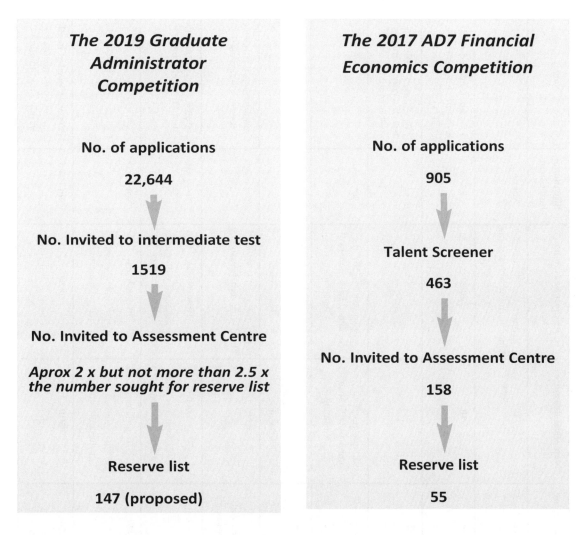

The 2019 Graduate Administrator Competition

No. of applications

22,644

No. Invited to intermediate test

1519

No. Invited to Assessment Centre

Aprox 2 x but not more than 2.5 x the number sought for reserve list

Reserve list

147 (proposed)

The 2017 AD7 Financial Economics Competition

No. of applications

905

Talent Screener

463

No. Invited to Assessment Centre

158

Reserve list

55

plan where you allocate sufficient time for the upcoming weeks and months for practice, revision, simulation and preparation. Simply saying "I'll find the time whenever I have nothing else to do" will not lead to tangible results, as watching the next episode of your favourite Netflix series will always seems more fun than dealing with rhombuses in abstract reasoning questions.

Scoring

As can be seen from the table on the next page, the rules for scoring vary from one competition to another. Making sure you know and understand the rules for your particular competition is essential if you are going to focus on the critical areas for practice.

As the table shows, the various tests have "pass marks". **Three important aspects of pass marks need to be taken into account**.

- **A pass mark is precisely that, a pass mark. Anything below it is a fail**. If you don't achieve the pass mark in any test where one is stipulated, then you are out of the competition however superbly you might perform in all the other tests. Thus in preparing for a competition you cannot afford to ignore your

Competition	Reference	Verbal Reasoning	Numerical Reasoning	Abstract Reasoning	Situational Judgement	Note
AD 7 in 1. Financial economics 2. Macroeconomics	EPSO/AD/339/17	20 questions. 15/30 combined with abstract reasoning	6/10	10 questions. 15/30 combined with verbal reasoning	Not used	
AD5 Graduate Administrators 2019	**EPSO/AD/373/19**	**5/10**	**5/10**	**10/20**	24/40	**Pass mark needed in all tests but only abstract + SJTs count to score**
AD5 Audit	EPSO/AD/357/18	5/10	5/10	10/20	24/40	Pass mark needed in all tests but only abstract + SJTs count to score
AD7 in 1. Customs, 2. Taxation	EPSO/AD/363/18	10/20	10 questions, 10/20 combined with abstract reasoning	10 questions, 10/20 combined with numerical reasoning	Not used	
AD6 Building Management Engineers	EPSO/AD/342/17	10/20	10 questions, 10/20 combined with abstract reasoning	10 questions, 10/20 combined with numerical reasoning	Not used	
AD5 Italian language translators	EPSO/AD/345/17	20 questions. 15/30 combined with abstract reasoning	4/10	10 questions. 15/30 combined with verbal reasoning	Not used	Computer-based language test MCQs also used
AD7 Danish lawyer-linguists	EPSO/AD/349/17	10/20	10 questions. 8/20 combined with abstract reasoning	10 questions. 8/20 combined with numerical reasoning	Not used	Computer-based language test MCQs also used
AD6 Food Safety Policy and Legislation	EPSO/AD/341/18	10/20	10 questions. 10/20 combined with abstract reasoning	10 questions. 10/20 combined with numerical reasoning	Not Used	
AD5 Graduate Administrators 2017	**EPSO/AD/338/17**	**10/20**	**5/10**	**10/20**	**Not Used**	**Pass mark needed in all tests but only abstract + verbal count to score**

areas of weakness in a vague hope that you will be saved by doing well in other areas.

- A pass mark is a **minimum requirement** and NOT a ticket to go on to the next stage of a competition. EPSO will be selecting the "best X" candidates for the next stage. So, for example, if EPSO is planning to invite 120 candidates to the next stage and 500 candidates achieve the pass marks in every test, only the 120 with the best scores will get the invitation.

- **The results of two tests may be combined** to create a pass mark for the combined tests. For example, looking at the table on the page opposite, for the AD5 Italian language translators the marks for the verbal reasoning and abstract reasoning tests were added together to produce a combined pass mark. So, if a candidate was very good at verbal reasoning and got 15/20 and very poor at abstract reasoning and got no marks at all they would still reach the pass mark because their combined score for verbal and abstract reasoning was 15. This can take a little bit of the pressure off candidates if they find that the results of one of their strongest tests are to be combined with one of their weakest. Of course, in the case of the translators they would still have the problem that other candidates might themselves get 15/20 on verbal reasoning but also accumulate points on abstract reasoning, thus getting a higher combined score. As already said, it is not just a matter of achieving the pass marks, you have to be among the "best X" in scores.

Another important factor is that in totalling your scores EPSO *sometimes disregards altogether the results of some tests*, provided of course that you have reached the pass mark in those tests.

Look, for example, at the scoring rules for the 2019 AD5 graduate competition. You had to achieve the pass mark of 5/10 in both the verbal and numerical reasoning tests. However, when it came to determining the "best X" scores, EPSO disregarded the verbal and numerical reasoning scores and simply added together the scores for abstract reasoning and situational judgement. With those rules, it made sense for a candidate to make sure they were "good enough" to get the pass marks in the verbal and numerical reasoning and then focus all their efforts and energies on becoming the "very best possible" in the other two tests. In the real world it is hard to become brilliant at everything so how your competition is scored should influence where you make the most intensive effort to improve.

Finally, you should be aware that EPSO *can and does change the scoring rules from one similar competition to another*. Just because a particular type of competition was scored one way one year it does not mean the same rules will apply the next. A notable example was the scoring for the AD5 graduate Administrator competition pre-selection round in the 2017, 2018 and 2019 competitions (see the table). For 2018 and 2019 the abstract reasoning and situational judgement test scores were the ones added together to decide the "best X". In 2017, in contrast, it was the abstract and verbal reasoning and there was not even a situational judgement test at all! While the EPSO system is relatively stable compared with the huge upheaval of 2010 everything

> ## *Scoring Rules of the 2019 AD5 Graduate Competition*
>
> Pass marks were 5/10 for both the verbal and numerical reasoning tests, 10/20 for the abstract reasoning and 24/40 for the situational judgement test. The minimum pass mark had to be reached in ALL the tests but ONLY the abstract reasoning and situational judgement test scores were used to qualify for the next stage, the intermediate test.

is by no means set in stone and you therefore need to keep alert as to what changes are made.

Computer Screens

As all tests in the pre-selection phase are administered on computers located in accredited exam centres, you should be prepared for the difficulties this entails. Reading a text is always slower on a computer screen than on paper, speed being also influenced by the font size and screen resolution. Adding comments on screen is technically not available, therefore you need to take notes on the scrap paper or erasable slate that the exam centres provide. (This is even more relevant when it comes to the case study, which is formally part of the Assessment Centre, even if it is usually organised separately for logistical reasons.) For the numerical reasoning test an on-screen calculator is available and candidates are also provided with a fairly standard physical calculator such as a Sharp EL-240 SA or similar.

Computer-based exams do have a few advantages however. These include: the mark and highlighter features; the display of the available time (which is not meant to put pressure on you but rather to help time management); the automatic registration of answered and unanswered questions (which should help you keep track of the questions); the flexibility of choosing a convenient exam day for all candidates (as opposed to having a single exam day for all candidates); and the faster (and more reliable) correction of your answers given the electronic evaluation.

Verbal and Numerical Reasoning Tests

The verbal and numerical reasoning tests, along with abstract reasoning, are commonly known as **psychometric tests**. These are one of the most popular methods to evaluate cognitive skills and the intelligence of prospective employees. They are widely used by multinational companies and civil service recruiters around the world given their flexible application, cost-effectiveness and proven relevance to gauge candidates' skills. The relevant chapters of this book provide a full methodology and hundreds of practice exercises: what follows here is more of a description of how these tests are administered along with some general advice on how to tackle them.

Verbal reasoning tests are essentially reading comprehension tests where you are required to answer a question based on a text. A fundamental rule is to only consider information contained in the text.

Numerical reasoning, on the other hand, is a calculation exercise using statistical charts, tables and graphs, based on which you are required to find a certain percentage, figure, or decide on relative values (e.g. "Based on the table, which country had the highest birth rate in 2018?"). Questions can be tricky as sometimes no or minimal exact calculation is required given that you can simplify the riddle by applying calculation methods and shortcuts. A comprehensive toolkit is offered in the relevant chapters of this book.

EPSO has been using verbal and numerical reasoning tests for some years in its competitions and they have proven to be one of the most challenging parts of the exam procedure. While EU knowledge, as tested before 2010, could to some degree be memorised by dedicating sufficient time to this end, succeeding in verbal and numerical reasoning requires a completely different approach. Learning the methodology, and then plenty of practice in using it, is therefore crucial to succeed.

As mentioned in the section on languages above, since 2011 all verbal and numerical reasoning tests can be taken in your first language (along with abstract reasoning, but there the choice of language has no relevance). Linguists can expect to have two or three different verbal reasoning tests: one in their main language (which depends on which linguistic profile they had applied for, e.g. Bulgarian translator or German interpreter); while the other two depend on the source languages available for that given exam (English, French and German have privileged status and almost always appear among the languages).

Work as hard as you can to improve your overall vocabulary in the exam's language by reading quality news websites, boost your spelling skills for complex words, your understanding of measurement units (billions vs. millions, how many litres in one cubic metre, etc.) and revise basic mathematical operations. In addition to the extensive resources in this book, you will find verbal reasoning tests in 19 different languages on the EU Training website.

Abstract Reasoning Tests

Abstract reasoning is another test type that various international employers commonly use; it is a common feature of popular IQ tests as well. Abstract reasoning is different from the other two tests as it requires no linguistic skills: there is only one main question for all tasks, such as "Which figure is the next in the series?"

Using these questions for personnel selection is practical for EPSO given that there is no need to translate the exercise into any language and also because abstract reasoning tests have been scientifically proven to be culture-neutral while effectively testing candidates' so-called "fluid intelligence". This latter term refers to the capability to solve new problems and understand the relationship between various concepts, independent of any acquired knowledge.

The main skill you need to efficiently resolve abstract reasoning tests is "imagination" – that is, the ability to mentally rotate, flip or turn certain figures according to a certain logic or rule. This rule is one of the main challenges of this question type as you should be able to "dissect" a figure and identify its component elements. Those capable of performing such tasks are likely to be able to cope with unknown or new situations in the workplace: this skill therefore does have more practical value for predicting actual job performance than may seem at first glance. You can find a large number of abstract reasoning test questions along with an in-depth methodology in chapters 9, 10 and 11 of this book.

Situational Judgement Tests

The objective of situational judgement tests (or SJTs for short) is to create **realistic work-related scenarios** in which you must determine the most appropriate course of action given the parameters and situation.

An important element of SJTs is that there are no absolutely "right" or "wrong" answers when using your judgement. Rather, judgement is about your ability to assess a given situation and make clearly defined decisions on how to proceed from there, based on your own unique set of experiences in life and understanding of the EU institutions' culture and ethical rules, while applying a certain common

Key point

Many AD competitions do not involve situational judgement tests as such. The competencies they measure are instead evaluated at the Assessment Centre. Very importantly, however, such tests are often used for the big "generalist" AD5 graduate competitions: Although dropped for the 2017 competition they were used again in the 2018 and 2019 competitions (see table on page 26).

sense to workplace situations. This is closely linked to the competencies, summarised in chapter 1, that EPSO is seeking to find in future EU officials.

Since there are no right or wrong answers as such, the decision whether one answer is better than another lies in the hands of the test administrators; however, the benchmark for deciding the value of each answer is the competency list that EPSO has established and against which it evaluates candidates. This is explained more fully in chapter 12.

It is important to point out that while real world situations can certainly be summarised into brief sentences or paragraphs, rarely do we come across situations in life that resemble these questions precisely. For example, you could be confronted with a colleague who may be stealing but who may also be a friend, or someone with whom you are in direct competition for a promotion. Such factors would certainly influence your judgement and response.

Professional Skills Tests

Skills specifically related to the field of the competition (for specialists and linguists) may be tested either at the pre-selection stage or the Assessment Centre, or both. For convenience these types of tests are discussed in a separate section below.

Notification of Results

After the pre-selection phase, candidates are notified both of their positive or negative results. The scores and the answers you had given are communicated to you in all cases though for practical reasons EPSO cannot disclose the multiple choice questions themselves, only the answers you had marked.

Since the number of applicants in the pre-selection phase can run into the tens of thousands, EPSO decided to require the submission of supporting documents only for those who have passed the pre-selection or were specialists short-listed on the basis of their CV. This means that even those who have already cleared the first hurdle may not take their eligibility for the assessment phase for granted.

Key point

The feedback from EPSO on your pre-selection test results is of limited value if you have failed the test and are planning to retake. EPSO tell you what the correct answer options were and what you chose but because they don't repeat the actual questions it is impossible to work out where you went wrong. You need to practise with the tests in this book to see where you are making mistakes.

Phase 3: Intermediate Test

The intermediate test is a fairly recent addition to the EPSO selection process and consists of an e-tray exercise. It was brought in specifically for the AD5 graduate competition, always the biggest of the year in terms of number of applications, but was also used in the 2018 (but not 2019) Audit competition. The test takes place on computers at testing centres around the Member States.

The intermediate test is designed to compensate for a fairly obvious difficulty with the pre-selection tests in generalist competitions where there are very large numbers of candidates. If there are many thousands of candidates – bearing in mind that an

AD5 graduate competition will attract well over 20,000 – of whom only a small proportion will be invited to the Assessment Centre, there is a risk that only those who are exceptional performers in tests like abstract reasoning will ever be seen for personal evaluation by the assessors. Such candidates may not always be the ones possessing the ideal range of "soft skills" – the EPSO competencies, listed in chapter 1 – that are needed for a "rounded" EU civil servant.

> ### Key point
>
> The intermediate test provides a useful "second chance" in some competitions with a lot of candidates. But you still need to get a very good score in the pre-selection tests.

It is logistically impossible (and would in any case be prohibitively expensive) to invite thousands of candidates to an Assessment Centre, so the intermediate test is a filtering process, designed to let some of those who did well, but not quite well enough, in the pre-selection tests have a second chance. The e-tray exercise, like the pre-selection tests, is computer-based so is logistically practicable but it shifts the emphasis to real-world office skills, calling to some degree on the competencies that will be thoroughly measured at the human level at the Assessment Centre.

The general principle is that EPSO will invite to the intermediate test around 10 to 11 times the number of candidates sought for the reserve list. Thus, for example, of the 22,666 who applied for the 2018 AD5 graduate competition, 1639 were invited to take the intermediate test as compared with an intended reserve list of 158 successful candidates. Similarly, for the 2018 AD5 in the field of Audit, 803 of the 4755 candidates who applied for the competition were invited to the intermediate test as compared with an intended reserve list of 80.

Three important points should be noted about the intermediate test.

- Firstly, as the above figures show, although the intermediate test provides a useful second chance for those who might not be absolutely brilliant at, for example, numerical or abstract reasoning, the great majority of candidates in such competitions will nevertheless drop out at pre-selection. In other words, *you still need to get a very good score in the pre-selection tests* so cannot in any way ease back your preparation for those tests in the hope of "saving yourself" at the intermediate test.

- Secondly, once the intermediate test is reached, *your pre-selection scores are forgotten*. In other words, even if you had the maximum score on everything in the pre-selection tests, this will not help you if you do badly in the intermediate test.

- Thirdly, the intermediate test e-tray is, formally speaking, part of the Assessment Centre. This means that if you do get to the Assessment Centre proper, *your e-tray scores will be added to the scores you get in the Assessment Centre exercises* in evaluating how you do in the competencies of analysis and problem solving, delivering quality and results, prioritising and organising, and working with others. So, once again, you can't afford to do "just enough" – you must aim for the best score possible.

The e-tray exercise is covered in *The Ultimate EU Test Book Assessment Centre* edition.

Phase 4: Assessment Centre

Generic Assessment Centre Exercises

An Assessment Centre is used as the **second full round of exams** for Administrators (including linguists) and Assistants (but in most cases, the first round for specialists). At the Assessment Centre several trained observers called "assessors" evaluate your performance throughout half a day or a full day of exercises that have been developed specifically for this purpose. EPSO uses multiple types of exercises based on their competency framework: the idea is that each competency (listed in chapter 1, such as "Delivering quality and results") will be tested by two types of exercises to make sure that the observations are valid.

The core generic exercises currently used at the Assessment Centre for Administrators are:

1. The Case Study

2. The Group Exercise

3. The General Competency-based Interview

4. The Oral Presentation

The above exercises are generic in the sense that they test personal behaviours and qualities in ways which are relevant to the wide range of roles that candidates may be called on to undertake in the course of their career. For administrative reasons, the Case study may be done separately.

A new test of "EU motivation", basically evaluating your commitment to working for the EU was introduced for the 2018 generalist Administrator competition.

In addition to these "core" elements of assessment, for more specialised roles the competition will involve other tests focusing on specialised knowledge, as will be explained in the following section.

All about the Assessment Centre

The exercises used at the Assessment Centre and the competencies they measure are fully described in *The Ultimate EU Test Book Assessment Centre*, which is regularly updated.

These exercises are very different from the psychometric (reasoning) tests we focus on in this book. They are instead designed to test the "soft skills" like "working with others" needed to perform effectively as an EU civil servant.

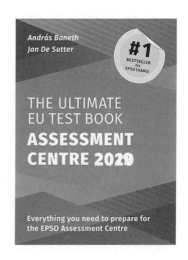

András Baneth
Jan De Sutter

#1 BESTSELLER for EPSO EXAMS!

THE ULTIMATE EU TEST BOOK
ASSESSMENT CENTRE 2029

Everything you need to prepare for the EPSO Assessment Centre

AD Professional Skills Tests

Candidates in linguist and specialist competitions face a double challenge. They have much the same range of reasoning tests and Assessment Centre exercises as generalists but are also intensively tested in their skills specific to the profile they are applying for.

Linguists' Skills Tests (Translators, Interpreters, Lawyer-Linguists)

Linguists are typically tested in their language skills in three phases, the pre-selection round, a second round of translation tests in an accredited EPSO centre, and then the Assessment Centre. But they also must tackle the other types of tests faced by all candidates. This means, for example, that however good at translating texts a translator might be, they will not get past the first pre-selection round of computer-based tests unless they achieve the necessary marks in their verbal, numerical and abstract reasoning tests. The pass marks may not seem particularly daunting per se (e.g. 4 out of 10 in numerical reasoning – see sample scoring in table on page 26) but it is not just a question of achieving the pass mark because only the "best X" number of candidates with the highest total marks will be invited to the next stage of translation tests. Beyond that, they will also be tested in their generic competencies at the Assessment Centre, so if their "soft skills" are unsatisfactory then, again, skill in translating texts will not save them. This underlines the importance for linguists of preparing "across the board", especially as language skills rather than the other tests may be their real strength.

> ### *Key point*
>
> It doesn't matter how good a translator you are if you can't pass the verbal, numerical and abstract reasoning tests.

Linguists need to offer 3 languages and the language requirement will be quite precise. For example, in the 2017 AD5 translators competitions, for the German-language translators your language 1 had to be the language of the competition (i.e. German), language 2 had to be either English or French and so too did language 3. In other words, the only 3 languages you could offer were English, French and German. If you were an Italian language candidate your language 1 had to be Italian, language 2 one of English, French or German and language 3 one of English, French or German. Similarly, for the 2016 AD7 lawyer-linguists competition your language 1 had to be one of the languages of the competition (in this case Spanish, Greek, Italian, Lithuanian, Maltese or Swedish), language 2 had to be English, and language 3 one of French, German, Italian, Polish or Spanish.

The most widely applicable combination of languages is native language (if not English or French) + English + French. The key is knowledge of the working languages. There is no point being able to offer half-a-dozen languages if they do not include at least one and usually two of the working languages.

For the 2017 AD5 translators competition at the pre-selection computer-based testing round candidates faced (as well as verbal, numerical and abstract reasoning in their language 1 – the language of the competition) tests in their two source languages (languages 2 and 3). Provided they achieved the pass mark in numerical reasoning, the numerical reasoning score was not added in to the calculation of their total score.

As the next phase, the translators faced translation tests from languages 2 and 3 into language 1 and again the "best X" were invited to the Assessment Centre where they took the competency exercises (oral presentation, competency-based interviews and group exercise, but no case study) in their language 2, the scores in those exercises then

---

Create your own competency passport!

You can carry out your own self assessment using the EPSO competencies at:

www.johnharperpublishing.co.uk/the-ultimate-eu-career-development-toolkit/

This tool kit will automatically generate your own personal competency passport. It's a great way to start your preparations for an Assessment Centre and is absolutely free to use.

---

being added together with those brought forward from the translation tests.

In the lawyer-linguists competition mentioned above, at the first round a language comprehension test was taken in language 2 and verbal, numerical and abstract reasoning tests in language 1. Those invited to the next round, the translation test, had to translate a legal text from language 2 into language 1. At the Assessment Centre, in addition to a general competency-based interview and group exercise in language 2, candidates had to summarise in language 1 a legal text in language 3 and do an oral presentation including their field-specific competencies (i.e. knowledge of EU law in particular) in their language 1.

Specialists' Tests

As noted previously, for specialists, the pre-selection verbal, numerical and abstract reasoning tests may be moved into the Assessment Centre stage, depending on the number of applicants.

As a general rule, EPSO says that if the number of specialist applicants (e.g. nuclear scientist, cohesion policy expert, competition lawyer etc.) exceeds X times the number of places available on the reserve list, it will organise a pre-selection round for them as well. If not, then these tests will be included in the assessment phase. The use of the Talent Screener means that in that case all those applying will not necessarily be called to any test at all. This is different to other Administrator competitions where the default rule is that every candidate who meets the formal eligibility criteria will be invited to take the pre-selection tests.

Specialist knowledge is tested in the assessment phase mainly in the form of a practical exercise, a special field-specific and targeted interview, and/or in the framework of the case study. This latter is closely related to the competition profile and the sub-profile or domain that the candidate chose at the time of application.

The importance of field-specific knowledge in specialist competitions is reflected in the fact that this may account for 55% (or even more in some cases) of the final score at Assessment Centre, as opposed to 45% for the "general" competencies.

Specialist knowledge is tested for all profiles, as no capable candidate who otherwise lacks the proper knowledge of the chosen field can be recruited, given EPSO's wish that all new officials should be operational from "day one". Moreover, even specialists need a solid understanding of EU institutions, procedures and stakeholders, which can add valuable points to your performance in the assessment phase of the exam. For instance, if you are familiar with the overall context of the EU's environmental policy, know which institutions and agencies are involved, which are the formal rules to enact policy in this field, which European associations and NGOs are taking an active part in influencing decision-makers and what the strategic thinking is on this policy's future, you are immediately in a position to make more out of the group exercise, the case study or the oral presentation than many other candidates who lack such knowledge would be able to do.

CAST Permanent Selection

Key point

CAST Permanent selections offer an alternative route to an Administrator type of job without being a permanent official. But you still have to pass the EPSO verbal, numerical and abstract reasoning tests.

So-called "CAST Permanent" selections ("Calls for expressions of interest") are organised by EPSO and attract many applicants as an alternative to the open competitions for permanent officials.

Contract Agents for Specific Tasks are divided into four "function groups" designated with Roman numerals, I to IV. **Function Group IV** is the highest. Function Group IV contract agents will include profiles such as administration/human resources, budgeting and financial planning, law, political affairs/EU policies, translators, and communication, which are very much classic Administrator tasks. CAST positions have in effect increasingly been used to cover roles which might otherwise have been taken by permanent officials: more than one-fifth of the European Commission staff are now contract agents.

Type 3(b) contract agents, found in the lager institutions, have contracts for fixed periods but with the advantage that they are usually eligible to take part in internal competitions for permanent posts, and internal competitions are generally easier than open ones. Thus a 3(b) contract agent post can potentially be a stepping stone to a job as an Administrator permanent official.

Type 3(a) contract agents, found for example in the executive agencies, have contracts that become indefinite on second renewal, providing job security. Although this type of contract does not give access to internal competitions, in practice long careers are possible for 3(a) contract agents.

In some respects the CAST Permanent procedures are very different from the competitions for permanent officials.

- There is **no planned number of successful candidates** to fill a more-or-less defined number of actual jobs. Instead this is a way for the institutions to have a reservoir of candidates they can call on from time to time as need arises. There is therefore no way at the time of applying to calculate your chances of succeeding.

- There is **no deadline for applications**; the whole process is very open-ended and you need to renew your application (to show you are still interested/available) every six months.

- Applying for a competition **does not mean you will actually be invited** to take any tests. Instead, only candidates short listed (pre-selected) by the recruiting service on the basis of information provided in applications will be invited, as and when vacancies arise. As there are often large numbers of applicants, this means you may never get to take any tests.

- **If you pass the EPSO tests, the recruiting service will then use its own selection procedure** to see if you are suitable for the post. If you pass the tests, the recruiting service is obliged to interview you. Once you have passed the EPSO tests you are available for further testing/recruitment by other services too, so you do not have to start the process all over again.

- The computer-based multiple-choice tests administered by EPSO are similar to the "regular" EPSO competitions. They include numerical, verbal and abstract reasoning tests (in your language 1) and a specific competency test for the profile and function group you have applied for (in your language 2). Languages 1 and 2 are defined as in the regular competitions. These tests are, however, **held on a rolling basis at intervals** (usually every one or two months) rather than in one window as with regular competitions. The recruiting service will not wait for you so if you are offered the chance to take the exam, you should do so as soon as possible.

The EPSO CAST tests are easier in the sense that your marks just produce a straight pass or fail – you do not have to be among a "best X" top slice of candidates, which is a big challenge in many regular competitions. For example, the pass marks in a currently still open CAST Permanent procedure, which started back in January 2017, are 10/20 in verbal reasoning and 10/20 in abstract and numerical reasoning combined. Thus you can afford to do rather poorly on abstract reasoning, say, as long as you can compensate for this in numerical reasoning, and you don't have to worry about the impact on your aggregate score. You also have to get a pass mark in your specific competency test (16/25 for FG IV).

> ### *Key point*
>
> In CAST Permanent competitions if you get a pass mark in the EPSO verbal, numerical and abstract reasoning tests it remains valid for 10 years. That is different from the regular open competitions each of which is a stand-alone.

If you pass the EPSO tests your scores are not taken into any further account (and remain valid if successful for 10 years for the numerical, verbal and abstract reasoning and 5 years for the competency test). It then becomes a question of whether you can pass any additional tests or interviews required by the recruiting service. It is also possible that if you fail the EPSO tests you will get a further chance to take them after 6 months, if the recruiting service liked your profile enough. In other words, all through the process the recruiting service is very much in the driving seat, to a far greater extent than in the regular open competitions.

Assessment of Heads of Unit

The assessment for Head of Unit and Director posts has traditionally been carried out via an Assessment Centre. Potential Heads of Unit should prepare along the same lines as Administrators, even though the competency model against which they are evaluated is somewhat different, having a strong focus on management-related issues. This means that questions testing the candidate's skills in variously managing people, time, teams, finance, operations and conflict feature prominently in the competency based interview and possibly impact other exam items such as the group exercise and the case study as well. Moreover, candidates for these exams are advised to be familiar with the EU Financial Regulations and general principles of handling budgets and funds. Besides the Assessment Centre, these candidates would also have normal interviews with the recruiting services as the second step in the procedure.

Assessment Report

After both the Assessment Centre and other forms of assessment, a report with a **competency passport** will be drawn up by the assessors to evaluate you against the preestablished competencies. This also means that first and foremost you will not be judged against other candidates but rather against the objective behavioural criteria

EPSO seeks in candidates. The ranking of suitable candidates will come afterwards and will be influenced by your performance in professional knowledge metrics.

Based on a streamlined and structured methodology, assessors draw up a report that summarises your performance, along with your strengths and weaknesses. EPSO provides this report to all candidates regardless of whether or not they were successful in the assessment phase. This report can add a lot to your self-development as it provides a comprehensive analysis of your personality traits as observed during the assessment. It can also be very helpful in deciding which of your skills or competencies may need to be developed.

Phase 5: Reserve List, Recruitment

For those candidates who successfully passed the Assessment Centre, a notification including the words "we are happy to inform you" arrives in their virtual EPSO account's mailbox. This also means that your name will be published in the reserve lists that appear in the EU's Official Journal and on EPSO's website (unless you opt out) and your competency passport, based on the above assessment, will be added to your profile once you take up employment. Those who did not succeed this time should not despair as they can re-apply for any later exam with the advantage of being familiar with the working methods of the system.

Validity of the Reserve List

Once a reserve list is published, it is always clearly indicated when it expires, meaning until which date you can be recruited from it. However, EPSO has in practice regularly extended the validity period of a reserve list to make sure that all available candidates are recruited from it.

The idea is to have the Administrator and Assistant competitions' reserve lists valid until the next annual cycle results in a new list; for linguists it is the same approach but instead of the next annual cycle, it will be the next competition in the same language that replaces the previous list; for specialists, the lists are valid for at least three years as long as they still contain recruitable (available) laureates.

Recruiter Portal

Once on the reserve list, candidates (or as they are called at this stage, "**laureates**") are available for recruitment by the institutions. The recruiter portal enables recruiters to generate multi criteria searches for candidates across the lists of available laureates. The recruiting services also have access to the competency passports of laureates. It is advisable to upload your CV into the portal to share more information about yourself.

Job Interview

When you pass an EPSO competition, EPSO will activate a "show vacancies" button in your account, which will allow you to see the available vacancies. Once on the reserve list, you can try to lobby for yourself by indicating your exam's reference number and presenting your CV to targeted Heads of Unit; this, however, is of mixed effectiveness: while it works for some, it may yield no result at all for others. Those candidates who are already working in one of the EU institutions (e.g. as a temporary agent) can also-have direct access to the internal vacancy list. Application to these posts is sometimes limited to "internal" candidates; however, sometimes "external" candidates are also considered if they meet the specific requirements of the post.

Finally, if you have a chance to make personal contacts, it can go a long way as you can make a good impression on a Head of Unit or demonstrate your abilities instead of depending on an impersonal message. Friday afternoons may be your best bet to manage to talk to or meet with a person in charge, but you may need to travel to Brussels at your own expense in the hope of effective networking. And if you know people in the institutions, personal recommendations can also be very useful.

Any time between a few weeks and several months, you may receive a phone call or e-mail asking whether you would be interested in an interview for a position at x or y EU institution. Always make sure your contact data is up-to-date and that you regularly check your EPSO profile as well in order not to miss such important events.

Once offered the chance to attend a job interview, it is highly recommended to participate even if the job itself may not be the most appealing. You can always decide to decline and wait for a better or different offer, but it is better to have such options than decline flatly in the first place and take a gamble. You can also gain useful interview experience and find out more about the position; you might even realise that the job is in fact meant for you.

The job interview itself is different from other parts of the selection competition as it is focused on your suitability for the specific position and it may only include some basic general EU questions. If you apply for a consumer health expert position, for example, you can expect a number of technical questions on this specific topic but nothing on e.g. the Treaty of Lisbon or the EU's immigration policy (unless the job in question is in the Commission's DG Home).

Your interviewers will most likely speak in English, French or German, unless you are applying for a translator or interpreter post where the rule is rather your second language (if different from the above three). Be aware, however, that questions may be put to you in any other language specified in your CV. Should you feel that you need to further clarify matters, take care not to patronise the interviewer and that your body language is also entirely respectful.

Travelling

You will most likely need to travel to Brussels or Luxembourg for the interview unless a video- or phone-conference call can be arranged at the EU representation or delegation office of your country of residence. Should you need to travel, all costs will be reimbursed and you will be given a modest daily subsistence allowance as well (based on strict formal conditions), but be prepared to receive the reimbursement only several weeks later.

Recruitment

If your interview was successful, you will be offered a job first by phone or e-mail, then formally by letter. Should this not arrive in time, make sure you ask your future EU institution's HR department or the unit in which you will work to send it to you.

A medical check is required of all new recruits. It takes place after a successful interview. Usually you will have received an "intention of offer" letter or email which will say that the service wishes to hire you, but this can be rescinded in the (rare) case of an unsuccessful medical check.

Generally you can agree on the starting date of employment with your future boss, so you can look for accommodation (if in Belgium, try *www.immoweb.be* or the

European Commission's Intranet also has a fine small ads section with real estate ads) and arrange paperwork in due course.

Moving costs are paid for unless you have lived in the country where you were recruited to for more than a certain period of time (e.g. if you had done an EU traineeship at the Commission in Brussels right before you got recruited, this may prevent you from having your moving costs paid, though the rule is generally six months of residence and for traineeships, the duration is five months). The detailed rules can be found in the EU officials' Staff Regulations.

Knowing Your Goals

Having bought this book shows that you are serious about starting an EU career. But it is still worth thinking on an ongoing basis about your goals. As well as working hard on the detail of the EPSO tests you face, you also need to make sure you are prepared to take a step back to *think strategically and long-term.*

The "holy grail" for most who seek a career in the EU administration is to become a permanent EU civil servant, an Administrator in one of the "core" EU institutions. It is this status that opens the widest opportunities, with the highest salaries and benefits, and opportunities for roles with great responsibilities and recognition. To achieve this goal, there is really only one *direct* route, and that is to pass an EPSO open competition. But even that route, though direct, is not really short: as we have seen above, from the time of submitting your application to getting on a reserve list can easily be 12 to 15 months, even if you pass your first competition, and then further months can go by before you actually get a job.

As always, the most direct route is not necessarily the easiest. The competition is fierce. This is especially so if you aspire to be a "generalist" Administrator. If you are looking for a more specialist role – and, of course, have the specialist skills – the competition may be a bit less intense, but it will still be considerable. If you take an open competition and pass it first time, you will have done well.

In practice many of those who do make it to become permanent EU civil servants are not starting from point zero. They have, rather, started in one of the many types of temporary or contract roles within the institutions and then proceeded by "stepping stones", sometimes taking an internal competition or an open competition where they benefit from the experience they have gained from working in the institutions.

There are plenty of people in the institutions who have "hopped" from one supposedly short-term stepping stone to another, never actually becoming permanent civil servants as such but in practice having many of the benefits and much of the security of permanent officials as their accumulated experience becomes increasingly valuable to the institutions that employ them. You can be sure that with the ever-increasing use of contract posts in the institutions, this sort of "semi-permanent" status will become ever more a feature, a sort of grey zone which is not exactly one thing or another.

You need therefore to consider your options carefully. Are you absolutely wedded to the idea of being a permanent civil servant? While the ideal, this is also the hardest goal to achieve. Might it make more sense to try in parallel to get a contract/temporary post? You will then be on the "inside", able to take advantage of opportunities that come along that are closed off to outsiders. There is absolutely nothing to prevent you from exploring multiple options simultaneously – indeed it is positively recommended. A CAST position might not be your ideal but there are many good jobs available in this category and it can also be a good springboard.

You will also need to think about where the jobs are. If you are aiming for a career in Brussels, you need to target career paths that will take you there. Bear in mind that most EU jobs do not involve working on top-level policy documents at the Berlaymont with EU Commissioners waiting in the wings. There are many back office roles which are essentially just the same as working in any large public administration. If you "want Brussels" you may need to explore many options before you get to where you want to be. That could well involve working in the "bubble" of NGOs, public affairs firms, consultancies, national and regional representations and media that surround the institutions.

Understanding how the system works and opportunities arise, the indirect "back routes" that most people do not know, the role of networking to be in the right place at the right time, and the need to always think strategically, are all of vital importance. Plenty of potentially excellent candidates never get the careers they are looking for because they do not understand this. This is a large and complex subject, and beyond the limits of this book. So do take the opportunity to read *Working for the EU: How to Get In* by Johannes de Berlaymont because it is packed with the information you need to help you with this.

Finally, bear in mind that, even if you decide at some point that the EU is not going to be where your career path takes you, the work you have done in preparing for and taking EPSO competitions will not be wasted. The EPSO tests are something of a "gold standard". Many big employers use tests with many similarities to those used by EPSO, so you will have a head's start in tackling them.

Our Top 10 Tips

Obviously there are many aspects to succeeding in an EPSO competition, and the importance of the different aspects can vary from one competition to another. However, we have picked out our "top 10 tips" – key things to keep in mind that apply to pretty much all competitions.

(1) **Think strategically and learn how the system works.** Are you taking the right competitions, can you get more experience that will help you, can you get a temporary position that will qualify you for internal competitions? Sometimes there is a back door as well as a front door. Read *Working for the EU: How to Get In* as soon as you can!

(2) **Don't hesitate to apply for multiple competitions,** if you are qualified for them. Each competition is independently organised and previous unsuccessful attempts, however many, don't count against you. You will also very likely get better at it the more competitions you take. Also consider becoming an EU trainee, available to 1200 people each year at the Commission, and several hundred options at the European Parliament, European Court of Justice and other institutions as well.

(3) **Try to calculate the odds, by reference to previous similar competitions.** By all means go for a competition which has very long odds, but if you can qualify for an "easier" competition, it makes sense to try for that instead or as well. And remember that if you pass a CAST competition, your numerical, verbal and abstract reasoning scores remain valid for 10 years.

(4) **Always read carefully the Notice of Competition.** Never assume you know what's in it because you have done a similar competition in the past – the rules can and do change, sometimes in big ways. Candidates can easily get confused about matters that are actually clearly spelled out in the Notice of Competition.

(5) **Observe the competition rules strictly.** The information you provide to EPSO must always be accurate so never make claims that are not true. Bear in mind that the deadlines are inflexible – and you need to be proactive in checking your EPSO account, because EPSO doesn't "chase" you.

(6) **Make sure you understand the scoring system for your competition.** Which elements require just a pass mark, which ones require you to be in the "best X"? Which elements are totalled and which are stand-alones? The rules vary from competition to competition and you need to understand which tests are most likely to be critical for you.

(7) **Never rely on just doing well in some tests** – you must prepare across the board because you will have to reach pass mark targets in everything even though some tests will carry more weight than others. But proceed one step at a time – for example, while it is worth knowing what the Assessment Centre exercises are at the outset, there is no point in preparing for them in detail if you are going to fail your pre-selection tests.

(8) **Practise as much as possible** with the aim of mastering the main techniques to make them instinctive. This will save you vital time under pressure because there is very little time for thinking in EPSO reasoning tests. This is especially relevant to numerical and abstract reasoning.

(9) **The best advice is usually to "get in" first.** If you succeed in becoming a laureate, you don't have to take the first job offer that comes along. You may have very good personal reasons for rejecting it. But remember that it is far easier to move on once you are already inside the system. And that second job offer may never come, or only come several months later when your personal situation may have already changed.

(10) **Finally, don't ever regard not succeeding in your EPSO competition as some sort of personal failure.** Not only are the mathematical odds very tough, you are up against ambitious and well prepared people from all over Europe. In most competitions a "second team" of candidates who just missed out could be selected who would be virtually as good as the "first team". The EU simply doesn't employ enough people to take in all the talent on offer. And remember, your experience with the EPSO system will also stand you in good stead to tackle the similar tests organised by many other employers.

3.   Verbal, Numerical and Abstract Reasoning Tests in EPSO Administrator Exams

Introduction

EPSO has, since its inception, used verbal reasoning and numerical reasoning tests in the pre-selection or admission phase of open competitions (while for some specialist profiles these are required in the assessment phase). Although such tests do not require specific knowledge, they have been dreaded by many candidates – and for good reason. From 2010 onwards, the so-called abstract reasoning test also became part of the pre-selection stage of the competitions.

When it comes to abstract, verbal and numerical reasoning tests (commonly referred to as "psychometric tests"), a number of questions arise:

- What exactly are these tests like?

- What do they measure?

- What is the concept behind their design?

- What is the rationale for their use?

- What are the factors determining success?

- How are these tests scored?

- And finally: how to prepare and practice for them?

An Overview of the Three Test Types

Each test type will be described in detail in the relevant upcoming chapters, but it is important to first get a sense of what these tests are like in general terms.

Format

All three test types, verbal, numerical and abstract reasoning, are in multiple-choice format. Based on EPSO's practice, all three "reasoning" tests have either four or five answer options for each question or text passage. In both cases, there is always only one correct answer and no penalty for wrong answers.

Verbal Reasoning

Verbal reasoning tests are designed to measure a candidate's ability to comprehend complex texts on various topics. These may vary from the description of an EU policy through current news, culture, history, or even natural sciences – in other words, the topic can be almost anything.

The length of the text is typically around 150 words and you are normally asked to decide which of four answer options is correct, based on the information in the text.

The answer options will then measure whether you:

- understood key concepts
- have the necessary vocabulary to comprehend a wide range of topics (believe it or not, this may be an issue in your native language as well)
- are able to deduce arguments from the text
- can accurately interpret key indicators (such as chronology, causality, quantities) in the text

For more information and practice tests, turn to chapters 4 and 5.

Numerical Reasoning

Numerical reasoning tests are designed to measure a candidate's ability to interpret data and numbers, with a special emphasis on the relationship between various data sets and on performing quick calculations based on intuitive insight. This means in practice that the focus is not on complex mathematics but on identifying how one can arrive at the correct answer in the most efficient way.

The data on which the test question is based is usually a table with several rows and columns. The rows usually indicate various groups (countries, age groups, regions, industries, and so on), while the columns often contain various metrics (GDP, average income, amount transported, percentages, and so on). Alternatively, the data can also be presented in the form of a chart or several charts (pie chart, bar chart, etc.), or any combination of the above-mentioned items.

The test question usually seeks either a figure ("200", "0.3", "45%", "1/5", etc.) or one of the groups in the data set ("France", "People aged between 15-64", "Europe", "Agriculture", etc.) as the answer.

By arriving at the answer in a timely manner, you can demonstrate your ability to:

- identify relevant data
- understand the relationship between various metrics
- determine the level of accuracy needed to answer the question
- perform quick mental calculations, and
- make fast but relatively accurate estimates

For more information and practice tests, turn to chapters 6, 7 and 8.

Abstract Reasoning

Abstract reasoning tests always involve geometric shapes. Although there are test types where the shapes are three-dimensional, EPSO has so far decided against using such tests and therefore candidates will only be given questions with two-dimensional objects.

The figures in the questions can be geometrical ones, such as circles, rectangles, triangles, lines, and combinations of these, but they can also be the simplified representations of real-life objects, for example bodies, faces, vehicles, animals, and so on. Another important aspect is to avoid any gender, nationality or other bias regarding candidates' abilities to solve them; EPSO (or, more precisely, the company that has created the tests) also makes sure that those with visual challenges are not being discriminated against either.

The tests are designed so that there is a linear relationship among the items in the set of illustrations included with the question. The figures in the test item form a series going from left to right and the test-taker is expected to select which of the five answer options would come next in the series.

Abstract reasoning tests measure your ability to:

• interpret abstract concepts that do not carry actual real-life meaning

• draw conclusions in new and unfamiliar scenarios

• discover relationships between seemingly unrelated concepts, and

• use your so-called "fluid intelligence" and apply it to any intellectual problem

For more information and practice tests, turn to chapters 9, 10 and 11.

Why these Tests are Used

When someone first looks at verbal or numerical reasoning test questions, and especially in the case of abstract reasoning, a thought that often comes to mind is *"How is this related to my potential performance as an Administrator in the European Commission?"* It is a fair question and one which deserves a good answer.

According to one approach, these tests are generic indicators of intelligence. Their results are standardized and are simply good predictors of performance in any work situation where intelligence, creativity and independent thinking is required. While this is certainly true, it is also easy to identify much more concrete work scenarios where the "skills" measured by these tests can actually be put to good use.

As mentioned above, **verbal reasoning** tests measure a general ability to interpret texts, regardless of the topic. One can easily imagine the wide array of topics, formats and styles an Administrator at the European Commission or the Committee of the Regions will be expected to read about and make sense of in the course of their career. One day you might be reading about some new internal procedures to follow, the next day you might be asked by your superior to skim through a report on the effects of the increasing price of fertilizers on the Latvian farmers' standard of living. Regardless of the topic, one thing is certain: you will need to be able to make sense of the text in a timely manner, draw the right conclusions, avoid common misunderstandings and eventually summarize your findings. Sounds familiar? Hopefully it does as this is exactly what you will be expected to do in the verbal reasoning test as well.

The same goes for the **numerical reasoning** tests. You might also be given a statistical report one day at work. It may contain a mind-numbingly large number of tables and charts, and although you are looking for one single figure or piece of data, it's just not in there. There may be a wealth of other (irrelevant) data, but not the bit you are looking for though you are expected to come up with an answer based on that report and nothing else. What you will need to do is sort through all the data, disregard everything you do not need and find a way to "extract" the useful information. This is exactly what you will do when taking the numerical reasoning tests.

When it comes to **abstract reasoning**, the above analogy will of course not work. Not even in an institution with as widespread responsibilities as the EU will you face a situation where you need to select a shape with four circles and one rectangle (as opposed to two rectangles) in order to get through the day! You do, however, stand a good chance of going to your office one Monday morning and facing a situation or being given a task that will be completely unfamiliar; it might be about something you have never even heard about. Situations like this are the ones where the above-mentioned "fluid intelligence", the ability to manage the "unfamiliar" and apply logic, patterns and common sense becomes useful and that is exactly what abstract reasoning tests measure, as proven by various psychological experiments.

The Factors Determining Success

Just as is the case with any other test, success and good performance in EPSO's pre-selection exam is determined by several factors. We will now briefly discuss the four most important ones:

- Motivation
- Educational background
- Habits and hobbies
- Preparation and practice (most important)

Motivation

EPSO's pre-selection exam is certainly an event that one must prepare for and set aside significant amounts of time for this purpose: expect to experience a lot of stress both in the process of preparing and in the exam itself. In short, it takes time and effort, and it is easy to be distracted or discouraged on the way. This is exactly why having a clear and strong motivation is so important.

One essential component of self-motivation is knowing why you are expected to carry out a given task and how you can benefit from the effort that must be dedicated to it. Even if performing well at these tests is just a means to an end, it is still much easier to put in the required effort if you have a clear sense of why you are expected to do them and understand their objective benefits, such as getting an EU job or performing much better in job tasks requiring psychometric skills.

The above section on how these test types can be related to actual work situations may be thought of as one component of the motivation needed to succeed – knowing why you are expected to do these tests at the exam rather than something else.

Motivation is also about setting clear and attainable goals. There is an acronym that nicely sums up this challenge: being SMART.

A SMART strategy is one that includes goals that are:

Specific – "I will practice X hours a day for X days a week in order to get the job I have always wanted. Each week I will do X number of tests and revise X previous tests. I will also start reading about EU affairs to familiarise myself with the institutions."

Measureable – "I will improve this or that much every week, and will be able to get X per cent at these tests by the time of the exam. I will do a benchmark test against which I can measure my progress."

Achievable – "I have never been particularly good with numbers so I will not try to score 100% at numerical reasoning, but I will make sure to score as much as possible above the 50% threshold and to make it up in the other test types."

Relevant – "I will do all of the above because my goal is to work in the Directorate General for Development of the European Commission. I would also like to get this job so I will have the financial means to pursue my long-time dream of visiting a friend in Australia. Even if I find these tests challenging or tedious at times, I understand that they are required for the exam and in any case I can improve my skills too."

Time-bound – "I will set aside this amount of time for the next X months to achieve this or that goal. I will have a clear timetable for the next two months where I indicate the days and hours I plan to spend on practicing. I will be able to stick to my schedule because I see the end of the tunnel."

Educational Background

Educational background is another important factor in success. In addition to the obvious fact that the quality of education one received can make a huge difference, there are various fields of study that provide a more relevant background for performing well at these tests than others. Mathematics or other disciplines that make use of logic and deduction may help in solving the test questions better under time pressure.

Obviously, your educational background is not something you can change at the time you decide to participate in an EPSO Administrator competition. If you have a more relevant background, so much the better – though if you do not, there is certainly no reason for despair either: there are numerous important factors in success, all of which you can improve significantly (see relevant tips below and in each consequent chapter).

Habits and Hobbies

Before turning to the "controllable" factors mentioned above, we must also mention that there are certain hobbies and activities that, if you are a fan of them, may provide some temporary advantage. When it comes to verbal, numerical and abstract reasoning, people who have done crossword puzzles, Sudoku and other mind games might be at some advantage.

Preparation and Practice

The factor, however, that is the single most important one is what this book is all about: *the quality and quantity of preparation and practice you complete in the run-up to the exam*.

In the following chapters, we will introduce in detail:

- the three test types and how they are designed
- the typical problems and challenges they pose
- the methods and skills that can greatly improve your performance
- the best ways to approach and interpret the test questions, and
- the optimal way to prepare and practice for these tests

With a clear grasp of the methods that can be used to efficiently take these tests and with the right amount of focused practice, powered by the correct motivation, even those candidates who feel that such tests are not their strong suit can improve significantly and pass this stage of the exam.

How these Tests are Scored

When you are preparing for the exam, you might often wonder exactly how well you are expected to perform in order to succeed. To answer this question, let us overview the marking system for these tests. The score candidates receive will have to satisfy two conditions:

Pass Mark – this is a simple "objective" barrier, usually 50% (but in some profiles, this is lowered to 40% for certain test types) that must be reached in each test separately, to be considered for the shortlist. It often happens, however, that for Administrator exams EPSO will set a pass mark for two or more tests combined (e.g. they will consider your numerical and abstract reasoning test scores as one and establish a 50% pass mark for the aggregate score of these two tests) – this is a somewhat easier situation because you can compensate for poorer performance in one test by excelling in the other one(s).

The Best X – this is a "relative" barrier, meaning that in addition to scoring higher than the objective pass mark, you must also be among a given number of best-performing candidates in all the tests combined. Some of the test results may be excluded from this relative barrier, meaning that numerical reasoning, for example, sometimes doesn't count toward your total score: all you need to do is achieve the pass mark.

Mixed Version –   EPSO may also use the "pass mark" approach to create a larger pool of potential candidates and then "sift in" a certain number whose qualifications or professional experience (in the case of "specialist" Administrator exams) match various objective, pre-determined criteria, though the "best X" may also be factored in the decision.

In Practice

- Although you can hope to compensate for your weakness in one test type by performing better in another and thus still reaching a relatively high overall score, this option is limited by the requirement to reach the pass mark in each test separately (except for the cases outlined above when two test types have a combined pass mark)

- A "good" score in the context of one group of candidates (e.g. those who sit exams for the human resources sub-profile) might be an insufficient score in another group (e.g. those who have chosen the financial management sub-profile) – so examples of "successful scores" from the past are not really relevant

The figure below shows what is known as a "bell curve". Although it is just an illustration and it is not based on statistics, it quite accurately shows the typical distribution of scores candidates get at such tests. As we can see, there are few candidates with very low scores and very high scores. Most of the candidates will get scores in a very narrow range, for example between 60% and 70%, or 70% and 80%.

If "successful" candidates are selected by the best X number of participants in the exam, you must certainly score higher than others. *Looking at the bell curve, it is easy to see that only a few percentage points of improvement can mean that you have beaten a large number of additional candidates!*

Why is this important? The way we must approach this information is that the goals you set when you start preparing and practicing for these tests do not have to be unrealistic or unattainable. Also, you can take comfort in the fact that every small improvement will make a huge difference at the exam and will improve your chances exponentially – all thanks to the bell curve.

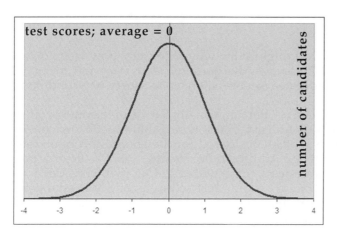

In the following chapters, we will see what the best methods and skills to achieve success are, accompanied by a large number of quality practice tests.

After all, the best way of learning things is by doing them a lot.

4. Succeeding in Verbal Reasoning Tests

In the world of standardized testing, the term "verbal reasoning" is commonly used to designate various test types relating to the interpretation and comprehension of texts. Although EPSO uses currently only one of these verbal reasoning test types, some of the models below measure skills that underlie the verbal reasoning tests EPSO uses to test candidates. It is therefore worth taking a quick look at each of them:

- **Spelling tests** are designed to test a person's ability to spell words correctly and also to differentiate between words with similar spellings yet completely or partially different meanings (for example, "steal" and "steel" or the correct spelling of "miscellaneous")
- **Word meaning tests** measure a person's vocabulary and their ability to select the best definition for words that have complex meanings (for example, to correctly identify the meaning of "exasperation" or "innuendo")
- **Word relationship tests** are designed to test a person's ability to determine the relationship between two concepts based on the analogy of another pair of concepts (for example, "what law is to anarchy, medicine is to …")
- **Comprehension tests** measure a person's ability to comprehend complex texts and determine whether statements about a text are correct, incorrect, or impossible to tell (this is the "classical" type used by EPSO)
- **Verbal deduction tests** are the most advanced form of verbal reasoning exercises – they measure the reader's ability to make correct and logical conclusions based on the information provided (for example, a text describing the mating habits of penguins followed by various questions such as "What are the right conditions for penguins to start mating?", "How do male penguins draw attention to themselves?" etc; this is a somewhat different approach from the "Which of the following statements is false?" question)

EPSO's verbal reasoning tests are closest in design to the comprehension test type. It is, however, easy to see how good performance in a comprehension test is based on the candidate's ability to identify correct spelling, the meaning of complex expressions and the relationship between various concepts. In this respect, this type of test is at the top in a hierarchy where success in comprehension depends on skills stemming from good performance on each of the lower levels.

In the following, we will overview several issues to look out for in a text, as well as a number of methods and skills that, once mastered, can greatly improve your performance. These include:

- How verbal reasoning tests are designed
- The role of familiar and unfamiliar topics
- Sources of information
- Assumptions
- Correct versus incorrect statements
- Near-equivalent versus identical statements
- Omission of information
- General versus particular
- Determiners and quantities

- Frequency
- Verbs: time and mode
- Causality versus chronology

We must mention here that a few of the methods and tips discussed in this chapter are discussed in the context of English-language test questions – this does not mean, however, that they cannot be applied in taking tests in other languages as well. In addition, the overwhelming majority of test-taking strategies discussed here are language-independent and are extremely useful in taking these tests in any language.

We will also discuss the best way to deal with each test question, the suggested order of reading the various components of the test (the text, the question and the answer options) and the recommended methods to practice for the test.

The sample test below is representative of the type of test questions EPSO currently uses as well as the expected level of difficulty at an EPSO competition. It consists of:

- A passage of text of between 100 and 200 words
- A standard question asking which of the supplied statements is correct or true
- Four statements as answer options, one being the right answer, i.e. the only correct statement

A Sample Test

Bacteria growing in near darkness use a previously unknown process for harvesting energy and producing oxygen from sunlight, a research team discovered. The discovery lays the foundation for further research aimed at improving plant growth and harvesting energy from the Sun.

"We have shown that some cyanobacteria, also called blue-green algae, can grow in far-red wavelengths of light, a range not seen well by most humans," said a researcher. "Most cyanobacteria can't 'see' this light either. But we have found a new subgroup that can absorb and use it, and we have discovered some of the surprising ways they manipulate their genes in order to grow using only these wavelengths," he said.

The experiments revealed that these cyanobacteria replace seventeen proteins in three major light-using complexes while also making new chlorophyll pigments that can capture the far-red light. The scientists also discovered that the organisms accomplish this feat by quickly turning on a large number of genes to modify cellular metabolism and simultaneously turning off a large number of other genes.
(*Science Daily*, 26 August 2014)

Which of the following statements is correct?

A. The mechanism by which some cyanobacteria capture far-red light may in the future be used to harness solar power.
B. Blue-green algae utilise far-red light by substituting three light-using proteins for chlorophyll pigments.
C. Some cyanobacteria cannot activate the genes necessary to absorb far-red light because they lack the necessary proteins.
D. The light-absorbing process described requires replacing 17 proteins but does not necessitate major genetic changes.

We will now consider the factors and methods listed above one by one. Before we do that, however, it is essential to gain some insight into how verbal reasoning tests are designed by their authors – if you understand the concepts and strategies behind the creation of verbal reasoning tests, taking those tests will become incomparably easier.

How are verbal reasoning tests designed?

When psychologists whose specialty is the creation of psychometric tests design verbal reasoning items, they essentially follow two design steps:

1. Selecting an appropriate piece of text.
2. Authoring appropriate answer options.

Let us see what considerations go into each of these two steps.

1. Selecting an appropriate piece of text

When selecting excerpts for a verbal reasoning text, several factors are considered, such as:

- Does the text include a good variety of verbs, nouns, adjectives, and so on?
- Is the difficulty of vocabulary appropriate for the purposes of the test (e.g. for assessing Assistant or Administrator candidates for an EU job?)
- Is the text free of jargon?
- Are abbreviations explained at least once in the text?
- Is the text free of topics that might be objectionable from a political, moral or ethical point of view?

The difficulty of the text and its vocabulary is a complex issue: suffice it to say that such things are considered as the length of the sentences (in number of words) or the length and complexity of the words themselves.

2. Authoring appropriate answer options

The creation of the answer options is the most difficult and most important task in the design of verbal reasoning tests. Let us overview what kind of answer options exist – being aware of the types of answer options that you might face will be highly useful in the EPSO pre-selection as well.

"Correct" or "True" statements: Such statements are clearly and demonstrably correct based on the information in the text. No outside knowledge is required to prove their correctness; it is possible to determine that on the basis of the excerpt and by drawing well-founded conclusions. Obviously, each verbal reasoning test item features only one such statement, and that statement will be the right answer. It is worth noting that the difficulty of the test item can be greatly influenced by how this statement is formulated:

- Does the right answer use similar expressions to those found in the text? The more similar the wording, the easier it is to spot that it is the correct statement.
- Is the right answer simply a reworded version of a statement in the passage, or is it a conclusion that can be drawn by utilizing several pieces of information from various parts of the excerpt?

"Incorrect" or "False" statements: Such statements are clearly and demonstrably incorrect based on the information in the text passage. It is important to point out that these statements are not simply unfounded (that is, no evidence exists as to whether they are correct or incorrect) but can be clearly disproved by utilizing information in the text. The difficulty of spotting such statements is, again, dependent on several factors:

- Is part of the statement correct? If so, it may be more difficult to realize that it is an incorrect statement, because only part of the information contained in it makes it so.
- Is the topic of the text expected to be familiar to test-takers? If so, it is much easier to decide a statement is incorrect, because most candidates will know it to be false and it will immediately "stand out".

You may now think that the above two statement types are all there is to verbal reasoning tests, but we will see very soon that there is one more statement type which makes the whole thing much more complicated. Nevertheless, we can already see that the degree of difficulty of test items that utilize only these two statement types can also vary greatly based on the factors listed above.

"Insufficient information" or "Cannot say" statements: This is the type of statement which usually causes the greatest confusion and represents the most dangerous trap when taking a verbal reasoning test. "Insufficient information" statements can belong to one of two categories:

- Statements that are *incorrect* if assessed using outside knowledge: such statements are easier to handle, because they will "feel" incorrect – you might know the statement to be incorrect based on your knowledge of facts, but it is impossible to classify the statement as incorrect based solely on information in the test passage. Fortunately, you are not expected to do that – just remember that **any statement which cannot be clearly proven by information in the excerpt is "incorrect"** in the context of a verbal reasoning test
- Statements that are *correct* if assessed using outside knowledge: such statements are the hardest to spot because they will "feel" correct upon first reading. The reason they are dangerous is exactly because you instinctively want to agree with the statement you know to be true. The important thing to remember here is that the **only correct statement in a verbal reasoning test is one that is fully supported and proven by information in the text passage**.

We can now easily realize that verbal reasoning tests can be designed using any mixture of the above statement types.

Here are a few:

- 1 true statement, 3 false statements: this is probably the easiest type, as true and false statements are easier to spot
- 1 true statement, 2 false statements, 1 "insufficient information" or "cannot say" statement: this test would be a bit harder, because in addition to the correct answer, one additional answer option might at first "feel" correct – remember the tips above and you will be able to easily avoid this trap
- 1 true statement, 3 "insufficient information" statements: this is the "crown jewel" of verbal reasoning tests – the most difficult type. This is because due to the nature of the statement types used, you might feel that *all four statements* are correct upon first reading, but, again, you can discard those with insufficient information by remembering the principles described above

Based on experience and consulting with occupational psychologists, the great majority of verbal reasoning test questions that you will encounter at an EPSO Administrator competition will feature at least one "insufficient information" statement and it is quite likely that you will face at least a few questions where three of the four answer options will be of this type. You should, however, be aware of the existence of the other combinations listed above as well – better safe than sorry, as the saying goes.

Let us now consider a concrete example and return to the sample test item above. Let us analyze the answer options based on the criteria we established.

A. The mechanism by which some cyanobacteria capture far-red light may in the future be used to harness solar power.

This is a true statement:

- the passage describes the way certain bacteria can absorb and use far-red light
- the passage states that this discovery lays the foundation for further research
- one of the future research areas mentioned is harvesting the energy of the sun
- we can draw the well-supported conclusion that the mechanism may in the future be used to harness the power of the sun

B. Blue-green algae utilise far-red light by substituting three light-using proteins for chlorophyll pigments.

This statement is false. Although all of the components of the statement have a basis in the text passage, things are completely mixed up. The number of proteins is 17, three is the number of light-using complexes. Also, chlorophyll pigments are not substituted, rather, new ones are grown. The only correct part of the statement is the one that states that it is blue-green algae that can utilise far-red light.

C. *Some cyanobacteria cannot activate the genes necessary to absorb far-red light because they lack the necessary proteins.*

This is a typical insufficient information type statement which is made even more difficult by the fact that the claim it makes feels logical and true.

- it is true that some cyanobacteria cannot use far-red light
- it seems logical that this may be caused by the necessary genes not being activated
- it also seems logical that this might be because the necessary proteins are missing

What we have to realise here is that we used several unfounded assumptions to arrive at this conclusion. In reality, we have no idea what causes some cyanobacteria not to be able to absorb far-red light, and we are not given enough information to make claims about what proteins are necessary to activate which genes.

D. *The light-absorbing process described requires replacing 17 proteins but does not necessitate major genetic changes.*

This statement is false. While it starts out making a correct claim (the process does require replacing 17 proteins), the last paragraph of the passage is in clear contradiction to the second part of the statement: it describes major genetic changes taking place in these bacteria and a large number of genes are activated and turned off to achieve this ability.

Now that we have analyzed the above four statements, we can see that our sample test item contains one true statement (the right answer), one "insufficient information" or "cannot say" statement, and two false statements. From a design perspective, the above test item is of medium difficulty, and the EPSO verbal reasoning test for Administrators will include items of comparable or greater difficulty.

Let us now turn our attention to the factors listed a few pages earlier – familiarity with such techniques as verb time and mode or generalizations will help you quickly determine which category each statement in a test belongs to, allowing you to find the correct answer in record time.

The Role of Familiar and Unfamiliar Topics

The topics of the texts in the verbal reasoning test can be varied. They may be closely EU-related (descriptions of policies, EU news) or they may be completely unrelated, dealing with history, art, nature, science and technology, music, and so on. Based on their interests or hobbies, most candidates have one or several preferred topics; however, the topic of the text should be completely irrelevant from the point of view of performing well in the test. While it is troubling to be faced with a topic that is completely alien to you, a familiar topic has its own dangers, because you must only use the information in the text, not your own knowledge.

Let us consider the pros and cons of familiar and unfamiliar topics.

As we can see, there is no significant argument either for or against wishing for familiar topics. Each has its distinct pitfalls and advantages.

As an example, if a candidate is very interested in space exploration and reads a text on a topic they know a lot about, for instance the New Horizons spacecraft launched to explore the solar system and beyond, it may seem a comfortable situation but may also backfire. Having a deep knowledge of a topic may make it hard to separate the information in the text from the information we already have about the subject – and, as we will see, it is one of the main mistakes test takers commit. In the above example, the candidate may, for instance, be aware that New Horizons initially travelled faster than any other space probe launched previously. This could lead the candidate to choose a statement about the spacecraft's speed as being correct when it is actually a "cannot say" statement because the speed is not mentioned in the text or any reference is ambiguous.

On the other hand, many candidates panic when faced with a text about a subject they have never been interested in. There may even be words and expressions that they have never even heard of. Yet it often happens that it is exactly the distance from the topic and "objectivity" that allows us to consider only the information in the text and select the right answer quickly and systematically.

Familiar Topic (space exploration)		Unfamiliar Topic (e.g. molecular biology)	
Pros	*Cons*	*Pros*	*Cons*
Mainstream vocabulary	*Bias*	*No bias*	*May be colloquial*
Familiarity	*Technical vocabulary*	*May be everyday topic*	*May include exotic vocabulary*
No colloquialisms	*Assumptions*	*No assumptions*	*Not familiar*

Sources of Information

When we discussed the familiarity of the subject, we touched upon the fact that it is crucial to always keep in mind what information we use when assessing whether statements in the answer options are correct.

Let us consider the following sentence from an imaginary verbal reasoning text passage: *"nearly one in five European adult males still smoke cigarettes on a daily basis"*.

Now let's look at a theoretical answer option where pre-existing knowledge could cause a problem: *"Almost 40 million European adult males still regularly smoke cigarettes."*

If the candidate happens to know that there are approximately 200 million adult males in Europe and uses that knowledge when taking the test, they might end up selecting the above answer option as correct – and lose a point, because the statement cannot be correct if the text does not contain information about the adult male population of Europe.

It is thus crucial to remember that statements in the answer options must be assessed based solely on the information in the text.

It can be particularly dangerous when a statement includes information of the sort that it may seem "everybody" knows, not just that is familiar to you because of your own specialist knowledge. Examples of this would be: "The German economy is bigger than that of Greece"; "the Olympic Games are held every four years"; "more of the Earth's surface is ocean than land". Be very alert to this risk. The test questions in the next chapter have many such examples.

Assumptions

In the previous example, we saw a situation where an assumption (regardless of whether true or false) was made about a statement based on "outside" knowledge. Let us consider another example.

"Performing specific physical exercises daily decreases the chances of developing certain movement-related difficulties in old age."

A possible answer option: *"Cycling for 30 minutes every day decreases the chances of developing rheumatism later."*

One might be tempted to select the above answer option as correct. If we do so, we make two assumptions:

1. Cycling is one of those specific physical exercises that are useful for such purposes.

2. Rheumatism is one of those movement-related difficulties that can be prevented in such a way.

Whether the above answer option is indeed the correct one depends entirely on what other information regarding the specific physical exercises and the types of movement-related difficulties is included in the text. For example, if there is no mention of cycling in the text, considering it as one of those exercises will be a false assumption which will cause us to lose a valuable point in the test. Also, it is merely our interpretation (assumption) that rheumatism is a movement-related difficulty that can be prevented this way – unless the text itself gives that information.

Correct versus Incorrect Statements

Although the verbal reasoning test in EPSO competitions almost exclusively includes items where the question is of the *"Which of the following statements is correct?"* type, it is important to mention another possibility – when the question is *"Which of the following statements is incorrect?"*.

The same principles that we discussed apply in this situation as well, but we will need to look for the false statement – that will be the right answer. It is also important to point out that if the question is seeking the incorrect statement, we can still encounter "insufficient information" statements – in this case, however, such statements will often be designed to "feel" incorrect – thereby leading you to think that they indeed are. Just remember: if you are expected to pick the incorrect answer option, look for a statement that can be clearly and unambiguously disproved based on the information in the text passage.

As a final point, it is worth mentioning something that may seem obvious, but must be noted. It is crucial to always carefully read the question (the one immediately after the text) and keep in mind whether you are supposed to look for the correct or incorrect statement. As simple as this may sound, many candidates have lost points in verbal reasoning tests by not taking the extra two seconds to read the question, especially under the stress and time pressure of the exam.

Near Equivalent versus Identical Statements

Consider the following example.

"Not many inventions last for more than a hundred years without major modifications. One of them is the barometer."

A possible answer option: *"Since it was invented, the barometer has not been modified."*

The statement in the answer option is very similar to the information in the excerpt. It uses many of the same words, and it essentially conveys a fairly similar meaning. Yet in the context of a verbal reasoning test, we cannot infer that "without major modifications" is equivalent to "has not been modified". The former implies *little* has been changed, the latter that *nothing* has been changed in the design of the barometer.

It is always dangerous to look for similar words and expressions in the answer option. Similarity can hide small but important differences in meaning and can prevent you from reading on and seriously considering other answer options among which the correct one can be found.

Another piece of advice is to always look for prefixes or adjectives that change the meaning or the scope of a statement, such as "some", "hardly", "almost", "not always", "any", "completely", "at all", "partially", "to some extent", "mostly", "generally", "exclusively", "sometimes", "largely", "arguably", "seemingly" and others (see more examples below).

Although since 2011 this problem has eased as you are now able to take the verbal reasoning test in your native (official EU) language, it is still worth taking some time to think about words and expressions in your own language that slightly modify the meaning of the sentence in which they are included. This is especially true because we use our native language much less consciously than a second language and slight shifts in meaning are often overlooked in everyday speech.

Omission of Information

Here is an excerpt from another text:

"Shakespeare's plays are still well-liked by audiences. In 2010, almost 100 countries had theatres where a Shakespeare play was in the programme and tickets to these productions were sold to nearly 15 million people."

A possible answer option: *"There are still theatres that stage Shakespeare productions."*

Note that this answer option has a completely different approach than the excerpt from the text. Having read the text, readers might be inclined to look for answer options that emphasize how well-liked Shakespeare's plays still are. Our example answer option does not do that, it simply states that Shakespeare productions are still being staged in an unspecified number of theatres.

At first reading, the statement in the answer option seems to be in conflict with the excerpt by not conveying the popularity of these plays. Yet it is a perfectly valid and correct statement.

We must, then, remember that the fact that a statement fails to convey all the information that was included in the text about something does not mean that it is an incorrect statement. In short and all other factors being equal, omission of information is not necessarily disagreement or contradiction.

General versus Particular

Another typical mistake many candidates make has to do with the difference between general categories and particular instances. This mistake can take one of two forms:

• Generalisation
• Over-specification

Let us consider an example.

"The oceanic climate is one of the wettest ones in the world. Average precipitation is significantly higher than in continental habitats. Some areas of the Atlantic Ocean do not go a full week without rain for decades."

A possible answer option: *"Oceanic areas do not have completely dry weeks for decades."*

The above statement is an example of a generalisation where a statement made about certain instances of a category (in this case, Atlantic areas) is assumed to be correct about the entire category (that is, all oceanic climate areas).

Let us consider another example.

"Some oceanic areas have wetter winters and springs while others experience more rainfall in the summer and autumn."

A possible answer option: *"The amount of rainfall in oceanic areas differs by season, depending on the geographical location."*

The above answer option is correct in stating that the amount of rainfall differs by season, but it is overly specific in stating that this depends on the geographical location – this is unfounded information not included in the text.

Determiners and Quantities

We now come to more language-specific problems. While most of the points raised so far are valid in all languages the test is administered in, there are always language-specific issues to consider. If the test is administered in English these tips will be directly useful to your preparation.

If you take your test in another language, the following few sections can serve as a guideline along which you can consider the peculiarities of your own language and come up with a list of things to look out for. A good way of doing this is to read newspaper articles with higher than usual attention – professional journalists are always careful about how they formulate their statements and use many of the linguistic devices demonstrated here to make their statements more accurate.

Determiners and words expressing certain or uncertain quantities can be hard to notice; many candidates tend not to attribute much meaning to them in everyday situations even though they may greatly alter the meaning of a statement in the context of a verbal reasoning test.

Be mindful of the exact meaning of some of the most common determiners:

- "the" usually signifies one concrete object or person, or one concrete group: "the apple","the fruit", "the pencils [on the table]", and so on.
- "a/an" and nouns without any determiner usually refer to one unspecified object or person, or an unspecified group of objects or persons: "an apple", "a fruit", "people in the United Kingdom", and so on.

When the answer option lacks the determiner found in the text or features a different one, we must always be suspicious and consider whether this distinction changes the meaning of the statement.

A similar pattern can be observed when it comes to quantities: "some", "many", "several", "a number of" refer to an unspecified number of objects of persons. "All", "the entire", "every", and "each" signifies that the statement is about every single member of a group, or an object in its entirety, without exception.

It is important to bear in mind that these determiners of quantity are not interchangeable and if the text mentions "many countries", an answer option that extends that claim to "all countries" will not be correct.

Frequency

A very similar situation can be created by the use of adverbs signifying the frequency at which an action takes place. Always pay special attention to the use of the adverbs "sometimes", "often", "usually", "frequently", "never", "hardly ever", "occasionally", "always" and so on.

Although the only two concrete indicators are "never" and "always", and it is very hard to define the difference between "sometimes" and "occasionally", we must be mindful of the fact that they do carry meaning and can significantly change the meaning of a statement.

The same also can be said about adjectives and adverbs expressing chronology:

- "before", "previously", "earlier", "prior to that" are hints that one event took place sooner than another one
- "meanwhile", "concurrently", "simultaneously", and others indicate that two events occured at the same time

- "after", "subsequently", "followed by", "later", and similar words help us establish that one event followed another event in time

Think of the following statements: "I occasionally go to work after eating breakfast" and "I sometimes eat breakfast after going to work". The implied sequence of actions and their frequencies are very different. Another example is "Birds have colourful feathers" versus "Some birds have colourful feathers": the scope and extent are very different.

Verbs: Time and Mode

Closely related to the previous point, the tense of verbs also plays a crucial role in re-creating a series of events. Take an example:

"Until his brother successfully launching his internet startup, Gerorge was the richest member of the family thanks to his burgeoning career as a successful attorney."

A possible answer option: *"George is the richest member of the family."*

The above option is incorrect because according to the text, he had been the richest member of the family only until his brother successfully launched his internet startup. This fact is indicated by the use of the expression "until" and also the past tense.

Verb mode also plays an important part in determining whether a statement is correct:

- Probability – "would happen" does not necessarily mean that something "will happen"; "would have happened" commonly means that the event did not in fact happen at all
- "Could happen" indicates that a certain event is only one of several possible outcomes
- "Should do something" indicates that a certain course of action is recommended or likely, but not necessarily unavoidable or mandatory
- "About to happen" shows that an event was going to take place but may or may not have actually happened
- "Was about to" (e.g. "he was about to go home when") refers to an intention or plan that was likely to take place when a certain event interrupted it or took place

Causality versus Chronology

As a last point, we must mention two phenomena that are frequently confused. Let us look at an example.

"The San Francisco Zoo has been visited by record numbers of visitors ever since 2005. In 2012, it received a gold medal from the World Zoological Society."

A possible answer option: *"Record numbers of visitors go to see the San Francisco Zoo every year, which resulted in it receiving the Gold Medal from the World Zoological Society."*

The statement in the above answer option incorrectly makes the assumption that there is a cause-and-effect relationship between the record number of visitors to the zoo in recent years and the receipt of the gold medal. As far as the statement goes, the relationship between the two things is merely chronological. There is no evidence that the gold medal was awarded because of the high number of visitors: it could just as well wave been given as a commendation for good animal keeping conditions or other factors, we simply do not know.

It is easy to mistake a merely chronological relationship for a cause-and-effect one, but one thing that will help decide is the verbal clues mentioned above. Since test-makers tend not to include ambiguous information in tests, we can always count on indicators of a cause-and-effect relationship ("led to", "consequently", "resulted in") or a mere chronological relationship to appear in the text.

Methods for Approaching the Test Questions

Let us return to our sample text:

> Bacteria growing in near darkness use a previously unknown process for harvesting energy and producing oxygen from sunlight, a research team discovered. The discovery lays the foundation for further research aimed at improving plant growth and harvesting energy from the Sun.
>
> "We have shown that some cyanobacteria, also called blue-green algae, can grow in far-red wavelengths of light, a range not seen well by most humans," said a researcher. "Most cyanobacteria can't 'see' this light either. But we have found a new subgroup that can absorb and use it, and we have discovered some of the surprising ways they manipulate their genes in order to grow using only these wavelengths," he said.
>
> The experiments revealed that these cyanobacteria replace seventeen proteins in three major light-using complexes while also making new chlorophyll pigments that can capture the far-red light. The scientists also discovered that the organisms accomplish this feat by quickly turning on a large number of genes to modify cellular metabolism and simultaneously turning off a large number of other genes.
> (*Science Daily*, 26 August 2014)
>
> *Which of the following statements is correct?*
> A. The mechanism by which some cyanobacteria capture far-red light may in the future be used to harness solar power.
> B. Blue-green algae utilise far-red light by substituting three light-using proteins for chlorophyll pigments.
> C. Some cyanobacteria cannot activate the genes necessary to absorb far-red light because they lack the necessary proteins.
> D. The light-absorbing process described requires replacing 17 proteins but does not necessitate major genetic changes.

When somebody first looks at a verbal reasoning test like the one above, the natural instinct is to start reading the text, then read the question, and finally read the four answer options. If we wish to consider all the factors we discussed in this chapter and make mental "notes" of them by underlining the key expressions in the text using the above method, it would look like this:

> Bacteria growing in <u>near</u> darkness use a <u>previously</u> unknown process for harvesting energy and producing oxygen from sunlight, a research team discovered. The discovery lays the foundation for <u>further</u> research aimed at improving plant growth and harvesting energy from the Sun.
>
> "We have shown that <u>some</u> cyanobacteria, also called blue-green algae, <u>can</u> grow in far-red wavelengths of light, a range not seen <u>well</u> by most humans," said a researcher. "Most cyanobacteria can't 'see' this light either. But we have found a <u>new</u> subgroup that <u>can</u> absorb and use it, and we have discovered <u>some</u> of the surprising ways they manipulate their genes in order to grow using <u>only</u> these wavelengths," he said.
>
> The experiments revealed that these cyanobacteria replace <u>seventeen</u> proteins in <u>three major</u> light-using complexes <u>while</u> also making new chlorophyll pigments that can capture the far-red light. The scientists also discovered that the organisms accomplish this feat by <u>quickly</u> turning on a <u>large number</u> of genes to modify cellular metabolism and simultaneously turning off a <u>large number</u> of other genes.

Which of the following statements is correct?

A. The mechanism by which some cyanobacteria capture far-red light <u>may in the future</u> be used to harness solar power.
B. Blue-green algae utilise far-red light by substituting <u>three</u> light-using proteins for chlorophyll pigments.
C. <u>Some</u> cyanobacteria cannot activate the genes necessary to absorb far-red light <u>because</u> they lack the necessary proteins.
D. The light-absorbing process described requires replacing 17 proteins but does <u>not</u> necessitate <u>major</u> genetic changes.

The underlined expressions are "suspect phrases" because of the various factors we discussed.

But what if most of the factors that we concentrated on when reading the text for the first time later turn out to be completely irrelevant because the answer options do not relate to those bits of the text? In order to avoid wasting time on irrelevant information, it is a good idea to read the question and the answer options first, looking for keywords and key concepts, and then read the text, already focusing on and searching for those bits that we know we need to answer the question.

Our mental notes using this recommended method would therefore look like this:

Bacteria growing in near darkness use a previously unknown process for harvesting energy and producing oxygen from sunlight, a research team discovered. The discovery lays the foundation for further research aimed at improving plant growth and harvesting energy from the Sun.

"We have shown that some cyanobacteria, also called blue-green algae, can grow in far-red wavelengths of light, a range not seen well by most humans," said a researcher. "Most cyanobacteria can't 'see' this light either. But we have found a new subgroup that can absorb and use it, and we have discovered some of the surprising ways they manipulate their genes in order to grow using only these wavelengths," he said.

The experiments revealed that these cyanobacteria replace seventeen proteins in three major light-using complexes while also making new chlorophyll pigments that can capture the far-red light. The scientists also discovered that the organisms accomplish this feat by quickly turning on a large number of genes to modify cellular metabolism and simultaneously turning off a large number of other genes.

Using this method, we can immediately discard option B when we read that chlorophyll pigments are not substituted, but capture far-red light. Option D can be discarded when we read that significant genetic changes take place to allow for the absorption of far-red light. Option C is a bit trickier, but when we realise that the text passage does not actually explain why certain cyanobacteria can not absorb far-red light, the entire explanation given in the statement becomes an unfounded assumption and we can discard that quickly as well.

Let us summarize the above method in a few points:

1. Read the question first – are we looking for the correct or incorrect statement?
2. Read the answer options and make a mental note of the important keywords and themes included in those statements.
3. Read the text by focusing on the themes and keywords you made a mental note of when reading the answer options.
4. If you encounter a statement in the text that is clearly in agreement with an answer option (or in clear disagreement, if you are looking for the incorrect statement), and you are sure about your assessment, you can even stop reading and move on, thereby saving precious time.
5. If you are not sure about your assessment, you can continue reading and then eliminate the answer options one by one. This is where your knowledge of the possible statement types (true, false, insufficient information) will prove extremely useful – if you apply this knowledge right, and factor in the methods we discussed in this chapter, no amount of "witchcraft" on the part of the test item's author will confuse you.

Practice Methods

As a last point, it might be useful to make a few suggestions as to what the best methods are for preparing for the verbal reasoning test.

- Start practicing by taking your time, reading all kinds of high level English texts, making mental notes of the "suspect phrases" we covered in this chapter
- Continue by doing the same, this time with the actual test questions in this book (for

the sake of practicing, you may wish to underline or outline these concepts and also write down in your own words why a certain answer option is wrong)
- Once you have established the necessary routine in identifying the key phrases and concepts, you can start timing yourself – begin by simply measuring how much time it takes for you to answer one test question
- Check how much time you will have at the exam, and how many questions you will need to answer (**as a general rule, you will have 35 minutes for 20 questions**).
- Start decreasing the amount of time you let yourself use for answering one question – ideally, by the time of the exam, you should be able to answer more questions in the given time than required in the exam (this is necessary because you cannot re-create the stress of the exam, which can decrease performance, not to mention the slower pace when reading texts on a computer screen for the pre-selection exams)
- Try to re-create as much of the atmosphere and infrastructure of the exam as you can – do not interrupt the test, go to a quiet place, use an alarm clock, and so on
- If you have access to such a service, practice tests online, e.g. the *www.eutraining.eu* site – since the EPSO exam will also be computer-based, and it is a good idea to get used to the "interface" before going to the exam. Most such websites also offer the opportunity to revise the practice tests you took and look at detailed statistics, comparing your performance to others and measuring your improvement in a test type over time – experience shows that such statistics can have an extremely positive psychological effect as well as help to reveal the weaknesses and strengths of your skills in various tests.
- Try to read as much as possible on screen and measure the time it takes to read texts of comparable length (e.g. one page copied into Word) so you can measure and improve your performance.

For advice and tips on tackling verbal reasoning questions – see the previous chapter.

For the answers to this test – see at end of questions.

5.   Verbal Reasoning Test

150 QUESTIONS – ANSWERS follow questions

In each question below, you have to decide which of 4 statements, A, B, C or D is correct, based on the preceding passage of text.

The is only one correct answer to each question, *which is "True" in terms of the information given in the text: The other statements will either be "False" or "Cannot say" from the information given in the text. Each question must be considered without any other knowledge you may have of the subject matter – **only information included in the passage itself may be used** in deciding your answer.*

For practice purposes, you should try to complete 20 questions in 35 minutes.

1.   In the 1960s, the U.S. started vaccinating kids for measles. As expected, children stopped getting measles. But something else happened. Childhood deaths from all infectious diseases plummeted. Scientists saw the same phenomenon when the vaccine was introduced elsewhere around the world. Now there's an obvious answer to the mystery: children who get the measles vaccine are probably more likely to get better healthcare in general. But Michael Mina and his colleagues have found there's more going on than that simple answer. "We found measles predisposes children to all other infectious diseases for up to a few years," Mina says. Like many viruses, measles is known to suppress the immune system for a few weeks after an infection. But previous studies in monkeys have suggested that measles takes this suppression to a whole new level: it erases immune protection to other diseases. (*National Public Radio*)

A.   Children who catch measles will also catch other diseases.

B.   Children who received the measles vaccine receive better healthcare overall.

C.   Scientists have found evidence that measles may reduce immunity to other diseases.

D.   While studies have found what measles did to monkeys, the same cannot be said for humans.

2.   How can cheese be aged so long, but when it's in the refrigerator for longer than a few weeks it goes mouldy? Aged cheese wheels have something called a "rind." Rinds are most obvious on a cheese like brie. Some cheeses are also waxed on the outside (think gouda.) It's basically an outer dehydrated shell that is maintained by the cheesemakers, and either one certain type of edible mould is allowed to flourish on it (like brie,) or it is wiped with saline regularly to keep mould from growing on it (cheddar). Once you penetrate the rind (slice the cheese into blocks) and stop maintenance, the "inner" non-dehydrated cheese is susceptible to mould it picks up from the environment. (*Reddit*)

A.   Once untreated cheese is exposed to the environment it will eventually go bad.

B.   It makes no difference to how long a cheese lasts if the outer layer of mould on cheese is edible or not.

C.   The mouldy rind found on cheddar is the most effective for preserving its cheese.

D.   Cheese only expires in a refrigerator once its rind has been breached.

3.   Acute kidney injury (AKI) is where your kidneys suddenly stop working properly. It can range from minor loss of kidney function to complete kidney failure. AKI normally happens as a complication of another serious illness. It's not the result of a physical blow to the kidneys, as the name might suggest. This type of kidney damage is usually seen in older people who are unwell with other conditions and the kidneys are also affected. It's essential that AKI is detected early and treated promptly. Without quick treatment, abnormal levels of salts and chemicals can build up in the body, which affects the ability of other organs to work properly. If the kidneys shut down completely, this may require temporary support from a dialysis machine, or lead to death. (*National Health Service*)

A.   Acute kidney injury is widely believed to be the result of a physical blow to the kidneys.

B.   Acute kidney injury is limited to older people who have other health conditions.

C.   Without dialysis, acute kidney injury may lead to death.

D.   It cannot be said that acute kidney injury means that your kidneys stop working.

4.   Individuals with high levels of psychopathy, narcissism, and Machiavellianism — known as the "dark triad" of personality traits — do not appear to have an impaired ability to empathize, according to new research. But these individuals are not inclined to use this ability. "Sometimes psychopaths (people with dark traits) are understood as callous persons, not being able to empathize with others, while at other times they are understood as fully functional in that regard, but just don't care," said Petri Kajonius. "We wanted to find out what the data in a HR-community sample, purposed to be in tune with personnel, would say?" The study of 278 participants found that dark personality traits were negatively related to the disposition to empathize, but had no relationship with the ability to empathize. "The results show that overwhelmingly, HR-people with dark traits, are not lacking the ability to empathize, but score low in their dispositions to do so," Kajonius told PsyPost. (*psypost.org*)

A.   The study used HR people because of the higher rates of the dark triad found among them.

B.   Human resources professionals who can empathise can be psychopaths.

C.   People who do not care for others' feelings are for the most part those who are unable to empathise.

D.   Researchers discovered that many people with the dark triad behaved in an empathetic way.

5.   The Assyrian empire was built during a time of heavy precipitation and successful harvests. But now we can tell, from climate records, that the civilization experienced a series of megadroughts that likely triggered the collapse of the empire—weakening agriculture and amplifying conflict. The impact of drought in this region was dependent on where the Assyrians were located in northern Iraq. The Tigris River is so deeply cut into the surrounding soil that you can't do large scale-irrigation there. That's why rainfall was so crucial to their lives. The Assyrians were much more vulnerable to

the impacts of prolonged and severe drought than people downriver. (*colorado.edu*)

A. The Assyrians by the Tigris lacked the irrigation skills of the Egyptians by the Nile.

B. Geological features cannot be said to exacerbate or diminish the impact of climatic changes.

C. It is possible that the Assyrian Empire rose during a climatological anomaly.

D. Had the Assyrians built their empire further downriver it would not have fallen when it did.

6. Patricia Goodhines and colleagues at Syracuse University examined how 83 university students' sleep was affected on days when they did and didn't take marijuana over a two-week period. Each day, the students filled in questionnaires asking how often they had used marijuana or alcohol the previous day, and their reasons for taking the drug. Participants also rated the quality and duration of their sleep that night, and how fatigued they felt during the day. The team found that 29 of the students used cannabis specifically as a sleep aid on at least one night of the 14-day study period. Using the drug was related to longer duration of sleep and less time spent awake during the night, suggesting that there are some elements of sleep that cannabis may improve. But importantly, the drug didn't help participants get to sleep any faster or improve their perceived quality of sleep – and worse, it actually increased their levels of fatigue the following day. (*British Psychological Society*)

A. The study found marijuana to be an effective aid for falling asleep.

B. Marijuana was found to be an effective aid for keeping a person asleep.

C. Only a minority of participants felt more fatigued the day after smoking marijuana.

D. Marijuana was found to be a more effective sleeping aid than alcohol.

7. Drinking red wine may be better for your microbiome than drinking other types of alcohol, according to a study of 3,000 people. Caroline Le Roy and colleagues at King's College London found that red wine

drinkers had a greater diversity of bacteria living in their guts, compared to people who drank beer, cider, white wine or spirits. The team found that this held true even when the age, wealth, diet and socioeconomic status of the participants were taken into account. The team think red wine drinkers may have more of a mix of microbes than other drinkers because of polyphenols, defence chemicals in red wine that act as antioxidants. The findings may partly explain why red wine is linked to heart health, says Le Roy. Drinking red wine rarely, such as once every two weeks, seemed to be enough to observe an effect on gut microbiota, she says. (*New Scientist*)

A. Drinking alcohol will make a positive impact on a person's gut bacteria.

B. Drinking wine more frequently than once every two weeks will enhance its effects.

C. Drinking wine in and of itself was not found to be beneficial for gut bacteria.

D. Drinking red wine will improve your health.

8. Little is known about the difficulties experienced by those with high intelligence. Specifically, those with a high intellectual capacity (hyper brain) possess overexcitabilities in various domains that may predispose them to certain psychological disorders as well as physiological conditions involving elevated sensory, and altered immune and inflammatory responses (hyper body). A study surveyed members of American Mensa in order to explore psychoneuroimmunological (PNI) processes among those at or above the 98th percentile of intelligence. Participants were asked to self-report prevalence of both diagnosed and/or suspected mood and anxiety disorders, attention deficit hyperactivity disorder (ADHD), autism spectrum disorder (ASD), and physiological diseases that include environmental and food allergies, asthma, and autoimmune disease. High statistical significance and a remarkably high relative risk ratio of diagnoses for all examined conditions were confirmed among the Mensa group when compared to the national average. (*Science Direct*)

A. The Mensa study found that people with above average intelligence have more psychological disorders.

B. Being highly intelligent appears to make

people inclined to have certain mental health issues.

C.   Highly intelligent people appear to have higher rates of nut allergies.

D.   People who had average intelligence were found to have below average rates of these conditions.

9.   Patients were 390 percent more likely to say their pain was well-controlled when the person taking their blood was courteous, according to a new study. "It's not surprising that a courteous healthcare provider can improve the patient experience, but we were shocked at just how powerful that factor was," said lead author Mario Moric. "We thought the more needle sticks, the higher the pain perception, but we found that effect was small. It turns out the experience of pain is much more significantly affected by the attitude of the people treating you," Moric said. Patients were asked about the pain they experienced while having blood taken and about the courtesy of the people who took the blood samples. The results showed that pain was significantly lower when the healthcare worker taking blood was courteous – for example, asking about patients' previous experiences with needles and taking their preferences into account. (*UPI*)

A.   Sometimes drawing blood is painless.

B.   Being pricked with a needle twice can be less painful than being pricked once.

C.   Courteous people drawing blood reduced the amount of pain by 390 percent.

D.   Asking about previous experiences with needles is the best way to reduce pain levels.

10.   Previous research has found that people born in January were 13 percent more likely to develop schizophrenia and at 17 percent greater risk of bipolar affective disorder. Scientists have been puzzled about the finding, with some suggestions that a lack of Vitamin D from sunlight could be driving the higher incidence. But now researchers at the University of Cardiff have discovered that mothers who gave birth in autumn or winter had 20 percent more cortisol – the stress hormone – in their saliva than those who gave birth in the spring or summer. Professor Ros John said:

"As higher levels of cortisol in pregnant women have previously been associated with a higher risk of children developing mental health disorders, the new findings could explain why these disorders are more common in people born during the winter months. (*The Telegraph*)

A.   The lack of Vitamin D from sunlight has been shown not to cause depression in winter babies.

B.   Women have higher stress levels in winter due to a lower level of sunlight at that time.

C.   A woman's stress levels during late pregnancy may influence psychological risks in her children.

D.   Children born in January are the most likely to develop mental health disorders.

11.   A study by Cancer Research UK reveals that while the number of people smoking has fallen by 15 percent since 2011, the total number of cigarettes smoked has dropped by 24 percent. Around 14.7 percent of UK adults smoke, down from 20.2 percent in 2011, official figures show. And the new research shows that the average smoker now has 10.6 cigarettes a day – down from 12.4 a day in 2011. It comes in the wake of the ban in smoking indoors in 2007, and the ban on billboards and print adverts four years earlier. Meanwhile, the number of adults vaping has risen by 70 percent in just two years, with one in four children trying e-cigarettes. Public Health England say vaping is now the most popular and effective way for smokers to quit. (*The Telegraph*)

A.   Vaping is the main reason for the fall in the number of smokers.

B.   There is reason to believe that the indoor smoking ban had a knock-on effect.

C.   It cannot be said that today's smokers are lighter smokers than those of yesterday.

D.   Soon more adults will be vaping than smoking cigarettes.

12.   A study of 352 Olympic and professional athletes found high rates of dental problems, even though they brushed their teeth on average twice a day. Researchers believe the relentless intake of sports drinks, energy gels and bars are to blame, due to their high sugar content. Intensive exercise may also prompt

changes in saliva and the immune system that further exacerbates the damage. Published in the British Dental Journal, the study found that 49.1 per cent had untreated tooth decay, with a large majority showing early signs of gum inflammation. Dr Julie Gallagher said: "We found that a majority of athletes in our survey already have good oral health related habits in as much as they brush their teeth twice a day, visit the dentist regularly, don't smoke and have a healthy general diet. However, they use sports drinks, energy gels and bars frequently during training and competition." (*The Telegraph*)

A.   Brushing your teeth on average twice a day can be insufficient to prevent tooth decay.

B.   The changes to saliva prompted by intensive exercise is what primarily causes tooth decay.

C.   Non-British athletes were not found to have as high rates of dental problems.

D.   Sports drinks and energy gels and bars were found to produce bad oral health in athletes.

13.   Fasting every other day could be the secret to losing weight while staying healthy because it mimics humans' caveman diet, a new study suggests. A trial showed that people who ate no food at all for 36 hours then anything they felt like for 12 hours lost more than three kilograms within a month. Crucially, their immune systems remained stable, even after six months, in contrast to many diets which aim to restrict calorie intake consistently each day. Scientists at the University of Graz in Austria believe the strength of alternate-day fasting (ADF) may lie in its adherence to hunter-gatherers' patterns of eating thousands of years ago, when food was not available every day. However, they warn that it may not be suitable for everyone and that further studies need to prove its safety over the long-term. (*The Telegraph*)

A.   Alternate day fasting is effective for weight loss because it is the same as the caveman diet.

B.   Participants on the alternate-day fasting diet lost more than three kilograms without exercise.

C.   Scientists at the University of Graz have pioneered a diet called alternate-day fasting.

D.   Because it mimics earlier human eating pat-

terns, alternate-day fasting may be a healthy option.

14.   Ethan Bernstein and Stephen Turban, two Harvard Business School academics, set out to test the impact of open plan offices. At the first company, the authors found that face-to-face interactions were more than three times higher in the old, cubicle-based office than in an open-plan space where employees have clear lines of sight to each other. In contrast, the number of e-mails people sent to each other increased by 56% when they switched to open-plan. In the second company, face-to-face interactions decreased by two-thirds after the switch to open-plan, whereas e-mail traffic increased by between 22% and 50%. Why did this shift occur? The authors suggest that employees value their privacy and find new ways to preserve it in an open-plan office. They shut themselves off by wearing large headphones to keep out the distractions caused by nearby colleagues. Indeed, those who champion open-plan offices seem to have forgotten the importance of being able to concentrate on your work. (The Economist)

A.   The ability to quickly speak to each other in open plan offices resulted in a drop in emails.

B.   Workers in offices with cubicles are more productive than those in open-plan offices.

C.   Open plan offices encourage employees to find new ways to be left alone.

D.   The cost savings of an open plan layout were cancelled out by the adverse effect on communication.

15.   In a new study published in American Sociological Review, Asst. Prof. Mathijs de Vaan and Prof. Toby Stuart show that the likelihood of someone using opioids increases significantly once a family member living in the same household has a prescription. They also find that the chances of a relative obtaining a prescription for opioids within a year after a relative they live with gets one rises by 19 percent to over 100 percent, depending on family circumstances. Individuals from low-income households, for example, are the most likely to secure their own prescription after a family member does. De Vaan and Stuart suggest two reasons for this contagion:

when a family member takes painkillers, other relatives in the home observe first-hand its effects. Patients also typically receive more pills than they need, which means relatives may be tempted to experiment with leftovers sitting in the medicine cabinet. (*University of California, Berkeley*)

A. The majority of people getting new prescriptions for opioids are from households where opioids are already used by other family members.

B. It cannot be said that the wealthier have easier access to obtaining opioids.

C. It would be wrong to say that if doctors were to prescribe fewer pills, then other family members would be less likely to try them.

D. It would be wrong to say that the impact of family circumstances on prescribing of opioids cannot really be measured.

16. Boosting a single molecule in the brain can change "dispositional anxiety," the tendency to perceive many situations as threatening, in nonhuman primates, researchers from the University of California, Davis, and the University of Wisconsin-Madison have found. The molecule neurotrophin-3 stimulates neurons to grow and make new connections. The finding provides hope for new strategies focused on intervening early in life to treat people at risk for anxiety disorders, depression and related substance abuse. Current treatments work for only a subset of people and often only partially relieve symptoms. "There are millions of people worldwide who suffer from debilitating anxiety and depressive disorders," said Andrew Fox. "These disorders are also some of the leading causes of disability and days lost to disability." Anxiety disorders often emerge around adolescence and can continue to affect people for most of their lives. (*University of California, Davis*)

A. Scientists have discovered a way to relieve dispositional anxiety in humans.

B. Once anxiety emerges at adolescence, it will continue to affect people all their lives.

C. The study may indicate a new avenue for treating anxiety in humans.

D. Currently available treatments for anxiety are largely ineffective.

17. Electronic cigarettes (e-cigarettes) are a relatively new form of nicotine delivery device and the prevalence of their use is rapidly growing in many countries. E-cigarettes have been put forth as a way to reduce nicotine dependence and have been reported to be less addictive than traditional cigarettes. However, there have been numerous reports of people who become addicted to e-cigarettes and report typical symptoms of nicotine addiction, including with a dose-response effect. E-cigarette use has even been suggested to lead to an increased risk of addiction, especially among young people, with higher exposure to doses of nicotine compared to people who smoke traditional cigarettes, as e-cigarettes are used in times and places where smoking is prohibited. While some suggest e-cigarettes will help to quit smoking or reduce this addiction, others have reported that using e-cigarettes has a negative impact on successfully quitting. Using e-cigarettes may have little effect on reducing the frequency of nicotine use. (*MDPI*)

A. There is reason to believe that e-cigarettes may be achieving the opposite of their stated intent.

B. The prevalence of e-cigarette use is rapidly growing all around the world.

C. E-cigarettes help people give up traditional cigarettes because they are a socially acceptable alternative.

D. E-cigarettes actually contain more nicotine than traditional cigarettes.

18. The bystander effect occurs when the presence of others discourages an individual from intervening in an emergency situation. The greater the number of bystanders, the less likely it is for any one of them to provide help to a person in distress. People are more likely to take action in a crisis when there are few or no other witnesses present. Social psychologists Bibb Latané and John Darley popularized the concept of the bystander effect following the infamous 1964 Kitty Genovese murder in New York City. As 28-year-old Genovese was stabbed to death outside her apartment, neighbours failed to step in to assist or call the police. Latané and Darley attributed the bystander effect to the perceived diffusion of responsibility (onlookers are less likely to intervene if there are other witnesses who seem

likely to do so) and social influence (individuals monitor the behaviour of those around them to determine how to act). (*Psychology Today*)

A. Having no witnesses to a person's actions increases their likelihood of acting.

B. The bystander effect only presents itself in modern disconnected societies.

C. A person's likelihood of intervening is directly proportional to the number of others present.

D. People are more likely to remain bystanders if they are worried about being affected themselves.

19. In many cases, having high standards can drive success, but for some people, diligence and motivation can shift into perfectionism, a sorely misunderstood personality trait that can have dangerous consequences. Perfectionism has increased significantly over the past three decades, a recent analysis shows. Young people in particular place higher demands on themselves and on others. Our dog-eat-dog world, full of impeccable images of what our bodies, careers and aspirations should look like, is creating a rising tide of millennials who may be putting themselves at risk of mental and physical illness in their search for the perfect life. An epidemic of perfectionism poses a serious, even deadly problem, according to those researching the trend. (*New Scientist*)

A. Older people are largely unaffected by the increase in perfectionism seen over the past three decades.

B. Perfectionism is driving millennials to behave in rash and unpredictable ways.

C. The increase in perfectionism over the past 30 years can be mainly blamed on the media.

D. Unrealistic expectations are considered to be an essential reason why perfectionism has increased.

20. Looking at data from two large annual surveys of college undergraduates covering the years 2007-2018, researchers found a broad worsening of mental health indicators, particularly in the second half of the study period. "It suggests that something is seriously wrong in the lives of young people

and that whatever went wrong seemed to happen around 2012, or 2013," said study co-author Jean Twenge. She noted that this was around the time smartphones became common and social media moved from being optional to mandatory among youngsters. "It's difficult to think of any other event that began around that time, and then got stronger on until 2018," Twenge said. The rate of moderate to severe depression rose from 23.2% in 2007 to 41.1% in 2018, while rates of moderate to severe anxiety rose from 17.9% in 2013 to 34.4% in 2018. (*Reuters*)

A. The study found that depression and anxiety rates increased at a steady rate between 2007 and 2018.

B. Smartphones and social media are the reasons why mental health worsened after 2012-2013.

C. It cannot be said for certain that social media and smartphones increased mental health issues.

D. The increase in anxiety among college undergraduates was greater than among others of the same age.

21. Researchers randomly selected a group of 1,769 residents of Brno, in the Czech Republic. None had a history of cardiovascular illness, and 42 percent owned pets. They then scored them on the American Heart Association's seven measures of heart health and compared scores of the 24 percent of the people who owned dogs and the 18 percent who owned other pets with those of the rest who owned none. Owners of any pet scored higher than those who didn't own a pet, but dog owners scored higher than both. The authors do not conclude that owning a dog by itself assures protection against cardiovascular disease. Instead, the physical activity that dog ownership requires may be the key. Other factors may play a role as well. "Owning a dog increases the sense of well-being in general, decreases loneliness and decreases rates of depression," said Dr. Francisco Lopez-Jimenez. (*New York Times*)

A. Dogs are the best animal for improving cardiovascular health in humans.

B. Pets other than dogs were not found to increase the sense of well-being.

C.   Owning a physically demanding pet has positive benefits for your health.

D.   Owning a dog is probably enough by itself to protect against cardiovascular disease.

22. **The human desire for companionship may feel boundless, but research suggests that our social capital is finite—we can handle only so many relationships at one time. Social scientists have used a number of ingenious approaches to gauge the size of people's social networks; these have returned estimates ranging from about 250 to about 5,500 people. Looking more specifically at friendship, a study using the exchange of Christmas cards as a proxy for closeness put the average person's friend group at about 121 people. However vast our networks may be, our inner circle tends to be much smaller. The average American trusts only 10 to 20 people. Moreover, that number may be shrinking: From 1985 to 2004, the average number of confidants that people reported having decreased from three to two. This is both sad and consequential, because people who have strong social relationships tend to live longer than those who don't. (*The Atlantic*)**

A.   There is reason to believe that Americans are becoming less-trusting people.

B.   The average person has between 250 and 5,500 friends in their social networks.

C.   Christmas cards are an excellent way to determine the number of friends a person has.

D.   As the average number of confidants that people have has decreased, so have life spans.

23. **A study found that a given person, in 2006, eating the same amount of calories, taking in the same quantities of macronutrients like protein and fat, and exercising the same amount as a person of the same age did in 1988 would have a BMI that was about 2.3 points higher. "Our study results suggest that if you are 25, you'd have to eat even less and exercise more than those older, to prevent gaining weight," Jennifer Kuk said. "However, it also indicates there may be other specific changes contributing to the rise in obesity beyond just diet and exercise." Just what those other changes might**

be **are still a matter of hypothesis. First, people are exposed to more chemicals that might be weight-gain inducing. Second, the use of prescription drugs has risen dramatically since the '70s and '80s. Finally, Kuk and the other study authors think that the microbiomes of people might have somehow changed between the 1980s and now. (*The Atlantic*)**

A.   Gaining weight involves factors that may well be outside the average person's immediate control.

B.   Losing weight was much easier 20-30 years ago than it is today.

C.   Average BMI was 2.3 points higher in 2006 than in 1988 among people of the same age.

D.   Chemicals and prescription drugs are to blame for today's slower metabolisms.

24. **Today's children spend more time gazing at screens than ever, with smartphones and tablets competing with the television for their attention. But while some argue that technology can support child development, industry experts suggest that too much screen time could in fact result in a loss of imagination. According to a poll by daynurseries.co.uk, almost two-thirds of childcare professionals believe that screens are making children less creative. The survey found that fewer than half (48 percent) of nursery workers said there are children at their nursery with imaginary friends. Furthermore, a total of 72 percent agreed that far fewer children have imaginary friends now than five years ago, while 63 percent of those questioned said they think screens are to blame for this decline of inventiveness. David Wright agreed with the findings, explaining that there is a "general issue with children's creativity and development of imagination". (*The Independent*)**

A.   A consensus has been reached on how technology harms child development.

B.   Screen time appears to negatively impact on children's imaginations.

C.   Over two-thirds of childcare professionals think screens make kids less creative.

D.   Fewer than half of children today were reported to have an imaginary friend.

25. It wasn't just the coastline and the ocean surface that was drenched in oil after the Deepwater Horizon spill in 2010. Craig McClain and his colleagues used remotely operated underwater vehicles to survey the Gulf of Mexico around the site of the disaster. They did the survey in June 2017 and compared their findings with surveys done in the two months directly after the oil spill. While the number of animals increased in that time, the diversity was lower. There has also been a change in which animals inhabit the area. The communities seen in 2010 and 2017 were less than 20 percent similar in composition. Surprisingly, they found an abundance of arthropods, including red shrimp, a white caridean shrimp, and the Atlantic deep-sea red crab. McClain says they may be attracted to the site because the hydrocarbons that break down in the wake of an oil spill can mimic the chemicals in sex hormones that they use to find mates. (*The Independent*)

A. A survey of the Gulf of Mexico seven years after an oil spill found that some crabs were plentiful.

B. Animal diversity is lower and overall numbers have not yet recovered to pre-spill levels.

C. The lower diversity in animals is due to how the oil irreversibly changed the area.

D. The types of animals that inhabit the area have been permanently changed.

26. As devastating as forest fires are in the rainforest, the destructive power of fire is necessary for the preservation of other ecosystems, where parts of the natural fauna and flora develop only thanks to the fires. Animals and plants often have a natural capacity for resistance in such fire-dependent ecosystems. The nature of the fires varies, however. In grasslands, savannahs, some forests and wetlands, only a moderately intense ground fire sweeps through, ensuring that the open landscape structure is maintained. Rare but very intense fires are characteristic of bush landscapes or forests. They consume old and diseased trees, create new habitats and ensure an ecological rejuvenation of the tree population. Intervening in these ecosystems, for instance by preventing small fires in order to protect the population, can have fatal consequences. Over time, more and more combustible material accumulates. Even harmless fires can quickly turn into highly destructive walls of flames. (*Deutsche Welle*)

A. Fires are a natural part of the life cycles of all forests around the world.

B. Human attempts to control fires have actually made some worse when they occur.

C. Mild fires can be beneficial but intense fires are always damaging.

D. The reason some trees are resistant to fires is because of their thick barks.

27. In a new set of studies, researchers found that people showed greater goal commitment and performance when they told their goal to someone they believed had higher status than themselves. It didn't help people at all to tell their goals to someone they thought had lower status, or to keep their objectives to themselves. "Contrary to what you may have heard, in most cases you get more benefit from sharing your goal than if you don't – as long as you share it with someone whose opinion you value," Howard Klein said. Results showed that people were motivated by sharing a goal with someone they thought had higher status because they cared about how that higher-status person would evaluate them. "You don't want them to think less of you because you didn't attain your goal," Klein said. In these studies, higher-status people were those who the participants thought had more prestige and respect than they did. (*Ohio State University*)

A. People got the best advice on achieving their goals from those of higher status than themselves.

B. People who do not share their goals with others do not achieve them.

C. The fear of being looked down upon was found to be an excellent motivator.

D. The study found the opinions of those with lower status do not matter.

28. A panic attack is when your body experiences a rush of intense mental and physical symptoms. It can come on very quickly and for no apparent reason. A panic attack can be very frightening and distressing. Most panic attacks last for between 5 and 20 min-

utes. Some panic attacks have been reported to last up to an hour. The number of attacks you have will depend on how severe your condition is. Some people have attacks once or twice a month, while others have them several times a week. Although panic attacks are frightening, they're not dangerous. An attack won't cause you any physical harm, and it's unlikely that you'll be admitted to hospital if you have one. Be aware that most of these symptoms can also be symptoms of other conditions or problems, so you may not always be experiencing a panic attack. (*National Health Service*)

A.   The triggers for panic attacks are well understood.

B.   In bad cases people can experience several panic attacks per day.

C.   While most panic attacks are brief, some can last over an hour in duration.

D.   A person may think they are having a panic attack when something else is wrong.

29.   It's not uncommon to accidentally ingest expired medication, but not to fear: In general, most of them are not toxic when expired, but they can lose their effectiveness over time. When a drug is made, the time it takes to break down (known as its shelf life) is determined. Drug makers guarantee that if their product is used within the shelf life, it will work to its maximum potency and safety. This being said, even when medication passes its shelf life, it remains partially effective – but quantifying when and how fast the potency decreases is difficult. A study done by the U.S. military measured how ineffective medications actually become after their expiry date and found that of over 100 drugs tested, over 90 percent were sufficiently effective several years after their expiry date. The bottom line: Expiry dates are a conservative measure to make sure you're using medication of the highest potency possible. (*The Globe and Mail*)

A.   Although gradually losing effectiveness, most expired medications are still good enough.

B.   The main risk from taking medication beyond its shelf life is that it might not work, not that it might do you harm.

C.   Studies have found that all medications are still safe to take even after they have expired.

D.   Ninety percent of medications are still sufficiently effective years after they expire.

30.   Scientists combined data from two large, long-term studies: one including 69,744 women and another of 1,429 men, all of whom completed questionnaires that assessed their feelings about the future. After controlling for health conditions, behaviours like diet and exercise, and other demographic information, the scientists were able to show that the most optimistic women (top 25%) lived an average of 14.9% longer than their more pessimistic peers. For the men the results were a bit less dramatic: The most optimistic of the bunch lived 10.9% longer than their peers, on average, the team reported. The most optimistic women were also 1.5 times more likely to reach 85 years old than the least optimistic women, whereas the most optimistic men were 1.7 times more likely to make it to that age. (*Science Magazine*)

A.   Optimistic men were more likely to reach 85 years old than optimistic women.

B.   The study on women is more accurate due to its larger sample size.

C.   Optimists had higher life expectancy because they also lead healthier lives.

D.   Optimism had a greater impact on life expectancy in women than in men.

31.   Impostor syndrome is a psychological pattern in which an individual doubts their accomplishments and has a persistent internalized fear of being exposed as a "fraud". Despite external evidence of their competence, those experiencing this phenomenon remain convinced that they are frauds, and do not deserve all they have achieved. Individuals with impostorism incorrectly attribute their success to luck, or as a result of deceiving others into thinking they are more intelligent than they perceive themselves to be. While early research focused on the prevalence among high-achieving women, impostor syndrome has been recognized to affect both men and women equally. (*Wikipedia*)

A. An essential part of impostor syndrome is dismissing your own achievements.

B. At one time impostor syndrome was believed to only affect women and not men.

C. Impostor syndrome is a mental illness in which people do not recognise their achievements.

D. People who have achieved their success through luck will not feel like impostors.

32. **Psychosis, which is not a disease but a symptom of a brain illness, usually begins in late adolescence and young adulthood. The causes are not known. The disorder, which is genetically complex, tends to run in families — more than 100 genes have been linked to schizophrenia, for example. Its onset is often precipitated by episodes of intense stress or severe chronic stress. There are many possible signs that someone is at risk of developing a psychotic break, but too often they are often dismissed as symptoms of typical adolescent behaviour, experts say. Psychosis rarely comes on suddenly. Rather, the person gradually experiences changes in thoughts and perception, making it difficult for the person to recognize what is real and what is not, the National Alliance on Mental Illness points out. (*New York Times*)**

A. Psychosis has been found to be exclusively passed on through families.

B. Intense or severe chronic stress will precede a psychotic break.

C. Signs of impending psychosis are frequently dismissed as normal behaviour.

D. A psychotic break can be averted if the signs are recognised in time.

33. **Teenagers are twice as likely to be hyperactive if their mothers were anxious during pregnancy and their early years, a new study has shown. While around five percent of youngsters usually experience some symptoms of Attention Deficit Hyperactivity Disorder (ADHD) by the age of 16, the number jumped to 11 percent of those whose mothers suffered anxiety. Although some anxiety is natural during pregnancy and the early years of motherhood, the researchers measured extreme symptoms such as trembling, insomnia, dizziness and sweating. In the study around** one quarter of the women tested showed medium to high anxiety. Researchers say they cannot be sure of a causal link, but have speculated that high levels of stress hormones may have an impact on brain development. (*The Telegraph*)

A. The majority of youngsters with ADHD symptoms have mothers who were anxious in pregnancy or early childhood.

B. High levels of stress hormones in the mother affects the way a child's brain develops.

C. Having an anxious mother roughly doubles the chances of a child having ADHD.

D. Anxious mothers had higher rates of children with Attention Deficit Disorder.

34. **The IWSR, in conjunction with BDS Analytics, says a growing number of consumers are showing a preference to consume both booze and marijuana. "Our research shows that up to 40% of adults 21 and over consume cannabis in states where it's legal," said Jessica Lukas. "Cannabis presents substantial opportunities across consumer industries, including new occasions in which alcohol cannot and will not play. Consumers will continue to look to cannabis products over alcohol for occasions when they are feeling creative, need to get motivated, or seeking health, medical or wellness benefits." The IWSR is warning that makers of adult beverages need to begin anticipating consumers' shifting demands now if they want to avoid trouble down the road. Last year, Americans drank 3.345 billion cases of alcohol, a 0.8% decline from 2017. That worked out to about 7.9 billion gallons of booze, roughly 160 million bathtubs full. (*Fortune*)**

A. Drinking has declined since 2017 due to people smoking more legal marijuana.

B. Alcohol companies have so far proved reluctant to diversify to cannabis products.

C. Consumers prefer cannabis to alcohol in certain situations although they increasingly consume both.

D. More adults consume alcohol than cannabis even in states where cannabis is legal.

35. **South Korean imports of beer from Japan plunged 97% in August from a year earlier amid a popular backlash against Japanese**

products that has spread as relations between the two countries sour. South Korea imported just $223,000 worth of Japanese beer in the month, down from $7.57 million a year earlier, the Maeil Business Newspaper said, citing preliminary data from Korea Customs Service. Japan has held the largest share of South Korean beer imports every year since 2010, with sales surging more than sixfold by 2018 to $78.3 million. The boycott of Japanese goods has spread since Tokyo first imposed export restrictions on key chip materials in July. The trade dispute may not be without its winners, however – shares in South Korean brewer Hite Jinro Co. have risen to the highest level in more than a year amid swift sales of its new beer. (*Bloomberg*)

A. South Korea is no longer the biggest importer of Japanese beer.

B. Changes in tariffs on Japanese beer have seen imports to South Korea drop.

C. The boycott of Japanese beers is meant to increase consumption of South Korean beer.

D. It is not unreasonable to believe that Japanese beers may no longer lead South Korean beer imports.

36. Most earthquakes occur along faults, or deep cracks in the crust, where blocks of Earth slide against each other and create friction. This process builds stress and strain in the crust until the tension releases suddenly as seismic energy, producing an earthquake. Geologist Wendy Bohon compares an earthquake to breaking a pencil: You can see the pencil bend a little bit as you apply more pressure, but at some point, enough tension builds up so that the pencil snaps. Almost 75 percent of earthquakes occur along tectonic plate boundaries, which cover thousands of miles of Earth's surface. We know earthquakes are constantly rattling our planet, so much so that geologists can confidently say that there is a 100-percent chance that an earthquake will strike somewhere in the world each day. In Southern California alone, the data show that an earthquake occurs almost every three minutes, on average. (*National Geographic*)

A. A majority of earthquakes occur along specific parts of the Earth's surface.

B. Earthquakes can occur anywhere.

C. In some places, such as South Carolina, earthquakes occur on a very regular basis.

D. There is a 100% chance of an earthquake occurring somewhere along the tectonic plates each day.

37. One of the hottest times in Earth's history came 56 million years ago, during the Palaeocene-Eocene Thermal Maximum, or PETM. The crux of the issue is the fact that Earth's orbit actually looks like a very slightly squashed circle, or ellipse. Astronomers call this eccentricity, and it varies predictably over time, becoming more or less squashed in a regular cycle. But the degree of eccentricity has noticeable, if subtle, effects on the climate, says Richard Zeebe the co-author of a study on the topic: "If we look at the past 100 million years, we see distinct relationships between changes in eccentricity and climate". Scientists were able to pinpoint the sudden temperature spike of the PETM at 56 million years ago, right when Earth's orbit was at its most eccentric, or elliptical. A more eccentric orbit would mean that more solar radiation is hitting Earth, so it makes sense that it would cause warming. (*astronomy.com*)

A. The study suggests that the Earth's elliptical orbit is a factor in current global warming.

B. A spike in the Earth's temperature 56 million years ago was not caused by greenhouse gases.

C. The Earth's orbit around the sun is becoming increasingly elliptical over time.

D. Scientists found that the hottest the Earth has ever been was 56 million years ago.

38. Samsung's smartphone shipments in Central and Eastern Europe during Q2 2019 grew a significant 21% year-on-year (YoY), and 8% quarter-on-quarter (QoQ), solidifying the OEM's lead in the market, according to the latest research from Counterpoint's Market Monitor service. The growth in Samsung's shipments came even as the overall smartphone market in CEE remained flat. Samsung benefitted from the drop in Huawei's volumes after the US trade ban. Excellent traction for its refreshed A-series also helped the company's performance in the region. Samsung

ended the quarter with a 40% market share, twice that of its nearest competitor, Huawei. Commenting on Samsung's performance, Peter Richardson said, "Samsung has been the main beneficiary of the drop in Huawei (and Honor) volumes, as it could offer a comparable range of smartphones and fill the portfolio gaps with its recent launches under the A-series. The refreshed A-series was the star performer for Samsung." (*counterpointresearch.com*)

A. Samsung doubled the size of its market share in Central and Eastern Europe.

B. Samsung's smartphones are comparable to Huawei's but cost a little more to buy.

C. Samsung is the market leader in a part of the world where smartphone sales have not been increasing.

D. Without the refreshment of its A-series, Samsung would not have seen the growth that it did.

39. Smell happens when the receptors in your nose pick up aromatic molecules in the air. These molecules ooze out of objects and living organisms in the environment around you. You smell more aromatic molecules during the summer because hot, muggy air holds more of the molecules and enables them to move through the atmosphere more quickly. The opposite happens when it's cooler and drier in the fall: air molecules contract together and leave less space for odour molecules to move through. "In summer, we have just more of a mixture of scent and sort of a wide blend of scent ... we smell a lot more of everything around us," said Rachel Herz, a neuroscientist. "When it gets cooler and drier, specific scents tend to stand out more — we're able to kind of pull out the scent of leaves, the scent of bark, the scent of grass in more distinct ways." (*CBC*)

A. It is more difficult to smell specific scents in the summer since we are bombarded by smells.

B. Scents are easier to pick out in the autumn because they are stronger in that season.

C. When the air is hotter scents can move through the atmosphere more quickly.

D. Humidity levels are more important than temperature for transmitting scents.

40. The spotlight effect is a cognitive bias that causes people to overestimate the degree to which they are observed and noticed by others, as well as the degree to which others care about the things that they notice about them. The spotlight effect is something that we all experience frequently in our everyday life. We experience the spotlight effect because when we think about how other people see us, we suffer from an egocentric bias, which is the tendency to anchor other people's viewpoints to our own. Essentially, since we are so used to seeing things from our own perspective, we struggle to accurately judge what other people's perspectives are like. Since we are so focused on our own appearance and actions, it's difficult for us to remember that other people are not as focused on what we look like or on what we do, since they are already preoccupied with their own lives for the most part. (*effectiviology.com*)

A. People who keep to themselves will experience the spotlight effect more than others.

B. Our tendency not to consider others' perspectives is the root cause of the spotlight effect.

C. It is mainly people who are self-obsessed that experience the spotlight effect.

D. We experience the spotlight effect because we cannot consider other perspectives.

41. Many planets across the universe probably end up falling into their stars, either because they stray too close, or because the stars expand as they age. We have seen some evidence of this, like clouds of leftover debris and stars full of elements they couldn't maintain on their own. Alexander Stephan and his colleagues calculated how planets could affect the stars that eat them. They found that a planet falling into a star can make the star brighten for anything from centuries to millennia. And that the star can spin faster as the planet deposits its energy. "The interactions between the planet and star may not be able to kill the star as such, but they can certainly mess it up," Stephan says. Often, when a star eats a planet, the star can start to spin so quickly that it begins to rip apart, throwing its outer layers off into space. (*New Scientist*)

A. Planets close to a star will be swallowed when the star expands as it ages.

B.   By providing it with more energy, a planet can make a star grow larger.

C.   When a star eats a planet, it will cause it to spin so quickly that it rips apart.

D.   A star's swallowing of a planet may in fact be a self-destructive act.

42.   **The so-called "casual dining crunch" has led to customers turning their backs on chains such as Byron, Strada, Gourmet Burger Kitchen and Jamie Oliver's restaurant empire. The number of restaurants falling into insolvency in the year to the end of June 2019 increased by 25% to 1,412 compared to 2018, according to research by the accountancy firm UHY Hacker Young. It is the highest number of insolvencies since at least 2014 and is said to reflect tightened consumer spending on the back of concerns about Brexit and rising costs because of the collapse in the value of the pound. UHY Hacker Young said the rapid growth of the casual-dining sector since the 2008 financial crisis had resulted in an oversaturated mid-market, which is still going through a dramatic shakeout. The research found that hundreds of small independent restaurants had collapsed as well as big chains, such as those owned by the celebrity chef Oliver. (The Guardian)**

A.   The casual dining crunch saw customers turn away from chains to independent restaurants.

B.   Over-expansion in the mid-market sphere is a reason why such restaurants are closing.

C.   The fall in the value of the pound caused by concerns about Brexit tightened consumer spending.

D.   Small independent restaurants saw more closures than chain restaurants.

43.   **Europe will likely be a large growth market for air conditioners despite the outsized costs of retrofitting older buildings with new cooling systems, said Nicholas Heymann. Currently, only about 20% of European households have air conditioning, compared with 87% percent of U.S. households and 90% in Japan, due in part to greater emphasis on less energy-intensive forms of cooling in Europe. The number of European households that buy and install a new air conditioning system will increase**

by an average of 4.3% a year through 2040 as more people move to cities, according to a study published in Environmental Science & Policy. Overall, global air conditioner sales will increase by 700 million units by 2030 and 1.6 billion by 2050, driven mostly by sales in developing countries such as India, according to estimates from the U.S. Department of Energy. (Reuters)

A.   Europeans use air conditioning less than Americans since they are more environmentally conscious.

B.   Japan has the highest rate of households with air-conditioning in the world.

C.   Most European households do not have air conditioning but the biggest increase in sales will be elsewhere.

D.   Increasing temperatures are why Europeans will buy more air conditioning systems.

44.   **The euro area annual inflation rate was 1.0% in August 2019, stable compared to July. A year earlier, the rate was 2.1%. European Union annual inflation was 1.4% in August 2019, stable compared to July. A year earlier, the rate was 2.2%. The lowest annual rates were registered in Portugal (-0.1%), Greece (0.1%) and Spain (0.4%). The highest annual rates were recorded in Romania (4.1%), Hungary (3.2%), the Netherlands and Latvia (both 3.1%). Compared with July, annual inflation fell in nine Member States, remained stable in six and rose in twelve. In August, the highest contribution to the annual euro area inflation rate came from services (+0.60 percentage points, pp), followed by food, alcohol & tobacco (+0.40 pp), non-energy industrial goods (+0.08 pp) and energy (-0.06 pp). (Eurostat)**

A.   Inflation rates fell throughout the European Union.

B.   In August 2019 services made a higher contribution to the annual EU inflation rate than did non-energy industrial goods.

C.   Although inflation was the general trend, deflation was also observed.

D.   Inflation within the Eurozone was over one percent in August 2019.

45.   **In July 2019 compared with June 2019, seasonally adjusted production in the construction sector decreased by 0.7% in the euro**

area (EA19) and by 0.1% in the EU28, according to first estimates from Eurostat, the statistical office of the European Union. In June 2019, production in construction increased by 0.6% in the euro area and by 0.1% in the EU28. In July 2019 compared with July 2018, production in construction increased by 1.1% in the euro area and by 1.7% in the EU28. Among Member States for which data are available, decreases in production in construction were recorded in France (-4.2%), Slovakia (-2.0%) and Poland (-0.6%). The highest increases were observed in Hungary (+9.6%), Romania (+4.1%) and Portugal (+2.3%). (*Eurostat*)

A. Month-on-month production in construction increased by 1.1% in the euro area in July 2019.

B. Production in construction saw greater increases in June among countries using the euro.

C. From states with available data, Hungary led the European Union in terms of construction.

D. Only three EU Member States saw decreases in production.

46. Both NASA and the European Space Agency are reporting that a newly discovered comet zooming toward the sun is likely from another star. Astronomers said that it's traveling at 150,000 kph, so fast it likely originated outside our solar system. It's 420 million kilometres from the sun and getting closer. Scientists predict the comet will hurtle past the sun in December and keep going until it's back in interstellar space. Its nucleus is estimated between 2 kilometres and 16 kilometres across. With another comet from outside our solar system so soon, these interstellar passers-by could be more common than thought. Marco Micheli of ESA said "We need to wait a few days to really pin down its origin with observations that will either prove the current thesis that it is interstellar, or perhaps drastically change our understanding." (*AP News*)

A. The speed of the comet is what proves that it originated from outside our solar system.

B. Comets originating from outside our solar system are more common than we thought.

C. The comet's speed is why astronomers believe the comet is an interstellar object.

D. Comets from our own solar system only travel at slower speeds.

47. In optics, an aperture is a hole or an opening through which light travels. The aperture size of a photographic lens can be adjusted to control the amount of light reaching the film or image sensor. In combination with variation of shutter speed, the aperture size will regulate the film's or image sensor's degree of exposure to light. Typically, a fast shutter will require a larger aperture to ensure sufficient light exposure, and a slow shutter will require a smaller aperture to avoid excessive exposure. Reducing the aperture size increases the depth of field, which describes the extent to which subject matter lying closer than or farther from the actual plane of focus appears to be in focus. In general, the smaller the aperture (the larger the f-number), the greater the distance from the plane of focus the subject matter may be while still appearing in focus. (*Wikipedia*)

A. Aperture size is what determines the amount of light that reaches film or an image sensor.

B. F numbers on a lens are directly proportional to the size of the aperture.

C. A fast shutter speed with a small aperture will produce a worse image than a slow shutter speed with a large aperture.

D. Aperture is what determines how much of an image is in focus.

48. As the world warms, ocean temperatures will also increase—a process which, scientists predict, will lead to an increase in the intensity of hurricanes. The warmer the temperature of the sea surface that a hurricane is moving over, the stronger the storm will become, because heat energy in the water acts almost like a fuel. Furthermore, global sea level rises—which are being driven by climate change—could mean that coastal storms become more destructive, due to the increased risks of storm surges. This will only be exacerbated by the fact that climate change is expected to lead to a rise in hurricane rainfall. While hurricanes are expected to become more intense in future, scientists are still not sure whether climate change will lead to an increase or decrease in their frequency. (*Newsweek*)

A. It cannot be said for certain that hurricane intensity will increase as the world warms.

B. Climate change will lead to an increase in the number of hurricanes.

C. Hurricanes are now producing more rainfall than they did in the past.

D. Scientists believe the rise in global sea levels will probably lead to more intense hurricanes.

49. **ISO is a camera setting that will brighten or darken a photo. As you increase your ISO number, your photos will grow progressively brighter. For that reason, ISO can help you capture images in darker environments, or be more flexible about your aperture and shutter speed settings. However, raising your ISO has consequences. A photo taken at too high of an ISO will show a lot of grain, also known as noise, and might not be usable. So, brightening a photo via ISO is always a trade-off. You should only raise your ISO when you are unable to brighten the photo via shutter speed or aperture instead (for example, if using a longer shutter speed would cause your subject to be blurry). Although ISO initially defined only film sensitivity, it was later adopted by digital camera manufacturers with the purpose of maintaining similar brightness levels as film. (*photographylife.com*)**

A. ISO is the setting that determines how bright or dark a photograph will be.

B. Photographs taken at high ISO levels will be too grainy to be usable.

C. It cannot be said that ISO solely determines a camera sensor's sensitivity to light.

D. In addition to light sensitivity, ISO can also determine the quality of an image.

50. **Capsaicin is an active component of chili peppers, which are plants belonging to the genus Capsicum. It is an irritant for mammals, including humans, and produces a sensation of burning in any tissue with which it comes into contact. The seeds of Capsicum plants are dispersed predominantly by birds: in birds, the TRPV1 channel does not respond to capsaicin or related chemicals (avian vs. mammalian TRPV1 show functional diversity and selective sensitivity). This is advantageous to the plant, as chili pepper seeds consumed by birds**

pass through the digestive tract and can germinate later, whereas mammals have molar teeth which destroy such seeds and prevent them from germinating. Thus, natural selection may have led to increasing capsaicin production because it makes the plant less likely to be eaten by animals that do not help it disperse. (*Wikipedia*)

A. Capsicum plant seeds are only dispersed by birds, which is why they need to be spicy.

B. A bird's inability to chew Capsicum seeds is why it is better suited to dispersing them.

C. The increase of capsaicin in peppers was the result of evolution.

D. Capsaicin only provides a burning sensation to animals that do not help it disperse.

51. **Occupational asthma is asthma that's caused by breathing in chemical fumes, gases, dust or other substances on the job. Occupational asthma can result from exposure to a substance you're sensitive to — causing an allergic or immunological response — or to an irritating toxic substance. Like other types of asthma, occupational asthma can cause chest tightness, wheezing and shortness of breath. People with allergies or with a family history of allergies are more likely to develop occupational asthma. Avoidance of occupational triggers is an important part of management. Otherwise, treatment for occupational asthma is similar to treatment for other types of asthma and generally includes taking medications to reduce symptoms. If you already have asthma, sometimes treatment can help it from becoming worse in the workplace. If it's not correctly diagnosed and you are not protected or able to avoid exposure, occupational asthma can cause permanent lung damage, disability or death. (*mayoclinic.org*)**

A. Occupational asthma is a leading cause of workplace-derived illness.

B. People do not have to be sensitive to particular substances to develop occupational asthma.

C. People with a genetic predisposition to asthma are the ones who also have the workplace type.

D. Occupational asthma is limited to people who work under certain conditions.

52. A boycott of The Sun in Liverpool led to people in Merseyside having more positive attitudes towards the European Union, a study has claimed. The report on tabloid media influence over attitudes towards the EU claims the boycott cut Euroscepticism in the county by more than ten percent. It also noted a "substitution effect of Sun readership to pro-EU papers", particularly rival tabloid the Daily Mirror. The Sun has faced a boycott in Merseyside ever since its coverage of the 1989 Hillsborough Disaster, which saw it wrongly claim fans of Liverpool FC had behaved despicably during the crush that claimed 96 lives. The report, authored by Florian Foos and Daniel Bischof, says the long-standing Sun boycott lowered Euroscepticism among the "unskilled" working class who "made up a large share of Sun readers before the disaster". The report said "attitudes towards the EU got significantly more positive in Merseyside during the boycott". (*pressgazette.co.uk*)

A. The boycott of The Sun was a factor in Merseyside voting Remain in the EU referendum.

B. People who avoided tabloid media were found to be better informed.

C. The most popular choice of people who boycotted The Sun was to switch to the Daily Mirror.

D. A single media actor can have significant influence on opinion on a particular subject.

53. Scientists at the University of Dundee found that hunger can significantly alter how people make important decisions and lead to impatience. Hunger may also change preferences for rewards completely unrelated to food, the study suggested. It was also found to affect other types of decisions such as financial or interpersonal ones. When hungry, people expressed a stronger preference for smaller hypothetical rewards to be given immediately instead of larger ones that would arrive at a later time. Leader of the study Benjamin Vincent said it is important that people know that being hungry can affect their preferences. He also believes it is a danger for those in poverty who may make decisions that entrench their situation. "Say you were going to speak with a pensions or mortgage adviser – doing so while hungry might make you care

a bit more about immediate gratification at the expense of a potentially more rosy future." (*Sky News*)

A. People who make short-sighted decisions are probably hungry at the time.

B. People living in poverty will be unable to escape their position so long as they are hungry.

C Hunger was found to be one of the reasons why people ended up in poverty.

D. Being hungry was found to negatively impact a person's patience.

54. While the environmental case for going vegetarian is unequivocal and powerful, the long-term health impacts of adopting a vegetarian or vegan diet are still poorly understood. To help fill the gap, Tammy Tong at the University of Oxford and her colleagues grouped 48,000 people in the UK by diet and followed them over 18 years. The results showed vegetarians had a 22 percent lower risk of heart disease than their meat-eating counterparts. The finding, which is in line with some previous research, could be explained by vegetarians generally having lower cholesterol levels. But the analysis has a sting in the tail: vegetarian diets were also associated with a 20 percent higher risk of stroke than that seen in meat-eaters. The reason could be vegetarians missing out on some nutrients only found in meat, such as the B12 vitamin. But that deficiency can be addressed with supplements, says Tong. (*New Scientist*)

A. The vegan diet is overall the healthiest, the vegetarian the second healthiest, and the meat-eating diet the least healthy.

B. Vegans run a lower risk of heart disease than do meat-eaters.

C. Vegetarians run a greater risk of a serious medical condition than do meat-eaters.

D Lower cholesterol levels from not eating meat reduce the risk of heart disease.

55. The number of motorists and cyclists receiving compensation for injuries and damage caused by potholes on London's main roads has quadrupled in a year. A total of 281 claims — 244 from drivers and 37 from cyclists — were accepted by Transport for London in 2018. Almost £350,000 was paid

to cyclists alone in 2018 — taking the total over the past five years paid to cyclists to £1.7 million. The increase in claims follows a controversial decision by TfL commissioner Mike Brown to "pause" non-safety-critical road repairs on TfL's "red route" network for two years to ease a cash crisis. The number of successful claims last year was more than four times the 68 on which TfL paid out in 2017, according to figures obtained by the London Assembly. A total of 571 claims were made in 2018, up from 342 the previous year, just under half of which were successful. TfL was unable to provide a figure for the amount paid to motorists. (*Evening Standard*)

A.   The costs of claims has reduced potential savings from suspending repair works.

B.   Claims costs are rising because there are more problems with the roads today.

C.   Less than half the claims made in 2018 were successful.

D.   More was paid out to cyclists in claims in 2018 than in any of the previous four years.

56.   The euro area (EA19) seasonally-adjusted unemployment rate was 7.4% in August 2019, down from 7.5% in July 2019 and from 8.0% in August 2018. This is the lowest rate recorded in the euro area since May 2008. The EU28 unemployment rate was 6.2% in August 2019, down from 6.3% in July 2019 and from 6.7% in August 2018. This is the lowest rate recorded in the EU28 since the start of the EU monthly unemployment series in January 2000. Eurostat estimates that 15.432 million men and women in the EU28, of whom 12.169 million are in the euro area, were unemployed in August 2019. Compared with July 2019, the number of persons unemployed decreased by 111,000 in the EU28 and by 115,000 in the euro area. Compared with August 2018, unemployment fell by 1.189 million in the EU28 and by 960,000 in the euro area. (*Eurostat*)

A.   The EU unemployment rate is the lowest that it has ever been.

B.   In terms of unemployment, the non-euro area is performing better than the euro area.

C.   Since records began in 2000, this is the lowest number of people unemployed in the EU28.

D.   The number of unemployed men outnumbered the number of unemployed women in the EU28.

57.   Russian alcohol consumption decreased by 43% from 2003 to 2016, a World Health Organization (WHO) report says. It attributed the decline to a series of alcohol-control measures implemented under former President Dmitry Medvedev and a push towards healthy lifestyles. The WHO said the drop in alcohol consumption was linked to a significant rise in life expectancy. It noted that Russia had previously been considered one of the heaviest-drinking countries in the world. "Alcohol consumption has long been recognised as one of the main driving factors of mortality in the Russian Federation, especially among men of working age," the report said. But from 2003 to 2018, alcohol consumption and mortality decreased, with the most significant changes occurring in causes of death linked to alcohol. In 2018, life expectancy in Russia reached a historic peak, at 68 years for men and 78 years for women. (*BBC News*)

A.   Russia formerly led the world in terms of alcohol consumption.

B.   Alcohol-related deaths unevenly impacted working age men.

C.   In 2016 Russians drank less than half the alcohol they did in 2003.

D.   Russian women have higher life expectancy because they drink less alcohol.

58.   People treated for several days in an intensive care unit had their stomachs quickly colonised by harmful pathogens, tests show. Healthier gut microbes were pushed out – a shift that may have long-term effects after someone is discharged. Heavy use of broad-spectrum antibiotics, feeding people through a tube and using a ventilator to help them breathe could all contribute to the effect, say the team who carried out the study. "It's quite disconcerting," says Mark Pallen. "I suspected that something like this was going on, but I was quite taken aback at the scale of the changes." To assess the impact of intensive care treatment on the gut microbiome, the team tracked 24 people admitted to Queen Elizabeth Hospital Birmingham, UK, over a 10-month period. Two-thirds of the patients showed a marked reduction in microbial diversity at some

stage during their stay. The biggest changes were associated with intravenous use of the antibiotic meropenem. (*New Scientist*)

A.   A trip to the hospital has the potential to play havoc with a person's gut bacteria.

B.   A person may leave the hospital worse off than before they were admitted.

C.   Two-thirds of patients left the hospital with a significant reduction in microbial diversity.

D.   Using antibiotics inevitably reduces microbial diversity in the gut.

59.   After surveying more than 6,000 people in the US, Germany, France and the UK, Swiss bank UBS found that 21% had reduced the number of flights they took over the last year due to environmental concerns. Only 16% of British respondents said they were cutting back on flying, but 24% of US travellers were worried enough to change their flying habits. The bank now expects the number of flights in the EU will increase by just 1.5% per year, which is half the rate expected by plane maker Airbus. The bank forecasted that growth in US flights would fall from the 2.1% expected to just 1.3%. And that could have a big impact on aircraft manufacturers. UBS estimates it could reduce the number of smaller planes ordered from Airbus and rival Boeing by 110 each year. The bank said that would reduce revenues at Airbus, which controls around 57% of the market, by around €2.8bn a year. (*BBC News*)

A.   Airbus and Boeing expect they could lose 110 orders of smaller planes per year.

B.   American respondents were more concerned about the environment than British ones.

C.   British respondents were found to be the least likely to change their flying habits.

D.   An aircraft manufacturer is more optimistic than a bank about future flight numbers in the European Union.

60.   An experiment in Germany has made the most precise measurement yet of the maximum mass of neutrinos — light subatomic particles that are so devilishly difficult to measure that physicists have only been able to estimate the upper limit of their mass. The first results from the Karlsruhe Tritium Neutrino (KATRIN) experiment in south-

western Germany reveal that neutrinos weigh at most 1.1 electronvolts (eV). This measurement is a two-fold improvement over previous upper-bound measurements of 2 eV. Guido Drexlin, co-spokesperson for the KATRIN collaboration, presented the results on 13 September at a conference in Toyama, Japan. Neutrinos are among the most abundant particles in the Universe. They are also the lightest of all the known subatomic particles that have mass — weighing around 500,000 times less than an electron. But they tend to cross matter undetected, which makes it extremely challenging to take direct measurements of these particles. (*Nature*)

A.   Neutrinos are the lightest materials in the universe.

B.   Scientists cannot estimate how light neutrinos may be.

C.   Neutrinos make up most of the mass of the universe.

D.   Neutrinos are difficult to measure because of their small weight.

61.   Emma Garnett and her colleagues at the University of Cambridge collected data on more than 94,000 meals sold in 3 of the cafeterias at the university in 2017. When the proportion of meatless options doubled from one to two of four choices, overall sales remained about constant. But sales of meat-containing meals dropped, and sales of vegetarian meals rose 40–80%. Increases in plant-based dining were largest among people with the lowest baseline rates of vegetarian-meal consumption. The researchers found no evidence that higher sales of vegetarian dishes at lunch led to lower vegetarian sales at dinner. Other variables that influenced dining choices included the relative prices of vegetarian and non-vegetarian options, and the outdoor temperature. The authors suggest that an increase in vegetarian options could encourage consumers to move away from meat-heavy diets, potentially reducing greenhouse-gas emissions linked to animal-derived food. (*Nature*)

A.   The lower price of vegetarian meals may have made them a more desirable option.

B.   Providing better-tasting vegetarian meals saw an increase in their consumption.

C.   The increasing amount of vegetarian options will have a positive impact on the environment.

D.   Cafeterias which added a second vegetarian option saw vegetarian sales nearly double.

62.   **Demographers study populations to determine their size and composition and to predict how they are likely to change in years to come. In all countries, this knowledge is key to meeting the population's present and future needs, for example, to decide how many new kindergartens, schools or retirement homes are needed. Demographers analyse data collected by the national statistical offices and organise surveys on specific themes. To become a demographer, you need a Master's degree in demography or a related discipline, such as sociology, statistics, geography, biology etc. You can also study for a PhD to specialise in research or to teach demography at university level. (*ined.fr*)**

A.   No country should disregard its demographers.

B.   Demographers know how populations will change in the future.

C.   Most demographers have earned a degree in demography.

D.   Demographers assemble data for statistical purposes.

63.   **In a new study, Penn State researchers found that people who were more sensitive to shifts in negative emotion — quickly moving from a relaxed state to one of fear, for example — were more likely to feel anxious while being led through relaxation exercises. Michelle Newman, professor of psychology, said the results could help benefit people who experience "relaxation-induced anxiety," a phenomenon that occurs when people actually become more anxious during relaxation training. "People may be staying anxious to prevent a large shift in anxiety, but it's actually healthier to let yourself experience those shifts," Newman said. "The more you do it, the more you realize you can do it and it's better to allow yourself to be relaxed at times. Mindfulness training and other interventions can help people let go and live in the moment." (*Penn State University*)**

A.   People with anxiety may actively resist efforts to calm them down.

B.   Preventing relaxation for stressed people is healthier in the long run.

C.   Mindfulness training is the best way to deal with anxiety.

D.   A large shift in anxiety levels can be harmful to people.

64.   **The resource curse is a paradoxical situation in which countries with an abundance of non-renewable natural resources experience stagnant economic growth or even economic contraction. The resource curse occurs as a country begins to focus all of its production means on a single industry, such as mining, and neglects investment in other major sectors. As a result, the nation becomes overly dependent on the price of commodities, and overall gross domestic product becomes extremely volatile. Additionally, government corruption often results when proper resource rights and an income distribution framework are not established in the society, resulting in unfair regulation of the industry. The resource curse is most often witnessed in emerging markets following a major natural resource discovery. (*Investo-pedia*)**

A.   The resource curse overwhelmingly affects less democratic countries.

B.   Revenues from mining are volatile primarily because of fluctuations in demand.

C.   Focusing on a single resource exposes a country to price fluctuations.

D.   Government corruption is necessary for the resource curse to occur.

65.   **Q fever is an infection caused by the bacterium Coxiella burnetii. Q fever is usually a mild disease with flu-like symptoms. Many people have no symptoms at all. In a small percentage of people, the infection can resurface years later. This more deadly form of Q fever can damage your heart, liver, brain and lungs. Q fever is transmitted to humans by animals, most commonly sheep, goats and cattle. When you inhale barnyard dust particles contaminated by infected animals, you may become infected. High-risk occupations include farming, veterinary medicine and animal research. Mild cases of Q fever clear up quickly with**

antibiotic treatment. But if Q fever recurs, you may need to take antibiotics for at least 18 months. (*mayoclinic.org*)

A.   An infection that can cause brain damage can often go unnoticed.

B.   Like chicken pox, Q fever tends only to be dangerous the second time.

C.   Antibiotics can deal quickly with Q fever.

D.   Sheep are the animal most likely to pass Q fever on to humans.

66.   Exposure Compensation allows photographers to override exposure settings picked by a camera's light meter, in order to darken or brighten images before they are captured. Since camera meters work by evaluating light reflected off subjects and are standardised on middle grey, any time a camera is pointed at something very dark, the meter will work the opposite way by brightening up the exposure, whereas a very bright subject will cause the meter to darken the exposure. This is done in order to get as close to the middle grey as possible, so that the resulting image is not too dark or too bright. While this works out quite well in most cases, one might experience overexposure or underexposure in more challenging lighting conditions, where the camera meter might be adjusting the exposure too aggressively. This is where Exposure Compensation comes into play, with the photographer manually taking control of the brightness of the image and overriding it using the exposure compensation feature of the camera. (*photographylife.com*)

A.   Exposure compensation is a setting that is best left to experienced photographers.

B.   Exposure compensation is only to be used in more challenging lighting conditions.

C.   Exposure compensation is used because camera light meters are too often unreliable.

D.   Exposure compensation allows photographers to manipulate an image's darkness.

67.   The current scientific view of Venus holds that, at some point in the past, the planet had much more water than its bone-dry atmosphere suggests today. But as the Sun grew hotter and brighter, surface temperatures rose on Venus, eventually vaporizing any oceans and seas. With ever more water vapor in the atmosphere, the planet entered a runaway greenhouse condition from which it couldn't recover. Whether Earth-style plate tectonics ever operated on Venus is unknown. Water is critical for plate tectonics to operate, and a runaway greenhouse effect would have effectively shut down that process had it operated there. But the ending of plate tectonics wouldn't have spelled the end of geological activity: The planet's considerable internal heat continued to produce magma, which poured out as voluminous lava flows and resurfaced most of the planet. Indeed, the average surface age of Venus is around 700 million years – very old, certainly, but much younger than the multi-billion-year-old surfaces of Mars, Mercury or the Moon. (*The Conversation*)

A.   Venus has the youngest surface of any planet in the solar system.

B.   Venus is much younger than Mars, Mercury or the Moon.

C.   It is uncertain if the vaporising of water stopped plate tectonics on Venus.

D.   As the Sun grew hotter and brighter, it eventually vaporised Venus.

68.   The number of children who have smoked has fallen to a record low, an NHS survey revealed today. Sixteen percent of secondary school pupils said they had tried cigarettes last year, down from 19 percent two years earlier. This is the lowest level ever recorded by the two-yearly survey and continues the decline from 49 percent in 1996. The percentage of pupils who had ever smoked was similar for boys (16 percent) and girls (17 percent). It increased with age, from two percent of 11-year-olds to 31 percent of 15-year-olds. Five percent of 15-year-olds were regular smokers. Rates were lowest in London (three percent) and highest in Yorkshire and the Humber, at more than seven percent. A quarter of pupils said they had used e-cigarettes, the same as in 2016. (*Evening Standard*)

A.   The number of children who have smoked has fallen to the lowest annual level since the survey began.

B.   It cannot be said that boys were more likely to have smoked than girls.

C.   There is a good chance that e-cigarettes will

eventually reduce smoking among the young.

D. Current figures are a huge drop from the days when the majority of secondary school pupils smoked.

69. Researchers at Newcastle University ran tests with full-scale washing machines to show that a delicate wash, which uses up to twice as much water as a standard cycle, releases on average 800,000 more microfibres than less water-hungry cycles. "Our findings were a surprise," said Prof Grant Burgess. "You would expect delicate washes to protect clothes and lead to less microfibres being released, but our careful studies showed that in fact it was the opposite. If you wash your clothes on a delicate wash cycle the clothes release far more plastic fibres. These are microplastics, made from polyester. They are not biodegradable and can build up in our environment." The finding challenges the assumption that more aggressive washing cycles, which use less water, change direction more frequently and spin at higher speeds, release more fibres into wastewater. Instead, the volume of water used per wash appears to be the most important factor in dislodging fibres from clothing, the study found. (*The Guardian*)

A. Delicate washes were found to destroy clothes more often than standard cycles.

B. Washing machine manufacturers did not properly test how their machines work.

C. Standard wash cycles are better for the environment than delicate cycles.

D. The amount of water used had little bearing on the amount of microplastics released.

70. A new study has suggested that ear infections were responsible for the Neanderthals' extinction. Today they can be simply treated with modern medicines like antibiotics, but the Neanderthals contracted many complications from ear infections, including respiratory infections, hearing loss and pneumonia. The study found that the ears of Neanderthals were comparable to those of human children and did not change with age, as children's do. While the shape of a human child's ear begins to change around the age of five, meaning that they are less likely to contract ear infections, this did not happen with Neanderthals, the study found. "It's not just the threat of dying of an infection," Prof. Samuel Marquez said. "If you are constantly ill, you would not be as fit and effective in competing with your Homo sapien cousins for food and other resources." He added: "In a world of survival of the fittest, it is no wonder that modern man, not Neanderthal, prevailed." (*The Independent*)

A. Complications from ear infections are what killed off the Neanderthals.

B. Modern humans do not have ears shaped like those of Neanderthals.

C. Neanderthals were doomed because they failed to evolve.

D. Neanderthals' ears appear to have predisposed them to becoming ill.

71. After taking other related factors into account, a new study has revealed that living in large towns and cities near to England's coastline is linked with better mental health for those in the lowest earning households. Approximately one in six adults in England suffer from mental health disorders such as anxiety and depression, and these are far more likely in people from poorer backgrounds. The findings suggest that access to the coast could help to reduce these health inequalities in towns and cities close to the sea. The research used data from the Health Survey for England and compared people's health to their proximity to the coast; from those living less than 1km away, to those more than 50km away. Its findings add to the growing evidence that access to blue spaces—particularly coastal environments—might improve health and wellbeing. (University of Exeter)

A. The study showed there is something to be said about the benefits of sea breezes.

B. The poor near the coast had better mental health than richer people further inland.

C. The study adds to the growing evidence of the benefits of having access to green spaces.

D. It cannot be said that proximity to the coast was linked with better mental health for the wealthy.

72. The Sahm Rule was invented by Federal Reserve economist Claudia Sahm to flag the onset of recessions more quickly than the current process. It also aims to be more dependable than some of the financial market metrics known to throw off false signals. Sahm said the unemployment rate can cut through all that. It is a widely used and easily understood statistic that captures why recessions matter. It also turns out that when the three-month average unemployment rate rises half a percentage point above the low of the previous year, the economy has just or is about to enter a period of contraction. It has happened every time since the 1970s, Sahm noted in recommending her rule be used as a way to automatically trigger stimulus payments to households to help offset the sting of rising joblessness and potentially shorten the recession without waiting for politicians to sort through the data and vote on a stimulus package. (*Reuters*)

A. The Sahm Rule is a widely adopted and easy to understand statistic.

B. The Sahm Rule is intended to be a more reliable indicator of an upcoming recession.

C. The Sahm Rule is more reliable than some of the metrics the financial market uses.

D. The Sahm Rule is going to be used to automatically trigger stimulus payments to households.

73. Sleep deprivation combined with long haul trips are a common cause of truck accidents. A new report suggests truck drivers across Europe are more likely to succumb to obstructive sleep apnoea (OSA) as a result of not getting enough shut eye and living a sedentary lifestyle on the road. Obesity is a main risk factor of OSA. Over 70% of participants in a study by the European Lung Foundation were reported to be overweight and as a result had sleep-related breathing problems. Between 30-50% of road accidents in Germany are caused by truck drivers who fall asleep momentarily at the wheel, the Intersom Cologne Center for Sleep, Medicine and Research reports. These are the most serious accidents, Hans-Günter Weess remarks, because "the driver doesn't realise what is happening and cannot react. Deadly accidents due to sleep deprivation happen quite frequently — perhaps twice as often as accidents as a result of drunk driving." (*Deutsche Welle*)

A. It cannot be said that a majority of road accidents in Germany are caused by truck drivers falling asleep.

B. Accidents caused by drivers falling asleep are more frequent but less serious than those caused by drunk drivers.

C. People with sleep-related breathing problems are likely to be overweight.

D. It cannot be said that sleep-deprived drivers caused more deadly road accidents than drunk drivers.

74. A Korean study suggests that people who flush after drinking could be more vulnerable to the harmful effects of alcohol on blood pressure. The study compared the risk of high blood pressure in men who flush after consuming alcohol, compared with "non-flushers". It found that when "flushers" have more than four drinks a week their risk of high blood pressure was increased to a potentially hazardous level. While in non-flushers the risk only increased when they had more than eight drinks weekly. Researchers speculate that "flushers" may have a faulty version of a gene ALDH2, which, when working, breaks down a substance in alcohol called acetaldehyde. And it could be excess amounts of acetaldehyde that is causing both facial flushing and high blood pressure. However, a causal relationship between the two remains unproven. It would also be dangerous to conclude that, if you are not a flusher, you can happily booze with impunity. (*National Health Service*)

A. "Non-flushers" can have up to eight alcoholic drinks a week without health risks.

B. Women "flushers" were found to be at greater risk than men "non-flushers".

C. An inability to break down acetaldehyde may carry greater risks for high blood pressure.

D. Excess amounts of acetaldehyde are what cause facial flushing and high blood pressure.

75. An ARkStorm (for Atmospheric River 1,000 Storm) is a hypothetical but scientifically realistic "megastorm" scenario developed

and published by the Multi Hazards Demonstration Project of the United States Geological Survey, based on historical occurrences. It describes an extreme storm that could devastate much of California, causing up to $725 billion in losses (mostly caused by flooding), and affect a quarter of California's homes. The event would be similar to exceptionally intense California storms that occurred between December 1861 and January 1862, which dumped nearly 10 feet of rain in parts of California, over a period of 43 days. The name "ARkStorm" means "Atmospheric River (AR) 1,000 (k)" as the storm was originally projected as a 1-in-1000-year event. However, more recent geologic data suggests that the actual frequency of the event is likely in the 100- to 200-year range. (*Wikipedia*)

A.   ARkStorms are known to occur about every 100 to 200 years.

B.   It would be wrong to think that ARkStorms are merely a wild theory.

C.   An ARkStorm would leave most of California underwater.

D.   An ARkStorm is less likely to occur in the neighbouring desert state of Arizona.

76.   Middle-aged adults who walk slowly are likely to have brains and bodies that have aged prematurely, researchers announced. They found that the walking speed of 45-year-olds was associated with physical and biological indicators of "accelerated aging". Walking speed was already a well-known indicator of functional decline and mortality in the elderly, but this is the first study to link it with midlife health. Senior author Professor Terrie Moffitt said: "Doctors know that slow walkers in their 70s and 80s tend to die sooner than fast walkers their same age. But this study found that a slow walk is a problem sign decades before old age." The study of 45-year-olds found those who had the fastest walking speeds were in the best health. Those who registered the slowest speeds tended to have lower total brain volume and lower average cortical thickness, an indicator of neurodegenerative and psychiatric disorders. (*Evening Standard*)

A.   Slow walkers were found to have neurodegenerative and psychiatric disorders.

B.   A person's walking speed is inversely related to how their aging is progressing.

C.   A child's walking speed can determine how they will age later in life.

D.   Slow walkers in their 70s and 80s will die sooner than fast walkers.

77.   Technology frequently inspires ambivalence: we know that Facebook and Google know too much about us, yet we continue to use their services because they're so convenient. Voice assistants, however, are unusually polarising. People who consider them sinister and invasive regard enthusiasts as complacent, while those who find them useful and benign see the sceptics as paranoid technophobes. (*The Guardian*)

A.   People use Facebook and Google because they aren't worried about privacy.

B.   Voice assistants are more polarising because they are invasive.

C.   People who are sceptical of voice assistants are technophobes.

D.   Opinions regarding voice assistants are especially divided.

78.   Glaucoma is a common eye condition where the optic nerve, which connects the eye to the brain, becomes damaged. It's usually caused by fluid building up in the front part of the eye, which increases pressure inside the eye. Glaucoma can lead to loss of vision if it's not diagnosed and treated early. It can affect people of all ages, but is most common in adults in their 70s and 80s. Glaucoma does not usually cause any symptoms to begin with. It tends to develop slowly over many years and affects the edges of your vision (peripheral vision) first. For this reason, many people do not realise they have glaucoma, and it's often only picked up during a routine eye test. If you do notice any symptoms, they might include blurred vision, or seeing rainbow-coloured circles around bright lights. Both eyes are usually affected, although it may be worse in 1 eye. (*National Health Service*)

A.   If a person makes it to their 90s without developing glaucoma, they probably will not develop it at all.

B.   Once glaucoma affects peripheral vision, it is already too advanced to reverse.

C.   Fluid building up in the front part of the eye is occasionally the cause of glaucoma.

D.   The danger with glaucoma is that many people are unaware they are developing it.

79. **Pulmonary hypertension is high blood pressure in the blood vessels that supply the lungs (pulmonary arteries). It's a serious condition that can damage the right side of the heart. The walls of the pulmonary arteries become thick and stiff, and can't expand as well to allow blood through. The reduced blood flow makes it harder for the right-hand side of the heart to pump blood through the arteries. If the right-hand side of your heart has to continually work harder, it can gradually become weaker. This can lead to heart failure. Pulmonary hypertension is a rare condition that can affect people of all ages, but it's more common in people who have another heart or lung condition. (***National Health Service***)**

A.   Pulmonary hypertension essentially leads to heart fatigue, which can cause death.

B.   It cannot be said that pulmonary hypertension primarily affects the elderly.

C.   It is rare for someone to have pulmonary hypertension without other conditions.

D.   Pulmonary hypertension primarily affects the right side of the heart.

80. **Exercising for 30 minutes four times a week may delay brain deterioration in people likely to develop Alzheimer's, scientists have shown. Researchers from the University of Texas found that people who had an accumulation of amyloid beta protein in the brain – an early sign that Alzheimer's disease is on the way – experienced slower degeneration in a region of the brain crucial for memory if they exercised regularly for one year. Scientists say the findings suggest that aerobic workouts can at least slow down the effects of the disease if intervention occurs in the early stages. "What are you supposed to do if you have amyloid clumping together in the brain? Right now, doctors can't prescribe anything," said Dr Rong Zhang. "If these findings can be replicated in a larger trial, then maybe one day doctors will be telling high-risk patients to start an exercise plan. In fact, there's no harm in doing so now." (***The Telegraph***)**

A.   Exercising for 20 minutes six times a week may delay brain deterioration.

B.   It cannot be said that the researchers determined that exercise can slow the effects of Alzheimer's.

C.   Workouts at high intensity are more effective than gentle exercise.

D.   It cannot be said that the researchers think exercise may be a useful treatment for early Alzheimer's.

81. **"When the moon is low in the sky," astronomer Bob Berman says, "It is farther away from you than when it is directly overhead. Because of this, the light that's being reflected off of a horizon-hugging moon has to travel a farther distance—and through more particles of air—to reach your eyes. By the time we perceive this light, the shorter wavelengths of light, the 'blue' ones, have been scattered by the air, leaving only the longer wavelengths, the 'red' ones, to reach our eyes," he said. "Thus, to us, the bluish hues are filtered out, and the moon takes on an orange tinge!" On the other hand, when the moon is directly overhead, the light does not have to travel through as many air particles to reach us because the moon is closer, thus it is scattered less. This enables more of the blue wavelengths to reach our eyes, lending the moon a brighter, less orangey color. (***Newsweek***)**

A.   Shorter wavelengths do not travel through the atmosphere as well as longer ones.

B.   The moon appears larger on the horizon because of the way light waves are scattered.

C.   It cannot be said that the colour of the moon is more accurately observed when it is overhead.

D.   The moon appears smaller when it is closer because you can see the shorter light waves.

82. **Astronomers have spotted hints of water raining in the atmosphere of an exoplanet. Named K2-18 b, the planet is not much bigger than Earth and is located 34 parsecs (110 light years) away. Researchers pushed the limits of the Hubble and Spitzer space telescopes to observe how the light from K2-18 b's star filtered through the planet's atmosphere, revealing signs that water vapour was condensing into liquid water. Of course, the presence of water in the**

atmosphere of an Earth-size planet doesn't necessarily mean the world also has life: just look at Venus. (*Nature*)

A.   Astronomers have spotted water droplets on an exoplanet far away.

B.   It's possible that a distant planet has more rainwater than planet Earth.

C.   The planet is unlikely to have life, just as is the case for Venus.

D.   A planet needs to be Earth-sized for it to have water in its atmosphere.

83.   **The 1992 Framingham Heart Study, which still stands as the gold standard for long-term health studies, tracked workers over 20 years. It found that "men who don't take vacations were 30% more likely to have a heart attack and for women it went up to 50%," according to Brigid Schulte. Those numbers hold true even after researchers took into account other health factors like diabetes, cigarette smoking, income levels and obesity. The conclusions from the study have been backed up by other similar research studies. "It shows how the body reacts to a lifestyle of stress. This is real evidence that vacations are important to your physical health," Elaine Eaker, a co-author of the study, told the New York Times. (*CNN Travel*)**

A.   An annual vacation is enough to reduce stress and improve health.

B.   It cannot be said that women were affected more by not having vacations.

C.   Heart attack risk rates were found to be the same even when adjusting for exercise.

D.   It cannot be said that not taking vacations affected men and women equally.

84.   **Instances of rain—not to mention typhoons, flooding or heat—stopping play in sports are likely to become more common as climate change makes some weather events more severe. In the case of storms such as Typhoon Hagibis, a warmer atmosphere holds more water vapour, which makes them more intense. 2018 saw more natural disasters than any year going back to 1980, according to Munich Re, a reinsurer. In the future, coastal regions will become more prone to storms and flooding, while inland regions will face heatwaves and flash flood-**

ing, according to Piers Forster, a professor of climate physics. A study in 2016 found that over the past 40 years, Asian typhoons such as the one that hit Japan have become 50% stronger. The tropical storms hitting America are becoming more potent, too. When it comes to sporting events, Mr Forster points out, "nowhere is safe." (*The Economist*)

A.   The typhoons that strike Asian countries are more potent than the tropical storms that hit America.

B.   Storms such as the one that hit Japan have become half as strong over the past 40 years.

C.   Asian typhoons have become stronger faster than tropical storms that hit America.

D.   It cannot be said that all weather events are becoming more severe with climate change.

85.   **A new study published in the Lancet Respiratory Medicine found smoking just a handful of cigarettes per day causes lung damage similar to smoking more than a pack per day. Having fewer than five cigarettes per day was associated with about two-thirds as much lung damage as puffing on 30 or more cigarettes per day, according to the study. Put another way, a light smoker could expect to lose about as much lung function in a year as a heavy smoker would in nine months. Study co-author Dr. Elizabeth Oelsner says that the finding should dissuade people from taking up any amount of smoking—but it shouldn't discourage current smokers from reducing their daily cigarette use. Doing so can be an important step toward quitting entirely, and can come with significant health benefits. (*Time*)**

A.   Halving their cigarette consumption won't make a big difference to heavy smokers' risk of lung damage.

B.   Light smoking was found to cause just as much lung damage as heavy smoking.

C.   Those who cut back their smoking are more likely to eventually quit entirely.

D.   Doctors said there was not much to be gained from cutting back cigarette consumption.

86.   **Despite their shortcomings, impact factors continue to be a primary means by which academics "quantify the quality of science".**

One side effect of impact factors is the incentive they create for editors to coerce authors to add citations to their journal. Coercive self-citation does not refer to the normal citation directions, given during a peer-review process, meant to improve a paper. Coercive self-citation refers to requests that give no indication that the manuscript was lacking in attribution; make no suggestion as to specific articles, authors, or a body of work requiring review; and only guide authors to add citations from the editor's journal. This quote from an editor as a condition for publication highlights the problem: "you cite Leukemia [once in 42 references]. Consequently, we kindly ask you to add references of articles published in Leukemia to your present article". Gentler language may be used, but the message is clear: Add citations or risk rejection. (*Science Magazine*)

A. Impact factors are not a good method for quantifying the quality of science.

B. Academic articles were generally found to include unnecessary citations.

C. Coercive citations occur when journal editors ask authors to add more citations or risk rejection.

D. In order to be published, some articles may need to include superfluous citations.

87. A new study has found that "cartilage in human joints can repair itself through a process similar to that used by creatures such as salamanders and zebrafish to regenerate limbs". These findings could open the door to new treatments for joint injuries and diseases like osteoarthritis -- and perhaps even lead to human limb regeneration one day. Scientists have known for years that humans do have some regenerative capabilities -- when children's fingertips are amputated, the tip can regenerate when treated correctly. But it was widely believed that these capabilities were limited, and that humans were "unable to counteract cumulative damage" to their joints, the study said – which these new findings disprove. This has potentially huge implications for athletes or people with joint injuries. MicroRNA could be injected into joints or developed into medicines that prevent or reverse arthritis, the study said. In the more distant future, it could even "establish a basis for human limb regeneration." (*CNN Health*)

A. The study found new treatments for repairing joint injuries.

B. The study has opened the door to human limb generation.

C. Humans already have some limited abilities to regenerate.

D. Human cartilage repairs itself the same way as salamanders regenerate limbs.

88. Scientists found that openness to experience — a trait related to greater curiosity and imagination — stood out as separating politicians who won elections from those who lost. Candidates with greater openness were less likely to win their seat, and on average those who won scored 0.24 points lower on the seven-point openness scale. So even though higher openness to experience was associated with running for election, amongst candidates it was related to a reduced chance of winning. Why might that be? The trait is associated with holding left-wing views, so politicians who score higher could alienate right-leaning voters — though the researchers didn't find that the "penalty" of greater openness was any worse in traditionally conservative areas. Another possibility is that people who are particularly open to new ideas are just not that great at sticking to their political messages — and consistency in messaging is important to voters. (*British Psychological Society*)

A. People with higher levels of openness to experience hold left-wing views.

B. Politicians who lack imagination are better at winning elections.

C. People who are open to experience have difficulty staying on message.

D. The less open to experience a particular candidate is, the better their chances of victory.

89. Teenagers are less likely to use cannabis in places where the drug has been legalised, a new study suggests. While overall use among US youth went up between 1993 and 2017, the likelihood of teen use declined by nearly 10% in states where recreational use was legalised. Lead study author Mark Anderson said that the study "should help to quell some concerns that use among teens will actually go up". Dr Anderson said it was usually harder for teens to buy from

licensed dispensaries – where proof of age is required – than from dealers, which could partly explain the drop. Cannabis sold in dispensaries is also often more expensive. Dr Anderson said that the researchers did not find a change after medical cannabis was legalised – only when the drug was legalised for recreational purposes. (*BBC News*)

A.   Among teenagers it was legalising recreational, not medical, cannabis that made the difference.

B.   The price of cannabis became too expensive for teens after legalisation.

C.   It cannot be said that legalising cannabis is the solution to ending teen use.

D.   Where cannabis is legal, it loses its cool factor, leading to less use.

90.   **In astronomy, the barycentre is the centre of mass of two or more bodies that orbit one another and is the point about which the bodies orbit. If one of two orbiting bodies is much more massive than the other and the bodies are relatively close to one another, the barycentre will typically be located within the more massive object. In this case, rather than the two bodies appearing to orbit a point between them, the less massive body will appear to orbit about the more massive body, while the more massive body might be observed to wobble slightly. When the two bodies are of similar masses, the barycentre will generally be located between them and both bodies will orbit around it. When the less massive object is far away, the barycentre can be located outside the more massive object. (*Wikipedia*)**

A.   The barycentre of Jupiter's orbit is outside the Sun.

B.   A barycentre outside a celestial object means the distance is huge.

C.   It cannot be said that an object orbits around the centre of another.

D.   The Earth's orbit causes a slight wobble in the Sun.

91.   **It has been argued that an interstellar mission that cannot be completed within 50 years should not be started at all. Instead, assuming that a civilization is still on an increasing curve of propulsion system** velocity and not yet having reached the limit, the resources should be invested in designing a better propulsion system. This is because a slow spacecraft would probably be passed by another mission sent later with more advanced propulsion (the incessant obsolescence postulate). On the other hand, Andrew Kennedy has shown that if one calculates the journey time to a given destination as the rate of travel speed derived from growth (even exponential growth) increases, there is a clear minimum in the total time to that destination from now. Voyages undertaken before the minimum will be overtaken by those that leave at the minimum, whereas voyages that leave after the minimum will never overtake those that left at the minimum. (*Wikipedia*)

A.   A spacecraft launched today will be overtaken by one launched in 25 years.

B.   It is increasingly accepted that interstellar missions that cannot be completed in 50 years should not be started.

C.   Not enough resources are spent on improving propulsion systems.

D.   So long as technology is rapidly improving, newer missions may overtake older ones.

92.   **Researchers asked 76 female undergrads (half of them were diagnosed with depression) to listen to various classical music clips. The scientists found that, like in a 2015 study, participants with depression indicated they would rather listen to sad music than happy music. Then, the researchers gave the participants new clips of happy and sad instrumental music and asked them to describe how the tracks made them feel. Again, the depressed participants preferred the sad music, but they also stated that the sad music made them feel happier. "They actually were feeling better after listening to this sad music than they were before," study co-author Jonathan Rottenberg said. It seemed to have relaxing and calming effects. This challenges the assumption that sad people listen to sad music to make themselves feel worse, when, in fact, it may be a coping mechanism. (*The Verge*)**

A.   Happy music has no impact on making people feel better.

B.   There is reason to believe that sad music makes the depressed feel better.

C. Depressed people preferred sad music since it would not cheer them up.

D. Vocal sad music was not found to have benefits like instrumental music.

93. The US has fallen behind several countries around the world in terms of educational mobility and university-level educational attainment. The number of young people attending and graduating from university has in the past surpassed the numbers of the previous generation. Today, however, that is not always true, and fewer young adults are getting a higher education than their parents. Several factors contribute to this trend. One of the biggest reasons that fewer individuals are going to university is the cost. Tuition costs at public universities have drastically increased over the last few decades, leading to less equitable access to education. This indicates that those from lower socioeconomic classes have a more difficult time paying for and attending university. (*worldatlas.com*)

A. It cannot be said that the rise in tuition fees has been felt evenly across society.

B. The United States formerly led the world in terms of university education attainment.

C. The cost of tuition is the biggest reason why less people are going to university.

D. Despite a recent drop, more are going to university today than in their parents' time.

94. Auto-brewery syndrome or gut fermentation syndrome is a condition in which ethanol is produced through endogenous fermentation by fungi or bacteria in the gastrointestinal system. Patients with auto-brewery syndrome present with many of the signs and symptoms of alcohol intoxication while denying an intake of alcohol and often report a high-sugar, high-carbohydrate diet. The production of endogenous ethanol occurs in minute quantities as part of normal digestion, but when fermenting yeast or bacteria become pathogenic, extreme blood alcohol levels may result. Auto-brewery syndrome is more prevalent in patients with co-morbidities such as diabetes, obesity, and Crohn disease, but can occur in otherwise healthy individuals. Several strains of fermenting yeasts and rare bacteria are identified as the pathogens.

While auto-brewery syndrome is rarely diagnosed, it is probably underdiagnosed. (*ncbi.nlm.nih.gov*)

A. Auto-brewery syndrome is most commonly linked to diabetes.

B. Everyone produces alcohol in their system as a normal part of digestion.

C. People with auto-brewery syndrome produce methanol in their digestive system.

D. Auto-brewery syndrome is inconvenient, but not potentially dangerous.

95. In a study published in the journal Proceedings of the National Academy of Sciences, a team of scientists showed that socioeconomic advantage can be mapped by wastewater. Specifically, the wastewater from wealthier communities where people had higher educational achievement showed higher levels of vitamins, citrus, and fibre, while the waste from poorer communities where people were generally less educated showed higher levels of prescription pain relievers and antidepressant medications. "Although [wastewater-based epidemiology] has primarily been used for measuring drug consumption, our results demonstrate that it can be used to identify sociodemographic patterns or disparities which associate with consumption of specific chemicals or food components," the team wrote. (*inverse.com*)

A. It cannot be said that higher educational achievement was associated with a better diet.

B. A correlation between prescription pain reliever use and less education appears to exist.

C. People who took anti-depressants did so because of their socioeconomic status.

D. It cannot be said that the study of wastewater can be used to indicate school attainment patterns.

96. The World Health Organisation (WHO) defines gaming disorder as a pattern of gaming behaviour characterised by "impaired control over gaming, increasing priority given to gaming over other activities to the extent that gaming takes precedence over other interests and daily activities, and continuation or escalation of

gaming despite the occurrence of negative consequences". The decision to classify gaming disorder as a mental health condition for the first time was heavily criticised by leading video game firms, who argued the move was not based on sufficiently robust evidence and created a risk of misdiagnosis for patients. Neuroscientist Nastasia Griffioen recently warned of the dangers of stigmatising people as being addicted to video games. "If we do stigmatise people basically as being addicted to video games, we might take away those video games when they might be a coping mechanism for a deeper, underlying problem like depression or anxiety", she said. (*videogameschronicle.com*)

A. Video game makers oppose classification of a gaming disorder due to potential loss of profits.

B. Video games are a coping mechanism for other underlying problems.

C. The decision to classify a video game disorder caused widespread controversy.

D. Something that has been classified as a mental health condition might just be a coping mechanism.

97. The Roche limit is the distance within which a celestial body, held together only by its own force of gravity, will disintegrate due to a second celestial body's tidal forces exceeding the first body's gravitational self-attraction. Inside the Roche limit, orbiting material disperses and forms rings whereas outside the limit material tends to coalesce. Typically, the Roche limit applies to a satellite's disintegrating due to tidal forces induced by its primary, the body about which it orbits. Parts of the satellite that are closer to the primary are attracted more strongly by gravity from the primary than parts that are farther away; this disparity effectively pulls the near and far parts of the satellite apart from each other, and if the disparity (combined with any centrifugal effects due to the object's spin) is larger than the force of gravity holding the satellite together, it can pull the satellite apart. (*Wikipedia*)

A. Saturn's rings were created by a moon that fell inside the Roche limit.

B. A larger planet's gravity is enough to pull a satellite apart.

C. A satellite can create tidal forces that rip it apart.

D. The Roche limit applies when an object's own gravitational pull is weaker than tidal forces.

98. Tidal heating occurs through tidal friction processes: orbital energy is dissipated as heat in either the surface ocean or interior of a planet or satellite. When an object is in an elliptical orbit, the tidal forces acting on it are stronger near periapsis than near apoapsis. Thus, the deformation of the body due to tidal forces (i.e. the tidal bulge) varies over the course of its orbit, generating internal friction which heats its interior. This energy gained by the object comes from its gravitational energy, so over time in a two-body system, the initial elliptical orbit decays into a circular orbit (tidal circularization). Sustained tidal heating occurs when the elliptical orbit is prevented from circularizing due to additional gravitational forces from other bodies that keep tugging the object back into an elliptical orbit. In this more complex system, gravitational energy still is being converted to thermal energy; however, now the orbit's semimajor axis would shrink rather than its eccentricity. (*Wikipedia*)

A. Tidal heating occurs due to the erratic nature of tidal forces.

B. Tidal heating can be sustained when an orbit becomes circular.

C. An elliptical orbit is necessary for tidal heating.

D. Tidal heating is most intense at the periapsis of the orbit.

99. Synaesthesia is a neurological condition in which the stimulation of one sensory or cognitive pathway (for example, hearing) leads to automatic, involuntary experiences in a second sensory or cognitive pathway (such as vision). Simply put, when one sense is activated, another unrelated sense is activated at the same time. This may, for instance, take the form of hearing music and simultaneously sensing the sound as swirls or patterns of colour. The most common type of synaesthesia is grapheme-colour synaesthesia, in which individual letters and numbers are associated with specific colours and sometimes colourful patterns.

Some synesthetes perceive texture in response to sight, hear sounds in response to smells, or associate shapes with flavours. Many synesthetes have more than one type of synaesthesia. It is estimated that approximately 3 to 5 percent of the population has some form of synaesthesia, and the condition can run in families. (*Psychology Today*)

A.   Synaesthesia is a hereditary neurological condition.

B.   Although any sense can trigger it, synaesthesia only produces visual responses.

C.   The majority of synaesthesia cases are visual.

D.   Smelling sounds would be one form of synaesthesia.

100. In a recent study, 85% of respondents believed that their mothers had a favourite among their siblings. The finding chimes with many years of research about parental favouritism, which has found that many parents admit to having a favourite child. Dig a little deeper, though, and it turns out that most favouritism has less to do with love and more to do with like: the same parents say that they love their children equally, but that one child's personality resonates more with them than those of their siblings. (*The Guardian*)

A.   Eighty-five percent of study respondents thought their parents had a favourite child.

B.   Parents may show favouritism towards a child even when they love all of their kids equally.

C.   Eighty-five percent of mothers had a favourite among their children.

D.   Studies have shown that most parents do in fact have a favourite child.

101. A new study from Northwestern University found that toddlers with fewer spoken words have more frequent and severe temper tantrums than their peers with typical language skills. It is the first study to link toddlers' delayed vocabulary with severe temper tantrums, including children as young as 12 months old, which is much younger than many clinicians typically believe problematic behaviour can be identified. Similarly, both irritability and language delays are risk factors for later language and learning disorders, co-princi-pal investigator Elizabeth Norton said. About 40% of delayed talkers will go on to have persistent language problems that can affect their academic performance, Norton said. This is why assessing both language and mental health risk in tandem may accelerate earlier identification and intervention for early childhood disorders because children with this "double whammy" are likely to be higher risk. (*news.northwestern.edu*)

A.   Half of delayed talkers will go on to have persistent language problems later in life.

B.   Children with mental health risks are more likely to have delayed language skills.

C.   The study explored the established link between temper tantrums and delayed talking.

D.   Many clinicians do not believe problematic behaviour can be identified in young toddlers.

102. Children born during the summer are more likely to suffer depression than their fellow pupils, a study has revealed for the first time. The youngest children in the academic school year are 30 percent more likely to develop mental health problems. Scientists used electronic GP records for a sample of one million school-aged children in the UK and found children born in the last three months of the school year were prone to being 30% more likely to develop depression compared to those born in the first three months. Dr Joseph Hayes, co-author of the study and clinical research fellow consultant, at University College London, said: "It makes sense that as a child, if you're comparing yourself to someone a year older, even something as simple as kicking a football – the difference in size between a four-year-old and a five-year-old is stark, so it's most likely similar for mental development. Teachers also have expectations of certain behaviours." (*The Telegraph*)

A.   Children born in the first three months of the school year do not usually suffer from depression.

B.   Being born in autumn has some advantages.

C.   Younger children should be held back a year to improve their mental well-being.

D.   The youngest children in a school year were frequently found to develop mental health problems.

103. Whether napping during the daytime is healthy or unhealthy is unclear. Some previous studies found a reduced risk of heart and circulation problems, while others found a higher risk. A study of 3,462 Swiss adults aimed to see whether the number of naps a week, and the length of time spent napping, could explain the conflicting results. While researchers found no link between length of naps and heart or circulation problems, they found that 1 or 2 naps might reduce risks, but having more than 1 or 2 naps did not reduce risk. Sleeping in the daytime on most days could be a sign of a health problem, such as sleep apnoea, which disrupts night-time sleep. (*National Health Service*)

A. It may be the case that people who take more frequent naps have other problems.

B. Frequent sleeping during the daytime is a sign of a more serious health problem.

C. It cannot be said that there is a lack of a consensus on the healthiness of daytime napping.

D. Taking more than 1 or 2 naps a week was found to increase heart and circulation risks.

104. Researchers asked more than 450,000 adults from 10 European countries about their consumption of soft drinks. Soft drinks included sugary and artificially sweetened fizzy drinks such as cola as well as diluted cordial. The researchers followed up with the participants for an average of 16 years and found that people who drank 2 or more glasses of any type of soft drink a day were 17% more likely to have died during the study, compared to people who drank less than 1 soft drink a month. Sugary drinks were linked to deaths from digestive diseases (such as liver disease), while artificially sweetened drinks were linked to deaths from cardiovascular diseases such as heart disease. While the link between sugar consumption and health problems is well established, it is unclear why artificially sweetened drinks could have an adverse effect on health. (*National Health Service*)

A. Researchers found that the longer they studied a person, the more health issues they had.

B. Artificially sweetened drinks were found to be just as bad as sugary drinks.

C. The study compared frequent soft drink

drinkers to those who generally abstained from them.

D. Artificially sweetened drinks were found to be worse for digestive diseases.

105. Matthew Gallagher led a study that examined the role of hope in predicting recovery in a clinical trial of 223 adults in cognitive behaviour therapy (CBT) for one of four common anxiety disorders: social anxiety disorder, panic disorder, generalized anxiety disorder and obsessive-compulsive disorder. "In reviewing recovery during CBT among the diverse clinical presentations, hope was a common element and a strong predictor of recovery," said Gallagher who reports that moderate-to-large increases in hope and changes in hope were consistent across the five separate CBT treatment protocols. In terms of psychotherapy, hope represents the capacity of patients to identify strategies or pathways to achieve goals and the motivation to effectively pursue those pathways. Significantly, the results of this study indicate that hope gradually increases during the course of CBT, and increases in hope were greater for those in active treatment than for those in the waitlist comparison. (*uh.edu*)

A. Feelings of hopelessness were found to be strongest among the sufferers from panic disorder.

B. Patients without a change in their hope levels were not expected to recover.

C. Sufferers from panic disorder got more hopeful once treatment started.

D. Hope was found to promptly increase during the course of cognitive behavioural therapy.

106. People with long-term health conditions are 20 percent more likely to suffer from pain on days that are humid and windy with low atmospheric pressure according to new research from University of Manchester scientists. According to the research, the most important factor associated with worsening pain is high relative humidity. Using a smartphone app developed by healthcare software company uMotif, participants recorded daily symptoms while the local weather was determined from location data provided by the smartphone's GPS. Humid days were most likely to be painful,

whereas dry days were least likely to be painful. Low pressure and higher wind speed were also linked to more painful days, although to a lesser extent than humidity. Despite many people believing pain to be influenced by temperature, there was no association observed, when averaged across the population. That said, cold days that were also damp and windy could be more painful. Rainfall was not associated with pain. (*manchester.ac.uk*)

A. A cold and windy day is worse for pain than a warm day with low atmospheric pressure.

B. Most cold days result in more pain in people with long-term health conditions.

C. A cold and dry day causes less pain than a warm and damp one.

D. Days that are dry are when patients will not experience pain from humidity.

107. A recent study has identified a new marker for autism that could facilitate earlier diagnosis. The marker is a difference in the autistic brain's capacity for binocular rivalry, which describes the visual cortex's ability to process one image at a time when presented with multiple images at once. The brain's inability to ignore one of several competing stimuli is tied to the hypersensitivity to sensory input that is characteristic of autism. Autistic participants were much less able to toggle their focus between the two images, compared to neurotypical participants. Amazingly, the researchers found that the rate of binocular rivalry they measured was predictive of the severity of one's symptoms, and using the data they could diagnose autism in study participants with 87% accuracy. A clear benefit of this study is that this marker is non-verbal, which means it can be used to evaluate young children who have not started talking yet as well as non-verbal adults. (*massivesci.com*)

A. Even if it doesn't prove to be the most accurate method of diagnosis, binocular rivalry has a potential benefit.

B. Binocular rivalry is better for diagnosing autism than assessments using language.

C. The study showed that people without autism did not have binocular rivalry.

D. The rate of binocular rivalry was inversely related to the severity of a person's symptoms.

108. A study examined the long-term impact of co-authorship with established, highly-cited scientists on the careers of junior researchers in four scientific disciplines. Using matched pair analysis, it found that junior researchers who co-author work with top scientists enjoy a persistent competitive advantage throughout the rest of their careers, compared to peers with similar early career profiles but without top co-authors. Such early co-authorship predicts a higher probability of repeatedly co-authoring work with top-cited scientists, and, ultimately, a higher probability of becoming one. Junior researchers affiliated with less prestigious institutions show the most benefits from co-authorship with a top scientist. As a consequence, it can be argued that such institutions may hold vast amounts of untapped potential, which may be realised by improving access to top scientists. (*Nature*)

A. The study found that who you write with is more important than what you write.

B. Co-authorship with an established scientist was not as significant for those at top universities.

C. Junior researchers who co-author with established names will themselves become established.

D. Some junior researchers enjoy an unfair competitive advantage.

109. Our hands touch all sort of things during the course of the day, and we don't always have the opportunity to wash them. If you bite your fingernails, you're constantly ingesting microorganisms, and that can have consequences. Nail-biters get colds, gastrointestinal infections and skin rashes more frequently. Your teeth and oral cavity can suffer as well, because pathogens can also establish themselves there. If you gnaw your nails down to below the quick, it can lead to bleeding and damage the nail bed. Constantly open wounds on your fingers can also become infected. In addition, nail biters often suffer psychologically. They feel stigmatized and hide their fingers because they're embarrassed. Many people think chewed fingernails are a sign of being weak-willed and lacking self-discipline. (*Deutsche Welle*)

A.   Biting one's nails will lead to catching a cold or gastrointestinal infection.

B.   Chewed fingernails are a sign of weak willpower and a lack of self-control.

C.   It cannot be said that nail biters are stigmatized because of their behaviour.

D.   A distressing habit can result in problems with the digestive system.

110.   On a scale from 0 ("not satisfied at all") to 10 ("fully satisfied"), the mean (average) life satisfaction of EU residents aged 16 and over was 7.3 in 2018, an increase compared with 7.0 in 2013. Since 2013, the mean level of satisfaction with the financial situation of their own household in the EU also increased, from 6.0 in 2013 to 6.5 in 2018, whilst the mean satisfaction with personal relations remained nearly stable, 7.8 in 2013 and 7.9 in 2018. In 2018, the mean life satisfaction varied significantly between EU Member States. With an overall average of 8.1, inhabitants of Finland were the most satisfied with their lives in the EU, closely followed by those in Austria (8.0), Denmark, Poland and Sweden (all 7.8). At the opposite end of the scale, residents in Bulgaria (5.4) were by far the least satisfied, followed by those in Croatia (6.3), Greece and Lithuania (both 6.4), Hungary (6.5), Latvia and Portugal (both 6.7). (*Eurostat*)

A.   Life satisfaction rates in the EU appear to correlate with the wealth of a given country.

B.   Life satisfaction rates increased across the board in the EU between 2013 and 2018.

C.   The study found that within the EU, the inhabitants of Finland were the happiest.

D.   While mean life satisfaction increased in the EU, it may have decreased in some countries.

111.   Whiplash is a neck injury due to forceful, rapid back-and-forth movement of the neck, like the cracking of a whip. Whiplash most often occurs during a rear-end auto accident, but the injury can also result from a sports accident, physical abuse or other trauma. Common signs and symptoms of whiplash include neck pain, stiffness and headaches. Most people with whiplash get better within a few weeks by following a treatment plan that includes pain medication and exercise. However, some people have chronic neck pain and other long-lasting complications. **Whiplash may be called a neck sprain or strain, but these terms also include other types of neck injuries. (*Mayo Clinic*)**

A.   Whiplash occurs when the neck is propelled very suddenly in one direction.

B.   The overwhelming cause of whiplash is from rear-end auto accidents.

C.   A neck sprain or strain is another term for whiplash.

D.   A rear-end auto accident can lead to years of pain.

112.   A mosquito-transmitted virus causes most cases of West Nile infection. Most people infected with West Nile virus either don't develop signs or symptoms or have only minor ones, such as fever and mild headache. However, some people develop a life-threatening illness that includes inflammation of the spinal cord or brain. Mild signs and symptoms of a West Nile virus infection generally go away on their own. But severe signs and symptoms — such as a severe headache, fever, disorientation or sudden weakness — require immediate attention. Exposure to mosquitoes where West Nile virus exists increases your risk of getting infected. Protect yourself from mosquitoes by using mosquito repellent and wearing clothing that covers your skin to reduce your risk. (*Mayo Clinic*)

A.   Most people who are infected with the West Nile virus do not know they have it.

B.   Mosquito repellent and covering your skin with clothes will save you from getting the virus.

C.   West Nile infection is always caused by a mosquito-transmitted virus.

D.   Many people who are infected with the West Nile virus may not know they are.

113.   An increase in wind speed in recent years is good news for renewable energy production. Average global wind speed had been dropping since 1978, but this trend has reversed over the past decade. Researchers found that from 2010 to 2017, average global wind speed over land increased by 17 percent – from 3.13 to 3.30 metres per second. Before this, from 1978 to 2010, wind speed had been falling by 0.08 metres per second –

or two percent – every decade. The reversal came as a surprise, says Zeng. Wind speed was thought to be declining because of increasing urbanisation resulting in more barriers, such as buildings, that slow down moving air. Why average global wind speed has been increasing since 2010, despite no reduction in urban development, isn't known, says Zeng. (*New Scientist*)

A.   Wind speed is expected to continue to increase over the next few years.

B.   Climate change is believed to have contributed to the increase in wind speed.

C.   The change in global wind speed has challenged a theory proposed by scientists.

D.   Despite what scientists thought, urban development does not impact wind speed.

114.   Children are growing up in a warmer world that will hit them with more and different health problems than their parents experienced, an international report said. "A child born today, as they go through their lives, they will be increasingly exposed to more and more harms that I did not experience," said study co-author Dr. Renee Salas. Already, the number of days when conditions are ripe for the spread of the waterborne bacteria Vibrio, a major cause of debilitating diarrhoea, have doubled since 1980 with last year ranking second highest on record, the report said. Because of the warming climate, 29% more of the U.S. coastline is vulnerable to Vibrio. Nine of the top 10 years where conditions were most ripe for dengue fever transmission have occurred since 2000, the report said. Those diseases hit children harder, the report said. (*AP News*)

A.   It cannot be said that climate change will impede the spread of diseases.

B.   The number of days that favour the spread of Vibrio has increased each year since 1980.

C.   Today's children will grow up in a wetter world exposing them to more health problems.

D.   Children growing up today will have higher rates of catching Vibrio or dengue fever.

115.   Ash dieback is caused by the fungus Hymenoscyphus fraxineus, which originated in Asia. In its native range, it causes little damage to trees, but when the fungus was introduced to Europe about 30 years ago, it caused widespread destruction. Recent estimates suggest that the disease can kill up to 70% of ash trees. In the UK, this means 70 million trees could be lost, which would cost the economy £15bn, according to an analysis published this year. In a bid to halt this seemingly unstoppable disease, scientists have been studying the DNA of hundreds of ash trees. A small number of trees are showing some natural resistance to ash dieback – and the researchers have identified the parts of their genome that are helping this fightback. "We've discovered about 3,000 locations in the DNA of these ash trees that are contributing to the resistance," explained Prof Richard Buggs. (*BBC News*)

A.   Finding what makes Asian ash trees resistant could help European ash trees.

B.   Ash dieback runs the risk of wiping out the ash trees found in Europe.

C.   Scientists are racing to stop ash dieback due to the potential economic costs.

D.   There are approximately 100 million ash trees within the United Kingdom.

116.   Husbands are least stressed when their wives earn up to 40 percent of household income but they become increasingly uncomfortable as their spouse's wages rise beyond that point and are most stressed when they are entirely economically dependent on their partner, new research from the University of Bath shows. The study of over 6,000 American heterosexual couples over 15 years showed husbands are at their most anxious when they are the sole breadwinner, shouldering all the burden of responsibility for the household's finances. Stress levels decline as their wives' earnings approach 40 percent of household income. But as women's earnings go above that point, the study showed husbands' stress levels gradually increasing. "These findings suggest that social norms about male breadwinning – and traditional conventions about men earning more than their wives – can be dangerous for men's health. They also show how strong and persistent are gender identity norms," said Dr Joanna Syrda. (*bath.ac.uk*)

A.   Men do better as the sole breadwinner than when entirely economically dependent.

B.   The study found men do best as the primary breadwinner in a household.

C.   According to the study, it did not matter whether the spouse was of the same gender or not.

D.   Men felt increased anxiety when they were not following traditional gender norms.

117.   Researchers have found that, on average, children who had an older sibling had worse language skills than those who didn't. The sex of an older sibling was important, however: kids with older sisters had better language skills than those with older brothers. In fact, a subsequent analysis showed that children with an older sister didn't actually differ in their language skills from those with no older sibling. It's not yet clear why children perform better when they have older sisters, the researchers write. It could be that sisters have better language abilities or are more nurturing than brothers — but another possible explanation is that sisters are less demanding on their parents, taking less parental attention away from their younger siblings than do brothers. Whatever the reason, the authors say, "it ... might be more accurate to think of the well-established negative older-sibling effect as an older-brother effect." (*British Psychological Society*)

A.   Girls learn faster at younger ages, hence the difference in language skills.

B.   Boys' behaviour towards their parents is why their younger siblings have worse language skills.

C.   Only older brothers were found to be detrimental to younger siblings' language skills.

D.   Older brothers spend more time with younger siblings and keep them from their parents more.

118.   More and more Americans are trying to lose weight, but few are finding success, a new study has found. According to figures published Wednesday in the journal JAMA: Diabetes and Endocrinology, the percentage of U.S. adults 20 and older that have attempted a weight-loss regimen has increased from 34.3 percent in 1999 to 42.2 percent in 2016. However, over the same period, researchers found increases in weight and weight gain – an indication that their efforts may be in vain. Notably, over the 18-year study period, mean weight of the participants increased from approximately 176 pounds to roughly 184 pounds. And, though a minimum of one in four participants reported trying to lose weight in each of the two-year periods, they appeared to be unsuccessful. For example, among those trying to lose weight within the 2015-16 time frame, there was a reported mean weight gain of eight pounds. (*UPI*)

A.   Efforts to lose weight by Americans cannot be generally said to correlate with actual weight loss.

B.   For some unknown reason, Americans were not able to lose weight despite trying.

C.   The study found that too many Americans lacked the willpower to lose weight.

D.   A minimum of a quarter of the participants in the study attempted to lose weight.

119.   A nationwide poll of 819 parents with at least one child in middle school, junior high or high school found that while one-third were confident they could detect depression in their children, two-thirds said certain things would make it difficult. About 30 percent of parents said their child is good at hiding feelings and 40 percent said they struggle to differentiate between their child's normal mood swings and signs of depression. "In many families, the preteen and teen years bring dramatic changes both in youth behaviour and in the dynamic between parents and children," poll co-director Sarah Clark explained. "These transitions can make it particularly challenging to get a read on children's emotional state and whether there is possible depression," she added. "Some parents may be overestimating their ability to recognize depression in the mood and behaviour of their own child," Clark noted. "An overconfident parent may fail to pick up on the subtle signals that something is amiss." (*UPI*)

A.   Less confident parents were more likely to pick up on subtle signals that something is wrong.

B.   About 70 percent of parents could not read their children's feelings well.

C.   Roughly two-thirds of parents did not

express confidence in detecting depression in their kids.

D.   Nearly one-third of parents overestimated their ability to detect depression in their children.

120.   New research finds that a person's risk of atrial fibrillation (a-fib) increases by about 3 percent for every inch over the average height of 5-foot-7. Further, it appears that certain genes linked to height also are associated with a-fib, said lead researcher Dr. Michael Levin, a cardiology fellow at the University of Pennsylvania Perelman School of Medicine. Atrial fibrillation is a quivering or irregular heartbeat that increases a person's risk of stroke fivefold. It also raises risk of blood clots, heart failure and other heart-related diseases, the American Heart Association says. Knowing that tall folks are at increased risk of a-fib could help prevent deaths and disease related to the heart condition, Levin said. "While we can't change your height, we may be able to modify other risk factors for a-fib in taller individuals and be more aggressive about controlling blood pressure or diabetes or cholesterol," Levin said. (*UPI*)

A.   The reason the risk of atrial fibrillation increases in tall people is that their hearts work harder.

B.   According to the study, the taller a person is, the greater the risk of having a stroke.

C.   Atrial fibrillation increases the risk of a stroke because it raises the risk of blood clots.

D.   Aggressive control of blood pressure and diabetes can reduce tall people's risk of stroke to normal levels.

121.   There are many myths about unwanted intrusive thoughts. One of the most distressing is that having such thoughts mean that you unconsciously want to do the things that come into your mind. This is simply not true, and, in fact, the opposite is true. It is the effort people use to fight the thought that makes it stick and fuels its return. People fight thoughts because the content seems alien, unacceptable, and at odds with who they are. So, people with violent unwanted intrusive thoughts are gentle people. People who have unwanted intrusive thoughts about suicide love life.

And those who have thoughts of yelling blasphemies in church value their religious life. A second myth is that every thought we have is worth examining. In truth, these thoughts are not messages, red flags, signals or warnings--despite how they feel. (*Anxiety and Depression Association of America*)

A.   Most of the common knowledge surrounding intrusive thoughts is mistaken.

B.   By not fighting an intrusive thought, a person will come to actually act them out.

C.   Having an intrusive thought is the subconscious showing what a person really wants to do.

D.   Paradoxically, fighting intrusive thoughts only serves to make them stronger.

122.   Why do people get tired when they travel long distances in certain vehicles? When you're traveling on a road, your car/bus is bound to accelerate/decelerate countless times, thanks to the natural flow of traffic. In addition to that, the vehicle will also take many turns, which are bound to repeatedly sway you from one side to another. In addition to the umpteen turns, swaying and constant changes in speed, there are a few other factors at play, such as the condition of the automobile, passenger seats and even the quality of the roads. All of these factors have a cumulative effect on passenger comfort. You don't realize it actively, but the constant sways and changes in speed cause you to remain upright. Your brain keeps your muscles engaged to account for these movements of the vehicle to ensure that your posture is properly maintained. These small movements cause your muscles to constantly work, which makes them tired over a long journey. (*scienceabc.com*)

A.   Long journeys in old cars are usually more tiring than those in new ones.

B.   It's generally more tiring to travel by car than by train.

C.   Long car journeys tire people because they are using their muscles throughout.

D.   Driving on a straight road is less tiring than driving on a twisting road.

123.   This might seem like a no-brainer, but when you stand still, you don't actually stand

absolutely still. The body has the tendency to sway a little (thus shifting the body-weight on either leg) almost constantly. In order to keep you upright, therefore, certain leg muscles, particularly in the calves, must constantly make small adjustments. In contrast, when you're walking, a greater number of muscles in both the legs are engaged. Additionally, they also get assistance from the core muscles, which keep your gait stable. That's one of the primary reasons why walking doesn't hurt nearly as much as standing still for the same amount of time. When one is walking, the body weight is borne alternatively by either leg. This way, both legs get rest very frequently, even if it lasts for only a second. (*science-abc.com*)

A.   Certain leg muscles are more prone to becoming painful from extended use than others.

B.   The core muscles are what make walking less painful than standing.

C.   Using less muscles made an activity more painful than one that uses more muscles.

D.   Walking is less painful than standing because it involves both legs as opposed to standing.

124.   Urban dwellers who live in close proximity to greenery are less likely to die before their life expectancy, per the findings of a new study. Green spaces like parks are excellent venues for physical activity, another health-boosting activity, David Rojas-Rueda said. Vegetation can act as a buffer between residents and blaring city racket, even if it's as simple as a tree-lined street. Plants also help regulate temperature and extremity of environments, tempering the effects of climate change, he said. More research is needed to determine the most evident benefit of urban green spaces. Narrower studies have already outlined a few significant improvements. That study's authors laid out specifics: Women who lived among lush greenery had a 41% lower death rate for kidney disease, 34% lower death rate for respiratory disease (trees' leaves trap air pollutants) and 13% lower death rate for cancer. (*CNN*)

A.   Urban dwellers living near greenery will reach the end of their life expectancy.

B.   The study found that the mere presence of

some greenery already provided benefits to people.

C.   The greatest benefit of green spaces was how they increased life expectancies in people.

D.   People living among lush greenery had a bigger reduction in death rate for kidney disease than for respiratory disease.

125.   People with lactose intolerance are unable to fully digest the sugar (lactose) in milk. As a result, they have diarrhoea, gas and bloating after eating or drinking dairy products. The condition, which is also called lactose malabsorption, is usually harmless, but its symptoms can be uncomfortable. A deficiency of lactase — an enzyme produced in your small intestine — is usually responsible for lactose intolerance. Many people have low levels of lactase but are able to digest milk products without problems. If you're actually lactose intolerant, though, your lactase deficiency leads to symptoms after you eat dairy foods. Most people with lactose intolerance can manage the condition without having to give up all dairy foods. (*Mayo Clinic*)

A.   A deficiency of lactase is in most cases the culprit in lactose malabsorption.

B.   Being lactose intolerant means that a person has to avoid eating dairy foods.

C.   Lactose intolerance occurs when people produce low levels of lactase.

D.   Lactose intolerance, while generally harmless, can also be quite dangerous in some cases.

126.   In the moments after a snowstorm concludes, leaving behind a landscape shrouded in white, the great outdoors often becomes noticeably quieter. As it turns out, there's a scientific reason behind the calming silence, with the characteristics of snow playing a big role in how sound can travel. When light, fluffy snow accumulates on the ground, it acts as a sound absorber, dampening sound waves much like commercial sound absorbing products. However, as the structure of snow changes, the amount of noise in the surrounding environment could increase. When the snow surface melts and refreezes, it can become hard and reflect sound waves, causing sounds to travel farther and become clearer, according

to the National Snow and Ice Data Center. (*Accuweather*)

A. The reason it becomes totally quiet after a snowfall is that the snow absorbs sound.

B. Refrozen snow is only half as effective at absorbing sound as freshly fallen snow.

C. The deeper the snow, the quieter it gets.

D. A big snowfall can end up making it noisier.

127. Sunspots are darker, cooler areas on the surface of the sun in a region called the photosphere. The photosphere has a temperature of 5,800 degrees Kelvin. Sunspots have temperatures of about 3,800 degrees K. They look dark only in comparison with the brighter and hotter regions of the photosphere around them. Sunspots can be very large, up to 50,000 kilometres in diameter. They are caused by interactions with the Sun's magnetic field which are not fully understood. But a sunspot is somewhat like the cap on a soda bottle: shake it up, and you can generate a big eruption. Sunspots occur over regions of intense magnetic activity, and when that energy is released, solar flares and big storms called coronal mass ejections erupt from sunspots. (*space.com*)

A. Despite appearances, sunspots are not actually dark areas on the sun's surface.

B. Sunspots are darker and cold spots on the sun's surface in an area called the photosphere.

C. Sunspots are cooler areas, usually a bit bigger than the size of the Earth, on the surface of the sun.

D. Solar flares and coronal mass ejections can only be launched from sunspots.

128. Red sprites and blue jets are flashes of light that occur above thunderstorms and that are associated with normal lightning in the thundercloud below. The causes of both phenomena are not known. Red sprites tend to form almost instantaneously over a broad region between 40 and 90 km in altitude. This region spans most of the mesosphere, the region of the atmosphere between about 50 and 80 km in altitude and which overlaps much of the ionospheric D region (between 70 and 90 km in altitude). Red sprites have a reddish colour on low-light television records, and blue tendrils have been observed trailing beneath them. Blue jets propagate out of the tops of thunderclouds at surprisingly low velocities (roughly 100 km per second) in the form of narrow cones of light that are blue in colour. Both phenomena are the subject of active research. (*britannica.com*)

A. Blue jets can reach greater altitudes than red sprites.

B. Blue tendrils trail at around 100 km per second.

C. An unexplained phenomenon occurs in the ionospheric D region.

D. Red sprites only form in the part of the atmosphere known as the mesosphere.

129. Glaciers are formed by the recrystallization of snow or other solid precipitation that does not significantly melt, even during melting season. The fallen snow compresses over many years (at a rate that depends on temperature and wetness) into ice. A glacier may also gain mass from the refreezing of meltwater at its base. Though glaciers are fed mainly by snowfall, they may also grow as a result of freezing of rain, hail, hoarfrost, and rime; avalanches may contribute snow to a glacier as well. Glaciers are found in Arctic areas, Antarctica, and on high mountains in temperate and even tropical climates. Glaciers that extend in continuous sheets and cover a large landmass, such as Antarctica or Greenland, are called ice sheets. If they are similar but smaller, they are termed ice caps. (*britannica.com*)

A. Elevation is not essential for determining if glaciers can form.

B. It cannot be said that glaciers can exist at all latitudes of the Earth.

C. The largest glaciers can be found in the Arctic and Antarctic regions.

D. Glaciers form the fastest in areas that are the coldest.

130. Eating two apples a day may reduce people's risk of suffering a heart attack or stroke, experts found. When 40 people with slightly high cholesterol ate two large apples a day for eight weeks, it lowered their levels of "bad" cholesterol by almost

four percent. That could help to reduce their risk of a stroke or heart attack, which can be caused by cholesterol hardening the arteries. Two large apples contain about a quarter of someone's recommended daily fibre, and a type of fibre that fuels bacteria in the gut which may reduce cholesterol. This could explain the traditional advice that "an apple a day keeps the doctor away". Researchers also found people had healthier, more relaxed blood vessels after eating apples daily, which is similar to an effect seen in other foods containing natural compounds called polyphenols, such as red wine and tea. (*Daily Mail*)

A.   Eating two large apples a day for eight weeks lowered bad cholesterol levels fourfold.

B.   Apples contain a type of fibre that fuels bacteria in the gut that reduce cholesterol.

C.   Drinking red wine or tea is as good for you as eating apples.

D.   Consuming two apples a day might make a positive impact on your cholesterol levels.

131.   While recent research has shown that cannabis access laws can reduce the use of prescription opioids, the effect of these laws on opioid use is not well understood for all dimensions of use and for the general United States population. Analysing a dataset of over 1.5 billion individual opioid prescriptions between 2011 and 2018, which were aggregated to the individual provider-year level, it was found that recreational and medical cannabis access laws reduced the number of morphine milligram equivalents prescribed each year by 11.8 and 4.2 percent, respectively. These laws also reduced the total days supply of opioids prescribed, the total number of patients receiving opioids, and the probability a provider prescribes any opioids net of any offsetting effects. Additionally, the study found consistent evidence that cannabis access laws have different effects across types of providers, physician specialties, and payers. (*sciencedirect.com*)

A.   Following this research, more US states will relax their restrictions on cannabis.

B.   A dataset of over 1.5 billion records has not led to certainty about the effects of cannabis access laws.

C.   Laws that allow access to cannabis have been

proven to reduce the use of prescription opioids.

D.   Cannabis laws were found to have a uniform effect on prescription opioid use.

132.   About 84% of official workplace social events involve alcohol, according to research carried out for the Chartered Institute of Personnel and Development. During the Christmas party season 40% of businesses that are planning a Christmas event say that alcohol will be freely available and paid for by the company, while 39% say alcohol will be available to buy with no limit. The impact can be positive and negative. Four out of 10 HR managers surveyed said that alcohol can cause problems at work. But almost 50% of the managers said having some drinks at social events had a positive effect on morale and team bonding. (*BBC News*)

A.   Drinking to excess is a common feature of workplace social events involving alcohol.

B.   It cannot be said that a minority of HR managers found that drinks at social events have positive effects.

C.   Only a minority of workplace social events appear to place limits on alcohol consumption.

D.   Christmas events with free alcohol cause more problems than those where employees pay.

133.   A third of the poorest countries in the world are dealing with high levels of obesity as well as under-nourishment, which leaves people too thin, according to a report in The Lancet. It says the problem is caused by global access to ultra-processed foods, and people exercising less. The report estimates that nearly 2.3 billion children and adults on the planet are overweight, and more than 150 million children have stunted growth. And many low and middle-income countries are facing these two issues at once – known as the "double burden of malnutrition". This means that 20% of people are overweight, 30% of children under four are not growing properly, and 20% of women are classified as thin. Communities and families can be affected by both forms of malnutrition, as well as individual people at different points in their lives, the report

says. According to the report, 45 out of 123 countries were affected by the burden in the 1990s, and 48 out of 126 countries in the 2010s. (*BBC News*)

A. Ultra-processed foods are the main reason why people in poor countries are becoming more obese.

B. Being overweight and also experiencing stunted growth are not mutually exclusive.

C. A combination of obesity and undernourishment causes people to be too thin.

D. The number of countries affected by the double burden has grown significantly.

134. A team collected hair from several mammal species, including humans, and pulled strands until they broke. The researchers examined the broken ends with scanning electron microscopy. They found that thin hair, such as human hair, tends to break in long cracks, with individual keratin fibres coming unstuck. Thicker hair, such as elephant hair, tends to break cleanly straight across. Counterintuitively, the researchers found that thin hair tends to be stronger than thick—a phenomenon they suggest is related to the size and quantity of flaws in the hair strand. One exception was capybara hair, the strands of which have an indent down the middle believed to help shed water. That hair tended to fail along that centre line, giving it a lower tensile strength than expected. (*cen.acs.org*)

A. Thick hair tends to be weaker because it has more flaws.

B. Researchers found the strength of hair was inversely proportional to its thickness.

C. Capybara hair is the one exception to the rule that thinner hair is stronger.

D. Human hair was found to be among the strongest types of hair.

135. Multiple systems that are designed to make driving safer and easier are placing drivers in danger, according to a new study. Adaptive cruise control and lane-keeping-assist technologies lull drivers into letting their guard down, which puts them at greater risk of crashing. When used correctly, the technologies can make people safer. But many drivers place too much trust in the systems, according to the study.

Evidence increasingly suggests that drivers often don't properly use or understand partially automated systems. The AAA study concluded that those two systems make drivers "nearly twice as likely to engage in distracted driving" as drivers who aren't using them. Perhaps counterintuitively, drivers who aren't as familiar with the systems are less likely to drive distracted while using them, according to the AAA. (*USA Today*)

A. The AAA thinks that two systems that increase the risk of crashes should be discouraged.

B. Cruise control and lane-keeping-assist technologies inevitably make driving more dangerous.

C. Driving assisting technologies were found to have the potential to increase driving risks.

D. When drivers use both technologies, they are almost twice as likely to not pay as much attention.

136. Universities are accused of being left wing bastions, unwelcoming to conservative and right wing professors. However, we know little about the political orientation of professors in comparison to other professionals, which would be the right comparison group if we want to know whether universities are potentially hostile environments to conservatives. Examining culturally and economically oriented political orientations in Europe, it is demonstrated that professors are more liberal and left leaning than other professionals. However, there is no greater homogeneity of political orientations among the professoriate relative to other specific professions, suggesting that there is a diversity of opinions which is similar to what professionals would find in other occupations. Importantly, the difference between professors and other professionals is not so clear within graduates from the social sciences, but emerges more clearly among graduates with a medical, STEM, economics or law degree. (*wiley.com*)

A. Professors in the United States were found to be more liberal and left-leaning than other professionals.

B. The study found that universities in Europe were hostile towards those with conservative values.

C.   The study found a lack of heterogeneity in beliefs by professors compared to other professionals.

D.   Professors and other professionals with social science degrees were found to have more similar political opinions than those with medical degrees.

137.   A new study found that people given accurate statistics on a controversial issue tended to misremember those numbers to fit commonly held beliefs. For example, when people are shown that the number of Mexican immigrants in the United States declined recently – which is true but goes against many people's beliefs – they tend to remember the opposite. And when people pass along this misinformation they created, the numbers can get further and further from the truth. "People can self-generate their own misinformation. It doesn't all come from external sources," said Jason Coronel. "They may not be doing it purposely, but their own biases can lead them astray. And the problem becomes larger when they share their self-generated misinformation with others." (*news.osu.edu*)

A.   The study found that people tended to create their own fake news.

B.   People will ignore the truth if it contradicts their opinions on things.

C.   The more information is passed on, the more it becomes distorted.

D.   People were found to deliberately distort the truth to their own beliefs.

138.   People distracted by their mobile phones are tripping, falling and hurting their heads and necks more often, with such injuries increasing "steeply" over a 20-year period, a new analysis has found. Most cases were mild, but some involved facial lacerations and traumatic brain injuries that could lead to long-term consequences, the authors warned. The study is believed to be the first to investigate the role smartphones play in injuries to these parts of the body. Previous studies have found that all types of "distracted walking" injuries have been on the rise. Head and neck injuries related to mobile phone use were relatively rare until the rate began to increase sharply in 2007,

the year the first iPhone was released, followed by a much steeper increase that peaked in 2016. Mobile phone users aged 13 to 29 made up almost 40 percent of the patients, and most of the injuries caused by distraction happened in this age group. (*NBC News*)

A.   Mobile phone distraction has resulted in a big increase in serious head and neck injuries.

B.   Older people were found to have higher rates of injury from distracted mobile use.

C.   The arrival of smartphones has led to medical problems.

D.   The ability of smartphones to browse the web or play games is why injuries increased.

139.   Puppies in pet stores appear to have transmitted a dangerous, antibiotic-resistant germ that's sickened 30 people across 13 states, the U.S. Centers for Disease Control and Prevention warned. The infection in question is a multidrug-resistant form of Campylobacter jejuni, the agency said. So far, of 24 patients interviewed by the CDC, 21 – 88 percent – said they had recently touched a puppy. "Four people have been hospitalized," the CDC said, although "no deaths have been reported. Interviews with ill people and laboratory evidence indicate that contact with puppies, especially those from pet stores, is the source of this outbreak. Puppies and dogs can carry Campylobacter germs that can make people sick, even while appearing healthy and clean," the CDC noted. So, "people who own, work with or come in contact with puppies or dogs should take steps to stay healthy." (*upi.com*)

A.   A puppy bought from a pet store is likely to be a carrier for an antibiotic-resistant germ.

B.   Despite looking healthy and clean, puppies and dogs carry a variety of germs.

C.   Puppies sold in pet stores were more likely to carry the Campylobacter germ.

D.   The CDC reported that the majority of those who had touched puppies had become sick.

140.   Tropical forests that have been heavily logged -- cleared and replanted, cleared and replanted -- may never recover. According to a new study, continually logging tropical forests depletes the reserve of vital nutri-

ents in the soil, diminishing the forest's odds of long-term recovery. "Old-growth tropical forests that have been the same for millions of years are now changing irreversibly due to repeated logging," lead study author Tom Swinfield said. When scientists surveyed the health of trees in previously logged forests on the island of Borneo, they found their leaves were thicker and featured lower concentrations of nitrogen and phosphorous. Soil nutrients are essential to healthy vegetation. When trees die and decompose naturally, the nutrients are returned to the soil. When forests are logged, the nutrients are carried away with trees. Logging also increases soil erosion, further depleting the land of nitrogen and phosphorous. Scientists estimated that as much as 30 percent of a forest's phosphorous is lost when it is logged. (*upi.com*)

A. Hopes that better tropical forest management can restore the previous ecosystem are misplaced.

B. It would be wrong to claim that repeated logging does damage.

C. The effects seen in tropical forests are unlikely to be as serious in temperate forests.

D. Repeated logging can be damaging, but a single cycle won't cause much real damage.

141. If you already have a cold, you're less likely to get the flu, and vice versa, a large new study shows. While this interaction between colds and the flu has been observed, a new study was large enough to provide strong evidence of it, according to its authors. The investigators tested for 11 types of respiratory viruses in more than 44,000 samples taken from more than 36,000 people with an acute respiratory illness. Of those people, 35 percent tested positive for a virus. Of those, 8 percent were infected with more than one type of virus. The most significant interaction was between influenza A viruses and rhinoviruses, a cause of the common cold. Computer modelling found that interactions between the two that inhibited infection with both appeared to occur in both individual people and the population as a whole. Patients with influenza A were about 70 percent less likely to also be infected with rhinovirus than patients infected with other virus types, according to the study. (*upi.com*)

A. The study showed that the common cold could be used as a vaccine to prevent the flu.

B. People who caught the flu or the rhinovirus were found to have immunity to the other.

C. Understanding how these viral infections work could pave the way to a common cold vaccine.

D. Catching one virus acts like a temporary vaccine to lower the risk of catching the other type.

142. Researchers studied the growth of the Italian broadcaster Mediaset, and found that those heavily exposed as children to its pabulum of cartoons, soap operas and quiz shows were almost 10% more likely to support populists, because poorer cognitive skills left them more susceptible to politicians peddling simplistic arguments. Kids in towns where it was harder to pick up the Mediaset signal were less affected than their peers. The result was that heavy Mediaset consumers ended up with poorer cognitive skills, and less of an orientation to civic life, as well as performing worse on maths and literacy tests. Still, it's crucial to grasp that this sort of "dumbing down" doesn't happen because bad TV somehow injects stupidity into people's heads. It's about the opportunity cost: every hour you're sitting in front of a rubbish cartoon is an hour you're not reading, exploring the physical world, or watching educational programming. (*The Guardian*)

A. For bad television to have a negative impact it simply has to replace something better.

B. People who watched less television were less inclined to support populists.

C. The study found that Italians were especially susceptible to being affected by television.

D. Watching low quality television is certain to make people more supportive of populists.

143. According to a study by the University of Manchester, we may have the wrong idea about blue light filters. Also referred to as night mode, the blue light filters on our devices are designed to help us sleep better at night by not messing with our circadian rhythm. It turns out this feature could be doing the exact opposite. Using specially designed lighting to adjust the colour temperature without changing the brightness,

the team exposed mice to various colours and observed the effects it had. The results suggested blue light produced fewer effects on the mice's body clock than yellow light. The research team says this makes sense since the evening is both dimmer and bluer than day time, and the body heavily relies on these two identifiers to determine appropriate asleep and awake times. Using dimmer, cooler lights in the evening and brighter, warmer lights in the day may be more effective at helping manage our bodies natural sleep cycle. (*androidauthority.com*)

A.   The colour of a light and not its brightness is what affected the mice's ability to fall asleep.

B.   The night time light filters on our electronic devices may be having an unintended effect.

C.   Evening use of dimmer, warmer lights is better for our sleep patterns than cooler, brighter ones.

D.   The study found that yellow lights were more likely to keep people awake later at night.

144.   Scientists say they have discovered a possible underlying cause of the neurological disorder, motor neurone disease (MND). The University of Exeter team says it has found evidence that MND is linked to an imbalance of cholesterol and other fats in cells. It says the research could lead to more accurate diagnosis and new treatments. MND affects around 5,000 people in the UK and causes more than 2,000 deaths a year. Scientists at the university say they had a "eureka moment" when they realised that 13 genes – which, if altered, can cause the condition – were directly involved in processing cholesterol. They say their theory could help predict the course and severity of the disease in patients and monitor the effect of potential new drugs. Lead author Prof Andrew Crosby said: "For years, we have known that a large number of genes are involved in motor neurone disease, but so far it hasn't been clear if there's a common underlying pathway that connects them." (*BBC News*)

A.   The scientists found evidence that high cholesterol levels are linked to motor neurone disease.

B.   Discovering how genes process cholesterol

could lead to a better understanding of the disease.

C.   If the 13 genes can be altered back, then they can be prevented from causing the disease.

D.   The researchers had expected only one defective gene would be involved in MND.

145.   In a recent study, children exposed to smoking in the first 4 years of life were more likely to exhibit symptoms of hyperactivity and conduct problems. The study found that the association remained even after controlling for family poverty level, parental education, parental history of attention deficit hyperactivity disorder, hostility, depression, caregiver IQ, and obstetric complications. The effects examined in the study, which included 1,096 children, were a function of the dosage of nicotine that children were exposed to, as quantified by the metabolic by-product cotinine in their saliva. The findings are consistent with animal models demonstrating an effect of exposure to nicotine on ongoing brain development in regions related to hyperactivity and impulsivity. "There is a lot of emphasis on the dangers of smoking during pregnancy, but our findings indicate that children continue to be vulnerable to the adverse effects of nicotine exposure during the first several years of life," said lead author Lisa Gatzke-Kopp. (*eurekalert.org*)

A.   Hyperactivity in children is frequently caused by exposure to smoking in the first 4 years of life.

B.   Children's exposure to smoking early in life is not as well understood as smoking during pregnancy.

C.   A child who exhibits hyperactivity could have been exposed to nicotine at a young age.

D.   It is the cotinine in the cigarettes that is thought to damage children.

146.   Northern Scotland registered a "remarkable" overnight temperature of 16.8°C in the early hours of 30 December, a record high for that time of year. Forecasters have attributed the unseasonably warm weather to a meteorological pattern called the Foehn Effect. It occurs in mountainous areas, creating wet and cold conditions on one side of a mountain and warm and dry conditions on the other. The phenomenon occurs when

humid air is pushed over high ground by strong winds. As the moisture-filled air rises, it cools and condenses, resulting in clouds and rain. This then releases dry air, which moves down the mountain's other side, heating up and raising ground level temperatures as it travels. The effect coincided with gusts of warm air arriving from the southern Atlantic, which have resulted in Britain being warmer than Athens and Rome. (*The Guardian*)

A. The Foehn Effect occurs when air hits a mountain and is diverted in a different direction.

B. On 30 December the Foehn effect raised the temperature by 16.8°C.

C. Wet and cold air is as much a part of the Foehn Effect as warm and dry air is.

D. The temperature of 16.8°C was remarkable because it occurred during the night-time.

147. The North Atlantic Current transports warm water from the Gulf of Mexico towards Europe, providing much of north-western Europe with a relatively mild climate. However, scientists suspect that meltwater from Greenland and excessive rainfall could interfere with this ocean current. Simulations by scientists from the University of Groningen and Utrecht University showed that it is unlikely that the current will come to a complete stop, due to small and rapid changes in precipitation over the North Atlantic. However, there is a 15 percent likelihood that there will be a temporary change in the current in the next 100 years. The current shows non-linear behaviour, which means that small changes can have large effects. Such temporary transitions may cause cold spells in the North Atlantic, although this needs to be verified in further studies. (*eurekalert.org*)

A. A small change in an ocean current could have large effects.

B. Much of north-western Europe has a warm climate due to the North Atlantic Current.

C. More studies are likely to find that temporary changes will cause cold spells in the North Atlantic.

D. It cannot be said that the possibility exists that the current will undergo a transitory change.

148. Autism spectrum disorder (ASD) is a developmental disorder that affects how a person behaves, interacts with others and learns. Previous studies have found that when one identical twin has ASD, chances are extremely likely that the other twin has it, too. A new study analysed data from three previous studies comprising a total of 366 identical twin pairs with and without ASD. The severity of autism traits and symptoms in the twins was measured by a clinician's assessment or by parents' ratings on a standardized questionnaire. Some cases were diagnosed by both methods. The researchers determined a 96% chance that if one twin has ASD, the other has it, too. However, symptom scores varied greatly between twins diagnosed with ASD. The researchers estimated that genetic factors contributed to only 9% of the cause of trait variation among these twins. In contrast, among pairs of identical twins without ASD, the scores for traits were very similar. (*eurekalert.org*)

A. Even if both twins had autism spectrum disorder, the severity could be very different.

B. If one twin does not have autism spectrum disorder, then neither twin will have the disorder.

C. Genetic factors were the leading single reason for the differing levels of severity in twins with ASD.

D. ASD traits for identical twins were found to be more similar than for non-identical twins.

149. The platypus is one of the few living mammals to produce venom. Males have a pair of spurs on their hind limbs that secrete venom that is active only in breeding season, supporting the hypothesis that the use of venom is for competition for mates, not for protection. While the spur remains available for defence, outside of breeding season the platypus's venom gland lacks secretion. While the venom's effects are described as excruciatingly painful, it is not lethal to humans. Many archaic mammal groups possess similar tarsal spurs, so it is thought that, rather than having developed this characteristic uniquely, the platypus simply inherited this characteristic from its antecedents. Rather than being a unique outlier, the platypus is the last demonstration of what was once a common mammalian characteristic, and it can be used as a

model for non-therian mammals and their
venom delivery and properties. (*Wikipedia*)

A.   Although today it is rare for mammals to
      have venom, it was once widespread.

B.   The platypus's venom, while extremely
      painful, is not lethal to other animals.

C.   The platypus is the last example of once
      common mammals that produce venom.

D.   It cannot be said that the venom of the female
      platypus is more painful than the male's.

150.   **The capacity of re-grown areas of the
       Amazon rainforest to draw carbon dioxide
       from the atmosphere and combat climate
       change may have been "vastly overesti-
       mated", scientists fear. The forest is a gigan-
       tic carbon sink, drawing the greenhouse gas
       from the atmosphere. Cleared areas that are
       re-planted are known as secondary forest,
       and have been seen as key to fighting cli-
       mate change, researchers at Lancaster
       University said. But a new study has found
       that those areas held just 40 percent as much
       carbon dioxide as sequestered by parts of
       the Amazon untouched by humans, casting
       doubt on their ability to aid in mitigating
       the crisis. And at the same time, global
       warming appeared to be hampering the re-
       growth of secondary forest. Scientists moni-
       tored forest regrowth over a period of 20
       years and revealed how the Amazon was
       affected by periods of drought. During
       times of "water deficit", regrown forests
       absorb less carbon from the atmosphere.
       (*The Independent*)**

A.   Secondary forests were found to have no
      effect in capturing carbon from the atmos-
      phere.

B.   Clearing areas in the Amazon has a lasting
      impact even when trees are later replanted.

C.   Rainforests are inherently more effective at
      capturing carbon than other forest types.

D.   Forests that go through cycles of replanting
      were found less able to absorb carbon.

ANSWERS

1. C

A.   Cannot say. While measles "predisposes chil-
      dren to all other infectious diseases for up to
      a few years" the passage does not say
      whether those who catch measles definitely
      will catch other diseases.

B.   Cannot say. The passage suggests that this is
      probably the case, but not that it is for certain.

C.   True. The passage says that "studies in mon-
      keys have suggested that measles ... erases
      immune protection to other diseases".

D.   Cannot say. While the passage only refers to
      monkeys, it does not exclude humans, mean-
      ing that it could also apply to them.

2. A

A.   True. While an outer protective layer will
      protect a cheese, once that is breached, the
      inner, untreated cheese will eventually go
      bad, even in a refrigerator.

B.   Cannot say. Although the passage mentions
      that brie has an outer layer of edible mould, it
      does not mention inedible types.

C.   False. Cheddar "is wiped with saline regu-
      larly to keep mould from growing on it".

D.   Cannot say. The passage does not discuss
      whether a cheese will remain preserved
      indefinitely if the rind is intact.

3. D

A.   Cannot say. The passage does not state if this
      is widely believed or not, only that the name
      may suggest it.

B.   False. The passage says that it is *usually* older
      people with other conditions who experience
      acute kidney injury, but that means that
      younger people do experience it as well, even
      if not as frequently.

C.   Cannot say. Without dialysis, kidney shut-
      down *may* lead to death, but as the passage
      states, acute kidney injury may also only
      result in a minor loss of kidney function,
      which would not be fatal.

D.   True. It CAN be said. Acute kidney injury is
      when your kidneys suddenly stop working

properly, and this can include a "minor loss" of kidney function.

4. B

A.   False. Human resources people were used because their job is to be in tune with other people.

B.   True. We are told in the passage that psychopaths are "people with dark traits". The study of HR personnel found those with dark traits who were "not lacking the ability to empathize", meaning they CAN empathize, but score low in their inclination to use this ability.

C.   Cannot say. People who do not actually empathise may be either able or unable to do so, and there is no information as to the relative proportions in the general population.

D.   False. Researchers found that "overwhelmingly" those with the dark triad were not inclined to behave in an empathetic way.

5. C

A.   Cannot say. There is no comparative assessment of the irrigation skills of the Assyrians and Egyptians.

B.   False. The Assyrians were affected more seriously by the megadroughts than those further downstream because the Tigris in northern Iraq was "so deeply cut into the surrounding soil" that it prevented large-scale irrigation.

C.   True. As the passage states, the empire was built during a time of heavy precipitation and successful harvests, which when they ceased spelled the end of the empire. While not saying that this was a "climatological anomaly", it also doesn't rule it out, thus making it possibly the case.

D.   Cannot say. We are told that it was "a series of megadroughts that likely triggered the collapse of the empire" and that "Assyrians were much more vulnerable to the impacts of prolonged and severe drought than people downriver". However that by itself does not necessarily mean the empire would not have fallen when it did if it had been further downriver. It could, for example, have fallen to invasion.

6. B

A.   False. The study found the drug did not help participants get to sleep any faster.

B.   True. The study found that using the drug was related to longer duration of sleep and less time spent awake during the night.

C.   Cannot say. The passage does not provide specifics on whether it was a minority or majority of participants who felt fatigued the day after smoking marijuana to help them sleep.

D.   Cannot say. The passage does not discuss how effective or ineffective alcohol was as a sleeping aid.

7. C

A.   Cannot say. The passage simply states that red wine is better for your microbiome than other types of alcohol, not that other types are necessarily good.

B.   Cannot say. Drinking red wine once every two weeks was enough to observe an effect, but we are not told if this could be increased by drinking more frequently.

C.   True. Drinking wine is not enough to be beneficial for gut bacteria, it has to be red wine.

D.   Cannot say. The passage refers to some possible health benefits of drinking red wine but does not discuss whether drinking red wine, regardless of amount or frequency, will improve your health.

8. B

A.   Cannot say. The study only looked at people "at or above the 98th percentile of intelligence", not all those who are "above average".

B.   True. According to the passage, "those with a high intellectual capacity (hyper brain) possess overexcitabilities in various domains that may predispose them to certain psychological disorders".

C.   Cannot say. The passage refers to highly intelligent people having higher rates of food allergies, but does not specifically mention nuts.

D.   Cannot say. The passage only provides specific rates for the highly intelligent.

9. B

A.   Cannot say. The passage does not say if drawing blood became painless in some cases, only that it was much less painful when the person taking the blood was courteous.

B.   True. The study found that "the experience of pain is much more significantly affected by the attitude of the people treating you" than by the number of needle pricks, whose effect was small.

C.   False. The figure refers to people being 390% more likely to say their pain was well-controlled, not that the actual pain reduced by 390%.

D.   Cannot say. This is mentioned as one way of helping to reduce pain levels, but not whether it is the *best* way.

10. C

A.   False. The new finding is a new possible explanation, but the passage does not say that it negates earlier possible explanations.

B.   Cannot say. This has been suggested as an explanation, but the passage does not discuss its likelihood.

C.   True. According to the passage, children born in the autumn and winter when pregnant women have higher cortisol rates may have higher risks for schizophrenia and bipolar disorder.

D.   Cannot say. Although the passage discusses the incidence of such disorders in January, it says only that "these disorders are more common in people born during the winter months", not whether January is the peak month.

11. B

A.   Cannot say. Although vaping is the single "most popular and effective way for smokers to quit" we are not told how many ways there are, or vaping's importance as a proportion of these. Nor are we told the relative importance of people not starting to smoke in the first place.

B.   True. Although the indoor smoking ban only prevented smoking inside, the number of smokers and cigarettes smoked fell subsequent to it coming into effect.

C.   False. This can indeed be said, as the average number of cigarettes smoked per day by smokers has decreased over time.

D.   Although vaping is increasing rapidly and cigarette smoking falling, we are not told the percentage of adults vaping, or indeed if present trends will continue.

12. A

A.   True. The study found high rates of dental problems among athletes despite their brushing twice a day.

B.   False. According to the passage, changes to saliva may "exacerbate the damage", but this is not the prime cause.

C.   Cannot say. There is nothing in the passage to indicate either way if British athletes had better or worse oral health than non-British athletes.

D.   Cannot say. The passage says researchers believe that to be the case, but it did not say it has been proven.

13. D

A.   Cannot say. Scientists think this may be the case but the passage does not say that this is known for certain.

B.   Cannot say. The passage does not mention what role, if any, exercise played in the weight loss.

C.   Cannot say. The research into the effects of alternate-day fasting was carried out at the University of Graz but there is nothing in the passage about who has pioneered the use of the diet.

D.   True. As the passage states, the reason alternate-day fasting appears to be a healthy option is because it is close to how humans ate thousands of years ago.

14. C

A.   False. Email traffic actually increased when offices switched to an open plan layout.

B.   Cannot say. The study looked at the comparative impact of open-plan and cubicle layouts on communication, not at the impact on productivity.

C.   True. The study found that in open plan offices, people were less likely to make face to face contact and found new ways to preserve their privacy.

D. Cannot say. The passage does not discuss cost savings.

15. D

A. Cannot say. While "the likelihood of someone using opioids increases significantly once a family member living in the same household has a prescription" we are not told whether or not the *majority of new users* come from such households.

B. Cannot say. The comparative ease of access of lower and higher-income households is not mentioned.

C. False. It would be right to say it. Because patients "typically receive more pills than they need" it creates a temptation for relatives to "experiment with leftovers sitting in the medicine cabinet".

D. True. The study found that the impact *could* be measured: "the chances of a relative obtaining a prescription for opioids within a year after a relative they live with gets one rises by 19 percent to over 100 percent, depending on family circumstances".

16. C

A. Cannot say. The test was conducted on non-human primates, so whether or not it would work on humans is not yet known.

B. False. The passage says that anxiety that emerges at adolescence *may* affect people all their lives, not that it will.

C. True. According to the passage, the finding provides hope for new strategies focused on intervening early in life to treat people at risk for anxiety disorders.

D. Cannot say. While stating that current treatments work for only a subset of people and often only partially relieve symptoms, we don't know the size of the subset or what percentage "partially" means.

17. A

A. True. According to the passage, e-cigarette use may in fact be leading to an increase in nicotine addiction.

B. Cannot say. The passage says that the "prevalence of their use is rapidly growing in many countries", but this could be limited to certain parts of the world.

C. Cannot say. The passage does not discuss the social acceptability of e-cigarettes.

D. Cannot say. The passage says that e-cigarettes can result in users having "higher exposure to doses of nicotine compared to people who smoke traditional cigarettes", but the reason given for this is that "e-cigarettes are used in times and places where smoking is prohibited". The comparative amounts of nicotine in traditional and e-cigarettes is not mentioned.

18. A

A. True. According to the passage, people are more likely to take action in a crisis when there are few or no other witnesses present.

B. Cannot say. The passage does not say if the effect only occurs in certain societies.

C. False. The more people are around, the *less likely* a person is to intervene in a situation, which means that it is inversely proportional.

D. Cannot say. While this may seem a plausible statement, there is nothing in the passage to indicate its validity.

19. D

A. Cannot say. While "young people in particular place higher demands on themselves", nothing is said about the effects on older people.

B. Cannot say. The passage states that millennials put themselves at risk of mental and physical illness, but it does not elaborate on their behaviour.

C. Cannot say. The passage hints that images in the media might be an important factor but does not explicitly evaluate its impact.

D. True. This is the main theme of the text.

20. C

A. False. Researchers "found a broad worsening of mental health indicators, particularly in the second half of the study period".

B. Cannot say. The authors indicate they believe this to be the case but do not state it as being for certain.

C. True. While the passage certainly suggests that to be the case, nonetheless it does not say it for certain.

D.   Cannot say. No comparable data is given for non-students in the same age group.

21. C

A.   Cannot say. According to the passage, they are the best pet, but there are other animals not considered pets that might be better.

B.   Cannot say. The passage only mentions dogs as increasing the sense of well-being, but it does not state that other animals do not also have this effect.

C.   True. According to the passage, what seemed to make dogs have the greatest positive impact on health is that they require their owners to be physically active.

D.   False. According to the passage, the researchers did not find that owning a dog by itself was enough to protect against cardio-vascular disease.

22. A

A.   True. The passage states that average Americans trust only 10 to 20 people, and that that number may be shrinking.

B.   False. According to the passage, a study put the average person's friend group at about 121 people. 250 to 5,500 people refers to a person's social network size.

C.   Cannot say. Although this was used in the study, that does not mean it is excellent, only that it was deemed suitable for the purposes of the study.

D.   Cannot say. The passage says there is a link between strong social relationships and living longer, but it does not say that life spans have decreased.

23. A

A.   True. The study found that several factors may make it harder to avoid gaining weight today than in the past such as exposure to chemicals, increased use of prescription drugs and changes in people's microbiomes.

B.   Cannot say. The passage only says that *not gaining* weight is more difficult today than 20-30 years ago, not that *losing* weight is.

C.   Cannot say. A person of the same age having the same diet and amount of exercise in 2006 would have a BMI 2.3 points higher than in 1988. However we are not told if *on average* people in 2006 ate or exercised more or less

than in 1988, and therefore what BMI was on average.

D.   Cannot say. The passage mentions these as possible factors, but only as a hypothesis.

24. B

A.   False. According to the passage, there are arguments over whether technology is good or bad for children's development.

B.   True. The study found that as children use more smart devices and televisions, their imaginations have suffered.

C.   False. The passage said "almost" two-thirds, not more than two-thirds.

D.   False. The "fewer than half" refers to the percentage of nursery workers who said that the children at their nursery had imaginary friends.

25. A

A.   True. The survey was in 2017 and the oil spill was in 2010 and the survey found "an abundance of … the Atlantic deep-sea red crab".

B.   Cannot say. The passage says there has been an increase in numbers since a survey two months after the spill, but does not indicate how this compares to numbers *before* the spill.

C.   Cannot say. Although saying the oil spill damaged the area, the passage does not say if it was *irreversibly* changed or not.

D.   Cannot say. The passage says that there has been a change, but it does not say if this is permanent or only temporary.

26. B

A.   False. Fires are part of the life cycles for certain types of forests, but not for all of them, such as rainforests.

B.   True. In certain situations, preventing small fires from occurring means that fuel for a fire accumulates so that when one does occur, it is much worse than it would be otherwise.

C.   False. Intense fires are sometimes necessary to consume old and diseased trees, create new habitats, and ensure an ecological rejuvenation of the tree population.

D.   Cannot say. While this might seem a possible explanation, the passage does not mention it.

27. C

A. Cannot say. Researchers found people showed "greater goal commitment" when they shared their goals with someone they believed had higher status. We are not told whether or not they got *better advice*.

B. Cannot say. The passage does not elaborate on the rates of goal attainment by those who do not share them.

C. True. According to the passage, people do not want perceived superiors to think less of them, which was their motivation for attaining a goal after they revealed it to someone with higher status.

D. Cannot say. The passage says that the opinions of those with a lower status were not beneficial for pushing people to achieve a goal, but not whether the opinions of those with a lower status matter or not.

28. D

A. False. According to the passage, panic attacks can come on for no apparent reason.

B. Cannot say. The highest frequency the passage mentions is several panic attacks a week, but it does not say that they cannot happen more frequently.

C. Cannot say. While saying some panic attacks have been reported to last up to an hour, it does not say that they cannot last longer.

D. True. As the passage states, most of the symptoms of a panic attack can also be symptoms of other conditions or problems.

29. A

A. True. The U.S. military found that 90 percent of expired medications were still sufficiently effective several years after their expiry date.

B. Cannot say. While a medicine used within its shelf life "will work to its maximum potency and safety", there is no indication whether it is the subsequent reduction of potency or of safety that is the more significant risk.

C. False. The passage tells us that "most of them are not toxic when expired", meaning that some of them are.

D. Cannot say. While the U.S. military study found that to be the case for the over 100 medicines they tested, that does not mean it applies to ALL medicines.

30. D

A. Cannot say. The passage compares the chances of reaching 85 of the most optimistic and the least optimistic women, and those of the most optimistic and the least optimistic men. It does not make a comparison between men and women.

B. Cannot say. While this *may* be the case, the passage does not declare one study to be more accurate than the other.

C. False. The studies controlled for health conditions and behaviours so that these would not impact the results.

D. True. The most optimistic women lived 14.9% longer than their peers, while men only lived 10.9% longer.

31. A

A. True. As the passage says, people experiencing impostor syndrome incorrectly attribute their success to luck or as deceiving others.

B. Cannot say. The passage states that early research focused on women, but does not say that men were believed not to be affected by impostor syndrome.

C. False. Impostor syndrome is described as a "psychological pattern", not a mental illness.

D. Cannot say. The passage says that people with impostor syndrome "incorrectly attribute their success to luck", but does not refer to how people *who actually did* achieve their success through luck will feel.

32. C

A. False. The passage says it tends to run in families, which means that it is not always the case.

B. False. The passage says that it is *often* the case, which also means that it is not *always* the case.

C. True. The signs of an impending psychotic break are often dismissed as symptoms of typical adolescent behaviour.

D. Cannot say. There is no information in the text as to whether a psychotic break can be prevented if its warning signs are recognised in time.

33. C

A. Cannot say. The passage tells us that 11 percent of youngsters whose mothers suffered anxiety have ADHD symptoms, compared with 5 percent of all youngsters. However we are not told what proportion of ALL mothers suffer anxiety. It could be that most children with ADHD are actually born to mothers who do not suffer anxiety.

B.   Cannot say. Scientists believe this may be the case, but say they are not certain.

C.   True. The study found that the rate for ADHD among children was 11% for those with anxious mothers, and only 5% for those without.

D.   Cannot say. The passage specifically refers to Attention Deficit Hyperactivity Disorder, not Attention Deficit Disorder, which is not mentioned.

34. C

A.   Cannot say. While the passage states that alcohol consumption has declined by 0.8% since 2017, it does not directly attribute this to increased legal marijuana sales. Other factors could be involved.

B.   Cannot say. The IWSR warns that companies will need to begin anticipating shifting demands, but we are not told if they have so far "proved reluctant" to do so.

C.   True. The passage tells us both these facts.

D.   Cannot say. Up to 40% of adults consume cannabis in states where it is legal but we are not told the proportion who consume alcohol.

35. D

A.   Cannot say. Although we are told South Korean imports of Japanese beer have plunged 97%, making this seem a likely conclusion, the text gives us no information about the scale of imports of Japanese beer by other countries.

B.   Cannot say. The passage suggests it is simply a case of South Koreans not buying Japanese beers in protest, but there is nothing said about tariffs.

C.   Cannot say. Although the passage mentions a South Korean brewer as benefiting, we are not told whether an aim of the boycott was to increase consumption of South Korean, as opposed to any other non-Japanese, beers.

D.   True. With a drop of 97% in August from a year earlier, it is perfectly reasonable to

believe that Japanese beer "may no longer" have the largest share of the South Korean beer import market, even if we are not definitively told as much.

36. A

A.   True. Almost 75 percent of earthquakes occur along tectonic plate boundaries.

B.   Cannot say. As 75 percent of earthquakes occur along tectonic plate boundaries, 25 percent must occur elsewhere. However that does not necessarily mean they can occur *anywhere*.

C.   Cannot say. The passage mentions *Southern California* experiencing earthquakes almost every three minutes, but does not say anything about whether earthquakes occur in *South Carolina*.

D.   Cannot say. We are told that "there is a 100-percent chance that an earthquake will strike somewhere in the world each day" and that almost 75 percent of earthquakes occur along tectonic plates. However that does not rule out the possibility of there being days on which earthquakes are experienced only in areas NOT on the tectonic plates.

37. B

A.   Cannot say. The passage tells us that the Earth's elliptical orbit can cause warming, but does not refer to it as a factor in current global warming.

B.   True. Scientists have found that the Palaeocene-Eocene Thermal Maximum was caused by an eccentricity in the Earth's orbit around the sun.

C.   False. The Earth's orbit around the sun goes through cycles where it is more circular or more elliptical.

D.   Cannot say. During the past 100 million years, the Earth was at its hottest 56 million years ago, but it may have been hotter before that.

38. C

A.   Cannot say. The passage does not state whether Samsung doubled its market share or not, only that it ended the quarter with twice the market share of its nearest competitor.

B.   Cannot say. While we are told that Samsung

offers smartphones that are indeed "comparable" there is no mention of what they cost to buy.

C.   True. While "the overall smartphone market in CEE remained flat" Samsung achieved a 40% market share, which was twice that of Huawei, its nearest competitor, meaning that it is the largest player in the market.

D.   Cannot say. While the passage tells us that the refreshed A-series was Samsung's "star performer", other factors such as the US trade embargo, marketing or pricing could also have produced such growth.

39. A

A.   True. In the summer there is "a wide blend of scent", while when it is cooler and drier "specific scents tend to stand out more".

B.   False. Scents are easier to pick out because there are not as many of them as in the summer.

C.   Cannot say. The passage says *hot and muggy* air enables scent molecules to move through the atmosphere more quickly. However the question refers only to the heat of the air, not whether it is also muggy. Since we are not told how scent travels in *hot but dry* conditions, we cannot say for sure.

D.   Cannot say. The relative importance of temperature and humidity are not discussed.

40. B

A.   Cannot say. The passage describes the spotlight effect as something everyone experiences, and does not discuss how it varies between different types of people.

B.   True. Our "tendency to anchor other people's viewpoints to our own", and not accurately consider what someone else's perspective might be, is the root cause of the spotlight effect.

C.   False. The spotlight effect is "something that we all experience frequently in our everyday life".

D.   False. The reason we experience the spotlight effect is because we *tend not to* consider other perspectives, not that we cannot.

41. D

A.   Cannot say. Planets that "stray too close" may be swallowed, but we are not told for

certain if that applies to any planets that are simply "close" when the star expands as it ages.

B.   Cannot say. The passage says that it can make a star grow brighter, but does not state either way if it can make the star grow larger.

C.   False. This situation may cause the star to spin too quickly, but it is not certain to.

D.   True. As the passage makes clear, this can certainly have detrimental effects for the star, such as causing it to rip itself apart.

42. B

A.   Cannot say. We are told that "hundreds of small independent restaurants had collapsed as well as big chains", so we do not know whether overall customers turned away from chains to independents or vice-versa.

B.   True. According to the passage, this market segment is oversaturated and there is simply more supply than demand.

C.   Cannot say. We are told that "tightened consumer spending on the back of concerns about Brexit" and "rising costs because of the collapse value in the value of the pound" are said to be factors in the insolvencies, but no direct link is suggested between the concerns about Brexit and the value of the pound.

D.   Cannot say. The passage tells us that 1,412 restaurants became insolvent in the year to the end of June 2019 and that "hundreds" of small independent restaurants had collapsed. However without more exact figures we cannot determine if "hundreds" represented a majority or minority of the restaurants that closed.

43. C

A.   Cannot say. The passage merely states that Europeans put greater emphasis on "less energy-intensive forms of cooling". This could be for other reasons, such as cost.

B.   Cannot say. Japan has the highest rate mentioned in the text, but there could be other countries with higher adoption rates.

C.   True. Only 20% of European households have air conditioning, but increased global sales will be driven mostly by sales in developing countries.

D.   False. According to the passage, increased European air conditioning system sales will be driven by more people moving to cities.

44. C

A.   False. Inflation *increased* in twelve Member States.

B.   Cannot say. The passage discusses two different sets of inflation rates, one for the whole of the EU and the other just for the euro area. The statement is true in respect of the annual euro area inflation rate, but we are not told whether this was also true of the inflation rate for the EU as a whole.

C.   True. Portugal had a negative annual inflation rate of -0.1% during the period observed.

D.   False. Inflation within the euro area was 1.0% exactly, and not over it.

45. B

A.   False. Euro area production in construction in July 2019 was 1.1% higher than in July 2018. Month-on-month, meaning comparing with June 2019, it decreased by 0.7%.

B.   True. "In June 2019, production in construction increased by 0.6% in the euro area and by 0.1% in the EU28." It follows therefore that production in construction must have increased by less, or most likely decreased, in the non-euro countries.

C.   Cannot say. The passage only says Hungary saw the largest percentage increase in construction, not construction outright.

D.   Cannot say. France, Slovakia and Poland are the only three countries *for which data was available* that saw decreases, but that does not rule out the possibility that other countries also had decreases.

46. C

A.   Cannot say. According to the passage, its speed means that the comet "likely originated" outside our solar system, meaning that it is probable but not certain.

B.   Cannot say. The passage says that such comets "could be more common than thought", but not that they definitely are.

C.   True. Astronomers said that speed of the comet was so fast that it likely originated from outside our solar system.

D.   Cannot say. The passage implies that comets from our own solar system are slower than those with an interstellar origin, but it does not say that they ONLY travel at slower speeds.

47. D

A.   False. Aperture only partially determines this, in combination with shutter speed.

B.   False. As the passage states, the smaller the aperture, the larger the f-number, meaning it is inversely proportional.

C.   Cannot say. The effects of these particular combinations of aperture size and shutter speed are not discussed.

D.   True. Aperture is what determines the depth of field of an image, or how much of the image is in focus.

48. A

A.   True. Scientists "predict" this, but that does not mean it is known for certain.

B.   Cannot say. Scientists "are still not sure whether climate change will lead to an increase or decrease in their frequency".

C.   Cannot say. Although "climate change is expected to lead to a rise in hurricane rainfall", there is nothing in the text to indicate that this is already occurring.

D.   False. Scientists believe the rise in global sea levels will lead to coastal storms being more destructive due to increased risks from storm surges, but not from more intense hurricanes.

49. D.

A.   False. ISO is ONE of the settings, along with aperture and shutter speed, that determines the brightness of a photograph.

B.   Cannot say. The passage states that as a possibility, not a certainty.

C.   False. ISO is in fact what determines a camera sensor's sensitivity to light.

D.   True. As the passage states, "a photo taken at too high of an ISO will show a lot of grain, also known as noise, and might not be usable".

50. B

A.   False. We are told that Capsicum plant seeds "are dispersed predominantly by birds", which means that seeds are also dispersed in other ways or by other animals.

B.   True. Mammals have molar teeth which destroy the seeds, thus preventing them from germinating, while birds simply pass the seeds through their digestive tracts unharmed.

C. Cannot say. It is only a theory that natural selection "may have led" to increased capsaicin production. It does not mean that it definitely did.

D. Cannot say. The passage only mentions birds and mammals, and does not refer to reptiles, for example.

51. B

A. Cannot say. The passage merely states that occupational asthma can cause a range of illnesses, not that it is a *leading cause* of them.

B. True. As the passage states, although occupational asthma can result from "exposure to a substance you're sensitive to", it can also result from exposure to "an irritating toxic substance".

C. False. Those with family histories are "more likely" to develop occupational asthmas, which means that some people who develop it do NOT have a genetic predisposition.

D. Cannot say. While it may well be the case that some jobs are far more likely to cause occupational asthma than others, the passage does not state that it ONLY affects people in certain lines of work.

52. D

A. Cannot say. The passage does not reveal how Merseyside voted in the referendum.

B. Cannot say. The passage does not discuss the avoidance of tabloid media as a whole, or how well informed people were.

C. Cannot say. While a "substitution effect" particularly benefitted rival tabloid the Daily Mirror, we do not know if this was the "most popular choice" of former Sun readers. Many may simply have stopped reading ANY newspaper.

D. True. The report says the boycott of a Eurosceptic newspaper for an entirely unrelated reason "cut Euroscepticism in the county by more than ten percent".

53. D

A. Cannot say. While it can be said based on the passage that it is possible that they are hungry, we cannot say if it is probable.

B. Cannot say. Benjamin Vincent said that "it is

important that people know that being hungry can affect their preferences", because of the "danger" of them making decisions that entrench their poverty. However while this is a danger it does not mean it will always happen.

C. Cannot say. The passage never discusses why people end up in poverty, only that going hungry may negatively impact their ability to escape it.

D. True. The scientists found that "hunger can … lead to impatience".

54. C

A. Cannot say. We are only given comparative data for two medical conditions, stroke and heart disease, and in any case only comparing vegetarians with meat-eaters.

B. Cannot say. This might seem a perfectly logical inference, given that vegetarians have a lower risk of heart disease than meat-eaters. But the risk of heart disease faced by vegans is not mentioned, and there could be additional factors, such as missing elements in the vegan diet, that make heart disease more likely, not less.

C. True. Vegetarian diets are associated with a 20 percent higher risk of stroke, a serious medical condition, than that seen in meat-eaters.

D. Cannot say. Vegetarians have a lower risk of heart disease than meat-eaters, but while this "could be explained by vegetarians generally having lower cholesterol levels" this is not given as a definite case of cause and effect.

55. A

A. True. Although the passage does not tell us by how much, the amount paid out in claims means less has been saved from suspending repairs than initially would have been the case.

B. Cannot say. While likely the case, it could also be that people are now more proficient at filing claims or simply file more of them.

C. Cannot say. We are told that 571 claims were made in 2018 and that the number of successful claims in 2018 was "more than four times the 68 on which TfL paid out in 2017". Four times 68 is 272, which is indeed less than half the total of 571 claims. However, because the number of successful claims was "more than" four times 68, we cannot be sure that the actual number of successful claims was less than half of the total of 571 claims.

D.   Cannot say. We are told that £1.7 million has been paid to cyclists over the past 5 years, of which almost £350,000 was in 2018. This means that at least £1,350,000 was paid in the other 4 years combined. This *could* have been paid out evenly, meaning no other year exceeded £350,000 (the average of £1,350,000 over 4 years being only £337,500), but it is also possible that the 2018 figure of £350,000 could have been exceeded previously.

56. B

A.   Cannot say. The passage says the unemployment rate is the lowest in the EU28 since the start of the EU monthly unemployment series in January 2000, but the statement does not exclude lower rates prior to that.

B.   True. While we are not given specific figures for the non-euro area, since the euro area is performing worse than the EU as a whole, it follows that the non-euro area is outperforming the euro area.

C.   Cannot say. The passage only says the *unemployment rate* was the lowest recorded since records began in 2000, not that the *number of people unemployed* was the lowest. If the workforce has grown since 2000, it is possible that the unemployment rate could have gone down while the number of unemployed went up.

D.   Cannot say. The passage does not break down the number of unemployed men or women, only providing a combined total.

57. B

A.   Cannot say. Russia was previously considered "one of" the heaviest-drinking countries, but that does not necessarily mean it was THE heaviest-drinking country.

B.   True. According to the WHO, alcohol consumption has long been recognised as one of the main driving factors of mortality in the Russian Federation, especially among men of working age.

C.   False. While Russian consumption has gone down, it is not 43% of what it was in 2003, but 43% less, meaning that it is still more than half the previous figure.

D.   Cannot say. While probably true, the passage never says this.

58. A

A.   True. Two-thirds of the patients showed a marked reduction in microbial diversity at some stage during their stay.

B.   Cannot say. While long-term effects could exist after a person has been discharged, that is not equivalent to saying they will be "worse off" than before they were admitted. Patients will have been admitted for treatment of some other condition.

C.   Cannot say. The passage tells us that two-thirds "showed a marked reduction in microbial diversity at some stage during their stay". This does not exclude the possibility of some patients leaving only after their microbial diversity was back to normal.

D.   Cannot say. Although "heavy use of broad-spectrum antibiotics" is something that could contribute to reduced microbial diversity in the gut, that does not necessarily mean that ANY use of antibiotics would inevitably have the same effect.

59. D

A.   Cannot say. This is what UBS estimates could happen, but we are not told what Airbus and Boeing expect.

B.   Cannot say. Although 24% of US travellers said they would change their flying habits due to environmental concerns compared to 16% of British respondents, this measures willingness to change flying habits, not concern for the environment. Other factors might be involved: for example, American respondents might more easily be able to substitute other forms of travel.

C.   Cannot say. Without the figures for French and German respondents, we cannot say if this is the case or not.

D.   True. UBS, which we are told is a Swiss bank, expects flights in the EU to increase by only 1.5% per year, while Airbus, which we are told is a plane maker, forecast a more optimistic rate double that.

60. B

A.   Cannot say. We are told only that neutrinos are "the lightest of all the known subatomic particles".

B.   True. Scientists have only been able to measure the upper limit of their mass, but not the lower limit.

C.   Cannot say. While neutrinos are "among the most abundant particles in the Universe", we are also told that they are the lightest of the known subatomic particles, so we cannot deduce if they make up most of the universe's mass.

D.   False. Neutrinos are difficult to measure because they tend to cross matter undetected.

61. A

A.   True. Although not definitely stating this as a fact, the passage suggests that dining choices may have been influenced by the relative prices of vegetarian and non-vegetarian options. This means that price "may" have been a factor.

B.   Cannot say. The passage does not provide information on the taste of the meals, only their quantity.

C.   Cannot say. This is a possibility, the passage states, but not one that is for certain.

D.   False. Sales of vegetarian meals rose 40–80%.

62. A

A.   True. As the passage states, in all countries, the information provided by demographers is key to meeting the population's present and future needs.

B.   False. Demographers *predict* how populations are likely to change; this does not mean they necessarily *know* how they will.

C.   Cannot say. The passage doesn't say what percentage of people working as demographers actually have a degree in demography, so we cannot say.

D.   False. According to the passage, demographers analyse data that has been assembled by national statistical offices.

63. A

A.   True. According to Professor Newman, some people with anxiety may stay anxious and avoid relaxation to prevent a later larger shift in anxiety.

B.   False. It is better to experience shifts in stress levels and to allow yourself to be relaxed at times.

C.   Cannot say. The passage says that mindfulness training *and other interventions* can help people let go and live in the moment. What sort of intervention is best is not stated.

D.   False. The text tells us that "it's actually healthier to let yourself experience those shifts".

64. C

A.   Cannot say. The passage mentions government corruption but not how democratic or undemocratic a country is.

B.   Cannot say. While GDP becomes extremely volatile because of over-dependence on the price of commodities, we are not told whether the price is primarily affected by fluctuations in demand or other factors such as fluctuations in output from the country's mines.

C.   True. As the passage states, when a country focuses on a single industry, its overall gross domestic product becomes volatile, which means that the price of the resource being focused on is not stable. Since the price of the resource on which the country has become over-reliant is not stable, the country is now exposed to price fluctuations.

D.   Cannot say. The passage does not elaborate on this either way, although of course it may play a role.

65. A

A.   True. In its more deadly form, Q fever can damage your brain but many people with the milder form have no symptoms at all, therefore are unaware they have it.

B.   Cannot say. The passage does not provide information on when chicken pox is dangerous or not.

C.   False. The passage says that "if Q fever recurs, you may need to take antibiotics for at least 18 months".

D.   Cannot say. Q fever is transmitted to humans by animals, "most commonly sheep, goats and cattle", but we are not told which of these is the most likely to pass it on.

66. D

A.   Cannot say. The passage only discusses its use by photographers in general terms, without reference to their experience.

B.   False. Since it is a manual override of an automatic feature, it can also be used when a photographer wants a photo to be lighter or darker than the camera's meter would other-wise allow.

C.   False. As the passage states, camera meters can usually be relied on, except in challenging lighting conditions.

D.   True. Exposure compensation allows a photographer to manually determine how bright, or how dark, a photograph will be.

67. C

A.   Cannot say. Although we are told it has a younger surface than Mercury or Mars that does not rule out other planets being younger.

B.   Cannot say. The passage only states that the surfaces of Mars, Mercury and the Moon are much younger than the surface of Venus, and does not provide information on the age of the planet itself.

C.   True. Since scientists do not know if Venus had plate tectonics to begin with, they also cannot know if the vaporising of the planet's water stopped plate tectonics or not.

D.   False. The Sun did not vaporise Venus, merely the surface water on the planet.

68. B

A.   Cannot say. The passage says this is the lowest level recorded by this *two-yearly* survey, so there could have been lower levels in intervening years.

B.   True. According to the passage, 16 percent of boys had smoked, compared to 17 percent of girls, therefore it CAN be said that boys were more likely to have smoked than girls.

C.   Cannot say. The only information provided on the use of e-cigarettes is that the number who said they had used e-cigarettes had remained stable.

D.   Cannot say. The highest proportion of smokers recorded by this survey was 49 percent, in 1996, which would have been just short of a majority. However there is no information as to whether a majority of children smoked at any time before 1996.

69. C

A.   Cannot say. The passage only states that delicate cycles released more microplastics than standard cycles, not that they destroyed

clothes (that is made them unwearable) more often.

B.   Cannot say. The passage says nothing on this topic.

C.   True. Contrary to expectations, delicate wash cycles released more plastic fibres into the environment than standard cycles.

D.   False. As the passage states, the volume of water appears to be the most important factor in dislodging fibres from clothing.

70. D

A.   Cannot say. Scientists suggest this may be the case, not that it is established for certain.

B.   False. According to the passage, "the ears of Neanderthals were comparable to those of human children". However they did not change with age, as children's ears do.

C.   Cannot say. The passage does not discuss the issue of failing to evolve and there may have been other factors involved in their extinction.

D.   True. Scientists found that Neanderthal ears were similar to children's ears, making them more susceptible to ear infections and complications.

71. D

A.   Cannot say. The passage does not mention sea breezes specifically, only proximity to the coast, so it could be something else that is actually beneficial.

B.   Cannot say. The passage tells us that "mental health disorders … are far more likely in people from poorer backgrounds". However it also tells us that proximity to the coast is linked to better mental health among the poor. It is possible, therefore, that this specific group among the poor have better mental health than richer people inland.

C.   False. The passage specifically mentions access to blue spaces, not green spaces.

D.   True. While it is quite possibly the case that proximity to the coast is also good for the mental health of richer people, nonetheless the passage only states this for those in the lowest earning households.

72. B

A.   False. The Sahm Rule is a rule for *interpreting*

the unemployment statistics, not itself a statistic.

B. True. Claudia Sahm invented it to flag oncoming recessions and the rule aims to be more dependable than metrics the financial market currently uses.

C. Cannot say. The passage says that the Sahm Rule is *intended* to be more dependable, but that does not necessarily mean that it is.

D. Cannot say. Sahm herself argues in favour of this, but there is no indication of whether it will actually happen.

73. A

A. True. The percentage of road accidents in Germany caused by truck drivers who fell asleep was between 30-50%, or less than a majority.

B. False. Accidents "caused by truck drivers who fall asleep momentarily at the wheel … are the most serious accidents".

C. Cannot say. The passage tells us that being overweight can lead to sleep-related breathing problems. However, that does not mean that having sleeping problems means that a person is likely to be overweight. There could be many other reasons for sleep problems.

D. False. According to the passage, "deadly accidents due to sleep deprivation happen quite frequently — perhaps twice as often as accidents as a result of drunk driving".

74. C

A. Cannot say. While "non-flushers" can have up to eight drinks a week without increasing their risk of high blood pressure, we are not told whether drinking more than this can have other types of health risk.

B. Cannot say. The study did not include women, so there is nothing said on this topic.

C. True. According to the passage, excess amounts of acetaldehyde may cause both facial flushing and high blood pressure, and since "flushers" were found to be at greater risk of high blood pressure, acetaldehyde may be the culprit.

D. Cannot say. The passage only says this could be the case, not that it is, and that "a causal relationship between the two remains unproven".

75. B

A. False. More recent data suggests only that this is "likely" to be the case, not that it is known for certain.

B. True. As the passage states, they are hypothetical but scientifically realistic, and it mentions the storms that affected in California in 1861-1862.

C. False. The passage says a quarter of California's homes could be affected, meaning that three-quarters would not. Thus we can conclude that most of California would NOT be underwater.

D. Cannot say. The passage gives no information on the factors that can cause such storms or whether or not they are more or less likely in Arizona or California.

76. B

A. False. The passage says the slowest walkers, not all slow walkers, tended to have indicators for neurodegenerative and psychiatric disorders, and having an indicator for a disease is in any case not the same as actually having it.

B. True. Doctors found that slower walkers were aging faster.

C. Cannot say. The passage discusses the middle-aged and elderly, but does not mention children.

D. Cannot say. Slow walkers in their 70s and 80s tend to die sooner, which is not the same as saying that they always do.

77. D

A. False. According to the passage, people use them because they're so convenient, even though "we know that Facebook and Google know too much about us".

B. Cannot say. The passage presents this opinion, but follows it up with a contradictory one.

C. Cannot say. This is what people who find such services useful and benign think about the sceptics, but that does not mean they are.

D. True. As the passage states, voice assistants are "unusually polarising".

78. D

A. Cannot say. While saying it is most common

for those in their 70s and 80s, the passage also says it can affect people of all ages.

B.   False. Loss of peripheral vision is the first sign of glaucoma, when it can still be treated.

C.   False. Fluid build-up in the front part of the eye is USUALLY the cause, not just occasionally.

D.   True. Because it tends to develop slowly over many years, i.e. gradually, many people do not realise that they have it.

79. A

A.   True. By overworking the muscles on the right-hand side of the heart, they weaken, and this can lead to heart failure.

B.   Cannot say. It "can affect people of all ages" but the passage does not reveal if certain age groups are more affected by it or not.

C.   Cannot say. The passage tells us that pulmonary hypertension is "a rare condition" and that it is "more common in people who have another heart or lung condition". However that does not necessarily mean that it is rare among those who have pulmonary hypertension for someone to be without other conditions.

D.   False. Pulmonary hypertension ONLY affects the right side of the heart.

80. B

A.   Cannot say. The findings are based on exercising for 30 minutes four times a week. While this is the same amount of exercise as 20 minutes six times a week, we do not know if the *frequency* or the *length of each session* could also be relevant factors.

B.   True. Researchers said it may be effective, but that more research needs to be done in a larger trial.

C.   Cannot say. We are told what the research found about the regularity of exercise, not its intensity.

D.   False. Doctors do in fact think that exercise may well be a useful treatment, even if not a cure, for early Alzheimer's: "the findings suggest that aerobic workouts can at least slow down the effects of the disease if intervention occurs in the early stages".

81. A

A.   True. The passage tells us that shorter or

"blue" wavelengths are scattered by the atmosphere unlike longer wavelengths.

B.   Cannot say. The passage only mentions how the scattering of light waves affects the moon's apparent colour, not its apparent size.

C.   False. The light reaching us scatters less when the moon is overhead, thus its appearance is distorted less.

D.   Cannot say. There is no information provided on how shorter or longer light waves affect how large the moon looks.

82. B

A.   False. Scientists did not see water droplets, but rather that light was being filtered in a way that would be caused by water vapour condensing into liquid water.

B.   True. K2-18 b is a distant planet and astronomers "have spotted hints of water raining in the atmosphere". There is no indication of *how much* rainwater there might be, so it is possible there could be more than on Earth.

C.   Cannot say. The passage only says having water in the atmosphere does not necessarily mean it also has life, and does not say if it is likely or unlikely.

D.   Cannot say. The passage does not state if planet size is important for having water in the atmosphere.

83. D

A.   Cannot say. The passage discusses the beneficial effects of taking vacations, but does not say whether or not an *annual* vacation would be sufficient.

B.   False. As the study noted, a woman's chances of having a heart attack when not taking vacations went up 50%, compared to only 30% for men.

C.   Cannot say. While the study took into account health factors such as diabetes, cigarette smoking, income levels and obesity, it is not mentioned if exercise was also controlled for, so we cannot say.

D.   True. Not taking vacations affected women more than it did men.

84. D

A.   Cannot say. The passage does not mention if

Asian typhoons or American tropical storms are stronger than the other.

B. False. The storms have become 50% stronger, which is 1.5 times their previous strength, not half as strong.

C. Cannot say. The passage does not provide a rate for how much stronger the storms hitting America have become, so we cannot say.

D. True. According to the passage, climate change makes SOME weather events more severe, which also means that it is not the case for ALL weather events.

85. A

A. True. According to the passage, even smoking five cigarettes a day is two-thirds as bad for lung damage as smoking 30 a day, meaning that cutting down from 30 to 15 won't make a big difference.

B. False. Light smoking caused two-thirds of the damage of heavy smoking.

C. Cannot say. The passage says that reducing daily cigarette use "can be an important step toward quitting entirely", but not that people who cut back first are more likely to quit entirely than those who don't.

D. False. Because cutting back can be an important step towards quitting entirely, it can still have significant health benefits.

86. D

A. Cannot say. The passage says they have their "shortcomings", but that can mean anything from being bad to being good but just needing some improvement.

B. Cannot say. The passage does not make clear if this is usually the case or if it only occurs within a minority of journals.

C. False. Coercive citations occur when an editor asks for more citations *to their own journal*, but not when they simply ask for citations to improve a paper.

D. True. As the passage makes clear, in some cases an article may only be published if it includes unnecessary citations referring back to the journal it is being published in.

87. C

A. False. The study "opens the door" tor new treatments for joint injuries, but did not itself produce new treatments.

B. Cannot say. While the study has opened the door to new treatments for repairing joint injuries, at best it can be said that it has made human limb generation perhaps more possible, which itself is far from certain.

C. True. As the passage states, children can regenerate their fingertips when treated correctly.

D. False. The process is similar, but not the same.

88. B

A. False. While the trait is "associated with holding left-wing views", that does not rule out that some hold other views.

B. True. Politicians who showed an openness to experience, "a trait related to greater curiosity and imagination" were found to be less likely to win.

C. Cannot say. This is raised as a possibility, but it is not stated for certain.

D. Cannot say. Openness to experience is just one of many factors in deciding any individual outcome, so we cannot say if it would be the determining factor or not.

89. A

A. True. There was no change after medical use was legalised, but contrary to some concerns, usage among teens declined by nearly 10% in states where recreational use was legalised.

B. Cannot say. The passage only suggests this as one possibility.

C. Cannot say. There is evidence that teen use falls when cannabis is legalised, but the passage does not say either way if this would be a solution.

D. Cannot say. The passage does not elaborate on this.

90. C

A. Cannot say. This seems quite possible, but the passage does not discuss Jupiter and the Sun.

B. Cannot say. A barycentre being located outside a celestial object may be due to distance, or it may be due to the similar size of the objects.

C. True. Even when there are differences in size,

the barycentre is not the exact centre of the larger object.

D.   Cannot say. The text says that when a less massive body orbits a more massive one "the more massive body might be observed to wobble slightly". However we are not told if this happens in the case of the Earth and the Sun.

91. D

A.   Cannot say. The passage does not discuss this specific possibility.

B.   Cannot say. While "it has been argued" that such missions should not be started, there is no indication that this is "increasingly accepted".

C.   Cannot say. This is given as a point of view, not as a fact.

D.   True. The passage highlights the risk of a newer mission overtaking an older one.

92. B

A.   Cannot say. The passage does not elaborate on the effects of happy music.

B.   True. Two studies have found that people with depression felt better after listening to sad music.

C.   False. Depressed people were found to feel better after listening to sad music.

D.   Cannot say. The passage only discusses the effect of instrumental music, not vocal music.

93. A

A.   True. The rise in tuition fees has impacted those from lower socioeconomic classes more significantly.

B.   Cannot say. The passage says the United States has fallen behind, but that does not mean it led formerly.

C.   Cannot say. The passage says that it is *one* of the biggest reasons, but not that it is *the* biggest.

D.   False: "fewer young adults are getting a higher education than their parents".

94. B

A.   Cannot say. The passage tells us that the syndrome "is more prevalent in patients with co-morbidities such as diabetes, obesity, and

Crohn disease, but can occur in otherwise healthy individuals". However, there is no indication of the likely relative frequency of any of these so the syndrome may or may not be most commonly linked to diabetes.

B.   True. Everyone produces alcohol, but in most people the amounts remains minute.

C.   False. The passage says such people produce ethanol, not methanol.

D.   False. Because it can produce extreme blood alcohol levels, auto-brewery syndrome is in fact potentially dangerous.

95. B

A.   False. The study did in fact find that people from wealthier communities with more education ate better diets.

B.   True. It was found that in poorer communities where people were less educated, there were higher rates of prescription painkiller use.

C.   Cannot say. The passage does not elaborate on this.

D.   False. That is precisely what the study *did* find.

96. D

A.   Cannot say. While loss of profits *may* be their concern, the passage never states this and the video game makers themselves cited other concerns.

B.   Cannot say. While a neuroscientist suggests that this might be the case, it is not given as a definite fact.

C.   Cannot say. The only group mentioned as opposed to this classification is the video game industry, so we do not know how widespread the controversy was.

D.   True. Gaming disorder has been classified as a mental health condition by the WHO, but a neuroscientist says it might be a coping mechanism for a deeper, underlying problem.

97. D

A.   Cannot say. The passage does not mention Saturn or its rings.

B.   False. As the passage states, centrifugal forces are also needed to pull a satellite apart, meaning that a larger planet's gravity is not enough.

C. False. It is not the tidal forces created by the satellite that are the issue, but those produced by the object that it orbits.

D. True. When the tidal forces exerted on a planet are greater than its gravitational self-attraction, then the Roche limit will apply and it will disintegrate.

98. C

A. Cannot say. While tidal forces may vary depending on the distance from the object being orbited, the passage does not state that they are erratic.

B. False. "Sustained tidal heating occurs when the elliptical orbit is prevented from circularizing."

C. True. The difference in tidal forces due to an elliptical orbit is what causes tidal heating.

D. Cannot say. The passage says that tidal forces "are stronger near periapsis", but that does not necessarily mean that tidal heating is at its most intense at periapsis. There could, for example, be a delayed reaction.

99. D

A. False. Although it *can* run in families that does not mean that it always does.

B. False. Synaesthesia can trigger senses other than sight.

C. Cannot say. While saying that a specific type of visual synaesthesia (grapheme-colour synaesthesia) is the most common, other types combined may still make up a majority of the cases.

D. True. When a person senses something and another sense is also activated, that is synaesthesia.

100. B

A. False. Eighty-five percent of respondents believed their *mother* had a favourite child, not both parents.

B. True. Some parents said they love their children equally, but may get along best with one in particular.

C. Cannot say. Eight-five percent of respondents thought their mothers had a favourite

child, but we do not know what percentage of mothers actually did.

D. Cannot say. The passage says that MANY parents admit to having a favourite child, which may or may not mean MOST.

101. D

A. False. The passage says the percentage of delayed talkers having persistent language problems later in life is 40%, which is less than half.

B. Cannot say. The passage only mentions that having mental health risks and delayed language skills can be a "double whammy", but does not say if one causes the other.

C. False. This was the first study to link the two, so it cannot have been already established.

D. True. The study investigated the link between toddlers' delayed vocabulary and severe temper tantrums, including in children as young as 12 months, "which is much younger than many clinicians typically believe problematic behaviour can be identified".

102. B

A. Cannot say. We are told only that those born in the last three months of the school year were 30% more likely to develop depression than those born in the first three months. There is no information about the *actual likelihood* of any of these children getting depression.

B. True. The passage identifies children born in the summer as being the youngest in their school year and tells us that "children born in the last three months of the school year were prone to being 30% more likely to develop depression compared to those born in the first three months", i.e. those born in the autumn.

C. Cannot say. The passage mentions how younger children may be more at risk of mental health issues, but does not provide any remedies or suggestions on how to avoid it.

D. Cannot say. The youngest children were 30% more likely to develop mental health problems, but as we do not know the actual frequency we cannot say if 30% is frequent or uncommon.

103. A

A.   True. According to the passage, sleeping in the daytime on most days could be a sign of a health problem.

B.   Cannot say. The passage indicates this could possibly be the case, but not that it is for certain.

C.   False. There is indeed a lack of a consensus on the healthiness of daytime napping, with different studies reaching contradictory conclusions.

D.   False. According to the passage, having more than 1 or 2 naps merely "did not reduce" risks.

104. C

A.   Cannot say. Logic may dictate as much, but the article does not elaborate on this.

B.   Cannot say. While stating that sugars and artificial sweeteners both caused health problems, of different types, there is no assessment of which problems were worst.

C.   True. The researchers compared people who drank 2 or more glasses of a soft drink per day to those who drank less than 1 per month, i.e. those who frequently drank them were compared with those who rarely did.

D.   False. Sugary drinks were linked to digestive diseases, while artificially sweetened drinks were linked to cardiovascular diseases.

105. C

A.   Cannot say. Panic disorder was one of the "four common anxiety disorders" studied, but there is no evaluation of which of the four involved the strongest feelings of hopelessness.

B.   Cannot say. While saying that increases in hope were a positive indicator in terms of recovery, the passage does not say that those whose hope levels remained unchanged were NOT expected to recover.

C.   True. The study looked at the use of CBT for four common anxiety disorders, including panic disorder, finding that hope was a "common element" in recovery for all types and that "increases in hope were greater for those in active treatment than for those in the waitlist".

D.   False. According to the passage, hope increased gradually, not quickly.

106. C

A.   Cannot say. No association with temperature was observed except in the case of cold days that were also damp as well as windy, therefore in this case the temperature is irrelevant. Both windiness and low atmospheric pressure are "linked to more painful days" but we are not told which of these is the more significant.

B.   Cannot say. Cold days can produce more pain if also damp and windy, and we do not know if that means *most* cold days.

C.   True. Cold makes no difference unless also accompanied by dampness and "the most important factor associated with worsening pain is high relative humidity". Therefore a cold and dry day will produce less pain than a warm and damp one.

D.   False. The passage says that dry days are when patients are "least likely" to experience pain, which means that they still might.

107. A

A.   True. There is nothing in the passage to say whether or not binocular rivalry will prove to be the most accurate method of diagnosis, but we are told that it "could facilitate earlier diagnosis", which is a benefit.

B.   Cannot say. While an advantage of binocular rivalry is that "it can be used to evaluate young children who have not started talking yet as well as non-verbal adults", it is not stated whether it is better overall. Verbal assessment might, for example, be more accurate in assessing most adults.

C.   Cannot say. Although the rate of binocular rivalry was predictive of the severity of symptoms, and the data meant autism could be diagnosed with 87% accuracy, this does not necessarily mean that people without autism never had binocular rivalry. It is possible that ALL the cases not in the 87% were where people had autism without showing binocular rivalry; likewise it is possible that ALL or SOME of them were where people had binocular rivalry but not autism.

D.   False. The rate was found to be directly, not inversely related.

108. B

A.   Cannot say. Although junior researchers who co-author with established, highly-cited scientists gain a "competitive advantage", the comparative importance of the quality of their work is not discussed.

B.   True. "Junior researchers affiliated with less prestigious institutions show the most benefits from co-authorship with a top scientist".

C.   Cannot say. The passage states this as a possible outcome, not a certainty.

D.   Cannot say. While some junior researchers do enjoy a competitive advantage "compared to peers with similar early career profiles but without top co-authors", the article does not consider if this is actually fair or not. Clearly, if the researchers studied had similar early career profiles, so were equally qualified, the selection of which of them got the top co-authors was not necessarily unfair.

109. D

A.   Cannot say. The passage says this is more likely to happen to nail-biters than non-nail-biters, but it does not say that it is for certain.

B.   Cannot say. The passage says that "many people" think this to be true, but does not say if it actually is or not.

C.   Cannot say. The passage only says nail-biters often feel stigmatized, but not whether they actually are.

D.   True. Nail biters "often suffer psychologically", so have a distressing habit, and they get gastrointestinal infections more frequently.

110. D

A.   Cannot say. The passage does not discuss any correlation of this sort.

B.   Cannot say. The passage only says that the average life satisfaction rate increased, but that could still allow for it to have decreased in some member states.

C.   Cannot say. The passage is about life satisfaction, not happiness.

D.   True. The passage does not state either way whether life satisfaction decreased in some countries, so it is possible.

111. D

A.   False. Whiplash occurs from a "rapid back-and-forth movement of the neck", not just in one direction.

B.   Cannot say. The text says whiplash "most often" occurs during a rear-end auto accident, but that does not necessarily mean this is the "overwhelming" cause.

C.   False. Whiplash is only a *type* of neck sprain or strain, much like how a square is a rectangle but a rectangle is not necessarily a square.

D.   True. Whiplash can be the result of a rear-end auto accident and can lead to chronic back pain and other long-lasting complications.

112. D

A.   Cannot say. The passage says that most people who are infected have no or only minor symptoms. It does NOT say, however, what proportion of these people actually know they have the virus, so we cannot be sure if most people know or do not know they have it.

B.   False. Mosquito repellent and covering your skin with clothes will only reduce your risk.

C.   False. A mosquito-transmitted virus causes "most" cases of West Nile infection, which means that some cases have other causes.

D.   True. Since most people infected with West Nile virus either do not develop signs or symptoms or have only minor ones, it is possible that many do not know they are infected.

113. C

A.   Cannot say. The passage says that wind speed has been increasing in recent years, but does not say if this trend will continue or not.

B.   Cannot say. The topic of climate change is not mentioned.

C.   True. Scientists believed that wind speed was falling due to increasing urbanisation creating more barriers to moving air, but despite continued urbanisation wind speed has *increased* in recent years. This has created a challenge to the former theory.

D.   Cannot say. While saying that scientists thought the earlier decline in wind speed was due to urban development, the passage does not say this was wrong. It leaves open the possibility that while urban development does indeed slow wind speed, other factors increasing wind speed have more recently counteracted this.

114. A

A.   True. According to the passage, climate change will not impede the spread of diseases, but instead will facilitate it.

B.   False. The period covered by the data is from 1980. Therefore if last year was the second highest on record, at some point in the period there must have been one year with more such days, meaning that the number of days did not increase each year.

C.   Cannot say. The passage only discusses the health impacts of warmer, not wetter, conditions, so we do not know if wetter conditions will also cause health problems.

D.   Cannot say. The passage says they will have higher exposure to it, which is different from saying they will have a higher rate of catching it. Children may become more resistant or drugs developed to prevent it being caught.

115. D

A.   Cannot say. While this might seem plausible, the passage does not state if this is being done, or if it is even possible.

B.   False. Current estimates say it could kill up to 70% of European ash trees, which while a huge proportion, is still not wiping them out.

C.   Cannot say. The passage does not state if scientists are trying to stop ash dieback due to the economic costs or simply to save the trees.

D.   True. If the fungus can kill up 70% of ash trees, and up to 70 million trees could be lost in the UK, that means that there are approximately 100 million ash trees in the United Kingdom.

116. B

A.   Cannot say. The passage says men are *most stressed* when they are entirely economically dependent on their partner, but then says husbands are at their *most anxious* when they are the sole breadwinner, so we cannot say.

B.   True. According to the study, men were least stressed when their spouse made 40% of the total household income, leaving them as the primary breadwinner.

C.   False. The study only looked at heterosexual couples, thus stating that the study found that gender did not matter would be false.

D.   Cannot say. The passage says the study suggests this may be the case, but not that it is known for certain. Men's anxiety could be being triggered by economic factors or the difficulties of juggling two careers.

117. C

A.   Cannot say. The passage does not mention anything about girls learning faster at younger ages, only that having an older sister does not impact a younger sibling's language skills.

B.   Cannot say. The passage mentions this as a possibility, but not as something that is definitely true.

C.   True. According to the passage, children with an older sister did not actually differ in their language skills from those with no older sibling.

D.   False. According to the passage, older brothers take up more of their parents' time, not spend more time with their younger siblings.

118. A

A.   True. As the passage states, of those trying to lose weight, few find success, and the mean weight of those studied actually increased.

B.   Cannot say. The passage does not state if there was an unknown reason for the weight gain or not. The reason might be known but simply not given here.

C.   Cannot say. While willpower might seem likely to have been a factor, the passage does not mention it one way or another.

D.   Cannot say. We are told that "a minimum of one in four participants reported trying to lose weight in each of the two-year periods". However we do not know if these were different sets of participants or if some people were surveyed in both periods. If the latter, it could be that less than a quarter of ALL the participants attempted to lose weight.

119. C

A.   Cannot say. The passage merely says that overconfident parents might not pick up on subtle signals, not what less confident ones might do.

B.   Cannot say. We are told that "30 percent of parents said their child is good at hiding feelings and 40 percent said they struggle to differentiate between their child's normal mood swings and signs of depression". We are NOT told, however, if these two subsets of parents overlap, with some in both groups, so the two figures cannot simply be added together.

C.   True. According to the passage, only a third of parents said they were confident they could detect depression in their children.

D.   Cannot say. The passage says that "one-third were confident they could detect depression in their children" but we are not told what proportion of these might overestimate their ability to detect depression.

120. B

A.   False. According to the passage, the increased risk appears to occur because the genes that are linked to height are also associated with atrial fibrillation.

B.   True. Since taller people have a higher risk of atrial fibrillation, and atrial fibrillation increases a person's risk of stroke, it follows that taller people are at higher risk of a stroke.

C.   Cannot say. The passage does not clarify if the two are related or coincidental.

D.   Cannot say. While aggressive control of blood pressure and diabetes could reduce risk, we are not told whether this could be reduced to normal levels.

121. D

A.   Cannot say. The passage says there are many myths surrounding them, but does not say if most of the common knowledge about them is wrong.

B.   False. According to the passage, not fighting an intrusive thought will make it go away.

C.   False. According to the passage, the opposite is the case.

D.   True. Rather than making intrusive thoughts go away, the effort people put into fighting the thought is what makes it stick and fuels its return.

122. C

A.   Cannot say. The age of a car is neither mentioned nor excluded as a factor.

B.   Cannot say. The passage discusses cars but there is no reference to trains.

C.   True. A person's muscles are in use throughout long car journeys to keep their posture properly maintained.

D.   Cannot say. While turns are cited as one factor, others are involved, such as the condition of the car and how often it brakes. On a straight road these other factors may outweigh the benefits from lack of turns.

123. C

A.   Cannot say. While the passage states that standing puts more strain on fewer muscles, particularly the calves, it does not say either way if they have a lower threshold for pain than others.

B.   False. The core muscles only contribute to, and are not the sole reason, why walking hurts less than standing still.

C.   True. We are told that "when you're walking, a greater number of muscles in both the legs are engaged" and also that "walking doesn't hurt nearly as much as standing still". Therefore standing still is an activity that uses fewer muscles than another activity, walking, that is less painful.

D.   False. The reason walking is less painful is because it involves frequently alternating which leg bears the load, while standing, although using both legs, involves longer periods of load bearing per leg.

124. B

A.   False. The passage says they are "less likely" to die before reaching the end of their life expectancy, meaning that some will die beforehand.

B.   True. As the passage states, even tree-lined streets held positives for people.

C.   Cannot say. As the text says: "more research is needed to determine the most evident benefit of urban green spaces".

D.   Cannot say. While this is true of women, the figures for men are not given and could be different enough to change the overall result.

125. A

A.   True. The passage tells us that another name for lactose malabsorption is lactose intolerance, and that *lactose* intolerance is usually caused by a deficiency of *lactase*.

B.   False. According to the passage, most people

with lactose intolerance can manage the condition without having to give up all dairy foods.

C. False. Some people with low levels of lactase can digest milk products without problems. Lactose intolerance is when these low levels lead to symptoms after eating dairy foods.

D. Cannot say. Although saying that lactose intolerance is generally harmless, the text does not say either way if it can be quite dangerous or not.

126. D

A. False. While snow does absorb sound, the passage says it becomes quieter, not totally quiet.

B. Cannot say. We are told that when snow refreezes "it can become hard and reflect sound waves, causing sounds to travel farther and become clearer". However the effect is not quantified.

C. Cannot say. While it may seem likely that there is some relationship of this sort, the passage does not refer to any.

D. True. Soft, fluffy snow acts as a sound absorber, but "as the structure of snow changes, the amount of noise in the surrounding environment could increase".

127. A

A. True. Sunspots "look dark only in comparison with the brighter and hotter regions of the photosphere around them."

B. False. While sunspots are relatively cooler, they are about 3,800 degrees Kelvin (3,527 degrees Celsius), which cannot be called cold.

C. Cannot say. We are told only that they "can be very large, up to 50,000 kilometres in diameter", and nothing about how their usual size compares to that of the Earth.

D. Cannot say. The passage says that sunspots can release flares and mass ejections, but does not say if these types of eruptions are limited to sunspots or not.

128. C

A. Cannot say. Both occur above thunderstorms, but we are not given any data on which can reach the highest altitudes.

B. Cannot say. We are told that *blue jets* propagate from the tops of thunderclouds at

around 100km per second but there is no information about the velocity of *blue tendrils*, which trail below red sprites.

C. True. Red sprites form between 40 and 90 km in altitude and this includes the ionospheric D region, which is between 70 and 90 km in altitude. The causes of both red sprites and blue jets are not known, therefore they are unexplained.

D. False. Red sprites form "over a broad region between 40 and 90 km in altitude" and as the mesosphere is "between about 50 and 80 km in altitude", this means they can form outside the mesosphere.

129. A

A. True. Glaciers form when water recrystallizes, that is freezes, meaning that cold temperatures are what is essential. If it is cold enough, elevation is not important.

B. False. According to the passage, glaciers can exist on high mountains even in tropical climates.

C. Cannot say. While this may seem very likely, the passage does not explicitly say where the largest glaciers are located.

D. Cannot say. According to the passage, temperature is only one thing that determines the glacier formation rate, wetness is another factor.

130. D

A. False. It lowered bad cholesterol by four percent.

B. Cannot say. The fibre fuels gut bacteria that *may reduce cholesterol*, so it's not known for certain.

C. Cannot say. The passage only refers to "healthier, more relaxed blood vessels" as a benefit that eating apples and drinking red wine or tea have in common; what other benefits any of them might have, or their relative value, is not discussed.

D. True. According to the passage, eating two apples a day lowered "bad" cholesterol levels in the study group, and the fibre in apples fuels gut bacteria that may reduce cholesterol.

131. B

A. Cannot say. The passage only discusses the

results of the research, not the possible effect on public policy.

B. True. Though the dataset of over 1.5 billion opioid prescriptions has indicated a correlation between easier access to cannabis and lower prescribing of opioids, "the effect of these laws on opioid use is not well understood for all dimensions of use and for the general United States population".

C. Cannot say. The passage says there is good reason to think this may be the case, but at the moment it is still not well understood.

D. False. As the passage states, "cannabis access laws have different effects across types of providers, physician specialties, and payers".

132. C

A. Cannot say. The passage only says that drinking is a common feature of workplace social events, but does not mention drinking to excess.

B. False. According to the passage, the percentage who said there were positive effects was "almost" 50%, which is less than half, so it is a minority.

C. True. If 40% of events have freely available alcohol and 39% have it for purchase with no limits, then only 21% of events have some sort of limit on consumption, which is a minority.

D. Cannot say. This may seem plausible, but the comparison is not made in the text.

133. B

A. Cannot say. The passage says that "the problem is caused by global access to ultra-processed foods, and people exercising less", so we cannot be sure what the *main* reason is.

B. True. As the passage states, individuals can experience both forms of malnutrition at different points in their lives.

C. False. Obesity means being very overweight, so by definition someone who is obese cannot be too thin at the same time.

D. False. 45 countries were affected in the 1990s and 48 in the 2010s, so the figure has actually been rather stable.

134. A

A. True. According to the passage, thin hair tends to be stronger than thick, which

researchers suggest is related to the size and quantity of flaws in the hair strand.

B. Cannot say. Although thin hair was found to be stronger than thick hair, we are not told whether the relationship was inversely proportional.

C. Cannot say. While capybara hair is "one exception" to the tendency for thin hair to be stronger than thick hair, we are not told if it is "the one exception", i.e. the ONLY exception.

D. Cannot say. While human hair is an example of thin hair, that does not rule out the possibility of there being many types of thinner hair that are stronger.

135. C

A. Cannot say. The AAA's study found that drivers' use of adaptive cruise control and lane-keeping-assist technologies "puts them at greater risk of crashing" but there is no indication of whether the AAA thinks their use should be discouraged.

B. False. According to the passage, "when used correctly, the technologies can make people safer".

C. True. According to the study, some drivers were prone to over-rely on these driving technologies and would not pay as much attention as they otherwise would.

D. Cannot say. The passage only says that those two systems make drivers almost twice as likely to drive distractedly, but it does not specify if that means using either of them, or both simultaneously.

136. D

A. Cannot say. The passage only says this in reference to *European* professors.

B. Cannot say. The passage says universities are accused of this, and that professors are more liberal and left-leaning than other professionals, but that cannot be equated with universities being hostile to conservative values.

C. False. The passage said there was no greater homogeneity, i.e. no less heterogeneity, among the professoriate relative to other specific professions.

D. True. According to the study, differences between professors and other professionals with a social science degree were not as clear as they were in other fields, such as medical, STEM, economics and law.

137. A

A. True. People who received accurate information nonetheless inadvertently modified it to more closely fit their own beliefs when they passed it on to other people.

B. Cannot say. The passage never says this, and only suggests that the misremembering is not actually an intentional ignoring of the truth.

C. Cannot say. The passage only says that when people pass misinformation on "the numbers can get further and further from the truth", but that does not necessarily mean it will always happen.

D. Cannot say. According to the study's author, people "may not be doing it purposely".

138. C

A. False. While there has been a steep increase in head and neck injuries due to being distracted by mobile phones, "most cases were mild".

B. False. According to the passage, most injuries happened to those aged 13 to 29.

C. True. Head and neck injuries are medical problems and the study found that mobile-related head and neck injuries "were relatively rare until the rate began to increase sharply in 2007, the year the first iPhone was released".

D. Cannot say. While this is likely the case, the passage never says so.

139. C.

A. Cannot say. The passage says that "puppies in pet stores appear to have transmitted a dangerous, antibiotic-resistant germ", but this is short of saying that any one puppy is likely to be a carrier.

B. Cannot say. While quite likely the case, the passage only specifically mentions Campylobacter.

C. True. As the passage says, laboratory evidence indicates that contact with puppies, *especially those from pet stores*, is the source of the outbreak.

D. False. The CDC reported that the majority of those who became sick had touched puppies. It did NOT report that the majority of those who had touched puppies had become sick.

140. A

A. True. Old-growth tropical forests that have been the same for millions of years are now changing *irreversibly* due to repeated logging.

B. False. The passage explains why it would in fact be RIGHT to claim that it does damage.

C. Cannot say. The passage does not make this comparison.

D. Cannot say. The passage focuses on the damage done by "continually logging" tropical forests but does not explicitly discuss how much damage might be done by a single cycle of logging.

141. D

A. False. The passage only states that one virus infection lowered the rates of catching another virus, but does not mention its use as a vaccine.

B. False. People could still catch both viruses, although their chances of catching one if they had been infected by the other were much lower.

C. Cannot say. This might be a possibility, but the passage does not mention it.

D. True. As the passage states, people who were infected with one virus were far less likely to also be infected by the other type.

142. A

A. True. As the passage states, "every hour you're sitting in front of a rubbish cartoon is an hour you're not reading, exploring the physical world, or watching educational programming".

B. Cannot say. The study specifically referred to low-quality television, not television overall.

C. Cannot say. The passage does not say whether Italians were more or less susceptible than others, simply that the study was performed in Italy.

D. False. The passage says people who watched low quality television were "almost 10% more likely to support populists", not that they would do so for certain.

143. B

A. Cannot say. The study only tested for colour, "without changing the brightness", so it did not provide results on the impact of brightness.

B. True. The passage says that "the blue light filters on our devices are designed to help us sleep better" but instead "could be doing the exact opposite".

C. Cannot say. The study suggests that "dimmer, cooler lights in the evening" may be better for our sleep patterns but does not indicate which might be the better option of "dimmer, warmer" or "cooler, brighter".

D. False. Since the study was conducted on mice, it could not have found results on humans.

144. B

A. Cannot say. The passage says that the scientists found "evidence that MND is linked to an imbalance of cholesterol and other fats in cells" but we are not told whether "imbalance" in this case refers to "high" levels.

B. True. As the passage states, the "eureka moment" in the research was realising that 13 genes, if altered, can cause the condition.

C. Cannot say. While this might seem a logical possibility, the passage does not mention it.

D. False. "For years, we have known that a large number of genes are involved in motor neurone disease".

145. C

A. Cannot say. The passage says only that children exposed in this way are "more likely" to be hyperactive.

B. Cannot say. The passage says "there is a lot of emphasis" on the dangers of smoking during pregnancy, but it does not say whether nicotine exposure in young children is not as well understood.

C. True. Since children exposed to nicotine in the first four years of life were found to be more likely to exhibit symptoms of hyperactivity, it is possible that a hyperactive child has been exposed to nicotine early in their lives.

D. False. It is nicotine that is thought to do the damage, not the cotinine, which is a metabolic by-product of nicotine in the saliva that is used to quantify the dosage of nicotine.

146. C

A. False. In the Foehn Effect the air is not diverted, it simply passes over a mountain before continuing in the same direction.

B. Cannot say. It raised the temperature TO, not BY 16.8°C but we do not what it would have been without the Foehn effect.

C. True. Wet and cold air is on the windward side of the mountain, while the warm and dry air is on the leeward side.

D. False. The passage says that what made the temperature remarkable was that it occurred at that time of year, not that it occurred at night.

147. A

A. True. The passage is about the North Atlantic Current and the current "shows non-linear behaviour, which means that small changes can have large effects".

B. False. The passage says "relatively mild", not warm. Relatively mild can still mean cold, but just not as cold as it otherwise would be.

C. Cannot say. The passage says that more studies are needed to verify this theory, not that they *will* verify it.

D. False. There is a 15 percent chance of a temporary change, so it CAN be said.

148. A

A. True. According to the passage, symptom scores varied greatly between twins diagnosed with ASD.

B. False. Although it is extremely likely (a 96% chance) that if one twin has ASD, the other will too, that also means that there are cases where only one twin has it.

C. Cannot say. According to the passage, genetic factors contributed to only 9% of the cause of trait variation among these twins, meaning that it is probably not the case. However it is still possible that there were many other small contributory factors, none of which was as great as 9%.

D. Cannot say. The passage only says that the scores for traits were very similar for identical twins without ASD, but does not mention the level of similarity for those with ASD, or non-identical twins with ASD.

149. D

A. Cannot say. Although we are told that many archaic mammal groups possess similar tarsal spurs to the platypus, that does not mean that most mammals were venomous, so we cannot say.

B. Cannot say. The passage only says that platypus venom is not lethal to humans, but that could still mean it is lethal to other animals.

C. False. As the first line states, the platypus is one of "the few living mammals" to produce venom.

D. True. Since only males have the spurs on their hind limbs that secrete the venom, female platypuses cannot produce painful venom.

150. B

A. False. Replanted areas still captured carbon from the atmosphere, just less effectively than areas that had been untouched.

B. True. As the passage states, replanted trees are not as effective at absorbing carbon as untouched forests.

C. Cannot say. The passage says untouched rainforests capture more carbon than secondary rainforests, but does not provide information on other types of forest.

D. Cannot say. The passage does not give any information as to whether repeated cycles of replanting, as opposed to one replanting, affected the absorption of carbon.

6. Succeeding in Numerical Reasoning Tests

Introduction

It is often said that the difficulty in taking numerical reasoning tests lies not in finding the actual answer to the question but doing it within the limited time available. This observation is correct inasmuch as these tests do not require complex mathematical calculations but rather the ability to:

- **identify data** relevant to answering the question from a larger set of information

- **identify the quickest way** to extract the answer from the relevant data

- discover one or several **possible shortcuts** that will allow us to arrive at the answer quickly

- determine the **level of accuracy** required to select the correct answer, and

- make **quick mental calculations**

In order to be prepared for the above, there are certain aspects of numerical reasoning tests that we must be aware of.

First of all, the "alternative reality" of a numerical reasoning test is different from what we are used to in everyday life – relevant data is not provided in a clean format but is rather hidden among other pieces of information that we may call "noise". Our first task is to always identify what we will need to work with from the information provided and avoid getting bogged down in wondering why other data might also be present.

Secondly, such tests have a surprising tendency to reach back to basic mathematical skills that may in fact come naturally to a secondary school student but are often lost during later academic stages and at the workplace. It is useful to refresh our basic calculus (see for instance www.calculus.org or www.sosmath.com and the "math refresher" Webinar on Online EU Training).

Also, many candidates dread the numerical reasoning test simply because it is based on mathematics and they have always considered this discipline their weakness. What we must realize here is that the "mathematical" aspect of numerical reasoning tests is rather basic – addition, subtraction, multiplication, division, ratios and percentages and simple equations will always be sufficient to perform the necessary calculations. As we will see, in some cases even such calculations are unnecessary and arriving at the correct answer is rather based on an intuitive insight or the realization of a relationship between figures that is in fact right in front of our eyes – we just need to learn to see it.

It is also useful to note here that, just like in the case of verbal reasoning, the broad term "numerical reasoning" may be used to designate various test types related to the handling of numbers, calculations and data, such as:

- **Computation tests** are basic tests that measure the speed at which the test-taker is able to make basic mental calculations such as addition, subtraction, multiplication and division (e.g. "how much is (15+65) / 2 ?").

- **Applied reasoning tests** represent a higher level where the focus is not on the actual ability to make calculations but rather the insight required to find out which calculations need to be performed to arrive at the answer. In other words, *applied reasoning* is tested. These tests are usually text-based in which a certain scenario involving numbers is described – it is this situation that the test-taker is expected to interpret in mathematical terms. To take an example of such a scenario: "There are 60 children at a camp site. Each child either wants to play hide and seek or go to the movies. Twice as many children want to play hide and seek. How many children want to go to the movies?"
- **Data interpretation tests** are similar to the above but instead of using a text, a "scenario" or story as the input, the basis of the exercise is a data set presented in the form of a table, a chart, or any combination of these (e.g. "Based on the data in the chart, by what percentage did the proportion of English-speaking people in cities change in France between 2000 and 2010?").
- **Estimation tests** resemble computation tests in that the calculations to be made are very similar, but the numbers with which you have to work may be greater. The point of the test is not to measure ability to perform the actual calculation but rather the speed and accuracy at which candidates can approximate the result of the calculation. The aim is to select an answer option that will be close to what the result would be if the actual calculation was performed (e.g. 3.98 times 997 is approximately 4000).

EPSO's numerical reasoning tests use elements of these four test types. Yet it is easy to see how each test type builds on skills and routines used in the other types. Quick estimations can only be made if we can make quick calculations as well. When you are faced with text-based numerical reasoning tests and you need to find a way to arrive at the answer, once you have done that, you must actually perform the required calculations or estimations to end up with the correct figure. When it comes to data interpretation based on tables and charts, the task is very similar to those in a text-based numerical reasoning test, with the added twist of having the data presented in a tabular or graphical format.

Let's now turn our attention to a real numerical reasoning test item and see how the above skills come into play.

High-Definition Television Sets in Various Countries (thousands)

	2000	2005	2010
Belgium	345	612	880
Slovakia	230	462	510
Netherlands	702	950	1002
Spain	810	1230	1600

Q. Approximately what percentage of total high-definition television sets across the four countries shown were in Belgium in 2010?

A.   10%   B.   15%   C.   22%   D.   30%   E.   35%

Using this sample test item, we can demonstrate how the above-described skills (data interpretation, applied numerical reasoning, estimation and computation) can be used to quickly and efficiently solve EPSO's numerical reasoning tests.

The first step is to interpret the data that we need to work with.

In the present case, the first step is to determine which figures from the table we actually need. The question concerns the number of high-definition television sets in 2010, so we can concentrate on the 2010 column in the table knowing that all the other figures are irrelevant to the task.

Next, we need to figure out what calculations we actually need to perform – in other words, we apply our numerical reasoning skills to the task at hand. Since the question is about Belgium's share of the total number of television sets in the four countries shown in the table, we need to calculate the total (by adding up the individual figures for the four countries), and then calculate Belgium's share in it (by dividing Belgium's number by the total). Finally, we need to convert the result of this division into a percentage figure (multiplying it by 100).

The next question we have to decide is whether we actually need to perform the exact above calculations at all. We can decide this by considering if there is any possibility of estimating certain results. Let's look at the four numbers we need to add up from this perspective:

880

510

1002

1600

Whenever making a decision about the use of estimation, we must take into account the answer options first. In our case, these are percentages which are quite far apart from one another: 10%, 15%, 22%, 30% and 35% – this will tell us that the level of accuracy required to answer the question is not too high and you can feel free to "guesstimate".

Looking at the numbers, we can see that they lend themselves quite nicely to rounding up and down. By doing this, we can arrive at some more "convenient" numbers:

900 (rounded up)

500 (rounded down)

1000 (rounded down)

1600 (stays the same)

Now that the numbers are easy to work with, we can perform some actual computation. Since all numbers end in 00, we can disregard those two digits and work with one and two-digit numbers as their relative proportions (percentages) will remain the same. Add up these four numbers to get to the total number of subscriptions:

9+5+10+16 = 40

Remember that we are looking for a percentage. This means that we do not need to add back the two zeroes – that would only be needed if we had to arrive at an actual value. Instead, we can just compare our total (40) with Belgium's number: 9. (The methodology for this calculation is under Ratios below.)

9 / 40 = 0.225

To convert this to a percentage, simply multiply the number by 100:

0.225 x 100 = 22.5%

Remember at this point that we rounded all the numbers up and down a bit – this explains why our result is not exactly the same as any of the answer options provided. It is, however, overwhelmingly clear that it is closest to Answer C (22%), which will be the correct answer.

Let's take stock of what we did in solving this test problem:

1. We interpreted the data in the table.

2. We applied our reasoning to determine what calculations we needed to perform.

3. We made estimations to simplify our calculations.

4. Finally, we performed the actual calculations.

Hopefully, this example demonstrates how the various skills required for succeeding in numerical reasoning depend on one another. If you keep these simple principles in mind and follow the steps laid out above, you will gain a systematic approach to solving all numerical reasoning tests successfully. There are, of course, lots of other things to look out for in test items, traps to avoid and tactics to use and become accustomed to and these are explored in the practice questions in Chapters 7 and 8.

Based on the required skills and the aspects introduced above, we will now provide an overview of the following:

- Mental calculus

- Ratio calculation

- Percentages and percentage points

- Per capita calculations

- Order of magnitude

- Calculations around speed, time and distance

- Estimation

- Equations

- Tables and charts

After reviewing these various methods and aspects, we will discuss how to approach numerical reasoning tests, what to focus on in each exercise and how to practice for the exam.

Mental Calculus

If you read through the information made available to candidates, it will be stated that a physical calculator will be available for you to use at the exam centre. In light of this, you might be doubtful as to why it is so important to be able to perform quick mental calculations. There are a few important reasons for this:

- There are some calculations that it is faster to perform in your head

- Overreliance on a calculator may make you less intuitive and prevent you from realizing whether certain calculations are really required to answer the question

- You will be able to make any necessary reality checks for every step of the solution, which can be useful, for example, when you are not finding a plausible answer (e.g. because of wrongly inserting numbers into the calculator)

Wherever possible, therefore, it is strongly advised to practise without using a calculator, saving the calculator for problems where its use is essential.

Fractions

As mentioned above, certain types of calculations can quite simply be performed more efficiently without any "technical assistance". One such example is the handling of fractions (as in the illustration below).

Consider the following scenario. We are looking for the proportion of households living in one-bedroom apartments with access to a garden from all households in the United Kingdom. Based on the data provided, let's say that you realize that approximately one in six households in the United Kingdom live in a one-bedroom apartment and among those, two out of three have access to a garden. One way of approaching this calculation would be to use the calculator to do the following:

$$\boxed{\text{Numerator}}$$

$$\frac{1}{6} \times \frac{2}{3}$$

$$\boxed{\text{Denominator}}$$

$1 \div 6 = 0.1667$ (proportion of UK households living in one-bedroom apartments)

$2 \div 3 = 0.6667$ (proportion of these that have access to a garden)

$0.6667 * 0.16667 = 0.1111$ (proportion of UK households living in one-bedroom apartments with access to a garden)

If we also have the total number of households, say 19,540,000, we then perform one additional calculation:

$0.1111 * 19,540,000 = 2,170,894$

Now, let's see how this calculation would go without the use of a calculator, by using fractions:

$$\frac{1}{6} \times \frac{2}{3} = \frac{2}{18} \quad \frac{\text{Numerator}}{\text{Denominator}}$$

How did we do this calculation? Fractions are multiplied by multiplying the first numerator by the second numerator and the first denominator by the second denominator.

We can then simplify the fraction by finding a number that both the numerator and the denominator can be divided by – in our case, this is the number 2:

$$\frac{2}{18} = \frac{1}{9}$$

It is easy to see that the above two calculations can be performed very quickly by mental arithmetic. Also, the final figure we arrive at is extremely convenient – now we know that one in nine UK households are one-bedroom apartments with garden access. If we consider that there are 19,540,000 households, the remaining calculation will also be very simple:

$19,540,000 / 9 = 2,171,111$

You can see that the number we get this way is slightly different from the number we get using the first method. We can be sure that the latter is more accurate because we did not have to do any rounding in the interim calculation stages.

There are two observations to make here:

• We arrived at the required figure by making extremely simple calculations with easy, round numbers
• Using fractions is actually more accurate than the calculator, because during the first method, we "truncated" many of the figures.

Calculations with Fractions

Multiplication: **Division:**   **Addition and subtraction:**

Lowest Common Multiple

$$\frac{3}{5} \times \frac{4}{6} = \frac{12}{30} \qquad \frac{4}{7} \div \frac{2}{3} = \frac{4}{7} \times \frac{3}{2} = \frac{12}{14} \qquad \frac{2}{3} + \frac{3}{7} = \frac{14}{21} + \frac{9}{21} = \frac{23}{21}$$

Multiplication

Method

If we need to multiply two fractions, we first multiply the two numerators (the numbers at the top) and then the two denominators (the numbers at the bottom).

Example of Application

Imagine that you are given a table showing IBM's 2013 revenues in billions. You are also given the following two pieces of information in the question text itself:

- 30% of revenue was made from selling datacenter components
- Of the datacenter revenue, 40% was generated in China

    Your task could be to calculate either how much or what percentage of revenue was generated from datacenter components in China. A quick answer to this question can be found using fractions.

    30% can be transcribed as a fraction, 3⁄10 and 40% as 4⁄10. Based on this, the calculation would go as follows:

$$\frac{3}{10} \times \frac{4}{10} = \frac{12}{100}$$

    If the question was "what percentage", we are extremely lucky because the fraction we arrived at after the multiplication is already "per hundred", so the answer is 12%. If the question was "how much", we simply calculate the 12% of the total revenue by multiplying it by 0.12.

Division

Method

If we need to divide a fraction by another fraction, our first task is to turn the operation into multiplication. We do this by "inverting" the numerator and the denominator in one of the fractions. This way, $^2\!/_3$ would become $^3\!/_2$, and so on.

    Next, we multiply the two numerators and then the two denominators in the same way as we do when multiplying fractions.

Example of Application

Q. 20% of France's annual wine production is equal to half of England's annual consumption. If all of the wine consumed in England were French, what percentage of France's production would be imported into England?

We can transcribe the above information with fractions as follows.

$$20\% = \frac{1}{5} \qquad\qquad half = \frac{1}{2}$$

We are looking for England's total consumption in terms of France's total production. We have the following information:

$$\frac{1}{5} \times Production_{France} = \frac{1}{2} Consumption_{England}$$

We want only England's total consumption on one side of the equation, so we need to divide both sides of the equation by one half:

$$\frac{1}{5} \div \frac{1}{2} \times Production_{France} = Consumption_{England}$$

We can now invert the numerator and the denominator (say, in the second fraction) and then perform the multiplication as described above:

$$\frac{1}{5} \times \frac{2}{1} \times Production_{France} = Consumption_{England}$$

$$\frac{1}{5} \times 2 \times Production_{France} = Consumption_{England}$$

$$\frac{2}{5} \times Production_{France} = Consumption_{England}$$

With a little practice, we can readily see that two-fifths is equal to four-tenths, or, in more familiar terms, 40%.

In the above very simple example, we could have calculated this even more easily by simply saying that if 50% of England's consumption is equal to 20% of France's production, then the full consumption (which is twice as much), will represent twice as much of France's production, or 40%. In other situations, however, things are not as self-evident and fractions can serve a very useful purpose.

Addition and Subtraction

Method

When adding or subtracting fractions, we need to make sure first that the denominators are the same in both fractions. We can do this by finding the smallest number that can be divided by both denominators. If our two denominators are 3 and 7, as in the illustration at the start of this section on Calculation with fractions, that number will be 21. Once we have done that, we need to multiply the numerators by the same number as the one with which we had to multiply the denominator in the same fraction. In the illustration, the numerator in the left fraction needs to be multiplied by 7 and the numerator in the right fraction needs to be multiplied by 3.

The last step is to simply add up the two numerators.

Example of Application

Imagine that you have the following three pieces of information:

- 30% of Italians believe that the minimum wage must be increased
- three in five Italians believe that the minimum wage must remain unchanged
- the rest believe it should be eliminated to increase competitiveness

Based on the wording of the above, we can be sure that there is no overlap between the groups – one group believes in an increase, the other in maintaining the current level, the third in eliminating it.

We have to answer the following question:

Q. What percentage of Italians believe that the minimum wage must remain unchanged or increase?

To answer the above question with fractions, we need to express "30%" and "three in five" in the form of fractions and then add up the two.

"30%" = 3 / 10

"three in five" = 3 / 5

The proportion we are looking for, then, is as follows:

3/10 + 3/5

You will notice that in this particular case, only the second fraction will need to be "converted". If we multiply both the numerator and the denominator of that fraction by 2, the two denominators will be identical and we can perform the addition.

3/10 + 6/10 = 9/10

By using fractions, we can answer the question by saying that 90% of Italians believe the minimum wage needs to be retained or increased, and 10% believe it should be eliminated. When solving numerical reasoning tests, it is always worth considering for a second whether we can take advantage of fractions – they are an extremely powerful tool in reducing seemingly complex relationships into the simplest of calculations.

Calculating Ratios

The two major mathematical concepts used during the exam are ratio and percentage calculations.

What, then, is a ratio? Let's take the following example:

Q. There are 120 people working in a company of whom 24 are Hungarian. What is the percentage of Hungarians in the company?

In such calculations there are three elements: the total (in this case the 120 employees), the subgroup we are looking at (here the 24 Hungarians), and the ratio, which is the relationship between the other two elements. In the exam you will be given two of these elements and have to find the third.

Scenario 1: Calculating the Ratio

The formula for this is:

Ratio = Subgroup divided by the Total Group.

If, again using our example, you divide the subgroup (24) by the total group (120) with your calculator you will get 0.2. This is the ratio expressed as an absolute number; to turn it into a percentage you simply multiply it by 100, so 20%.

Scenario 2: Calculating the subgroup

This is a common type of question. A typical question would be:

Q. In a company with 150 employees, 12% are Norwegians. What is the number of Norwegians?

Here the formula becomes:

Total x Ratio = Subgroup

In other words, 150 x 12% = 18 Norwegians (or 150 x 0.12 if we use the ratio as an absolute number)

Scenario 3: Calculating the Total

Perhaps the least common type of question is where we are asked to find the total. In this case Total = Subgroup divided by the ratio.
Here is a typical question of this type:

Q. In a company, 20 people are Irish, and they represent 5% of the company's workforce. How many people work for the company?

The calculation is 20 / 5% = 400, or put another way: 20 / 0.05

Scenario 4: Dividing a group into subgroups in a certain proportion to each other

Let us consider the following question:

Q. In a class of 32 children there are 5 boys to every 11 girls. How many boys and how many girls are there in the class?

This sort of problem is much more straightforward than it can sound. Think of the class as our group. To make one complete subgroup of boys and girls we need 5 boys and 11 girls, i.e. 16 children. We know there are 32 children in the class. If we divide 32 by 16, the size of our subgroup, we get 2, which is the number of subgroups in the class. To get the number of boys in total in the class we therefore simply multiply 2 x 5 and to get the number of girls we do 2 x 11. Therefore, there are 10 boys and 22 girls in the class.
This method also works when we are dealing with 3 or more subgroups. Let's say we have to divide 50 people into 3 subgroups that have a proportion to each other of 2 to 3 to 5. We first total 2 + 3 + 5 = 10, and then divide 50 by 10, giving us 5. We then multiply back with every number, to get 5 x 2 = 10, 3 x 5 = 15 and 5 x 5 = 25. In other words there will be 3 subgroups, one of 10 people, one of 15 people and one of 25.

Percentages

Consider the following example:

Q. Profits in a company were 80,000 euro in June. They increased by 50% between June and July and then decreased by 50% between July and August. What were the profits in August?

Previously we were looking at ratios in static situations but here we have a dynamic situation where we need to calculate more than one value to get to the answer – in this case, we need to find out what the profits were in July before we can get to the figure for August.

June	July	August
80,000 EUR		

Here we start with the known value (80,000 euro) to which we add the relevant percentage change: 80,000 + (80,000 x 50%) = 80,000 + 40,000 = 120,000.

Let's name all the elements in this equation: our starting value will be called Basis, the percentage change called Change and the resulting value the New Value. Using these, our formula is therefore like this:

Basis + Basis x Change = New Value

We can notice that Basis is part of both elements on the left side, therefore, we can group these elements. By pulling out Basis, we get the following formula:

Basis x (1 + Change) = New Value

This formula can be our starting point for any calculation. As mentioned above, we will always be asked to calculate one of the three elements of this formula.

Scenario 1: Calculating the New Value (both increase and decrease)

As shown above, the first half of the problem can be solved like this:

80,000 x (1 + 0.5) = 80,000 x 1.5 = 120,000

Continuing from here, we can use the formula again for the second half to calculate August, but this time applying a minus for the 50% because profits decreased:

120,000 x (1 – 0.5) = 60,000.

Scenario 2: Calculating the Change

Calculating the Change in the case of an Increase

Remember our formula: Basis x (1 + Change) = New Value

To calculate Change we have to rearrange the formula:

1 + Change = New Value / Basis

Let's return to our previous example, but assume we instead know the profits for June and July and have to calculate the percentage increase:

June	July	August
80,000 EUR	120,000 EUR	

1 + Change = 120,000 / 80,000

Change = (120,000 / 80,000) – 1

Change = 1.5 – 1

Change = 0.5 = 50%

A more challenging case is where the increase is bigger than 100%, but the formula can handle this as well:

June	July	August
40,000 EUR	180,000 EUR	

In this case 1 + Change = (180,000 / 40,000)

Change = (180,000 / 40,000) − 1

Change = 4.5 − 1

Change = 3.5 = 350%

A word of warning here: you might easily think that 350% is wrong because 180,000 is four-and-a-half times as much as 40,000. However, it is the correct answer. Think of 350% this way: to get to the 180,000 figure for July profits you add 40 to the initial 40 (our initial 100%) three times, plus an additional 20, which is 50%. In total, we have: 40 + (3 x 40) + 20 = 180, which is the correct amount for July profits.

Calculating the Change in the case of a Decrease

June	July	August
180,000 EUR	135,000 EUR	

In our example here the profit has dropped from 180,000 euro in June to 135,000 euro in July, but the formula works the same way.

Change = (135,000 /180,000) − 1

Change = 0.75 − 1

Change = −0.25 = −25%

In other words, profits decreased by 25%.

Scenario 3: Calculating Basis

A typical question here would look like the following:

Q. The value of profits in July was 144,000 EUR which was 20% higher than in June. What was the value in June?

June	July	August
	144,000 EUR	

Remember again our formula: Basis x (1 + Change) = New Value

We can rearrange this as follows: Basis = New Value / (1 + Change)

So in the case of our sample question:

Basis = 144,000 / (1 + 20%)

Basis = 144,000 / 1.2

Basis = 120,000

Therefore profits in June were 120,000 euro.

Be careful with this sort of question. You can't simply deduct 20% from the July figure. In that case you would calculate 144,000 x 0.8 which is 115,200. This sort of pitfall can often appear in a numerical reasoning test and there are lots of examples with full explanations in the questions later in this book.

Percentages and Percentage points

Mixing up these two concepts (percentage change and percentage point change) is a common source of error for candidates taking a numerical reasoning test.

Let us consider the following example (some lines are blocked out):

Bus Companies in the United States, 2013

Company	Profit (in million USD)	Number of Passengers (in millions)	Number of vehicles	Average vehicle utilization (%)
Greyhound	46	289	4560	73

In many numerical reasoning tests, you will be faced with data where calculation of the correct answer will require working with percentages. A straightforward case is where one figure (for example the number of cars in Italy) is an amount, and the other figure (for example the proportion of foreign-made cars) is a percentage. In such cases, the calculation is obvious:

No. of cars in Italy * % of foreign-made cars = No. of foreign made cars in Italy

Let us, however, consider another example. There are cases when *both* figures are proportions or percentages. What happens when the first piece of data (in the table, the average utilization of Greyhound buses) and the second piece of data (the % change in average utilization, for example) are both percentages?

Suppose that the question based on the above table is the following:

Q. What was the average vehicle utilization of Greyhound in 2012 if its vehicle utilization was 22% worse than in 2013?

In this example, where average utilization in 2013 is 73%, and it was 22% worse in 2012, our natural instinct might well be to perform the following calculation:

73% - 22% = 51%, therefore the average utilization in 2012 was 51%.

However, this would not be the correct answer. For comparison, keep in mind how we would calculate a 22% decrease of a regular amount, for example 1200:

1200 * (100% − 22%) = 1200 * 78% = 1200 * 0.78 = 936

Now apply the above logic to capacity utilization:

73% * (100% − 22%) = 73% * 78% = 73% * 0.78 = 56.94%

We can see that the correct calculation yields a significantly different result from what our initial instinct suggested.

When it comes to percentage changes in values that are themselves percentages, what many people think of as a 22 per cent change (for example 62% to 40%) is in fact a 22 percentage point change.

Through an intuitive example, we will be able to appreciate the fundamental difference between the two concepts.

Suppose that a bank in Switzerland pays 10% interest on deposits (we wish!). Now let's take a look at possible changes to this interest rate:

- If the interest rate drops by 5 percentage points, the new interest rate will be 5%
- If the interest rate drops by 5 percent, the new interest rate will be 9.5%
- A 10% interest rate can decrease by a maximum of 10 percentage points, but it can decrease by as much as 100 per cent – both resulting in a 0% interest rate

Per Capita Calculations

Per capita calculations are quite often needed, so it is important to be confident about them.

Let's imagine a country with the following parameters:

Population:	12 million people
Area:	60,000 km^2
Production of apples:	15 million

Let's now answer the following two questions:

Question 1: what is the population per km^2?

Question 2: what is the production per capita?

These calculations are always asking for the creation of an average, meaning that we need to find how many of a certain thing we have for one unit of another thing. A simple way to think of this is to always divide with what comes after the word per. Following this principle, we can answer both questions:

Q1: 12 million people / 60,000 km^2 = 200 people per km^2

Q2: 15 million apples / 12 million people = 1.25 apples per person

Order of Magnitude

	Apple Production in Various European Countries			
		Apple Production (thousands of tonnes)		
	Population in 2000 (thousands)	1990	2000	2010
Slovakia	4 895	31	25	35
Croatia	4 290	103	98	112
Bulgaria	8 930	120	90	134
Austria	10 354	546	490	560

Note: 1 tonne=1000kg

Q. What was the production of apples per person in Croatia in 2000?

A. 0.23 kg   B. 2.29 kg   C. 22.84 kg   D. 228.4 kg   E. 2.28 tonnes

An order of magnitude is a scale of amounts where each amount is in a fixed ratio to the amount preceding it. The most common ratio is 1:10, which means that the next amount in a scale can be calculated by multiplying the previous figure by 10.

For example: 1, 10, 100, 1000, 10000 …and so on…

If we look at the above answer options, we can see that that is exactly the situation we have here:

0.23, 2.29, 22.84, 228.4, 2.28 tonnes, (which is 2280 kg) – with some small variations from exact multiples of ten which slightly disguise the relationship.

When we are faced with a set of numbers like the ones above, it gives us an important hint that the actual calculation of the figure may not really be necessary – all we need to figure out is the order of magnitude of the correct answer.

Let us consider the above sample test from the perspective of whether we can take advantage of this observation.

We have the following information:

• The amount of apples produced in Croatia in 2000 in thousands of tonnes – 98
• The population of Croatia in thousands – 4290

Since the answer options only differ in their order of magnitude, we can be quite flexible in rounding our numbers up or down to simplify our calculations.

Let us round 98 up to 100 and 4290 down to 4000. You can disregard the exact number of digits for a second. What is the relationship between the numbers 100 and 4000? If you think about that for a second, you will realize that 100 and 4000 are in a relationship to each other that is similar to that between 1 and 4 – that is, to one quarter. Expressed in decimal terms, this is 0.25. Our answer options are close to this (this is especially apparent in option A – the difference of 0.23 versus 0.25 is caused by having rounded down the numbers). Remember – we do not need to be particularly accurate in this case, all that we are looking for is the number of digits in the correct answer. Now turn your attention to those zeroes we disregarded so far.

Apple Production: 98 thousand tonnes – we will add 6 zeroes here to make it kilogrammes: 98 000 000 kg

Population: 4 290 thousand – we will need to add three zeroes here: 4 290 000

If we turn back to our simplified figures, our calculation would look like this:

100 million divided by 4 million

We could use a calculator to obtain the result here, but let us recall what we said earlier – this is very close to one quarter of 100, which is 25.

25 is closest to Option C and that is the correct answer.

Calculations with Speed, Time and Distance

Questions involving the calculation of speed, time and distance can be expected at the exam. Let's have a look first at the three elements and how they interact with each other.

Speed = distance / time

From this, we can deduce the other two formulas.

Distance = speed x time
Time = distance / speed

You can also remember them by thinking of real-life situations, e.g. driving for 3 hours at 100 km/h will take us a distance of 3 x 100 = 300 kms.

A major pitfall with these questions can be converting between different units, as in the following example: Let's assume that we drove 180 kilometers and it took us 2 hours and 15 minutes. What was our average speed?

To answer this, it might be tempting to divide 180 kilometers by 2.15 hours. However 2 hours and 15 minutes is not 2.15 hours, because there are 60 minutes in an hour not 100. Therefore, we need to find what part of an hour is represented by 15 minutes. This we can get as a simple ratio calculation, dividing 15 minutes / 60 minutes, which is 0.25 hours. Here we don't need to further convert this into a percentage, we simply add it to the number of hours, giving us 2.25 hours. Our calculation becomes 180 kilometers / 2.25 hours, resulting in 80 km/h

Estimation

In a previous section, when calculating the per-capita apple production of Croatia, we applied a sort of estimation to get to the correct answer. In that case, the estimation took the form of concentrating only on the number of digits in the correct answer. There are cases, however, where we need to be a little more precise than that

Let's go back to our table and ask a different question:

Bus Companies in the United States, 2013				
Company	Profit (in million USD)	Number of Passengers (in millions)	Number of vehicles	Average vehicle utilization (%)
Greyhound	46	289	4560	73

Q. How many passengers would Greyhound carry in 2014 if its average vehicle utilization improves by 10% and its number of vehicles doesn't change?

a) 317.9 million

b) 356.6 million

c) 232.07 million

d) 260.1 million

Again, let us first consider the less innovative (and therefore more time-consuming) way of calculating the correct answer.

The data we will work with are:

- Number of passengers in millions in 2013: 289
- Average vehicle utilization in 2013: 73%
- The fact that average vehicle utilization in 2014 is forecast to increase by 10%

The first thing we would do is calculate the new utilization. An important point to remember here is the difference between percentage change and percentage point change, as discussed above.

New capacity utilization = 73% * (100% + 10%) = 73% * 110% = 73% * 1.1 = 80.3%

One mistake we could make here is equating the 2014 figure for passengers carried with the following (i.e. confusing the Basis and New Value discussed earlier):

289 million * 80.3% = 289 million * 0.803 = 232.07 million (note that this is one of the answer options)

Why is the above calculation incorrect? We must bear in mind that the number 289 million is actually equal to 73% of the total vehicle capacity of Greyhound, since its average utilization according to the table was 73%.

We also know the new capacity utilization figure (80.3%), but we must also calculate total capacity, the Basis (X). We know the following:

X * 0.73 = 289 million (73% of the total capacity is 289 million passengers)

Let's solve the equation for X:

X = 289 million / 0.73 = 395.9 million

We can now calculate the number of passengers transported at 80.3% capacity utilization:

395.9 * 0.803 = 317.9 million

Answer A is in fact the correct answer.

While the above series of calculations were all correct, we must always be suspicious when so many raw calculations are required to get to the correct answer. Do not forget that numerical reasoning in EPSO exams is not primarily a mathematical exercise, so this might be a hint that an easier solution may exist.

We need to make two observations here:

- Some of the data is irrelevant
- The "distance" between the values in the answer options allows for estimation

Let's go back to the problem. As the question referred to average vehicle utilization, we immediately started to work with that number. However, we should reconsider the meaning of this term. If average vehicle utilization increases by 10%, and the number of vehicles does not change, is this not just another way of saying that Greyhound carried 10% more passengers? This immediately simplifies our calculation:

289 million + 10% = 289 million * 110% = 289 million * 1.1

Now let us look at the answer options again:

a)   317.9 million

b)   356.6 million

c)   232.07 million

d)   260.1 million

Answers C and D can be immediately ruled out because those numbers are smaller than the 289 million in the table, which is impossible when the utilization increases.

Answer B has a greater number than in the table, but if we estimate 10% of 289 million (about 30 million, or exactly 28.9 million) we will immediately see that Answer B's 356.6 million is simply too large an amount, which leaves only Answer A as a feasible option.

The correctness of Answer A can also be verified very quickly, with a simple subtraction:

317.9 million – 28.9 million = 317.9 million – (17.9 million + 11 million) = 300 million – 11 million = 289 million

The above calculation also shows an example of how to make subtractions easier. In this example, we reformulated 28.9 million as 17.9 million + 11 million so it became much easier to first subtract 17.9 million from 317.9 million (leaving the round number of 300 million), and then deal with the rest.

Equations

Equations might sound too mathematical, yet they are a brilliantly inventive way of dealing with problems where multiple calculations must be made. Consider this:

Q. There are 13 600 customers in a café in a month. Out of them, 45% order coffee; of these, 30% opt for coffee with milk, of whom 200 ask for soy milk. Of the other customers, 25% ask for espresso macchiato, for which 60 millilitres of regular milk is used per customer. How much regular milk is used in a month for espresso macchiatos?

A.   245.4 litres

B.   245.4 millilitres

C.   24.54 litres

D.   29.54 litres

One way of approaching the problem would be to perform a series of individual calculations. First, we would calculate 45% of 13 600 customers to get 6120, then 30% of 6120 to get 1836, then we would subtract 200 from that to get 1636, then we would calculate 25% of this to get 409. Finally, we would multiply 409 by the amount of milk (60 ml, or 0.06 litres) and get the correct result, which is answer C. This is all perfectly reasonable.

However, by denoting the amount of milk used for macchiatos (which is the answer we are looking for) by X, we can create an equation which will make the calculation faster:

X = (13 600 * 0.45 * 0.3 – 200) * 0.25 * 60 (where 0.45 equals 45%, 0.3 equals 30%, and 0.25 equals 25%)

We can further simplify the equation:

X = (13 600 * 0.135 – 200) / 4 * 60

X = (1836 – 200) / 4 * 60

X = 1636 / 4 * 60

X = 409 * 60

X = 24 540

The final thing we need to remember is that this is in millilitres. Since this doesn't match any of the available answer options, let's convert it into litres:

24 540 / 1 000 = 24.54 litres

This matches Answer C. By denoting the figure we are looking for as X and then using the data to find X, we can work systematically with all levels of difficulty in the figures and reduce the risk of "getting lost" in a jumble of numbers.

Tables and Charts

Bus Companies in the United States, 2013				
Company	Profit (in million USD)	Number of Passengers (in millions)	Number of vehicles	Average vehicle utilization (%)
Trailways	12	123	2140	71
National	14	150	2400	69
Roger's	7	65	1300	75
Greyhound	46	289	4560	73

Q. How many passengers would Greyhound carry in 2014 if its average vehicle utilization improves by 10% and its number of vehicles doesn't change?

A.   317.9 million   B.   356.6 million   C.   232.07 million   D.   260.1 million

The above table may seem familiar. This is because we previously used a version of this table with some rows "blacked out" for demonstrating certain methods. In real numerical tests, however, the table always contains lots of superfluous data that you will not need for your calculations – this is what we referred to as "noise" in the introduction. When starting to solve a numerical reasoning question, it is always important to first decide exactly what data is necessary for the calculation because the superfluous information will just confuse you and can take valuable time if you become distracted.

For this reason, it is good advice to mentally "black out" that data from the table which you will not need. In this instance, the first thing we will realize is that we don't need any of the data about the other three bus companies (Trailways, National, Roger's). So let's black out the data for the other companies.

Bus Companies in the United States, 2013

Company	Profit (in million USD)	Number of Passengers (in millions)	Number of vehicles	Average vehicle utilization (%)
Greyhound	46	289	4560	73

Since the question refers to the number of passengers carried, we will certainly not need profit data to answer the question, so let's black out that data:

Bus Companies in the United States, 2013

Company	Profit (in million USD)	Number of Passengers (in millions)	Number of vehicles	Average vehicle utilization (%)
Greyhound		289	4560	73

Based on our reasoning in the section on Estimation, we will also realize that the number of vehicles is a superfluous figure, as is average vehicle utilization, so let's black those out too:

Bus Companies in the United States, 2013

Company	Profit (in million USD)	Number of Passengers (in millions)	Number of vehicles	Average vehicle utilization (%)
Greyhound		289		

If we systematically exclude all superfluous data, the task will seem significantly less complicated. As it turns out, in our example, the table's only purpose is to tell us that Greyhound carried 289 million passengers in 2013!

How to Approach Numerical Reasoning Tests

This chapter demonstrated the number of factors we must consider in order to efficiently solve the problems posed in numerical reasoning tests. Consider aspects such as the required level of accuracy, the relevance of data or the possibility of estimation, then decide the approach to take – whether to perform raw calculations, apply estimates, draw up an equation, or simply read a relationship or a trend off a chart.

As is true in the case of verbal and abstract reasoning tests, a systematic approach will make your test-taking experience much more efficient. Below, you will find a a summary of the recommended approach:

1. Read the question and the answer options first as carefully as possible.
2. The question will help you identify which data sets will be relevant and necessary for answering the question and know what to ignore.
3. Looking at the answer options will help you decide the level of accuracy required. If, for example, the values in the answer options are very far apart, you may consider estimation.
4. Based on the question, determine the relevant information and mentally "black out" the unnecessary data.
5. Having looked at the answer options and the data in the table, you can now make a final decision about whether to go for an exact figure or make an estimate, whether to use an equation, and so on. Before you start, think through your calculation methodology step by step.
6. Make sure you exclude all unrealistic answer options (for example numbers representing an increase when the question refers to a decrease).
7. Once you have performed your calculations, you can match the result against the remaining answer options. If you estimated, look for the answer option closest to your estimated result. If the result is significantly closer to one answer option than to all others, you were probably on the right track.

Practice Methods

Finally, a few suggestions for how to practice for the numerical reasoning test:

• Start your practice by identifying your weaknesses. Percentages? Subtraction? Estimation? Equations? Calculus in general? Or is it instead deciding what data is relevant when there is a great deal of irrelevant "noise" in the tables and charts?
• Once you have identified your weaknesses, you should particularly practice these operations, all of which are tested in the next two chapters
• Make sure you check how many questions you will face in the actual exam and how much time you will have to answer them
• Start decreasing the time needed to answer the questions so it gets closer to the time available at the exam
• Ideally, by the time of the exam, you should be able to answer more questions in the time available than required at the exam, because you cannot account for stress and other outside factors are impossible to recreate at home
• The EPSO test will be administered on a computer, which will make it much more challenging (and stranger) to take than a paper-based test where you can scribble on the paper and make quick calculations, write down equations, underline key concepts and so on – so if you have access to such services, try to practice online

7.   Numerical Reasoning Warm-Up Exercise

Before starting on the mixed questions full numerical reasoning test in the next chapter, where different types of questions are mixed at random, we recommend you first practise specific operations in this "warm-up" exercise. The operations in sequence are (A) Order of Magnitude, (B) Per capita/Percentage Calculations, (C) Speed, Time and Distance, (D) Equations, (E) Ratios, with a final section (F) on Estimating techniques.

As this is a warm-up exercise rather than a test, we have kept the answer explanations immediately under the questions.

A.   ORDER OF MAGNITUDE QUESTIONS

Set A1 (Order of magnitude)

Total Population (millions)			
Country	2009	2012	2015
Belgium	10.75	11.08	11.24
Denmark	5.51	5.58	5.66
Norway	4.80	4.99	5.17
Spain	46.24	46.82	46.45
United Kingdom	62.04	63.50	64.88

Foreign-born Population (thousands)			
Country	2009	2012	2015
Belgium	1444	1678	1783
Denmark	486	532	596
Norway	489	615	746
Spain	6226	6295	5891
United Kingdom	6862	7762	8412

Q1. Which country had the second-highest percentage of foreign-born population in 2012?

A. Belgium
B. Denmark
C. Norway
D. Spain
E. United Kingdom

Correct Answer: D

Data Interpretation

From the tables we need:

- The 2012 total population figures for all countries

- The 2012 foreign-born population figures for all countries

Reasoning

We have to calculate the foreign-born population as a percentage of the total population for each of the 5 countries in 2012 and then select the second-highest.

Calculation

To get the foreign-born population percentage for each country, we need to divide its foreign-born population in 2012 by its total population in 2012.

The total population figures are provided in millions and the foreign-born population figures are in thousands. To get a comparable ratio for each country there is no need to use the figures with all the zeroes added, we can just use the figures as given. The result will not be the actual foreign-born percentage but since we only need to compare the numbers between countries, it will suffice.

Belgium:

1 678 / 11.08 = 151.444

Denmark:

532 / 5.58 = 95.341

Norway:

615 / 4.99 = 123.246

Spain:

6 295 / 46.82 = 134.451

United Kingdom:

7 762 / 63.50 = 122.236

If we arrange the above results in descending order (highest to lowest), we get:

1st   Belgium (151.444)

2nd Spain (134.451)

We do not need to go further as we now have the second-highest result, Spain.

Potential Shortcuts / Pitfalls

There is no need to calculate the exact foreign-born population percentages as we are only looking for the comparable ratios for each country, which are easy to calculate. If you add the zeroes for the millions and the thousands into your calculation, it will both take more time and make it more likely you will make a mistake.

There's also no need to waste time on writing down the resulting numbers with too many decimal places. The numbers before the decimal point are all different anyway and are relatively easy to compare.

Be careful to avoid reading the population figures of 2009 or 2015 from the tables or mixing up figures of different countries. It's easy to make that sort of mistake when rushing.

Q2. Given that the EU's total population in 2009 was 502.09 million and that Spain's non foreign-born population was 8% of the EU's total population in 2015, by how many millions did the EU's total population increase between 2009 and 2015?

A. 0.4898
B 4.898
C. 4.285
D. 40.285
E. 48.98

Correct Answer: B

Data Interpretation

From the table we need:

- The 2009 foreign-born population figure for Spain

- The 2009 total population figure for Spain

From the question text we need:

- EU's total population figure for 2009

- Spain's non foreign-born population as a percentage (8%) of EU's total population in 2015

Reasoning

We need to find the EU's total population in 2015 to determine the increase between 2009 and 2015. We can calculate the EU's total population for 2015 by using Spain's 2015 non foreign-born population percentage.

Calculation

To calculate the EU's total population for 2015 by using Spain's 2015 non foreign-born population percentage (which is provided), we must first find Spain's 2015 non foreign-born population. For that we must subtract Spain's 2015 foreign-born population (given in thousands) from Spain's 2015 total population (given in millions). We must however convert both figures to either thousands or millions before our calculations (remember, 1 million = 1 000 thousand). We are going to work with millions.

Spain's 2015 non foreign-born population (millions):

(46.45) − (5891 / 1 000) = 46.45 − 5.891 = 40.559

40.559 million people were equivalent to 8% of the EU's total population of 2015, therefore we can reverse-calculate the EU's total population in 2015 (in millions):

40.559 / 8% = 40.559 / 0.08 = 506.9875

We already know the EU's total popula-

tion for 2009, which is 502.09 million. By subtracting the EU's total population in 2009 from the EU's total population in 2015, we will get the increase (millions):

506.9875 − 502.09 = 4.8975

Potential Shortcuts / Pitfalls

There are two major pitfalls to avoid in answering this question.

Firstly, you must read the question very carefully. The question refers to the "non foreign-born population" whereas the table has figures only for the foreign-born and total populations. If you miss the key word "non" you will go wrong from the very outset.

Secondly, the foreign-born population (given in thousands) has to be subtracted from the respective total population (given in millions). You cannot simply subtract a figure in thousands from a figure in millions; therefore you need to do all the calculations in either thousands or millions. We could have also opted to perform our calculations by converting all figures to units, but this complicates matters unnecessarily.

By simply looking at the answer options, using common sense, you might intuitively realise that the answer is likely to be either B or C. However these answers are too close together to risk guessing which is right – unless, of course, you are completely out of time and need to take a 50/50 gamble.

Q3. Which of the following is the best estimate of Spain's foreign-born population in 2014 assuming that it changed by an even annual amount between 2012 and 2015?

A. 6.026
B. 6 341
C. 6 026
D. 6 341 000
E. 6 026 000

Correct Answer: E

Data Interpretation

From the table we need:

- The 2012 foreign-born population figure for Spain

- The 2015 foreign-born population figure for Spain

- From the question, the information that the foreign-born population changed by an even annual amount between 2012 and 2015

Reasoning

We can use the trend in Spain's foreign-born population between the years 2012 and 2015 to estimate its foreign-born population in 2014.

Calculation

We know Spain's foreign-born populations for the years 2015 and 2012. We can find the change between these two years (in thousands) by deducting the 2012 figure from the 2015 figure:

5 891 – 6 295 = -404

Thus Spain's foreign-born population decreased by 404 thousand during the 3 years between 2012 and 2015. Therefore, the approximate yearly change (in thousands) was:

-404 / 3 = -134.667

Spain's foreign-born population decreased by approximately 134.667 thousand every year after 2012. Based on this statistic, we can estimate the approximate change that took place in the two years from 2012 to 2014 (in thousands):

-134.667 * 2 = -269.334

If we add this approximate change to Spain's actual foreign-born population in 2012, we will get an estimate for Spain's foreign-born population in 2014 (in thousands):

6 295 + (-269.334) = 6 295 – 269.334

= 6 025.666

The question simply asks for the best estimate (and does not mention whether it should be in thousands or millions which means that it has to be in units). Therefore:

6 025.666 * 1 000 = 6 025 666

The result 6 025 666 can be rounded off to 6 026 000.

Potential Shortcuts / Pitfalls

The key to this question is the statement that the population "changed by an even annual amount between 2012 and 2015". Without this information it would be impossible to answer the question. Consider this example: someone earns 10,000 euro in Year 1 and 30,000 euro in Year 3. If you know their earnings increased by an even annual amount, it is obvious that in Year 2 they earned 20,000 euro. But if you don't have that information it is impossible to say what their earnings were in Year 2 – they might, for instance, have carried on earning 10,000 euro, or they might alternatively have gone straight to 30,000 or indeed any other figure.

The foreign-born population figures in the table are given in thousands, so it is simplest to keep the calculations in thousands too. However, you must be careful to provide the final answer in units, as required in the question, and not in millions or thousands. You would end up choosing Answer A if you were thinking in millions or C if you were thinking in thousands.

Set A2 (Order of Magnitude)

Fishing Catch (1000 tonnes)

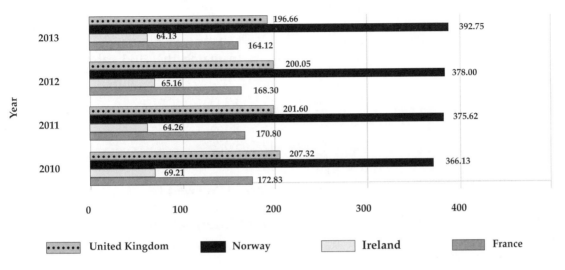

Fishing Fleet (Number of Vessels, hundreds)	2010	2011	2012	2013
France	72.2	72.1	71.4	71.2
Ireland	21.4	21.9	22.5	21.9
Norway	63.1	62.5	62.1	61.3
United Kingdom	64.6	63.9	63.6	63.0

Q1. In which year(s) did Ireland's fishing catch exceed 30 000 kgs per vessel?

A. 2010 only
B. 2011 and 2013 only
C. 2013 only
D. 2010, 2011, 2012 and 2013
E. None of these years

Correct Answer: A

Data Interpretation

From the table and chart we need:

- The fishing catch of Ireland for all four years

- The size of the fishing fleet of Ireland for all four years

From the question text we need:

- The benchmark with which to compare Ireland's fishing catch per vessel

Reasoning

We must compute Ireland's fishing catch per vessel figures for all four years and compare them to the 30 000 kgs per vessel benchmark.

Calculation

To calculate the catch per vessel (in kgs per vessel), we must divide the total fishing catch (in kgs) by the number of vessels (in units) for each year. To convert the total fishing catch from 1 000 tonnes to kgs, we must multiply by 1 000 (as the figures are given in thousands) and then again multiply by 1 000 (1 tonne =1 000 kgs). To convert the number of vessels from hundreds to units, we must multiply by 100. The catch per vessel (in kgs per vessel) is as follows:

2010:

(69.21 * 1 000 * 1 000) / (21.4 * 100) = 69 210 000 / 2 140 = **32 340**

2011:

(64.26 * 1 000 * 1 000) / (21.9 * 100) = 64 260 000 / 2 190 = **29 342**

2012:

(65.16 * 1 000 * 1 000) / (22.5 * 100) = 65 160 000 / 2 250 = **28 960**

2013:

(64.13 * 1 000 * 1 000) / (21.9 * 100) = 64 130 000 / 2 190 = **29 283**

Thus the calculations show that Ireland exceeded the 30 000 kgs per vessel mark in 2010 only.

Potential Shortcuts / Pitfalls

Not confusing the units in which the data is provided is key to this problem. As we saw above, we must first convert the units of the fishing catch from 1 000 tonnes to kgs and the number of vessels from hundreds to units. An order of magnitude error could lead to the selection of options D or E.

Flicking between chart and table can be tricky at speed, so beware of using another country's data instead of Ireland's.

There is a useful shortcut which you might spot if you read the answer options carefully. Once we have worked out the 2010 figure, we know that the correct answer cannot be options B, C or E. At this point, D could still be right. However, once we have worked out the 2011 figure

that also eliminates answer D. In other words, *we don't actually need to calculate the 2012 or 2013 figures at all.*

Q2. How many more tonnes would Ireland need to have caught in 2012 to match the 2013 catch per vessel figure of the United Kingdom?

A. 3.203
B. 5.076
C. 3 203
D. 5 076
E. 50 760

Correct Answer: D

Data Interpretation

From the table and chart we need:

- The 2013 fishing catch of United Kingdom

- The 2013 fishing fleet of United Kingdom

- The 2012 fishing catch of Ireland

- The 2012 fishing fleet of Ireland

Reasoning

We need to calculate the United Kingdom's catch per vessel figure for 2013 and use it to find the additional catch Ireland would have needed to achieve this level in 2012.

Calculation

The formula for catch per vessel is:

$$\text{Catch per vessel} = \frac{\text{Total catch}}{\text{Number of vessels}}$$

In 2013, the United Kingdom's catch per vessel (in tonnes per vessel) was:

(196.66 * 1 000) / (63.0 * 100) = 196 660 / 6 300 = 31.2159

Using the formula for catch per vessel we can write:

Total catch = Catch per vessel * Number of vessels

By using Ireland's number of vessels in 2012 we can calculate the catch Ireland needed in 2012 to match the United Kingdom's 2013 catch per vessel figure:

(31.2159) * (22.5 * 100) = 70 235.8

Therefore, the additional catch (in tonnes) Ireland needed was the required catch minus the actual catch:

(70 235.8) – (65.16 * 1 000) =
70 235.8 – 65 160 = **5 076**

Q3. Which of the following is the best estimate for Norway's average monthly fishing catch between July 2010 and June 2012?

A.   20.769 tonnes
B.   31.154 tonnes
C.   Impossible to say
D.   31 104 tonnes
E.   31 154 tonnes

Correct Answer: C

Reasoning

You have to think carefully about this question because a vital piece of information is missing. If you don't spot this, you will end up doing a large number of complicated calculations and most likely end up choosing Answer E.

Remember question 3 in the previous set. In that case we could make a similar sort of estimate because we knew what the trend was in the data. But in this case we don't have any information of that type (for example that that the monthly fishing catch was more or less balanced over this period). If the yearly fishing catch was spread out evenly across the 12 months of a year, we could make a calculation, but we don't know that to be the case. Suppose that most of the catch in 2010 was in the *first* 6 months of the year and most of the catch in 2012 was in the *last* 6 months. That would result in a much lower average monthly catch for the period July 2010 to June 2012 than if most of the catch in 2010 was in the *last* 6 months of the year and most of the catch in 2012 was in the *first* 6 months.

"Impossible to say" type questions can occur in EPSO exams so you need to be alert to this.

B.   PER CAPITA/PERCENTAGES CALCULATIONS

Set B1 (Per Capita / Percentages)

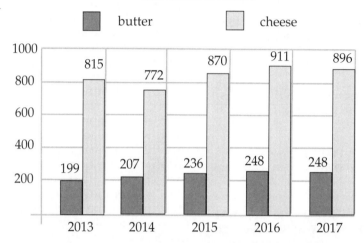

Netherlands Butter and Cheese Production
(Thousands of tonnes)

Netherlands Total Population (millions)	
2013	16.78
2014	16.83
2015	16.90
2016	16.98
2017	17.08

Q1. If the average price of butter in 2016 was €3.25 per kg, what was Netherlands' per capita turnover for butter in 2016?

A.   €14.61
B.   €47.47
C.   €53.65
D.   €806
E.   €14 605

Correct Answer: B

Data Interpretation

From the table and chart we need:

• The 2016 butter production figure for Netherlands

• The 2016 total population figure for Netherlands

From the question text we need:

• The average price of butter in 2016

Reasoning

We must calculate the per capita production of butter in 2016, in kilograms, and multiply it by the average price to get the per capita turnover of butter.

Calculation

To calculate the 2016 per capita production of butter, we need to divide the total production of butter in 2016 by the population of the Netherlands in 2016.

The population figures are provided in millions (which has six zeroes), whereas the butter production is given in 1 000 tonnes. Since 1 tonne = 1 000 kgs the production figure also has six zeroes when converted to kgs. Therefore, to get the per capita production of butter in kgs we can simply divide the butter production figure by the population figure.

248 / 16.98 ≈ 14.605

So, in 2016 Netherlands produced 14.605 kgs of butter per capita (per person). To convert this into per capita turnover, we must multiply the per capita production by the average price:

14.605 * 3.25 ≈ 47.47

Therefore Netherlands produced butter worth €47.47 per person in 2016.

Potential Shortcuts / Pitfalls

It is easy to end up using the wrong year's production figure or the figure for cheese instead of butter. You need to be careful in this regard when working at speed.

As indicated earlier, it isn't necessary to convert the production quantity of butter to kgs and the population from millions to units before calculation. The same order of magnitude (six zeroes) in each figure cancels out. You will waste precious time as well as risk making a mistake if you don't spot this.

Another typical mistake would be to consider the per capita production of butter in kilograms as the final answer. It is the per capita *turnover* and not the per capita *production* that is being asked for.

Q2. The total production of butter and cheese in Netherlands declined from 2013 to 2014. What percentage increase in the total production in 2014 would have been required for the per capita production of butter and cheese to have been the same as in 2013?

A.   0.3%
B.   3.6%
C.   3.7%
D.   3.9%
E.   5.5%

Correct Answer: A

Data Interpretation

From the table and chart we need:

- The 2013 total population figure for Netherlands

- The 2014 total population figure for Netherlands

Reasoning

We must work out the percentage increase in the combined production of butter and cheese that would offset the increase in population from 2013 to 2014, such that the combined per capita production of butter and cheese remains constant.

Calculation

There is a simple solution to this problem for which we need to understand how the per capita production is calculated. It is the ratio of the combined production of butter and cheese and the corresponding total population:

$$\text{Per capita combined production in 2013} = \frac{\text{Combined production in 2013}}{\text{Total population in 2013}}$$

We know that we want the per capita value for 2014 to be the same as in 2013. We also know that the population changed from 16.78 million to 16.83 million between 2013 and 2014, a percentage change of:

([16.83 – 16.78] / 16.78) * 100% = 0.3%

To offset a 0.3% increase in the denominator (population), the numerator (production) should also have increased by the same percentage. Therefore, the total production should have increased by 0.3% for the per capita combined production to remain constant from 2013 to 2014.

Per capita combined production in 2013 = $\dfrac{\text{Total production in 2013 * 100.3\%}}{\text{Total population in 2014}}$

Potential Shortcuts / Pitfalls

The major pitfall to this question is thinking it is a lot more complicated than it is. Because the question starts with the information that "the total production of butter and cheese in Netherlands declined from 2013 to 2014" it is natural to assume that we should be doing a lot of calculations with butter and cheese, whereas this is not necessary. As we have seen, all we actually needed was the population figures.

A more obvious but far longer method involves calculating the per capita combined production of butter and cheese in 2013 and then using the population of 2014 to find the necessary level of combined production in 2014. The required percentage change in production from 2013 to 2014 would be found by subtracting the two values and calculating the percentage. As we have seen, a bit of smart numerical reasoning can save us a lot of unnecessary calculations.

It is also important to realise that the 6 zeroes from production (1 000 tonnes) and population (millions) can be ignored to simplify calculations or you will make more work for yourself.

Q3. Which of the following hypothetical situations will definitely result in an increased per capita production of butter in Netherlands?

A. Decrease in production of butter and decline in population.
B. Decrease in production of butter and an increase in population.
C. Increase in production of butter and decline in population.
D. Increase in production of butter and an increase in population.
E. No change in production of butter and an increase in population.

Correct Answer: C

Data Interpretation

The answer is found by straight numerical reasoning; we do not require any specific information from the table or the question.

Reasoning

We must consider each option separately to ascertain the situation in which the per capita production of butter will definitely increase.

Calculation

The per capita production of butter is calculated by dividing the production of butter by the total population.

Per capita production of butter = $\dfrac{\text{(Production of butter)}}{\text{(Total population)}}$

Option A: Decrease in production of butter and decline in population.

The numerator and denominator of our ratio are both decreasing. The resulting per capita production can decrease or increase depending upon the percentage decrease in production and population. Only specific numbers can tell us what will actually happen. Therefore, this option will not definitely result in an increase in per capita production of butter.

Option B: Decrease in production of butter and an increase in population.

The numerator is decreasing while the denominator is increasing. This will result in a definite decrease in per capita production.

Option C: Increase in production of butter and decline in population.

The numerator is increasing while the denominator is decreasing. Both of these changes cause the per capita production to increase. Therefore, this situation will definitely lead to an increase.

Option D: Increase in production of butter and an increase in population.

As with option A, the per capita production can increase or decrease depending on the percentage increase in production and population. Only specific numbers can tell us the exact outcome. Therefore no definite predictions can be made.

Option E: No change in production of butter and an increase in population.

The numerator stays constant while the denominator increases. This will lead to a definite decrease in the per capita production.

Potential Shortcuts / Pitfalls

The qualitative nature of this question (i.e. no specific numbers involved) should not prevent us from believing that there can be a definite answer to this problem.

Options A and D can possibly result in an increase in the per capita production but since the problem asks us to be definite in our assessment we must reject these two options.

Finally, if you look at the options in sequence (A, B, C…) you will get to the correct answer as soon as you reach C. As there can only be one correct answer in this test, you would be wasting your time to go any further.

Set B2 (Per Capita / Percentages)

Artificial land cover (million square metres)	2009	2012	2015
European Union	160 770	166 733	173 295
Finland	5 134	5 326	5 531
France	27 847	28 574	29 415
Italy	19 815	20 346	20 837
Slovakia	1 272	1 361	1 461

Artificial land cover (square metres per capita)	2009	2012	2015
European Union	347.3	357.0	367.2
Finland	966.6	983.8	1 009.4
France	444.7	449.7	456.2
Italy	335.3	341.7	343.1
Slovakia	236.2	251.7	269.4

Q1. What was the difference in the populations of Finland and Slovakia in 2015?

A. 56 330
B. 168 092
C. 5 189 398
D. 5 423 163
E. 56 330 000

Correct Answer: A

Data Interpretation

From the tables we need:

- The 2015 artificial land cover of Finland

- The 2015 artificial land cover per capita of Finland

- The 2015 artificial land cover of Slovakia

- The 2015 artificial land cover per capita of Slovakia

Reasoning

We need to calculate the populations of Finland and Slovakia in 2015 by using the respective artificial land cover areas and per capita figures. We can then calculate the difference in population.

Calculation

$$\text{Artificial land cover per capita} = \frac{\text{Artifical land cover}}{\text{Total population}}$$

Hence

$$\text{Total population} = \frac{\text{Artifical land cover}}{\text{Artificial land cover per capita}}$$

Substituting the data from the table, the total population (in millions) of Finland in 2015 was:

5 531 / 1 009.4 5.47949

Since the artificial land cover area was provided in million square metres, the total population we calculated is also in millions.

The total population (in millions) of Slovakia in 2015 was:

1 461 / 269.4 5.42316

Therefore the difference (in millions) in the populations of Finland and Slovakia in 2015 was:

5.47949 – 5.42316 = 0.05633

We need to convert our answer to units by multiplying by 1 million:

0.05633 * 1 000 000 = 56 330

Potential Shortcuts / Pitfalls

We need to be careful in applying the per capita formula. If we multiply the per capita figure with the area, our answer will be incorrect.

The artificial land cover area is provided in million square metres. We must account for this in our calculations. We can solve our problem in millions but the answer choices are provided in units. We must therefore convert the final population figure from millions to units.

Q2. What was the European Union's artificial land cover per capita (in square metres per capita) in 2009 excluding France?

A. 322.8
B. 332.1
C. 342.4
D. 347.3
E. 353.1

Correct Answer: B

Data Interpretation

From the tables we need:

- The 2009 artificial land cover for the EU

- The 2009 artificial land cover for France

- The 2009 artificial land cover per capita for the EU

- The 2009 artificial land cover per capita for France

Reasoning

We need to calculate the EU's artificial land cover and population, excluding France, in 2009, and use those figures to calculate the EU's per capita artificial land cover in 2009.

Calculation

The EU's artificial land cover excluding France in 2009 was (in million square metres):

160 770 – 27 847 = 132 923

The EU's population in 2009 (in millions):

160 770 / 347.3 ≈ 462.91391

France's population in 2009 (in millions):

27 847 / 444.7 ≈ 62.61974

Therefore the EU's population excluding that of France in 2009 was (in millions):

462.91391 – 62.61974 = 400.29417

Now we know the EU's artificial land cover excluding France in 2009 as well as the EU's population excluding France in 2009.

We use the formula:

$$\text{Artificial land cover per capita} = \frac{\text{Artifical land cover}}{\text{Total population}}$$

The EU's artificial land cover per capita (in square metres per capita) in 2009 excluding France was:

132 923 / 400.29417 ≈ 332.1

Potential Shortcuts / Pitfalls

It is vital to realise that you cannot simply subtract the per capita land cover of France from that of the European Union. You must first find the two components, area and population, separately and then use them to find the new per capita value.

Remember that since we calculated all the population figures in millions and the areas we used were also in million square metres, the effect of both sets of zeroes cancels each other out in the per capita formula.

Q3. **The population of Italy was approximately 340 000 larger in 2016 than in 2015. If the artificial land cover per capita remained unchanged from 2015, what was the percentage change in the artificial land cover in 2016 from 2015?**

A. Increase of 0.15%
B. Increase of 0.56%
C. Increase of 5.60%
D. Decrease of 0.56%
E. Decrease of 5.60%

Correct Answer: B

Data Interpretation

From the tables we need:

- The 2015 artificial land cover of Italy

- The 2015 artificial land cover per capita of Italy

From the question text we need:

- The increase in population of Italy from 2015 to 2016

- The change (none) in artificial land cover per capita of Italy from 2015 to 2016

Reasoning

We need to calculate the population of Italy in 2016 and use the per capita figure for 2015 to estimate the artificial land cover in 2016. The percentage change in artificial land cover area can then be calculated using the figures for 2015 and 2016.

Calculation

Population of Italy in 2015 (in millions):

20 837 / 343.1 ≈ 60.731565

The population of Italy in 2016 was equal to the population in 2015 plus the increase in 2016:

60.731565 + (340 000 / 1 000 000)

≈ 61.071565 million

Italy's artificial land cover per capita in 2016 was the same as that in 2015.

Artificial land cover = Artificial land cover per capita * Total population

Italy's artificial land cover in 2016 was (in million square meters):

343.1 * 61.071565 ≈ 20 954

The percentage change in Italy's artificial land cover from 2015 to 2016 will be:

([20 954 – 20 837] / 20 837) * 100%

≈ 0.56%

Potential Shortcuts / Pitfalls

It is convenient to solve this problem by keeping the population figures in millions. The population growth for 2016 has, however, been provided in units. Therefore, we must convert this figure to millions before adding it to the population of 2015.

There is also a quicker way of solving this problem. Since the per capita figure does not change from 2015 to 2016, we know that the percentage change in the population (denominator) will be equal to the percentage change in the artificial land cover (numerator).

The percentage change in the population of Italy from 2015 to 2016 was:

(340 000 / [60.731565 * 1 000 000]) * 100%

≈ 0.56%

Therefore, the percentage change in the artificial land cover must also have been 0.56% for the per capita figure to have remained unchanged.

C.   SPEED, TIME AND DISTANCE QUESTIONS

Set C1 (Speed, Time and Distance)

Distance-Time Chart

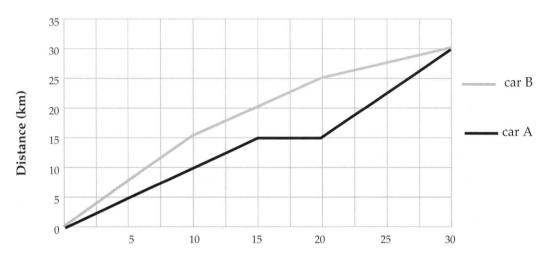

Time (minutes)

Q1. What was the average speed of Car B between minutes 10 and 20?

A.   1 km/h
B.   30 km/h
C.   60 km/h
D.   75 km/h
E.   90 km/h

Correct Answer: C

Data Interpretation

From the chart we need:

- The distance travelled by Car B at time = 10 minutes

- The distance travelled by Car B at time = 20 minutes

From the question text we need:

- The time interval for which the speed needs to be calculated

Reasoning

We must calculate the speed by dividing the distance Car B travels, during the specified time interval, by the duration of the time interval.

Calculation

At time 10 minutes, the total distance travelled by Car B was 15 km while at time 20 minutes the total distance travelled was 25 km. Therefore, the distance travelled between 10 and 20 minutes was:

25 – 15 = 10 km

We now have to divide this distance (10 km) by the time taken, which is:

20 – 10 = 10 minutes

Since the required answer is in km/h, we need to convert the time taken into hours by dividing by the number of minutes in an hour.

10 / 60 = 0.16667 hours

Recall the formula from chapter 6:

$$\text{Speed} = \frac{\text{Distance}}{\text{Time}}$$

The speed of Car B between 10 and 20 minutes was:

10 / 0.16667 ≈ 60 km/h

Potential Shortcuts / Pitfalls

There is a very simple shortcut to this problem. Remember what was said in looking at methodologies about sometimes being able to use fractions as a way that is both quicker (you can do it in your head) and more accurate? That's the case here. 10 minutes is 1/6 of an hour, so simply multiplying the distance (10 km) by 6 would result in the correct km/h value.

As for the pitfalls, it is easy to overlook the units and divide the distance travelled (10 km) by the time taken (10 minutes) and choose the incorrect answer of 1 km/h, which is given as answer option A. Always be careful about the units. It is also possible to misunderstand the problem and subtract the average speed for the first 10 minutes from the average speed during the first 20 minutes.

Q2. Had Car A not stopped during the journey but instead continued at its initial speed for the entire journey, how many minutes earlier would it have reached its destination?

A.   0 minutes
B.   5 minutes
C.   10 minutes
D.   25 minutes
E.   30 minutes

Correct Answer: A

Data Interpretation

From the chart we need:

•   The distance travelled by Car A at time = 15 minutes

•   The total distance for the entire journey of Car A

Reasoning

We need to calculate the speed of Car A before it stopped and use this to calculate the time it would have taken for it to travel 30 km. We must then find the difference between this calculated time and the actual time taken.

Calculation

Car A stopped when the time was 15 minutes (or 15/60 = 0.25 hours). It had travelled 15 km at this time. Therefore the speed of Car A before it stopped was:

15 / 0.25 = 60 km/h

We can use this speed to calculate the time it would have taken Car A to travel 30 km without stopping. Since:

$$\text{Speed} = \frac{\text{Distance}}{\text{Time}}$$

Then:

$$\text{Time} = \frac{\text{Distance}}{\text{Speed}}$$

Therefore:

30 / 60 = 0.5 hours

The time taken without stopping would have been 0.5 hours (or 0.5 * 60 = 30 minutes) which is exactly equal to the actual time taken by Car A with the stop. Therefore, Car A would not have arrived any earlier. This is of course because the speed of the car after it stopped and then resumed its journey was greater than the initial speed.

Potential Shortcuts / Pitfalls

You have to be careful with the units involved. To calculate the speed in km/h you must convert all times to hours. The calculated time will be in hours and that has to be converted back to minutes.

There is an easy visual shortcut to this problem. If you look at the graph you can see that Car A travels 15 km (3 gridlines vertically) in 15 minutes (6 gridlines horizontally) during the first half of the journey. Extend this straight line upwards and to the right, up to the 30 km mark on the vertical axis (length of the journey). You will see that the line meets with the original graph at time equals 30 minutes.

Q3. **If both cars continue their journey for an extra 10 minutes, at the same speed they are travelling at time = 30 minutes, what would be the ratio between Car A to Car B of the total distance travelled over the whole journey?**

A. 1 : 1
B. 2 : 1
C. 9 : 7
D. 5 : 3
E. 3 : 1

Correct Answer: C

Data Interpretation

From the table we need:

- The distance travelled by Car A at time = 20 minutes

- The distance travelled by Car A at time = 30 minutes

- The distance travelled by Car B at time = 20 minutes

- The distance travelled by Car B at time = 30 minutes

- The total distance travelled in the first 30 minutes

From the question text we need:

- The additional time for the journey (10 minutes)

Reasoning

Both cars travelled 30 km during the first 30 minutes. We must therefore calculate the additional distances both cars will travel in the next 10 minutes and then find the ratio of the total distances travelled.

Calculation

Car A's speed at 30 minutes can be calculated from the time interval 20 to 30 minutes. The distance travelled during these 10 minutes (0.16667 hours) was:

$30 - 15 = 15$ km

We could then calculate the speed as:

$15 / 0.16667 \approx 90$ km/h

In the additional 10 minutes (0.16667 hours), Car A will travel:

$90 * 0.16667 \approx 15$ km

Similarly, Car B's speed after 30 minutes can be calculated from the time interval 20 to 30 minutes. The distance travelled during these 10 minutes (0.16667 hours) was:

$30 - 25 = 5$ km

Therefore its speed was:

$5 / 0.16667 \approx 30$ km/h

In the additional 10 minutes (0.16667 hours), Car B will travel:

$30 * 0.16667 \approx 5$ km

We can now calculate the total distance travelled by Car A in 40 minutes as:

$30 + 15 = 45$ km

And for Car B:

$30 + 5 = 35$ km

The ratio of these total distances is:

45:35

This can be simplified to:

9:7

Potential Shortcuts / Pitfalls

The ≈ signs in the calculations above tell you that the figures are approximations, even if they are very close approximations. It's actually easier (and totally accurate) in this case to use fractions, like in question 1: instead of considering 10 minutes as 0.16667 of an hour you can simply say it is 1/6 of an hour. All the calculations can then be done very rapidly in your head.

You can also work out the answer just by using your eyes. By looking at the graph you can see see that Car A travelled 15 km (3 gridlines vertically) in the last 10 minutes. Therefore it will travel another 15 km in the additional 10 minutes bringing the total distance to 45 km. Similarly, Car B travelled only 5 km (1 gridline vertically) in the last 10 minutes, therefore it will travel another 5 km in the additional time. Car B's total distance travelled will be 35 km. In this case using the graph can help avoid time consuming calculations.

Set C2 (Speed, Time and Distance)

London Underground Metropolitan line timetable	
Time	*Station*
06:56	Aldgate
07:01	Barbican
07:10	Great Portland Street
07:27	Wembley Park
07:39	North Harrow
07:49	Moor Park
07:56	Watford

Q1. **If the average speed of trains on the Metropolitan line is 34 km/h, what is the approximate distance from Aldgate to Moor Park?**

A.   28 km
B.   30 km
C.   34 km
D.   49 km
E.   53 km

Correct Answer: B

Data Interpretation

From the table we need:

- The clock time at Aldgate
- The clock time at Moor Park

From the question text we need:

- The average speed on the Metropolitan line

Reasoning

We need to calculate the time taken to travel from Aldgate to Moor Park and use it in the speed formula, along with the average speed, to give us the approximate distance between the two stations.

Calculation

The train travels between Aldgate and Moor Park from 06:56 to 07:49. It took:

4 minutes between 6:56 and 7:00

49 minutes between 7:00 and 7:49

4 + 49 = 53 minutes

Convert the time to hours, since the average speed is given in km/h:

53 / 60 ≈ 0.88333 hours

Recall the speed formula:

$$Speed = \frac{Distance}{Time}$$

Multiply both sides by Time to get a formula for the distance:

Distance = Speed × Time

Substitute the values to calculate the approximate distance between Aldgate and Moor Park:

34 * 0.88333 ≈ 30.03 km

Potential Shortcuts / Pitfalls

You have to read the question carefully; it asks for the distance between the first and the *second last* stations and not for the length of the whole route.

The time difference is calculated in minutes which must be converted to hours since the average speed for the journey has been provided in km/h.

You can also eliminate answer options C, D and E straight away. If the journey had taken one complete hour, the train would have travelled 34 km. Since the time taken was less than an hour, it means that the train must have travelled less than 34 km. You still have to do the calculations to be sure of getting the right answer because answer options A and B are so close together. However, if you spot this and have no time left at all for calculations, it means you have a 50/50 chance if you just guess either A or B.

Q2. The distance from Barbican to Watford is 30.94 km. The train was delayed for 3 minutes due to a technical problem at Wembley Park. If the train continued the rest of the journey at the usual time intervals, what was the average speed of the train between Barbican and Watford?

A. 32 km/h
B. 33.75 km/h
C. 36 km/h
D. 44 km/h
E. 58 km/h

Correct Answer: A

Data Interpretation

From the table we need:

- The clock time at Barbican station

- The clock time at Watford station

From the question text we need:

- The distance from Barbican to Watford

- The time delay at Wembley Park

Reasoning

We must calculate the total time taken for the journey, including the delay, and use it along with the distance provided to find the average speed of the journey.

Calculation

Had there been no delay, the train would have travelled from 07:01 till 07:56, i.e. for 55 minutes. However with the delay, the total time taken was:

55 + 3 = 58 minutes

We have to convert this time to hours:

58 / 60 ≈ 0.96667 hours

The total distance travelled was 30.94 km. Therefore, by using the speed formula, the average speed of this trip including the delay was:

30.94 / 0.96667 ≈ 32 km/h

Potential Shortcuts / Pitfalls

You must remember that the time interval has to be converted to hours before using it in the speed formula as the speed has been given in km/h.

Q3. If the management decides to operate the trains at 20% higher average speed, what percentage of time will be saved between Great Portland Street and North Harrow?

A. 10.00%
B. 16.67%
C. 20.00%
D. 33.34%
E. 83.33%

Correct Answer: B

Data Interpretation

From the question text we need:

- The change in average speed of the train

Reasoning

Since the distances remain the same, we must find the percentage change in time taken based on the percentage change in speed. We will use the percentage change in time to find the time saving.

Calculation

Recall the speed formula:

$$\text{Speed} = \frac{\text{Distance}}{\text{Time}}$$

Or:

$$\text{Time} = \frac{\text{Distance}}{\text{Speed}}$$

This can be re-written as follows:

New Time as a percentage of old Time = (New Distance as a percentage of old Distance)/(New Speed as a percentage of old Speed)

Therefore, our new journey time based on the 20% higher speed will be as follows:

100% / (100% + 20%) = 100% / 120%

≈ 0.8333 or 83.33%

This means that on average, all distances on the Metropolitan line will now be covered in 83.33% of the original time. Hence the time saving will be:

100% − 83.33% = 16.67%

Potential Shortcuts / Pitfalls

We could very easily have wasted time by taking a long route to solve this problem. We could have calculated the time taken to travel between Great Portland Street and North Harrow at the old speed and then used it to compute the distance between the two stations. We would then have used the distance and the new speed to calculate the time for the quicker journey. Finally, we would have used the old and the new times to find the percentage time saving.

In contrast, in the method we used in the calculation section above, we realised that since the speeds have been increased throughout the Metropolitan line, the specific stations involved do not matter; the percentage time savings will be the same all along the line irrespective of the stations of departure and arrival.

D. EQUATIONS

Set D1 (Equations)

GDP of Germany by sector
(total GDP = $3 700 billion)

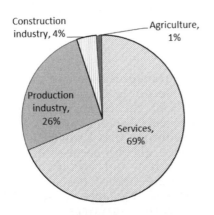

Turnover of Services Sector in Germany

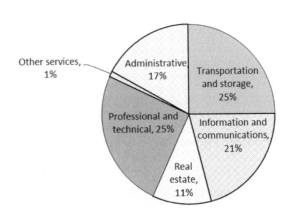

Turnover of Transportation Sector and Storage Sector

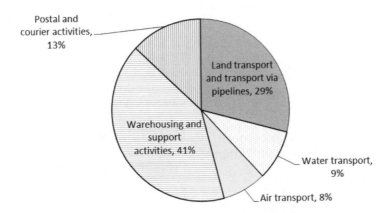

Q1. What is the turnover of the air transport sector in Germany?

A. $51 billion
B. $83 billion
C. $185 billion
D. $638 billion
E. $2 553 billion

Correct Answer: A

Data Interpretation

From the charts we need:

- The percentage share of services in Germany's GDP

- The percentage share of the transportation and storage sector in the turnover of Germany's services sector

- The percentage share of the air transport sector in the turnover of the transportation and storage sector

Reasoning

We need to form an equation to calculate the turnover of the air transport sub-sector (2 levels down) using Germany's GDP.

Calculation

Let X be the turnover of the air transport sector, in billions $.

From the three pie charts, we know that 69% of Germany's GDP is based on services, of which 25% is based on the transportation and storage sector, of which 8% comes from air transport. We can write this in an equation as follows:

X = ([{3 700 * 0.69} * 0.25] * 0.08)

Note that 0.69 equals 69%, 0.25 equals 25% and 0.08 equals 8%. When we solve the inner-most parentheses, we get the turnover of the services sector of Germany as follows:

X = ([{**2 553**} * 0.25] * 0.08)

The number inside the second set of parentheses gives us the turnover of the transportation and storage sector:

X = ([**638.25**] * 0.08)

Finally, we can find the turnover of the air transport sector when we solve the outer-most parentheses:

X = 51.06

Therefore, the turnover of Germany's air transport sector is approximately $51 billion.

Potential Shortcuts / Pitfalls

The calculation above was done in full, working out the actual turnover at each stage. However, that full calculation is not really necessary here. You can get to the answer much faster simply by multiplying the percentage of the services sector in the GDP with the percentage of the transportation and storage services in the services sector and then multiplying with the percentage of air transport in the transportation and storage services.

(0.69 * 0.25 * 0.08) = 0.0138

This can then be multiplied by the total GDP to find the answer:

0.0138 * 3 700 = 51.06 (billion)

Much quicker!

Q2. The transportation and storage service sector is forecast to contribute 30% of the turnover of the entire service sector after 2 years. Assuming that growth is uniform across all sub-sectors of the transportation and storage sector and that the size of the services sector remains the same, what will be the increase in turnover of the air transport sector after 2 years?

A. $10 billion
B. $15 billion
C. $51 billion
D. $61 billion
E. $128 billion

Correct Answer: A

Data Interpretation

From the charts we need:

- The percentage share of services in Germany's GDP

- The percentage share of the air transport sector in the turnover of the transportation and storage sector

- The current turnover of the air transport sector (solution to the last question)

From the question text we need:

- The new percentage share of the transportation and storage sector in the turnover of Germany's services sector

Reasoning

We need to form an equation to work out the increase in turnover by subtracting the forecast turnover from the current turnover of the air transport sector.

Calculation

Let Y be the increase in the turnover of the air transport sector, in billions $.

We know that the size of the services sector is 69% of Germany's GDP, which is:

(3 700 * 0.69)

We also know that after 2 years 30% of this is forecast to come from the transportation and storage sector. Since growth will be uniform across all the subsectors, the air transport sector will still be 8% of the transportation and storage sector. This will let us work out the forecast turnover of the air transport sector. To find the increase we must then subtract the current turnover of the air transport sector ($51 billion, the solution to question 1 above) from the forecast figure. We can write this in an equation as follows:

Y = ([{3 700 * 0.69} * 0.30] * 0.08) − 51

Note that 0.69 equals 69%, 0.30 equals 30% and 0.08 equals 8%.

Y = 61.272 − 51

Y = 10.272

Solving the above equation gives the increase in turnover of Germany's air transport sector as approximately $10 billion.

Potential Shortcuts / Pitfalls

A quicker, though slightly complicated, way to solve this problem is to find the percentage change in the total turnover of the transportation and storage sector and use it directly to calculate the increase in turnover of the air transport sector. The percentage change in the turnover of the transportation and storage sector is:

([0.30 − 0.25] / 0.25) * 100% = 20% or 0.20

Therefore the increase in turnover of the air transport sector is:

0.20 * 51 = 10.20

To put both of the above steps into one equation:

Y = ([0.30 − 0.25] / 0.25) * 51 = 10.20

Note that since the GDP is provided in billions $ and the solution required is also in billions $, we should keep our figures in billions $ to simplify the calculation and to avoid any mistakes.

Q3. The information and communications sector can be subdivided into telecommunications and "other information services". If the other information services sector contributes three times as much as the telecommunications sector, what is the turnover generated by the other information services sector?

A. $134 billion
B. $179 billion
C. $357 billion
D. $402 billion
E. $536 billion

Correct Answer: D

Data Interpretation

From the charts we need:

- The percentage share of services in Germany's GDP

- The percentage share of the information and communications sector in the turnover of Germany's services sector

From the question text we need:

- The relationship between the share of the other information services sector and the telecommunications sector (i.e. three times as large)

Reasoning

We need to form an equation to calculate the turnover of the other information services sector by using Germany's GDP and sector percentages and relationships.

Calculation

Let Z be the turnover of the telecommunications sector, in billions $. The turnover of the other information services sector is then 3Z. The combined GDP of these two subsectors is equal to the GDP of the information and communication services sector. The information and communications services sector is 21% of the services sector, which is 69% of Germany's GDP. We can write this as:

$Z + 3Z = 0.69 * 0.21 * 3700$

$4Z = 536.13$

$Z \approx 134$

Solving the equation gives the value of Z as 134 billon. The other information serv-

ices sector is, however, 3Z. Multiply 134 billion by 3 to get the answer:

$134 * 3 = 402$

The turnover of Germany's other information services sector is approximately $402 billion.

Potential Shortcuts / Pitfalls

You need to read this question particularly carefully because of the multiple layers so you do not end up calculating the wrong thing.

There is also a very simple shortcut. Based on the information in the question, the information and communications sector can be subdivided into telecommunications (25%) and other information services (75%). This can be written as:

$3700 * 0.69 * 0.21 * 0.75 = 402.1$

D2 (Equations)

Number of shares			
Company	Alex	Bob	Charles
Xancom	1000	0	250
Yayvo	0	1500	70
Zem	800	0	1200

Current unit share prices (Price of 1 share)	
Company	Unit share price
Xancom	$86.00
Yayvo	?
Zem	$22.00

Q1. Charles's total investment in Xancom and Yayvo is equal in value to his investment in Zem. What is the current unit share price of Yayvo?

A. $4.08
B. $19.60
C. $54.00
D. $70.00
E. $108.00

Correct Answer: D

Data Interpretation

From the tables we need:

- The number of Charles's shares in all three companies

- Current unit share price of Xancom

- Current unit share price of Zem

From the question text we need:

- The relationship between Charles's

investments in Xancom, Yayvo and Zem

Reasoning

We must equate Charles's investment in Xancom and Yayvo with his investment in Zem to work out the current unit share price of Yayvo.

Calculation

We first form an equation as follows:

Charles's investment in Xancom + Charles's investment in Yayvo = Charles's investment in Zem

Then:

(Charles's shares in Xancom * Current unit share price of Xancom) + (Charles's shares in Yayvo * Current unit share price of Yayvo) = (Charles's shares in Zem * Current unit share price of Zem)

Let y be the variable for the current unit share price of Yayvo. When we substitute figures in the equation we get:

(250 * $86.00) + (70 * y) = (1 200 * $22.00)

(**$21 500**) + (70 y) = (1 200 * $22.00)

($21 500) + (70 y) = (**$26 400**)

70 y = $26 400 - $21 500

70 y = **$4 900**

y = $4 900 / 70

y = **$70.00**

Therefore, the current unit share price of Yayvo is $70.00.

Potential Shortcuts / Pitfalls

You have to be careful with the equation to make sure you do not mix up the companies and the share prices. This can easily happen in switching from one table to the other.

Q2. After one year, the value of Alex's total investment grew by 26% but the unit share price of Zem fell to $19.36. Assuming Alex did not purchase or sell any shares during the year, what was the new unit share price of Xancom?

A. $190.19
B. $115.05
C. $108.36
D. $86.00
E. $26.00

Correct Answer: B

Data Interpretation

From the tables we need:

- Number of Alex's shares in all three companies
- Current unit share price of Xancom
- Current unit share price of Zem

From the question text we need:

- Alex's total investment percentage change

- New unit share price of Zem

Reasoning

To work out the new unit share price of Xancom we must create an equation where we set the increased total of investments as equal to the sum of the new investment amounts in each company.

Calculation

The new value of Alex's total investment is made up of (a) his 800 shares in Zem, which we know fell in unit value from $22 to $19.36, and (b), his 1000 shares in Xancom, whose unit price was $86 and whose new unit price we are trying to calculate. We also know that the value of his total investment increased by 26%, so it can be expressed as 1.26.

Let us designate the new unit share price of Xancom as x.

By substituting values we get:

(1.26 * [{1 000 * $86} + {800 * $22}])

= (1 000 * x) + (800 * $19.36)

Where 1.26 is equivalent to 126%

We have to simplify this equation:

(1.26 * [{**$86 000**} + {**$17 600**}])

= (1 000 * x) + (800 * $19.36)

$130 536 = (1 000 * x) + (800 * $19.36)

$130 536 = (1 000 * x) + (**$15 488**)

$130 536 = (**1 000x**) + ($15 488)

1 000x = $130 536 - $15 488

1 000x = **$115 048**

x = $115 048 / 1 000

x = $115.048 ≈ **$115.05**

Potential Shortcuts / Pitfalls

You have to do these rather complex calculations to be sure of getting the right answer. However, if you need to take a guess, notice that since the total investment amount *increased* and the new unit share price of Zem *decreased*, the unit share price of Xancom must have increased as Alex only has these two types of shares. This immediately eliminates options D & E without any calculations.

You can also eliminate Option C with one simple calculation because it only increases the unit share price of Xancom by 26% whereas we know the total value of his investment increased by 26% and the value of his other shares fell.

Q3. **Alex plans to purchase some Yayvo shares from Charles so that the total value of his investment becomes equal to Bob's total investment. How many Yayvo shares should Alex purchase from Charles if the current unit share price of Yayvo is $70?**

A. 0
B. 20
C. 22
D. 70
E. 1500

Correct Answer: B

Data Interpretation

From the tables we need:

- Number of Alex's shares in all three companies

- Number of Bob's shares in all three companies

- Current unit share price of all three companies

From the question text we need:

- The new relationship between the total investments of Alex and Bob

Reasoning

We need to formulate an equation based on the new relationship between the total investments of Alex and Bob to find the number of Yayvo shares Alex should purchase from Charles.

Calculation

The new relationship can be written in the form of an equation:

Alex's new total investment = Bob's existing total investement

Let z be the variable for the number of Yayvo shares Alex purchased from Charles.

Substituting values into the equation:

$(1\ 000 * \$86) + (z * \$70) + (800 * \$22) = (1\ 500 * \$70)$

$(\$86\ 000) + (z * \$70) + (\$17\ 600) = (1\ 500 * \$70)$

$(\$86\ 000) + (z * \$70) + (\$17\ 600) = (\$105\ 000)$

$z * \$70 = \$105\ 000 - \$86\ 000 - \$17\ 600$

$z * \$70 = \$1\ 400$

$z = \$1\ 400 / \$70$

$z = 20$

Therefore, Alex needs to purchase 20 Yayvo shares from Charles in order for his total investment to equal Bob's total investment.

Potential Shortcuts / Pitfalls

Note that Bob's investment remains unaffected from the sale of shares; hence his total investment stays constant. Also remember that Alex is purchasing Yayvo shares from Charles but his total investment is being compared to Bob's. Comparing Alex's new investment to Charles's new investment by mistake will lead to the wrong answer.

E.   RATIOS

Set E1 (Ratios)

Statistics for 2017	GDP: Gross Domestic Product (billions €)	Tax Revenue (billions €)	Public Debt to GDP Ratio
Croatia	49.0	22.44	0.784
Greece	180.2	86.68	1.819
Iceland	21.7	9.22	0.409
Norway	354.3	194.87	0.367
Portugal	194.6	83.09	1.256

(The Public Debt to GDP ratio is the ratio of a country's public debt to its GDP and the Tax-to-GDP ratio is the ratio of a country's tax revenue to its gross domestic product)

Q1.   What is the difference in the Tax-to-GDP ratios of Norway and Iceland?

A.   0.125
B.   0.425
C.   0.550
D.   0.558
E.   0.773

Correct Answer: A

Data Interpretation

From the table we need:

- The 2017 tax revenue of Norway
- The 2017 tax revenue of Iceland
- The 2017 GDP of Norway
- The 2017 GDP of Iceland

Reasoning

We need to work out the Tax-to-GDP ratios of the two countries separately and then find the difference.

Calculation

The information at the foot of the table tells us that the Tax-to-GDP ratio is the ratio of a country's tax revenue to its gross domestic product (GDP).

Since all currency values are in billions €, we do not need to convert them to €.

Norway's Tax-to-GDP ratio is:

$194.87 / 354.3 \approx 0.55$

Similarly, Iceland's Tax-to-GDP ratio is:

$9.22 / 21.7 \approx 0.425$

Subtract the Tax-to-GDP ratio of Iceland from that of Norway:

$0.55 - 0.425 = 0.125$

Potential Shortcuts / Pitfalls

Since the GDPs and the tax revenues are provided in billions $ and you need to divide one by the other (the zeroes will cancel each other out), you should keep your calculation in billions $ to keep things simple and to avoid any mistakes.

You must find the two Tax-to-GDP ratios separately. If you try to find the ratio of the difference in tax Revenues and the difference in the GDPs, your solution will be incorrect.

Since you need to calculate the *Tax-to-GDP* ratio you must remember to divide the tax revenue by the GDP instead of the other way around.

Q2 By how much does the public debt of Greece exceed that of Croatia?

A. €36.6 billion
B. €38.4 billion
C. €135.8 billion
D. €289.4 billion
E. €327.8 billion

Correct Answer: D

Data Interpretation

From the table we need:

- The 2017 Public Debt to GDP ratio of Greece

- The 2017 Public Debt to GDP ratio of Croatia

- The 2017 GDP of Greece

- The 2017 GDP of Croatia

Reasoning

We must calculate the public debts for Greece and Croatia separately using the Public Debt to GDP ratios and the GDPs of the two countries, and then find the difference.

Calculation

The Public Debt to GDP ratio is the ratio of a country's public debt to its GDP:

$$\text{Public Debt to GDP Ratio} = \frac{\text{Public Debt}}{\text{GDP}}$$

To find the public debt using the Public Debt to GDP ratio and the GDP, we can rearrange the above formula as follows:

$$\text{Public Debt} = \text{Public Debt to GDP Ratio} \times \text{GDP}$$

Greece's public debt (billions €) is:

$1.819 * 180.2 \approx 327.78$

Croatia's public debt, in billions €, is:

$0.784 * 49 \approx 38.42$

Greece's public debt exceeds Croatia's public debt by:

$327.78 - 38.42 = 289.36$

Which is rounded to 289.4

Potential Shortcuts / Pitfalls

The public debts of both countries must first be calculated separately and then subtracted. If you subtract the two Public debt to GDP ratios and the two GDPs, your answer will be incorrect. Also, make sure you use the GDP in the calculation and not the tax revenue by mistake.

Q3. If Portugal's Tax-to-GDP ratio increases by 10% to approximately 0.4697, its tax revenue increases by 5% to €87.2445 billion, and its Public Debt to GDP ratio remains constant, what will be the percentage change in its public debt?

A. Decreases by 4.6%
B. Increases by 4.6%
C. Increases by 4.8%
D. Increases by 7.5%
E. Increases by 95.5%

Correct Answer: A

Data Interpretation

From the table we need:

- The 2017 Public Debt to GDP Ratio of Portugal
- The 2017 GDP of Portugal

From the question text we need:

- Portugal's new Tax-to-GDP ratio (0.4697)
- Portugal's new tax revenue (€87.2445 billion)

Reasoning

We need to calculate the new GDP using the new Tax-to-GDP ratio and the new tax revenue and then use it to find the percentage change in public debt using the Public Debt to GDP ratio.

Calculation

Recall that:

Hence:

Portugal's new GDP is:

$$\text{Tax to GDP Ratio} = \frac{\text{Tax Revenue}}{\text{GDP}}$$

$87.2445 / 0.4697 \approx 185.745$

$$\text{GDP} = \frac{\text{Tax Revenue}}{\text{Tax to GDP Ratio}}$$

Now, we can use the public debt formula:

Public debt = Public Debt to GDP ratio * GDP

Since Portugal's Public debt to GDP ratio

remains constant, Portugal's new public debt is:

$1.256 * 185.75 \approx 233.296$

Portugal's original public debt was:

$1.256 * 194.6 \approx 244.418$

The percentage change in Portugal's public debt is:

$([233.296 - 244.418] / 244.418) * 100\% \approx -4.6\%$

The negative percentage change tells us that Portugal's public debt has *decreased* by 4.6%.

Potential Shortcuts / Pitfalls

Another, slightly quicker, way of solving this problem is to evaluate all unknowns in terms of percentage changes. First, we can find the new GDP as a percent of the original GDP:

$1.05 / 1.10 = 0.9545$

Note: 1.05 equals 105%, 1.10 equals 110% and 0.9545 equals 95.45%.

Now we can find the new public debt as a percentage of the original public debt value:

Public debt = Public Debt to GDP ratio * GDP

Since the Public Debt to GDP ratio remains constant, we get:

$1.00 * 0.9545 = 0.9545$

Note: 1.00 equals 100% and 0.9545 equals 95.45%.

Therefore, we know that the Public debt has decreased by:

$1.00 - 0.9545 = 0.0455 \approx 4.6 \ (\%)$

Q1. How many more (or less) Swiss

Set E2 (Ratios)

Average Exchange rates versus various currencies (1 Euro =)			
Year	2011	2014	2017
US Dollar	1.39200	1.32850	1.12970
Pound Sterling	0.86788	0.80612	0.87667
Swiss Franc	1.23260	1.21460	1.11170
Russian Rouble	40.88460	50.95180	65.93830

Francs would we get in exchange for 100 Pounds Sterling in 2017 as compared to 2014?

A. 15.21 more Swiss Francs
B. 23.86 more Swiss Francs
C. 10.29 fewer Swiss Francs
D. 15.21 fewer Swiss Francs
E. 23.86 fewer Swiss Francs

Correct Answer: E

Data Interpretation

From the table we need:

* The 2014 exchange rate for Pounds Sterling

* The 2017 exchange rate for Pounds Sterling

* The 2014 exchange rate for Swiss Francs

* The 2017 exchange rate for Swiss Francs

From the question text we need:

* The amount of Pounds Sterling to convert

Reasoning

We must calculate the Swiss Francs equivalent to 100 Pounds Sterling in 2014 and compare it with the amount of Swiss

Francs that could be exchanged for 100 Pounds Sterling in 2017.

Calculation

To convert from Pounds Sterling to Swiss Francs we must use the Euro exchange rates.

In 2014:

0.80612 Pounds Sterling = 1 Euro = 1.21460 Swiss Francs

Hence:

0.80612 Pounds Sterling = 1.21460 Swiss Francs

Therefore:

1 Pound Sterling = (1.21460 / 0.80612) Swiss Francs

1 Pound Sterling ≈ 1.50672 Swiss Francs

100 Pounds Sterling = 100 * 1.50672 Swiss Francs

100 Pounds Sterling = 150.672 Swiss Francs

Similarly, in 2017:

0.87667 Pounds Sterling = 1 Euro = 1.11170 Swiss Francs

1 Pound Sterling = (1.11170 / 0.87667) Swiss Francs

1 Pound Sterling ≈ 1.26809 Swiss Francs

100 Pounds Sterling = 100 * 1.26809 Swiss Francs

100 Pounds Sterling = 126.809 Swiss Francs

The change in the number of Swiss Francs that 100 Pounds Sterling would get in 2017 as compared to 2014 is therefore:

126.809 − 150.672

= −23.863

The negative sign signifies that the number of Swiss Francs we get in 2017 will be less than in 2014.

Potential Shortcuts / Pitfalls

A typical error in rushing would be to use the exchange rates for the wrong years or the wrong currencies. Another potential pitfall is to convert the 100 Pounds Sterling to Euros in both the given years, calculate the difference and then convert the amount back to Swiss Francs from Euros at the 2017 rate.

You can clearly see from the currency table that, from 2014 to 2017, the Pound Sterling has depreciated (got weaker) against the Euro while the Swiss Franc has appreciated (got stronger). This can only mean that the Pound Sterling will be able to buy fewer Swiss Francs. Hence, answer options A & B can be easily ruled out. If you can't do any calculations and have to guess the answer, this at least improves your odds to 1 in 3 from 1 in 5.

Q2. In 2011, the sum of 50 US Dollars and 249 Russian Roubles was closest in value to which of the following?

A. 36 Euros + 10 Pounds Sterling
B. 48 Swiss Francs + 125 Roubles
C. 101 Pounds Sterling
D. 50 US Dollars + 199 Russian Roubles
E. 42 Euros + 32 Swiss Francs

Correct Answer: B

Data Interpretation

From the table we need:

- The 2011 exchange rates for all currencies

From the question text we need:

- The original amounts in US Dollars and Russian Roubles to compare

- All amounts provided in each option

Reasoning

Since Euros is the common currency in the table, we need to calculate the Euro equivalent of the sum of currencies in the question and then evaluate all options, one at a time, to find a similar Euro value.

Calculation

The 2011 equivalent Euro value of 50 US Dollars and 249 Russian Roubles was:

(50 / 1.39200) + (249 / 40.88460)

≈ 35.92 + 6.09

≈ 42.00

If we examine the available options, we can eliminate options C, D and E for various reasons.

Option C is 101 Pounds Sterling. We already know that 1 Pound Sterling was more valuable than 1 Euro. Therefore, 101 Pounds Sterling would have a much greater value than 42 Euros.

Option D has exactly the same amount of US Dollars but a different amount of Roubles as compared to the amounts mentioned in the question. Hence this option cannot result in an amount equivalent to 42 Euros.

Option E has 42 Euros (exactly the target amount) plus some Swiss Francs. This sum will definitely be greater than 42 Euros.

We are left with options A & B, which we will now evaluate.

Option A (36 Euros + 10 Pounds Sterling):

36 + (10 / 0.86788)

= 36 + 11.522

= 47.522

Option B (48 Swiss Francs + 125 Roubles):

(48 / 1.23260) + (125 / 40.88460)

≈ (38.942) + (3.057)

≈ 41.999

Option B was therefore closest in value to 50 US Dollars and 249 Russian Roubles in 2011.

Potential Shortcuts / Pitfalls

As explained in the calculations section, we can avoid unnecessary calculations for options C, D & E if we use pure numerical reasoning to eliminate the unlikely options.
Beware of multiplying with the exchange rate when you need to divide and vice versa during conversions.

Q3. **In 2011, a businessman converted 1000 Euros into Russian Roubles and invested them into Russian bonds. His investment had grown by 50% in value after 6 years. In 2017, he withdrew all his Roubles and converted them back to Euros. How many Euros more or less did he have in 2017 as compared to 2011?**

A. He had 500 more Euros in 2017
B. He had 930 more Euros in 2017
C. He had 70 fewer Euros in 2017
D. He had 930 fewer Euros in 2017
E. He had the same amount of Euros in 2017

Correct Answer: C

Data Interpretation

From the table we need:

*   The 2011 exchange rate for Russian Roubles
*   The 2017 exchange rate for Russian Roubles

From the question text we need:

*   The original amount of Euros
*   The investment return for 6 years

Reasoning

We need to calculate the equivalent in Roubles in 2011 and then add the increment after 6 years. We will then convert the total amount back to Euros as per the exchange rate in 2017 and compare.

Calculation

1 000 Euros converted to Roubles in 2011:

1 Euro = 40.88460 Russian Roubles

1 000 Euros = 1 000 * 40.88460 = 40 884.60 Russian Roubles

After six years, the Russian Roubles grew by 50%. The total amount of Russian Roubles in 2017 was:

40 884.60 + (40 884.60 * 50%)

= 40 884.60 + 20 442.30

= 61 326.90 Russian Roubles

In 2017 the businessman withdrew all the Roubles and converted them back to Euros:

1 Euro = 65.93830 Russian Roubles

61 326.90 Russian Roubles = 61 326.90 / 65.93830 Euros

61 326.90 Russian Roubles ≈ 930.06 Euros

We must subtract the amount of Euros in 2017 from the amount of Euros in 2011 to find the overall change:

930.06 Euros − 1 000 Euros

= -69.94 Euros ≈ −70 Euros

The negative sign indicates a decrease of 70 Euros.

Potential Shortcuts / Pitfalls

The major pitfalls to avoid in this problem are the use of incorrect exchange rates. Exchange rates for 2011 must be used for the start and 2017 exchange rates must be used for the end of the 6 year period.

The significant fall in the value of Russian Rouble as compared to the Euro over six years led to an overall loss on investment despite an increase in the amount of Roubles.

Be careful, the question asks for the *difference* in Euros from 2011 to 2017, not the *amount* of Euros in 2017.

F. ESTIMATING AND MENTAL ARITHMETIC

The practice questions in this section involve extensive use of estimating and sums you can do in your head, without using a calculator. In numerical reasoning tests you can sometimes solve what might appear quite tricky problems in these ways, but it means you need to apply reasoning to work out what the question is actually asking and how to use the information you are provided with.

SET 1

	2016			2017		
Employee Satisfaction Survey Results, ABC Company Share of employees in the 'satisfied' category						
	Marketing	Sales	Engineering	Marketing	Sales	Engineering
Pay	65%	68%	79%	78%	75%	49%
Facilities	49%	51%	50%	51%	52%	49%
Morale	80%	70%	75%	88%	76%	90%
CEO	66%	79%	78%	48%	50%	52%

Departmental Headcount

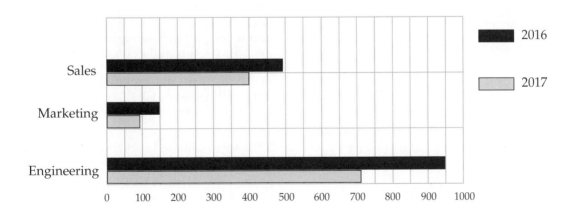

Q1. What was the difference between the number of marketing and sales employees satisfied with the CEO in 2016 and 2017?

A.   44
B.   79
C.   205
D.   243
E.   437

Correct Answer: D

Explanation

While the CEO satisfaction rates across various departments are given as exact percentages, the head count in each department is given in the form of a bar chart without exact figures. This is always a strong indication that we are encouraged to estimate the result.

If we look at the CEO satisfaction rates, we can observe the following:

Marketing: about two-thirds are satisfied in 2016 and about a half in 2017

Sales: about 4/5th are satisfied in 2016, and about half in 2017

Turning to the head counts:

Marketing: about 150 in 2016, less than 100 in 2017

Sales: less than 500 in 2016, about 400 in 2017

Let's combine the two.

Employees satisfied with the CEO in 2016:

Marketing: two-thirds of 150, about 100

Sales: 4/5th of 500, about 400

Total: 500

Employees satisfied with the CEO in 2017:

Marketing: half of 100, about 50

Sales: half of 400, about 200

Total: 250

The question was about the difference between the 2016 and 2017 numbers, so the estimated answer is 500 − 250 = 250.

The closest answer to this is 243 (option D), and all the other answer options are too far from our estimate.

It is important not to confuse which departments and which satisfaction metric we are calculating with as some of the other answer options match results that you would arrive at if you did so.

Q2. What was the change in the total number of employees satisfied with the facilities from 2016 to 2017?

A.   Increased by 198
B.   Increased by 393
C.   Decreased by 198
D.   Decreased by 393
E.   Decreased by 98

Correct Answer: C

Explanation

As in the previous problem, we need to rely on the departmental head count bar chart, hinting at a relatively low level of required accuracy and telling us that we can estimate.

Another important thing to notice is that the facilities satisfaction rates were very similar in all departments and across both years: 49, 51, 50, 51, 52 and 49, i.e. about one half across the board. Using this insight, we can make the assumption that the total difference between employees satisfied with the facilities in 2016 and 2017 will be about half of the difference between the total head counts in the two years.

2016 approximate head count: 500 + 150 + 950 = 1600

2017 approximate headcount: 400 + 100 + 700 = 1200

Difference: 400

The correct answer is approximately half of this, about 200, and a decrease, which is option C.

It is important to keep in mind the direction of change and that only half of the difference is to be counted, as both of these mistakes are represented by incorrect answer options.

Q3. If we assume that everyone who was dissatisfied with their pay in 2017 leaves the company within the same year, and nothing else changes, how many employees will the company have at the beginning of 2018?

A. 482
B. 592
C. 512
D. 719
E. 981

Correct Answer; D

Explanation

We already know that the departmental head count figures from the bar chart can only be estimated, so we will continue to do so.

Turning to those who are dissatisfied with their pay in 2017, we must first remember that the figures given represent the *satisfaction* rate, so to get the number of those who are *dissatisfied*, we need to subtract these percentages from 100:

Marketing: $100 - 78 = 22\%$, less than one quarter

Sales: $100 - 75 = 25\%$, one quarter

Engineering: $100 - 49 = 51\%$, about half

If all these people leave, that means:

Marketing: (less than) one quarter of (less than) 100 = less than 25

Sales: one quarter of about 400 = about a 100

Engineering: about half of (more than) 700 = 350

Total: about 475

We know from the previous problem that the approximate number of employees in 2017 was 1200. If 475 of them leave, about 725 remain, and answer option D is the closest to this.

We could save even more time by calculating instead the number of employees who are satisfied with their pay and will consequently stay at the company. The percentages for this category are directly available from the table. We can calculate the total and subtract that from overall headcount, saving us a bit more time.

SET 2

Government digital transformation						
Government services accessed through digital and non-digital channels						
	2005			2015		
	Digital	Non-digital		Digital	Non-digital	
		Phone	Post		Phone	Post
Passport applications	33%	39%	28%	80%	5%	15%
Tax returns	20%	21%	59%	67%	16%	17%

Number of transactions (thousands)

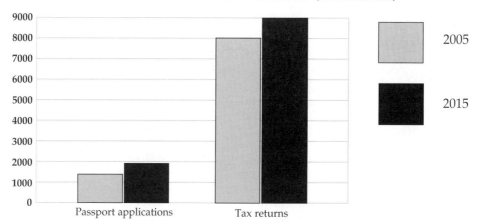

Q1. Digitally submitted tax returns cost 25% as much to process for the government as it does to process those returned in the post, and half as much as those submitted on the phone. If each digital tax return costs the government 1 euro, how much did they spend on processing tax returns in 2015?

A.   11 897 euros
B.   14 962 euros
C.   11.897 million euros
D.   14.962 million euros
E.   17.846 million euros

Correct Answer: D

Explanation

Here again we are faced with a problem where some of the figures we need can only be approximated as they appear in a chart, so estimation is required.

We know that processing each digitally submitted tax return costs the government 1 euro, so let's start there.

We can estimate the number of digitally submitted tax returns to be:

9 million x 67% (about two thirds) = about 6 million

We can apply a shortcut at this point. We know that the number of tax returns using the other two methods must then be 9 – 6 = about 3 million.

If we look at the percentages for phone and post, we see that they are 16% and

17%, i.e. approximately the same, so to simplify things, we will assume that there were 1.5 million phone and 1.5 million postal tax returns.

We know that a digital tax return (1 euro) costs half as much as a phone tax return, so that must be 2 euros; and it costs 25% (one quarter) as much as a postal return, so that must be 4 euros.

We can now calculate the cost of the other two methods:

1.5 million x 2 euros = 3 million euros

1.5 million x 4 euros = 6 million euros

And altogether:

6 + 3 + 6 million = 15 million euros, which means that option D is correct.

Q2. If the cost of digitally submitted passport applications is 61% higher than the cost of digitally submitted tax returns (which stands at 1 euro), what is the difference between the amount spent on each in 2005?

A. 793 729 euros
B. 988 529 euros
C. 1 103 530 euros
D. 1 215 040 euros
E. 1 611 400 euros

Correct Answer: A

Explanation

The approximate number of passport applications submitted digitally in 2005 was:

1.5 million x 33% (about one third) = 0.5 million

Since they cost 61% more than digitally submitted tax returns (which are 1 euro each), the cost of processing these passport applications must be:

0.5 x 1.61 = about 0.8 million euros

The approximate number of digitally submitted tax returns in 2005 was 8 million x 20% = 1.6 million, and since each of those costs 1 euro, this represents a 1.6 million euro cost.

The difference is about 1.6 – 0.8 = 0.8 million, or 800 000 euros, which is closest by far to option A.

Q3. How many fewer people used the phone to submit a tax return or apply for a passport in 2015 than in 2005?

A. 158 790
B. 503 610
C. 753 500
D. 1 628 810
E. 2 291 210

Correct Answer: C

Explanation

This problem can be approached in either of two ways. It is perfectly reasonable to *calculate* the correct answer accurately, but this requires 4 multiplications (to calculate the number of people who used the phone channel for each service and for each year), two subtractions (to subtract the 2015 number from the 2005 number for each service) and one addition (to calculate the difference for the two services combined).

The other option is to *estimate*. Although this requires practice and the ability to make quick mental calculations, it is still faster than the calculation method.

Here is what this method looks like.

Around 40% of about 1.5 million users used the phone channel in 2005, which is about 600 000, and 5% of about 2 million, about 100 000, did so in 2015, giving a difference of around 500 000.

For tax returns, this was 21% of about 8 million. We need to recognise here that the 1% from the 21% figure cannot be disregarded because of the high number (8 million) of transactions. 20% of 8 million is 1.6 million, 1% is 80 000, so this gives us 1.68 million.

In 2015, the total was about 9 million,

and 16% used the phone channel. Similarly to the above, we cannot round 16% down to 15% because of the high number of transactions. What we do is estimate that 15% of 9 million is about 1.35 million, and 1% is about 90 thousand, leaving the total at 1.44 million.

The approximate difference is then about 240 000.

Adding up the two "difference" figures (which are both decreases) gives us about 740 000 as the estimated result, which is clearly closest to option C.

SET 3

CO_2 emissions of various production methods kg / unit of production		
Product / Production Method	Method A	Method B
Dishwasher	101	50
Washing Machine	95	47
Fridge-freezer	197	98

Carbon tax rates USD/ton of CO_2 emissions per company		
	2010-2014	2015 onwards
First 1000 tonnes	2	3
For each additional tonne	3	5

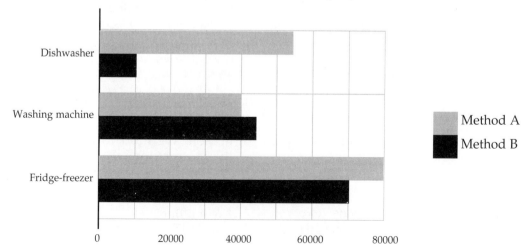

Production volumes in 2015, ABC Company (units)

Q1. **XYZ company produces 10 000 dish-washers, 10 000 washing machines and 5 000 fridge-freezers a year using production method A exclusively. How much higher/lower will their carbon tax bill be in 2015 than in 2014 if they switch exclusively to production method B?**

A.   2535 USD
B.   4455 USD
C.   5300 USD
D.   7835 USD
E.   8125 USD

Correct Answer: A

Explanation

It is key in this problem to notice that the tables are generic, i.e. not specific to one company, and that the chart is about ABC company's production volume whereas the question talks about another company, XYZ. By using approximate figures we can get to the answer doing any calculations in our head, without using a calculator.

To answer the question effectively, we should notice that the carbon emission of production method A is roughly twice as much as that of production method B. Also, production method A has carbon emissions at around 0.1 t (around 100 kg) per unit for dishwashers and washing machines and around 0.2t (around 200 kg) per unit for fridge-freezers.

First, we should calculate the total carbon emissions for 2014:

10 000 dishwashers x about 0.1tonnes = 1000 t

10 000 washing machines x about 0.1 t = 1000 t

5000 fridge-freezers x about 0.2t = 1000 t

That adds up to about 3000 tonnes. In 2014, this is taxed at:

2 USD/t for the first 1000 tonnes = 2000

3 USD/t for the remaining 2000 tonnes = 6000

Total = 8000

If they switch exclusively to production method B in 2015, their emissions will be about half, i.e. 1500 tonnes, and new tax rates will apply. This will add up to:

3 USD/tonne for the first 100 tonnes = 3000

5 USD/tonne for the remaining 500 tonnes = 2500

Total = 5500

The difference is 2500 USD, which is an estimate, but it is clearly closest to option A.

We must take care not to forget about the tax changes and the fact that half as many fridge-freezers are produced as dishwashers and washing machines, as there are answer options matching the results of these mistakes.

Q2. **What was ABC company's carbon tax bill in 2015 on its production of dish-washers and washing machines?**

A.   11 970.3
B.   34 910.9
C.   35 912.7
D.   59 851.5
E.   71 834.5

Correct Answer: D

Explanation

This question is about ABC company, which is a clue that information from the chart now has to be used. As the chart is purely visual, without providing exact figures, we will be using approximate figures to get to the closest estimate we can.

The approximate production volumes of dishwashers for ABC company for each production method are:

Production method A: 55 000
Production method B: 10 000

For washing machines:

Production method A: 40 000
Production method B: 45 000

Looking at the carbon emissions of the two methods for the two products, we can make the simplification that each method has the same emissions for both products, 0.1t/unit for method A and 0.05t/unit for method B.

With this, we can calculate the total emissions:

Method A: (55 000 + 40 000) x 0.1 = 9500 tonnes

Method B: (10 000 + 45 000) x 0.05 = 2 750 tonnes

Total = 12 250 tonnes

Using the 2015 tax rates, this adds up to:

3000 USD for the first 1000 tonnes

5 USD/tonne for the remaining 11 250 tonnes = 56250

Total = 59 250 USD

The answer option closest to this estimate is D.

It is essential in this question to use the correct tax rates, kg/tonne conversions and the correct products because there are incorrect answer options exploiting these mistakes.

Q3. In 2016, ABC company increased its production volumes by 10% compared to 2015 levels across all of its products and switched its entire operation to production method B. What percentage of the total number of units produced did dishwashers represent in 2016?

A.   19.76%
B.   21.74%
C.   25.78%
D.   28.36%
E.   52.13%

Correct Answer: B

Explanation

For this problem, we must first notice that the information in the question about the company switching its entire operation to method B is a distractor – we do not actually need this to answer the question. We

can get to the answer just by using mental arithmetic if we use a little bit of approximating in the final step.

Since the production method doesn't matter, we can add up all of the 2015 production volume figures from the chart to calculate the total volume and the total dishwasher volume. Once we have increased both of these figures by 10%, we can easily calculate what percentage dishwashers represent in the total number of units produced by the company in that year.

Total production in 2015:

Dishwashers: 65 000 units
Washing machines: 85 000 units
Fridge-freezers: 150 000 units
Total: 300 000 units

The 10% increase (for both dishwashers separately and for the total volume) account for:

Dishwashers: 65 000 + 10% = 71 500 units
Total: 300 000 + 10% = 330 000 units

The final calculation will give us what percentage 71500 represents of 330 000:

71 500/330 000 = 21.67%

We would need to use a calculator to give us this exact percentage figure, but we can get our answer even faster without a calculator by using a little bit of rounding and fractions. Simplify 71 500/330 000 to 7/33. Then, given that 33 is about one-third of 100, we only a have to multiply the 7 by 3 to get 21, which is close enough to give us the correct answer.

There is also one more trick we can use to save even more time: calculating the 10% increase is actually superfluous. The question is about the *percentage* one product represents of total production, and this is not affected if both the numerator and denominator are increased by the same percentage.

We can demonstrate this as follows:

$(X \times 1.1) \div (Y \times 1.1) = X \div Y$

Since the 10% increase (represented by the multiplication by 1.1) is on both sides of the fraction, they cancel each other out, resulting in the same percentage as using the original 2015 figures.

Regardless of whether we use this shortcut or not, we can see that while some of the answer options were quite close, this estimate is clearly closest to option B.

SET 4

Cost and speed of various shipping methods			
	Cost / haul (€)	Speed	Haul (units)
Rail	200	17	500
Road	8	11	10
Boat	1000	50	5000
Speed is defined as the number of hours needed to travel 1000 kilometers			

Order details for Company X				
	Unit price	Number sold	Delivery distance	Priority bonus
Order A	200 USD	20 000	3 000 km	0.5%
Order B	500 USD	30 000	8 000 km	5%
Priority bonus is paid to the supplier if delivery is made within 2 days. It is a percentage of the total price paid. Revenue = sales price minus delivery costs plus priority bonus (if applicable)				

Q1. Company X has to deliver Order A to the customer. What is the maximum revenue it can generate from this order?

A. 3.984 million USD
B. 3.992 million USD
C. 3.996 million USD
D. 4.004 million USD
E. 4.012 million USD

Correct Answer: D

Explanation

To solve this problem, we need to carefully consider all the information available in the tables and in the question. The first thing to establish is that the question is about maximum revenue. This is a prompt for us to look at the definition of revenue in the second table. This tells us that revenue includes any priority bonus we can earn by delivering the items quickly, which in turn will prompt us to consider the speed as well as the price of each delivery method. With a little bit of confidence, the calculations can be done without a calculator.

We can start by calculating the sales price of the items in Order A. This is:

200 USD/item x 20 000 items = 4 000 000 USD

Next, we need to consider the cheapest delivery option, taking into account the priority bonus (0.5%) we might earn if we deliver within 2 days. Looking at the delivery distance, only road delivery would allow the company to earn the priority bonus. If we disregard the priority bonus, the cheapest delivery option is by boat, so these are the two methods we should compare.

Boat: 4 hauls of 5 000 items each (total 20 000 items) would cost 4 x 1 000 USD = 4 000 USD.

Road: 2 000 hauls of 10 items each would cost 2000 x 8 USD = 16 000 USD.

However, if the delivery is made by road, the priority bonus is applied, earning the company:

4 000 000 USD x 0.5% = 20 000 USD

After evaluating the two methods, we find:

Revenue with transport by boat: 4 000 000 – 4000 USD = 3.996 million USD

Revenue with transport by road: 4 000 000 – 16 000 + 20 000 = 4.004 million USD

The correct answer, then, is option D.

In this question it is essential to take account of the speed of delivery, as the train would be a cheaper option than by road, but that is just outside the priority bonus timeframe.

Q2. What is the minimum cost of delivering both orders to the customer, irrespective of speed?

A.   4 000 USD
B.   8 000 USD
C.   10 000 USD
D.   20 000 USD
E.   400 000 USD

Correct Answer: C

Explanation

In this problem, the hint is the statement in the question text that we should only consider the cost of delivery *and nothing*

else. A second important observation is that the two deliveries must be considered separately as the two different distances for the two orders indicate that they do not go to the same location.

This problem can now be solved with some simple mental arithmetic.

As speed does not matter, we should look for the cheapest delivery option, and that is by boat.

Order A has 20 000 units, which takes up 4 hauls by boat. Order B has 30 000 units, accounting for 6 hauls.

A total of 10 hauls by boat costs 10 000 USD, so option C is the correct answer.

Q3. If order A has to be delivered on land and both orders must be delivered within 5 days, what is the minimum cost of delivery?

A.   10 000 USD
B.   20 000 USD
C.   32 000 USD
D.   40 000 USD
E.   42 000 USD

Correct Answer: C

Explanation

The actual calculations involved in this problem are quite easy and can be done by mental arithmetic. This problem is all about carefully weighing all the constraints set in the question itself:

Both orders must be delivered in less than 5 days

Order A can only be delivered by land (i.e. excluding the boat option)

Based on these constraints, we can consider the cost and speed of rail and road transport options. We should look at speed first, focusing on whether both modes can make the delivery in 5 days (or 120 hours)

Order A (3000 km), by rail: 17 x 3 = 51 hours

Rail can deliver within 5 days and it is

cheaper than by road, so we should use this for Order A. This will cost:

20 000 units / 500 = 40 hauls
40 x 200 USD = 8000 USD

Order B's delivery destination is 8000 km away, so we must again consider the delivery speeds:

Rail: 17 x 8 = 136 hours (this takes too long)

This leaves us with the road delivery option. Order B contains 30 000 units, so the delivery cost is:

30 000 units / 10 = 3 000 hauls
3 000 x 8 USD = 24 000 USD

The total, then, is 32 000 USD, making option C the correct answer option.

SET 5

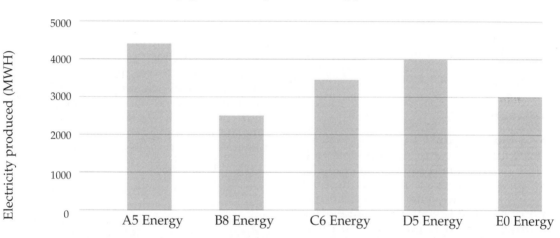

Electricity produced by various suppliers (MWh)

Q1. **15% of the electricity produced by A5 Energy is from renewables, 5% from B8 Energy, 10% from C6 Energy, 15% from D5 Energy, and 20% from E0 Energy. Which supplier produces the most electricity from renewable sources?**

A.   A5 Energy
B.   B8 Energy
C.   C6 Energy
D.   D5 Energy
E.   E0 Energy

Correct Answer: A

Explanation

If we look carefully at the chart and the percentages in the question, it is clear that by using estimation we can eliminate answer options one by one:
- B8 Energy has the lowest total electricity produced and the lowest renewable share as well – it can't be the correct answer
- D5 Energy has the same renewable share as A5 Energy, but a lower total, so it can't be the correct answer either
- C6 Energy has a lower share and a lower total than the already eliminated D5 Energy, so we can eliminate it as well
- While E0 Energy has a higher share of renewables than A5 Energy, this does

not fully compensate for the lower total, so it can't be the correct answer

This leaves A5 Energy as the only remaining possibility.

Q2. If B8 Energy increased the share of renewable energy in its electricity production by a factor of five, where would it rank among the five suppliers in terms of the share of renewable energy in electricity production?

A. First
B. Second
C. Third
D. Fourth
E. Fifth

Correct Answer: A

Explanation

This problem requires only the simplest mental arithmetic, but it is possible to go wrong by misinterpreting the question. The question asks us to rank the suppliers in a hypothetical scenario based on their *share* of renewable energy in their electricity production. It is important to distinguish this from a ranking based on the *amount* of electricity produced from renewable sources as this would result in a different answer being selected.

B8 Energy's current share of renewables is 5%. If they increased this share by a factor of 5, this would take their share to 25%, which is the highest among the 5 suppliers, making option A the correct answer.

If, however, we misinterpret the question and calculate the amount of electricity produced from renewable sources, we would get:

2500 x 25% = 625 MWh

This would place B8 Energy ahead of C6, D5 and E0 Energy, but it would still be behind A5 Energy, whose corresponding figure is 4500 x 15% = 675 MWh

This misinterpretation would lead us to pick option B, which would be incorrect.

Q3. What is the total amount of electricity produced by the five suppliers from non-renewable energy sources?

A. 2 350 MWh
B. 3 150 MWh
C. 14 350 MWh
D. 15 150 MWh
E. 17 500 MWh

Corrrect Answer: D

Explanation

The total amount of electricity produced by the 5 suppliers can be easily read off the chart. We also know the share of renewable energy for each supplier, expressed as percentages. One way to calculate the share of non-renewable energy is to calculate the remaining percentage. For example, for A5 Energy, this would be:

$$100\% - 15\% = 85\%$$

Some may find this method unnecessarily time-consuming. As an alternative, we can instead calculate the total amount of electricity produced by the 5 suppliers from renewable sources, and subtract this from the grand total.

Grand total for all suppliers: 4 500 + 2 500 + 3 500 + 4 000 + 3 000 = 17 500

Then, we can calculate the total from renewable sources, summing up as we go:

15% x 4 500 = 675
5% x 2 500 = 125 (800)
10% x 3 500 = 350 (1150)
15% x 4 000 = 600 (1750)
20% x 3 000 = 600 (2350)

The correct answer will be the difference between 17500 and 2350 = 15150, i.e. option D.

It is essential not to forget about this last step, as the interim calculation steps are among the answer options.

8. Numerical Reasoning Mixed Questions Test

40 Sets – Total 120 Questions
ANSWERS follow Set 40

This test consists of mixed question types, testing all the operations and techniques we practised in the previous chapter.

You should aim to eventually be able to answer these questions at a rate of 10 in 20 minutes, which is a typical EPSO scenario. However you will most likely struggle to achieve these speeds at first. Read the answer explanations carefully and focus on the range of strategies they give for speeding up your calculations until they become second nature to you.

Remember, too, to check the exact rules of your competition for the number of questions, time allowed and pass mark and use those for your practice.

Note: the symbols × and * are both used for multiplication.

Set 1

Intra-EU air traffic at country level, top-5 country pairs						
Rank	Country pairs		2015		2016	
			Passengers carried (in 1000)	Share in total intra-EU (%)	Passengers carried (in 1000)	Share in total intra-EU (%)
1	United Kingdom	Spain	35922.6	9.10	41637.8	9.60
2	Spain	Germany	25063.9	6.35	27581.6	6.36
3	United Kingdom	Germany	13302.7	3.37	13877	3.20
4	United Kingdom	Italy	12711.3	3.20	14123.5	3.24
5	Italy	Germany	12427.1	3.15	13296	3.07

Q1. What was the increase in total intra-EU traffic between 2015 and 2016 (*rounded to the nearest million*)?

A. 11 million
B. 39 million
C. 13 million
D. 73 million
E. 4 million

Q2. What was the percentage increase in traffic for the three top destinations from the United Kingdom between 2015 and 2016 (*rounded to one decimal place*)?

A. 0.9%
B. 8.9%
C. 11.2%
D. 12.4%
E. 0.4%

Q3. In 2015 the average cost of a Spain-Germany flight was €147.60, and it increased by 2.1% in 2016. What was the increase in the total amount spent by Spain-Germany passengers between 2015 and 2016 (*rounded to the nearest thousand euros*)?

A. €457 thousand
B. €364 thousand
C. €457115 thousand
D. €2108 thousand
E. €364091 thousand

Set 2

Trips, nights spent and expenditure of EU residents, EU-28, 2016			
	All trips (Thousand)	Domestic trips (Thousand)	Outbound trips (Thousand)
Trips	1 206 953	898 331	308 622
Nights	6 126 026	3 530 916	2 595 110
Expenditure in million €	428 198	192 949	235 249

Top 5 destinations for outbound trips made by EU residents outside the EU, in terms of number of trips, EU-28 2016 (%)

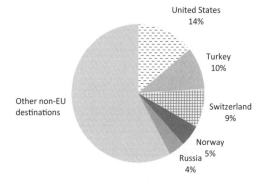

Q1. What was the difference between the numbers of outbound trips made by EU residents in 2016 to the U.S. and to Switzerland (*to the nearest million*)?

A. 60 million
B. 39 million
C. 15 million
D. 15431 million
E. 18934 million

Q2. The number of outbound trips made by EU residents to Turkey decreased by 0.6% between 2016 and 2017, and the total number of outbound trips increased by 1.8% during the same period. What was the share of outbound trips made by EU residents to Turkey in 2017 (*rounded to one decimal place*)?

A. 9.2%
B. 9.4%
C. 10.2%
D. 9.8%
E. 10.8%

Q3. The share in the expenditure of outbound trips made by EU residents to Norway in 2016 was 1.4 times larger than the share of Norway in the number of outbound trips, and the share in the expenditure of outbound trips made by EU residents to Russia in 2016 was by 25% less than the share of Russia in the number of outbound trips. What was the ratio between the expenditures of outbound trips made by EU residents to Norway and to Russia in 2016?

A. 4 : 5
B. 7 : 5
C. 5 : 4
D. 3 : 7
E. 7 : 3

Set 3

Health care expenditure, top-5 EU member states, 2015		
	Million EUR	EUR per inhabitant
France	241 366	3 623
Germany	338 207	4 140
Italy	148 029	2 437
Spain	98 586	2 123
United Kingdom	254 827	3 913

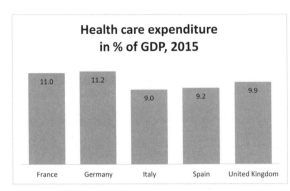

Health care expenditure in % of GDP, 2015

France 11.0 | Germany 11.2 | Italy 9.0 | Spain 9.2 | United Kingdom 9.9

(GDP = Gross domestic product)

Q1. The average health care expenditure of the top-5 EU members increased by 4.5% between 2015 and 2017. What was the average expenditure of the top-5 EU members in 2017 *(rounded to the nearest billion euros)*?

- A. 226 billion
- B. 39 billion
- C. 216 billion
- D. 236708 billion
- E. 225932 billion

Q2. What was the difference between the GDP of the United Kingdom and France in 2015 *(rounded to the nearest billion euros)*?

- A. €13461 billion
- B. €380 billion
- C. €415561 billion
- D. €379774 billion
- E. €13 billion

Q3. The population of Spain increased by 3.1% in 2016, and by 3.4% in 2017. What was the population of Spain by the end of 2017 *(rounded to the nearest million)*?

- A. 49 million
- B. 49505 million
- C. 50 million
- D. 49501 million
- E. 46 million

Set 4

Dataset: Generation of waste by sector							
Variable	01-03: Agriculture, forestry and fishing						
Unit	Tonnes, Thousands						
Year	2004	2005	2006	2007	2008	2009	2010
Country							
Austria	469	..	513	..	459	..	550
Belgium	1 187	..	361	..	288	..	231
Chile	1 515	1 393	1 367	1 470	1 435	1562	..
Hungary	4 000	..	1 998	..	337	..	488
Ireland	9	..	0	..	19	..	101
Italy	710	..	554	..	341	..	302
Japan	89 300	87 584	87 945	87 837	87 992	88 446	85 109
Korea	..	..	..	..	..	..	152
Latvia	208	..	96	..	75	..	68
Netherlands	2 393	..	2 659	..	3 468	..	4 978
Sweden	314	..	314	..	314	..	309
United Kingdom	719	..	666	..	681	..	495
Data extracted on 11 Oct 2018 15:40 UTC (GMT) from OECD.Stat							

Q1. If the generation of waste in the agriculture, forestry and fishing sector in Chile had been 500,000 tonnes less in both 2005 and 2007, what percentage would this decrease have represented in the total waste generated in this sector in Chile in the period from 2004 to 2007?

A. 11.4%
B. 17.4%
C. 18.9%
D. 21.1%
E. 174%

Q2. In which country did the generation of waste in this sector decrease at the greatest rate between 2006 and 2008, Austria, Belgium or Italy?

A. Austria
B. Belgium
C. Italy
D. Belgium and Italy (the difference between them is negligible)
E. The difference between all three is negligible

Q3. In which year did Japan's waste generation in this sector deviate the most from the average amount of waste it generated in the 2004–2010 period?

A. 2004
B. 2006
C. 2008
D. 2009
E. 2010

Set 5

Distribution of people aged 25–64 by knowledge of foreign languages, 2011 and 2016								
(%)	No foreign language		One foreign language		Two foreign languages		Three or more foreign languages	
	2011	2016	2011	2016	2011	2016	2011	2016
Czech Republic	30.9	21.0	39.6	44.7	22.4	26.9	7.1	7.4
Poland	38.1	32.9	38.7	45.0	19.2	19.2	4.0	2.8
Slovakia	14.7	11.8	30.2	24.5	33.5	35.7	21.6	28.0
Slovenia	7.6	20.0	15.0	17.6	32.6	24.7	44.9	37.7

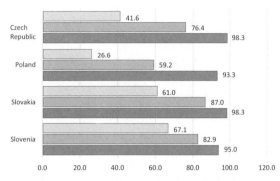

People aged 25–64 reporting they knew one or more foreign languages, by educational attainment level, 2016, %

☐ Less than primary, primary and lower secondary education (levels 0-2)
▨ Upper secondary and post-secondary non-tertiary education (levels 3 and 4)
▪ Tertiary education (levels 5-8)

Q1. What was the average percentage change between 2011 and 2016 of people aged 25–64 reporting they knew three or more foreign languages across the four countries shown (*rounded to three decimal places*)?

A. −0.48%
B. −0.425%
C. 0.425%
D. 0.48%
E. 0.34%

Q2. What was the ratio of the share of Slovenian people aged 25-64 and having tertiary education reporting that they knew one or more foreign languages, to the share of all Slovenian people of this age reporting that they knew one or more foreign languages in 2016?

A. 15 : 13
B. 10 : 9
C. 4 : 19
D. 19 : 4
E. 19 : 16

Q3. The population of Poland aged 25-64 changed from 31.2 million to 30.7 million between 2011 and 2016. What was the difference between the number of Polish people aged 25–64 reporting they knew just one foreign language in 2016 and in 2011 (*rounded to one thousand*)?

A. 2 thousand

B. 174 thousand

C. –1741 thousand

D. 1741 thousand

E. –174 thousand

Set 6

Marathon Results 2010 (42.2 km)	
Runner	Time (h:mm:ss)
Anderson	2:12:14
Benoit	2:12:38
Canard	2:13:31
Dennis	2:14:12
Ekimov	2:14:20

Q1. Canard passed the halfway marker at 1:07:50. What was his average speed for the second half of the race?

A. 15.20 km/h

B. 17.38 km/h

C. 18.63 km/h

D. 19.27 km/h

E. 20.31 km/h

Q2. Dennis and Ekimov passed the "1km to go" marker at exactly the same time, 2:11:00. How much faster than Ekimov did Dennis run in the last kilometre?

A. 1%

B. 4.2%

C. 6.6%

D. 8%

E. 12.5%

Q3. Benoit ran the last 150m at a speed 5% faster than his overall average for the race. How far was Benoit from the finishing line when Anderson finished?

A. 84m

B. 92m

C. 100m

D. 133m

E. 149m

Set 7

Tobacco Use Amongst High School Students in 2017			
Tobacco Product	Overall	Females	Males
Any tobacco product	19.6%	17.5%	21.6%
Electronic cigarettes	11.7%	9.9%	13.3%
Cigarettes	7.6%	7.5%	7.6%
Cigars	7.7%	6.3%	9.0%
Smokeless tobacco	5.5%	3.0%	7.7%
Hookahs	3.3%	3.2%	3.3%
Pipe tobacco	0.8%	0.5%	1.0%
Bidis	0.7%	0.6%	0.7%

Q1. If 60 male students in a high school use any kind of tobacco product, how many female students does the school have?

A. Fewer than 250

B. Around 260

C. Around 280

D. Around 290

E. More than 320

Q2. In a high school with 300 male students, of whom 20 use both electronic and regular cigarettes, how many male students use only one of them?

A. 15

B. 63

C. 20

D. 23

E. 43

Q3. If there are 100 students using any kind of tobacco product in a school where the number of male students is twice the number of female students, how many of the school's female students are using electronic cigarettes?

A. 7

B. 34

C. 12

D. 17

E. 39

Set 8

Meat consumption Beef and veal / Pork meat / Poultry meat / Sheep meat, Kilograms/capita 2017			Source: OECD-FAO Agricultural Outlook (Edition 2017)	
Location	Beef and veal	Pork	Poultry	Lamb
Algeria	3.9	0.1	6.3	7.1
Argentina	41.2	8.8	37.5	1.2
Australia	20.9	20.7	44.5	8.5
Bangladesh	0.9	0.0	1.2	1.2
Brazil	26.5	11.8	39.9	0.4
BRICS	4.5	15.5	10.8	1.7
Canada	18.4	15.9	34.9	0.9
Chile	18.1	18.6	34.8	0.4
China (People's Republic of)	4.1	30.8	12.3	3.1
Colombia	11.7	4.7	27.3	0.2
Egypt	9.3	0.2	9.2	1.3
Ethiopia	2.4	0.0	0.5	1.2

Q1. The carcass weight to retail weight conversion rate for beef and veal is 0.7. Assuming that Argentina had a population of 44.27 million people in 2017, what was the weight of bovine carcasses necessary to meet the beef and veal consumption?

A. 2.6 million kg

B. 2.6 million tonnes

C. 1.8 million kg

D. 1.8 million tonnes

E. None of the above

Q2. Assuming that Brazil has a population of 209.3 million people, what would be the overall rate of decrease of meat consumption in that country if both beef and veal, and poultry consumption decreased by 20%?

A. 15.3%

B. 16.9%

C. 18.7%

D. 20.3%

E. 22.2%

Q3. Australia's population is 24.6 million. Assuming that the weight of carcasses required to meet the country's pork consumption is 652.85 million kg, what is the carcass weight to retail weight ratio for pork?

A. 1 to 0.62

B. 1 to 0.72

C. 1 to 0.78

D. 1 to 0.88

E. None of the above

Set 9

Acme Closing Share Prices (€)		
	Buy	Sell
Monday	2.37	2.32
Tuesday	2.41	2.37
Wednesday	2.39	2.34
Thursday	2.28	2.25
Friday	2.34	2.29

Q1. You buy 2000 shares on Tuesday at 1.4% below the previous day's closing price. There is a €15.95 dealing charge. How much does it cost you?

A. €4673.64

B. €4689.59

C. €4734.37

D. €4761.47

E. €4768.47

Q2. You sell 2000 shares on Friday which incurs a €15.95 dealing charge. Your total proceeds amount to €4664.05. By what percentage had the price risen since yesterday's close?

A. 2%

B. 3%

C. 4%

D. 5%

E. 6%

Q3. The difference between the buying price and the selling price on a given day is known as 'the spread'. If the percentage spread is calculated as a percentage of the higher value, which day has the largest percentage spread?

A. Monday

B. Tuesday

C. Wednesday

D. Thursday

E. Friday

Set 10

Costs of Introducing New Accounting Software				
	Accounts Pro 10	BSheet 12	BSheet Lite	BookKeeper Standard
Licence fee (€)	4500 / year	3500 / year	8000 / year	9000 one-time fee
Installation fee (€)	130	150	200	550
Staff needed to operate*	4	4	3	5
Working hours needed to operate / person (monthly)	20	20	25	15
* The hourly wage of staff operating the accounting software is 20 (€)				

Q1. Which of the accounting software shown in the table is projected to cost the least to acquire and operate over a two-year period?

A. Accounts Pro 10

B. BSheet 12

C. BSheet Lite

D. BookKeeper Standard

E. BSheet 12 and BookKeeper Standard

Q2. If the company manages to negotiate a 15% discount on the licence fees and the installation is done free of charge, how much would it cost to introduce and operate the BSheet 12 software for 5 years?

A. 16 475 €

B. 19 100 €

C. 110 875 €

D. 113 500 €

E. 111 025 €

Q3. How much money will the company save or lose over 3 years if it introduces BookKeeper Standard instead of Accounts Pro 10?

A. 2 605 € in savings

B. 6 840 € in savings

C. 7 680 € in savings

D. 10 320 € in losses

E. 13 820 € in losses

Set 11

Crop Production in France (thousands of tonnes)			
	2005	*2010*	*2015*
Corn	12 107	12 211	12 409
Rapeseed	4 541	5 472	5 801
Sugar	2 814	2 920	2 702
Sunflowers	18 442	19 194	21 199
Wheat	7 422	7 719	7 792

Q1. If the table were ordered by percentage increase in production between 2010 and 2015, which crop would be in the middle of the table?

A. Corn

B. Rapeseed

C. Sugar

D. Sunflowers

E. Wheat

Q2. How many more tonnes of sugar would France have needed to produce in 2010 for its percentage increase from 2005 (to the nearest whole percentage point) to be the same as the corresponding increase for wheat?

A. 245.6

B. 6560

C. 191

D. 224.7

E. 2926.6

Q3. The yield (tonnes produced per hectare) of rapeseed is 3.1 tonnes per hectare in 2005. This improves by 6% by 2015. What is the percentage increase in land usage for rapeseed production between 2005 and 2015?

A. 27.7%

B. 13.7%

C. 35.4%

D. 26.2%

E. 20.5%

Set 12

Top-5 total production of fishery products, 2008 and 2015			
	(*1 000 tonnes live weight*)		*Share of EU-28, %*
	2008	*2015*	*2015*
Denmark	728	905	14.1
Spain	1,106	1,195	18.7
France	728	661	10.3
Netherlands	422	427	6.7
United Kingdom	768	913	14.3

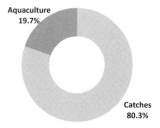

Aquaculture production and fish catches, EU-28, 2015
(% of total fisheries production)

Q1. What was the total EU-28 aquaculture production in 2015 (*in million tonnes, rounded to one decimal place*)?

A. 1.3 million tonnes

B. 5.1 million tonnes

C. 1264.4 million tonnes

D. 1189.3 million tonnes

E. 0.8 million tonnes

Q2. The French fish catch was 271 thousand tonnes greater than its aquaculture production in 2015. What was the share of French aquaculture production in the total EU-28 production of fishery products (*rounded to the nearest whole percent*)?

A. 6%

B. 4%

C. 7%

D. 3%

E. 1%

A. 14.8%

B. 22%

C. 19.3%

D. 13.8%

E. 96%

Q3. By what percentage was the increase in the total production of fishery products in the United Kingdom from 2008 to 2015 greater than that in Spain in the same period (*rounded to one decimal place*)?

A. 86.1%

B. 71.2%

C. 18.0%

D. 56.0%

E. 10.8%

Q2. Which form of power generation shows the greatest percentage increase in the percentage of total power generated between 2010 and 2015?

A. Fossil fuel

B. Wind

C. Solar

D. Tide/Wave

E. Nuclear

F. Other

Set 13

Percentage of Total Power Generated in the UK				
Source	2000	2005	2010	2015
Fossil Fuel	85.2	78.8	66.4	53.0
Wind	1.7	3.7	9.8	15.4
Solar	0.3	0.9	7.8	12.3
Tide/Wave	0.1	1.3	1.8	3.3
Nuclear	10.9	12.4	10.4	9.8
Other	1.8	2.9	3.8	6.2

Q1. The total power generated in the UK increased by 7.25% between 2000 and 2005. What was the percentage increase in nuclear power generation over the same period?

Q3. In 2005, 20% of the 'Other' power was generated by biomass. By 2010 this amount had increased by 50%. If the total power generated in the UK had increased by 10% over the same period, what percentage of 'Other' power was generated by biomass in 2010?

A. 30%

B. 63.6%

C. 22.9%

D. 48.6%

E. 20.8%

Set 14

The Natural Disasters That Inflict The Most Economic Damage Economic damage by disaster type and region from 1995 to 2005

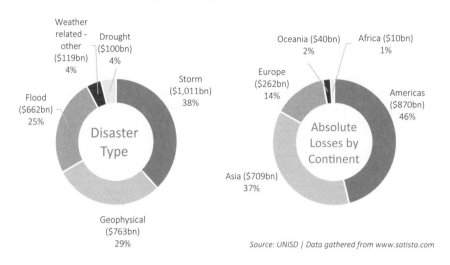

Source: UNISD | Data gathered from www.satista.com

Q1. If the economic damage caused by storms had doubled, what percentage of the total economic damage would have been caused by storms?

A. 55.2%

B. 62%

C. 71.8%

D. 76%

E. 83.7%

Q2. If the total cost of economic damage had stayed the same, but Asia had suffered 45% of it, what would have been the absolute loss of Asia?

A. Approximately 820 to 835 bn USD

B. Approximately 835 to 850 bn USD

C. Approximately 850 to 865 bn USD

D. Approximately 865 to 880 bn USD

E. Approximately 880 to 895 bn USD

Q3. What was the cost of economic damage caused by storms in the Americas?

A. $292 billion

B. $314 billion

C. $387 billion

D. $455 billion

E. There is not enough information

Set 15

100m Men's Final	
Runner	*Time (s)*
Adams	9.95
Best	9.98
Carter	10.03
Davies	10.07

Q1. Davies ran the last 10m at a speed 8% faster than his overall average speed. By what distance, to the nearest centimetre, did he miss out on the bronze medal (3rd place)?

A. 43

B. 37

C. 32

D. 26

E. 18

Q2. How much faster did Adams run than Best on average?

A. 0.1%

B. 0.3%

C. 0.7%

D. 1.0%

E. 1.2%

Q3. Carter ran the final 1.3% faster than he ran in the semi-final which was 1.8% faster than his performance in the heat (the race before the semi-final). He won his heat by 3 hundredths of a second. What was the finishing time of the runner who came second in Carter's heat?

A. 10.09

B. 10.18

C. 10.29

D. 10.34

E. 10.37

Set 16

Sold production and trade of chemical products, EU-28, 2017				
	EUR billion			
	Sold production	Extra-EU-28		Intra-EU-28
		Exports	Import	Exports
Total Chemicals	674	333	195	527
51-Organic chemicals	102	44	45	81
52-Inorganic chemicals	32	10	12	17
53-Dyeing,tanning&colouring materials	41	12	5	23
54-Medical and pharmaceutical products	168	156	77	171
55-Essential oils, resinoids and perfume materials	57	32	10	48
56-Fertilizers (other than those of group 272)	14	3	4	7
57-Plastics in primary forms	93	27	17	76
58-Plastics in non-primary forms	68	15	9	39
59-Chemical materials and products	98	34	16	66

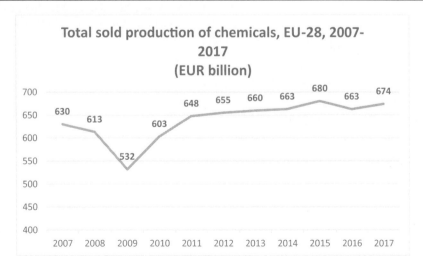

Total sold production of chemicals, EU-28, 2007-2017 (EUR billion)

Q1. What was the ratio of the percentage change
of the total EU sold production of chemicals
between 2016 and 2017 to the percentage
change between 2014 and 2015?

A. 674 : 663

B. 11 : 17

C. 17 : 11

D. 2 : 5

E. 16 : 17

Q2. The amount sold of medical and
pharmaceutical products increased by 5.2%
between 2016 and 2017. What was the share of
medical and pharmaceutical products in total
sold production of chemicals in 2016 (*rounded
to one decimal place*)?

A. 23.8%

B. 24.4%

C. 26.7%

D. 25.6%

E. 24.1%

Q3. What was the difference between the organic
and inorganic shares in intra-EU-28 exports
of chemicals in 2017 (*rounded to one decimal
place*)?

A. 12.1%

B. 18.6%

C. 64.0%

D. 29.5%

E. 63.6%

Set 17

Netherlands Population	
Year	Pop ('000)
2005	16 316
2010	16 492
2015	16 714

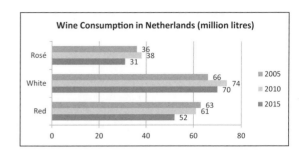

Q1. If the average cost of a 75cl bottle of red wine
in the Netherlands was €6.63 in 2015, what
was the per capita spending on red wine in
2015?

A. €18.15

B. €27.87

C. €20.62

D. €27.50

E. €37.02

Q2. If the change in consumption of white wine
between 2010 and 2015 had been the same
as the change for rosé wine over the same
period, what would the consumption figure
for white wine have been in 2015?

A. 56

B. 60

C. 67

D. 14

E. 66

Q3. What was the percentage change in per capita
consumption of red wine between 2005 and
2010?

A. −4.2%

B. −4.4%

C. −5.1%

D. −3.2%

E. −3.9%

Set 18

Participation rates of young people in education, 2015				
(%)	15-29 years	15-19 years	20-24 years	25-29 years
EU-28	45.0	86.4	41.4	13.3
Germany	50.2	88.4	49.3	20.8
Spain	48.4	87.1	49.1	16.1
France	42.8	85.2	35.6	6.8
Italy	41.1	83.9	33.8	10.6
United Kingdom	40.2	84.3	32.0	10.0

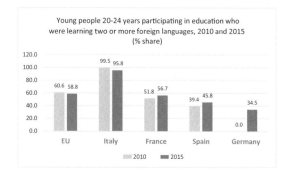

Q1. What was the ratio of the share of Italian young people aged 20-24 years participating in education and learning two or more foreign languages in 2015 to the share for the EU-28? Choose the closest option.

A. 8 : 5
B. 17 : 10
C. 4 : 3
D. 3 : 2
E. 96 : 59

Q2. The number of French young people aged 20-24 years participating in education was 1.365 million in 2010, and it increased by 3.6% between 2010 and 2015. Find the increase between 2010 and 2015 of French young people aged 20-24 years who were participating in education and learning two or more foreign languages (*in thousands*).

A. 95 thousand
B. 67 thousand
C. 94747 thousand
D. 56 thousand
E. 765 thousand

Q3. The German population aged 15-29 years in 2015 was 23% greater than that of Italy. By what percentage was the number of German young people aged 15-29 years participating in education in 2015 larger than that in Italy (*rounded to one decimal place*)?

A. 9.1%
B. 50.2%
C. 64.2%
D. 29.5%
E. 12.2%

Set 19

U.S. energy consumption by energy source, 2017

Total = 97.7 quadrillion

British thermal units (Btu)

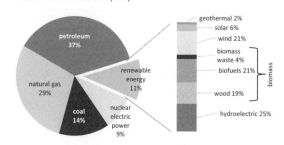

Note: Sum of components may not equal 100% because of independent rounding.

Q1. What percentage of biomass energy did bio fuels account for in 2017 in the US?

A. Around 21%
B. Around 36%
C. Around 48%
D. Around 54%
E. There's not enough information

Q2. If all the percentage values had stayed the same and the amount of hydroelectric energy produced had been 2 quadrillion Btu, what would have been the total amount of energy produced in 2017 in the US?

A. 18.2 quadrillion Btu
B. 33.4 quadrillion Btu
C. 57.6 quadrillion Btu
D. 72.7 quadrillion Btu
E. 91.9 quadrillion Btu

Q3. If the amount of petroleum based energy had decreased by 10%, and energy from the other sources had increased by equal amounts so that the total amount of energy produced stayed the same, what would have been the amount of energy produced from coal?

A.   13.2 quadrillion Btu

B.   14.2 quadrillion Btu

C.   14.6 quadrillion Btu

D.   16.1 quadrillion Btu

E.   17.3 quadrillion Btu

Set 20

Number of books in the subcategories of Teen and young adult books	
Annuals, Anthologies & Poetry	10 096
Education	390 686
Fiction	371 140
Non-fiction	310 547
Reference	15 387
Society & Social Issues	81 664
Total number of books in the Teen & young adult category: 1 017 540 *(Each book may belong to one or two subcategories)*	

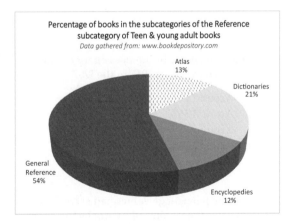

Percentage of books in the subcategories of the Reference subcategory of Teen & young adult books
Data gathered from: www.bookdepository.com

Atlas 13%
Dictionaries 21%
General Reference 54%
Encyclopedies 12%

Q1. What percentage of Teen & young adult books belong to more than one subcategory?

A.   12.3%

B.   15.9%

C.   17.2%

D.   20.4%

E.   22.8%

Q2. What percentage of Teen & young adult books belong to the general reference subcategory?

A.   0.45%

B.   0.7%

C.   0.82%

D.   1.51%

E.   1.12%

Q3. What percentage of the reference subcategory would dictionaries represent if we added another 1000 atlases?

A.   15.67%

B.   16.8%

C.   18.21%

D.   19.72%

E.   25.82%

Set 21

European Rail Travel – normal journey times		
Brussels to ...	Distance (km)	Time (hours:mins)
Amsterdam	210	1:24
Berlin	770	5:20
Luxembourg	220	1:35
Paris	320	2:40
Strasbourg	435	3:45

Q1. You travel from Brussels to Strasbourg, departing and arriving on time. The cruising speed of your train is 15% faster than its overall average speed. What is its cruising speed to the nearest kilometre per hour?

A.   100

B.   116

C.   125

D.   133

E.   150

Q2. You are travelling from Brussels to Luxembourg but due to adverse conditions the train travels 10% slower than normal. How late do you arrive in Luxembourg?

A. 5m 35s

B. 9m 30s

C. 10m 31s

D. 12m 45s

E. 15m 10s

Q3. Trains leave Brussels for Berlin every 2 hours starting at 0600 and similarly from Berlin starting at 0500. If you depart Brussels at 0800, how many Brussels-bound trains do you pass on your journey to Berlin?

A. 4

B. 5

C. 6

D. 7

E. 8

Set 22

	Pop 2015 ('000)	Workforce (% of Pop)	
		2010	2015
Croatia	4887	41.9	42.1
Hungary	11086	46.1	46.7
Ireland	4606	48.7	48.5
Portugal	11602	41.8	42.1
Ukraine	51629	46.1	47.6

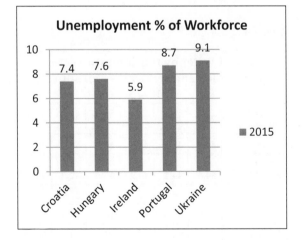

Q1. In 2015 the number of unemployed in Ireland was 10000 more than in 2010 and the percentage of the workforce unemployed was 0.1 percentage points less in 2010 than 2015. What was the percentage change in population in Ireland between 2010 and 2015?

A. −0.5%

B. 0%

C. 5.7%

D. 6.8%

E. −3.8%

Q2. What percentage of the number of unemployed people in Portugal is the number of unemployed in Hungary in 2015?

A. 87.4%

B. 92.6%

C. 96.9%

D. 96.6%

E. 103%

Q3. The percentage of the workforce unemployed in Croatia rose by 5% between 2010 and 2015 and the population rose by 3.3% over the same period. What was the rise in the number of unemployed in Croatia between 2010 and 2015?

A. 5715

B. 18912

C. 7939

D. 104680

E. 12542

Set 23

Population in Hungary in the years 2007–2017	
Year	Population
2007	10 023 887
2008	9 991 201
2009	9 958 942
2010	9 927 840
2011	9 898 204
2012	9 869 684
2013	9 841 697
2014	9 813 335
2015	9 783 925
2016	9 753 281
2017	9 721 559

Unemployment rate (in the population aged 15-74)

7.0% 8.0% 9.8% 11.8% 11.8% 11.9% 11.6% 8.3% 7.8% 6.0% 4.5%

2007 2008 2009 2010 2011 2012 2013 2014 2015 2016 2017

Q1. Assuming that 66% of the population is of working age, in what year in the 2007-2011 period was the number of unemployed people of working age at its peak?

A. 2007
B. 2008
C. 2009
D. 2010
E. 2011

Q2. Assuming that 66% of the population is of working age from 15 to 74, and that every age group is equally represented in the unemployed working age population, how many of those unemployed people who are of working age in 2017 will be older than 74 years in 2020?

A. Less then 14000
B. Around 14500
C. Around 15000
D. Around 15500
E. More then 16000

Q3. At what rate did the number of people (of any age) who were not working change from 2007 to 2017, assuming that 66% of the population is of working age, and that nobody outside the 15-74 age group has a job?

A. Around a 7% increase
B. Around a 38% increase
C. It stayed roughly the same
D. Around a 38 % decrease
E. Around a 7% decrease

Set 24

Use of water by the domestic sector (households and services) — all sources, 2010–15						
(m³ per inhabitant)	2010	2011	2012	2013	2014	2015
Bulgaria	44.7	45.1	45.9	46.7	45.4	47.1
Czech Republic	44.4	44.2	43.9	42.6	42.2	43.0
Hungary	38.9	39.0	39.2	38.0	37.5	38.9
Latvia	57.4	93.6	64.8	44.1	44.8	56.8
Lithuania	34.5	35.5	35.0	37.8	40.6	50.9

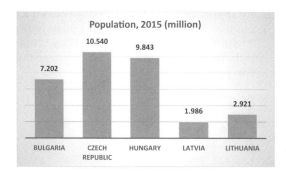

Set 25

Populations	
	2005 ('000)
Croatia	4 443
Denmark	5 417
Portugal	10 547
Sweden	9 293

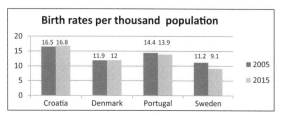

Q1. What was the total water usage of the domestic sector in Latvia in 2015 as a percentage of that of Lithuania (*rounded to one decimal place*)?

A. 68.0%

B. 75.9%

C. 87.4%

D. 111.6%

E. 115.1%

Q2. What was the difference in the average per capita water usage of each of the five countries in 2015 and 2010 (*in m³, rounded to one decimal place*)?

A. 3.4 m³

B. 17.4 m³

C. 13.2 m³

D. 16.8 m³

E. 5.9 m³

Q3. Total water usage by the domestic sector in Lithuania increased by 40.3 million m³ between 2011 and 2015. What was the population of Lithuania in 2011 (*in millions, rounded to one decimal place*)?

A. 4.2 million

B. 2.9 million

C. 2.4 million

D. 2.7 million

E. 3.1 million

Q1. The population of Croatia increased by 7.5% between 2005 and 2015. How many more births were there in Croatia in 2015 than in 2005 (*rounded to the nearest whole number*)?

A. 6931

B. 1433

C. 1333

D. 73310

E. 80241

Q2. What is the average number of births across all four countries shown in 2005 (*rounded to the nearest whole number*)?

A. 92704

B. 102314

C. 98433

D. 96154

E. 100238

Q3. In Portugal there were 4 more births in 2015 than there were in 2005. What was the percentage change in population of Portugal over this time?

A. 5%

B. −5%

C. 0.1%

D. −0.1%

E. 3.6%

F. −3.6%

Set 26

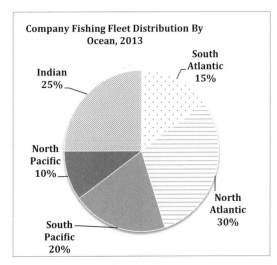

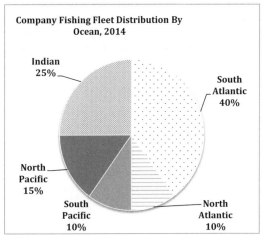

* *The Indian Ocean is not considered part of the Pacific Ocean.*

Q1. The company is realigning its fishing fleet distribution according to changing catch expectations. If, in 2013, the company had 42 fishing boats in the South Atlantic and the company increases its total fleet size by 15% in 2014, how many fishing boats will it have overall in the Atlantic Ocean in 2014, rounded to the nearest whole boat?

    A.   105

    B.   112

    C.   129

    D.   140

    E.   161

Q2. By approximately what percentage does the number of the company's fishing boats in the Pacific Ocean change between 2013 and 2014 if the overall fleet grows by 15% between the two years?

    A.   -16.67%

    B.   -5.00%

    C.   -4.17%

    D.   -1.25%

    E.   +27.78%

Q3. If the Pacific Ocean is 2.3 times as large as the Indian Ocean, by what percentage is the company's number of boats per square kilometer in the Indian Ocean greater than in the Pacific Ocean in 2014?

    A.   30%

    B.   92%

    C.   130%

    D.   230%

    E.   Impossible to tell

Set 27

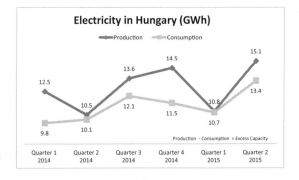

Q1. If 5% of production in Quarter 1 2014 came from 50 wind farms and the same percentage of Quarter 2 2014 production was also contributed by wind farms, how many wind farms produced electricity in that quarter? You should assume that all operational wind farms produce identical amounts of electricity as each other and in each quarter.

    A.   42

    B.   48

    C.   52

    D.   55

    E.   Cannot say

Q2. In 2014, Hungary exported 79% of its excess capacity. How many GWh of excess electricity does Hungary still need to generate in the rest of 2015 to achieve the same export volume in 2015 if in the first half of 2015 it exported 50% of its excess capacity?

A. 4.2 GWh

B. 5.1 GWh

C. 5.8 GWh

D. 6.7 GWh

E. It cannot achieve the same export volume

Q3. The Paks nuclear power plant in Hungary produces 14.8 GWh annually and its rate of production is constant. In how many of the quarters shown was Paks's production more than 30% of total production?

A. In none of them

B. 1

C. 2

D. 4

E. In all of them

Set 28

	Total		Couple		Couple	
	(thousand)		with children (%)		without children (%)	
	2007	2017	2007	2017	2007	2017
EU-28	200 974.5	221 326.2	21.2	20.0	24.1	24.9
Germany	39 290.5	40 722.6	16.5	15.7	28.1	28.4
Spain	16 643.0	18 512.5	22.3	23.1	20.3	21.8
France	26 456.5	29 314.4	23.7	21.2	27.5	26.2
Italy	23 710.7	25 864.7	23.5	20.9	20.4	20.7

Private households by household composition, 2007-2017 (number of households in 1 000 and % of household types)

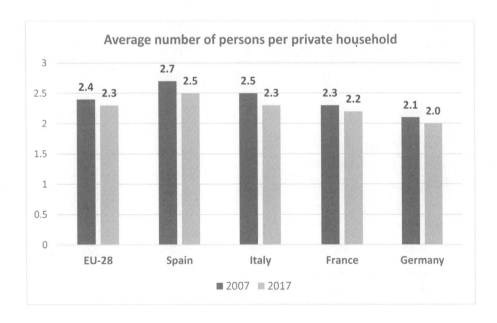

Q1. What was the difference between 2017 and 2007 in the total number of persons living in French private households (*in millions, rounded to one decimal place*)?

    A. 2.9 million

    B. 3.6 million

    C. 9.2 million

    D. 6.3 million

    E. 8.0 million

Q2. What was the percentage change between 2007 and 2017 in the number of couples with children living in private households in Italy (*rounded to two decimal places*)?

    A. 3.40%

    B. 9.08%

    C. –2.98%

    D. –2.60%

    E. 5.91%

Q3. The total number of EU-28 private households increased by 0.65% in 2018, and the share of couples without children didn't change. What was the EU-28 total number of persons without children in 2018 (*rounded to the nearest million*)?

    A. 110 million

    B. 55 million

    C. 111 million

    D. 27 million

    E. 1 million

Set 29

The Planets		
Planet	Distance from Sun (million km)	Orbital Period (Earth Days)
Mercury	58	88
Venus	101	224.7
Earth	150	365.25
Mars	228	687

Q1. As a planet travels around the Sun (orbital period), the distance it covers is 6.3 times its distance from the Sun. At what speed does the Earth travel around the Sun in km/sec?

    A. 0.03

    B. 0.3

    C. 3

    D. 30

    E. 300

Q2. How much faster than Venus is Mercury travelling? The distance travelled by a planet around the Sun is the distance of the planet from the Sun multiplied by 6.3.

    A. 24%

    B. 47%

    C. 67%

    D. 85%

    E. 125%

Q3. A future astronaut on Mars has to wait at least 8m 40s to get a response from Earth to his messages. This minimum delay occurs when the distance of Mars from Earth is the distance of Mars from the Sun minus Earth's distance from the Sun. At what speed do his messages travel (in km/sec)?

    A. 120,000

    B. 150,000

    C. 210,000

    D. 270,000

    E. 300,000

Set 30

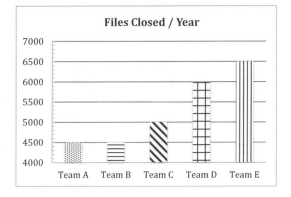

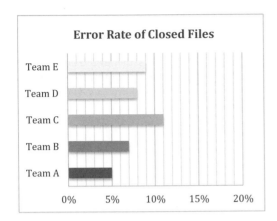

Error Rate of Closed Files

Team E
Team D
Team C
Team B
Team A

0%   5%   10%   15%   20%

Set 31

Tax Systems		
SYSTEM 1 Tax free allowance: 10000 10001–30000: 15% 30001–50000: 25% 50001+: 31% Insurance tax: 100 per month	**SYSTEM 2** Tax free allowance: Nil 0–30000: 15% 30001+: 21% Insurance tax: 50 per month	**SYSTEM 3** Tax free allowance: 15000 15001–30000: 17% 30001–60000: 22% 60001+: 28% Insurance tax: 200 per month
All amounts are in euro and are annual except where otherwise indicated. Tax rates are marginal (the percentage indicated is levied only on that part of the income falling in the given range). *Effective tax rate (%) = tax / income × 100*		

Q1. Five teams work on closing financial audit files and each team sometimes makes errors. Which team closes the lowest number of files per year without errors?

A. Team A

B. Team B

C. Team C

D. Team D

E. Team E

Q2. If Team C's error rate deteriorated to 17% and Team B's improved to 2%, how many fewer files would Team C be able to close without errors than Team B?

A. 35

B. 250

C. 260

D. 350

E. 500

Q3. If teams progress through files at a constant rate from month to month, how many files will the five teams close by the end of September?

A. 16525

B. 17667

C. 18258

D. 19875

E. 22083

Q1. A country is considering the adoption of a new tax system. Under which system does a person earning 55 000 € / year owe the least in taxes?

A. System 1

B. System 2

C. System 3

D. Systems 1 and 2 are the same

E. All Systems are the same

Q2. What is the effective tax rate of a person earning 62 000 € annually under System 3?

A. 15.66%

B. 15.98%

C. 19.53%

D. 19.77%

E. 23.65%

Q3. A person earns 75 000 € a year. By what percentage is their after-tax income greater or smaller under System1 than under System 3?

A. Approximately 1% smaller

B. Approximately 2% smaller

C. Approximately 2% greater

D. Approximately 3.9% smaller

E. Approximately 3.9% greater

Set 32

Power Station	Country	Annual Electricity Production (TWh)
Itaipu Dam	Brazil	98.30
Three Gorges Dam	China	98.50
Krasnoyarsk	Russia	20.40
Grand Coulee	USA	20.00
Guri	Venezuela	53.41

Country Annual Electricity Consumption Statistics (MWh)	
Brazil	455 700 000
China	5 322 300 000
Russia	1 016 500 000
USA	3 886 400 000
Venezuela	85 850 000
1 TWh = 1 000 000 MWh	

Q1. If they are ranked by the percentage that a power station generates of the total electricity consumption of the given country, which station would be in the middle?

A. Three Gorges Dam

B. Itaipu Dam

C. Guri

D. Grand Coulee

E. Krasnoyarsk

Q2. Venezuela plans to build another power station of the same production capacity as that of Guri. If existing power stations produce 78% of the electricity consumed in Venezuela, how much electricity will Venezuela have available for export after completion of the new power station?

A. 20.97 TWh

B. 34.523 MWh

C. 34 523 MWh

D. 20 970 000 MWh

E. 34 523 000 MWh

Q3. If the electricity produced by the Three Gorges Dam would be enough to cover 3.24% of the electricity consumed in the EU, and the EU produces 30% of the electricity it consumes from nuclear power, how much electricity in the EU is produced from nuclear power?

A. 912.04 MWh

B. 91.20 TWh

C. 912.00 TWh

D. 912.04 TWh

E. 3040.12 TWh

Set 33

Energy Ratings of Selected Household Appliances, 2014					
Appliance	A+ / A	B	C	D	Total units
Air conditioners	10%	45%	20%	25%	3 400
Washing machines	45%	35%	10%	10%	5 500
Dryers	25%	10%	50%	15%	2 000
Refrigerators	40%	25%	25%	10%	9 000

Appliances with A+, A and B energy ratings are considered energy-efficient.

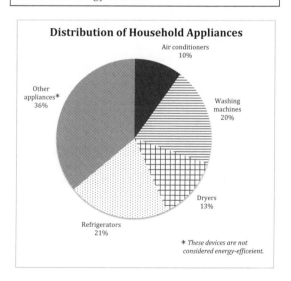

Distribution of Household Appliances

Air conditioners 10%

Other appliances* 36%

Washing machines 20%

Dryers 13%

Refrigerators 21%

* These devices are not considered energy-efficeient.

Q1. What percentage of all household appliances are energy-efficient washing machines?

A. 9%

B. 13%

C. 16%

D. 20%

E. 80%

Q2. If the share of energy-efficient units among refrigerators and air conditioners rose by 20%, how many energy-efficient refrigerators and air conditioners would there be?

A. 4 728

B. 6 024

C. 6 420

D. 9 264

E. 10 200

Q3. If D-rated household appliances are ranked by the number of such units in a highest-to-lowest list, which one would be at the top of the list?

A. Air conditioners

B. Washing machines

C. Dryers

D. Refrigerators

E. Impossible to tell

Set 34

Population age structure by age groups, 2007 and 2017						
	(% of the total population)					
	0–14 years old		15–64 years old		65 years old or over	
	2007	2017	2007	2017	2007	2017
Denmark	18.6	16.6	66.1	64.3	15.3	19.1
Finland	17.1	16.3	66.5	62.8	16.5	20.9
Iceland	21.3	19.7	67.1	66.2	11.6	14.0
Norway	19.4	17.8	66.0	65.5	14.6	16.6
Sweden	17.0	17.6	65.6	62.6	17.4	19.8

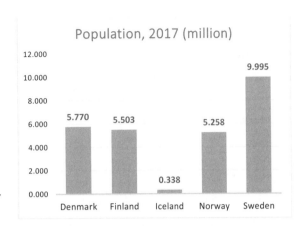

Population, 2017 (million)

Q1. The population of Norway increased by 577 thousand between 2007 and 2017. By how much did the number of persons aged 0-14 in Norway change between these years (*rounded to the nearest thousand*)?

A. –39 thousand

B. –84 thousand

C. 28 thousand

D. 103 thousand

E. 112 thousand

Q2. By what percentage was the number of persons 15 years old or over in Denmark in 2017 larger than the number of persons belonging to the same age group in Finland (*rounded to two decimal places*)?

A. 3.52%

B. 4.48%

C. 7.36%

D. 2.61%

E. –0.30%

Q3. What was the average change per country in the 5 countries in the share of persons aged 15-64 between 2007 and 2017?

A. –1.98%

B. –9.90%

C. –2.99%

D. –4.60%

E. –1.14%

Set 35

Factory annual production and wood supplier figures, tonnes				
		Utilisation of forestry production volume for:		
Forestry (number of employees)	Production Volume	Roofing	Outdoor Furniture	Indoor Furniture
Craybourne Woodlands (50)	8 000	2 000	4 000	850
Stirling Forest (80)	14 000	3 800	5 900	2450
Woodcombe Hills Woods (30)	3 000	1 600	1 200	0
Hampton Forest (30)	3 000	1 600	1 300	55
Frasier Green (40)	8 000	4 000	2 800	1 045

Q1. Which forestry has the most productive employees?

  A.   Craybourne Woodlands
  B.   Stirling Forest
  C.   Woodcombe Hills Woods
  D.   Hampton Forest
  E.   Frasier Green

Q2. If 50 tonnes of wood are needed for each outdoor furniture shipment, how many shipments could have been manufactured in total relying on all forestries if 10% of the wood used for roofing had been shifted to outdoor furniture?

  A.   26
  B.   88
  C.   114
  D.   304
  E.   330

Q3. Based on the average of all five forestries, how much roofing wood is supplied by each forestry employee?

  A.   56.52 tonnes
  B.   66.09 tonnes
  C.   156.52 tonnes
  D.   565.2 tonnes
  E.   156.2 tonnes

Set 36

Restaurant Wine List		
	Glass (€)	Bottle (€)
Chablis	8.95	31.95
Chardonnay	7.50	28.50
Margaux	7.15	27.00
Sancerre	9.20	34.80
Tavel	7.95	29.50

Q1. Assuming a glass is a fifth of a bottle, which wine provides the most extra profit in euro terms when sold by the glass?

  A.   Chablis
  B.   Chardonnay
  C.   Margaux
  D.   Sancerre
  E.   Tavel

Q2. The restaurant makes 220% profit on all bottles of wine. In one evening they make €287.10 profit on Sancerre alone. How many bottles of Sancerre did they sell?

  A.   6
  B.   10
  C.   12
  D.   15
  E.   18

Q3. If a glass is 187.5ml and a bottle is 750ml, what is the percentage increase in revenue on a bottle of Tavel when sold by the glass?

  A.   5.9%
  B.   7.8%
  C.   8.3%
  D.   9.4%
  E.   11.1%

Set 37

Results for Swimming Championships (m:ss.ss)			
In medley races, the swimmers swim equal distances in four different styles: butterfly, backstroke, breaststroke, freestyle.			

	100m Freestyle	200m Backstroke	400m Medley	100m Breast-stroke
Gold	50.91	1:58.31	3:48.7	1:03.41
Silver	50.99	1:59.72	3:49.6	1:04.06
Bronze	51.31	1:59.88	3:53.2	1:04.92

Q1. In the medley, the winner spent 26.2% of the time on the butterfly section of the race. What was his average speed during that leg of the race?

A.   1.67 m/s

B.   1.75 m/s

C.   1.8 m/s

D.   2.0 m/s

E.   2.25 m/s

Q2. How much faster was the gold medal winner than the bronze medal winner in the 200m backstroke event?

A.   0.1%

B.   1.0%

C.   1.3%

D.   1.5%

E.   2.0%

Q3. From the moment that the gold medallist finished until he himself finished, the freestyle silver medal winner swam 10% faster than his overall average. To the nearest centimetre, by what distance did the gold medallist beat the silver medallist?

A.   14

B.   17

C.   25

D.   36

E.   51

Set 38

Country	Export (2014,% of production)	Export Volume (2014, million t)	Change from 2013 (volume)
China	34%	279.5	+ 3%
USA	27%	23.8	+ 5%
Japan	19%	21	− 2 %
EU	34%	55.9	−
Rest of World	62%	285.4	+ 9%

Domestic consumption = Production – Export + Import

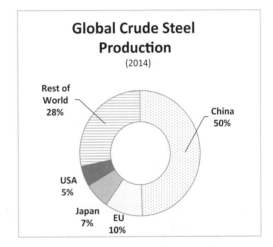

Global Crude Steel Production
(2014)

Q1. If China exported 30% of its steel production to the United States in 2014, how much steel did the US use in that year?

A.   143.85 million tonnes

B.   166.05 million tonnes

C.   310.97 million tonnes

D.   328.82 million tonnes

E.   Cannot say

Q2. How much more steel did the EU export in 2013 than Japan?

A.   66.2% more

B.   71.6% more

C.   161% more

D.   166.2% more

E.   171.6% more

Q3. Approximately what percentage of global steel production did 2013 exports make up if production in every region was the same in 2013 as in 2014?

    A.   Around 6%

    B.   Around 14%

    C.   Around 38%

    D.   Around 50%

    E.   Around 70%

Set 39

Electricity Generation in the Netherlands (%)		
	2005	*2010*
Fossil Fuel	81.1	76.4
Wind	6.8	8.1
Solar	3.4	5.2
Nuclear	3.9	3.8
Other	4.8	6.5

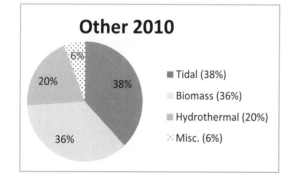

Other 2010

- Tidal (38%)
- Biomass (36%)
- Hydrothermal (20%)
- Misc. (6%)

Q1. Generation of electricity rose by 10% between 2005 and 2010. Tidal power generation doubled over that period. What percentage of the electricity was generated by tidal power in 2005?

    A.   1.12%

    B.   1.36%

    C.   1.59%

    D.   1.73%

    E.   1.94%

Q2. In 2010, 2.4 million kWh of electricity was generated from biomass. How much was generated from solar power (in millions of kWh)?

    A.   5.3

    B.   5.9

    C.   6.2

    D.   6.8

    E.   7.3

Q3. If total electricity generation rose by 10% between 2005 and 2010, what was the percentage change in fossil fuel generated electricity over that time?

    A.   +3.6%

    B.   +1.8%

    C.   No change

    D.   -1.8%

    E.   -3.6%

Set 40

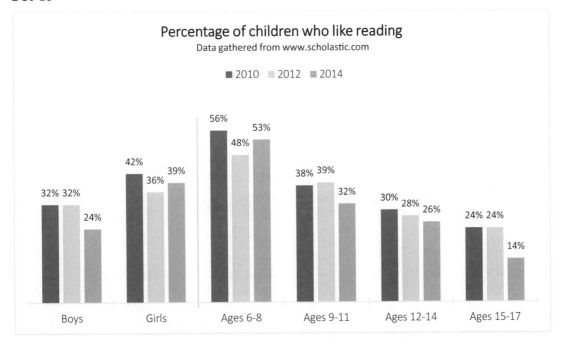

Percentage of children who like reading
Data gathered from www.scholastic.com

■ 2010 ■ 2012 ■ 2014

Q1. Assuming a sample size of 1000 children, where each gender is represented equally, by what percentage did the number of boys who like reading decrease from 2010 to 2014?

A. 8%

B. 12%

C. 17%

D. 21%

E. 25%

Q2. What was the sample size if in 2012 the number of boys and girls who liked reading were both 150?

A. 792

B. 823

C. 833

D. 886

E. 938

Q3. Assuming an overall sample size of 1000 children where the four different age groups are equally represented, and in each age group the genders are also equally represented, what was the number of boys aged 9 to 11 who liked reading in 2010?

A. 41

B. 48

C. 58

D. 64

E. There's not enough information

ANSWERS

SET 1, Q1. Correct Answer: B

Reasoning

We need to calculate the total intra-EU traffic in both 2015 and 2016, and then the difference between the two figures.

Calculation

We will use the data from the first pair in the table (UK-Spain), though the figures for *any* of the pairs in the table would yield the same result.

In 2015 the UK-Spain share of total traffic was 9.1%, so total intra-EU traffic was:

35922.6 / 0.091 = 394753.846

In 2016 the UK-Spain share of total traffic was 9.6%, so total intra-EU traffic was:

41637.8 / 0.096 = 433727.083

Finally, we calculate the difference, and round it to the nearest million.

Total intra-EU traffic increase:

433727.083 – 394753.846 = 38973.237 thousand ≈ 39 million

Potential Shortcuts / Pitfalls

Don't make the mistake of simply adding up the top-5 pairs in the table, instead of calculating the total intra-EU traffic. This would give the incorrect figure of 11 million, which is option A.

SET 1, Q2. Correct Answer: D

Reasoning

We need to calculate the total number of passengers carried from the UK in 2015 and 2016 using the 3 relevant pairs in the table. We then calculate the percentage increase by dividing those numbers, subtracting 1, and multiplying the result by 100%.

Calculation

First, we must calculate the total number of passengers carried from the UK to the three top destinations in both 2015 and 2016.

Number of passengers in 2015:

35922.6 + 13302.7 + 12711.3 = 61936.6

Number of passengers in 2016:

41637.8 + 13877 + 14123.5 = 69638.3

Finally, we calculate the percentage increase, and round the answer to one decimal place:

(69638.3 / 61936.6 – 1) * 100% = 12.43% = 12.4%

Potential Shortcuts / Pitfalls

If you make the mistake of adding up all the pairs in the table, rather than just the UK traffic, you will get the incorrect figure of 11.2%, which is given as option C.

Another, and more common error, would be to add up the *percentage shares* rather than the *actual number* of passengers. In other words, to add 9.10 + 3.37 + 3.20 to get 15.67, and 9.60 + 3.20 +3.24 to get 16.04. This would give you a difference of 16.04 minus 15.67, which is 0.37. Rounded to one decimal space, as the question asks, this would give you 0.4% – which is answer option E. To understand why this is wrong, take a simple example. 50% of 100 is 50 and 20% of 50 is 10. However 50 + 10 is not 70% of 150, it is 40%.

SET 1, Q3. Correct Answer: C

Reasoning

First, we need to calculate the average 2016 cost of a Spain-Germany flight using the 2015 average cost and percentage increase for 2016. Then we have to work out the total amount spent by passengers on Spain-Germany flights in 2015 and in 2016. Finally, we calculate the increase as the difference between the amounts spent in 2016 and in 2015.

Calculation

The average cost of a Spain-Germany flight in 2016:

$147.60 * 1.021 \approx €150.70$

The amount spent by passengers for the flights between Spain and Germany in 2015 (in thousand euros):

$25063.9 * 147.60 \approx €3699432$

Note that the number of passengers is given in the table in thousands, so we don't need to multiply it by 1000.

Amount spent in 2016:

$27581.6 * 150.70 \approx €4156547$

Finally, we need to calculate the difference:

$4156547 - 3699432 \approx €457115$ thousand

Potential Shortcuts / Pitfalls

You can go wrong if you miss that the numbers of passengers are given in the table in thousands. If you make this mistake, you would get the incorrect figure of 457 thousand (answer option A).

A possible shortcut is to combine all the steps shown above by factorizing: $1000 * 147.60 * (27581.6 * 1.021 - 25063.9)$, which would reduce the number of keystrokes and multiplications. This would, because of rounding errors, give only the approximately correct figure of 457104. However this would not be a problem in this case as the answer options are all sufficiently far apart.

SET 2, Q1. Correct Answer: C

Reasoning

We need to work out the numbers of outbound trips made by EU residents in 2016 to the U.S. and to Switzerland, and then calculate the difference. The number of outbound trips is the total number of outbound trips by EU residents multiplied by the respective percentages.

Calculation

First, we must calculate the number of outbound trips made by EU residents in 2016 to the U.S. given the total number of trips and the U.S. share of 14% (in thousands of trips):

$308622 * 0.14 = 43207.08$ thousand

Second, we calculate in the same way the number of outbound trips made by EU residents in 2016 to Switzerland:

$308622 * 0.09 = 27775.98$ thousand

Finally, we calculate the difference, and round it to the nearest million:

$43207.08 - 27775.98 = 15431.1$ thousand ≈ 15 million

Potential Shortcuts / Pitfalls

If you miss that the numbers of passengers are presented in the table in thousands you will get the incorrect answer of 15431 million, which is given as answer option D. And If you use the total number of trips made by EU residents in 2016 instead of the number of outbound trips only, you will get 60 million (option A).

A shortcut is to combine all the steps shown above by factoring out the total number of outbound trips:

$308622 (0.14 - 0.09) = 308622 * 0.05 = 15431.10$ (thousands)

This would significantly reduce the number of keystrokes and arithmetical operations.

SET 2, Q2. Correct Answer: D

Reasoning

We need to calculate the total number of outbound trips made by EU residents in 2017, then the number of outbound trips to Turkey in 2016 and 2017, and then the Turkey percentage share. The number of outbound trips to Turkey in 2016 is the total number of outbound trips multiplied by the Turkey share in 2016, and the number of outbound trips to Turkey in 2017 is the number of outbound trips to Turkey in 2016 adjusted by the percentage decrease.

Calculation

First, we calculate the total number of outbound trips made by EU residents in 2017 (in thousands of trips), using the number in 2016 and the percentage increase between 2016 and 2017:

$308622 * 1.018 = 314177.196$ thousand

Second, we calculate the number of outbound trips made by EU residents in 2016 to Turkey:

$308622 * 0.1 = 30862.2$ thousand

Third, the number of outbound trips made by EU residents in 2017 to Turkey using the number of trips in 2016 and the percentage of decrease of 0.6%:

30862.2 * (1 – 0.006) = 30677.0268 thousand

Finally, we calculate the Turkey share in 2017, and round it to one decimal place:

30677.0268 / 314177.196 ≈ 0.09764 ≈ 9.8%

Potential Shortcuts / Pitfalls

If you make a calculator mistake and decrease the number of trips to Turkey by 6% instead of 0.6% you would get the incorrect figure of 9.2% (option A). Another possible error would be to calculate Turkey's share as 10% – 0.6% = 9.4% (option B), ignoring the increase in the total number of trips made by EU residents between 2016 and 2017.

It is possible to do the calculation faster by combining all the steps shown above by using the expression 308622 * 0.1 * (1 – 0.006) / 308622 / (1 + 0.018), and, after cancelling the total number of outbound trips, 0.1 * 0.994 / 1.018, which would significantly reduce the number of keystrokes and arithmetical operations.

SET 2, Q3. Correct Answer: E

Reasoning

We need to work out the percentage shares in the expenditure made by EU residents in 2016 for Norway and Russia, then calculate their ratio. The percentage share of the expenditure is the share in the number of outbound trips to Norway and Russia, multiplied or divided by the respective scale factor.

Calculation

First, we must calculate the percentage share of the expenditure made by EU residents in 2016 for Norway:

5% * 1.4 = 7%

Second, the percentage share of the expenditure made by EU residents in 2016 for Russia:

4% * = 4% * 0.75 = 3%

Finally, we need to calculate the ratio between Norway and Russia shares in 2016:

7% : 3% = 7 : 3

Potential Shortcuts / Pitfalls

The length of this question can make it seem a lot more complicated than it really is. You just have to take it step by step and, as we have seen, it actually requires only a few calculations.

A possible mistake would be to swap the places of Norway and Russia in the ratio. This would give the incorrect ratio of 3 : 7, and as this is given as answer option D you would not realise the error. Another potential error would be to calculate the ratio between Norway and Russia using their respective shares in the number of trips instead of expenditure. This would give the incorrect ratio of 5 : 4 (option C).

SET 3, Q1. Correct Answer: A

Reasoning

We need to calculate the average health care expenditure of the top-5 EU members in 2015, and then increase it by the given percentage. The average health care expenditure of the top-5 EU members is the sum of their expenditures divided by five.

Calculation

First, we must calculate the sum of the top-5 EU members' health care expenditures in 2015 (in million euros):

241366 + 338207 + 148029 + 98586 + 254827 = 1081015 (million euros)

Second, we calculate the average health care expenditure of the top-5 EU members in 2015:

1081015 / 5 = 216203 (million euros)

Finally, we calculate the average health care expenditure of the top-5 EU members in 2017, rounded to the nearest billion euros:

216203 * (1 + 0.045) = €225932.135 million ≈ €226 billion

Potential Shortcuts / Pitfalls

If you miss that the average expenditure is required to be given in billion euros, instead of millions, you would get the incorrect figure of 225932 (option E). Likewise, if you ignore the fact that average expenditure increased between 2015 and 2017 you would get the incorrect figure of 216 billion (option C).

SET 3, Q2. Correct Answer: B

Reasoning

We need to calculate the GDP of the United Kingdom and France in 2015, and then calculate the difference. The GDP of a country is its health care expenditure divided by its health care expenditure percentage share in GDP.

Calculation

First, we must calculate the GDP of the United Kingdom given the health care expenditure and the respective share in GDP of 9.9% (in million euros):

254827 / 0.099 ≈ €2574010 million

Then we calculate the GDP of France in the same way:

241366 / 0.11 ≈ €2194236 million

Finally, we calculate the difference, and round it to the nearest billion:

2574010 – 2194236 = €379774 million ≈ €380 billion

Potential Shortcuts / Pitfalls

If you miss that the health care expenditures are presented in the table in million euros you would get the incorrect figure of 379774 (option D). If you calculate the difference in health care expenditures instead of the GDP (i.e. 254827 – 241366 = 13461), you would get either answer option E (after rounding to the nearest billion) or, if you forget the figures in the table are in millions not billions, option A.

SET 3, Q3. Correct Answer: C

Reasoning

We need to calculate the population of Spain in 2015, and then in 2016 and 2017 using the percentage increases for each year. The population of Spain in 2015 is the health care expenditure divided by the health care expenditure per inhabitant.

Calculation

First, we must calculate the population of Spain in 2015:

98586 / 2123 ≈ 46.437 (million)

Note that the health care expenditure is presented in the table in million euros, and the health care expenditure per inhabitant is presented in euros, so we don't need to scale the resulting number.

Second, we calculate the population of Spain by the end of 2016 given the population increase of 3.1%:

46.437 * (1 + 0.031) ≈ 47.877 (million)

Finally, we calculate the population of Spain by the end of 2017 given the population increase of 3.4%, and round it to the nearest million:

47.877 * (1 + 0.034) ≈ 49.505 million ≈ 50 million

Potential Shortcuts / Pitfalls

If you simply add the annual percentage population increases together, i.e. 3.1% + 3.4% = 6.5%, and then use 6.5% to calculate the population of Spain in 2017 directly from 2015, you would get 49.455 million, which you would then round down to 49 million. This is given as option A and also looks a very plausible answer, given that it is very close to the correct answer.

SET 4, Q1. Correct Answer: B

Reasoning

We need to calculate the total waste generated in Chile in the agriculture, forestry and fishing sector by adding together the figures for each year of the 2004-2007 period. Then we have to divide the hypothetical decrease in generated waste by our total, and multiply by 100 to get the percentage.

Calculation

First, we add together the annual figures:

1515 + 1393 + 1367 +1470 = 5745 (thousand tonnes)

The total hypothetical decrease is 500 + 500 = 1000 (thousand tonnes)

The percentage decrease is then: (1000 / 5745) * 100 ≈ 17.4%

Potential Shortcuts / Pitfalls

This question is very straightforward provided you are careful in reading the data off the table. For instance, if you add up ALL the figures in the Chile row rather than just 2004 to 2007, you would end up with answer option A.

SET 4, Q2. Correct Answer: C

Reasoning

We need to calculate the amount of decrease from 2006 to 2008 in each country, and then what percentage this amount is of the generated waste in 2006.

Calculation

For Austria the decrease from 2006 to 2008 is: 513 – 459 = 54

Let us call the percentage change X

As 54 is X% of 513, that means that 513 * (X / 100) = 54
X = (54 / 513) * 100
X ≈ 10.53%

We can in the same way calculate the decrease in Belgium ([73 / 361] * 100) and in Italy ([213 / 554] * 100) as around 20.2% and 38.45% respectively. From this we can see that the greatest rate of decrease, 38.45%, was in Italy, answer C.

Potential Shortcuts / Pitfalls

Since the initial (2006) amount of waste was *larger* in Italy than in Austria, and the final (2008) amount of waste was *smaller* in Italy than in Austria, we know without any calculation that the rate of decrease must be higher in Italy. We don't know the exact difference, but looking at the numbers, we can estimate that it's not negligible. This means that we only have to compare Belgium and Italy.

SET 4, Q3. Correct Answer: E

Reasoning

We need first to calculate the average amount of waste generated in each year, by dividing the total waste by the number of years, and then calculate the difference for each year.

Calculation

The total amount of waste generated is:

89300 + 87584 + 87945 + 87837 + 87992 + 88446 + 85109 = 614213

We then divide by the number of years, 7, to get our average amount, which is 87745 (thousand tonnes). Therefore the deviation from the average amount in the first year of the series, 2004, was 89300 – 87745 = 1555

We *could* now calculate the *exact* deviation for each year in turn and then compare all the resulting figures one by one. But do we really need to do all those calculations? In fact we can get to the answer very rapidly just with a bit of rounding and simple mental arithmetic.

We know that to beat our 2004 figure the deviation for any other year has to be more than 1555. Simplify the average amount to 87.7 and the 2004 deviation to 1.5 (it is slightly larger).

You can instantly see that the 2004 figure can only be beaten either by an amount more than 1.5 *smaller* than 87.7, i.e. less than 86.2, or *bigger* than the 89.3 for 2004. It is immediately apparent that the answer has to be 85.1, the figure for the year 2010.

SET 5, Q1. Correct Answer: B

Reasoning

We need to calculate the percentage change between 2011 and 2016 of people aged 25–64 reporting they knew three or more foreign languages for each country, and then calculate their average.

Calculation

Percentage change in Czech Republic = 7.4 – 7.1 = 0.3%
Percentage change in Poland = 2.8 – 4.0 = –1.2%
Percentage change in Slovakia = 28 – 21.6 = 6.4%
Percentage change in Slovenia = 37.7 – 44.9 = –7.2%

Now we calculate the average of the percentages above:

Average = (0.3 – 1.2 + 6.4 – 7.2) / 4 = –0.425%

Potential Shortcuts / Pitfalls

This is a simple enough question as long as you remember you have a percentage decrease at the end and not an increase, which would give you answer option C.

SET 5, Q2. Correct Answer: E

Reasoning

We need to calculate the total share of Slovenian people aged 25-64 reporting they knew one or more foreign languages in 2016, which is the sum of the shares for one, two, and three or more foreign languages, and then find the ratio to the share of such people having tertiary education.

Calculation

We first calculate the share of ALL Slovenian people aged 25-64 reporting they knew one or more foreign languages in 2016:

17.6 + 24.7 + 37.7 = 80%

The bar chart tells us that 95% of those aged 25 to 64 *with tertiary education* reported they knew one or more foreign language. Therefore the ratio to all people of that age reporting one or more language is 95 : 80. This ratio can be simplified since both sides of it are multiples of 5. By dividing each side by 5, we will reduce the ratio to the lowest terms, i.e. to 19 : 16.

Potential Shortcuts / Pitfalls
The most likely mistake would be to use the figure for those knowing *exactly* one foreign language (17.6) instead of all those knowing *one or more*. This would lead you to the incorrect ratios of either 19 : 4 (option D) or 4 : 19 (option C).

There is an easy shortcut. The table tells us that 20% don't know ANY foreign language, therefore those who know 1 or more must be 100% less this 20%. Our calculation then becomes 95 / (100 − 20). You can most likely do this straight away in your head without any need for a calculator.

SET 5, Q3. Correct Answer: D

Reasoning

We need to calculate the number of Polish people aged 25–64 reporting that they knew just one foreign language, for both 2016 and 2011. This is the total population of that age multiplied by the respective percentage share. We then work out the difference between the two years.

Calculation

First, we must calculate the number of Polish people aged 25–64 reporting they knew just one foreign language in 2016 (in thousands):

30700 * 0.45 = 13815 thousand

Note that the Polish population is given in millions in the question, so we needed to multiply the number given us by 1000 to convert it to thousands.

Second, we do the same for 2011:

31200 * 0.387 = 12074.4 thousand

Finally, we calculate the difference, and round it to the nearest thousand:

13815 − 12074.4 = 1740.6 ≈ 1741 thousand

Potential Shortcuts / Pitfalls
You have to be careful not to get the population figures for 2011 and 2016 the wrong way round. If you do, you would get the negative figure of (option C). And if you don't convert the Polish population figure from millions to thousands, you would get the incorrect figure of 2 thousand (option A).

SET 6, Q1. Correct Answer: D

Reasoning

We need to calculate the average speed of the runner, which is the distance divided by the time taken. We also need to figure out a way to convert the time given in hours, minutes and seconds into decimals.

Calculation

The distance run in the second half of the race is simply half the total distance:

42.2 / 2 = 21.1

The time taken to run this is the total time taken less the time taken to run the first half of the race:

2:13:31 − 1:07:50 = 1:05:41

The calculation of distance / time is simple enough but here, the time is not in an easily usable form so we must first convert it. To do this, take the seconds and divide by 60 (seconds per minute) to convert it to minutes and then add in the minutes. Now divide the minutes by 60 (minutes per hour) and add in the hours:

41 / 60 = 0.683
0.683 + 5 = 5.683
5.683 / 60 = 0.0947
0.0947 + 1 = 1.0947

Now calculate the average speed:

21.1 / 1.0947 = 19.27 km/h.

SET 6, Q2. Correct Answer: B

Reasoning

We need to calculate the average speed for each of the runners, which is distance / time. We then need to calculate the percentage difference.

Calculation

We first need to calculate the time taken by each of the runners for the last kilometre. For Dennis it was:

2:14:12 – 2:11:00 = 3:12 minutes
3:12 minutes = 3 × 60 seconds + 12 seconds = 192s

For Ekimov it was:

2:14:20 – 2:11:00 = 3:20
3:20 = 3 × 60 + 20 = 200s

Their speeds can now be calculated as distance (1000m) divided by the time taken. For Dennis:

1000 / 192 = 5.21m/s

Note that the calculated speed is in metres per second. If we had written 1 km as 1 km rather than 1000 metres, the unit would have been kilometres per second and the number would have been 0.00521 km / s. These are unusual units but we don't even have to write them out. Since we are going to calculate only the *percentage difference between them*, we can just take note of the number itself.

And for Ekimov:

1000 / 200 = 5m/s

The percentage difference is the difference divided by the slower speed and then multiplied by 100:

100 × (5.21 – 5) / 5 = 4.2%

Potential Shortcuts / Pitfalls
Because both runners are covering the same distance (1km) then their percentage difference in

speed is actually the same as their percentage difference in *time*.

Why is this important? The reason is that *it is not necessary to calculate the two runners' speeds at all.* Once we know the time they took to cover the last kilometre (and this was the first calculation we performed), we can directly proceed to the difference in time, which is 200-192 = 8 seconds and so the percentage difference is:

100 × (8 / 192) = 4.2%

SET 6, Q3. Correct Answer: D

Reasoning

First, we need to work out Benoit's overall average speed. Then we calculate his speed in the last 150 metres. Once we have done this, we can calculate how far he was from the finishing line when Anderson finished.

Calculation

Benoit's overall average speed is distance divided by time but the time first needs converting to decimal form to make it easier to use. As above, divide the seconds by 60, add in the minutes and divide by 60 again and add in the hours:

38 / 60 = 0.633
0.633 + 12 = 12.633
12.633 / 60 = 0.211
0.211 + 2 = 2.211

Benoit's overall average speed is therefore:

42.1 / 2.211 = 19.04 km/h

He ran the final 150m of the race at a speed 5% faster than this, which is:

19.04 × 1.05 = 20 km/h

The time gap between Anderson and Benoit was:

2:12:38 – 2:12:14 = 24 seconds

The distance by which Anderson beat Benoit is then *the distance run by Benoit in 24 seconds at 20km/h.* We have a mismatch of units here, because the speed is given in kilometres / hour and the time difference in seconds, so we can *either* convert the time difference to hours by dividing by 3600 (60 minutes × 60 seconds) *or* convert Benoit's speed to metres/second by multiplying by 1000 (metres in a kilometre) and dividing by 3600 (seconds in an hour). Let's do the latter.

Why is this the way to convert km/m to m/s, you might ask? Let's see.

20 km / h = 20 000 m / hour

But we want to establish how many metres the runner can cover in *one second* (because the unit we are looking for is metres / second, not metres / hour). 1 hour is 60 × 60 seconds. 60 × 60 is 3600, so the speed is:

20 000 m / 3600 seconds

There is one last step to take, because we are interested in how many metres are covered in 1 second, so we divide by 3600:

5.56 m / second

Benoit ran for 24 seconds at this speed from the moment Anderson finished until the moment he himself crossed the finishing line.
The distance is then:

5.56 m * 24 = 133m

SET 7, Q1. Correct Answer: B

Reasoning

We need to form an equation with only one variable. To do this, let X be the number of male and Y be the number of female students in the school. The overall number of smokers is 19.6% of all students, i.e.19.6% of X + Y. It is also 21.6% of all male students (X) plus 17.5% of all female students (Y). Since the two are equal, we can formulate an equation. After substituting the number of male students and the number of male smokers, we are left with an equation that contains only one variable (Y). We solve this to get the result.

Calculation

The starting equation looks like this:

$(X + Y) * 0.196 = X * 0.216 + Y * 0.175$

We know that $X * 0.216 = 60$ (from the question) and from this we can easily deduce that $X \approx 278$

Substituting these values we get:

$(278 + Y) * 0.196 = 60 + Y * 0.175$

If we move every term that contains Y onto the left side, and the rest onto the right we get:

$Y * (0.196 – 0.175) = 60 – 278* 0.196$
$Y* 0.021 = 5.512$

The solution for this equation is $Y \approx 262$, which corresponds to answer B as being around 260.

Possible Shortcuts / Pitfalls

If by mistake you calculate the number of males instead of females, you would get 278 (option C, around 280). Or if you calculate the number of females directly as 60 / 17.5%, you get 343 (option E, more than 320).

There is a shortcut if you calculate the number of male students as 60 / 0.216 = 278, and then compose the equation for only one variable, Y = number of female students. This gives the equation 0.196 (Y + 278) = 0.175Y + 60, which would significantly reduce the time taken.

SET 7, Q2. Correct Answer: D

Reasoning

To calculate the number of male students who use ONLY electronic cigarettes, we must first calculate the *total* number of male students who use electronic cigarettes, and then subtract the number of male students who use *both* types of cigarette. Then we do the same calculations with regular cigarettes and add the results together.

Calculation

Using the percentage from the table, male students using electronic cigarettes: 300 * 0.133 ≈ 40

We know from the question that 20 use both electronic and regular cigarettes, therefore the number using ONLY electronic cigarettes is 40 – 20 = 20.

Male students using regular cigarettes: 300 * 0.076 ≈ 23. Again, as the question tells us that 20 use both types, the number using *only* regular cigarettes is 23 – 20 = 3.

The number of male students using only one type is therefore 20 for electronic and 3 for regular, total 23.

Potential Shortcuts / Pitfalls

The calculations here are fairly straightforward provided you do not get confused by the data. For example, if you calculate the total number of male students using *either* type, forgetting that the number of students using *both* types must be subtracted, you would get 63 (option B).

SET 7, Q3. Correct Answer: D

Reasoning

We can calculate the number of students based on the number and percentage of students using any kind of tobacco product. Since there are twice as many males as females in the school, this means that one-third of the students are female, of whom 9.9% use electronic cigarettes.

Calculation

The table tells us that 19.6% of students use some kind of tobacco product. Therefore the total number of students in the school is 100 /0.196 ≈ 510

There are then 510 / 3 = 170 female students, of whom 170 * 0.099 ≈ 17 use electronic cigarettes.

Potential Shortcuts / Pitfalls
If you reverse the ratio between the male and female students, you would get the incorrect figure of 34 (option B). If you take 100 as the total number of students in school, instead of the students using any kind of tobacco product, you would get the incorrect figure of 7 students (option A).

SET 8, Q1. Correct Answer: B

Reasoning

We must calculate the total weight of beef and veal consumed in Argentina. To do this we multiply the population by the amount of meat consumed per capita in 2017. Since this only gives us the retail weight, we also have to divide the result by 0.7 to get the carcass weight required to meet the consumption.

Calculation

Total amount of beef and veal consumed in Argentina in 2017:

44.27 million * 41.2 =1823.924 million kg.

The carcass weight required to produce this amount of meat:

1823.924 /0.7 ≈ 2605.606 million kg, which is roughly 2.6 million tonnes.

Potential Shortcuts / Pitfalls
If you forget to convert the calculated result from kilograms to tonnes you would get 2.6 million kg (option A). And if you fail to divide the total amount of beef and veal consumed by 0.7, you would get 1.8 million tonnes (option D), or 1.8 million kg (option C) if you also forget to convert the result into tonnes.

SET 8, Q2. Correct Answer: B

Reasoning

Total meat consumption would decrease by the same percentage as total meat consumption *per capita*, so we don't need to bother with the former. The total meat consumption per capita is the sum of all the data in Brazil's row of the table. We can then calculate the amount that meat consumption would decrease, and determine what percentage this change would represent.

Calculation

The total per capita meat consumption is 26.5 + 11.8 + 39.9 +0.4 = 78.6 kg

The decrease is (26.5 + 39.9) * 0.2 = 13.28

If 13.28 is X% of 78.6 then 78.6 * (X / 100) =13.28

X = (13.28 / 78.6) * 100
X ≈ 16.9%

Potential Shortcuts / Pitfalls
With this problem you need to avoid being distracted by the data into making unnecessary calculations. EPSO numerical reasoning tests will make use of *distractors* which can overload you with data and make the problem seem more confusing than it really is. As mentioned, in this question there is no need to calculate the actual total Brazilian meat consumption. And the reference in the question to the population of Brazil being 209.3 million is a red herring as you do not need to know it.

You can go wrong if you try to calculate the rate of decrease by dividing the initial consumption by the decreased consumption. This would lead to 78.6 / (78.6 – 13.28) –1 = 20.3% (option D).

SET 8, Q3. Correct Answer: C

Reasoning

The total amount of pork consumed in the country in 2017 is the population times the pork consumed per capita. We need to convert this total to a percentage of the carcass weight required in order to get to the conversion ratio for pork.

Calculation

The total amount of pork consumed: 24.6 million * 20.7 kg = 509.22 million kg.

This number is (509.22 / 652.85) * 100 ≈ 78% of the total carcass weight, which means a 1 to 0.78 ratio.

Potential Shortcuts / Pitfalls

If you incorrectly calculate the ratio by dividing the carcass weight by the retail weight, thus doing 1– (652.85/509.22–1) ≈ 0.72, you would get 1 to 0.72 (option B).

SET 9, Q1. Correct Answer: B

Reasoning

We need to calculate the price at which we purchased 1 share, work out the total for 2000 shares and then add the dealing charge.

Calculation

Monday's closing price is given as 2.37 and we purchase at 1.4% below this so we have to multiply by (1-0.014) or 0.986. This is so because, remember, 100% is 1, so 1.4% must be 0.014. If the price is 1.4% below another value, another way of saying that is that the price was 98.6% of that:

$2.37 \times 0.986 = 2.33682$

The total cost is then the number of shares multiplied by the price:

$2000 \times 2.33682 = 4673.64$

We also have to pay the dealing charge:

$4673.64 + 15.95 = 4689.59$

Potential Shortcuts / Pitfalls

The actual price is 1.4% below yesterday's price. This means that we needed to multiply yesterday's closing price by 1 – 0.014. If the actual price had been 1.4% *above* yesterday's closing price, we would have multiplied by 1 + 0.014 – this is an important difference not to mix up.

SET 9, Q2. Correct Answer: C

Reasoning

We need to calculate the price at which we sold the shares and hence the rise since yesterday's close. In order to calculate the selling price, we must add the dealing charge to our proceeds.

Calculation

We are told how much we got from the sale of the shares, but we must remember that that amount was already reduced by the dealing charge of 15.95. This means that the actual selling price was 15.95 *higher* than the figure given in the question text:

$4664.05 + 15.95 = 4680$

This was the amount we got for selling 2000 shares so the amount per share was:

$4680 / 2000 = 2.34$

Yesterday, the closing selling price was 2.25 and so the percentage rise is the difference divided by the starting value and then multiplied by 100:

$2.34 – 2.25 = 0.09$
$100 \times (0.09 / 2.25) = 4\%$

Potential Shortcuts / Pitfalls

First of all, there are a couple of small but important issues to notice:

The question again talks about Friday but we need to compare our selling price to that of Thursday

There is a temptation to say that in order to calculate the price increase, we simply compare the Thursday selling price to the Friday selling price. This would be wrong because we did not sell at Friday's *closing* price but at an another price that we must calculate from our total proceeds

These were the pitfalls. There's also a shortcut. *You should be able to do this question without a calculator at all.* When dividing by 2000, be aware that this is basically division by 2 and then by 1000. Division by 2 simply means halving the number. Division by 1000 is moving the decimal point 3 places to the left.

When calculating the percentage, note that 2.25 is 2¼ which is the same as 9/4 (2 = 8/4). Remember that when we divide by a fraction it is the same as multiplying by the inverted version of that fraction, so when we divide 0.09 by 9/4 this is the same as multiplying by 4/9:

$(100 \times 0.09 \times 4) / 9$

When you multiply by 100 you can just move the decimal point 2 places to the right so 0.09 becomes 9 and now the 9s cancel out, leaving just 4:

$$\frac{9 \times 4}{9} = 4$$

SET 9, Q3. Correct Answer: E

Reasoning

We need to calculate the spread for each day as a percentage of the buy price.

Calculation

This is in essence a very easy problem because all the numbers are very similar. We can readily see the difference between the buy and sell price just by mentally subtracting the sell from the buy to get 0.05, 0.04, 0.05, 0.03 and 0.05 respectively. We can then calculate the percentage of the buy price by dividing the spread by the buy price and multiplying by 100:

Monday: $100 \times 0.05 / 2.37 = 2.11\%$
Tuesday: $100 \times 0.04 / 2.41 = 1.66\%$
Wednesday: $100 \times 0.05 / 2.39 = 2.09\%$
Thursday: $100 \times 0.03 / 2.28 = 1.32\%$
Friday: $100 \times 0.05 / 2.34 = 2.14\%$

From this we can clearly see that Friday has the largest percentage spread.

Potential Shortcuts / Pitfalls

Because we only want to know which is the largest spread we don't need to concern ourselves with the actual value, just whether it is larger or smaller than the others. Consequently, there is *no need to do all the '100 x' operations* which are common to all the calculations.

Furthermore, as all the numbers are very similar, then the largest result is going to come from the largest numerator, that is, the largest spread value. There are three which are equal at 0.05 and so only these need to be considered. Secondly, the largest result will come from the smallest denominator. Why is that?

Let's say you have some apples, you eat 5 of them and you want to work out what that 5 represents as a percentage of the total number of apples. If you had 10 apples in total, you ate half (50%) of the apples. If you had 100 apples, you ate 5% of the apples. This illustrates that the smaller the total (here 10 instead of 100), the higher the percentage a fixed number of apples represent.

On the same principle, since Friday's Buy price was the lowest, the fixed spread (0.5) will represent a higher percentage of that than of any other day's Buy price.

This can be determined without a single keystroke of the calculator!

SET 10, Q1. Correct Answer: E

Reasoning

First, we must determine how to work out the total cost of acquiring and operating the software and then calculate this amount for all of the software options. The total cost is calculated by adding up the licence fee for the given period, the one-off installation fee and the total working hours spent operating the software multiplied by the hourly wage of the operating staff.

Calculation

We can start by writing out the formula for calculating the total cost for each of the options.

Total cost = Installation Fee + Licence Fee (Year 1) + Licence Fee (Year 2) + (Staff Number × Working Hours × Number of Months × Hourly Wage)

Let's now calculate this for each of the options.

Accounts Pro 10:

$130 + 4\,500 + 4\,500 + (4 \times 20 \times 24 \times 20) = 47\,530$

BSheet 12:

$150 + 3\,500 + 3\,500 + (4 \times 20 \times 24 \times 20) = 45\,550$

BSheet Lite:

$200 + 8\,000 + 8\,000 + (3 \times 25 \times 24 \times 20) = 52\,200$

BookKeeper Standard (remember that this software has a one-off licence fee only to be counted once):

$550 + 9\,000 + (5 \times 15 \times 24 \times 20) = 45\,550$

We can now pick BSheet 12 and BookKeeper Standard as the two options that represent the lowest cost.

Potential Shortcuts / Pitfalls

One obvious pitfall to avoid is calculating BookKeeper Standard's one-off fee twice (once for each year). Also, there are a few opportunities where we can save time.

If you use a calculator, it is much better to start by calculating the total cost of the operating staff and only then adding the licence fees and the installation fee. Why? Because of the order of precedence between the various operations. The staff cost is the only factor which involves multiplication. Since multiplication is "higher priority" in a calculator than addition, we would either run into an error or would have to take note of an interim result – both of which make us lose time.

Let's take the BookKeeper Standard calculation to illustrate this. We started by adding up the licence fee and the installation fee:

$550 + 9000$

We then have to stop, memorize or write down this result, clear the calculator, calculate the staff costs and then add the above result in at the end. So what happens if we don't do that, and just continue with the calculations?

$550 + 9000 + 5$

A simple calculator will not wait to see which operation comes next, nor does it support the use of parentheses – it would simply add 5 to 550 + 9000, and then perform the multiplications, which would result in an obviously wrong answer.

SET 10, Q2. Correct Answer: C

Reasoning

We must first calculate the total licence fees for 5 years and then subtract the discount. We will then calculate the total cost of staff for 5 years and add up these two figures.

Calculation

Let's calculate the discounted licence fees for 5 years first. We do this by multiplying the yearly licence fee by the number of years and then calculating the discounted figure. A 15% discount can be expressed by saying that the new price is 85% of the original:

$3\,500 \times 5 \times 85\% = 3\,500 \times 5 \times 0.85 = 14\,875$

We now calculate the total staff cost, which is the number of staff needed multiplied by the monthly working hours and the number of months ($5 \times 12 = 60$), multiplied by the hourly wage:

$4 \times 20 \times 60 \times 20 = 96\,000$

The total cost is the sum of the above two figures:

$96\,000 + 14875 = 110\,875$ EUR

Potential Shortcuts / Pitfalls

Important to avoid:
- do not forget about the 15% reduction in licensing costs (if you do, you get option D)
- do not forget that the installation fee was waived (if you do, you get option E)
- do not forget about multiplying the staff costs by the number of months (if you do, you get option A or B, depending on whether you perhaps also forget about the licence fee discount)

SET 10, Q3. Correct Answer: C

Reasoning

We need to work out the total cost of introducing and operating each of the two software options for three years and then calculate the difference.

Calculation

The total cost of operating either software option for three years is as follows:

(Staff needed to operate × Working hours × Number of Months × Hourly Wage) + Licence fees + Installation fee

For BookKeeper Standard, this is:

$(5 \times 15 \times 36 \times 20) + 9\,000 + 550 = 63\,550$

For Accounts Pro 10, this is:

$(4 \times 20 \times 36 \times 20) + (4500 \times 3) + 130 = 71\,230$

Since the question was about the savings or losses if the company introduces BookKeeper Standard *instead of* Accounts Pro 10, we should subtract the costs of BookKeeper Standard from Accounts Pro 10, not the other way around:

71 230 – 63 550 = 7 680

Since the total cost of BookKeeper Standard is lower (the result of the above subtraction is positive), this represents a net saving, so option C is the correct answer.

SET 11, Q1. Correct Answer: A

Reasoning

The percentage increase in production for each crop is calculated by taking the difference in production between the two given years and then dividing this by the starting (2010) value and finally multiplying the answer by 100 to make it a percentage.

Calculation

Corn: (12409 – 12211) / 12211 x 100 = 1.62%
Rapeseed: (5801 – 5472) / 5472 x 100 = 6.01%
Sugar: (2702 – 2920) / 2920 x 100 = -7.47%
Sunflowers: (21199 – 19194) / 19194 x 100 = 10.45%
Wheat: (7792 – 7719) / 7719 x 100 = 0.95%

The correct answer is therefore Corn (A)

Potential Shortcuts / Pitfalls

If you perform all the calculations above with a calculator you will use well over 100 keystrokes. This can be shortened considerably and even eliminated completely just by taking a few moments to think about the data.

The question asks for the middle crop so we don't actually need an exact figure, just a relative figure compared to the other crops. A quick look at the data shows that sugar production has actually fallen and so without any calculation we know that this will be at the bottom of the new table. Next, try rounding all the figures to the nearest hundred. Now we can see that corn goes up 2 from 122, rapeseed goes up 3 from 55, sunflowers go up 20 from 192, and wheat goes up 1 from 77. From this we can see that sunflowers have risen enormously compared to the others and will be at the top of the table, with rapeseed close behind. The remaining two are a little bit closer, and you could use your calculator if you are

unsure, but given that the rounding would overestimate the wheat growth then corn is clearly going to be higher. This will make corn the third highest and hence in the middle of the table.

SET 11, Q2. Correct Answer: B

Reasoning

The percentage increase in production for wheat is calculated by taking the difference in production between the two given years and then dividing this by the starting (2005) value, finally multiplying the answer by 100 to make it a percentage. We can then reverse this process for sugar to calculate what value we should use for the 2010 production to get this same figure. Finally we need to subtract the actual amount produced to get the difference.

Calculation

Wheat: (7719 – 7422) / 7422 x 100 ≈ 4.0016%

This can be called 4% to the nearest percentage point

Let the 2010 figure for sugar be X, then:

(X – 2814) / 2814 x 100 = 4.0%
X / 2814 – 2814 / 2814 = 4.0% / 100
X / 2814 – 1 = 0.04
X = (1 + 0.04) x 2814 = 2926.56

Now subtract the actual production value to obtain the difference or increase as mentioned in the question.

2926.56 – 2920 ≈ 6.56 which is in thousands of tonnes.

Potential Shortcuts / Pitfalls

This problem can be simplified considerably by initially setting the two calculations to be equal to each other:

(X -2814) / 2814 = (7719 – 7422) / 7422

We can simplify this further because when you expand the bracketed parts of the equation we get 2814/2814 and 7422/7422; these are both equal to one and since they appear on each side of the equation then they just disappear.

Now we have:

X / 2814 = 7719 / 7422

And so:

X = 7719 x 2814 / 7422 = 2926.605

You will note that this is not the same as the answer given because this method has effectively used an exact figure for the percentage increase (7719/7422). To circumvent this, do that part of the calculation first and then only use the first two decimal places of the answer to continue with the rest of the calculation.

Don't forget to subtract the actual production figure to get the difference and remember that the figure is in thousands of tonnes.

SET 11, Q3. Correct Answer: E

Reasoning

The amount of land used for rapeseed production is the number of tonnes produced divided by the yield. We need to calculate this for 2005 and then can increase the yield by 6% and use this figure to calculate the land usage in 2015. We can then calculate the percentage increase by taking the difference and dividing by the 2005 figure.

Calculation

First, calculate the amount of land given over to rapeseed production. This is 4541 (thousand) tonnes divided by 3.1 tonnes per hectare:

4541 / 3.1 ≈ 1464.84

Increase the yield by 6%:

3.1 x 6% = 3.1 x 1.06 = 3.286

Now use this yield to calculate the land usage in 2015:

5801 / 3.286 = 1765.37

As a percentage of the 2005 rapeseed land use this is:

(1765.37 − 1464.84) / 1464.84 x 100 ≈ 20.5%

Potential Shortcuts / Pitfalls

Some things leap out as obvious and some things are really quite well hidden. If we write out the whole procedure above as one equation it looks quite messy...

((5801 / (3.1 x 1.06)) − (4541 / 3.1)) / (4531 / 3.1)

However, there are effectively three terms in the equation (B − A) / A, and you can see that all of them have the yield (3.1) as a common term as a divisor. As a result, this cancels out and can be eliminated

from the equation entirely. *So, in a question that, at first, seems to focus on the crop yield, it turns out that it is not even required.*

SET 12, Q1. Correct Answer: A

Reasoning

We need to calculate the EU-28 total production of fishery products in 2015, and then the aquaculture production using its share of the total. The EU-28 total production of fishery products can be calculated using *any* country's production divided by its share.

Calculation

First, we must calculate the EU-28 total production of fishery products in 2015. We can use any country to do this, so let's use Denmark and its share of 14.1%:

905 / 0.141 ≈ 6418 thousand tonnes

Second, we must calculate the EU-28 aquaculture production in 2015, in millions, and round it to one decimal place:

6418 / 1000 * 0.197 ≈ 1.3 million tonnes

Note that since the EU-28 total production is represented in *thousand* tonnes, we needed to divide it by 1000 to convert to *million* tonnes.

Potential Shortcuts / Pitfalls

If you miss that fishery production is given in the table in thousand tonnes, and don't convert to millions, you would get 1264.4 million tonnes (option C). If you simply added up the production figures for the 5 countries in the table, without calculating the entire EU-28 production, you would get 0.8 million tonnes (option E).

SET 12, Q2. Correct Answer: D

Reasoning

We need to calculate French aquaculture production in 2015, and then find what percentage of all EU-28 fishery production this represented.

Calculation

We must first calculate the aquaculture production of France in 2015.

We know from the table that fishery products totaled 661 (thousand tonnes). There are two elements to this total, aquaculture and fish catches. The question text tells us that the fish catch of France was 271 thousand tonnes greater than its aquaculture production.

Therefore total production of fishery products in 2015 was:

(aquaculture) + (aquaculture + 271)

Hence, aquaculture = (total − 271) / 2

= (661 − 271) / 2 = 195 thousand tonnes

Now we must calculate the aquaculture production share of total EU-28 production, using the information given in the table that the total French production of 661 thousand tonnes represents a 10.3% share of the EU-28 total.

Aquaculture production share = 195 / 661 * 10.3 ≈ 3%

Potential Shortcuts / Pitfalls

You have to be careful in this question to realise that in the first calculation you must use the 271 thousand figure twice. Also, if you incorrectly calculate the amount of French aquaculture production, swapping it with catches, you would get 7% (option C).

SET 12, Q3. Correct Answer: E

Reasoning

We need to calculate the percentage increase from 2008 to 2015 in the total production of fishery products for both the United Kingdom and Spain, and then calculate the difference.

Calculation

First, we must calculate the percentage increase from 2008 to 2015 in total production of fishery products for the United Kingdom:

(913 / 768 − 1) * 100% ≈ 18.88%

Now the equivalent calculation for Spain:

(1195 / 1106 − 1) * 100% ≈ 8.05%

Finally, we find the difference and round it to one decimal place:

Difference = 18.88 − 8.05 ≈ 10.8%

Potential Shortcuts / Pitfalls

You can go wrong with this question if you confuse the *percentage* of increase with the *amount* of increase. If you use the amount you will calculate the UK as 913 − 768 = 145 and Spain as 1195 − 1106 = 89, resulting in 145 − 189 = 56. This is answer option D.

A shortcut lies in combining all the steps shown above, and doing (913 / 768 − 1195 / 1106) * 100%, which would significantly reduce the number of keystrokes and arithmetical operations.

SET 13, Q1. Correct Answer: B

Reasoning

The percentage increase in nuclear power generation is calculated by taking the difference in generation figures between the two given years and then dividing this by the starting (2000) value and finally multiplying the answer by 100 to make it a percentage. However we first need to increase the 2005 figure by 7.25% to take account of the increase in the total amount of energy being generated.

Calculation

First, calculate the total amount of electricity generated in 2005. This is 7.25% higher than in 2000. Let us assume that the total in 2000 was X. Then:

2005: Total = X * 1.0725

So the increase is:

(X * 1.0725 * 12.4 − X * 10.9) / X * 10.9

As there is a common term (X) in every element of the calculation both above and below the dividing line we can cancel it out, leaving:

(1.0725 * 12.4 − 10.9) / 10.9 = 0.22

Multiply this by 100 to make it a percentage:

0.22 * 100 = 22%

Potential Shortcuts / Pitfalls

This question is far more straightforward than it first looks. The main problem is what to do with the 7.25% increase given that there is no total power generation figure to use. However, provided there is a common base figure (the 2000 total power generation) that is being worked from, then it is always going to cancel out and need not even be considered.

Make sure you apply the increase to the 2005 figure before you calculate the difference for the increase rather than applying it to the increase itself.

SET 13, Q2. Correct Answer: D

Reasoning

The percentage increase in generation for each form of energy generation is calculated by taking the difference in percentage generated between the two given years and then dividing this by the starting (2010) value and finally multiplying the answer by 100 to make it a percentage.

Calculation

First, calculate the percentage change in percentage of total energy generated for each of the forms.

Fossil: (53.0 – 66.4) / 66.4 * 100 = 20.2%
Wind: (15.4 – 9.8) / 9.8 * 100 = 57.1%
Solar: (12.3 – 7.8) / 7.8 * 100 = 57.7%
Tide: (3.3 – 1.8) / 1.8 * 100 = 83.3%
Nuclear: (9.8 – 10.4) / 10.4 * 100 = -5.8%
Other: (6.2 – 3.8) / 3.8 * 100 = 63.2%

The correct answer is Tide/Wave (D)

Potential Shortcuts / Pitfalls

Virtually all the calculations can be made redundant just by taking a moment to examine the data and do a little bit of estimation and approximation. First and foremost, the question asks for the *largest increase* and so we can immediately eliminate Fossil and Nuclear because they have actually fallen.

The others are a little closer but other work that need not be done is the multiplication by 100 to make percentages. You only want the *relative* values of these figures and so any identical operation is going to do the same thing to all of them and make no difference to their relative values.

Take Wind: it starts at about 10% and increases to about 16% which is an increase of about 60%. Solar increases 4.5 from a starting value of about 8. This is clearly more than 50% but less than 2/3. Tide and wave power increases by 1.5 from a base of 1.8 which is 5/6 – which leaves the previous 2 way behind. Finally, 'Other' increases 2.4 from a base of 3.8 which is less than ¾, so Tide/Wave is left as the clear winner.

SET 13, Q3. Correct Answer: E

Reasoning

We need to calculate the percentage of the total power generated by biomass in 2005 and increase this by 50%. We then need to calculate the amount generated by 'Other' in 2010 and work out the proportion of this generated by biomass.

Calculation

First, calculate the percentage of total power generated by biomass in 2005. If we say the total amount generated is X, then the amount generated by 'Other' is:

X * 2.9% = 0.029X

The amount generated by biomass is:

0.029X * 20% = 0.029X * 0.2 = 0.0058X

This increases in 2010 to:

0.0058 * 150% = 0.0058 * 1.5 = 0.0087X

In 2010 the total power is 10% higher than 2005, which is:

X * 110% = 1.1X

So, in 2010 the percentage of total power generated by 'Other' is:

1.1X * 3.8% = 1.1X * 0.038 = 0.0418X

The percentage of this generated by biomass is:

(0.0087X / 0.0418X) * 100 = 20.8%

Potential Shortcuts / Pitfalls

As you can see from the calculation, the total power generated in 2005 (X) is unspecified and cancels out so needn't be considered at all. It is used primarily to explain the process. However, we can shorten this calculation considerably if we stop and think about the data in question and what we are trying to achieve.

In 2010 'Other' accounts for 3.8% of the total generation, which increases by 10% to about 4.2 when applied to the 2005 base (X). So 'Other' rises from 2.9 to 4.2. This is very close to 50%, which is the same rise that has applied to biomass and so they pretty much cancel each other out.

SET 14, Q1. Correct Answer: A

Reasoning

Only the data in the left-side diagram is needed. We must first add together the economic damage costs for all the disaster types, counting the damage dealt by storms twice to get our new total. We can than work out what the doubled amount caused by storms is as a percentage of this new total.

Calculation

The cost of the total damage would have been:

763 + 662 + 119 +100 + (2 * 1011) = $3666 billion

The damage caused by storms would have been 2 * 1011 = $2022 billion

2022 is (2022 / 3666) * 100 ≈ 55.2 percent of 3666

Potential Shortcuts / Pitfalls
If you simply double the percentage damage caused by storms, 38%, you would get 76% (option D).

SET 14, Q2. Correct Answer: C

Reasoning

For this question we only need information from the right-side diagram. First we calculate the total cost of economic damage, then what 45% of this number is. Another method is to calculate what 1% of the total economic damage is, and multiply it by 45.

Calculation

The total cost of economic damage:

709 + 262 + 40 + 10 + 870 = $1891 billion
45% of this is 1891 * 0.45 ≈ $851 billion

The alternative solution: If 709 billion dollars is 37 percent of the total economic damage, then 1% is 709 / 37 ≈ 19.16 billion dollars. The absolute loss of Asia would have been 19.16 * 45 = 862 billion dollars.

Notice how the two different methods lead to different results, although both produce answer option C. This is because the percentages and the dollar values are individually rounded. This is anticipated in the answer options which refer to approximate ranges rather than specific numbers.

SET 14, Q3. Correct Answer: E

Reasoning

We cannot do this calculation as there is not enough information. Although we have a figure for total global storm damage in the left-side diagram ($1.011 bn), and a figure for all types of damage in the Americas ($870 bn), there is no information as to *what proportion* of the damage in the Americas was caused by storms. It could have been all the damage or none at all, or anything in between.

Possible Shortcuts / Pitfalls
The danger with this question is that you assume a calculation can actually be made and waste time on trying to find a way to do it. If you make the mistake of using the fact that globally $1011 bn of damage was done by storms, and apply the same proportion to the Americas, you would calculate 1101 * 0.45 = $455 billion and choose the incorrect answer option D.

SET 15, Q1. Correct Answer: A

Reasoning

We need to calculate the speed of the runner and then the distance he would cover at that speed over the time difference between the two runners. We also need to remember when calculating the speed that Davies ran the last 10 metres (when the fate of the bronze medal was decided) 8% faster than his overall average.

Calculation

First, we calculate Davies' overall average speed, which is the distance covered divided by the time taken:

100 m / 10.07 s = 9.93m/s

In the closing 10 metres, he was actually running 8% faster than this, which is:

9.93 × 1.08 = 10.72m/s

He finished 4th, just 0.04s behind the 3rd placed runner. In those 0.04 seconds he ran the following distance:

10.72 * 0.04 = 0.43m

which is 43cm.

Potential Shortcuts / Pitfalls
A risk in this question is that of confusing speeds and times because they are very similar in value. A runner covering 100m in 10s is travelling at 10m/s. As the times chosen are very close to 10 then so are the speeds, so care must be taken to ensure you keep track of each step.

Another thing to be careful about is the fact that we need to work with the 8% increased speed to calculate the distance covered in the last 0.04 seconds as this was the speed Davies ran at in the final 10 metres.

SET 15, Q2. Correct Answer: B

Reasoning

We need to calculate the speed of each runner and then the percentage difference between these speeds.

Calculation

The speed of the runner is calculated by dividing the distance run by the time taken. For Adams this is:

100 / 9.95 = 10.05 m/s

And for Best it is:

100 / 9.98 = 10.02 m/s

The percentage difference is the difference divided by the slower speed and then multiplied by 100 to make it a percentage:

100 × (10.05 – 10.02) / 10.02 = 0.3%

Potential Shortcuts / Pitfalls
If you try and do this in one step then you would get:

$$\frac{100 / 9.95}{100 / 9.98}$$

When we divide by a fraction (we have a fraction in the denominator as well) we invert it and then multiply instead:

$$\frac{100}{9.95} \times \frac{9.98}{100}$$

Now we can see that the 100s cancel out and we are simply left with:

9.98 / 9.95 = 1.003

Remember that this is not the percentage increase of one speed compared to other but rather how much faster the first place finisher was than the second. To get the percentage, you subtract 1 and multiply by 100. This way, you get the same answer of 0.3%.

SET 15, Q3. Correct Answer: E

Reasoning

We need to calculate the speed of the runner in the final, and from that calculate his speed in the previous races. Then we calculate his time in the heat (the first race) and hence the time of the unnamed runner-up in that heat. To calculate this last step, we use the information from the question text.

Calculation

First we need to calculate Carter's speed in the final. This is the distance run divided by the time taken:

100 / 10.03 = 9.97m/s

This was 1.3% faster than in the semi-final. The easiest way to calculate the semi-final speed from this is by imagining what we would have done if we had been provided the semi-final speed instead. If we knew the semi-final speed and the fact that Carter became 1.3% faster in the final, we would calculate his speed in the final as follows:

Semi-final speed × 1.013 = Final speed

Since we already have the final speed and we actually need to calculate the semi-final speed, we can work backwards:

Final speed / 1.013 = semi-final speed

With actual numbers:

9.97 / 1.013 = 9.84m/s

Similarly, this is 1.8% faster than in the heat which was:

9.84 / 1.018 = 9.67m/s

So he ran the heat at 9.67m/s. This would take:

100 / 9.67 = 10.34s

Don't forget that he beat the runner-up by 0.03 seconds:

10.34 + 0.03 = 10.37s.

SET 16, Q1. Correct Answer: B

Reasoning

We need to find the percentage change in the total EU sold production of chemicals between 2016 and 2017, then the change between 2014 and 2015, and then calculate the ratio.

Calculation

This problem can be solved very easily if you notice that the total EU sold production of chemicals is the same in both 2014 and 2016, i.e. 663, so this provides a common denominator. We therefore only need to subtract the denominator from the nominator.

The change in the total EU sold production of chemicals between 2016 and 2017:

674 – 663 = 11

And for 2014 and 2015:

680 – 663 = 17

The denominator, 663, is the same in both cases so the ratio is simply 11 : 17.

Potential Shortcuts / Pitfalls
You have to be careful here not get the ratio the wrong way round. If you do that then you will get answer C, 17 : 11.

SET 16, Q2. Correct Answer: E

Reasoning

We need to calculate the amount sold of medical and pharmaceutical products in 2016, and then calculate its share in the total sold production of chemicals in 2016. The amount sold of medical and pharmaceutical products in 2016 is the respective amount in 2017 adjusted by the percentage change between the two years.

Calculation

First, we must calculate the amount of medical and pharmaceutical products sold in 2016 using the amount sold in 2017 and the increase of 5.2% between 2016 and 2017 (in billion euros):

168 / (1 + 0.052) ≈ €159.7 billion

Second, we must calculate the share of medical and pharmaceutical products in total sold production of chemicals in 2016, and round it to one decimal: place:

159.7 / 663 * 100% ≈ 24.1%

Potential Shortcuts / Pitfalls
If you mistakenly assume that the total sold production of chemicals between 2016 and 2017 increased by the same amount as the medical and pharmaceutical products you would get the incorrect figure of 24.9% (option B). If you calculate the amount of medical and pharmaceutical products sold in 2016 as the respective amount in 2017 divided by (1 – 0.052) instead of (1 + 0.052), thus mixing the percentages of increase and decrease, you would get the incorrect figure of 26.7% (option C).

SET 16, Q3. Correct Answer: A

Reasoning

We need to calculate the shares of organic and inorganic chemicals in intra-EU-28 exports in the total intra-EU-28 exports of chemicals in 2017, and then calculate their difference. The percentage shares of organic and inorganic chemicals are their respective intra-EU-28 export amounts divided by the total intra-EU-28 exports of chemicals in 2017.

Calculation

First, we must calculate the share of *organic* chemicals in intra-EU-28 exports in the total intra-EU-28 exports of chemicals:

81 / 527 * 100% ≈ 15.37%

Second, the equivalent share of *inorganic* chemicals:

17 / 527 * 100% ≈ 3.23%

Finally, we need to calculate the difference between organic and inorganic shares, and round it to one decimal place:

15.37% – 3.23% ≈ 12.1%

Potential Shortcuts / Pitfalls

If you calculate the difference between organic and inorganic chemicals in intra-EU-28 exports, instead of their respective shares you would get the incorrect answer of 64.0% (option C).

You can do the whole calculation even faster by factoring out the division by the total intra-EU-28 exports of chemicals, thus: (81 – 17) / 527 * 100%

SET 17, Q1. Correct Answer: D

Reasoning

We need to calculate the number of bottles of red wine consumed in 2015, which is the total consumption divided by the size of a bottle. From this we can work out the total spending on red wine, which is the number of bottles multiplied by the cost. Finally we can calculate the per capita spending, which is the total spending divided by the population.

Calculation

First, let's calculate the total number of bottles consumed (and as wine consumption is in litres, we need to convert 75cl into litres, which is 0.75):

52 / 0.75 = 69.333

Remember that this figure is in millions of bottles.

Therefore the total spending on red wine in 2015 is:

69.333 * 6.63 = 459.678

This figure is millions of euros.

Now calculate the per capita spending:

459.678 / 16714 = 0.0275

Now we need to think about the order of magnitude. The total spending was in millions and the population is in thousands, so we need to multiply the answer by 1000 to get a per capita value:

0.0275 * 1000 = 27.50

Potential Shortcuts / Pitfalls

This problem can seem a bit more complicated than it really is. You just need to be methodical in following each step, converting litres to bottles, to money, etc. and you also need to be careful to keep an eye on the different magnitudes of the data items.

SET 17, Q2. Correct Answer: B

Reasoning

We need to calculate the percentage change in consumption of rosé wine between 2010 and 2015 and then apply this change to the white wine to calculate what the consumption would have been with the same percentage change.

Calculation

First, calculate the change in consumption of rosé wine between 2010 and 2015. This is the difference in consumption divided by the starting value (2010 figure) and then multiplied by 100:

(31 – 38) / 38 * 100 = –18.42%

Now we apply this change to the white wine figure:

74 * –18.42% = 74 * –0.1842 = –13.63

Now add this to the original 2010 figure for white wine:

74 + –13.63 = 60.37

Given that all the answer options are in millions then this can be rounded to 60.

Potential Shortcuts / Pitfalls

This question gives you the opportunity to make a quick estimation of the answer. If you look at the data you can see that the 2010 starting value for white wine (74) is very close to twice that of rosé wine (38). So, given that rosé wine reduced by 7 (million litres), then white wine will decline by pretty much double that, i.e. 14 (million litres), from 74 to 60.

SET 17, Q3. Correct Answer: A

Reasoning

We need to calculate the per capita consumption of red wine in 2005 and 2010. Then we can calculate the percentage change, which is the difference between the two figures divided by the starting value and multiplied by 100.

Calculation

First, calculate the per capita consumption in 2005:

63 (million) / 16316 (thousand) = 3.8612

The 2010 per capita consumption is:

61 (million) / 16492 (thousand) = 3.6988

Now calculate the percentage change in consumption:

(3.6988 – 3.8612) / 3.8612 * 100 = –4.2%

Potential Shortcuts / Pitfalls

Although it's often necessary to be aware of the difference in magnitude of the different data items, it is not actually necessary in this particular case as they cancel out.

However, we do have the little difficulty of keeping track of enough significant digits in each of the intermediate answers to ensure enough accuracy in the final answer. If you aren't accurate enough you can arrive at answers between 4.0% and 5.1% even using the correct procedure, leaving 3 of the answer options as possibly right. To get around this difficulty, you can do the calculation slightly differently. When calculating the percentage change you can use (final value / starting value) – 1 and multiply this by 100. This method is less intuitive but it has the advantage that you can do the whole calculation in one go. Remember when you divide by a fraction then you invert the divisor and multiply instead. This leads to:

61 / 16492 * 16316 / 63 * 100 = 95.8

This eliminates the need to record partial answers and gives full accuracy.

SET 18, Q1. Correct Answer: C

Reasoning

We need to calculate, for both Italy and the EU-28, the share of young people aged 20-24 years who were participating in education and learning two or more foreign languages in 2015, and then calculate the ratio. The share is the product of two percentage shares, i.e. of young people participating in education, and of young people learning two or more foreign languages.

Calculation

First, we must calculate the percentage share of Italian young people aged 20-24 years who were participating in education and learning two or more foreign languages in 2015:

0.338 * 0.958 = 0.323804

The same way, the percentage share for the E-28:

0.414 * 0.588 = 0.243432

Finally, we calculate the ratio, and simplify it to the lowest terms:

0.323804 : 0.243432 ≈ 32 : 24 = 4 : 3

Notice that although the initial ratio is 32 : 24, it can be simplified since both sides of it are multiples of 8. By dividing each term of the initial ratio, 32 : 24, by 8, we reduce the ratio to the lowest terms, i.e. to 4 : 3.

Potential Shortcuts / Pitfalls

A risk here is of trying to calculate the ratio using only the values from the bar chart, i.e. 95.8 and 58.8. If you do you would end up choosing either 8 : 5 (answer option A) or 96 : 59 (option E).

As always in using data from tables and bar charts, you have to be careful in flicking between the two that you do not by mistake take data from the wrong table row or column or the wrong bar. This is an easy mistake to make when working at speed.

SET 18, Q2. Correct Answer: A

Reasoning

We need to calculate the number of French young people aged 20-24 years who were learning two or more foreign languages in 2010 and 2015, and then calculate the difference.

Calculation

First, we must calculate the number of French young people aged 20-24 years who were learning two or more foreign languages in 2010 (in thousands):

1.365 * 1000 * 0.518 = 707.07 thousand.

Note that the number of young people is given in the question in millions, so we needed to multiply it by 1000 to work in thousands.

Second, we calculate the number of French young people aged 20-24 years participating in education in 2015 (in thousands):

1.365 * 1000 * (1 + 0.036) = 1414.14 thousand

Third, we calculate the number of French young people aged 20-24 years who were learning two or more foreign languages in 2015 (in thousands):

1414.14 * 0.567 = 801.81738 thousand

Finally, we calculate the difference between 2015 and 2010, and round it to thousands:

801.81738 – 707.07 ≈ 95 thousand

Potential Shortcuts / Pitfalls
If you ignore the increase in the number of young people participating in education between 2010 and 2015, thus using the same number of 1.365 million for both years, you would get the incorrect figure of 67 thousand, which is given as option B.

If you forget that the number in the question is presented in millions, you would get the incorrect figure of 94747 thousand (option C). Common sense would normally tell you that answer must be wrong as 94747 thousand is more than the entire population of France, but when you are rushing in a numerical reasoning test you can end up blindly following your calculations and not step back and think if the answer makes sense.

SET 18, Q3. Correct Answer: B

Reasoning

We need to use the ratio between the German and Italian populations of people aged 15-29 years in 2015, to calculate the shares of German and Italian young people aged 15-29 years participating in education in 2015. We then convert the ratio to the percentage of increase.

Calculation

The question text tells us that the German population of young people aged 15-29 years in 2015 was 23% greater than that of Italy: Therefore the ratio was 1.23 : 1.

We must now multiply the sides of the ratio by the respective shares of German and Italian young people aged 15-29 years who were participating in education in 2015:

1.23 * 0.502 : 1 * 0.411 = 0.61746 : 0.411

Finally, we need to convert the ratio to the percentage, and round it to one decimal place:

(0.61746 / 0.411 – 1) * 100% ≈ 50.2%

Potential Shortcuts / Pitfalls
If you ignore the fact that the German population aged 15-29 is larger than that of Italy, and only calculate the difference between young people participating in education, you would get the incorrect figure of 9.1% (option A).

SET 19, Q1. Correct Answer: C

Reasoning

We need to use the biomass waste to bio fuels to wood ratio as these are the energy sources that count to biomass energy. Using this ratio we can then calculate the bio fuels share as a percentage.

Calculation

The diagram tells us that the biomass waste to bio fuels to wood ratio is 4 to 21 to 19. This means that out of every 4 + 21 + 19 = 44 quadrillion Btu of biomass energy, 21 quadrillion Btu was supplied by bio fuels.

By calculating what percentage 21 is of 44, we get what percentage of biomass energy was supplied by bio fuels. 21 expressed as a percentage of 44 is:

(21 / 44) * 100 = 47.72 ≈ 48%, which gives us answer C.

Potential Shortcuts / Pitfalls
If you simply use the biofuel energy percentage of renewable energy straight from the diagram as the answer you would get 21% (option A).

SET 19, Q2. Correct Answer: D

Reasoning

First we calculate what would have been the amount of *renewable energy* by dividing 2 (quadrillion Btu), the amount given in the question, by the percentage of renewable energy that is produced by hydroelectric (25%). Then we determine the *total amount of all energy* by dividing the total of renewable energy by the percentage (11%) coming from renewable energy.

Calculation

The amount of *renewable energy* produced would have been 2 / 0.25 = 8 quadrillion Btu

The total amount of *all energy* produced would have been 8 / 0.11 ≈ 72.7 quadrillion Btu

Therefore the correct answer is D.

Potential Shortcuts / Pitfalls
Be careful not to skip the first step of the calculation. If you do, you would calculate 2 / 0.11 = 18.2 quadrillion Btu (option A).

SET 19, Q3. Correct Answer: C

Reasoning

We must calculate what amount of energy was actually produced from petroleum by multiplying the total for all energy types by the petroleum share of 37%. We then reduce this amount by 10%. In order for the total amount of energy produced to stay the same, we have to make up for this decrease by increasing the other 4 sources by equal amounts, so we divide the previous result by 4 to get what those amounts are. We then have to add this number to the original amount of energy produced via coal, which we can calculate by multiplying the total amount by 0.14.

Calculation

The amount of energy produced from petroleum originally: 97.7 * 0.3 7 ≈ 36.15

The amount of decrease is then 10% of this number which is 36.15 * 0.1 ≈ 3.62

That means that energy from other sources must increase by 3.62 / 4 ≈ 0.9 each

The amount of energy produced from coal originally is 97.7 * 0.14 ≈ 13.68

The answer to the question is therefore 13.68 + 0.9 = 14.58 quadrillion Btu

Potential Shortcuts / Pitfalls
This question can seem rather complex and needs to be read carefully. The phrase "energy from the other sources had increased by equal amounts" means that energy from all the other sources increased by a *combined* total of 3.62 and therefore *each* source increased by 3.62 / 4 ≈ 0.9. If you mistakenly calculate at 3.62 each you would get a total increase of 4 * 3.62, leading to 97.7 * 0.14 − 3.62 = 17.3 quadrillion Btu (option E).

A further risk is that you interpret the question in such a way as to increase the energy produced from each source by an equal *percentage* instead of an equal *amount*. This would give the incorrect figure of (97.7 + 3.62) * 0.14 = 14.2 quadrillion Btu (option B).

SET 20, Q1. Correct Answer: B

Reasoning

The number of books belonging to two subcategories is the sum of the books in each subcategory minus the total number of books in the Teen & young adult category. Once we have this figure, we can determine the percentage.

Calculation

The number of books belonging to two subcategories is:

10096 + 390686 + 371140 + 310547 +15387 + 81644 = 1179500

Now we deduct the figure for the total number of books in the Teen & young adult category:

1179500 −1017540 = 161960

If X is the percentage that this number represents, then

1017540 * (X / 100) = 161960
X = (161960 / 1017540) * 100

Solving the equation we get that X ≈ 15.9%, which is answer B.

SET 20, Q2. Correct Answer: C

Reasoning

We need to calculate the number of general reference books, using data from both the table and the pie chart. We can then convert this number to a percentage of the total number of Teen & young adult books.

Calculation

There are 15387 reference books, of which 54% belong to the general reference subcategory. So the number of books in the general reference subcategory is:

15387 * 0.54 ≈ 8309

If 8309 is X percent of 1017540 (the total number of books in the Teen & young adult category) then the equation is:

$1017540 * (X / 100) = 8309$
$X = (8309 / 1017540) * 100$

Solving for X we get that $X \approx 0.82\%$, giving us answer option C.

Potential Shortcuts / Pitfalls
Although the actual calculation here is not too difficult, it is very easy to get confused between the different categories and subcategories and end up calculating with the wrong values. If you use the sum of the books in each subcategory, 1179500, instead of the total number of Teen & young adult books, 1017540, you would end up with 0.7% (option B). Or if you use the number of books in the *reference* subcategory, 15387, instead of the number of books in the *general reference* subcategory (one level further down), you would get 1.51% (option D).

SET 20, Q3. Correct Answer: D

Reasoning
We must first calculate the number of dictionaries and then the percentage of reference books this represents after the addition of 1000 atlases.

Calculation
The number of dictionaries is $15387 * 0.21 \approx 3231$

The number of reference books after the addition of 1000 atlases:

$15387 + 1000 = 16387$

The percentage the dictionaries represent after the addition:

$(3231 / 16387) * 100 \approx 19.72\%$

Potential Shortcuts / Pitfalls
Again, you can go wrong by confusing the data. For instance, if you increased by 1000 the number of dictionaries, instead of atlases, you would end up with 25.82% (option E).

SET 21, Q1. Correct Answer: D

Reasoning
We need to calculate the overall average speed of the train. Speed is distance divided by time. Once we have the average speed, we can easily calculate the cruising speed by adding 15% to this value.

Calculation
The calculation of speed (distance / time) is quite straightforward, but here the time is not in an easily usable form. The hour component of the journey time is simple enough: 3 hours. The problem is with the minutes, as we do not express time in the decimal system. This means that 45 minutes is not equal to 0.45 hours, so we must first convert the minutes to a decimal value.

To do this, take the minutes, divide by 60 (minutes per hour) and then add the hours:

$45 / 60 = 0.75$
$0.75 + 3 = 3.75$

Now calculate the average speed:

$435 / 3.75 = 116$

The cruising speed is actually 15% faster than this. Remember how we convert a 15% increase to 1.15:

$116 \times 1.15 = 133.4$

Which, to the nearest whole number, is 133 km/h.

Potential Shortcuts / Pitfalls
The first part of this problem can be done more quickly without a calculator.

The time taken is 3:45, which is 3 whole hours and 3 quarters of an hour. This is a total of 15 quarter hours ($3 \times 4 = 12$, plus 3 quarters), so when we calculate the average speed we can use:

$435 / (15 / 4)$

But remember, if we are dividing by a fraction then we *invert* it and *multiply* instead:

$435 \times (4 / 15)$

This next step is difficult to spot but if you do, it can save a lot of time. 45 is 3x15 and so 450 is 30x15. So what? Well, notice that 435 is just 15 less than 450. Since 450 is 30x15, then 435 must be 29x15. Our division then looks like this:

(29 × 15 × 4) / 15

Notice how the 15 is both in the numerator and in the denominator – this means that they will cancel each other out, reducing the calculation to:

29 × 4 = 116

There is one last thing we should not forget about in dealing with minutes. 45 minutes is three quarters of an hour. We are trying to convert this into the decimal system, so what is three quarters of one hundred? The answer is of course 75, with or without using a calculator.

SET 21, Q2. Correct Answer: C

Reasoning

We need to calculate the normal average speed for the train. Once we have this, we can calculate the actual average speed of the train and then the delay caused by the slowdown.

Calculation

We first need to convert the time into a usable format. To do this, take the minutes, divide by 60 and add the hours back in:

35 / 60 = 0.583
0.583 + 1 = 1.583

Now calculate the normal average speed:

220 / 1.583 = 138.98

Because of adverse conditions, our *actual* average was only 90% of this (which is just another way of saying that it was 10% slower):

138.98 × 0.9 = 125.1

So, if we travelled all 220km at this speed it would take:

220 / 125.1 = 1.7586

This answer is in the decimal format, which we need to convert back to hours and minutes. Subtract the whole hours and then multiply the decimal part by 60:

0.7586 × 60 = 45.516

This is what we know so far: the journey took 1 hour and 45.516 minutes. This is still not good enough, as now it is the minutes that is in the decimal format.

Now subtract the minutes and repeat the above step to get the seconds:

0.516 × 60 = 30.96s

This is 1:45:31 which is 10m 31s late.

Potential Shortcuts / Pitfalls

There may be a temptation to take the time of 1 hour and 35 minutes and convert it to minutes. This would be 95 minutes. Some candidates would then take 10% of this and add it to the original 95 minutes to calculate the delay. This would give an answer of 9m30s delay, which is wrong. What this actually calculates is *how far you would be from your destination at the normal arrival time*, if you continued your journey at the normal average speed.

A shortcut we can take is *checking the level of accuracy needed* to answer the question. We initially calculated that the new journey time would be 1 hour and 45.516 minutes. We can see from the data in the table that 1 hour and 45.516 minutes is 10 minutes and × seconds longer than the normal journey time. As it turns out, this level of accuracy is more than enough, as option C is the only one which starts with 10 minutes – so we do not actually need to convert 0.516 of a minute into seconds.

SET 21, Q3. Correct Answer: B

Reasoning

We need to work out the number of trains we will pass. The easiest way to do this is to make note of when we depart and arrive and then calculate how many trains either (1) arrive after our departure time or (2) depart before our arrival time.

Calculation

To calculate our arrival time:

08:00 + 5:20 = 13:20

The first train leaving Berlin set off at 05:00 and so it will arrive at:

05:00 + 5:20 = 10:20

So, the first train of the day from Berlin to Brussels will still be en route when we set off. This means that we will pass every train leaving after 05:00 and before 13:20, when we arrive in Berlin.

Since trains leave from Berlin every two hours, this will add up to 5 trains:

05:00, 07:00, 09:00, 11:00 and 13:00, 5 in total.

Potential Shortcuts / Pitfalls

There may be a temptation to say that the journey is 5 hour and 20 minutes long and the trains set off every two hours, so we must pass only two trains (one after 2 hours, the second after 4 hours). This would only be true if we simply sat in a stationary train for 5 hours and 20 minutes! This incorrect approach disregards the fact that our train is also moving in the opposite direction.

SET 22, Q1. Correct Answer: D

Reasoning

The number of unemployed is the population multiplied by the size of the workforce as a percentage of the population, multiplied by the percentage of the workforce that is unemployed. We need to calculate this for 2015, subtract 10000 from it, adjust the percentages by the given values and calculate the population of Ireland in 2010. We can then calculate the percentage change in the population.

Calculation

First, calculate the number of unemployed in 2015:

4606 * 0.485 * 0.059 = 131.8

This number is in thousands because the population is given in thousands. Therefore before we subtract 10000 from it we need to convert it to the same units. You can either multiply the above answer by 1000 or divide the change in unemployed figure by 1000:

131.8 – 10000 / 1000 = 121.8

The percentage of the workforce that is unemployed rose by 0.1 percentage points (*not* 0.1%) and so in 2010 it would have been:

5.9 – 0.1 = 5.8

So, the population that would have this level of unemployed people is:

121.8 / (0.058 * 0.487) = 4312.12

This means that the percentage rise in population is therefore:

(4606 – 4312.12) / 4312.12 * 100 = 6.8%

Potential Shortcuts / Pitfalls

This is relatively straightforward but there are a lot of steps to it. Also, there are a few units that don't match up very easily. When you have calculated the number of unemployed in 2015, you cannot simply multiply in a percentage change because the change in the number of unemployed is given as an *absolute figure* rather than a percentage change. Also the change in the percentage of the workforce unemployed is given as a change in the figure rather than as a percentage change even though the data item itself is a percentage. This sort of thing is often a source of confusion.

SET 22, Q2. Correct Answer: B

Reasoning

The number of unemployed is the population multiplied by the size of the workforce as a percentage of the population, multiplied by the percentage of the workforce that is unemployed. We need to do this calculation for both Hungary and Portugal and then work out the percentage that the former is of the latter.

Calculation

First, calculate the number of unemployed in Hungary:

11086 * 0.467 * 0.076 = 393.5

Now do the same for Portugal:

11602 * 0.421 * 0.087 = 425

Now calculate the percentage Hungary is of Portugal:

393.5 / 425 * 100 = 92.6%

Potential Shortcuts / Pitfalls

Just be careful to get the fraction for the final percentage the correct way round and that you don't use the wrong year for the percentage of population figure.

SET 22, Q3. Correct Answer: E

Reasoning

The number of unemployed is the population multiplied by the size of the workforce as a percentage of the population, multiplied by the percentage of the workforce that is unemployed. We need to work this out for Croatia in 2015, then modify the figures for the population and the percentage of the workforce unemployed as indicated and calculate the number of unemployed in 2010. Finally, we can calculate the difference between the two.

Calculation

First, calculate the number of unemployed in Croatia in 2015:

4887 * 0.421 * 0.074 = 152.25

The percentage of the workforce who are unemployed rose by 5% from 2010 to 2015, so the 2010 figure would be:

0.074 / 1.05 = 0.0705 or 7.048%

The population of Croatia rose by 3.3% and so the population in 2010 would have been:

4887 / 1.033 = 4730.88

The number of unemployed in 2010 was:

4730.88 * 0.419 * 0.07048 = 139.708

The difference in numbers of people unemployed is then:

152.25 – 139.708 = 12.542

This is in thousands and so the answer is 12542.

Potential Shortcuts / Pitfalls
Try and avoid too many intermediate results as these can rounding errors if too few significant digits are used. Also note that although the percentage of the workforce unemployed is a percentage (7.4%), when this changes by a percentage then you must treat the figure if it were any other piece of data and multiply or divide as appropriate. The fact that it is a percentage is irrelevant. Do not just add or subtract 5 percentage points.

SET 23, Q1: Correct Answer: D

Reasoning

For each year we have to find the number of unemployed people of working age. We calculate the number of working age people for a given year by multiplying the population by the percentage of working age people. Then we multiply the result by that year's unemployment rate to get the number of unemployed people of working age.

Calculation

We can combine the steps of the calculation as follows:

For 2007: 10023887 *0.66 * 0.07 ≈ 463104
For 2008: 9991201 *0.66 * 0.08 ≈ 527535
For 2009: 9958942 *0.66 * 0.098 ≈ 644144
For 2010: 9927840 *0.66 *0.118 ≈ 773180

We do not need to do any calculation for 2011. Since the unemployment rate was the same in 2010 as in 2011, the year with the higher population will automatically have more unemployed people. The chart tells us that the population was higher in 2010 than in 2011, therefore the correct answer is 2010.

Potential Shortcuts / Pitfalls
Remember that we are not looking for an absolute number but to find which is the largest number in a range. As we are told that 66% of the population are of working age in every year, we do not actually need to use this 66% figure at all in the calculation, because its proportional effect will be the same in every year.

SET 23, Q2. Correct Answer: B

Reasoning

The people who are older than 74 years in 2020 are those who are aged 74, 73 or 72 in 2017. Since every age group is equally represented, the number of unemployed people for any given age group is one-sixtieth of the number of unemployed working age people in 2017. To calculate the latter figure we have to multiply the population by the percentage of working age people and the percentage of unemployed people of working age.

Calculation

The number of unemployed working age people in 2017:

9721559 * 0.66 * 0.045 ≈ 288730.3

The number of unemployed people at any given age between 15 and 74:

288730.3 / 60 ≈ 4812.2

The number of unemployed people at the age of 74, 73 or 72:

3 * 4812.2 = 14436.6

The answer options don't ask for exact figures, so 14436.6 corresponds to answer option B, around 14500.

Potential Shortcuts / Pitfalls

If you don't apply the scale factor of 0.66, you would end up with the incorrect figure of 21900 (option E).

You can also combine all of the calculations above, using the fact that 3 years out of 60 (i.e. those aged 15 to 74) is exactly one twentieth of the respective population:

9721559 * 0.66 * 0.045 / 20 = 14436.6

SET 23, Q3. Correct Answer: E

Reasoning

To calculate the number of people of any age who were not working in 2007 we need to calculate the number of unemployed working age people, and the number of people not of working age, and add them together. We will have to do the same for 2017. To calculate the rate of change, we must divide the number of people not working in 2017 by the number of people not working in 2007.

Calculation

The number of unemployed working age people in 2007:

10023887 * 0.66 * 0.07 ≈ 463104

The number of people not of working age in 2007:

10023887 * (1 − 0.66) ≈ 3408122

Now the number of people not working in 2007:

463104 + 3408122 = 3871226

With a similar calculation, we get the number of not working people in 2017:

9721559 * 0.66 * 0.045 ≈ 288730
9721559 * (1 − 0.66) ≈ 3305331
288730 + 3305331 = 3594061

If 3594061 is X% of 3871226, then 3871226 * (X / 100) = 3594060

X = (3594060 / 3871226) * 100
X = 92.84%, which means a (100 −92.84) = 7.16% decrease.

Potential Shortcuts / Pitfalls

If you calculate the rate of change of unemployed people aged 15-74 years, instead of using the total number of not working people, you would calculate a decrease of approximately 38% (option D).

The last steps of the calculation can also be shortened to:

3871226 − 3594061 = 277165
277165 / 3871226 = 7.16%, which is the rate of decrease

SET 24, Q1. Correct Answer: B

Reasoning

We need to calculate the total water usage of the domestic sector in both Latvia and Lithuania in 2015, and then the percentage difference between the two countries. The total water usage by the domestic sector in each country is the water usage per inhabitant multiplied by the population in 2015.

Calculation

First, we must calculate the total water usage by the domestic sector in Latvia in 2015:

56.8 * 1.986 = 112.8048

Note that since we only need to calculate a *percentage* difference between two numbers using the same unit of measurement, we don't need to determine the *actual units*.

Now we do the same calculation for Lithuania in 2015:

50.9 * 2.921 ≈ 148.6789

Finally, we need to calculate the percentage, and round it to the one decimal place:

112.8048 / 148.6789 * 100% ≈ 75.9%

Potential Shortcuts / Pitfalls

If you mistakenly calculate the percentage difference between the water usage *per inhabitant* by the domestic sectors in Latvia and Lithuania in 2015, instead of the *total* water usage, you would get the incorrect percentage of 111.6% (option D).

If you calculate the percentage difference between the populations of Latvia and Lithuania in 2015, instead of the total water usage you would get 68.0% (option A).

SET 24, Q2. Correct Answer: A

Reasoning

We need to calculate the average water usage per inhabitant for each of the five countries in both 2015 and 2010, and then calculate their difference. The average water usage per inhabitant per country is the sum of the average water usages per inhabitant in each of the 5 countries divided by 5.

Calculation

First, we must calculate the average water usage per inhabitant in each of the five countries in 2015 (in m³):

(47.1 + 43.0 + 38.9 + 56.8 + 50.9) / 5 = 47.34 m³

The same for 2010:

(44.7 + 44.4 + 38.9 + 57.4 + 34.5) / 5 = 43.98 m³

Finally, we need to calculate the difference between 2015 and 2010, and round it to one decimal place:

47.34 – 43.98 ≈ 3.4 thousand m³

Potential Shortcuts / Pitfalls
If you calculate the difference between the *totals* of water usage instead of *averages* you would get 16.8 m³ (option D).

A small shortcut lies in combining all the water usages per inhabitant, and only then dividing the difference by 5:

(47.1 + 43.0 + 38.9 + 56.8 + 50.9 – 44.7 – 44.4 – 38.9 – 57.4 – 34.5) / 5

SET 24, Q3. Correct Answer: E

Reasoning

We need to calculate the total water usage in Lithuania in 2011, then divide it by the water usage per inhabitant to get the population in 2011. To find the total water usage in Lithuania in 2011 we need to calculate the amount in 2015 by multiplying the

water usage per inhabitant by the population, and then decrease it by the amount given in the question.

Calculation

First, we must calculate the total water usage by the domestic sector in Lithuania in 2015:

50.9 * 2.921 = 148.6789 million m³

Note that the population of Lithuania is represented in millions in the figure, so we don't need to scale the resulting amount.

Now we calculate the equivalent figure for 2011:

148.6789 – 40.3 = 108.3789 million m³

Finally, we need to calculate the population of Lithuania in 2011, in millions, and round it to one decimal place:

108.3789 / 35.5 ≈ 3.1 million

Potential Shortcuts / Pitfalls
If you ignore the increase of the total water usage in Lithuania, and just scale its population to the total water usage in 2015, you would get the incorrect figure of 4.2 million (option A).

SET 25, Q1. Correct Answer: A

Reasoning

We need to work out the number of births in Croatia in 2005 and 2015 and then calculate the difference. The number of births is simply the population multiplied by the birth rate. However, before we can calculate the number of births in 2015 we must first calculate the population given the population has increased since 2005.

Calculation

First, calculate the population in 2015 given the increase from 2005 is 7.5%:

Population = 4443 * 1.075 = 4776.225

Now calculate the number of births in 2015:

4776.225 * 16.8 = 80241

Note that the population is in thousands and the birth rate is per thousand and so these cancel each other out. Also we can round to an exact number as this is a number of births and you cannot have a fractional birth.

Now calculate the number of births in 2005:

4443 * 16.5 = 73310

The difference is:

80241 − 73310 = 6931

Potential Shortcuts / Pitfalls

You must remember to take into account the scale of the units in the data tables. On this occasion they cancel each other out but this is not always the case.

Also, you can combine all the steps above by doing (16.8 * 1.075 − 16.5) * 4443. This is not quite as intuitive but it reduces the number of keystrokes and also saves the need to store partial results, which can lead to errors.

SET 25, Q2. Correct Answer: C

Reasoning

We need to calculate the total number of births for each country, add them together and then divide by 4, which is the number of countries.

Calculation

First, calculate the number of births for each country (rounding *each number of births to the nearest whole number*):

Croatia:	4443 * 16.5 = 73310
Denmark:	5417 * 11.9 = 64462
Portugal:	10547 * 14.4 = 151877
Sweden:	9293 * 11.2 = 104082

Now add all these together:

73310 + 64462 + 151877 + 104082 = 393731

And then divide this by the number of countries to get the average:

393731 / 4 = 98433

Potential Shortcuts / Pitfalls

It is important to understand that the average number of something is the total number of things divided by the number of data items. In this case it is births and countries. This is not the same as adding up all the populations and dividing by 4 (the average

population) and multiplying this by the total of all the birth rates divided by 4 (the average birth rate). This would give the incorrect figure of 100238, and as this is given as one of the answer options you might easily think you had got the calculation right.

SET 25, Q3. Correct Answer: E

Reasoning

We need to calculate the number of births in Portugal in 2005 then add in the increase in births for 2015. From this we can calculate the population of Portugal in 2015 and hence the increase in population from 2005.

Calculation

First, calculate the total number of births in 2005:

10547 * 14.4 = 151877

Therefore the total number of births in 2015 is:

151877 + 4 = 151881

Now calculate the population in 2015 that would give rise to this number of births:

Population * 13.9 = 151881
Population = 151881 / 13.9 = 10927

Now calculate the percentage change in population:

Change = (10927 − 10547) / 10547 *100 = 3.6%

Potential Shortcuts / Pitfalls

The increase in the number of births is obviously tiny (4 extra births out of a total of some 150,000). However, this small increase comes despite the birth rate having fallen between 2005 and 2015, and this means that the population must have grown. Therefore *you can immediately dismiss 3 of the possible answers*, because they have the population falling. Furthermore, as the growth in births is virtually nothing you can deduce that the fall in birth rate is basically equal to the rise in population. So, by simply calculating the fall in birth rate (13.9 − 14.4) / 14.4 = −3.6% we know that the population increased by this much.

SET 26, Q1. Correct Answer: E

Reasoning

We need to use the figures for the number of boats in the South Atlantic and the share this represents of the total to work out the total fleet size in 2013. Once we have done that, we calculate the increased fleet size in 2014 and, from that, the number of boats stationed in the Atlantic Ocean in that year.

Calculation

We know from the question that in 2013 the company had 42 fishing boats in the South Atlantic, and from the chart that this was equal to 15% of its total fleet.

Let us call the total 2013 fleet size F:

$42 = 0.15 \times F$

We now need F to be alone on one side of the equation, and everything else on the other side. We achieve this by performing the same operations on both sides of the equation. In this case, if we divide both sides by 0.15, we get there in one step:

$F = 42 / 0.15 = 280$

Now we can calculate the 2014 fleet size by increasing the 2013 size by 15%:

$280 \times 1.15 = 322$

We know that 40% of the fleet is in the South Atlantic in 2014 and 10% is in the North Atlantic, so a total of 50% of the fleet is in the Atlantic Ocean:

$322 \times 0.5 = 161$

Potential Shortcuts / Pitfalls
A couple of things to look out for:
- make sure you read off the correct data from the pie chart, as it is easier to confuse things here than in a table
- do not forget about the 15% fleet increase: disregarding this results in picking Option D

SET 26, Q2. Correct Answer: C

Reasoning

The chart does not tell us the number of fishing boats the company operates in 2013, only the proportions in each ocean. However we do not need to know the *actual 2013 fleet size* to answer the question.

We simply take the 2013 *proportion* of the fleet that is in the Pacific Ocean (10% North Pacific + 20% South Pacific = 30%) and compare that to the share it has in 2014 in a 15% increased overall fishing fleet.

Calculation

Even with an unknown 2013 fleet size, we can express how many boats the company had in the Pacific Ocean in that year:

$30\% \times \text{Fleet} = 0.3 \times \text{Fleet}$

Now for 2014. We know that the fleet size increased by 15%:

$\text{Fleet in 2014} = 1.15 \times \text{Fleet}$

We also know that the Pacific Ocean share of this total is 25%:

$25\% \times 1.15 \text{ Fleet} = 0.25 \times 1.15 \times \text{Fleet} = 0.2875 \times \text{Fleet}$

We therefore have values of 0.3 Fleet in 2013 and 0.2875 Fleet in 2014. We can calculate the difference in the usual way, by taking the difference between the two values and dividing by the originating (2013) value:

$$\frac{0.2875 \text{ Fleet} - 0.3 \text{ Fleet}}{0.3 \text{ Fleet}} = \frac{-0.0125 \text{ Fleet}}{0.3 \text{ Fleet}}$$

Notice that the unknown Fleet size is present in both the numerator and the denominator. This means that they cancel out, leaving us with a simpler calculation:

$-0.0125 / 0.3 = -0.0417$ (rounded)

Multiply this by a 100 to get a percentage:

$-0.0417 \times 100 = -4.17\%$

Potential Shortcuts / Pitfalls
The major pitfall here is the possibility of getting bogged down in the issue of how to frame the calculation when you do not have any figures for the number of boats, only proportions.

One other mistake not to make is to confuse a percentage change and a percentage point change. If you calculate the difference between 30% and 28.75% by simply subtracting one from the other, it would result in 1.25%, which is wrong – but since it is one of the answer options, it is easy to think you have got it right.

SET 26, Q3. Correct Answer: C

Reasoning

Since both oceans are home to 25% of the fishing fleet in 2014 and therefore have the same number of boats, the difference in the number of boats per square kilometre is the same as the difference in ocean size.

Calculation

To calculate the difference in ocean size, we simply subtract the size of the smaller ocean (the Indian Ocean) from the size of the larger ocean (the Pacific) and divide by the size of the smaller ocean.

Since we do not know the actual size of either ocean, only that the Pacific is 2.3 times as large as the Indian Ocean, we can think of the size of the latter as being 1. The advantage of this is that the size of the Pacific will then simply be 2.3.

Based on this, the calculation is as follows:

(2.3 – 1) / 1 = 1.3

To convert this to a percentage, we simply multiply by 100:

1.3 × 100 = 130%

Potential Shortcuts / Pitfalls

In this case it is essential to realize that you can in fact do the calculation just with the ocean sizes, without knowing the actual number of boats. If that is not immediately obvious, you might be tempted by answer option E, "impossible to tell".

A further key thing to bear in mind is that the question text states that the Pacific Ocean is 2.3 times as large as the Indian Ocean (i.e. 2.3 times larger) – this is not the same as saying that the Pacific Ocean is 230% larger than the Indian Ocean.

This distinction is nicely illuminated by using the alternative method of calculating a percentage increase. In the calculation section of chapter 6, we took the difference in size and divided by the smaller area. When it comes to percentage differences, we can also use the formula where we simply divide the larger value by the smaller value, in our case:

2.3 / 1 = 2.3

If we multiply this by 100, we get a percentage. In this case, however, we must remember that this merely gives us the *ratio* of the two values. To get the *percentage difference*, we must subtract the originating value, which is the size of the Indian Ocean in this case, which we denoted by 1 – or, in other words, by 100%:

230 – 100 = 130%

Even when the values are different, using the above calculation and then subtracting 1 or 100% works, and some people will prefer this method.

SET 27, Q1. Correct Answer: A

Reasoning

First, we must calculate 5% of the total electricity production in Q1 2014, and then work out the production per wind farm. We then calculate the total wind farm production in Q2 2014 and from that, the number of operational wind farms in that quarter.

Calculation

5% of the total Q1 2014 production gives us the production from wind farms:

12.5 x 0.05 = 0.625 GWh

There were 50 wind farms operating in this quarter, so the production of one wind farm is:

0.625 / 50 = 0.0125 GWh

Now let's calculate the total wind farm production in Q2 2014:

10.5 x 0.05 = 0.525 GWh

We now know the total wind energy production in this quarter and the production value for 1 wind farm, so we can calculate the number of wind farms that were operating in this quarter:

0.525 / 0.0125 = 42

Potential Shortcuts / Pitfalls

First, it is important to make sure to use the production figures from the chart, not the consumption figures.

Secondly, a moment's reflection will show that no real calculations are required at all in this case. We are told in the question text that that all operational wind farms produce identical amounts of electricity as each other and in each quarter. This means we can immediately rule out Answer E, as we have all the data we need to answer the question. We also know from the chart that production fell between the two quarters, which means therefore that the total number of operational wind farms must also have fallen – which rules out Answers C and D. The scale of the drop, from 12.5 to 10.5 GWh, is also clearly bigger than that from 50 to 48 (answer B), leaving answer A as the only possible option.

SET 27, Q2. Correct Answer: B

Reasoning

The definition of excess capacity as production minus consumption is given in the chart. Using this, we must first calculate the excess capacity for 2014, and from that calculate the amount exported.

We then calculate the excess capacity in the first half of 2015 and from that the amount exported.

Finally, we calculate the difference between the two export amounts to see how much more electricity Hungary needs to export in the second half of 2015 to match the 2014 export amount.

Calculation

The total excess capacity for 2014 is the sum of the excess capacities for the 4 quarters:

$12.5 – 9.8 + 10.5 – 10.1 + 13.6 – 12.1 + 14.5 – 11.5 = 7.6$ GWh

The exported amount is 79% of this:

$7.6 \times 0.79 = 6.004$ GWh

The excess capacity in the first half of 2015 was:

$10.8 – 10.7 + 15.1 – 13.4 = 1.8$ GWh

50% of this was exported:

$1.8 \times 0.5 = 0.9$ GWh

In order for the country to export as much as it did in 2014, it needs to export a total of 6.004 GWh. To achieve this, it still needs to generate the following excess capacity:

$6.004 – 0.9 = 5.104$ GWh

Which is Answer B (rounded).

Potential Shortcuts / Pitfalls
This question is basically straightforward but it involves a sequence of calculations which you have

to do systematically to avoid getting lost: excess capacity first, then the export amount, then the difference between the two years, and so on. The incorrect answer options are deliberately designed so that if you forget any of these steps, your incorrect result might match one of the incorrect answer options.

SET 27, Q3. Correct Answer: C

Reasoning

First we must calculate the quarterly production figure for Paks. Then we calculate 30% of each quarterly production value and count the number of quarters in which the Pak production figure was higher.

Calculation

The quarterly production figure for Paks is:

$14.8 / 4 = 3.7$ GWh

We now calculate 30% of the total quarterly production figures:

Q1 2014: $12.5 \times 0.3 = 3.75$ GWh
Q2 2014: $10.5 \times 0.3 = 3.15$ GWh
Q3 2014: $13.6 \times 0.3 = 4.08$ GWh
Q4 2014: $14.5 \times 0.3 = 4.35$ GWh
Q1 2015: $10.8 \times 0.3 = 3.24$ GWh
Q2 2015: $15.1 \times 0.3 = 4.53$ GWh

We can see that the Paks production figure of 3.7 GWh is greater than 30% in the case of two of the quarterly production figures.

Potential Shortcuts / Pitfalls
There is no real need to calculate 30% of each quarterly production figure. We know that Paks always produces 3.7 GWh per quarter. Therefore it will produce more than 30% of the total in any quarter in which total production is less than $3.7 / (100 / 30) = 12.33$ GWh. A glance at the chart shows that this is the case in two quarters. We have replaced six calculations with one.

SET 28, Q1. Correct Answer: B

Reasoning

We need to calculate the total number of persons in French private households in both 2007 and 2017, and then the difference between the two figures. The total number of persons is the number of households multiplied by the average number of persons per household for each year.

Calculation

First, we must calculate the total number of persons in French private households in 2017 (in thousands):

29314.4 * 2.2 = 64491.68 thousand

Now we do the same calculation for 2007:

26456.5 * 2.3 = 60849.95 thousand

Finally, we need to calculate the difference, in millions, and round it to one decimal place:

64491.68 – 60849.95 ≈ 3.6 million

Potential Shortcuts / Pitfalls
If you calculate only the difference between the number of French households in 2017 and 2007, forgetting the difference in the number of persons per household, you would get 2.9 million (option A). If you used the 2017 number of persons per household, 2.2, and then didn't adjust for the 2007 figure, you would get 6.3 million (option D). Finally, if you have the number of persons per household in 2017 and 2007 the wrong way round, you would get 9.2 million (option C).

SET 28, Q2. Correct Answer: C

Reasoning

We need to calculate the number of Italian couples with children in 2007 and 2017, and then the percentage of change between 2007 and 2017. The number of Italian couples with children for a particular year is the total number of private households in that year multiplied by the percentage of couples with children.

Calculation

First, we must calculate the number of Italian couples with children in 2017 given its share of 20.9%:

25864.7 * 0.209 = 5405.7223 thousand

Then the number of Italian couples with children in 2007 given its share of 23.5%:

23710.7 * 0.235 = 5572.0145 thousand

Finally, we calculate the percentage of change between 2007 and 2017, and round it to two decimal places:

([5405.7223 – 5572.0145] / 5572.0145) * 100 ≈ –2.98%

Potential Shortcuts / Pitfalls
If you calculate the percentage increase between the total number of households instead of the couples with children you would get 9.08% (option B). If you simply calculate the percentage of decrease as the difference between the shares in 2017 and 2007, ignoring the change in the total number of households, you would get 2.60% (option D).

SET 28, Q3. Correct Answer: C

Reasoning

We need to calculate the total number of EU-28 private households in 2018, and then multiply it by the doubled percentage share of the couples without children. The total number of EU-28 private households in 2018 can be calculated using the 2017 number and the percentage of increase.

Calculation

First, we must calculate the total number of EU-28 private households in 2018:

221326.2 * (1 + 0.0065) = 222764.820 thousand:

Second, we must calculate the number of EU-28 couples without children in 2018, then multiply it by 2 to get the number of persons, and round the answer to the nearest million:

Total number of persons without children in 2018:

222764.820 * 0.249 * 2 = 110.936880 thousand ≈ 111 million

Remember that we must multiply the number of couples by 2 if we want to get the number of persons, since obviously a couple is two persons.

Potential Shortcuts / Pitfalls
The most likely mistake in this question would be to fail to multiply the number of couples by two, forgetting that each couple consists of two persons. This would give the incorrect figure of 55 million (option B).

If you ignore the percentage of increase between 2017 and 2018, you would get the incorrect figure of 110 million (option A).

SET 29, Q1. Correct Answer: D

Reasoning

The speed is the distance travelled divided by the time it takes. When coming to the final result, we need to take into account the order of magnitude of the distance and the unit of time given in the table.

Calculation

The Earth is 150 million km from the Sun and the question tells us that the distance round its orbit is 6.3 times this, which is:

150 m × 6.3 = 945m km

The speed is then calculated as distance divided by time:

945m / 365.25 = 2.587 m km/day

This is how far the Earth travels in 1 day. For the purpose of calculating the speed per hour, then minutes, then seconds, let's add in the zeroes representing the million:

2,587,000 km/day

Divide this by 24 to calculate its speed per hour:

2,587,000 / 24 = 107,791.67 km/day

Next divide this by the number of seconds in an hour (60 minutes × 60 seconds = 3600):

107,791.67 / 3600 = 29.94 km/sec

Which is about 30 km/sec.

SET 29, Q2. Correct Answer: B

Reasoning

We need to calculate the speed of each planet, which is the distance travelled divided by the time taken. We then need to do the percentage calculation of the difference.

Calculation

The speed is distance travelled divided by time taken. The distance travelled is the distance of the planet from the Sun multiplied by 6.3.

Mercury = 365.4 million
Venus = 636.3 million

The time it takes to make these journeys is the orbital period. From this, we can calculate the speeds of both planets.

Speed of Mercury = 365.4 million / 88 days = 4.152 m km / day
Speed of Venus = 636.3 million / 224.7 days = 2.832 m km / day

Since we are going to calculate the percentage difference between these two speeds, we don't really care about what unit they are in, so we can leave them in the unusual million km / day format.

The question is how much faster Mercury is than Venus, so the percentage difference will be the difference in speeds divided by Venus's speed, multiplied by 100:

(4.152 − 2.832) / 2.832 × 100 = 46.61 %, or cca. 47%.

Potential Shortcuts / Pitfalls

The above calculation is a perfectly good way of arriving at the correct answer, but we in fact performed a couple of completely unnecessary calculations. Let's write out all the calculations we performed in one formula to see what I mean.

Mercury speed calculation: 58 × 6.3 / 88
Venus speed calculation: 101 × 6.3 / 224.7

What do we notice? The × 6.3 is present in both calculations. Since we are going to use the results of these calculations in a division, we can completely omit the × 6.3 from our process. Let's observe:

$$\frac{58 \times \cancel{6.3} / 88}{101 \times \cancel{6.3} / 224.7}$$

What does this mean? It means that *we do not need to waste our time calculating the actual speeds* when all we need for a percentage difference is their *relative* speeds in the same units.

The relative speed of Mercury is: 58 / 88 = 0.66
The relative speed of Venus is: 101 / 224.7 = 0.45

Now we can calculate the percentage difference by calculating the actual difference:

0.66 – 0.45 = 0.21

The percentage rise is this difference divided by the starting point and multiplied by 100:

100 × 0.21 / 0.45 = 47%

SET 29, Q3. Correct Answer: E

Reasoning

We need to calculate the distance between Mars and Earth and then the speed of the messages travelling between them.

Calculation

We are told that the delay in response is a minimum of 8m 40s and that this occurs when their distance is at a minimum. We are also told how to calculate this minimum distance, namely by subtracting the Earth – Sun distance from the Mars – Sun distance. This is simply:

228m – 150m = 78 million km

So, each message has to travel 78m km from Mars to Earth. But remember, the question is not about how much time it takes for the message to travel from Mars to Earth but how much time it takes to get a response. If we assume that Earth begins to reply immediately, that response still needs to travel the same distance as well, so the total distance travelled is twice as much as the Earth – Mars distance:

78m × 2 = 156m km

It takes a total of 8m 40s to do this journey. We need first to convert this into seconds which is:

8 × 60 seconds + 40 seconds = 520 seconds

So the speed is now calculated as distance divided by time:

156 million / 520 = 300,000 km/sec

Of course if you remember from school, you'll know that this is the speed of light.

Potential Shortcuts / Pitfalls
You might already know that radio signals travel at the speed of light and what the speed of light is – you should NOT, however, mark that as the correct answer without doing the calculations since the test designer is under no obligation to use realistic data (even though this is *mostly* the case).

SET 30, Q1. Correct Answer: B

Reasoning

The lowest number of error-free files is calculated by subtracting the erroneous files from the total number of files closed for each team and picking the lowest number.

Calculation

The error rate denotes the percentage of files that were closed with errors, so in order to calculate the number of error-free files, we must subtract this percentage from 100% and calculate with those figures.

The number of error-free files for the five teams are as follows.

Team A:

4 500 × (100% - 5%) = 4 500 × 95% = 4 500 × 0.95 = 4275

Team B:

4 500 × (100% - 7%) = 4 500 × 93% = 4 500 × 0.93 = 4 185

Team C:

5 000 × (100% - 11%) = 5 000 × 89% = 5 000 × 0.89 = 4450

Team D:

6000 × (100% - 8%) = 6 000 × 92% = 6 000 × 0.92 = 5 520

Team E:

6 500 × (100% - 9%) = 6 500 × 91% = 6 500 × 0.91 = 5 915

We can clearly see that Team B closed the smallest number of files without errors.

Potential Shortcuts / Pitfalls
If you take a moment to consider the two charts, you can easily figure out the correct answer without performing any calculations. The first thing to notice is that Teams A and B closed the smallest number of files (with or without errors). The only way one of those two didn't close the smallest number of error-free files is if their error rate was very low and the other three teams' error rates were disproportionately higher. This doesn't seem to be the case.

Teams D and E closed many more files and their error rates are only slightly higher, so we can safely disregard them. Team C closed only slightly more files and its error rate is much higher, so it is worth looking at it.

Team C closed 500 more files than either Team A or Team B, and its error rate is 11% compared to 5% for Team A and 7% for Team B. The only way Team C can be worse than A or B is if the difference in the error rates accounts for more files than the difference in the total number of files – this, again, doesn't seem to be the case.

The maximum difference in erroneous files is between Team A (7% of 4 500) and Team C (11% of 5 000). That is 4 percentage points, and 4 percentage points of 5 000 is never going to make up for the 500-file difference between Teams A and B on the one hand, and Team C on the other.

This leaves us with Teams A and B. Since they closed the same number of files, the correct answer is the team which has the higher error rate, namely Team B.

SET 30, Q2. Correct Answer: C

Reasoning

We need first to calculate the number of error-free closed files for Team B and Team C, and then the difference between the two values.

Calculation

The number of error-free files closed by Team B:

$4\,500 \times (100\% - 2\%) = 4\,500 \times 98\% = 4\,500 \times 0.98 = 4\,410$

The number of error-free files closed by Team C:

$5\,000 \times (100\% - 17\%) = 5\,000 \times 83\% = 5\,000 \times 0.83 = 4\,150$

The difference between the two figures is:

$4\,410 - 4\,150 = 260$

Option C is the correct answer.

Potential Shortcuts / Pitfalls

Since the answer options are quite close to each other, there isn't much leeway for shortcuts and estimations in this exercise. On the other hand, you must be careful when interpreting the changes in the error rates: contrary to how a lot of EPSO numerical

reasoning questions are worded, it is not the *change* in error rates that is given, but the *actual* new error rates – and this saves you a set of calculations which you don't have to perform.

SET 30, Q3. Correct Answer: D

Reasoning

We must first calculate the total number of files closed by the five teams throughout the year, and then what proportion of this total was closed by the end of September.

Calculation

The total number of files closed is simply the sum of the number of files closed by each team:

$Total = 4\,500 + 4\,500 + 5\,000 + 6\,000 + 6\,500 = 26\,500$

Since teams progress through files at a constant rate from month to month, we can calculate how many files they close in one month:

$26\,500 / 12 = 2\,208.33$

Since September is the 9th month of the year, we can multiply the above value by 9 to get the number of files closed by the end of that month:

$2\,208.33 \times 9 = 19\,875$ (rounded up)

Potential Shortcuts / Pitfalls

There is an alternative way of calculating this which might be quicker and could yield an even more accurate result.

If we think of September as the 9th month in a 12-month year, we can say that the teams closed 9/12th of the files. We can then use this fraction in our calculations:

$26\,500 \times 9 / 12 = 19875$

As it turns out, this method yields exactly 19 875 and there was no need for it to be rounded to match option D.

SET 31, Q1. Correct Answer: B

Reasoning

We work out the total tax owed on 55 000 EUR of income by calculating the tax owed in each tax bracket and then adding on the total insurance tax for 12 months.

Calculation

First, let's calculate the tax owed on 55 000 EUR in each of the three systems.

System 1

First 10 000 EUR: tax free

10 001 – 30 000 EUR: The tax is the amount of income falling within this range multiplied by the percentage. Since the person's income is more than 30 000 EUR, we need to calculate the tax for the full range. This is done by subtracting the top of the previous range from the top of the current range:

30 000 – 10 000 = 20 000

The tax is then:

20 000 × 15% = 20 000 × 0.15 = 3000

30 001 – 50 000 EUR:

Using the same formula as above, the tax is:

20 000 × 0.25 = 5000

We still have 5 000 EUR left to account for. This falls into the 50 001+ range.

50 001+ EUR:

5 000 × 0.31 = 1550

We must also not forget about the insurance tax, which is a flat fee of 100 EUR / month:

100 × 12 = 1200

The total tax owed is then:

3000 + 5000 + 1550 + 1200 = 10 750 EUR

We now have to do the calculations for the other two systems as well.

System 2

System 2 has no tax free allowance.

0 – 30 000 EUR: 4500 EUR tax

30 001+ EUR: 5250 EUR tax

Insurance tax: 600 EUR

Total: 10 350 EUR

System 3

System 3 has a tax free allowance of 15 000 EUR.

15 001 – 30 000 EUR: 2 550 EUR tax

30 001+ EUR: 5 500 EUR tax

Insurance tax: 2400 EUR

Total: 10 450 EUR

From the above, we can see that the person owes the smallest amount in taxes under System 2.

Potential Shortcuts / Pitfalls

Unfortunately there aren't really any shortcuts you can use for this question. However there are some potential pitfalls to watch out for. You must make sure to check whether there is a tax free allowance in the system, and it is crucially important to read and understand the description of marginal tax rate – namely that only the amount falling within the range must be taxed at the given rate.

If, for example, you look at the table for System 3 and conclude that 62 000 EUR must be taxed at 28%, and you calculate the tax at 28% for the entire amount, you will get an incorrect result.

SET 31, Q2. Correct Answer: C

Reasoning

First we must calculate the total tax owed on 62 000 EUR, and then we will divide that amount by the income and multiply by 100 to get a percentage.

Calculation

For the general logic of how to work with tax brackets, see the previous explanation.

Let's calculate the tax owed in each bracket.

0 – 15 000 EUR: no tax

15 001 – 30 000 EUR: 2 550 EUR

30 001 – 60 000 EUR: 6 600 EUR

60 001+ EUR:

There are 2 000 EUR left to tax at this rate, so the tax is:

2 000 EUR × 28% = 2 000 × 0.28 = 560

We must also not forget about the insurance tax, which is 200 EUR / month, so:

200 × 12 = 2400 EUR / year

The total tax is then:

2 550 + 6 600 + 560 + 2400 = 12 110 EUR

Now to the effective tax rate, which is calculated by dividing the above value by the person's income and multiplied by 100:

12 110 / 62 000 × 100 = 19.53%

Potential Shortcuts / Pitfalls

One error that people sometimes make is to try to calculate the effective tax rate by adding up the rates of tax in the various tax brackets and then dividing the total by the number of tax brackets: this is obviously wrong because of the different weights of the ranges.

SET 31, Q3. Correct Answer: B

Reasoning

We must first calculate the tax owed under each of the two systems using the already familiar method. We can then calculate the difference in after-tax income under the two systems and divide that difference by the value under System 3.

Calculation

Let's first calculate the tax owed under System 1.

System 1

0 – 10 000 EUR: no tax

10 001 – 30 000 EUR: 3 000 EUR tax

30 001 – 50 000 EUR: 5 000 EUR tax

50 001+ EUR: 7 750 EUR tax

Insurance tax: 1200 EUR

Total tax:

3 000 + 5 000 + 7 750 + 1 200 = 16 950 EUR

The after-tax income is then:

75 000 – 16 950 = 58 050 EUR

And now under System 3.

System 3

0 – 15 000 EUR: no tax

15 001 – 30 000 EUR: 2 550 EUR

30 001 – 60 000 EUR: 6 600 EUR

60 001+ EUR: 4 200 EUR

Insurance tax: 2 400 EUR

Total tax:

2 550 + 6 600 + 4 200 + 2 400 = 15 750 EUR

The after tax income is:

75 000 – 15 750 = 59 250 EUR

Here we must be careful to get our figures the right way round. The question asks "by what percentage is their after-tax income greater or smaller under System 1 than under System 3". If you look at the figures for Systems 1 and 3, this will tell you that the after-tax income is smaller under System 1 so we are dealing with a negative figure:

58 050 (System 1) - 59 250 (System 3) = -1 200 EUR

We must now divide this by the after-tax income for System 3, since the question compares System 1 to System 3, and multiply that by 100 to get a percentage:

-1 200 / 59 250 = -2% (rounded)

This corresponds to answer option B.

Potential Shortcuts / Pitfalls

The risk here is that if you get the comparison the wrong way round, you will calculate:

1 200 / 59 250 = 2% (rounded)

This will "look right" because it is indeed one of the answer options, C.

SET 32, Q1. Correct Answer: E

Reasoning

We must calculate the percentage each power plant's electricity production represents of the total for that country and then see which one is in the middle.

Calculation

To calculate the proportion the production of a power plant represents in the total consumption of that country, we simply divide its production by the country's consumption.

Since all of the operations we will perform are divisions, and there are five zeroes at the end of almost all consumption figures, we can simply disregard those. In the case of Venezuela, this means that we will divide by 858.5.

Itaipu Dam / Brazil:

98.3 / 4 557 = 0.02157121

Three Gorges Dam / China:

98.5 / 53 223 = 0.001850704

Krasnoyarsk / Russia:

20.4 / 10 165 = 0.002006886

Grand Coulee / USA:

20 / 38 864 = 0.0005146151

Guri / Venezuela

53.41 / 858.5 = 0.06221316

The numbers above are a little hard to compare because they are so small, but with a bit of care it is possible. We can see that Grand Coulee is the only one with 3 zeroes after the decimal point, so that will be the smallest proportion. Also, Guri and Itaipu Dam only have one zero after the decimal point, and the next number is greater (6 versus 2) in the case of Guri, so that will be the largest proportion, followed by Itaipu Dam.

This is what we have so far, from smallest to largest proportion:

Grand Coulee / USA
?
?
Itaipu Dam / Brazil
Guri / Venezuela

We are now left with Three Gorges Dam / China and Krasnoyarsk / Russia – one of them will be in the middle. Both of them have two zeroes after the decimal point, but the next number is greater in the case of Russia (2 versus 1), so we have our final order:

Grand Coulee / USA
Three Gorges Dam / China
Krasnoyarsk / Russia
Itaipu Dam / Brazil
Guri / Venezuela

Krasnoyarsk is clearly in the middle.

Potential Shortcuts / Pitfalls

There is a great opportunity to estimate here.

We can quite easily see that Guri tops the list for generating the highest proportion of its country's electricity. The Guri power plant generates more than half the electricity of either the Brazilian or Chinese power stations, but Venezuela's consumption is far smaller than that of Brazil or China.

The next smallest consumption figure belongs to Brazil, yet Itaipu Dam has the second largest production, so it must come second (while Itaipu Dam produces almost twice as much electricity as Venezuela's Guri, Brazil's consumption is about 5 times as large as Venezuela's).

If we compare the USA's consumption to China's, we see that they are fairly comparable (3.9 to 5.3) but the Grand Coulee generates only a fifth of the electricity generated by the Three Gorges Dam, so it must be in the last position.

We are now again left with Russia and China, but without having performed any calculations. The way to compare the Russian and Chinese power stations is to look at the relationship between their production and their national consumptions.

Krasnoyarsk to Three Gorges is 1 to slightly less than 5.

Russia to China, however, is 1 to slightly more than 5.

This means that the Three Gorges percentage will be lower, so it will be the fourth in the list, leaving Krasnoyarsk in the middle.

SET 32, Q2. Correct Answer: E

Reasoning

We must first calculate how much electricity is currently produced in Venezuela from the total consumption and the percentage which current production contributes to this. We will then add the capacity of the new power station to this total and subtract Venezuela's total consumption to see how much is left for export.

Calculation

To find the current total production, we calculate 78% of the total consumption of Venezuela. To keep things consistent, we should decide whether we are going to perform all calculations in TWh or MWh. We will use TWh on this occasion.

The electricity consumption of Venezuela is then:

85 850 000 MWh / 1 000 000 = 85.85 TWh

78% of this is produced by the existing power stations:

85.85 × 78% = 85.85 × 0.78 = 66.963 TWh

After the completion of the new power station (which has the same capacity as that of Guri), the new total production will be:

66.963 TWh + 53.41 TWh = 120.373 TWh

If we subtract the current total consumption from the above figure, we get the amount available for export:

120.23 TWh – 85.85 TWh = 34.523 TWh

Since this is not among the answer options, we must also convert this into MWh and check if that is correct:

34.523 TWh × 1 000 000 = 34 523 000 MWh

which is answer option E.

Potential Shortcuts / Pitfalls
There are two major issues to be careful with here.

First, we must notice and then not get confused by the different orders of magnitude represented by the two different units of measurement, as defined in a footnote to the table. In situations like this, it is advisable to make a decision about which one you will use and then consistently convert all values to that unit before performing the actual calculations.

Also, it is tempting to simply double the capacity of the Guri power station (since the new one has the same capacity) and compare that to the consumption of Venezuela. That, however, would disregard the information given in the question text, namely that current production represents 78% of the total consumption (which means there must be other power stations in the country).

SET 32, Q3. Correct Answer: D

Reasoning

The electricity consumption of the EU is unknown at the beginning of this exercise, but we know that the capacity of the Three Gorges Dam is equal to 3.24% of this, from which we can calculate the total (100%). Once we have that, we simply take 30% of this total to get the amount generated from nuclear power.

Calculation

Since the total electricity consumption of the EU is unknown, let's call it X. We do know that 3.24% of this is equal to the capacity of the Three Gorges Dam, and this capacity is a known value:

$3.24\% \times X = 98.5$ TWh

Let's convert 3.24% to a decimal:

$0.0324 \times X = 98.5$ TWh

Our aim is to find the total consumption of the EU, or X. Remember, in equations like this, we want 1 X to be alone on one side, and we achieve that by performing the same operations on both sides. Here, all we have to do is divide by 0.0324:

$X = 98.5 / 0.0324 = 3\ 040.12346$ TWh

This is the total consumption of the EU, 30% of which is produced from nuclear power:

$3\ 040.12346 \times 30\% = 3\ 040.12346 \times 0.3 = 912.04$ TWh (rounded)

Potential Shortcuts / Pitfalls
There are several things to watch out for in this question.
- do not stop after having solved the equation – that is the *total* consumption of the EU, not the share of nuclear power
- do not round prematurely: if you round the total consumption to the nearest whole number and you calculate 30% of that, you would erroneously mark option C as the correct answer
- watch out for the units of measurement: all throughout the calculations, we only worked with TWh, so be careful with the answer options expressed in MWh

SET 33, Q1. Correct Answer: C

Reasoning

We need to calculate what percentage of all washing machines are energy-efficient, and then what percentage this represents of all household appliances.

Calculation

To find the percentage of washing machines that are energy-efficient, we simply add up the percentages of A+/A and B-rated washing machines:

45% + 35% = 80%

We know that washing machines (energy-efficient and non-efficient together) represent 20% of the total of all household appliances, and 80% of these are energy-efficient:

80% × 20% = 0.8 × 0.2 = 0.16 = 16%

SET 33, Q2. Correct Answer: D

Reasoning

We need to work out the current number of refrigerators and air conditioners that are energy-efficient from their percentage share of all refrigerators and air conditioners, and then increase this number by 20%.

Calculation

The current share of energy-efficient refrigerators:

40% + 25% = 65%

And that of air conditioners:

10% + 45% = 55%

We can now calculate the number of energy-efficient units.

Refrigerators:

9 000 × 65% = 9 000 × 0.65 = 5 850

Air conditioners:

3 400 × 55% = 3 400 × 0.55 = 1 870

The current total of energy-efficient units is:

5 850 + 1 870 = 7 720

If this increases by 20%, we get:

7 720 + 20% = 7 720 × 120% = 7 720 × 1.2 = 9 264

Potential Shortcuts / Pitfalls

The key issue here is not to confuse what the question is asking and end up calculating a 20 percentage point increase rather than a 20% increase. Remember: if your share of a cake is one-half and your share increases by 20%, you will have 60% of the cake, not 70%.

If you make this mistake you will calculate as follows:

Refrigerators:

9 000 × 85% = 9 000 × 0.85 = 7 650

Air conditioners:

3 400 × 75% = 3 400 × 0.75 = 2 550

This will give you a combined total (7650 + 2550) of 10200, and as this is one of the answer options you will think you have got the question right.

SET 33, Q3. Correct Answer: D

Reasoning

We need to calculate the number of D-rated units for each of the four appliances, and then see which number is the largest.

Calculation

The number of D-rated units is the total of appliances multiplied by the percentage share that are D-rated.

Air conditioners:

25% × 3 400 = 0.25 × 3 400 = 850

Washing machines:

10% × 5 500 = 550

Dryers:

15% × 2 000 = 300

Refrigerators:

10% × 9000 = 900

From the above, we can see that D-rated refrigerators would be at the top of this list.

Potential Shortcuts / Pitfalls

It is easy to solve this question without using a calculator at all – let's see how.

10%

There are two values where 10% needs to be calculated – we can do this by simply taking away a 0 from the end of the figure.

15%

First we calculate 10%. Then we take half of that value and add it to the 10%. 15% of 2 000 then becomes 200 + 100 = 300.

25%

Calculating 25% of 3 400 seems to be the hardest of the four to calculate, but if you think of 25% as one quarter, it becomes much simpler. But how much is one quarter of 3 400? Again, if you think of 3 400 as 3 200 + 200, then you can take one quarter of both and add these two numbers up.

One quarter of 3 200 is the same as one quarter of 32 (plus the zeroes). Since 32 is 8 × 4, this is 800. One quarter of 200 is 50, so the result here is 850.

SET 34, Q1. Correct Answer: C

Reasoning

We need to calculate the number of persons in Norway aged 0-14 in 2007 and in 2017, and then work out the difference. The number of persons aged 0-14 is the total of the Norwegian population multiplied by the share who are 0-14. The population of Norway in 2007 can be calculated using the population in 2017 and the amount of increase between 2007 and 2017.

Calculation

First, we must calculate the number of persons in Norway aged 0-14 in 2017 (in thousands):

5.258 * 1000 * 0.178 = 935.924 thousand

Note that since the population of Norway is represented in millions in the diagram, we needed to multiply it by 1000 to get our results into thousands.

Second, we calculate the population of Norway in 2007:

5.258 * 1000 – 577 = 4681 thousand

Third, the number of persons in Norway aged 0-14 in 2007:

4681 * 0.194 = 908.114 thousand

Finally, we need to calculate the difference, and round it to the nearest thousand:

935.924 – 908.114 ≈ 28 thousand

Potential Shortcuts / Pitfalls

If you calculate the difference between the numbers aged 0-14 in the two years, ignoring the change in share from 19.4% in 2007 to 17.8% in 2017, you would get the incorrect figure of 103 thousand (using the 2017 share, option D), or 112 thousand (using the 2007 share, option E). If you calculate the difference while ignoring the increase in the total Norwegian population referred to in the question text, you would get –84 thousand (option B).

A shortcut lies in combining all the steps shown above, and factoring out the population of Norway in 2017:

577 * 0.194 – 5258 * (0.194 – 0.178)

This would reduce the number of keystrokes and arithmetical operations.

SET 34, Q2. Correct Answer: B

Reasoning

We need to calculate the number who are 15 years old or over in both Denmark and Finland in 2017, and then the percentage difference between these numbers. The number who are 15 years old or over is the total population multiplied by the sum of the shares of two age groups, 15-64 years old, and 65 years old or older.

Calculation

First, we must calculate the number who are 15 years old or over in Denmark in 2017 (in millions):

5.77 * (0.643 + 0.191) = 4.81218 million

Now the equivalent figure for Finland:

5.503 * (0.628 + 0.209) = 4.606011 million

Finally, we calculate the percentage difference between Denmark and Finland, and round it to two decimal places:

(4.81218 / 4.606011 – 1) * 100% ≈ 4.48%

Potential Shortcuts / Pitfalls

A likely mistake would be to use just the figure for those aged 15-64, rather than adding in the 65+ age group. This would give you 7.36% (option C).

If you did your calculations by treating the percentage change just as the difference between the respective shares of the major groups, ignoring the population of the countries, you would get –0.30% (option E).

SET 34, Q3. Correct Answer: A

Reasoning

We need to calculate the change in the share of persons aged 15-64 years for each of the five countries shown in the table, and then calculate the average as the sum divided by five. The change of share for a country is the difference between the respective shares in 2017 and 2007.

Calculation

First, we must calculate the change of the share of persons aged 15-64 years for each of the five countries shown in the table (in percent):

Denmark = 64.3 – 66.1 = –1.8
Finland = 62.8 – 66.5 = –3.7
Iceland = 66.2 – 67.1 = –0.9
Norway = 65.5 – 66.0 = –0.5
Sweden = 62.6 – 65.6 = –3.0

Second, we must calculate the average of the values calculated in the previous steps:

Average = (–1.8 – 3.7 – 0.9 – 0.5 – 3.0) / 5 = –1.98

Potential Shortcuts / Pitfalls

If you simply add up the different percentage changes and forget to average them, you would get the incorrect figure of –9.90 (option B).

You can combine all the steps shown above to reduce the number of keystrokes:

(64.3 – 66.1 + 62.8 – 66.5 + 66.2 – 67.1 + 65.5 – 66.0 + 62.6 – 65.6) / 5

SET 35, Q1. Correct Answer: E

Reasoning

The productivity of the employees is calculated by dividing the production volume by the number of employees.

Calculation

Craybourne Woodlands: 8 000 / 50 = 160 tonnes
Stirling Forest: 14 000 / 80 = 175 tonnes

Woodcombe Hills Woods: 3000 / 30 = 100 tonnes
Hampton Forest: 3000 / 30 = 100 tonnes
Frasier Green: 8000 / 40 = 200 tonnes

The correct answer is therefore Frasier Green (E).

Potential Shortcuts / Pitfalls

The above calculations are straightforward enough but we can reduce the number of calculations further. Just by looking at the ratio of production to employees, we can see straight away that Hampton Forest and Woodcombe Hills Woods employees each contribute half as much as those of Frasier Green (30:3 versus 80:4). Also, Craybourne Woodlands' employees clearly produce less than those of Frasier Green as the total production is the same but the number of employees is greater.

Be careful here to perform the calculations on production volume, not the volume actually utilised / sold.

SET 35, Q2. Correct Answer: E

Reasoning

First, we calculate the number of outdoor furniture shipments that were actually produced. Then, we calculate the total production volume for roofing, take 10% of it, and calculate how many outdoor furniture shipments that would have made up. We get the total by adding up the two numbers.

Calculation

The total volume used for outdoor furniture:

4 000 + 5 900 + 1 200 + 1 300 + 2 800 = 15 200

The total volume used for roofing:

2000 + 3800 + 1600 + 1600 + 4000 = 13 000

10% of the roofing figure is:

13 000 / 10 = 1300

The new total volume to be utilised for outdoor furniture:

15200 + 1300 = 16 500

With 50 tonnes per shipment, this adds up to:

16 500 / 50 = 330 shipments, which is Answer E.

Potential Shortcuts / Pitfalls

Notice how we saved time by only calculating the number of shipments (dividing by 50 tonnes) using the grand total, i.e. not twice, once for the original volume and once for the overall volume.

SET 35, Q3. Correct Answer: A

Reasoning

Similarly to how we calculated productivity, we need to divide the total production utilised for roofing by the total number of employees across all forestries.

Calculation

The total production utilised for roofing is:

$2\,000 + 3\,800 + 1\,600 + 1\,600 + 4\,000 = 13\,000$

The total number of employees is:

$50 + 80 + 30 + 30 + 40 = 230$

The roofing production of one employee, on average, is then:

$13\,000 / 230 = 56.52$ tonnes (rounded)

Potential Shortcuts / Pitfalls

An important thing to notice is that we calculated the average by adding up all the production volumes and we divided it by the total number of employees.

A typical mistake would be to divide each production volume by the corresponding number of employees. This is incorrect because it does not take into account the relative weight of each forestry in the average. For example, Frasier Green produces twice as much roofing wood as Craybourne Woodlands but with fewer employees.

SET 36, Q1. Correct Answer: A

Reasoning

We need to calculate the difference in revenue between 5 glasses of wine and a whole bottle.

Calculation

Calculate the price of 5 glasses of each wine and subtract the price of the whole bottle:

Chablis – $5 \times 8.95 - 31.95 = 12.80$
Chardonnay – $5 \times 7.50 - 28.50 = 9.00$
Margaux – $5 \times 7.15 - 27.00 = 8.75$
Sancerre – $5 \times 9.20 - 34.80 = 11.20$
Tavel – $5 \times 7.95 - 29.50 = 10.25$

From this we can see that Chablis is clearly the highest.

Potential Shortcuts / Pitfalls

Unlike with many questions of this type, you *cannot* omit the '5 x' that appears on each line because it is not applied to the bottle price as well. If the bottle price was multiplied or divided by the glass price (for example if the question had been about the highest *percentage* of extra profit) then the '5 x' would be common to all terms and could be omitted.

SET 36, Q2. Correct Answer: C

Reasoning

We need to calculate the profit on 1 bottle of Sancerre and then work out the number of bottles sold by dividing the total profit by the profit on one bottle.

Calculation

The first thing to do is to figure out what the unknown is in the question. We can set this to be *either* the profit on one bottle *or* the price of a bottle before profit. Whichever we choose, we will end up being able to determine the profit on one bottle of Sancerre.

If the cost of a bottle of Sancerre before profit is B then:

$B + Profit = 34.80$

We know that the profit rate is 220%. What does this mean? It means that the profit is 2.2 times as much as the cost of a bottle before profit, so:

$B + 2.2 \times B = 34.80$

We can now perform various operations to get 1 B (price of a bottle before profit) on one side:

$3.2 \times B = 34.8$
$B = 34.80 / 3.2 = 10.875$

This is the cost of a bottle before profit, and so the profit on each bottle is the selling price minus this cost price:

$34.8 - 10.875 = 23.925$

If the profit on one bottle is 23.925 then the number of bottles needed to produce 287.10 profit is:

287.1 / 23.925 = 12

Potential Shortcuts / Pitfalls

This question may appear more difficult than it really is simply because the profit is more than 100%. Treat it in the same way as any other profit margin. The crucial juncture at which you could go down the wrong path is how you define the price of the bottle before profit: if you say that it is the selling price divided by 2.2, that is incorrect: it would only be correct if the profit rate was 120%.

SET 36, Q3. Correct Answer: B

Reasoning

We need to calculate the revenue from one bottle of wine when sold by the glass and then calculate the percentage difference from the point of view of the revenue when sold by the bottle.

Calculation

We first need to calculate the number of glasses in one bottle:

750 / 187.5 = 4

The revenue from 4 glasses will be:

4 × 7.95 = 31.80

The percentage increase in revenue is the difference in revenue when sold by the glass compared with when sold by the bottle, divided by the revenue when sold by the bottle and multiplied by 100:

100 × (31.80 – 29.50) / 29.50 = 7.8%

Potential Shortcuts / Pitfalls

Most of this could be done by mental arithmetic for speed. Let's see how this can be accomplished.

750 / 187.5 – this seems to be quite close to 800 / 200, which is 4 – so let's assume this is 4 as well.

4 × 7.95 – this is almost the same as 4 × 8, so let's work with that – the result is 32. We only need to subtract 4 × 0.05 to get the accurate result, which is 31.8.

The revenue from a bottle is 29.50. The difference in revenue would then be 2.30 and the percentage

difference can then be calculated using a calculator.

With some practice and confidence, this method can be significantly faster than typing everything in.

SET 37, Q1. Correct Answer: A

Reasoning

Speed is calculated as distance divided by time. Since the answer options are in metres / second, and the distance is already given in metres, the easiest thing to do is convert the winning time into seconds.

Calculation

The total time taken for the medley was 3 minutes and 48.7 seconds, which we need to convert to seconds before we can use it. To do this, multiply the minutes by 60 and add in the seconds:

(3 × 60) + 48.7 = 228.7

The winner spent 26.2% of the total time doing the butterfly leg of the race, which is:

228.7 × 0.262 = 59.92s

So, he travelled 100m (one fourth of the total distance of 400 metres) in 59.92 seconds, which gives an average speed of:

100m / 59.92s = 1.67 m/s

SET 37, Q2. Correct Answer: C

Reasoning

The speed is calculated by dividing the distance covered by the time taken. The percentage difference is then the difference divided by the *slower* speed (since the question was how much faster the gold medallist was) and then multiplied by 100.

Calculation

Before we can calculate the speeds we must first convert the times into seconds. This is done by multiplying the minutes by 60 and then adding in the seconds:

1m 58.31s = 60 + 58.31 = 118.31
1m 59.88s = 60 + 59.88 = 119.88

The winner's speed is then:

200 / 118.31 = 1.6905 m/s

And the bronze medal winner's speed is:

200 / 119.88 = 1.6683 m/s

The percentage difference is:

100 × (1.6905 – 1.6683) / 1.6683 = 1.3%

Potential Shortcuts / Pitfalls
Because the men are racing over the same distance (200 metres), we do not actually need to calculate their speeds – the percentage difference in the *times* it took to swim the distance will be the same as the percentage difference between their *speeds* would be.

Following this logic, we can simply our calculation to:

$$\left(\frac{119.88\ 0\ 118.31}{119.88}\right) * 100 = 1.3\%$$

Note that we divided the difference by the higher number. Why? The higher number represents the time of the slower swimmer (the bronze medallist). Since the question asked how much faster the gold medallist was than the bronze medallist, we need to calculate the percentage increase on the basis of the slower swimmer's time.

SET 37, Q3. Correct Answer: B

Reasoning

The calculation for speed is distance divided by time and the calculation for distance is speed multiplied by time. We will use the first to calculate the silver medallist's speed in the last segment of the race, and the latter to calculate the distance he covered after the gold medallist completed the race.

Calculation

The overall average speed of the silver medal winner is calculated by dividing the distance by the time taken:

100m / 50.99s = 1.96 m/s

In the last few metres of the race he was travelling 10% faster than this:

1.96 × 1.1 = 2.16 m/s

The difference in time between the gold and silver medallists is:

50.99 – 50.91 = 0.08s

So, he was swimming at 2.16 m/s for 0.08 seconds; therefore in that time he travelled:

2.16m/s × 0.08s = 0.173m

which to the nearest centimetre is 17.

SET 38, Q1. Correct Answer: E

Reasoning

Domestic consumption is defined in the note to the table as production minus exports plus imports so we need to establish how much of its own production the US used itself and how much was added to this by imports.

From the table we know what 27% of US production amounts to, so we can calculate the quantity that the US does not export, which will be 100% - 27% = 73% of its production:

23.8 / 27 x 73 = 64.35 million tonnes

We can also establish the amount of imports to the USA from China. The Chinese export quantity, 279.5 million tonnes, is known, and we also know that this represents 34% of Chinese production. Further, we are told in the question text that 30% of Chinese production is exported to the US:

279.5 / 34 x 30 = 246.62 million tonnes

We now have a total of 64.35 + 246.62

= 310.97 million tonnes

At this point, however, we hit a problem because we do not have any data on the proportion of exports from any of the other regions that went to the USA. Without this information we cannot complete the calculation and so must choose Answer option E, "Cannot say".

Calculation

Following the reasoning above, we cannot do this calculation.

Potential Shortcuts / Pitfalls

The risk with this question is that you assume it must be possible to determine the quantity and waste valuable time in trying to make the data do this.

A particular danger is that you successfully calculate the amount of US production used domestically and the quantity of imports from China, as above, but forget about the lack of data for imports from other regions. If you do this you will choose Answer C, which is 310.97 million tonnes.

SET 38, Q2. Correct Answer: C

Reasoning

We must calculate the 2013 export volume for both Japan and EU by using the % change between 2013 and 2014 shown in the table.

Calculation

The 2013 export volume for the EU is identical to the 2014 export volume: 55.9 million tonnes.

To calculate the 2013 export volume for Japan, we need to consider the % change from 2013 to 2014. If we think of the 2013 export volume as X, we can write the following equation:

2013 export volume (X) – 2% = 2014 export volume = 21 million tonnes

In more usable terms:

98% of 2013 export volume = 21 million tonnes

From this, it is easy to calculate the 2013 export volume by dividing by 98 and multiplying by 100:

21 / 98 x 100 = 21.43 million tonnes (rounded)

We can now calculate the difference between the EU and Japanese export volumes:

55.9 – 21.43 = 34.47

And from this, the percentage difference:

34.47 / 21.43 = 1.6085 x 100 = 160.85%

Rounded, this is 161%.

Potential Shortcuts / Pitfalls

Be careful with data expressed as a percentage change between two years. Imagine we know a value for 2014 is 50 and that it is 20% higher than the figure for 2013.

The temptation is to simply deduct 20% from the 2014 value to get the 2013 value. If we do that we get a 2013 value of 40, which is incorrect. Think of the problem in terms of having an unknown number (X = the 2013 value) that increases by 20% to result in the known value (50). Thus we calculate X + 20% = 50, which becomes 50/120 x 100, giving us 41.66 (rounded). If you approach the problem this way, you can ensure that you will perform the correct calculation.

SET 38, Q3. Correct Answer: C

Reasoning

Using data from both the chart and the table, and the statement in the question that production in every region was the same in 2013 as in 2014, we need to calculate the 2013 share of exports from the production of the various regions in 2013 and then what percentage total exports make up of total global production.

Calculation

To calculate the 2013 share of exports in the various regions, we need to take into account the percentage changes. To do this, the easiest thing to do is to think of the 2013 export percentages as unknown values (X) and see how they compare to the 2014 percentages. In the case of China, this would be:

X + 3% of X = 34%
1.03X = 34%

The 2013 export share in China is then:

X = 34 / 1.03 = 33%

For the other regions:

USA: X = 27/1.05 = 25.7% (rounded)
Japan: X = 19 / 0.98 = 19.4% (rounded)
EU: X = 34% (as there was no change between 2013 and 2014)
Rest of World: X = 62 / 1.09 = 56.9% (rounded)

Next, we can calculate what share of global production each of the above export shares makes up by multiplying the share of each region's production from the global total by the export share. For example, for China, this is:

50% x 33% = 50% x 0.33 = 16.5%

For the other regions the figures are:

USA: 5% x 0.257 = 1.285%
Japan: 7% x 0.194 =1.358%
EU: 10% x 0.34 = 3.4%
Rest of World: 28% x 0.569 = 15.9% (rounded)

To get the total export share, we simply add up the above percentages:

16.5 + 1.285 + 1.358 + 3.4 + 15.9 = 38.443%

This is roughly 38%, so the correct answer is C.

Potential Shortcuts / Pitfalls

The calculations described above would be very time-consuming to perform, which you should take as a hint that they might not actually be necessary.

The key words in this question are "approximately" in the question text and "around" in the answer options. This should tell you that you can estimate the correct answer without calculating it to a high degree of accuracy. The level of accuracy you need to achieve depends on how much the answer options differ from each other so you need to make an initial judgement on this.

Let's look at the shortcuts.

1. We can see from the 4th column of the table that the export share of production while rising a bit didn't change radically from 2013 to 2014 overall. So we can try using the 2014 figures to aim for an approximate result, saving a lot of calculations. Very importantly, the answer options – 6%, 14%, 38%, 50%, 70% – are far apart, which suggests we can be fairly generous with our approximating.

2. The 3rd column of the table tells us that China and Rest of the World were overwhelmingly the dominant factors in exports so we can put aside the other regions unless we can't get a clear result from the China and Rest of the World data.

3. The 2nd column of the table tells us that in 2014 China exported 34% of its production and the Rest of the World 62%. Although the 2013 shares for each were lower, they are still in the same ballpark relative to the spread in the answer options. We can immediately tell therefore that answers A (6%) and B (14%) are far too low and E (70%) is far too high. That leaves us with just C (38%) and D (50%) to decide between.

4. At this point we can't avoid doing some calculations, but we can do some serious rounding:

Export % of Rest of World = ca. 60%

Global production share of Rest of World = ca. 30%
Share of exports from global production = ca. 60 x 0.3 = 20%
Export % of China = ca. 30%
Global production share of China = 50%
Share of exports from global production = ca. 30 x 0.5 = 15%
Total: 20% + 15% = 35%

The net result of all of this is very approximate, but it's close enough for our purposes to choose answer option C, 38%. We can get closer by calculating more of the variables but in this case it's unnecessary as the only alternative answer we were left with, 50%, is too far away.

SET 39, Q1. Correct Answer: B

Reasoning

We need to calculate the proportion of total electricity generated by tidal power and then determine that as a percentage of the 2005 total.

Calculation

We need to calculate the proportion of electricity generated by tidal power. Clearly, the big unknown in this exercise is the *total* electricity generated: we aren't told this number, so let us assume that the total power generated in 2005 was E. The question states that this rose by 10% in 2010 to:

$E \times 1.1 = 1.1E$

From the *table* we can see that 6.5% of this was generated by 'Other' means in 2010:

$1.1E \times 0.065 = 0.0715E$

The *pie chart* tells us that 38% of this was due to tidal power:

$0.0715E \times 0.38 = 0.02717E$

The *question* tells us that this doubled over the 5 years so in 2005 it was:

$0.02717E / 2 = 0.013585E$

To calculate this as a percentage of the total power generated in 2005, we need to divide by that total and then multiply by 100. We assumed that total was E at the beginning, so it is quite easy from this point on:

$(0.01358E / E) \times 100 = 1.3585\%$

which is rounded to 1.36%.

SET 39, Q2. Correct Answer: A

Reasoning

We need to calculate the total amount of electricity generated from 'other', and then calculate the solar power production.

Calculation

First, we need to calculate the total electricity generated from 'other'. The question tells us that 2.4 million kWh is the total generated from biomass, and the pie chart tells us this is 36% of 'other' generation. We can use this to calculate the total 'other' generation using the familiar 'reverse' method.

Other × 36% = 2.4
Other × 0.36 = 2.4
Other = 2.4 / 0.36 = 6.67

The table tells us that 'other' generation is, in turn, just 6.5% of the total generated which using the same method is:

6.67 / 0.065 = 102.62

5.2% of this total is generated by solar power, which is:

102.62 × 0.052 = 5.3mKwh

Potential Shortcuts / Pitfalls
It is usually good advice that you should *estimate whenever possible* to avoid the use of the clumsy calculator. This instance demonstrates that this advice has its limits. Let's say you decide to estimate the answer in this question. Quite quickly you would run into the problem that it is very hard to round up or down while also preserving at least a modest level of accuracy and therefore a chance to pick the correct answer at the end. This is made even more difficult by the fact that the answer options are quite close to each other.

Always consider these factors before deciding which method to use in calculating the answer.

SET 39, Q3. Correct Answer: A

Reasoning

We need to calculate the percentage change in fossil fuel generation.

Calculation

To calculate the total generated by fossil fuel, we need to know the overall total, which isn't given, so we can substitute the 2005 total with E. Then, the total generated by fossil fuel is:

E × 0.811 = 0.811E

In 2010, the overall total rose by 10% to:

E × 1.1 = 1.1E

So, in 2010, fossil fuel generation was:

1.1E × 0.764 = 0.8404E

This is a difference of:

0.8404E − 0.811E = 0.0294E

As a percentage of the 2005 generation this is:

100 × 0.0294E / 0.811E = 3.6%

Potential Shortcuts / Pitfalls
Once again, the *actual total figure is not required* as it cancels out in the last step.

There are, however, several pitfalls you can fall into along the way:

1. At first glance, you might look at the two fossil fuel percentages and say that the change is actually 81.1 − 76.4 = 4.7 %. This would be wrong on many fronts; for example it doesn't take into account the 10% rise in total generation or the fact that this would be a *percentage point* change.

2. You could also calculate the above by dividing the difference (4.7%) by the starting value (81.1), but again, this would not take into account the rise in total production.

SET 40, Q1. Correct Answer: E

Reasoning

Since the genders are represented equally, we know that there are 500 boys in the sample. The chart tells us that the percentage of boys who like reading was 32% in 2010 and 24% in 2014, so we have to turn those percentage shares into actual numbers. We then convert the 2014 number to a percentage of the 2010 number.

Calculation

The number of boys who like reading in 2010:

$500 * 0.32 = 160$

The equivalent number in 2014:

$500 * 0.24 = 120$

If 120 is X percent of 160 then $160 * (X / 100) = 120$

$X = (120 / 160) * 100, X = 75\%$

If the number in 2014 is 75% of the number in 2010, that means a 25% decrease, which is answer E.

Potential Shortcuts / Pitfalls

If you just subtract the 2014 percentage value, 24%, from the value for 2010, 32%, you would get the incorrect answer of 8% (option A).

There are two shortcuts.

Once you have done the first two calculations you can forget the calculator and do the rest in your head. The number of boys who like reading decreased from 160 to 120, i.e. by 40. You can see straight away that the decrease is one-quarter of the value in 2010. In other words, it is a 25% decrease.

Even better is simply to calculate the percentage decrease between the two given percentage values, 32% and 24%, using the formula $(32 - 24) / 32 = 25\%$. Doing it this way we don't actually need the sample size and indeed the calculation is instantly done with a bit of mental arithmetic.

SET 40, Q2. Correct Answer: D

Reasoning

To find the number of boys in the sample, we have to calculate the number of which 150 is 32% (the percentage of boys who like reading in 2012, according to the chart); then we do an analogous calculation for the girls. We then add the results together to get the full sample size.

Calculation

Let the number of boys in the sample be X:

$X * 0.32 = 150.$
$X \approx 469$

Now let Y be the number of of girls in the sample:

$Y * 0.36 = 150$, so $Y \approx 417$

Therefore the total sample size is $469 + 417 = 886$

Potential Shortcuts / Pitfalls

You can combinine all of the calculations above as $150 / 0.32 + 150 / 0.36$, or, after factorizing, as $150 (1 / 0.32 + 1 / 0.36)$, which would reduce the number of operations.

SET 40, Q3. Correct Answer: E

Reasoning

We don't have enough information to answer this question.

Since all four age groups are equally represented in the sample of 1000 children, we know that there were 250 children in each age group. And since in each age group the genders were equally represented, we also know that there were 125 boys and 125 girls in each age group.

We know from the chart that in the 9-11 age group 38% of children like reading, so we can work out that there were $250 * 0.38 = 95$ children who liked reading in that age group. However, we have no information about *how many of those were boys*. Likewise, while we know that there were 500 boys altogether in the sample, of whom $500 * 0.32 = 160$ liked reading, we have no information as to *which age group* they belonged.

Potential Shortcuts / Pitfalls

If you use the given percentage of 38% for the 9-11 age group in 2010 you would get $125 * 0.38 = 48$ boys. As this is answer option B you would assume that you had been able to solve the problem.

9.   Succeeding in Abstract Reasoning Tests

In an EPSO abstract reasoning test you are presented with a series of figures in a sequence which follows some rules you are not told. You are also given a second set of figures (A, B, C, D, E) as answer options, from which you must choose the correct one to answer the question "Which of the following figures comes next in the series?" (or similar).

It can certainly be a daunting experience to face such a test for the first time. Your eyes will tend to scan the shapes of the figures in a haphazard fashion. You finally get an idea about the possible rules, and then look at the figures in the answer options to see which one fits. And then you realise that the figure you carefully selected would only fit the series pattern if just one thing was a little bit different. So now you must start all over again...

But, just as in the case of verbal and numerical reasoning tests, understanding the principles involved and a systematic approach to applying them can produce results much more reliably and quickly.

As part of such a systematic approach, let us therefore first review the various abstract reasoning test types, which are based on:

- the use or avoidance of colours

- the logical relationship between the various figures, whether they are part of a series, a grid, or if there is one figure which is the odd-one-out

- the number of dimensions in the test (two- or three-dimensional tests both exist)

Fortunately, it is now known that EPSO have chosen a type of abstract reasoning test that is very well defined:

- only black-and-white images are used (possibly with various shades of grey)

A typical abstract question: *Which figure is next in the series?*

A   B   C   D   E

- only two-dimensional tests are given

- only series-type questions are used

- five items of the series are shown, and the candidate must select the next, sixth item

- there are usually five answer options (though EPSO may vary this).

In abstract reasoning tests, the most important skill is learning to identify the components. Let us look at these one-by one:

- Building blocks: the building blocks of abstract reasoning tests are the following:

  - **Shapes and patterns** are the actual visual objects that are used to construct the figures in the test: triangles, squares, circles and other geometric shapes, as well as the physical properties of these objects: striped, dotted or solid fill patterns

  - **Operations** are various visual changes that these objects can undergo, such as colour inversion, multiplication, rotation, change of position, and countless others

  - **Rules** are text-based descriptions of the relationship between the various shapes/patterns and the operations affecting them

  In this chapter, we will:

- Introduce how abstract reasoning tests are designed: insight into the thought process that is behind the creation of abstract reasoning tests will be very valuable when you are on the other side, that is, when taking such tests

- Introduce the various building blocks, typical shapes, patterns and operations that you will encounter in abstract reasoning tests

- Discuss how to approach abstract reasoning tests

- Provide tips on how to prepare for them

By identifying the building blocks of a test item and systematically looking for the above patterns and operations, you will quickly be able to identify the rules that the question author invented to create the figures and the answer options.

Consequently, you will be able to "generate" or "anticipate" the correct figure in your mind without even looking at the answer options. This method is highly reliable since you will not select one of the answer options as the correct answer just because it seems the best or most suitable option: you will also have independent confirmation – the figure you came up with yourself based on the rule(s) you have figured out.

How Are Abstract Reasoning Tests Designed?

In this section, we will provide a look into the "workshop" of abstract reasoning test designers and, through a real test example, introduce how abstract reasoning exercises are designed.

As mentioned earlier, EPSO exclusively uses the series type tests in its competitions. In this type of abstract reasoning test, the test taker is asked to find the figure that correctly completes a series.

If we identify the rule, we will not only be able to tell which figure will be the sixth one (as in the example above), but also the ninth or the sixteenth one.

When designing an abstract reasoning test, the designer has specific steps to take:

1. The designer decides what shapes and patterns will be used in the tests. Based on the sample test above, let's say we will use basic geometric shapes (circles and squares).

2. Next, the designer has to decide on the difficulty level of the test. The importance of this lies in the fact that the number of rules (generally) correlates with the difficulty of the test.

3. Once the rules and the shapes/operations are identified and drawn, the designer needs to come up with one correct and several incorrect answer options. The trick to keep in mind here is that the incorrect answer options are not random – they all follow the rules of the test item up to a point, then deliberately err in one or more respects, thus making them *almost* correct.

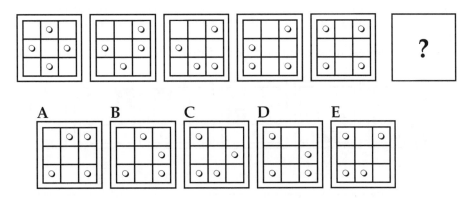

Consider the sample item above. We can identify the following building blocks:

- unshaded **circles**

- **squares** forming 3x3 areas.

    The first rule you may notice is the movement of the circles. We might describe this as follows:

***Rule #1**: One by one, the circles move in a clockwise direction.*

    Based on this rule we can quickly find the correct answer – which is **option D.**

    Let's see how we could make this test item a bit harder.

    If you look at the sample item below, you will immediately realize that a new building block was introduced: **shaded squares**.

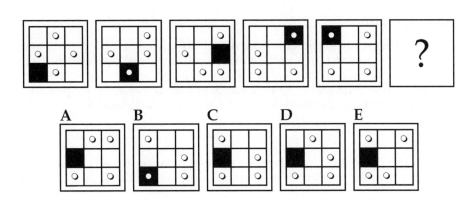

Before we try to find the rule governing the shading of certain squares, notice that the rule we came up with above still holds:

Rule #1: *One by one, the circles move in a clockwise direction.*

This rule, however, does not explain the appearance of shaded squares, as any number of different images could be correct from the answer options. We need to identify the second rule:

Rule #2: *The shading alternatingly takes one and two steps in an anticlockwise direction.*

The only answer option that matches both of these rules is **option C**.

Note how close option B is to be the correct answer, but deliberately misusing the second rule.

We can make the test item even harder by introducing another additional component:

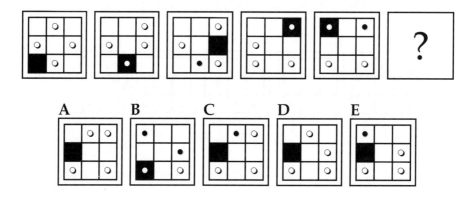

Notice that, again, a new building block and rule must have been introduced governing the appearance of the **shaded circle**. We can describe this regularity as follows:

Rule #3: *Circles that stood on a shaded square will become shaded themselves for a turn.*

The only answer option matching all three rules is **option E**.

As a summary, let us overview what techniques we can use to understand the thought process of the designer of the test items better:

- Determining what building blocks to use (unshaded/shaded squares and circles) and the number of rules governing their change
- Eliminating answer options based on each rule we have identified

Patterns and Operations

Now that we have seen the basic components of abstract reasoning tests and the way they are designed, it is time to turn to the various patterns and operations that you must be aware of and able to recognize in order to quickly and efficiently solve these tests.

It would be of course impossible to take stock of all the possible shapes and patterns, but we will try to give a comprehensive overview in the next section.

Rotation

Figs. 1 and 2 on the opposite page shows a simple rotation by 45° clockwise. You can gain the necessary routine in identifying rotations by taking the time to sit down with a piece of paper and a pencil, draw various shapes and then redraw them after rotating them various degrees in either direction, clockwise or counter-clockwise.

The example below shows a different kind of rotation. In strict geometrical terms, the relationship between the two figures is not rotation at all, yet for convenience's sake, we will discuss it in this section.

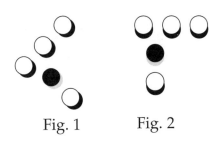

Fig. 1   Fig. 2

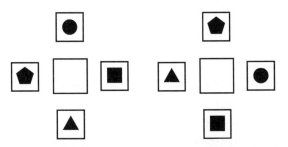

In the two figures, the small icons in the small squares around the larger one in the middle swap places with their neighbours in a clockwise direction. In a sense we can say that the icons "rotate" along an imaginary circle around the larger square.

Axial Reflection

The two examples on the right show the geometrical operation called "axial reflection". The thin lines between the two figures in each of the two sets represent an imaginary mirror. In the first set, the figure on the right is the reflection of the figure on the left in the "mirror" in the middle and vice versa. This is an example of a horizontal reflection.

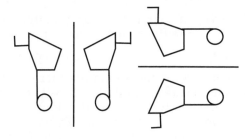

Horizontal reflection   *Vertical reflection*

The second set represents a so-called vertical reflection. While for demonstration's sake the examples show the horizontal reflection side by side and the vertical reflection with one figure below the other, in real tests this may not always be the case.

Vertical reflection

In the example on the left, the figure on the right is still the vertical "reflection" of the figure on the left, but the placement of the second figure does not correspond with where it would actually be in a strictly geometrical sense, that is, below the first image – this makes it harder to consider the relationship between the two figures as a reflection.

You can practice the recognition of this operation in the same cost-effective way as described above for rotations – all you need is paper, a pencil and loads of patience.

Patterns and Inversions

"Which of the following figures completes the series?"

In the example on the top right, a new building block component is introduced – patterns. The example features three of the next page shapes:

- Stars

- Circles
- Rhombuses

... and three distinct patterns or "fills":

- No fill (or solid white fill)
- Solid black fill
- Solid Grey fill

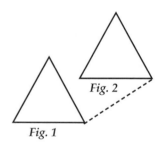

Looking at the sample test, we notice that two "operations" take place:

- The shapes in each figure change places according to some rule
- The patterns (or fill) of the rhombuses and the circle also change according to some rule
- The pattern (or fill) of the star never changes

After further observation, we can establish the following rules regarding the patterns:

Rule #1a: If a rhombus has a grey fill, change it to solid black in the next step. If it has a solid black fill, change it to a grey pattern in the next step.

Rule #1b: If a circle has a grey pattern, change it to solid white in the next step. If it has a solid white fill, change it to a grey pattern in the next step.

Rule #1c: Always leave the star's pattern unchanged.

There are of course many other combinations possible, involving more types of patterns and different relationships between them. Another typical case is so-called inversion. In such tests, the solid colour fill (usually black or white) of each shape and object turns into its exact opposite. Every shape with black fill becomes white, and vice versa.

The other component of our rule for the above example has to do with the positions of the shapes in relation to each other. We will discuss this in the next section.

Translation

In geometry, translation is an operation where each and every point of a shape is moved to a specified distance in a specified direction. In the example on the right, each point of the triangle is moved (or "translated") to the same distance and in the same direction, as indicated by the dotted line or "vector" connecting the two shapes. The vector is only shown here for demonstration purposes and would not be visible in a real exercise. We must also keep in mind that the movement sometimes occurs along an actual shape that is part of the figure:

Fig. 2

Fig. 1

In the example on the left, the handlebar line "migrates" around the other shapes in a counter-clockwise order. The movement is not a rotation or a reflection – the points of the handlebar line are simply moved at a certain distance in a certain direction in each step of the series.

Therefore the correct answer is a shape that is the same as the middle one in the top row.

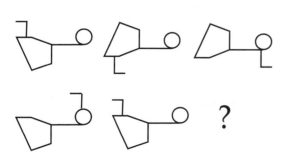

Similarly to rotation, there is also a geometrically less accurate meaning of the term "translation". Looking at the sample question with the star, the circle and the rhombus, we may notice the following rule governing the placement of the three shapes in the figures of the series:

Rule #2: Move each of the three shapes one position up. If the shape is already in the top position, it will now occupy the bottom position in the figure.

In the example, the six answer options were intentionally deleted. Based on the method described earlier in this chapter, we can mentally generate the correct figure based on the rules we have established for the series (repeated below for convenience).

Rule #1: "If a rhombus has a grey fill, change it to solid black in the next step. If it has a solid black fill, change it to a grey pattern in the next step. If a circle has a grey pattern, change it to solid white in the next step. If it has a solid white fill, change it to a grey pattern in the next step. Always leave the star's pattern unchanged."

In the fifth item in the series (the figure that will take the place of the question mark), then, the circle will become grey and the rhombus will become solid black. The star will remain white.

Rule #2: "Move each of the three shapes one position up. If the shape is already in the top position, it will now occupy the bottom position in the figure."

In the figure we are looking for, the now black rhombus will take the bottom position, the now grey circle will go to the middle, and the still white star will move to the top position.

Angles

In geometry, an angle is defined as a figure formed by two lines extending from the same point. In simple geometry, angles are usually given as being any number that is larger than zero and smaller than $360°$.

When it comes to abstract reasoning tests, we need to be aware of angles for various reasons. In the case of identifying rotations, the rotation is usually done at a certain angle: $45°$, $90°$ (also called a "right angle"), $180°$, or $270°$. Of course, rotation at any angle is possible, but due to the difficulty in identifying "custom" angles (say, $67°$), such rotations are not likely to appear in EPSO's abstract reasoning tests.

When establishing the "rule" for a test question, we must always think about angles as well.

Consider the example below:

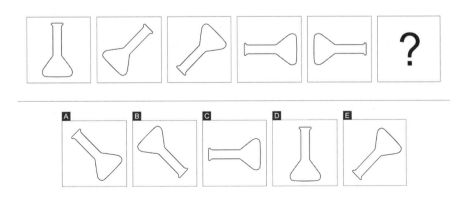

If we look at the images in the sample test above, we see a flask in various positions. After some further observation, we will notice that the flasks in the second, third and further figures are rotated at certain angles when compared to the flask in the first figure. We might describe this regularity based on angles as follows:

Rule #1: The flask is rotated around a fixed point 45 then 180 degrees, and then the cycle repeats.

Visual Arithmetic

The last typical abstract reasoning component we discuss here is sometimes referred to as visual arithmetic.

If we look at the figure extracted from a real abstract reasoning test, we see a large outer square with seven smaller squares along its sides. The top left square is black, and there are various shapes in the other squares (the fact that not all squares contain shapes is not relevant for our purposes now). What is the rule that could govern which kind of shape appears in each of the small squares? One tactic we can follow in items similar to this is to first count the number of sides the shapes have. Obviously, the triangle has three sides, the pentagon has five and the hexagon has six. How many sides should we "allocate" to the circle? Let's worry about that a bit later.

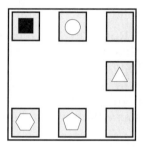

The other question is what determines why a certain shape is placed in a certain position in the figure. Counting can again help us out. If we count the distance (defined as the number of squares) between the shapes and the black square in a clockwise direction, we will notice that the position with the triangle, for example, is three steps away, the position with the pentagon is five shapes away, and so on.

We can now identify a rule:

Rule #1: The distance of a shape in any given square is governed by the number of sides the shape has.

It is important to bear in mind that EPSO's abstract reasoning tests, similarly to all such well-designed tests, attempt to measure the candidate's intuition and intelligence both visually (identification of shapes, patterns, and so on) and logically (e.g. identifying relationships and numerical regularities).

Summary and Approaches to Practice

In this chapter, we have overviewed various aspects of abstract reasoning tests:

- Test design, difficulty, rules and distractors
- Building blocks: operations, rules and patterns (rotation, reflection, angles, visual arithmetic, and so on)

Let us now add some suggestions on how to practice.

- If you feel that a geometrical operation (reflection, rotation, angles, etc.) is one of your weak points, do not shy away from sitting down with some paper and a pencil. Draw various shapes and perform the operations on them until they become routine and you are able to recognize a 90° clockwise rotation of a complex shape in a couple of seconds
- Once you are familiar with all of the typical rules and operations as detailed above, start practicing on the actual test questions in the next chapter of this book
- Since abstract reasoning tests are all about shapes, it is especially important to try to model the infrastructure of the exam while practicing – the EPSO test will be admin-

istered on a computer, which will make it harder (and stranger) to take than a paper-based test where you can scribble on the paper (even though you will be given scrap paper in the exam centre). If you have access to such services, try also to practice online

It is also important to develop a systematic approach when tackling abstract reasoning tests. One recommended approach is summarized below:

1. Quickly glance through the set of figures. Do not spend time looking at the answer options at this stage.

2. Run through all the rules, operations and patterns you familiarised yourself with during practice and try to apply them to the set of figures. Start with the one that, based on glancing at the figures, intuitively seems the most promising lead.

3. If you believe you have found the rule or rules governing the exercise, try to "generate" the correct answer figure in your mind or draw a sketch on a bit of scrap paper.

4. Look at the answer options provided and match them against the one you came up with yourself. If a test item is based on multiple rules, you may still be able to exclude one or two of the answer options based on only the first rule. If you are able to do that, you can continue looking for the second rule with a smaller set of answer options to work with – thereby speeding up the process one rule at a time.

5. If you have found a match (and only one), you can mark that as the correct answer. If there are no matches, or multiple matches to your rule(s), they probably have a flaw. Apply your rule to all the figures in the test – this will most likely reveal the flaw, which you can then correct and generate a new, hopefully correct, answer figure in your mind,

6. While practicing, you may consider writing every idea and step down for each exercise to make sure you are aware of the logic and rules at play.

In the next chapter there is a full warm-up exercise where you can follow detailed workings for 20 questions illustrating different rules and operations. Then in chapter 11 you will find a complete set of abstract reasoning questions that you can use to build up your your speed and accuracy.

10. Abstract Reasoning Warm-Up Exercise

In chapter 11 there is a full abstract reasoning practice test where you can time yourself. This warm-up chapter, in contrast, isn't about doing things fast, it's about learning how to get to the correct answer in a systematic way. So take your time, and make sure you work your way through every question step by step. You are given the correct answer right at the start of each question to help you follow the logic in an orderly way.

Ideally, of course, you will always want to systematically work your way through to the right answer. But as you will see, being systematic is not just about arriving at the right answer. It's also about simplifying your task by excluding the WRONG answers as soon as possible. You know your answer will always be one of the five answer options given. If you can rapidly eliminate two or three of them by spotting the easiest rule or rules, it becomes much easier and faster to check your theories about possible patterns against 2 or 3 answer options than it is comparing all 5. And, if all else fails, and you can't find the final elusive rule, run out of time and have to guess, by getting the easier rules quickly you will have given yourself a 1 in 2 or 1 in 3 chance of choosing the right answer – which is a lot better odds than 1 in 5.

What you have to do

In this exercise you have to decide which of the figures in the *bottom row* is the sixth in the series in the *top row*. The format is exactly the same as in the test in chapter 11.

Q1.

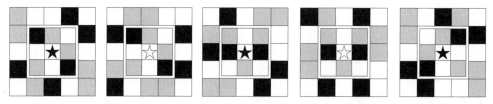

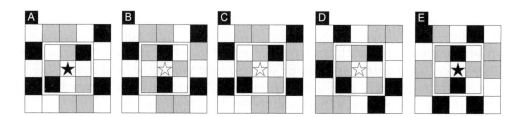

Rule 1: The star in the middle alternates black and white.

Rule 2: The shadings of the squares in the inner ring change in step every second turn.

Rule 3: The shadings around the outer ring of squares move 2 spaces clockwise each time.

The correct answer is C.

At first glance this is a visually very complex problem; there seems to be a lot going on. We need to simplify it. What are the elements that make up this question?

The most obvious is that there is a star in the middle. A quick look at this shows us that it alternates black and white each time. This gives us one rule already and means we can *immediately discard answers A and E* as possibilities as the correct answer must have a white star in the middle.

There are two other elements of the figure: an outer ring of squares (with 5 along each side) and an inner ring of squares (with 3 along each side). That there is a continuous white gap

between these two rings of squares suggests they are separate elements.

Let's take a look at each of these collections of squares. It makes sense to start with the inner ring because, with fewer potential configuration options, it should be easier to spot the pattern.

Look carefully and you can see that the shadings of the squares are exactly the same in figures 1 and 2, and they are also exactly the same in figures 3 and 4. This looks like a pattern. *The shadings of the squares in the inner ring change in step every second turn.* We can expect therefore that in the correct answer the squares in the inner ring will be exactly the same as in figure 5, because in figure 5 they are different than in figure 4.

Let's look at B, C and D (remember we have already eliminated A and E). C and D are the same as figure 5 but B is different so *we can now also discount answer B*.

Having reduced the possible options to two, C and D, our worst case scenario if we get bogged down or simply run out of time is a 50/50 guess, but here we will press on to get the correct answer.

The only difference between C and D is the configuration of the shading in the outer ring of squares. Let's work out which is right.

First, count the number of black, grey and white squares in the outer ring. Are they the same in each figure? Yes. This means that we are probably looking at a movement rule, where the position of the shading changes, rather than a rule where the shadings appear or disappear.

Quickly check across the figures to see if there is any obvious pattern. There is not – the squares change position each time and it all looks rather haphazard.

Let's try and find out what is going on. Rather than trying to examine the whole pattern in each figure, let's look for a visually distinct sub-section of the ring we are able to follow more easily. In figure 1, running down the left-hand side of the figure is a pattern of two grey squares, then white, black, white. Quickly check that this pattern isn't repeated elsewhere in figure 1. It isn't.

Now check figure 2 to see if that same pattern occurs. It does: working *anti-clockwise* from the middle of the top the squares appear in the same order. Is it also in figure 3? Yes, it is seen running along the top of the figure.

So what is the movement between figures 1 and 2? The shadings have moved two positions *clockwise*. Do they move two positions clockwise between figures 2 and 3? Yes they do. This looks like the pattern. Double check this across the other figures, does it hold true? Yes it does. This means that in the correct answer, our sub-section of grey, grey, white, black, white, which runs up the right side of figure 5, should have shifted two spaces clockwise. ***This is not observed in D so we can discount it***. It IS observed in figure C which must therefore be the correct answer.

Shortcuts and pitfalls

Shortcut – In this question we saved time by simplifying the problem twice. Firstly, when we were considering the inner ring, we observed that a change in the order of the shading occurred in every second figure. This gave us sufficient information to identify the correct answer, without needing to understand the rule that governed how the shading moved.

Secondly, we looked at *only part* of the outer ring when we were looking for a pattern. This reduced complexity and enabled us to find the pattern more quickly than looking at the whole outer ring – you can always check the rest of the pattern once you have confirmed the rule, but it may not be necessary.

Q2.

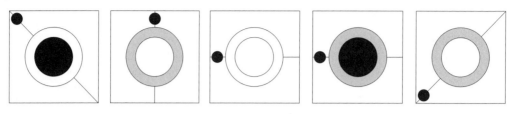

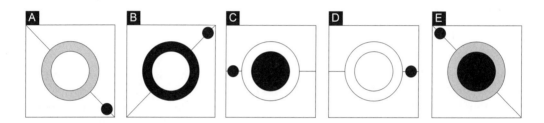

Rule 1: If the inner circle is black, the line will rotate clockwise by 45 degrees in the next figure.

Rule 2: If the outer circle is grey, the line will rotate anti-clockwise by 90 degrees in the next figure.

Rule 3: The effects of these circles are cumulative.

Rule 4: White circles have no effect.

The correct answer is A.

This is an interesting question because in order to solve the problem *you only actually need to understand the effect of an outer grey circle*, i.e. ONE rule. However, without first understanding the other rules that can apply to the problem you are extremely unlikely to be able to arrive at the correct answer by ever discovering that one rule.

Let's take a quick look at the question and answer options as a whole. We have a question that visually appears fairly "clean" – there are not a lot of different elements, just two large circles, a line and a small circle. However, at first

glance there is no obvious repeating pattern to the elements. We will have to examine them in more detail.

Let's look at the shading of the circles – is there a pattern there?

Outer circles are: white – grey – white – grey – grey. This tells us that the outer circles are always white or grey, but they occur in no particular order. We can *probably* discount answer B at this point as the outer circle is black.

Inner circles are: black – white – white – black – white. This tells us that the inner circles are always black or white, but they too are in no particular order.

Is there any specific relationship between the shadings? What possible relationships could there be?

Is a particular outer ring shade always associated with the same inner ring shade? No. Does a particular outer ring shade predict a particular inner ring shade in the next or preceding figure? No. There does not seem to be any pattern to the shading. Let's park this therefore and look at the line.

The line is in different configurations in each figure, but without an obvious pattern. This gives us three possibilities:
1. The orientation of the line is associated with another feature of the problem.
2. The line is rotating in an amount governed by some rule.
3. The direction of the line is arbitrary and therefore irrelevant.

There are only two figures where the shades of the circles are the same – figures 2 and 5. If the orientation of the line were governed by the shading of the circle we would expect the line to have the same orientation in these two figures. It does not, so we can therefore disregard this rule as a possibility.

The line has another feature that might be useful to us. The small black circle is always attached to the line. As it doesn't change independently of the line, we can assume that it might be there to give us a clue about how the line is moving (as it allows us to identify the different ends of the line).

Let's look at the movement of the line.
Figure 1 to 2 – the line moves 45 degrees clockwise.
Figure 2 to 3 – the line moves 90 degrees anti-clockwise (or 270 degrees clockwise)
Figure 3 to 4 – the line does not move.
Figure 4 to 5 – the line moves 45 degrees anti-clockwise (or 315 degrees clockwise).

There is no obvious pattern. This is clearly a complex problem.

There is one situation where the line does not change – between figures 3 and 4. Why? What is different about these figures to the others? Figure 3 is unique in that both circles are white. Perhaps the movement of the line is determined by the shading of the circles.

Let's consider this as a possibility – there are only two shaded circle types found (if we are excluding white) – black inner circles and grey outer circles. Let's look at these:

Black inner circle:
Figure 1 to 2 – the line moves 45 degrees clockwise
Figure 4 to 5 – the line moves 45 degrees anti-clockwise (or 315 degrees clockwise).

Grey outer circle:
Figure 2 to 3 – the line moves 90 degrees anti-clockwise (or 270 degrees clockwise)
Figure 4 to 5 – the line moves 45 degrees anti-clockwise (or 315 degrees clockwise).

There is no obvious pattern here. But look at figure 4. It has both a grey outer circle and a black inner circle. If both were impacting the movement of the arrow this would give a cumulative effect that would be hard to spot. Let's explore this as a possibility.
Following the figure with only a black *inner* circle, the line rotates 45 degrees clockwise.
Following the figure with only a grey *outer* circle, the line rotates 90 degrees anti-clockwise.

If these were added together you would get a movement of 45 degrees anti-clockwise in the next figure. This is exactly what we observe between figures 4 and 5.

With this as the rule, then we'd expect the grey outer circle in figure 5 to move the line 90 degrees anti-clockwise in the correct answer. *This means that only answer A can be correct*.

Shortcuts and pitfalls

Shortcut – This is a very difficult problem because of the lack of obvious patterns and the need to understand that rules can be cumulative. However, look at the first four figures: these show you the elements you need to understand in order to solve the puzzle in that they isolate the rules – this is often found in problems of this type. One rule is shown, then another, then neither and then both. Watch out for this pattern of showing rules in isolation then combined.

Q3.

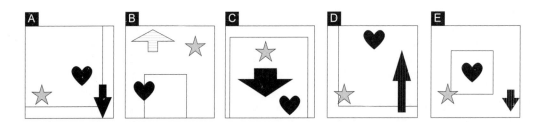

Rule 1: The arrow rotates 90 degrees clockwise each time.

Rule 2: The square moves around at random but gets bigger each time.

Rule 3: The star moves to the position occupied by the heart in the previous figure.

The correct answer is A.

So how do we work this out? A quick glance across the figures shows that they each look very different, but there are a number of common elements. In each figure there is a star, a heart, an arrow and a square. These are in different positions and are variously different shades, sizes and orientations.

Quickly check that each of the potential answer options includes all of these elements – they do, so there's nothing we can rule out at this stage. We will need to look at each of these elements individually:

The star – it is always the same size and it is always grey. It moves around but there is no obvious pattern governing this. This

doesn't help us select an answer.

The heart – it is always the same size and it is always black. It too moves around and again there is no obvious pattern governing this. This doesn't help us select an answer.

The arrow – this looks different in every figure. It is different colours, shapes and sizes, and the orientation is different. Check whether there is a pattern to the orientation. Yes there is, it rotates 90 degrees clockwise each time. ***This means that we can discount answers B and D as possibilities.***

The square – this is always white but it moves around and gets bigger each time. The correct answer would therefore include a white square that is larger than that in figure 5. ***This allows us to also reject answer E.***

This leaves us with only two potential answers: A and C. Which of these is correct? There is no obvious pattern governing where the square is positioned and both meet the requirements for the rules regarding the square and arrow. The only other elements are the heart and star

– there must be something about these that we have not yet understood.

Let's look at them again. The only way in which they change between the figures is where they are positioned. There must therefore be a rule about where they are, but it does look random. Let's break it down.

- In figure 1, the heart is in the top right and the star is next to it, in the middle at the top.
- In figure 2, the heart is in the bottom left corner, and the star is in the top right corner.
- In figure 3, the heart is towards the middle on the right of the figure, and the star is in the bottom left corner.

There appears to be a pattern here – *the star is always in the position the heart was in in the previous figure*. Does this hold true for figures 4 and 5? Yes it does.

We would therefore expect to see the star in the correct answer in the bottom left corner of the figure. ***This is found in answer A but not C***. Answer A must therefore be the correct answer.

Shortcuts and pitfalls

Shortcut – In problems like this where there are a limited number of elements but they seem to change between each figure, there is a need to look at each element individually. The patterns quickly emerged once we started to do this. Overall the problem looks difficult, but the individual rules are fairly easy to identify.

Q4.

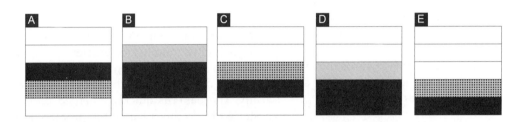

Rule 1: The black rectangles both move up by two positions each time, reappearing at the bottom when they get to the top.

Rule 2: The grey rectangle moves down alternately 1 or 2 positions each time, reappearing at the top when it gets to the bottom.

Rule 3: Where the black and grey rectangles overlap, the rectangle will become checkered.

The correct answer is C.

This is an unusual looking question. Each figure is split into 5 horizontal rectangles and these are of different shades.

How can we start to solve this? Let's start by looking at the shadings in each figure. Are they the same? No. Figures 1, 4 and 5 have two black, one grey and two white rectangles, whilst figures 2 and 3 have one black, one checkered, and three white rectangles. Since all of the answer options fall into one or other of these configurations, this is not very helpful for us.

What else could we consider? Are the rectangles changing shade in any particular order e.g. white becomes black, etc? No.

Are the shadings moving? Let's look at the black rectangles because there are two of them together in figure 1 and it is easy to follow.

> In figure 2, there is only one black rectangle, and it is two spaces above the top black rectangle in figure 1.
> In figure 3, there is only one black rectangle and it is at the bottom.
> In figure 4, there are two black rectangles again, they are in the second and third positions from the top.

In figure 5, there are two black rectangles again, they are at the top and bottom.

Are there any patterns here? Well, not really, but look at figures 2 and 3. If we were to view the checkered rectangles as 'black' then there *would* be a pattern: the two rectangles each move up by two positions each time, reappearing at the bottom when they disappear off the top. It's a bit of a logical stretch but it's worth considering. If this was true, then we'd expect to see black or checked rectangles in the third and fourth positions in the correct answer. ***This would allow us to discount answer D***. Let's keep this in mind as a possibility.

Let's look at the grey rectangle. What do you notice? There is NO grey rectangle in figures where there is a checkered rectangle. Why could this be? It's not clear. There's no obvious pattern to the position of the grey rectangles.

When we considered the black rectangles we found that a pattern emerged when we viewed the checkered rectangles as being *black*. What would happen if we viewed the checkered rectangles as being *grey*?

We find that a pattern once again emerges: the grey/checkered rectangle moves down by alternately 1 or 2 positions each time, reappearing at the top when it disappears off the bottom. If this were a pattern, we would expect to find a grey or checkered rectangle in the third position in the correct answer. The only remaining answer that includes this configuration is C. ***This means that C looks like it is the correct answer***.

Is our reasoning at this point sufficient to select answer C? *Probably*, although we still have not answered the question of why there are sometimes two black/one grey rectangles, and at other times one black/one checkered rectangle. If you wanted to be certain of the answer you would want to understand this, but if you were short on time, this might be something you came back to only if you had time left at the end.

So why are there sometimes two black/ one grey rectangles, and at other times one black/one checkered rectangle? Let's look at the logic we considered to identify the rules. We viewed the checkered rectangle as black to identify the rule governing the movement of the black rectangles, and we viewed the checkered rectangle as grey to identify the rule governing the movement of the grey rectangles. The checkered rectangles occur when a rectangle is both black and grey. This is why one black and one grey rectangle disappear in the figures where the checkered rectangle is present. This gives us our final rule *and the correct answer is therefore definitely C*.

Shortcuts and pitfalls

Shortcut – This is a difficult problem because to solve it you have to take a conceptual leap and view the checkered rectangle as being a combination of grey and black rather than a separate shade. It is not uncommon in abstract reasoning questions for items to change shading/pattern when they overlap one another like this, so bear this in mind when you see similar problems. Another indicator that this might be happening is if something only happens in the absence of other elements of the problem – for example, in this case, the checkered rectangles only appear when one black and one grey rectangle is missing.

Q5.

   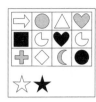 

 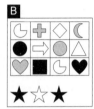  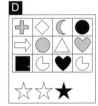 

Rule 1: The shading of the stars alternates black and white, including across figures.

Rule 2: The shapes move to the right, reappearing on the left of the row below when they leave the right side of a row, and at the top left when they leave at the bottom right.

Rule 3: The number of spaces the shapes move is determined by the number of stars on the bottom row e.g. 1 star means they move 1 space, 2 stars move 2 spaces etc.

The correct answer is B.

This is a complex question with a lot of data to process and understand in order to solve it. Let's try to break it down a little. There are two main components of the question: a 4 by 3 grid containing lots of different shapes, and some stars below this.

Let's look at the stars first because that looks simpler.

There are a different number of stars in each box, there is no apparent pattern to this and

some stars are black and some are white. Take a good look at the shading of the stars across the set of figures. What do you notice? The shading of the stars alternates between black and white across all of the figures (i.e. if the previous star was black, the next will be white, even if it is in a different figure).

Regardless of how many stars there are in the answer we therefore know that in the correct answer the FIRST star will be black and any subsequent stars will alternate white then black. *This means that we can discount answers D and E.*

Let's turn our attention now to the grid above the stars. How can we make any sense of this? First, check whether each figure contains the same shapes. They do, and if you read the grids from left to right, top to bottom, the shapes are in the same order: although their absolute position has changed, their relative position has not. So, for example, if you look at the crescent shape in the first figure its position relative to the black circle remains unchanged as it makes its tour around the grid.

Are there any answer options we can rule out based on this insight? Use the top four shapes from figure 5 to check. *Yes, we can rule out answer C because we would expect to see the black circle next to the crescent shape, but we actually find the grey heart. So now we are down to A and B.*

If the shapes are in the same relative positions but different absolute positions this tells us that they have moved. How have they moved? Use the black heart in the top left of figure 1 to track this:

- Figure 1 to 2 – it moves one space to the right.
- Figure 2 to 3 – it moves two spaces to the right.
- Figure 3 to 4 – it moves down one line and then three spaces to the right.

This suggests that the rule for movement is that shapes move to the right and reappear on the line below when they disappear on the right, and reappear at the top when they disappear at the bottom. Choose another shape and track its movements to double check this holds true. It does.

So we know how the shapes move, but the number of spaces the shapes move varies from figure to figure:

Figure 1 to 2 – shapes move one space.
Figure 2 to 3 – shapes move two spaces.
Figure 3 to 4 – shapes move three spaces.
Figure 4 to 5 – shapes move two spaces.

Look at the figures again, what do you notice? The number of spaces the shapes move between figures *equals the number of stars in the figure before*. Figure 5 has three stars, so we would therefore expect the shapes to move three positions in the next figure. *This can be seen in answer B but not A, so B is therefore the correct answer.*

Shortcuts and pitfalls

Shortcut – In this question the pattern for the shade of the stars operates across the figures as a whole. If you looked at each figure separately, without considering them within the context of the question as a whole, it would be difficult to identify the alternating pattern. Remember to check for repeating patterns that do not fit neatly within a figure.

Shortcut – Spotting that the shapes in the grid had the same relative pattern was key to solving this problem. In similar questions always check what the shapes are next to, bearing in mind that this could be above, below, left or right, and that sometimes "next to" could mean in a different line/column if the shape is on the end of a line of shapes.

Q6.

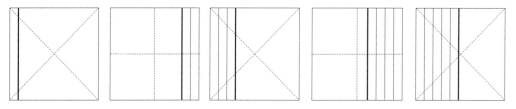

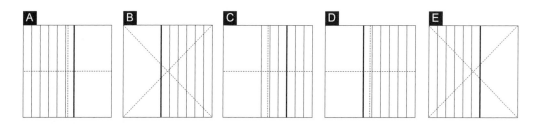

Rule 1: The dashed lines rotate by 45 degrees each time.

Rule 2: The vertical lines are positioned alternately on the left and right of the figure.

Rule 3: An extra vertical line in bold is added each time as the outer line of the group of lines.

The correct answer is D.

A quick glance at this question gives us some useful information to start to solve the problem. It is very obvious that:

1. The number of vertical lines is increasing.
2. There are two "groups" of lines: the vertical lines, and the dashed lines that split the figure into quarters.

Let's look at the dashed lines first as they are the easiest. There is a clear pattern whereby the dashed lines are alternately diagonal and perpendicular. As the lines in figure 5 are diagonal, we know that the dashed lines in the correct answer will be perpendicular. *This allows us to discount answers B and E.*

We also observed that the number of lines is increasing. Count the number of vertical lines in each box (not including any dashed lines): figure 1 = 1, figure 2 = 2, figure 3 = 3, figure 4 = 4, figure 5 = 5. It is clear that the number of lines increases by one each time. The correct answer will therefore include 6 vertical lines.

All of the remaining answers contain 6 lines so that does not help us solve the problem. What else can we observe? The vertical lines are *alternately* on the left and right of the figure. In figure 5 they are on the left, so in the correct answer they must be on the right. *This allows us to discount answer A.*

This leaves us answers C and D as possibilities. What is the difference between them? In answer D the bold line is on the left of the group of lines, in answer C the bold line is in the middle of the group of lines.

A quick look at the figures shows that the bold line is always the outer line of the group of lines, *D is therefore the correct answer*.

Q7.

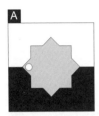 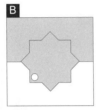 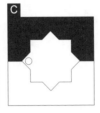 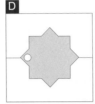 

Rule 1: The shading of the large central star follows the pattern: white, black, grey, white, etc.

Rule 2: The small white circle moves alternately 1 then 2 points clockwise around the star.

Rule 3: Each background is separated into 2 halves: a white and a shaded (grey or black) rectangle. The position of the shaded rectangle alternates between the bottom half and the top half. The actual shade is irrelevant.

The correct answer is E.

Let's break the problem down into chunks. What is in the figures? There is a star in the middle and this changes shading. Is there a pattern to the change? Yes, it goes white, black, grey, white, black. We can assume that the correct answer will have a grey star. *This allows us to discount option C.*

There is a small white circle which moves around the star. If you look at the figures as a whole it is clear that the circle is moving clockwise around the star. Compared to figure 5, the small circle has moved clockwise in all of the potential answers, so we need to work out *how much* it is moving

clockwise each time. Helpfully, it is moving around the points of the star so we can count how many points it moves.

Figure 1 to 2 = 2 points
Figure 2 to 3 = 1 point
Figure 3 to 4 = 2 points
Figure 4 to 5 = 1 point

There is clearly an alternating pattern there, and in the correct answer the circle will be 2 points more clockwise than the circle in figure 5. *This allows us to discount answer B.*

There are three options left, A, D and E. The only difference between them is that the bottom half of the figure is black in A, the top half is black in E, and the top half is white in D. Which one is right?

Look at the backgrounds of the figures. These are all split in half with one half being white and the other either black or grey. Is there any pattern to this? There is no obvious pattern to whether the background is shaded black or grey, but *which half of the figure* is shaded DOES follow a pattern: bottom, top, bottom, top, bottom. We can therefore conclude that the correct answer will be shaded at the top. *We can therefore discount A and D. The answer must be E.*

Q8.

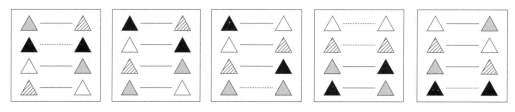

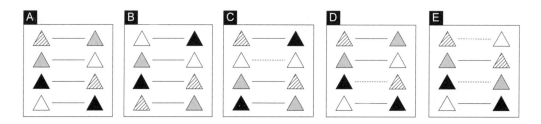

Rule 1: From odd-numbered to even-numbered figures, the triangles on the left move up one space.

Rule 2: From even-numbered to odd-numbered figures, the triangles on the right move down one space.

Rule 3: Where the shadings of the triangles match, the lines between them will be dashed.

The correct answer is A.

In this problem we have two vertical columns of four triangles and four horizontal lines between the columns that may or may not have something to do with the triangles.

A quick look across the figures tells us that both triangles and lines change. Let's find out why.

Start by checking whether the individual triangles change shading in any predictable pattern. Look at the triangle at the top on the LEFT side across the 5 figures. It is grey, black, black, white, white. This suggests that each shade is presented twice in succession. Let's check this with the next triangle below. It goes black,

white, white, striped, striped, which seems to confirm our assumption.

It also suggests there might be an order that the shading follows: grey, black, white, striped. Let's check the next triangle beneath: white, striped, striped, grey, grey. This too follows that pattern. We might therefore expect, that the correct answer would have triangles on the left of the figure with the following shading (top to bottom): striped, grey, black, white. *This would allow us to discount answers B and C.*

Let's check the triangles on the RIGHT side of the figures. Do they follow the same pattern? The top triangle is: striped, striped, white, white, grey. This is different. The order of the shades is different and unlike the triangles on the left-hand side they change on *odd numbered* (1, 3, 5) figures rather than *even numbered* figures (2, 4, 6). If they change on even numbered figures we don't need to work out what the pattern is to solve the problem, because we know that the shading of the right-hand set of triangles in the correct answer will be the same as those in figure 5. *This means that we can discount answer E.*

This leaves answers A and D as possibilities. The only difference between these is that in answer D the third line down is dashed. We need to work out whether or not it should be.

Let's look at the lines in the figures.

In figure 1 there is one dashed line, in the second position down.
In figure 2 there are no dashed lines
In figure 3 there is one dashed line, in the fourth position down.
In figure 4 there are two dashed lines in the top two positions.
In figure 5 there is one dashed line in the bottom position.

There is no obvious pattern there – the number of lines and the positions that the lines occupy looks random. Maybe there is a connection between the lines and the triangles. Is there anything special about the triangles linked by dashed lines? Yes, they are the same shade. Check whether there are ANY triangles of the same shading that are not linked by a dashed line. There are not. *This must therefore be the rule and the correct answer is A.*

Shortcuts and Pitfalls

Sometimes the rules of a problem might result in a different rule appearing. In this case, we solved the problem by following the changing shading of the triangles without needing to spot that the triangles on the right of the figure were moving up one space, and those on the left were moving down one space in alternating figures. If you are struggling to find an answer, consider how you could look at the same information differently.

Q9.

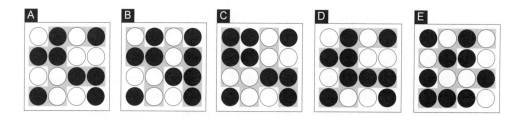

Rule 1: The pattern of grey squares in the background rotates 90 degrees clockwise each time.

Rule 2: An extra black circle is added at random each time.

Rule 3: The black circles move 1 space from right to left each time, reappearing on the right when they disappear on the left.

The correct answer is D.

So how do we get there? Just looking at this problem it is clear that there are two elements: there are 16 circles of which some are black and some are white, and there is a grey shape behind the circles.

Let's start by looking at the grey shape in the background. What do you notice about its movement? It is rotating by 90 degrees each time. This means that in the correct answer the grey background will have rotated another 90 degrees clockwise and will look the same as the background in figure 2. *This means we can discount answer options B and C.*

What else is obvious by looking at the figures? There are more black circles in later figures. Count how many black circles are in each figure:

    Figure 1 = 4
    Figure 2 = 5
    Figure 3 = 6
    Figure 4 = 7
    Figure 5 = 8

There is a clear pattern here and we would expect the correct answer for what is Figure 6, the continuation of the series, to contain 9 black circles. *This allows us to discount answer A.*

This leaves us with answers D and E. The only difference between these two figures is that the black circles are in different positions. So which is right?

There must be a rule that governs where the black circles are positioned, but what is it? As ever, let's start by considering the easiest options. The black circles could be moving up/down, left/right or diagonally (or some combination of these).

Let's look at the position of each of the circles in figure 1 and figure 2. Are there any similarities or relationships between these?

Yes, in figure 1 there are two black circles diagonally next to one another in the second and third rows, and another circle to the left of them in the bottom row. In figure 2, these circles retain this configuration but have moved one position to the left. The black circle in the top row has moved from the left to the right – this is something we commonly see when shapes moves from left to right: they reappear on the right when they disappear on the left (or vice-versa, of course).

Check figure 3. Have the black circles also moved one position to the left in this? Yes. This looks like a rule. Quickly check across the other figures, does this hold true? Yes it does.

The correct answer must therefore be D as the black circles in answer E are in the same place as in figure 5.

Shortcuts and Pitfalls

Since the questions are presented across five figures, any rule that repeats in fours will be repeated in the figures. This is evident in this question where the grey shape rotates by 90 degrees each time, meaning that its position in figure 1 and figure 5 is the same. This is particularly relevant when things are groups of fours, multiples of fours (like the circles in this case) or quarters. If you look at figure 5 you can see that the black circles in figure 1 are all in the same position in figure 5, but this is disguised by the addition of extra black circles. It can be useful to always quickly check for similarities between figure 1 and figure 5. If they are present then it is likely that the answer will be similar to figure 2.

Q10.

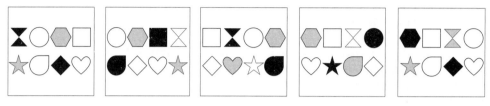

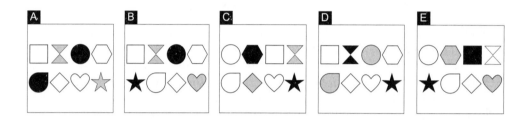

Rule 1: The shapes in the top row move an increasing number of spaces to the left each time.

Rule 2: The shapes in the bottom row move one position to the left each time.

Rule 3: The shadings rotate two spaces clockwise each time.

The correct answer is A.

What elements do we have in this problem? We have eight shapes arranged into two rows of four. Each shape is different. Shapes are either black, white or grey.

We need to break this problem down further in order to solve it. Look at each of the shapes in figure 1 and find them in figure 2. What do you see?

All of the shapes have moved and some have changed shade. Shapes have only moved along their own row, i.e. shapes at the top are still at the top. Check if this is true for all the figures. It is. This means that we can potentially treat the top and bottom rows as separate elements.

Let's look at the top row of shapes and try to understand how they are moving. Start by looking at the square on the right of figure 1. In figure 2 it has moved one space to the left. A quick check of the other shapes confirms they have too, except the hourglass which has moved from the left side to the right side.

How has the square moved in figure 3? It has moved two positions to the left, as have the other shapes (reappearing on the right when they disappear off the left).

What about in figure 4? It has moved three positions to the left.

However, it is in the same position in figure 5 as in figure 4. Why? Let's look at the movements so far; *it has moved one, then two, then three spaces*. Logically we would expect it to move *four* spaces in the next figure as it is moving by an increasing number of spaces each time. As there are only four shapes this would mean that all the shapes would appear in exactly the same position as in figure 4. They do.

We can therefore conclude that in the correct answer, the shapes in the top row will have moved FIVE positions to the left. In effect, they would each have done a complete circuit, disappearing off the left side and reappearing on the right side to end up 1 position to the left of where they are in figure 5. *This means that we can discount answers C and E.*

What about the shapes in the *bottom row*? Are they following the same pattern? Check the movement of the star. This is moving one space to the left each time, as are all the other shapes. *This means that we can discount answer B.*

We have two potential answers left: A and D. The only difference between these is the shading of the shapes.

Let's try to understand the rule governing the shading of the shapes. What are the possibilities?

Each shape *could* move through the different shades in a predictable way. Let's check this. The square is white, black, white, white, white. The hexagon is grey, grey, grey, grey, black. The hourglass is black, white, black, white, grey. There is certainly no predictable pattern in the top row. What about the bottom row? The teardrop is white, black, black, grey, white. The star is grey, grey, white, black, grey. Again, there is no predictable pattern.

Each position in the figure *could* however perhaps move through the different shades in a predictable way *regardless of the shape occupying that position.*

Look again at the shading of the figures. In figure 1 along the top the shapes are: black, white, grey, white. Look at figure 2. Does this same configuration of shades occur? Yes it does. *The shadings have moved two positions clockwise.* When a particular shade reaches the end of the top row it continues its clockwise journey around the bottom row. In figure 3, they have again moved two positions clockwise, confirming that the rule is that the shadings rotate two positions clockwise each time. *This means we can discount D and A must be the correct answer.*

Shortcuts and Pitfalls

Pitfall – This question has different rules governing the top and bottom line of shapes; this encourages you to look at them separately. However, the rule governing the position of the shading requires you to look at all eight shapes together. Take care to retain a holistic view of the problem even if there are sub-sets of data within it.

Q11.

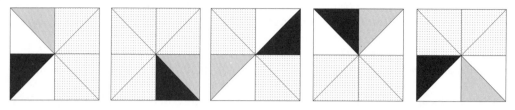

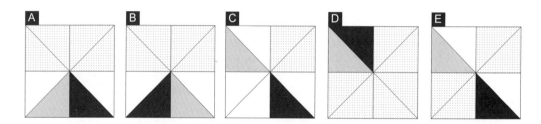

Rule 1: The black triangle moves two spaces anti-clockwise each time.

Rule 2: The grey triangle moves three spaces clockwise each time.

Rule 3: Quadrants where neither triangle is grey or black are spotty.

The correct answer is E.

This question is comprised of eight triangles. These can be black, white, grey or spotty, although not all shadings are present in all figures.

Check to see if there are any obvious patterns. Let's look at the black triangle first as it is the most visually distinct. It is clear that the position of the black triangle is moving anti-clockwise across the figure. It moves two spaces each time. *This means that we can discount answers D and B*.

Let's look at the grey triangle next. It too is moving each time, and although the pattern is less distinct than for the black triangles, it appears to be moving clockwise. Count how many triangles it has moved in a clockwise direction between figures 1 and 2. It has moved three spaces. What about between figures 2 and 3? Three spaces again. This looks like another rule. Quickly double check the other figures. It holds true, so *we can discount answer A*.

This leaves us with two potential answers, C and E. The difference between these is that both of the triangles in the bottom left quadrant are white in answer C and spotty in answer E. Which is correct? Take a look at the figures: the configuration of two white triangles next to one another in option C has not happened in ANY of the figures making up the question. This does not *necessarily* mean that it is incorrect, but if you were running short of time and needed to take a guess, then answer E looks more likely at this point.

However, let's continue and work out whether those triangles should be spotty or white. Look at the white triangles in the question figures. When they are next to a black or grey triangle, this is in a way that completes the square/ quadrant. Look at figure 2, there are no white triangles in this figure. Why is this? Maybe it is because the black and grey triangles complete the quadrant themselves?

Look at the spotty triangles this time, what can you observe? *They are always in pairs that together comprise a quadrant.* Whenever there is a quadrant that does not include either a black or grey triangle, both triangles in that quadrant are spotty. A quadrant cannot have two white triangles. This tells us that the triangles in the bottom left quadrant of the answer should therefore be spotty. **This rules out answer C, so the correct answer is E**.

Shortcuts and pitfalls

In this question the figures are divided into eighths with the triangles. However, in order to solve the problem it was necessary to look at the triangles in pairs and see them as quadrants. Remember, sometimes the combination of items is important for solving a question. In this question rules could potentially have applied to the individual triangles, the quadrants, or the halves.

When we had only two answer options left, we spotted that answer C had two white triangles next to each other and that this did not occur anywhere in the top row of figures. Whilst there is no guarantee that this answer is right, if you were struggling for time then in a situation like this you could make an informed guess and come back to check it later if you had time at the end.

Q12.

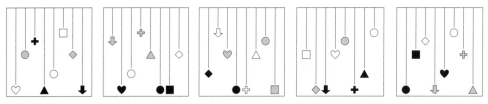

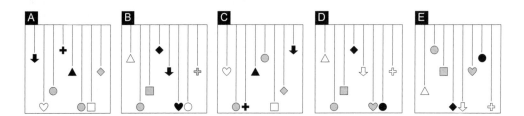

Rule 1: Lines move two spaces to the left each time, reappearing on the right when then disappear on the left.

Rule 2: Shapes move one position to the right each time, reappearing on the left when they disappear on the right.

Rule 3: Each figure contains objects in 3 different shades: black, white and grey in a 2-3-3 distribution. The shade that appears twice follows the pattern grey – white – black – grey – white etc.

The correct answer is D.

This is a visually "busy" question. There is obviously a lot going on with many lines of different lengths, and lots of shapes of different shades. At first glance there is so much going on it is a little intimidating. We need to break it down into its component parts to make it manageable.

Where should we start? Let's start with the lines.

There are eight lines in each figures, each with a shape at the end of them. Lines are of different lengths. A quick look across the figures shows us

that each figure includes lines of the same lengths in different configurations. Let's look at the longer lines because they are easiest to see. There are three lines in each figure that are longer than the others. In figure 1 they have a heart, a triangle and an arrow at the end of them. Is this true for the other figures? No. We know therefore that length of line is not connected to any particular shapes. We can see too that there is no particular shading or shape that is associated with length of line.

Let's consider where these lines are. If we numbered the lines 1 to 8 from left to right, the positions of the long lines are:

    Figure 1 – 1, 4, 8
    Figure 2 – 2, 6, 7
    Figure 3 – 4, 5, 8
    Figure 4 – 2, 3, 6
    Figure 5 – 1, 4, 8

The lines are moving. Are there any patterns? Sometimes two of the long lines are next to each other like in figures 2, 3 and 4. But if this is a pattern, why are there not two long lines next to one another in figures 1 and 5? There are two possibilities: either this is coincidental and not indicative of a real pattern, OR they have been split to each side of the figure.

If the lines were moving across the figure from right to left (as we can see that the two lines next to one another are moving towards the left in figures 2, 3 and 4), we would expect to see them reappear on the right as they disappeared off the left. In this instance we might end up with two lines that are theoretically next to each other, with one either side of the figure.

Is there any evidence to support this? Let's look at the relationship between the two long lines that are next to each other and the one that is separate. In figures 3 and 4, this line is three spaces after the two that are together. If this rule was true, we would expect to see a long line in position 3 where the other two long lines are in positions 1 and 8. This is exactly what we see.

So we know that the lines are *moving from right to left as a group* and reappearing on the right after they disappear off the left. Next we just need to work out how many spaces they are moving each time. It is easy to count that they are moving two spaces. Double check this pattern by following the shortest line across the figure. It holds true. This means that in the correct answer we would expect to see long lines in positions 2, 6 and 7. *This means we can rule out answers C and E.*

Next we need to look at the shapes. Are the same shapes in each of the figures? Yes and they are always in the same order. This tells us that they are moving across the figures in a predictable manner. Follow the heart across the figures and we can see that the shapes move one space to the right each time. This means that the heart would be in position 6 in the correct answer. *This means we can discount answer A.*

We are now left with answer options B and D. The difference between them is the shading of the shapes. Which is right?

What are the possibilities? Are particular shapes always the same shade? No. Are particular positions within the figure always the same shade? No. Is a particular shade associated with lines of particular lengths? No.

What else could be going on? Let's look at the first shape in each figure. What shade is that?
   Figure 1: White
   Figure 2: Grey
   Figure 3: Black
   Figure 4: White
   Figure 5: Black

There's no clear pattern there. How many times is each shade present in the figures?
   Figure 1: White = 3, Grey = 2, Black = 3
   Figure 2: White = 2, Grey = 3, Black = 3
   Figure 3: White = 3, Grey = 3, Black = 2
   Figure 4: White = 3, Grey = 2, Black = 3
   Figure 5: White = 2, Grey = 3, Black = 3

There is a pattern here around *which shade is only present twice*. It goes: grey, white, black, grey, white…

We can therefore conclude that the correct answer will have two black shapes, three white and three grey shapes. *This means we can discount B and the correct answer is D.*

Shortcuts and pitfalls

In this question we needed to understand the patterns of the lines. Having established that the same lines were present in each figure, just in different configurations, we simplified the data by only looking at the longest lines and looking for a pattern in them. If this hadn't worked we could always have considered more of the lines, but we were able to solve the problem without doing so. Looking for ways of simplifying problems can save you valuable time in solving problems.

The other way we simplified this question was by *numbering* the positions of the lines. This enabled us to understand how the lines were moving and what position the different shapes were in. Translating complex visual data into numerical data like this can be helpful for identifying patterns.

Q13.

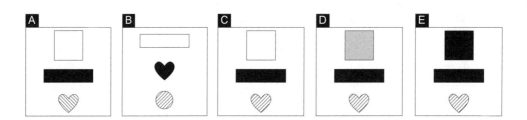

Rule 1: The order of the shapes rotates through circle, square, rectangle and heart.

Rule 2: The top shape alternates, black, grey, white.

Rule 3: The bottom shape is always stripy and the lines rotate through 45 degrees each time.

The correct answer is C.

This problem involves sets of three shapes, in various orders and with various shading. What do you observe when you take a quick look at the figures? The bottom shape is always striped and the middle shape is always black. However, this does not allow us to remove any of the answer options. We will need to look more closely at the different elements.

Let's break this problem down by looking at each of the layers in turn, starting with the top. There is no obvious pattern to the shapes although the first and the last shapes are the same: circle – square – rectangle – heart – circle. What about the shading? That goes black – grey – white – black – grey.

There is a repeating pattern in the shading and we would expect the correct answer to have a white shape at the top. *This allows us to discount answer options D and E.*

Let's look at the middle layer. These are all black so that doesn't help us solve the problem. What about the shapes? They go: square – rectangle – heart – circle – square. Again, the first and last shapes are the same. Interestingly, the shapes are also in the same order as the shapes on the top row. Check the bottom row, are they in the same order too? Yes they are. We would therefore expect the correct answer to have a square at the top, a rectangle in the middle, and a heart at the bottom. *This means we can discount option B.*

This leaves us with only two potential answers: A and C. These look very similar. What is the difference between them? Just one thing: *the diagonal stripes in the hearts slope in different directions.* So which is correct?

Look closely at the direction of the stripes in the bottom shapes in the five figures. It is clear that the stripes rotate by 45 degrees each time.

This eliminates A, meaning that the correct answer must be C.

Shortcuts and pitfalls

To solve this problem we needed to be able to spot a pattern that operates across more than one figure: only three of the four shapes are observed in each figure and the pattern continues in the next figure. However, if you look at this question you can see the pattern quite clearly in the shapes moving up from figure to figure, forming an almost diagonal pattern.

Q14.

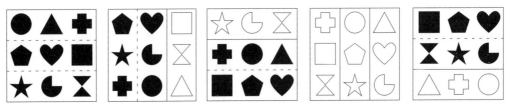

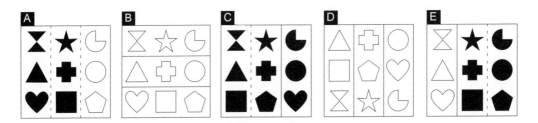

Rule 1: The lines rotate by 90 degrees each time.

Rule 2: The shapes on either side of a dashed line will be black.

Rule 3: Shapes move one position up each time, reappearing at the bottom of the column to the right when they disappear off the top, and reappearing on the left when they disappear off the right.

The correct answer is E.

Are there any obvious patterns that jump out straight away? Yes. There are two lines in each figure that alternate between being vertical and horizontal. We can very quickly see that the correct answer should have vertical lines. *This means that we can discount answer B.*

What else can you see? Some of the lines are dashed. Is there an obvious pattern to this? No: figure 1 has two dashed lines, figure 2 has one dashed line, figure 3 has one dashed line, figure 4 has no dashed lines and figure 5 has one dashed line. There doesn't seem to be any repeating pattern and it doesn't seem to matter

whether the lines are horizontal or vertical. Let's park this for now.

What else is obvious? One of the figures has shapes that are all black, three have black and white shapes, and one has shapes that are all white. There is no obvious repeating pattern to this, so what could be causing this? It could be something to do with the lines or it could be something to do with the shapes.

The lines are easier to look at, so let's consider them first. Is there a difference in the lines between figure 1, where all the shapes are black, and figure 4 where all the shapes are white? Yes. The lines are dashed in figure 1 and continuous in figure 4. The other shapes have one dashed line and some black shapes. It looks like dashed lines cause shapes to be shaded.

Is there any particular pattern to this shading? Look at figures 2, 3 and 5. Which shapes are shaded? *The shapes that are on either side of the dashed line.* This is a rule. If the correct answer includes a dashed line, it will have black shapes on either side of it. ***This means that we can exclude answers A and C.***

Since we don't know if the answer should include a dashed line or not we can't tell which of the remaining options, D and E, is correct. However, the presence of a dashed line is not the only difference between these two answers. They also have a different pattern of shapes.

Let's look at the shapes in more detail. Look at the shapes in figures 1 and 2. Is there any relationship between these? Any similarities? Yes. The middle row of shapes in figure 1 is at the top in figure 2, and the bottom row of shapes is now in the middle. It looks like the shapes are moving up by one space.

This being the case we would expect that the shapes leaving at the top might reappear at the bottom. Do they? Yes, but in a different order.

Look at figures 2 and 3. Does the same thing happen? Yes, the middle and bottom rows move up and the top row moves to the bottom but in a different order. This looks like a pattern – check across the other figures to be sure. Yes, it is true for all of them.

In that case we would expect to see an hour-glass, star and pac-man (sector) shape at the top of the correct answer. ***This means that the correct answer is E.***

Shortcuts and pitfalls

In this question we identified a rule (that the shapes were moving up by one space) but there was something a bit strange about this – the shapes on the bottom row were in a different order. In fact the reason for this is that shapes leaving from the top of the shape, moved into the next column to the right when they rejoined at the bottom, reappearing on the left when they left on the right. Understanding this element of the rule was not necessary to solve this problem as only one of the two remaining answer options included the correct shapes on the top line. If there is a rule that seems to hold true and allows you to identify an answer, go with that rather than wasting time trying to work out the rest of the rule.

Q15.

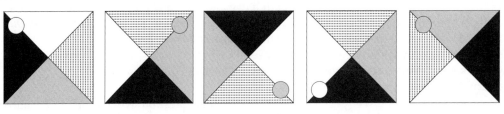

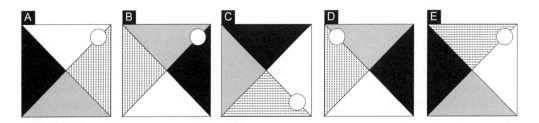

Rule 1: The circle moves from corner to corner in a clockwise direction one position each time.

Rule 2: If the circle is white, the shading of the triangles will rotate 1 space anti-clockwise in the next figure.

Rule 3: If the circle is grey, the shading of the triangles will rotate 2 spaces anti-clockwise in the next figure.

The correct answer is A.

How do we get to this solution? First, let's examine the circles. In the top row of figures some of the circles are grey and some are white. But now look at the answer options. What do you notice? *All of the circles are white*. This tells us straightaway that we do not need to try and work out what shade the circle in the answer will be.

What else do you notice about the circle in the figures? It moves from corner to corner in a clockwise direction one position each time. This means that it must be in the top right corner in the correct answer. *We can therefore discount options C and D straightaway*.

Let's move on to looking at the shading of the triangles. The same four shades are present in each of the figures. This gives two possibilities: the shading of a particular triangle changes in a predictable pattern e.g. black to grey to white to spotted etc, OR the shading moves around the figure (clockwise or anti-clockwise)

Check whether the shading changes in any predictable pattern. Look at the triangle at the top. It is successively white, spotted, black, spotted, grey – there's no apparent pattern. Just to be sure check another triangle, the triangle on the left. It goes black, white, grey, white, spotted. Again, there is no apparent pattern.

Let's look for movements instead:

> Figure 1 to figure 2 - the shades move 1 position anti-clockwise.
> Figure 2 to figure 3 – the shades move 2 positions clockwise/anti-clockwise (you can't tell which direction they are moving)
> Figure 3 to figure 4 – the shades move 2 positions clockwise/anti-clockwise.

Figure 4 to figure 5 – the shades move 1 position anti-clockwise

There's no clear pattern there either, but there are only 2 ways that the shades move: 1 position anti-clockwise, or 2 positions clockwise/anti-clockwise.

If the shades are not moving in any predictable pattern, what else could be causing them to change? The only other option left is that it has something to do with the circle. The shading or position of the circle could determine whether the shades move 1 or 2 positions anti-clockwise. Let's explore this.

Start with looking at the *shading* of the circle (because there are only 2 options this is easier than looking at where there circle is positioned, as there are 4 options for that). There are two figures with a white circle, figures 1 and 4. Look at the movements: following each of the white circles, the shades move 1 position in the next figure. When the circle is grey, the shades move 2 positions in the next figure.

The circle in figure 5 is grey, so we therefore expect a 2-position movement in the correct answer, which would mean white at the top, black on the left, grey at the bottom, and spotted on the right. *The correct answer is therefore A.*

Shortcuts and pitfalls

Pitfall – Sometimes, when in doubt, candidates look at the answer options and work out which answer is most likely based on similarities between the answers. For example, in this case they might conclude that since most of the circles are in the top right in the answers, therefore the circle is probably in the top right – and in this case they would be right. This is not a foolproof strategy, however, because sometimes the most repeated option is not correct. In this example, this approach might lead you to conclude that option B is correct because it has a circle in the top corner, and the same shading pattern is repeated in answer D.

Q16.

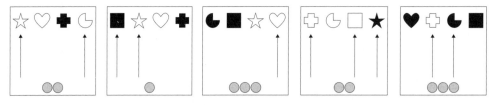

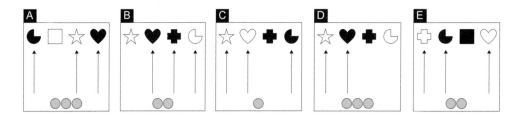

Rule 1: The number of arrows in a figure matches the number of circles in the previous figure.

Rule 2: The shapes on the top line rotate through the pattern: star, heart, cross, pac-man, square.

Rule 3: The number of arrows in the previous figure determines the number of black shapes in the next figure, and the black shapes are located where those arrows pointed.

The correct answer is B.

At first glance this looks like quite a difficult question. There is a lot going on and many different elements. A quick visual inspection of the figures does not give us any obvious patterns to start with. We therefore need to break the question down into the component parts.

There are some shapes along the top, some arrows in the middle and some circles at the bottom. We can see that there is no obvious repeating pattern in the arrows or circles. This means that the number of circles or arrows

must either be random or linked to another aspect of the figures.

Let's look at the arrows first. The presence/number of arrows could theoretically be determined by the presence of particular shapes, the shading of the shapes or the circles. These are the only other elements in the figures so logically these are the only possibilities.

Do the arrows all point at particular shapes? No, all of the shape types are pointed to by an arrow at some point. Do the arrows always point at shapes of a particular shade? No, they point at both black and white shapes, and there is no apparent pattern to this as in figure 1 there are two arrows and they both point at white shapes whereas in figures 2 and 5 there are also two arrows but they point at one black and one white shape.

Is there a relationship between the circles and the arrows? Let's consider this:

Figure 1 = 2 circles and 2 arrows
Figure 2 = 1 circle and 2 arrows
Figure 3 = 3 circles and 1 arrow
Figure 4 = 2 circles and 3 arrows
Figure 5 = 3 circles and 2 arrows

There is a pattern here. *The number of arrows in a figure matches the number of circles in the previous figure.* Figure 5 has three circles therefore the correct answer must contain three arrows. *We can therefore disregard answer D.*

There is no apparent pattern to the number of circles, however, so that is no help in identifying the correct answer. We need to look at the shapes along the top. Is there a pattern to the shapes? Let's take a look. In figure 1 the shapes are: star – heart – cross – pac-man. In figure 2 the shapes are: square – star – heart – cross. In figure 3 the shapes are: pac-man – square – star – heart. What do you notice? *The shapes are always in the same order.*

There is in fact a repeating pattern of five shapes: star – heart – cross – pac-man – square. As only four shapes are shown in a single figure it can be difficult to spot this pattern, but if you look across the figures as a set then it is clearly apparent. This means that the shapes across the top of the correct answer will be: star – heart – cross – pac-man. *This means we can discount answers A and E.*

This leaves us with two possible answers, B and C. Which is correct?

There are three differences between these options: the black shapes are in different positions, the arrows are in different positions, and there are a different number of circles. We haven't considered the black shapes at all yet, so let's look at them first.

Why might a shape be black? There might be a repeating pattern – a quick look shows that there is not. There is no obvious pattern to where in the figures the black shapes appear or how many white shapes there are between black shapes. It could be something to do with the arrows. What do the arrows and shapes have in common? Look at the number of black shapes:

> Figure 1 = 1 black shape and 2 arrows
> Figure 2 = 2 black shapes and 2 arrows
> Figure 3 = 2 black shapes and 1 arrow
> Figure 4 = 1 black shape and 3 arrows
> Figure 5 = 3 black shapes and 2 arrows

A pattern emerges. *The number of arrows in the previous figure predicts the number of black shapes in the next figure.* Look at figure 1 and figure 2. When you connect the arrows in the preceding figure to the black shapes in the next another clear pattern emerges. *The black shapes are located where the arrows pointed in the previous figure.* **This eliminates C, leaving B as the correct answer.**

Shortcuts and pitfalls

In this question we needed to spot that something in the previous figure influenced the occurrence of something in the following figure. Remember to check for patterns between items that cover more than one figure.

Q17.

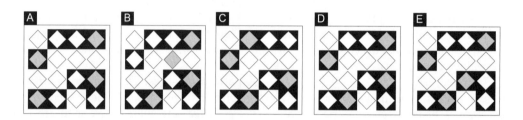

Rule 1: The grey diamonds move one position from left to right each time, reappearing on the left when they disappear on the right.

Rule 2: The grey diamonds will only move to positions against a black background and will skip over the position if the background is not black.

The correct answer is D.

In this question we have figures comprising 16 grey or white diamonds on a black and white background. A quick visual inspection tells us that the only thing that changes across the figures is the position of the grey diamonds. The key to solving this problem is therefore working out where the grey diamonds should be in the correct answer.

Let's look for a pattern. The most obvious patterns are those where the grey diamonds would be moving up/down, left/right or diagonally. Look at the diamonds in figures 1 and 2. Have they moved up or down? No – there are actually now two grey diamonds in the first column and that could not have happened if the rule was only about moving up or down.

What about left/right? The diamond on the top row has moved right, the second row has stayed the same, the third row has moved right and the bottom row has moved left. There is no obvious pattern there. The diamonds have obviously not moved diagonally either.

What are the other possibilities? There could be a more complex rule governing the movements, or different rules could apply to different rows.

To consider this, let's isolate the top row. What can we observe? The diamond moves one position to the right in figures 2 and 3, then it moves to the second column. After this it moves to the right again. It's not surprising that the diamond might appear on the left in figure 4 as often items that disappear off the right of a figure will reappear again on the left; it IS surprising, however, that it is in the second column rather than the first. If we ignore this aberration for now, it suggests that we have a general rule that the diamond moves from left to right.

Let's look at the second row. The grey diamond does not move at all in row 2 across any of the figures. This tells us that *we are going to be able to eliminate answer B*, the only answer option where the grey diamond in the second row moves.

In the third row the grey diamond appears to move backwards and forwards between the third and fourth columns. *This too looks like a clear pattern so we could discount answer E.*

Lastly, let's consider the bottom row. This does not have an obvious pattern in the way that the second and third rows did:

> Figure 1 to 2 – the grey diamond moves 3 spaces to the left (or one space to the right depending on your perspective.
> Figure 2 to 3 – the grey diamond moves 1 space to the right.
> Figure 3 to 4 – the grey diamond moves 2 spaces to the right.
> Figure 4 to 5 – the grey diamond moves 3 spaces to the left (or one space to the right depending on your perspective).

Again there seems to be a general movement towards the right but this is not a consistent pattern.

What else could be going on? The other element of the problem is the background. We know that the black and white squares are not moving, so what role are they playing in this problem? Is there a relationship with the grey diamonds? Yes there is – *grey diamonds only ever fall within the black squares.*

If that is a rule, how would that interact with our other observations? Let's look at the bottom row again. On the occasion where the grey diamond unexpectedly moved two spaces to the right, from figure 3 to figure 4, it would have fallen on a white square had it only moved one space. Maybe therefore it skipped the white square and moved to the next available black square.

This would also explain the pattern we observed in the top row whereby having disappeared off the right, the grey diamond reappeared in the second column. Had it rejoined in the first column, it would have fallen on a white square.

How would this rule affect the other rows? As there is only one black square in the second row, the grey diamond would be unable to move. This is what we observe. In the third row there are two black squares and we would therefore expect the grey diamond to move backwards and forwards between these. Again, this is what we see. This looks like a solid rule.

This would mean that in the correct answer we would expect to see grey diamonds on the right of the top row and in the second column of the bottom row (we already know where it will be in the second and third rows). *This means that the only answer that can be correct is D.*

Just to recap, there were two rules that we needed to identify to solve this tricky problem:

Rule 1: The grey diamonds move one position from left to right each time, reappearing on the left when they disappear on the right.

But that rule was itself modified by:

Rule 2: The grey diamonds will only move to positions against a black background and will skip over the position if the background is not black.

Shortcuts and pitfalls

Where there is a shaded/coloured background (or other item) that does not change, it is useful to ask WHY it is shaded/coloured. What is its purpose? This allowed us to notice that the grey diamonds only fell within black squares and this explained the unusual movements we had observed.

Q18.

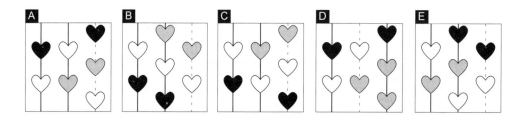

Rule 1: The dashed line moves one position at a time from left to right across the figures.

Rule 2: The groups of hearts move from right to left one position at a time across the figures, reappearing on the right when they disappear off the left.

Rule 3: The shading of the hearts moves one position up each time, reappearing at the bottom when it disappears from the top.

The correct answer is A.

What is going on in this question? We've got seven hearts of various shades arranged along three lines. It is clear from a quick glance that there are always two bold lines and one dashed line, although the order of these changes. Look across the figures, how is the dashed line moving? *It is moving one position to the right each time*, reappearing on the left when it disappears on the right. **This means that D cannot be the correct answer.**

Let's look at the hearts now. There are always two lines with two hearts on and one line with three hearts on. Once again the position of these

lines moves around. Does this also change in a predictable way? Yes, the line with three hearts on is clearly moving one position to the left each time, reappearing on the right when it disappears on the left. **This means that we can discount answer options B and E.**

This leaves us with answers A and C. The difference between these two options is the shading of the hearts. What rules can we identify about the shading of the hearts? In each figure there are always two black, two grey and three white hearts, however, as both answers A and C meet this criterion this doesn't help us.

The shades on each line are always the same: one line has one grey and one white heart, another has one black and one white heart, and the final line has one grey, one white and one black heart. Once again both answer options meet this criterion.

We can also observe that the positions of the different shades change across the figures. Let's just look at the lines with two hearts on them. *The different shaded hearts alternate in position from one figure to the next.* With this in mind, look at the line on the right of figure 5. The grey heart is above the right heart. This means they should be the other way round in the correct answer, the white heart above the grey heart, remembering that these two hearts will now be on the middle line. This happens in answer option A but not in C. *We can therefore eliminate C leaving A as the correct answer.*

Shortcuts and pitfalls

We managed to solve this problem just by seeing the pattern with the lines with TWO hearts. We didn't actually work out what happens to the positioning of the hearts on the lines with THREE hearts. It is possible that where there are two hearts on a line they simply alternate in position, which would not give us a pattern for a line with three hearts. However, you can see that where there are three hearts, the shadings move up one position each time (reappearing at the bottom when they disappear off the top). This confirms that there is one rule that applies to all the lines, regardless of the number of hearts, i.e. the shading of the hearts moves one position up each time, reappearing at the bottom when it disappears from the top.

Q19.

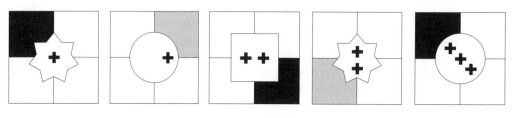

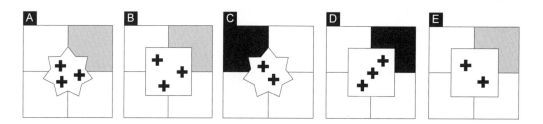

Rule 1: The shaded square moves 1 space clockwise each time, alternating between grey and black.

Rule 2: The large central shape alternates star, circle, square.

Rule 3: From odd-numbered to even-numbered figures, an extra cross is added to the central shape.

The correct answer is B.

What do we need to understand in order to identify the correct answer? Let's look at the different answer options. These tell us that there are four things we need to work out:

> Which corner of the figure should be shaded?
> What shade should the shaded corner be?
> Which shape should be in the centre of the figure?
> How many crosses should be included in the central figure?

Let's look at the first of these - which corner of the figure needs to be shaded? Look at the shaded corner across the figures. Is there any

pattern to the shading? Yes, the shaded corner rotates clockwise around the figure. *This means that we can discount answer C.*

What shade should the shaded corner be? Let's look at the pattern across the figures. The shaded corner is black – grey – black – grey – black. There is clearly a repeating pattern and in the correct answer the shaded corner will be grey. *We can therefore also eliminate answer D as a possibility*.

Next we need to work out which shape needs to be in the centre of the figure. Look at the shapes in the centre of the figures of the question:

> Figure 1 = star
> Figure 2 = circle
> Figure 3 = square
> Figure 4 = star
> Figure 5 = circle

There appears to be a pattern to this: star – circle – square, etc. This means that the next shape in the sequence will be a square. *We can therefore rule out answer A.*

This leaves us with only two possible answer options: B and E. E has two crosses in the central figure, while B has three. Which is correct?

Let's look at the crosses in the question figures. Figures 1 and 2 have one cross. Figures 3 and 4 have two crosses. Figure 5 has three crosses. It looks like the number of crosses is increasing by increments of one on odd numbered figures, meaning that each number of crosses is observed twice. This means that there will be three crosses in the correct answer. *Answer option E has only 2 crosses, so B is the correct answer.*

Shortcuts and pitfalls

We took a different approach to solving this problem in that we considered the differences between the answer options and used these to focus our attention on the problem. This was an effective way of honing in on the rules of the problem. If you are having difficulty working out what is going on in a problem, it can be very useful to look at the possible answers and identify the differences between them. This will help you identify the critical information within the question.

Q20.

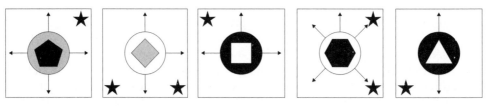

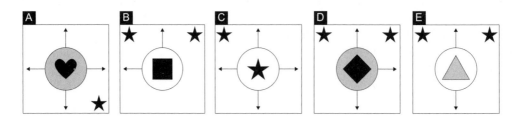

Rule 1: There are alternately 1 and then 2 stars in each figure.

Rule 2: There is always one arrow less than the number of corners of the central shape.

Rule 3: The shade of the central shape matches the shade of the circle in the previous figure.

The correct answer is D.

This is a question with lots of different elements – there is a large circle, of different shades, which contains a smaller shape, again with varying shades. There are arrows of varying number around the circle and stars in some of the corners.

Let's start with the stars to see if there is a clear pattern to them. There is one star in figures 1, 3 and 5, and two stars in figures 2 and 4. The number of stars therefore alternates between 1 and 2 so we can assume that in the correct answer there will be two stars. *This allows us to rule out answers A and C.*

Let's look at the arrows next. Is there any obvious pattern to the arrows? No, there are:

4 – 3 – 3 – 5 – 2 arrows. If there is not a pattern to the arrows, what is causing the difference in number? If it was the stars we could expect that the number of arrows would also alternate between even and odd numbers so we can discount that. *It must be something to do with the shapes in the middle.* Let's look at these more closely.

Each figure contains a circle. These are different shades but there is no obvious pattern to the shading: grey – white – black – white – black. It is possible that the number of arrows could be linked to the shading of the circle. However, if this was the case we would expect to see the same number of arrows in figures 2 and 4, where the circles are white, and 3 and 5, where the circles are black. We do not, so we can disregard that as a possibility.

The number of arrows must therefore have something to do with the shapes inside the circles. But what? The number of arrows could be associated with different shadings of the shapes, but as the shapes in figures 1 and 4 are both black but have different numbers of arrows, we have to discount this.

So other than their shading, what is different about these shapes? They are all the same size, but as they are different shapes they have different numbers of corners. Is there a connection between the number of corners and the number of arrows?

Figure 1 = 5 corners and 4 arrows
Figure 2 = 4 corners and 3 arrows
Figure 3 = 4 corners and 3 arrows
Figure 4 = 6 corners and 5 arrows
Figure 5 = 3 corners and 2 arrows

There is a clear pattern – there is always one less arrow than the number of corners. This means that answers A and B cannot be correct. We have already eliminated answer A but *we can now also eliminate answer B.*

This leaves us with only two potential answers, D and E. They contain different central shapes and different shadings. Is there a pattern around the central shapes in the figures? No – the number of corners they have appears to be random and there is no other obvious pattern to them.

The next rule must therefore be to do with the shading. We know that there is no repeating pattern in either the large circles or the inner shapes. We also know that shading is not related to the stars or the number of arrows. So what is left?

There must be a relationship of some description between the shades themselves. Let's see if we can spot it:

Figure 1 = the shape is black, the circle is grey
Figure 2 = the shape is grey, the circle is white
Figure 3 = the shape is white, the circle is black
Figure 4 = the shape is black, the circle is white
Figure 5 = the shape is white, the circle is black

When we break it down like this what can you observe? *The shade of the central shape matches the shade of the circle in the previous figure.* Thus in figure 1 the circle is grey and the shape inside the circle in figure 2 is also grey; in figure 2 the circle is white, which means that in figure 3 the shape is also white.

This means that the shade of the shape inside the circle in the correct answer will be black. *In answer E it is grey, so the answer must be D.*

Shortcuts and pitfalls

In a complicated question like this it can be hard to know where to start with solving the problem. Start by identifying the individual features of the problem and working out their significance.

Where there is a row of shapes that doesn't include circles or hearts or other "curvy" shapes, there is a possibility that the number of corners or edges might form part of the problem.

11. Abstract Reasoning Test

160 Questions – Answers follow on from Question 160

In each question you must choose which of the figures in the bottom line - A, B, C, D or E - completes the series in the top line.

For practice purposes, you should try to complete 10 questions in 10 minutes. If you can't identify the rules for a particular question within 1 minute, move straight on to the next question rather than wasting time. For the actual number of questions, time allowed and pass mark in your exam, always check the Notice of Competition.

Comparatively harder and easier questions are mixed at random through the test, but if you want to specially concentrate on hard questions the final 40 (i.e. questions 121 to 160) are mainly of that type.

1   Which figure completes the series below?

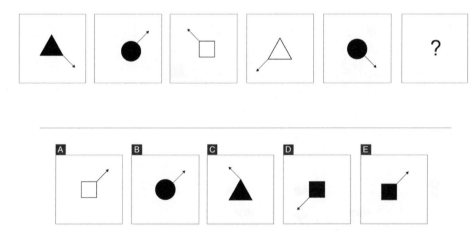

2   Which figure completes the series below?

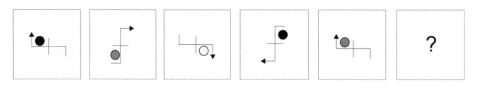

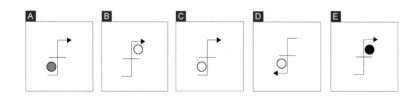

3   Which figure completes the series below?

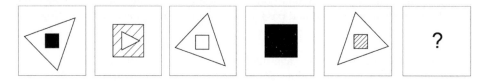

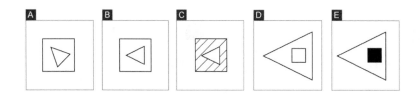

4   Which figure completes the series below?

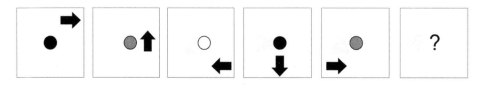

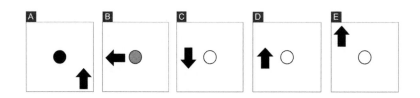

5   Which figure completes the series below?

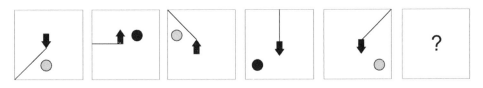

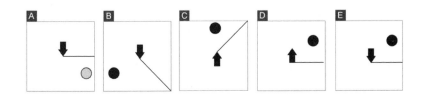

6   Which figure completes the series below?

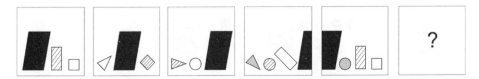

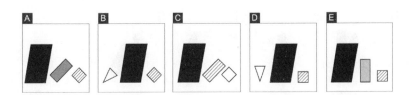

7   Which figure completes the series below?

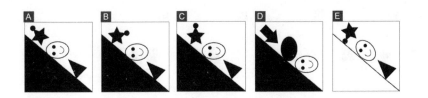

8   Which figure completes the series below?

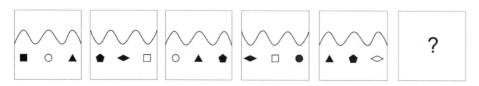

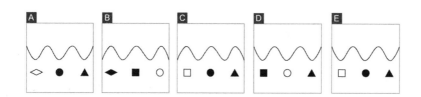

9   Which figure completes the series below?

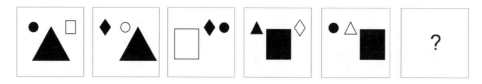

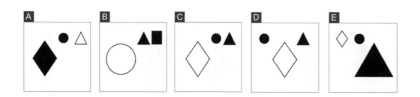

10   Which figure completes the series below?

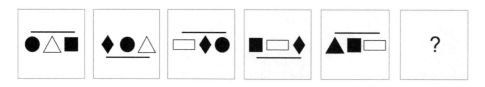

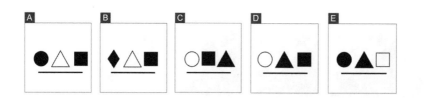

11 Which figure completes the series below?

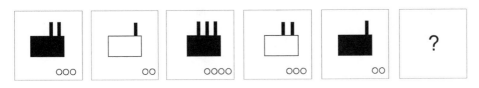

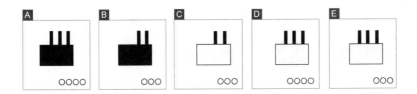

12 Which figure completes the series below?

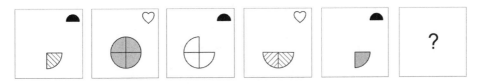

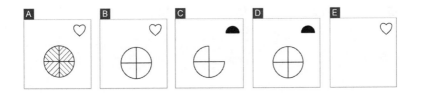

13 Which figure completes the series below?

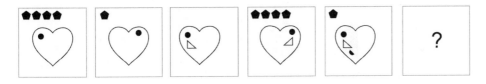

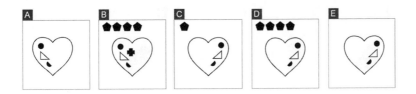

14   Which figure completes the series below?

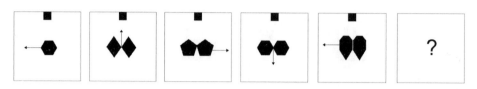

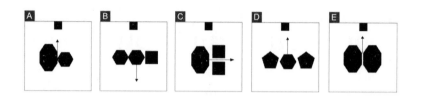

15   Which figure completes the series below?

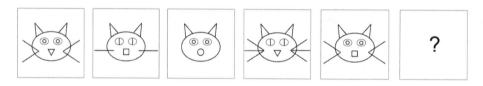

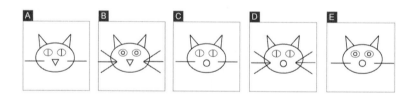

16   Which figure completes the series below?

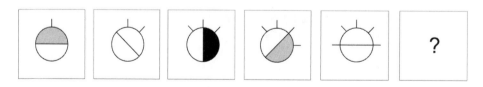

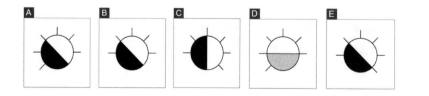

17 Which figure completes the series below?

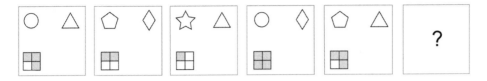

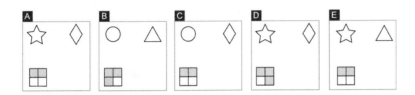

18 Which figure completes the series below?

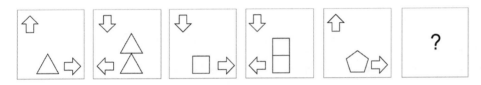

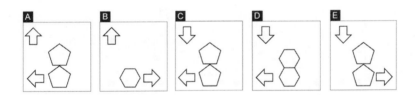

19 Which figure completes the series below?

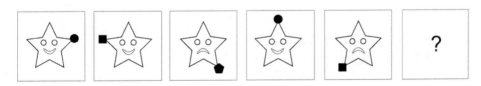

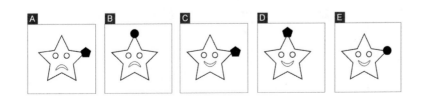

20 Which figure completes the series below?

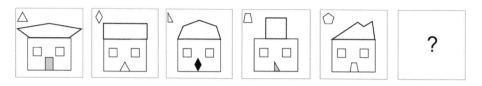

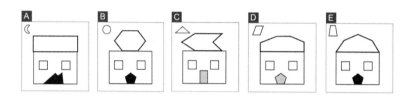

21 Which figure completes the series below?

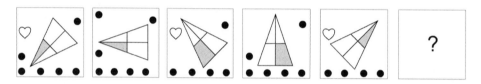

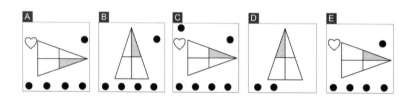

22 Which figure completes the series below?

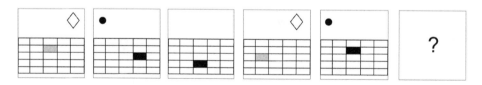

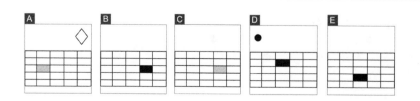

23 Which figure completes the series below?

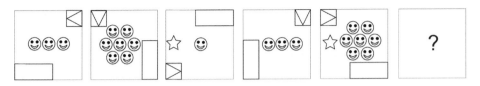

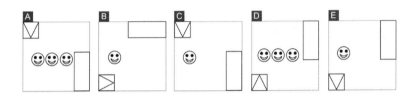

24 Which figure completes the series below?

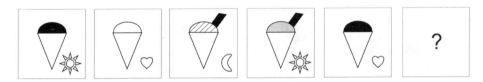

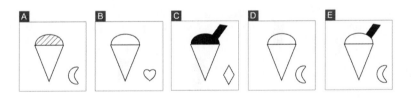

25 Which figure completes the series below?

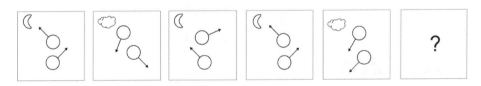

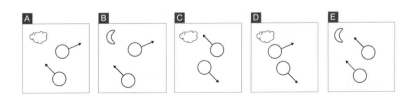

26   Which figure completes the series below?

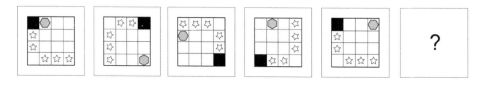

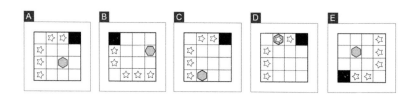

27   Which figure completes the series below?

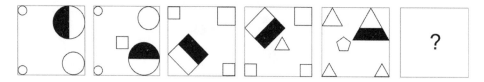

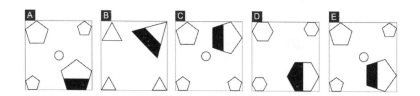

28   Which figure completes the series below?

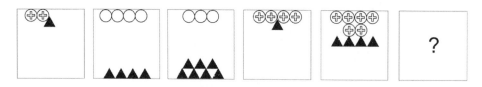

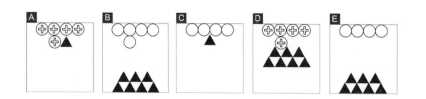

29   Which figure completes the series below?

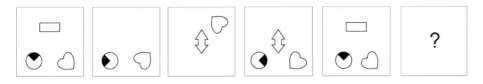

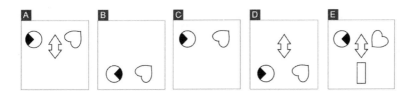

30   Which figure completes the series below?

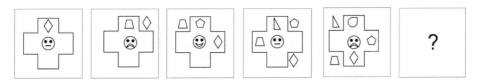

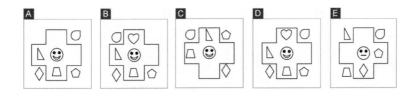

31   Which figure completes the series below?

32   Which figure completes the series below?

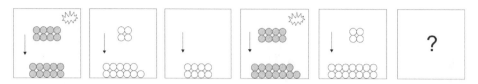

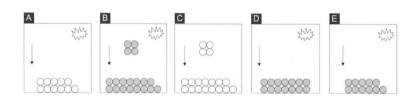

33   Which figure completes the series below?

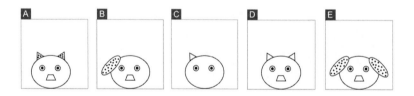

34   Which figure completes the series below?

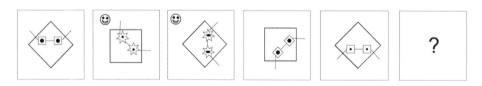

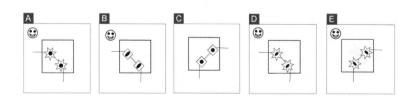

35   Which figure completes the series below?

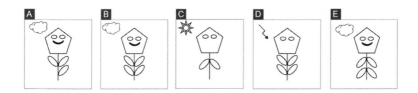

36   Which figure completes the series below?

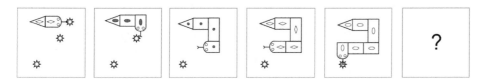

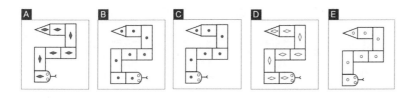

37   Which figure completes the series below?

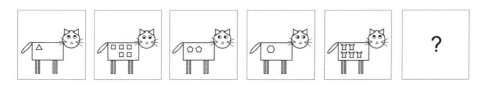

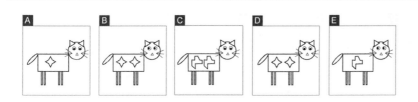

38   Which figure completes the series below?

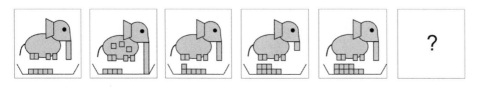

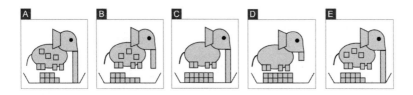

39   Which figure completes the series below?

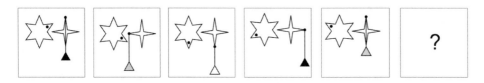

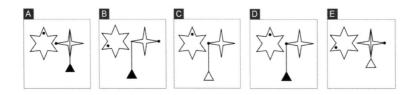

40   Which figure completes the series below?

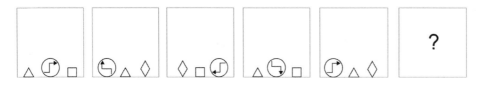

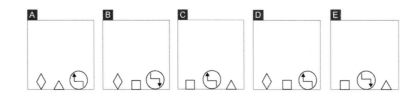

41   Which figure completes the series below?

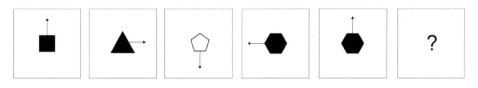

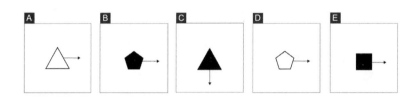

42   Which figure completes the series below?

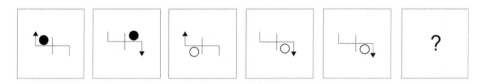

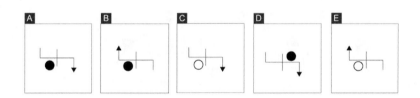

43   Which figure completes the series below?

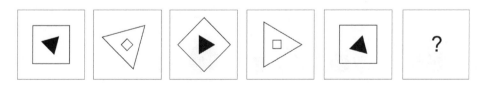

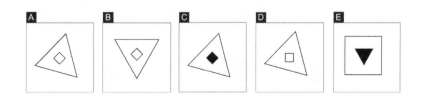

44   Which figure completes the series below?

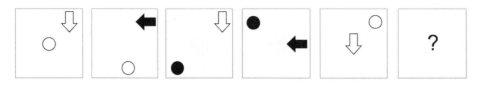

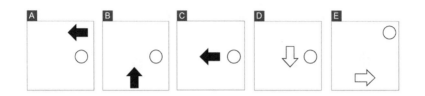

45   Which figure completes the series below?

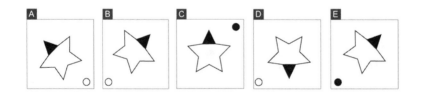

46   Which figure completes the series below?

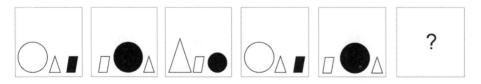

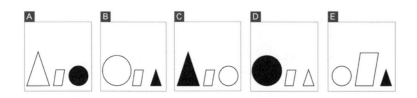

47   Which figure completes the series below?

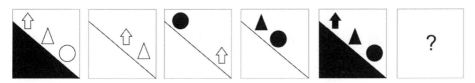

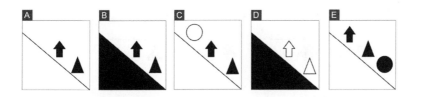

48   Which figure completes the series below?

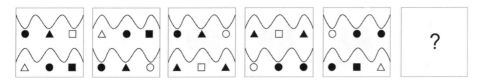

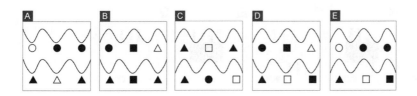

49   Which figure completes the series below?

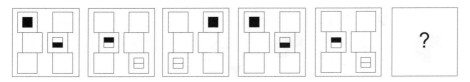

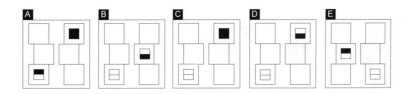

50   Which figure completes the series below?

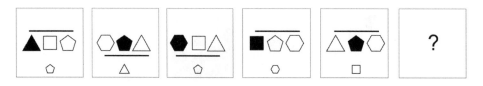

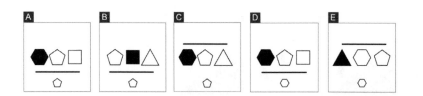

51   Which figure completes the series below?

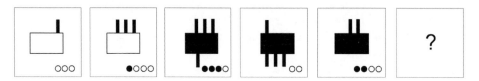

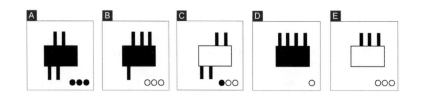

52   Which figure completes the series below?

53   Which figure completes the series below?

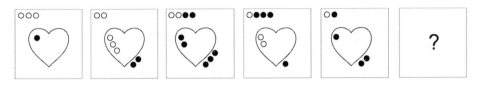

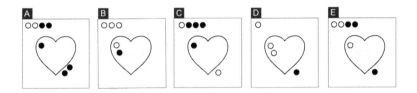

54   Which figure completes the series below?

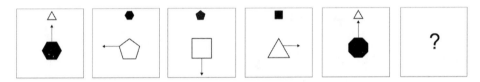

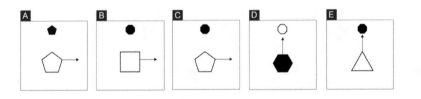

55   Which figure completes the series below?

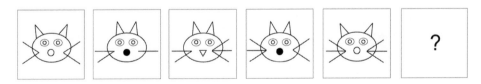

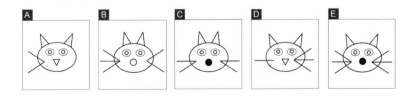

56   Which figure completes the series below?

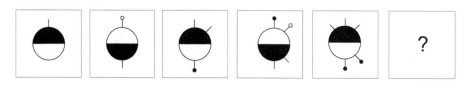

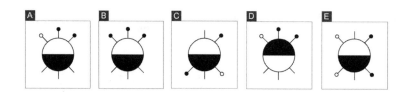

57   Which figure completes the series below?

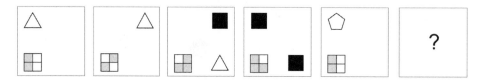

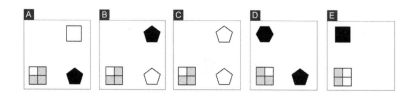

58   Which figure completes the series below?

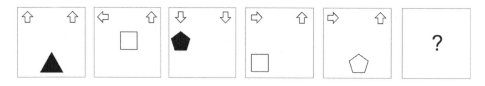

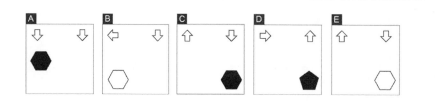

59   Which figure completes the series below?

60   Which figure completes the series below?

61   Which figure completes the series below?

62   Which figure completes the series below?

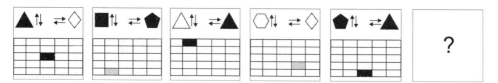

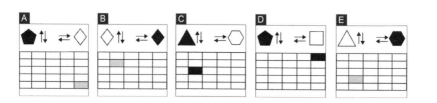

63   Which figure completes the series below?

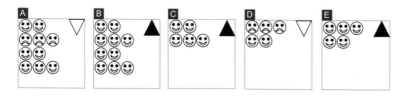

64   Which figure completes the series below?

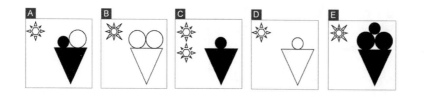

65 Which figure completes the series below?

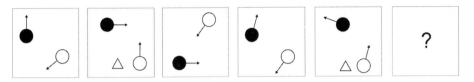

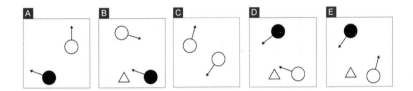

66 Which figure completes the series below?

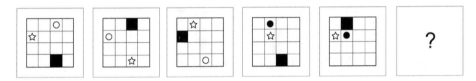

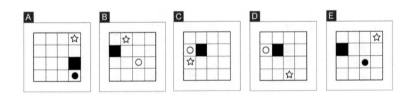

67 Which figure completes the series below?

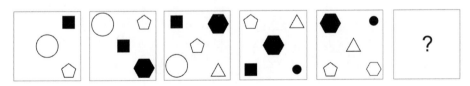

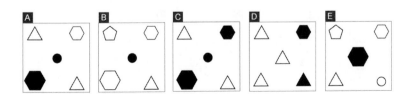

68   Which figure completes the series below?

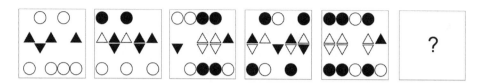

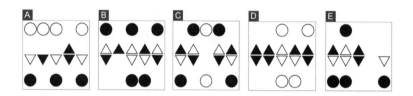

69   Which figure completes the series below?

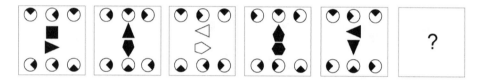

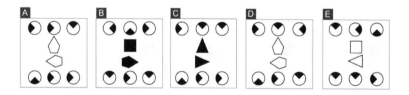

70   Which figure completes the series below?

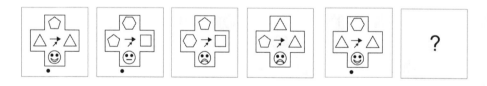

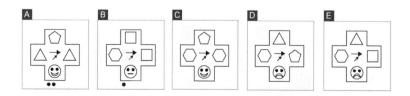

71 Which figure completes the series below?

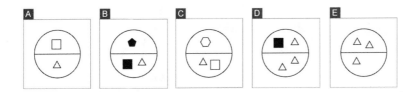

72 Which figure completes the series below?

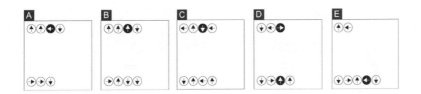

73 Which figure completes the series below?

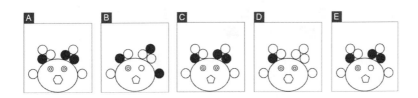

74 Which figure completes the series below?

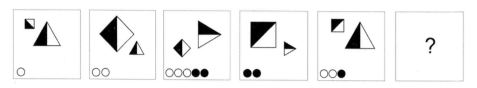

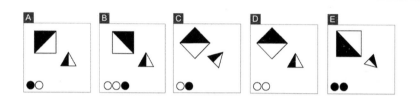

75 Which figure completes the series below?

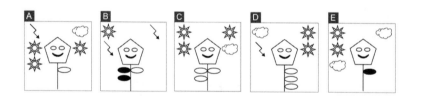

76 Which figure completes the series below?

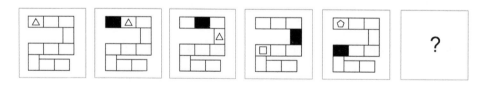

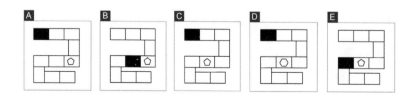

77 Which figure completes the series below?

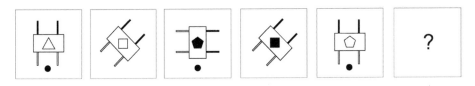

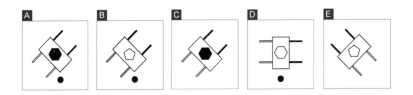

78 Which figure completes the series below?

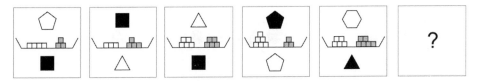

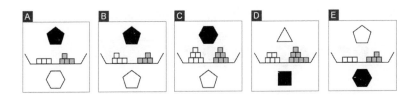

79 Which figure completes the series below?

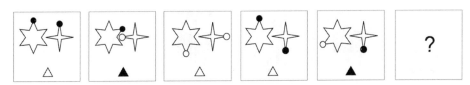

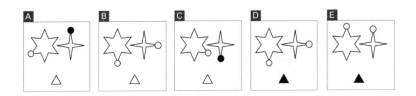

80   Which figure completes the series below?

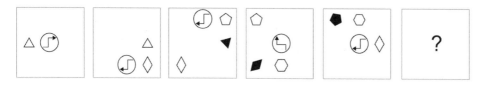

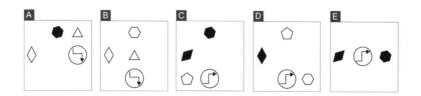

81   Which figure completes the series below?

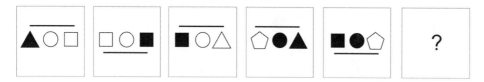

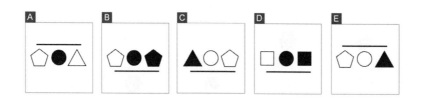

82   Which figure completes the series below?

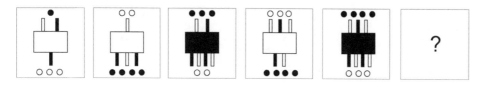

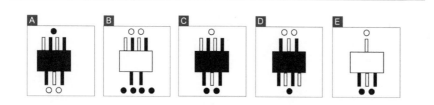

83 Which figure completes the series below?

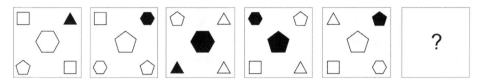

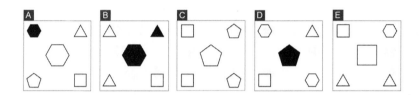

84 Which figure completes the series below?

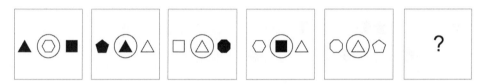

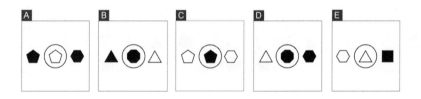

85 Which figure completes the series below?

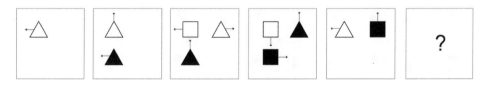

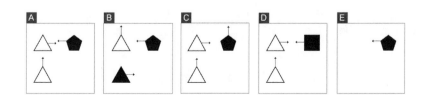

86　Which figure completes the series below?

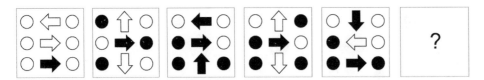

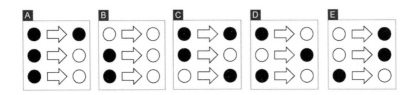

87　Which figure completes the series below?

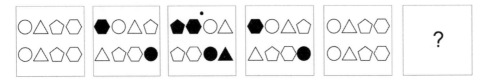

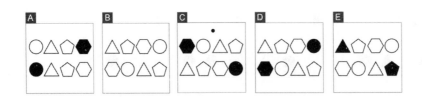

88　Which figure completes the series below?

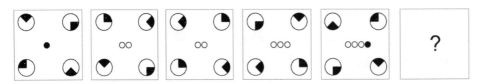

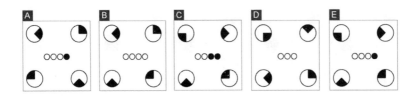

89 Which figure completes the series below?

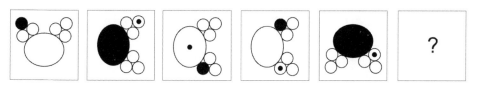

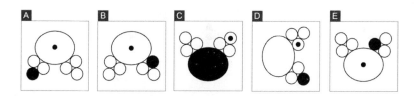

90 Which figure completes the series below?

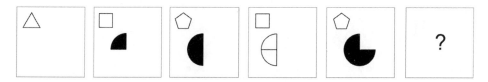

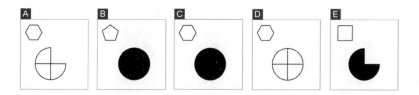

91 Which figure completes the series below?

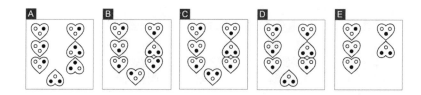

92   Which figure completes the series below?

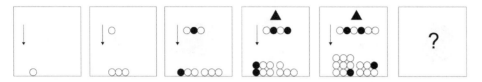

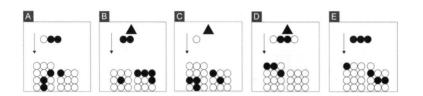

93   Which figure completes the series below?

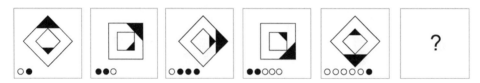

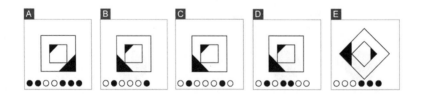

94   Which figure completes the series below?

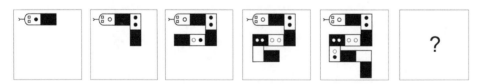

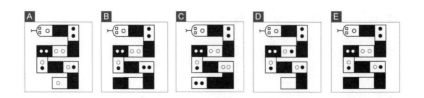

95   Which figure completes the series below?

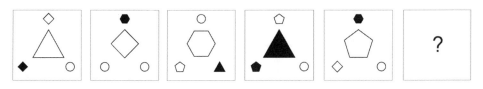

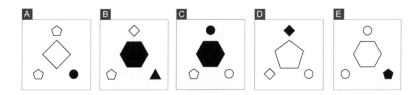

96   Which figure completes the series below?

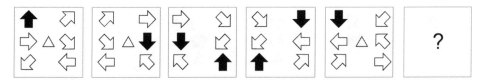

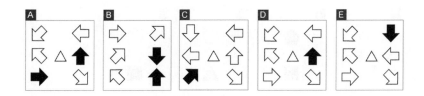

97   Which figure completes the series below?

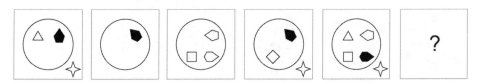

98   Which figure completes the series below?

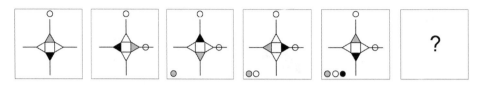

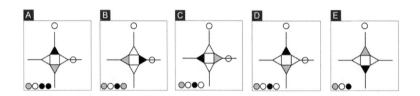

99   Which figure completes the series below?

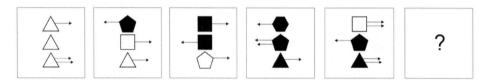

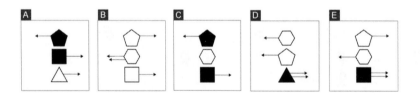

100   Which figure completes the series below?

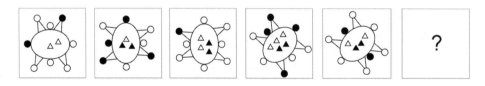

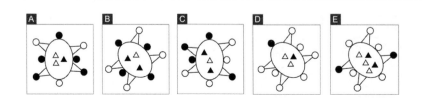

101 Which figure completes the series below?

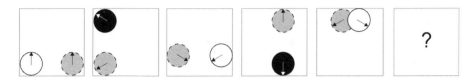

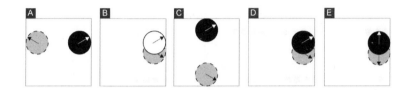

102 Which figure completes the series below?

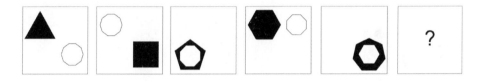

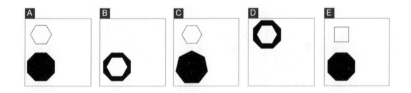

103 Which figure completes the series below?

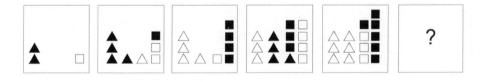

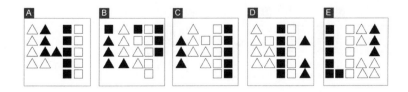

104 Which figure completes the series below?

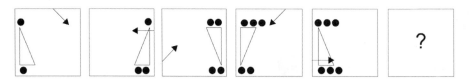

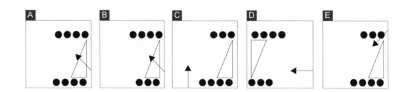

105 Which figure completes the series below?

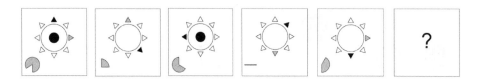

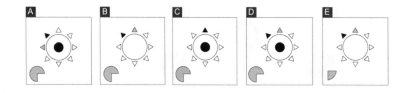

106 Which figure completes the series below?

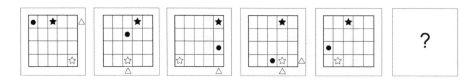

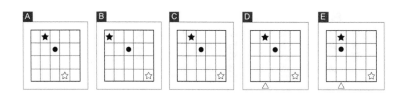

107 Which figure completes the series below?

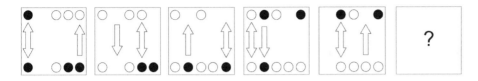

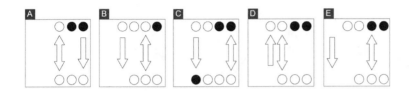

108 Which figure completes the series below?

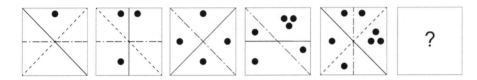

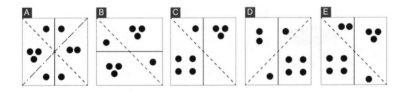

109 Which figure completes the series below?

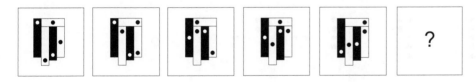

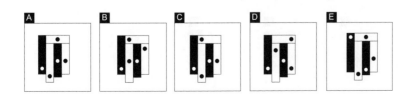

110 Which figure completes the series below?

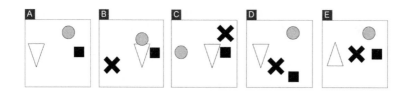

111 Which figure completes the series below?

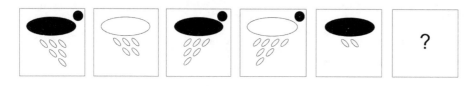

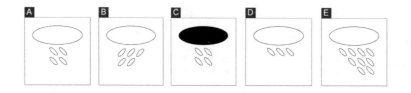

112 Which figure completes the series below?

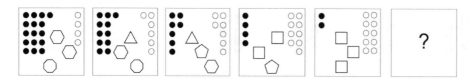

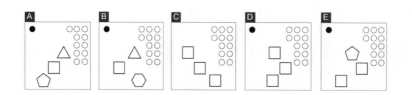

113 Which figure completes the series below?

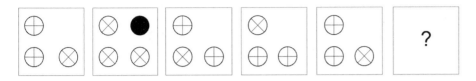

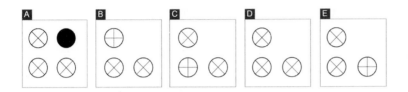

114 Which figure completes the series below?

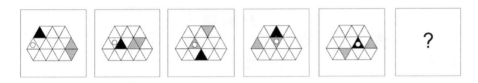

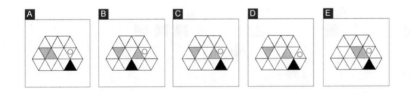

115 Which figure completes the series below?

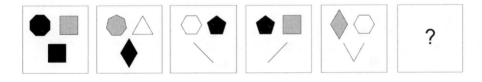

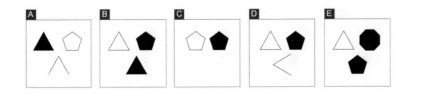

116 Which figure completes the series below?

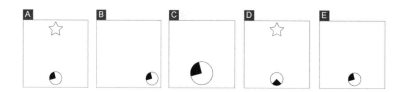

117 Which figure completes the series below?

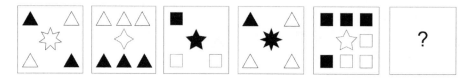

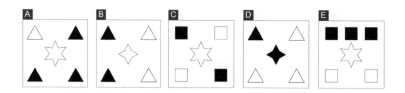

118 Which figure completes the series below?

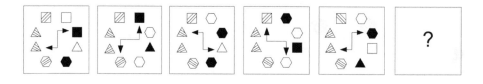

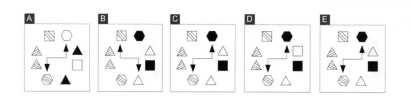

119 Which figure completes the series below?

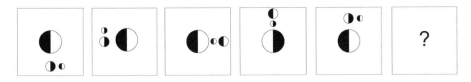

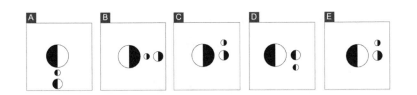

120 Which figure completes the series below?

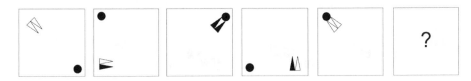

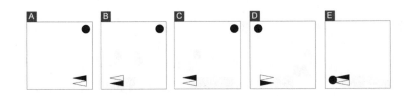

121 Which figure completes the series below?

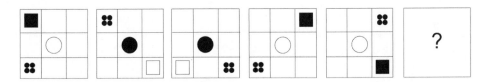

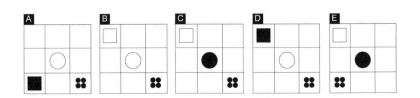

122 Which figure completes the series below?

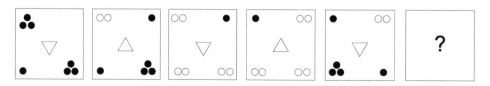

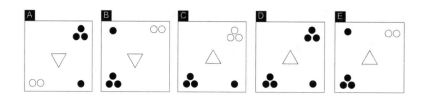

123 Which figure completes the series below?

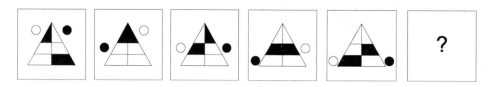

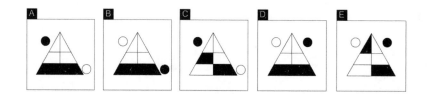

124 Which figure completes the series below?

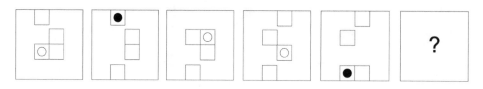

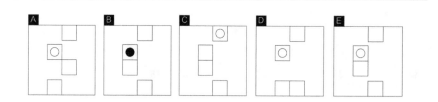

125 Which figure completes the series below?

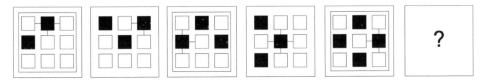

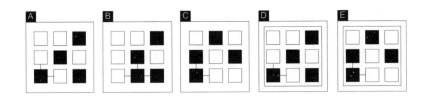

126 Which figure completes the series below?

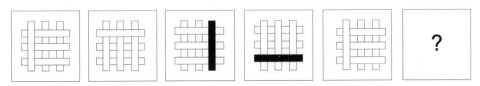

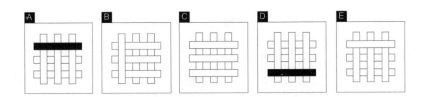

127 Which figure completes the series below?

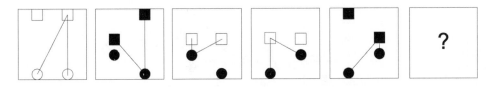

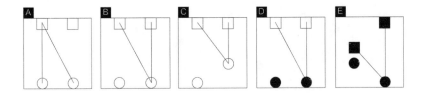

128 Which figure completes the series below?

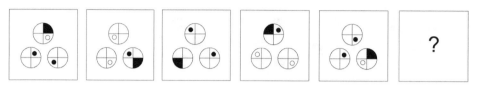

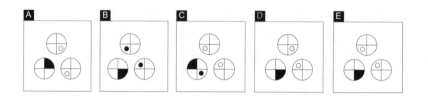

129 Which figure completes the series below?

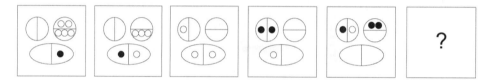

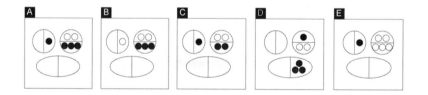

130 Which figure completes the series below?

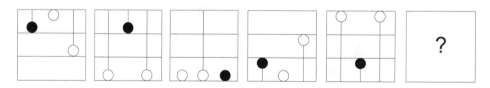

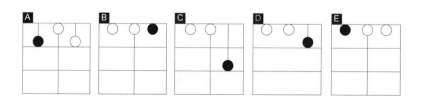

131 Which figure completes the series below?

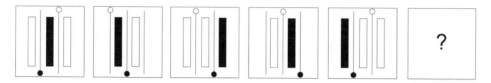

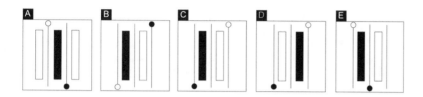

132 Which figure completes the series below?

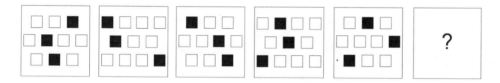

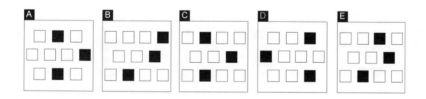

133 Which figure completes the series below?

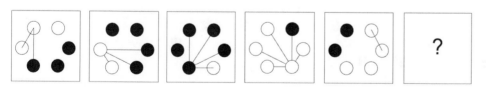

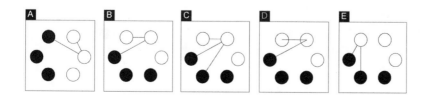

134 Which figure completes the series below?

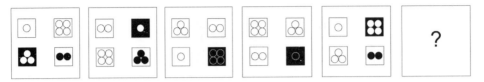

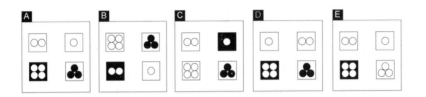

135 Which figure completes the series below?

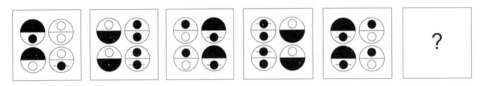

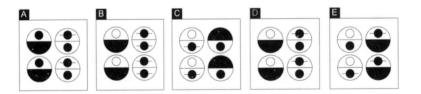

136 Which figure completes the series below?

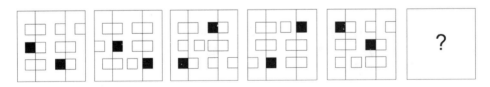

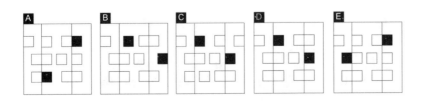

137 Which figure completes the series below?

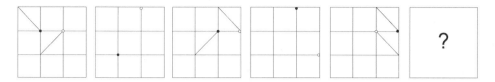

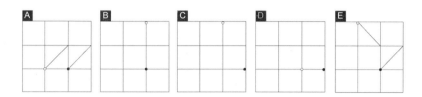

138 Which figure completes the series below?

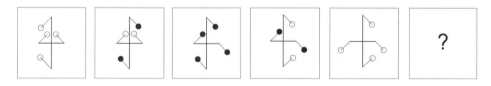

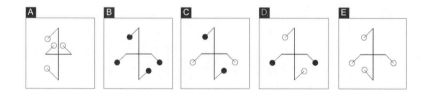

139 Which figure completes the series below?

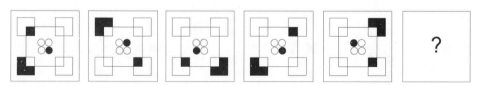

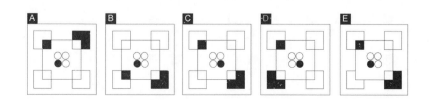

140 Which figure completes the series below?

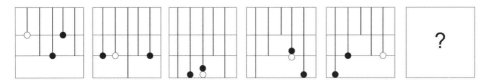

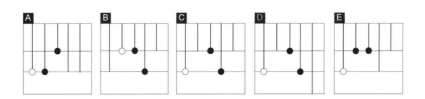

141 Which figure completes the series below?

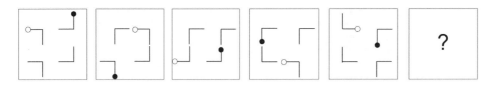

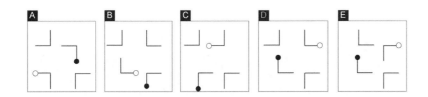

142 Which figure completes the series below?

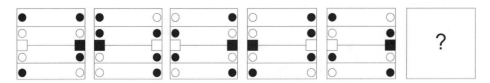

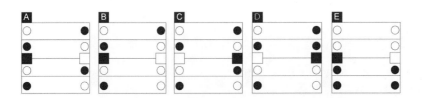

143 Which figure completes the series below?

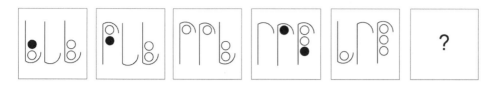

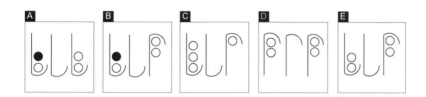

144 Which figure completes the series below?

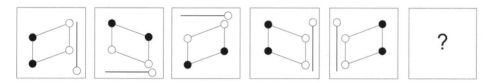

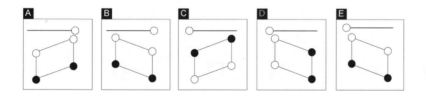

145 Which figure completes the series below?

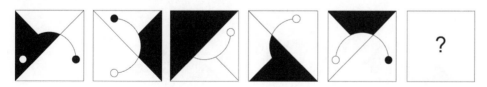

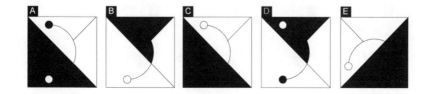

146 Which figure completes the series below?

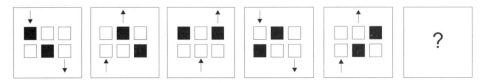

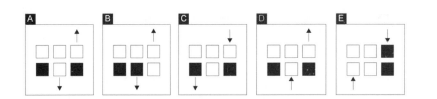

147 Which figure completes the series below?

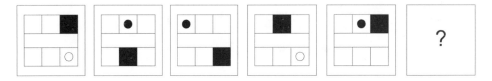

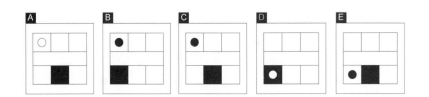

148 Which figure completes the series below?

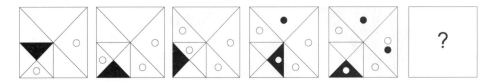

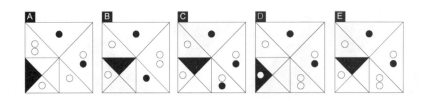

149 Which figure completes the series below?

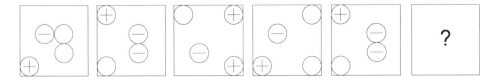

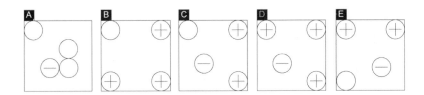

150 Which figure completes the series below?

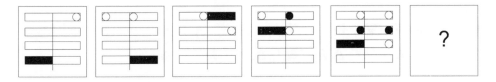

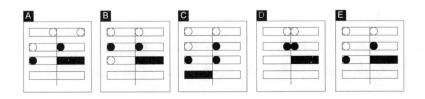

151 Which figure completes the series below?

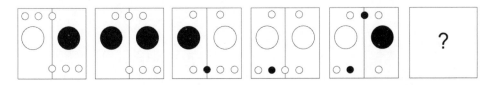

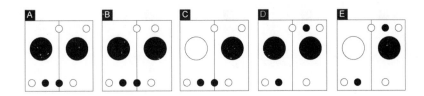

152 Which figure completes the series below?

153 Which figure completes the series below?

154 Which figure completes the series below?

155 Which figure completes the series below?

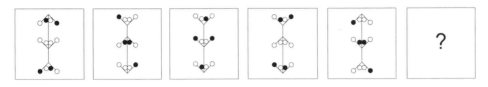

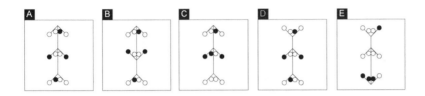

156 Which figure completes the series below?

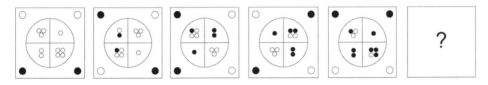

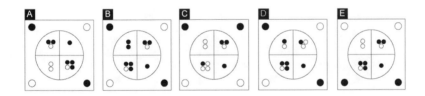

157 Which figure completes the series below?

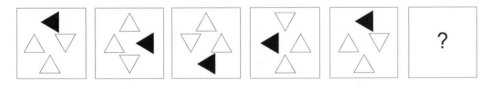

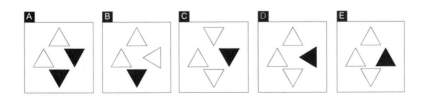

158 Which figure completes the series below?

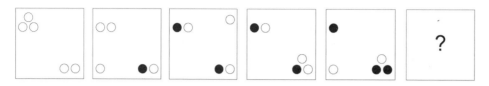

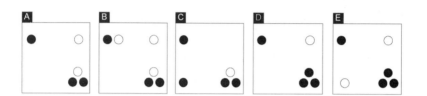

159 Which figure completes the series below?

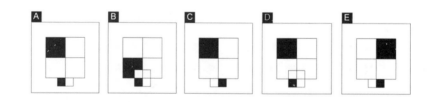

160 Which figure completes the series below?

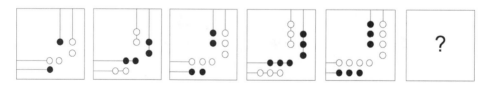

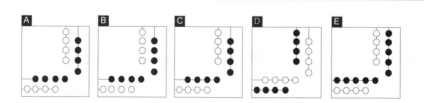

ANSWERS

1. E

Rule 1: The arrow rotates anti-clockwise 90° each time round the shape in the middle.

Rule 2: The shapes are shaded in the repeating pattern 2 black, then 2 white.

Rule 3: The shapes are in the repeating series triangle, circle, square.

2. C

Rule 1: The bent arrow rotates clockwise 90° each time round the centre.

Rule 2: The circles are shaded in the repeating pattern black, grey, white.

Rule 3: The circles move anti-clockwise around the centre, independently from the rotation of the bent arrow.

3. B

Rule 1: The triangle rotates 45° clockwise each time.

Rule 2: The fill of the square runs in the sequence black, striped, white (this leads to the square covering the triangle in the fourth of the series).

Rule 3: Which shape contains the other alternates (the square is big with triangle small, followed by triangle big with square small).

4. D

Rule 1: The arrow's position within the space moves around clockwise along the sides, progressing half the length of a side at a time (top right, middle right, bottom right, middle bottom etc.).

Rule 2: The arrow rotates anti-clockwise 90° each time.

Rule 3: The circle in the centre is shaded in the sequence black, grey, white.

5. D

Rule 1: The line connecting the arrow and the outside square rotates 45° clockwise each time.

Rule 2: The circle alternates between having a black and a grey centre.

Rule 3: The arrow points up if the circle is in the top half of the square and down if the circle is in the bottom half of the square.

6. A

Rule 1: The rhomboid moves left to right in equal steps, covering any shapes it passes over (two shapes when the rhomboid is fully visible, one shape when it is only half visible).

Rule 2: The small shapes rotate 45° each time (not visible for circle).

Rule 3: The small shapes alternate through the following shading sequence: white, striped, grey (they may have a fourth version as well but it never happens to be visible).

7. A

Rule 1: All the shapes rotate 45° each time even when not visible.

Rule 2: We move in the sequence star, smiley, triangle, arrow, ellipse one shape each time (only 3 are ever visible).

Rule 3: The slope alternates from white to black.

8. E

Rule 1: The waves move a half arc forward each time.

Rule 2: The shapes scroll horizontally two shapes at a time, through the sequence square, circle, triangle, pentagon, diamond.

Rule 3: The shapes are white in the repeating sequence second, third, first.

9. C

Rule 1: The shapes scroll one shape at a time through the sequence circle, triangle, rectangle, diamond (only 3 are ever visible).

Rule 2: The second visible shape is the largest, then the third, then the first, in a repeating pattern.

Rule 3: The shapes are white in the repeating sequence third, second, first.

10.   D

Rule 1: The shapes alternate between being below or above the line.

Rule 2: The shapes are white in the repeating sequence second, third, first.

Rule 3: The shapes scroll one shape at a time through the sequence circle, triangle, square, rectangle, diamond (only 3 are ever visible).

11.   D

Rule 1: The number of candles on the cake repeats through the sequence 2, 1, 3.

Rule 2: The number of circles is the number of candles plus 1.

Rule 3: The cake alternates between white and black.

12.   B

Rule 1: The number circle changes size in the repeating sequence whole, three quarters, half, one quarter.

Rule 2: The shape at the top right alternates between a semi-circle and a heart.

Rule 3: The circle parts progress through the repeating shading sequence striped, grey, clear.

13.   E

Rule 1: Starting with step one, every other step the number of shapes in the heart increases by one.

Rule 2: The heart is mirrored in the vertical plane after each step.

Rule 3: The number of pentagons changes in the repeating sequence 4, 1, 0.

14.   D

Rule 1: The number of sides of the shape or shapes in the centre increases by two each time (6, 8, 10, 12, 14, etc.).

Rule 2: The clock hand rotates 90° each time in a clockwise direction.

Rule 3: As the clock hand reaches the black square at the top, the number of shapes in the middle increases by one.

15.   C

Rule 1: The number of whiskers on each side of the animal's face goes through the sequence 2, 1, 0, 3.

Rule 2: The eyes alternate between slits and circles.

Rule 3: The nose changes shape in the sequence triangle, square, circle.

16.   E

Rule 1: The circle rotates 45° each time.

Rule 2: A line is added to the circle each time in equal spacing on the right side and then the left.

Rule 3: The circle is half shaded in the sequence grey, clear, black.

17.   A

Rule 1: The top left shape changes in the sequence circle, pentagon, star.

Rule 2: The top right shape alternates in the sequence between triangle and diamond.

Rule 3: The bottom left shape changes in the sequence 3 quarters shaded, 1 half shaded, 1 quarter shaded, all shaded.

18.   C

Rule 1: Each shape appears once on its own, then once stacked on top of its double.

Rule 2: When the total number of sides on the central shapes is even, the top left arrow points down. When they are odd, it points up.

Rule 3: The bottom arrows alternate between pointing right and left.

19.   C

Rule 1: The shapes on the star change in the sequence circle, square, pentagon.

Rule 2: The position of the shapes on the star moves two points anticlockwise each time.

Rule 3: The star smiles when the shape is on one of the top 3 points of the star.

20. B

Rule 1: The shape at the top left predicts the shape of the door of the house in the next figure.

Rule 2: The number of sides on the roof is the number of sides of the door plus one.

Rule 3: The doors are shaded in the sequence grey, clear, black.

21. E

Rule 1: The triangle rotates clockwise 45° each time.

Rule 2: If a heart is present, in the next figure the circles increase by one, otherwise they decrease by 2.

Rule 3: The shaded portion of the triangle shifts anti-clockwise each turn.

22. B

Rule 1. The shading of the grid piece changes in the repeating sequence grey, black, black.

Rule 2. The shapes in the upper parts of the figures are changing in the repeating sequence diamond, black circle and nothing.

Rule 3. The grid piece moves in a diamond pattern around the central rectangle.

23. E

Rule 1: The square, triangle and rectangle rotate 90° anti-clockwise and move along the following pattern around the corners. Rectangle: bottom left, bottom right, top right. Square/Triangle: top right, top left, bottom left, and then the cycle repeats.

Rule 2: If a star is present, the triangle is mirrored horizontally after the rotation from rule 1.

Rule 3: The number of smiley faces changes in the repeating pattern 3, 7, 1.

24. D

Rule 1: The ice cream colour changes in the repeating sequence black, light, stripy and grey.

Rule 2: The shapes at the bottom change in the sequence of sun, heart and moon.

Rule 3: A flake appears in the top of the ice cream in the sequence of no flake, no flake, flake, flake.

25. B

Rule 1: The top arrow rotates 120° anti clockwise each time (a third of a circle).

Rule 2: The bottom arrow alternates between rotating 90° and 180° clockwise each time.

Rule 3: If the arrows both point upwards, a moon is visible. If they both point downwards, a cloud is visible.

26. C

Rule 1: The hexagon jumps 2 spaces across the board each time, moving left to right, then down at the end of the row, before moving right to left until the end of the row. This is then repeated.

Rule 2: The board rotates 90° clockwise each turn.

Rule 3: If the hexagon would arrive on a star because of rule 1, it moves back 3 spaces, retracing where it came from.

27. E

Rule 1: The largest shape moves clockwise one each time.

Rule 2: If an extra shape appears near the middle, the shapes in the next turn change to be this shape, otherwise the shapes stay the same.

Rule 3: The largest shape alternates between rotating clockwise 45° and 90°, as seen via the shading.

28. B

Rule 1: The number of circles changes by the pattern: add two extra, take away one, add one.

Rule 2: If the number of circles is bigger than the number of triangles, crosses appear in the circles.

Rule 3: The number of triangles changes in the sequence 1, 4, 7.

29. A

Rule 1: The shapes (even when not visible) rotate 90° anti-clockwise each turn.

Rule 2: Presence of a double headed arrow in the centre means the shapes switch whether they are in the top half or bottom half within the same turn.

Rule 3: One shape vanishes each turn until there is just one shape. Then the other 2 reappear one by one (shapes continue to rotate while 'invisible'). The process then repeats.

30. D

Rule 1: A new random shape is added to the top of the cross each time.

Rule 2: The new shapes alternate between rotating clockwise around the cross and rotating anticlockwise.

Rule 3: The mouth on the face in the cross changes in the sequence straight, frowning, smiley.

31. B

Rule 1: If a star isn't present the circle and its internal shapes turn clockwise 45°, otherwise the shapes rotate anticlockwise 45°.

Rule 2: The number of triangles in the circle changes in the sequence 2, 4, 6.

Rule 3: The shapes inside the circle change in the repeating sequence clear, black, grey, stripy.

32. E

Rule 1: Balls shown at the top are added to balls at the bottom in the previous image in the repeating pattern 8, 4, 0.

Rule 2: After rule 1 is applied, balls at the bottom decrease by 3 each time.

Rule 3: If an explosion is present the balls are shaded grey.

33. A

Rule 1: The number of ears on the creature changes in the pattern 1, 4, 2.

Rule 2: Ears change shape in the pattern round, pointy, droopy, long.

Rule 3: If a nose is present, the ears go spotty.

34. D

Rule 1: The face rotates 45° clockwise each turn.

Rule 2: The eyes change shape in the pattern wide, point, slit.

Rule 3: If a smile appears, the glasses change to star shapes.

35. B

Rule 1: If the flower smiles, add a leaf.

Rule 2: The weather changes in the sequence sunny, cloudy, lightning, rain.

Rule 3: The angle of the leaves goes through the pattern down, middle, up.

36. C

Rule 1: The snake snakes down, adding a body section each time.

Rule 2: The shapes on the snake change in the repeating sequence diamond, oval, circle.

Rule 3: If the snake goes over (eats) a star, the shapes go grey.

37. D

Rule 1: The number of spots on the cat changes in the repeating sequence 1, 5, 2.

Rule 2: The number of sides of the cat's spots increases by one each time.

Rule 3: The cat's eyes look up, down, left, then right in sequence.

38. E

Rule 1: The elephant's trunk changes length from medium to long to medium to short in a repeating sequence.

Rule 2: The puddle in the dish grows by two squares each turn. See also Rule 3.

Rule 3: If the trunk reaches the puddle, it shrinks by 3 squares and the 3 squares appear in the elephant's stomach.

39. C

Rule 1: The 6-pointed star turns clockwise one point each turn.

Rule 2: The 4-pointed star turns anticlockwise one point each turn. The rope hangs off and moves with the 4-pointed star while holding onto the weight.

Rule 3: The weight changes colour in the pattern black, grey and clear.

40. D

Rule 1: The shapes scroll past one shape at a time through the sequence triangle, square, diamond.

Rule 2: The ball moves right to left covering one shape at a time until it reaches the far left and then reappears at the right.

Rule 3: The circle rotates 90° anticlockwise each time.

41. B

Rule 1: The arrow rotates 90 degrees in a clockwise direction in each turn.

Rule 2: If the arrow is at the top or left-hand side of the central shape, the central shape has an even number of sides. If the arrow is at the bottom or right-hand side of the central shape, the central shape has an odd number of sides.

Rule 3: If the arrow points to the bottom, the shape is unshaded.

42. E

Rule 1: The circle takes an increasing number of steps around the 'slots' of the central shape.

Rule 2: The circle is shaded if it's in one of the upper two 'slots'.

Rule 3: The arrow attached to the central shape points upwards if the circle is in one of the left-hand 'slots' – otherwise it points downwards.

43. A

Rule 1: The triangle and the square alternate between rotating 45 degrees in a clockwise direction and staying still: when the triangle rotates, the square stays still, and vice versa.

Rule 2: The shape which did not rotate from the previous turn is outside.

Rule 3: The triangle becomes shaded if it rotated compared to the previous turn.

44. C

Rule 1: The direction of the arrow shows in which direction the circle will move the following turn. If the circles reaches the edge of the image and is instructed by the arrow to move forward, it re-appears on the other side.

Rule 2: If the circle is shaded, the arrow itself will itself move in the direction in which it is pointing.

Rule 3: The arrow is shaded in every second turn.

45. E

Rule 1: The star rotates increasing multiples of 45 degrees in an anticlockwise direction.

Rule 2: The circle takes an increasing number of steps around the corners of the image in a clockwise direction.

Rule 3: The circle is shaded every time it's in one of the left corners.

46. A

Rule 1: The three shapes (triangle, circle and rhomboid) take one step to the right in each turn. When they reach the right edge of the image, they re-appear on the other side.

Rule 2: The shading starts at the rightmost shape and takes an increasing number of steps to the left in every turn.

Rule 3: The size of the leftmost shape is increased first. Then, the size increase moves an increasing number of steps to the right in every turn.

47. A

Rule 1: The four components (arrow, triangle, circle and empty space) move down the slope one step at a time.

Rule 2: The slope is shaded if all those three components that are actual, visible shapes, are visible.

Rule 3: The visible shapes become shaded the second time they appear.

48.   D

Rule 1: The direction of the bottom curvy line changes from turn to turn, while the shapes underneath change randomly, without any specific pattern.

Rule 2: The only unshaded bottom shape is first the left one, then the right one and, finally, the middle one. This pattern then repeats throughout the series.

Rule 3: The top half copies the bottom half (the direction of the curvy line and the shading and arrangement of the shapes) from the previous turn.

49.   C

Rule 1: The small square on the left-hand side alternates between being fully shaded, top-half shaded and unshaded.

Rule 2: The small square on the right-hand side alternates between being bottom-half shaded, unshaded and fully shaded.

Rule 3: The small squares are moving from the top to the bottom, reappearing at the top after reaching the bottom position.

50.   A

Rule 1: The shapes have increasing numbers of sides from left to right when the black line is above them. They have decreasing numbers of sides from left to right when the black line is below them.

Rule 2: The shading takes an increasing number of steps to the right. When the shading reaches the rightmost shape, it reappears on the leftmost one, and so on.

Rule 3: The shape that was shaded in the previous turn is shown at the bottom of the image.

51.   A

Rule 1: The circles at the bottom show how many candles will be on the cake in the following turn.

Rule 2: If a circle is shaded, the candle it represents will appear at the bottom of the cake.

Rule 3: The cake is shaded if it has an even number of candles on it (including candles at the bottom).

52.   B

Rule 1: The location of the small heart determines the number of quadrants the circle at the centre will have. The top left corner means one quadrant and every other corner in a clockwise direction means an additional quadrant added.

Rule 2: The heart is shaded if it's in either of the left corners.

Rule 3: If the heart is unshaded, the quadrants it creates will be shaded and vice versa.

53.   E

Rule 1: Unshaded circles outside the heart show how many circles will be inside the heart in the following turn.

Rule 2: If there are shaded circles outside the lower part of the heart, they will appear next to the unshaded circle(s) at the top in the following turn.

Rule 3: Circles inside the heart alternate between shaded and unshaded.

54.   C

Rule 1: The clock hand's position shows whether the shape in the centre will have an odd or even number of sides – 12 and 6 o'clock = even number of sides, 3 and 9 o'clock = odd number of sides.

Rule 2: The shape of the previous turn is shown at the top in the current turn.

Rule 3: Shapes in the centre are shaded if they have more sides than the small shape at the top and vice versa.

55.   D

Rule 1: If the cat has an even number of whiskers, its ears are farther away from each other – if it has an odd number of whiskers, the ears are closer to each other.

Rule 2: The cat's nose is shaded if it has more whiskers on the left side. It is unshaded in all other cases.

Rule 3: If the cat has more whiskers on the right side of its face, its nose turns into a triangle.

56. A

Rule 1: A new line is added to the circle in each turn, and the circle rotates in a way that the side which gets the line is always on top.

Rule 2: Every second line added gets a small circle on top of it.

Rule 3: The small circles turn shaded in their second turn of existence.

57. C

Rule 1: The shaded section of the square in the bottom left corner shows which corners of the figure have shapes in the same turn (the bottom left section of the square is always shaded as the square is always present).

Rule 2: Every shape in the corners starts as a triangle and they gain a side every consecutive turn they are present.

Rule 3: Shapes with an even number of sides are shaded.

58. E

Rule 1: The top left arrow shows which direction the shape will travel in the following turn.

Rule 2: If the top right arrow points upwards, the shape will gain a side, if it points downwards, the shape will lose a side.

Rule 3: If both arrows point in the same direction the shape is shaded in that turn.

59. B

Rule 1: Unshaded circles inside the star show how many steps (clockwise) along the points of the star the shape outside will take in the following turn.

Rule 2: Shaded circles inside the star mean an anti-clockwise movement.

Rule 3: Every time the shape crosses the top arm of the star, it gains a side.

60. D

Rule 1: The left 'window' of the house shows the shape of the 'door' in the following turn.

Rule 2: The right 'window' shows the shape of the left 'window' in the following turn.

Rule 3: 'Doors' with an even number of sides are shaded.

61. A

Rule 1: The number of circles by default shows how many 90 degree rotations the triangle will take in a clockwise direction in the following turn.

Rule 2: The number of hearts indicates how many steps the shading within the triangle will take in an anticlockwise direction in the following turn.

Rule 3: Shaded circles and hearts are 'disabled', that is, they do not exert any influence on the shape.

62. A

Rule 1: The number of sides the top left shape has indicates how many vertical steps the shaded section of the grid will take in the following turn. A shaded shape indicates moving upwards, an unshaded shape means moving downwards. When the shaded section reaches the edge of the grid, it re-appears on the other side.

Rule 2: The number of sides the top right shape has indicates how many horizontal steps the shaded section of the grid will take in the following turn. A shaded shape means moving left, an unshaded shape means moving right.

Rule 3: The shading alternates between black and grey.

63. E

Rule 1: The arrow in the top left corner shows whether a new line of smilies will be dropped on the current ones in the following turn (arrow pointing upwards) or an existing line will be removed (arrow pointing downwards) from the bottom. When new similies are added, they arrive in groups of 2-3-2-3.

Rule 2: Shaded arrows indicate that sad smilies will be dropped in the next figure.

Rule 3: Sad smilies will turn into happy smilies in the second turn of their existence.

64.   C

Rule 1: The number of 'snowflakes' indicates how many balls of ice cream the cone will consist of in the following turn. Every time a snowflake appears in a figure, the cone will get an extra ball of ice cream in the following turn. Whenever a 'sun' is present, the cone will lose a random ball of ice cream in the following turn.

Rule 2: An unshaded ball of ice cream turns shaded in the second turn of its existence and then disappears in the third.

Rule 3: As long as there is a shaded ball of ice cream present, the cone becomes shaded as well.

65.   B

Rule 1: The lower shape takes the posture (direction of arrow) of the upper one from the previous turn.

Rule 2: The upper circle is shaded for two turns, then the bottom one for one turn – this pattern then repeats.

Rule 3: Each time the arrow on the bottom circle is attached to the top half of the circle, a triangle appears in the image.

66.   D

Rule 1: The star shows where in the grid the circle will appear next.

Rule 2: In every turn, the previous position of the circle is shaded.

Rule 3: The circle is shaded if it's next to the star.

67.   A

Rule 1: The middle shape takes the form of the top right shape from the previous turn.

Rule 2: The bottom right shape shows what the middle shape will look like two turns from now.

Rule 3: The top and bottom shapes on the left do the same but with previous versions of the middle shape.

68.   C

Rule 1: In each turn, both the top and the bottom row of circles start with 5 – 5 circles, but some of these circles are 'destroyed' by the shaded triangles pointing at them.

Rule 2: Circles will become shaded if they have unshaded triangles pointing at them.

Rule 3: Figures in the series alternate between having more circles than triangles and vice versa.

69.   D

Rule 1: The shaded section of the circle in the top left corner shows where the shape in the middle was pointing in the previous turn. The shaded section of the circle in the middle shows where the shape is pointing in the current turn, while the shaded section of the last circle shows where the shape will be pointing in the following turn.

Rule 2: The shape in the middle is shaded for two turns then unshaded for a single turn. This pattern then repeats.

Rule 3: A second row of circles appears at the bottom, with the same rules applying to them.

70.   E

Rule 1: The shape in the top arm of the cross will appear in the left arm in the following turn. This shape then will be "judged" by the smiley face. If the face is smiling, the shape will transfer to the right arm without change. If the face is frowning, the shape will transfer with one fewer side, while if the face is sad, the shape will transfer with two sides taken away.

Rule 2: Each time the face is smiling, a small dot will appear at bottom of the cross which then stays there for the rest of the series.

Rule 3: Each time the face is sad, a dot is removed.

71.   E

Rule 1: The circle is divided into two halves with shapes in both. The total number of sides is always larger in the top half of the circle.

Rule 2: A shaded shape's sides are not counted towards the total number of sides.

Rule 3: In even-numbered turns (2,4, etc.), the total number of shapes (in both halves) is odd, while in odd turns, this number is even.

72. A

Rule 1: Vertical arrows within the circles indicate whether the given circle will appear/remain in the upper row or the bottom row in the following turn.

Rule 2: Circles with arrows pointing to the right will become shaded in the following turn.

Rule 3: Circles with arrows pointing to the left will be removed in the following turn.

73. E

Rule 1: The number of circles increases by two in each turn (eyes and eye segments are counted as circles).

Rule 2: In every even turn, a single circle becomes shaded.

Rule 3: The nose, starting as a triangle, gains an additional side in each odd turn.

74. D

Rule 1: The number of unshaded circles indicates how many times the smaller shape will rotate 45 degrees in a clockwise direction in the following turn, becoming the larger shape at the same time. In the next figure, the rule again applies to the smaller shape, the larger shape is always only the result of the rotation.

Rule 2: Shaded circles cause an anticlockwise 45 degree rotation similarly to the mechanism described in Rule 1.

Rule 3: The number of circles alternates between odd and even.

75. A

Rule 1: The number and location of the suns indicate how many leaves the flower will gain in the following turn. The side on which a given sun appears will determine the side on which the corresponding leaf will appear. The leaves are not cumulative, that is, leaves are removed before the new leaves are added in each turn.

Rule 2: Clouds have an effect opposite to that of suns. A sun and a cloud cancel each other out.

Rule 3: A lightning bolt will turn all the leaves black (if any) on the side on which it appears in the following turn.

76. C

Rule 1: The triangle takes an increasing number of steps down the shape. When it reaches the bottom of the shape, it re-appears at the top, continuing its movement.

Rule 2: The triangle gains a new side each time it lands on an odd section of the shape (counting from the top).

Rule 3: In each turn, the previous position of the triangle is shaded.

77. C

Rule 1: The shape within the structure gains an additional side for two turns then loses one in the third. This pattern then repeats.

Rule 2: The structure rotates 45 degrees in a clockwise direction after each turn where the shape within it was unshaded. If it was shaded, the structure rotates in an anticlockwise direction.

Rule 3: A circle appears under the structure each time the shape within has an odd number of sides.

78. A

Rule 1: In each turn, the shape above the bowl has as many sides as the number of unshaded squares in the bowl in the previous turn.

Rule 2: In each turn, the shape under the bowl has as many sides as the number of shaded squares in the bowl in the previous turn.

Rule 3: Shapes (with the exception of the squares in the bowl) change their shading from turn to turn.

79. B

Rule 1: The circle attached to the six-headed star takes an increasing number of steps around the points of the star in a clockwise direction, while the circle on the four-headed star does the same, but in an anticlockwise direction.

Rule 2: The circle on the six headed star is shaded if situated on any of the three upper arms of the star, while the circle on the other star is shaded when situated on the top or the bottom arm.

Rule 3: The triangle becomes shaded if one circle is shaded.

80.   A

Rule 1: The shape shown at the base of the arrow will appear in the following turn in the position where the arrow is pointing.

Rule 2: Shapes turn shaded and rotated 45 degrees clockwise in the third turn of their existence.

Rule 3: Shapes disappear in the fourth turn of their existence.

81.   E

Rule 1: A circle is surrounded by two other shapes, one of them shaded. The shaded shape will either gain a side in the following turn (when the straight line is above the shapes) or lose one (when the straight line is below the shapes).

Rule 2: If the circle is shaded, the shapes switch places in the following turn.

Rule 3: The shading goes left-right-left-right, etc.

82.   C

Rule 1: Circles at the top and the bottom indicate how many 'chimneys' will be visible in the following turn. The shading of the circles changes from turn to turn.

Rule 2: Counting from the left, even numbered chimneys are shaded at the top, and odd numbered ones are shaded at the bottom.

Rule 3: If three or more chimneys are shaded, the rectangle becomes shaded as well.

83.   A

Rule 1: The shape in the middle is the same as that shape from the corners from the previous turn which had the most sides (see also Rule 2).

Rule 2: Shaded shapes in the corners cannot become shapes in the middle.

Rule 3: The central shape becomes shaded every second time it appears.

84.   B

Rule 1: The shape within the circle is first the shape that was to the left from the circle then to the right of the circle in the previous turn. This pattern then repeats.

Rule 2: Shapes on the left are shaded if they have on odd number of sides, while shapes on the right are shaded when they have an even number of sides.

Rule 3: The shape within the circle is shaded in every second turn.

85.   A

Rule 1: An arrow pointing upwards shows that the shape will gain a side; if the arrow is pointing downwards, the shape will lose a side. An arrow pointing to the left signals that a new shape will appear, while an arrow pointing to the right shows that the shape will disappear. All transformations take place in the following turn.

Rule 2: Every second shape that appears is shaded.

Rule 3: No two arrows can point in the same direction in a given figure.

86.   B

Rule 1: If a horizontal unshaded arrow points to a circle, it will be shaded in the following turn.

Rule 2: If an arrow is pointing downwards, both circles will be shaded in the given row in the following turn, while if it's pointing upwards, neither of them will be.

Rule 3: If an arrow is shaded, its effect is the opposite of the default effect described above. In the case of horizontal arrows, this means that the circle 'behind' the arrow will become shaded.

87.   D

Rule 1: The top lane scrolls to the right, while the bottom one scrolls to the left. See also Rule 3.

Rule 2: Shapes change their shading if they disappear on one side and reappear on the other.

Rule 3: If a circle appears in the middle, the lanes switch scrolling direction from the next turn.

88.   E

Rule 1: The top left pie chart rotates 45 degrees in a clockwise direction in each turn, while the bottom left is showing the position of the top one from the previous turn. The pie charts on the right do the same but the rotations happen in an anticlockwise direction.

Rule 2: Each time a pie chart points upwards, a circle appears which then stays there for the rest of the series.

Rule 3: The number of shaded circles equals the number of pie charts pointing downwards in the current turn.

89. A

Rule 1: The shading switches between being on the left arm – in the middle – on the right arm of the structure.

Rule 2: Each time the big central oval is shaded, the whole construction rotates 90 degrees in a clockwise direction.

Rule 3: In each turn, a small circle appears in the circle that was previously shaded.

90. C

Rule 1: The small shape in the top right corner starts as a triangle, then gains a single side for two turns, then loses one on the third. This pattern then repeats.

Rule 2: For as long as the top left shape is gaining sides, a new section is also added to the circle.

Rule 3: The circle is shaded during the turns in which the top left shape is gaining sides.

91. D

Rule 1: An increasing number of circles appear within hearts. Once a heart has three circles, a new one appears.

Rule 2: Every second added circle (circles are added as following: Left – Bottom – Right) in a given turn will be shaded.

Rule 3: A heart with more shaded than unshaded circles stand upside down.

92. A

Rule 1: An increasing number of circles are added to the bottom each turn. The circles next to the arrow show how many circles will be shaded the following turn.

Rule 2: If a circle next to the arrow is shaded, it does not have a 'shading effect' on the circles in the bottom.

Rule 3: If the total number of circles next to the arrow is even, a large triangle is added to the image.

93. C

Rule 1: The inner square is rotating 45 degrees in an anticlockwise direction while the outer one is doing the same in a clockwise direction.

Rule 2: In each turn, the number of circles increases by one.

Rule 3: In even turns, there is an even number of shaded circles, while in odd turns there is an odd number of shaded circles.

94. E

Rule 1: The snake grows by two segments in each turn and the total number of circles in it also grows by two in each turn. There will always be an odd number of total circles as the circle in the first segment is alone.

Rule 2: First, an odd number of circles are shaded, then an even number. This pattern then repeats.

Rule 3: The snake segments alternate between being shaded and unshaded.

95. B

Rule 1: The large central shape assumes the form of the shape in the left then top then right position from the previous turn.

Rule 2: The small shape that will become the large shape in the following turn is shaded.

Rule 3: The big shape is shaded every second time it appears as the same shape.

96. D

Rule 1: The arrows on the left mirror the previous turn's arrows on the right, while the arrows on the right rotate 45 degrees in a clockwise direction every turn.

Rule 2: Arrows pointing upwards or downwards are shaded.

Rule 3: A triangle appears if only one arrow is shaded.

97.   A

Rule 1: Shaded shapes will rotate 45 degrees in an anticlockwise direction in the following turn, while unshaded shapes will rotate 45 degrees in a clockwise direction. There is no rule governing the shading of the shapes or which shape is removed.

Rule 2: First, two shapes are added, then one gets taken away. This pattern then repeats.

Rule 3: A star appears every time there is an even number of shapes in the image.

98.   C

Rule 1: The structure rotates 90 degrees in a clockwise direction in each turn while circles fall on the spikes (as shown by the single circle atop the construction).

Rule 2: A given spike loses its circle when facing downwards.

Rule 3: Circles that fell off the spikes are collected at the bottom of the figure and will have the shading of the spike they fell off of.

99.   E

Rule 1: The three shapes scroll vertically downwards one at a time.

Rule 2: Shapes switch their shading each time they reappear at the top.

Rule 3: The arrows show whether a shape will gain a side (pointing to the right), lose one (pointing to the left) or stay the same (no arrows) in the following turn. The number of arrows indicates how many sides the shape will gain.

100.   B

Rule 1: Based on how many circles were shaded in a given turn, the central shape is rotating that many times 45 degrees in the following turn.

Rule 2: During even-numbered turns, there is an odd number of unshaded triangles within the shape, while during odd-numbered turns, there is an even number.

Rule 3: The total number of shaded and unshaded triangles within the shape changes in the sequence 2, 3, 4, 5, 4, 3, etc.

101.   D

Rule 1: One clock hand and clock face alternate between black on white and white on black each time.

Rule 2: The hand of the alternating colour clock moves backwards by 2 hours (60°) each time.

Rule 3: When the hand is black and the clock face is white, the clock moves as far as possible within the figure in the direction indicated by the arrow on the hand. When the hand is white and the clock face is black, the clock moves as far as possible within the figure in the opposite direction to that indicated by the arrow on the hand. It always moves in a straight line in that direction from its current position.

Rule 4: The grey clock with the dashed outline mirrors the alternating colour clock face, with the mirroring alternating between mirroring in the vertical plane and mirroring in the horizontal plane. When overlap occurs, the grey clock is positioned behind the alternating colour clock.

102.   A

Rule 1: The number of sides on the black shape increases by 1 every time.

Rule 2: The number of sides on the white shape decreases by 2 every other time, beginning with staying the same the first time.

Rule 3: The black shape moves in the following pattern within the figure, which is then repeated: top left corner, bottom right corner, bottom left corner.

Rule 4: The white shape moves in the following pattern within the figure, which is then repeated: bottom right corner, top left corner, bottom left corner, top right corner. When the white shape and the black shape occupy the same space, the white shape is visible in front of the black shape.

103.   B

Rule 1: The overall number of squares increases by 2 each time.

Rule 2: The overall number of triangles increases by 3 then decreases by 1. This pattern is then repeated.

Rule 3: The number of black squares is 1 fewer than the overall number of triangles in the previous figure.

Rule 4: The number of white triangles in a figure is the same as the number of black squares in the same figure.

104.   E

Rule 1: The white triangle is reflected in a manner which alternates between the vertical plane and the horizontal plane.

Rule 2: The number of black circles increases by 1 every time.

Rule 3: The black circles are positioned at the same side as the triangle, starting from the edge of the figure. When there is an even number of circles, they are split equally above and below the triangle. When there is an odd number of circles, the extra circle is positioned near the shortest edge of the triangle rather than near the sharpest point.

Rule 4: The arrow points to the edge that the next arrow will start from.

105.   D

Rule 1: The black compass point moves round clockwise by 135° each time.

Rule 2: The grey point moves round anti-clockwise by 90° each time. When it occupies the same space as the black point, the grey point is completely obscured by the black one.

Rule 3: The grey pie chart slice in the bottom left reflects the angle in the previous figure, going clockwise, from the black compass point to the grey compass point. In the first figure shown, the pie chart slice reflects where the black and grey compass points would have been in the previous figure, based on Rules 1 and 2. Please note that as the black and grey compass points shared the same point on the compass in the third figure, there is an angle of 0° between them for that figure, so consequently the pie chart slice does not appear in the fourth figure in the sequence.

Rule 4: The shaded circle appears at the centre of the compass whenever the angle of the grey pie chart slice is greater than 180°.

106.   C

Rule 1: The black star moves 1 space horizontally each time. When it hits the edge of the grid it goes

back in the opposite direction, following the same rule.

Rule 2: The white star moves 2 spaces to the left every time. When it reaches the edge of the grid, it continues moving left by 2 spaces from the opposite edge of the grid.

Rule 3: The black circle moves 2 spaces horizontally and 1 space vertically each time. When it hits the edge of the grid it goes back in the opposite direction, still following this same rule.

Rule 4: A white triangle appears to the right of every row and underneath every column every time there are two symbols in that row or column.

107.   E

Rule 1: There are always three arrow heads, one on a single-headed arrow and two on a double-headed arrow. Whilst the left-to-right position of the arrows is arbitrary, the head of the single-headed arrow alternates between pointing up and pointing down.

Rule 2: If an arrow points to a black circle, that circle is changed into a white circle until pointed at again.

Rule 3: If an arrow points to a white circle, that circle vanishes until the space is pointed at again.

Rule 4: If an arrow points to a space, a black circle appears until that location is pointed at again.

108.   C

Rule 1: The solid black line rotates through 45° clockwise each time, joining either the opposite corners or the middle of the opposite edges of the figure.

Rule 2: The line comprising alternating long and short dashes rotates through 45° clockwise every other turn. Like the solid line, it joins either the opposite corners or the middle of the opposite edges of the figure. This line is not visible if it is in the same position as the solid line.

Rule 3: The dotted line of dashes of equal length rotates through 90° every time. It always joins the opposite corners of the figure. This line is not visible if it shares a position with either of the other lines.

Rule 4: When only two lines are visible in a figure, one or two additional circles are added in order to take the total number up to the first even number that is higher than the number of circles present in the last figure. When all three lines are visible, one or two additional circles are added in order to take the total number up to the first odd number that is higher than the total number of circles present in the last figure. The positioning of the circles is purely arbitrary.

109.   C

Rule 1: The circles move left to right in the top panel.

Rule 2: The circles move top to bottom in the rest of the panels.

Rule 3: The circles move in the shaded vertical panels on odd turns and in the unshaded vertical panels on even ones.

110.   B

Rule 1: The white triangle rotates through 90° anti-clockwise every time.

Rule 2: The black square always appears in the space that is just outside where the shortest edge of the white triangle was in the previous figure.

Rule 3: The grey circle always appears in the space to which the narrow point of the triangle was pointing two figures earlier. When the grey circle shares any space with the black square, the grey circle is positioned in front of the black square.

Rule 4: The black cross alternates between being absent and present.

111.   D

Rule 1: The cloud colour alternates between black and white.

Rule 2: White clouds produce an odd number of raindrops, whilst black clouds produce an even number of raindrops.

Rule 3: The rain falls on a diagonal from left to right for two figures then on a diagonal from right to left for two figures. This sequence then repeats.

Rule 4: The shaded circle next to the raindrops is present whenever there are 6 or more raindrops.

112.   B

Rule 1: The number of white circles is increased by 2 or 1 each time in an alternating sequence, starting with 2.

Rule 2: The number of black circles decreases by 1 less than the previous time every time, starting with 5, then 4, then 3, then 2, then 1.

Rule 3: The total number of sides on the three white shapes is equal to the combined number of white and black circles.

Rule 4: Reading from top to bottom, the three white shapes are always presented in order of their number of sides, with the lowest number at the top and the highest at the bottom. Shapes with an equal number of sides are presented consecutively in the downwards sequence rather than being positioned at the same height as each other.

113.   A

Rule 1: The circle with a cross in it that is located in the top left corner rotates by 45° every time.

Rule 2: The circle with a cross in it that is located in the bottom left corner of the figure rotates by 45° every other time, starting with the first time.

Rule 3: The circle with a cross in it that is located in the bottom right corner of the figure rotates by 45° every other time, starting with the second time.

Rule 4: The black circle appears in the top right corner whenever all 3 circles with a cross are oriented the same way.

114.   C

Rule 1: The black triangle moves one place at a time on a diagonal line down and to the right. When it reaches the bottom of the grid, it starts at the top of the next set of upward-pointing triangles to the right and follows the same type of diagonal movement as before.

Rule 2: The grey triangle pointing upwards moves by one place in a straight line from right to left. When it reaches the end of the grid, it starts again on the same line from the right hand side.

Rule 3: The grey triangle pointing downwards starts by moving by one place at a time in a diagonal up and to the left. When it reaches the top edge of the figure, it follows the path it would take if it was a snooker ball bouncing off the cushion of the table, and describes a diagonal down and to the left. Following the same logic, when it reaches the bottom of the figure it should next follow a diagonal that goes up and to the left.

Rule 4: The small white circle moves one triangle to the right every time, whether that triangle is pointing upwards or downwards. When it is positioned over a black or grey triangle, the circle remains visible over the top of it.

115.   D

Rule 1: Although they start at different points in the sequence, the top two shapes change colour in the order black, grey, white. This sequence then repeats. The bottom shape remains black at all times.

Rule 2: The shape at the top left has one fewer side each time.

Rule 3: The shape at the top right loses one side then gains two sides. This pattern then repeats.

Rule 4: The shape at the bottom has the same number of sides as the difference between the number of sides of the other two shapes. The orientation of the shape does not matter.

116.   E

Rule 1: The segmented circle alternates between being large and being small.

Rule 2: The segmented circle rotates by 120° anti-clockwise each time.

Rule 3: The segmented circle moves around the edge of the figure in an anti-clockwise direction, alternately taking up position at the corners and the mid-point of the edges. When the circle is large, it occupies the corners of the figure, when it is small it is half-way along the edge.

Rule 4: Whenever the shaded part of the segmented circle points down, a white star appears at the opposite edge or corner to the face.

117.   B

Rule 1: The number of points on the star determines the number of shapes in the next figure, including the star itself. There is no fixed sequence regarding which star will be in the next figure.

Rule 2: If there are an odd number of shapes (including the star), the non-star shapes are triangles. If there is an even number of shapes, the non-star shapes are squares.

Rule 3: Half of the shapes are black and half are white. If there are an odd number of shapes, the "extra" shape is always white.

Rule 4: The star alternates between being white for two figures and black for two figures.

118.   E

Rule 1: The arrow heads alternate between pointing left and right and pointing up and down. The position of the arrow heads is at the top right and bottom left for two figures, then at the top left and bottom right for two figures. After four figures, the sequence repeats.

Rule 2: The arrows on the left half of the figure have the effect of changing the fill of the shape they point to between a downward right diagonal stripe and a downward left diagonal stripe. The change itself takes place in the next figure in the sequence.

Rule 3: The arrows on the right half of the figure have the effect of changing the shape they point to. Triangles change into squares, squares change into hexagons and hexagons change into triangles. The change itself takes place in the next figure in the sequence.

Rule 4: The shapes on the right hand side of the figure all alternate between black and white each time.

119.   E

Rule 1: The small and medium circles take an increasing number of steps around the large one.

Rule 2: The small circle takes a single anti-clockwise step around the medium circle in each turn.

Rule 3: The large circle changes shading each time the medium circle is in the 12 o'clock position.

Rule 4: The medium circle changes shading in every second turn.

Rule 5: The small circle changes shading in every turn.

120.   C

Rule 1: The two triangles rotate by 45° anti-clockwise each time.

Rule 3: Looking at them from where their bases are joined (i.e. treating them like the left and right ears of a rabbit), the two triangles are both white, then white and black, then both black, then black and white. This sequence then repeats.

Rule 4: The black circle's position alternates between being at the corner of the figure that is closest to where the two triangles are pointing and being in the corner that is diagonally opposite to where the triangles are pointing.

121.   C

Rule 1: The square alternates between jumping diagonally between opposite corners and taking two clockwise steps.

Rule 2: The circle and the square swap their shading in every other step.

Rule 3: The group of dots follows the square, indicating the square's position in the previous step.

122.   D

Rule 1: The circles at the top left corner migrate from the left to the right corner one by one in every other step. The migration starts between the first and second steps.

Rule 2: The circles at the bottom right corner migrate from the right to the left corner one by one in every other step. The migration already started before the start of the series, and continues from between the second and third steps.

Rule 3: Circle clusters are shaded when there is an odd number of circles and unshaded when an even number.

Rule 4: The triangle alternates between pointing up and pointing down.

123.   A

Rule 1: The shading within the triangle moves from top to bottom, alternating between the left and right side between steps. When the shading reaches the bottom level, it resets to the top level in the next step (as on the right-hand side between the first and second steps).

Rule 2: The two circles show where the shading will be the following turn.

Rule 3: The circles' shadings are the opposite of the triangle segment they are next to in a given turn.

124.   E

Rule 1: The circle takes a clockwise step each turn.

Rule 2: The square the circle lands in will either move away from or towards the middle (based on its current position) the next turn.

Rule 3: The circle is unshaded when it is in squares that are in the middle.

125.   A

Rule 1: The square with the connector lines to neighbouring squares moves from left to right in each step. When it reaches the right edge of the figure, it moves onto the next row down.

Rule 2: The squares which were connected to the moving square in the previous step become shaded in the next step.

Rule 3: The 9-square grid is framed in every other step.

126.   E

Rule 1: The set of rectangles rotates 90 degrees clockwise in each step.

Rule 2: Every second time that either a single horizontal or vertical rectangle lies on top of the 2 lower layers of rectangles, it is shaded.

127.   B

Rule 1: In each step, one or two shapes move either to the middle or to the edge. Movement starts with the two shapes on the left, and then proceeds in a clockwise direction in a 2-1-2-1 sequence (two shapes move, then one shape moves…).

Rule 2: One shape in each figure is connected with lines to the two shapes in the opposite half (top or bottom) of the figure. This connection travels clockwise from one shape to the next, starting from the shape in the top right corner.

Rule 3: Shapes that are not aligned horizontally with their pairs (i.e. if the two rectangles or circles are not in the same horizontal line) are shaded, otherwise they are not.

128.   E

Rule 1: The shading of the larger circles takes a step clockwise each turn, moving from circle to circle to reach the next segment in the sequence.

Rule 2: The small circles within the circles take a clockwise step each turn.

Rule 3: The small circles are alternately either shaded or unshaded, based on whether the large circle they are in has the large shading or not.

129.   B

Rule 1: Small circles move clockwise as a group (not one by one) in each step from one segment of the large shapes to another.

Rule 2: As the small circles move to and through the segments of the top right shape, they increase by 1 in each step.

Rule 3: As the small circles move to the bottom shape, their number resets to 1.

Rule 4: As the small circles move to and through the segments of the top left shape, they change their shading.

130.   B

Rule 1: Circles hanging from the top move from top to bottom, stopping at the bottom for a step before starting to move upwards again.

Rule 2: The shading of the circles moves from left to right. Once it reaches the rightmost position, it reappears on the left side.

Rule 3: When a circle is shaded, it will move two positions (up or down) in the following step.

131.   C

Rule 1: The setup of shapes alternates between 3 columns with 2 dividing lines and 2 columns with 3 dividing lines.

Rule 2: The shading of the columns moves one space from left to right from each 3-column shape to the next 3-column shape, and one space from left to right from each 2-column shape to the next 2-column shape.

Rule 3: The circles also move from left to right along the top and bottom points of the dividing lines.

When they reach the rightmost point, they reset to the leftmost position.

132.   E

Rule 1: The setup of shapes alternates between 3/4/3 and 4/3/4 rows of squares.

Rule 2: The shading in each row moves left to right but only when the given row is visible.

133.   B

Rule 1: Going anticlockwise, a circle in each step has an increasing number of connections to subsequent circles in an anticlockwise direction. This resets to 1 connection after reaching 4.

Rule 2: The number of shaded circles increases by one and the shading moves in an anticlockwise direction in each step. When the number of shaded circles reaches 5, it resets to 1.

Rule 3: The connections alternate between reaching the middle or only the edge of the circles.

134.   A

Rule 1: In each square, the number of circles increases by 1 in each step, resetting to 1 after it has reached a maximum of 4.

Rule 2: Starting from 2 in the first figure, the number of shaded circles increases by 1 in each step from left to right, resetting to 1 after reaching a maximum of 4.

Rule 3: The number of shaded circles in a given step dictates how many anticlockwise steps the shading of the rectangle will take between the current and next steps.

135.   D

Rule 1: Each small circle can have the following states, in the following order: unshaded, shaded, shaded with an intersecting line. When a circle reaches the third state, it remains in that state until affected another rule.

Rule 2: The shading of the large half circles moves from top left to bottom left and top right to bottom right.

Rule 3: When a large half circle becomes shaded, the small circle in that sector resets to its starting (unshaded) state.

136.   D

Rule 1: The shading of the squares moves from left to right and from top to bottom in both columns. When the shading reaches the bottom, it resets to the top left positon and continues from there.

Rule 2: Shaded squares move away from the column in the following step.

Rule 3: Squares that moved away from the column in a given step move back to their original position in the next step.

137.   C

Rule 1: The shaded circle takes a diagonal step towards the bottom right, then a vertical step downwards, then a diagonal step towards the top right, then a vertical one upwards, and then this pattern repeats. Diagonal steps are indicated by diagonal lines pointing to where the circle was in the previous step. When the circle reaches the right edge of the figure, the left-right direction of movement switches to right-left (although this is not visible in the series).

Rule 2: The unshaded circle takes a diagonal step towards the top right, then a vertical step upwards, then a diagonal step towards the bottom right, then a vertical one downwards, and then this pattern repeats. Diagonal steps are indicated by diagonal lines pointing to where the circle was in the previous step. When the circle reaches the right edge of the figure, the left-right direction of movement switches to right-left (although this is not visible in the series).

138.   C

Rule 1: In even-numbered steps (e.g. 2,4), a circle on the vertical arm changes position, going from left to right or right to left, alternating between the top and bottom circles. In odd-numbered steps (e.g. 3,5), a circle on the horizontal arm changes position, going from top to bottom or bottom to top, alternating between the left and right circles.

Rule 2: The circles are shaded when they are in opposite positions on the same 'arm', i.e. when one is on the right, the other on the left, or when one is pointing to the bottom and the other to the top. Another way to think about it is to say that the circles follow the shading pattern of none shaded, outer two shaded, all shaded, inner two shaded, and so on.

139.   E

Rule 1: The square that is three-quarters shaded moves 1-2-1 positions clockwise between steps.

Rule 2: The square that is one-quarter shaded moves 2-1-2 positions clockwise between steps.

Rule 3: The shaded circle in the middle moves 1-2-1 positions anticlockwise between steps.

140.   C

Rule 1: The lines originating from the top of the figure lengthen until they reach the bottom, and then start to shorten again. The number of steps a line takes is equal to the numbers of circles on it and the line only changes length in the step after a circle has landed on it.

Rule 2: The unshaded circle jumps one step from left to right while the shaded circle jumps two steps from left to right. When circles reach the right edge of the figure, they reappear on the left side and the movement continues.

141.   D

Rule 1: The unshaded circle takes left-to-right and then diagonal steps across the left/right points of the right angles.

Rule 2: The shaded circle takes diagonal and then left-to-right steps across the top/bottom points of the right angles.

Rule 3: When an unshaded circle lands on a right angle, it is mirrored vertically in the next step.

Rule 4: When a shaded circle lands on a right angle, it is mirrored horizontally in the next step.

142.   A

Rule 1: Circles (both shaded and unshaded) move from top to bottom, reappearing at the top after they have reached the bottom.

Rule 2: The squares switch shading in every step.

Rule 3: When a circle 'jumps' through a square, it assumes the shading of the square in the next step. If it already had the same shading as the square, nothing changes.

143. B

Rule 1: The shapes containing the circles flip vertically one by one, going from left to right.

Rule 2: Once a shape has flipped, the circles contained in it start 'falling' out of it and into the next shape, one by one, starting with the bottom one first.

Rule 3: Falling circles change shading.

144. E

Rule 1: The line with the circle on the outside is rotated 90 degrees anticlockwise and then mirrored horizontally, then the pattern repeats.

Rule 2: The rectangular shape is mirrored vertically between each step.

Rule 3: The shaded circles at the points of the rectangle move clockwise in a 1-2-1 steps pattern.

145. A

Rule 1: The entire shape rotates 90 degrees clockwise in each step.

Rule 2: The shading takes a clockwise step across the three sections.

Rule 3: The shaded and unshaded circles swap positons in each step.

146. D

Rule 1: The arrows move from left to right between steps. Once they reach the rightmost position, they reappear on the left-hand side.

Rule 2: The arrows follow a down-up-up-pointing pattern.

Rule 3: Each shading takes one step in each row, from left to centre to right. When they reach the end of the row they move to the left position of the next row (top or bottom).

147. C

Rule 1: The shaded square moves from left to right along the row of squares in a 2-1-2 steps pattern, switching between rows when it reaches the right edge of the figure.

Rule 2: The circle is shaded while in the top row, unshaded while in the bottom row.

Rule 3: The circle moves around the rows, by two steps at a time from left to right when its starting position is in the bottom row, and by one step at a time from right to left when its starting position is in the top row.

148. E

Rule 1: The shaded triangle within the small square moves two positions and then one position clockwise between steps.

Rule 2: The circle in the small square moves clockwise around the four triangles.

Rule 3: A circle appears in a segment of the large square in each step going clockwise.

Rule 4: If the shading and the small circle appear in the same segment in a given step, the circle added to the large square will be shaded.

149. C

Rule 1: In successive steps, the blank circles become minus (–) circles, the – circles become plus (+) circles and the + circles become blank.

Rule 2: When blank circles become – circles, they move to the middle; when – circles become + circles they move to the corners, and stay in the corners when reset to blank, moving to the middle again when they become – circles.

150. E

Rule 1: In each step, a new circle is added, alternating between the left and the right columns. When a new circle is added in one of the columns, it pushes all previously added circles on that side down one row.

Rule 2: Each circle starts on the outside and then takes one step towards the centre, and then the cycle repeats.

Rule 3: The shading of the rectangle moves from left to right and top to bottom in a 1-2-1 pattern. When it reaches the bottom right corner, it continues from the top.

Rule 4: Circles become shaded when they are co-located with the shaded rectangle.

151.   D

Rule 1: The circle groups move according to the following pattern: (1) the circles at the top take a step from left to right; (2) the circle at the connecting vertical line drops to the bottom; (3) the circles at the bottom take a step from right to left; (4) the circle at the connecting vertical line ascends to the top. This cycle then repeats.

Rule 2: Circles that either dropped or ascended change their shading and stay that way.

Rule 3: The shading of the large circles changes (separately) in every other turn, i.e. the left circle changes shading in the second, fourth and sixth figure, while the right circle changes shading in the 3rd and 5th figures.

152.   C

Rule 1: The two shaded circles move one position clockwise in each step.

Rule 2: The short double lines at right angles to the main connecting lines flip direction when there are two shaded circles at either end of the main line they connect to.

Rule 3: Shaded / unshaded, shaded / shaded, unshaded / unshaded circles are connected (with a line in bold), then it repeats. An additional connecting line appears in each figure, connecting the shaded to the unshaded circle first, then shaded to shaded, and finally unshaded to unshaded, and then the cycle repeats.

153.   E

Rule 1: The shaded triangles in both the bottom and top rows alternatingly take a left to right step.

Rule 2: Those triangles in the top row that are pointed at by the shaded triangles in the bottom row rotate 90 degrees anticlockwise in the next step.

154.   E

Rule 1: The arms on the top side of the horizontal line change orientation one by one from left to right, and then right to left.

Rule 2: The arms on the bottom side of the horizontal line change orientation one by one from right to left, and then left to right.

Rule 3: Arms that are mirrored horizontally have circles on their endpoints.

155.   A

Rule 1: The inside shaded circle on the left travels from top to bottom. When it reaches the bottom, it resets to the top position.

Rule 2: The inside shaded circle on the right travels from bottom to top. When it reaches the top, it resets to the bottom position.

Rule 3: Outer circles next to shaded inner ones will become shaded themselves the following turn.

Rule 4: The direction of the arms changes whenever the two inside circles next to each other are both either shaded or unshaded.

156.   B

Rule 1: The groups of circles within the sectors of the large circle move clockwise from sector to sector.

Rule 2: The two shaded circles in the corners of the figure alternate in taking single steps clockwise.

Rule 3: One circle from each inner circle group that falls in the same position as either of the shaded outer circles becomes shaded in the next step. If a circle from the group is already shaded, an additional one becomes shaded (if there are additional circles in the group).

157.   D

Rule 1: Going clockwise, one triangle is rotated by 180 degrees in each step.

Rule 2: The shading travels along the triangles in a clockwise direction, starting from the top.

Rule 3: When the shading lands on a triangle, the triangle is rotated 90 degrees clockwise; then, in the subsequent step, it is rotated 90 degrees clockwise again.

158.   A

Rule 1: A single circle from the top left moves to the bottom left, then top right, then bottom right. Then another circle start its journey along the same path.

Rule 2: When a circle lands in the bottom left corner, a circle in the bottom right corner becomes shaded for the rest of the series.

Rule 3: When a circle lands in the top right corner, a circle in the top left corner (if available) becomes shaded for the rest of the series.

159.   A

Rule 1: The shaded quarters of both the large and small squares take alternating clockwise steps. This means that the shading in either square only moves every other step.

Rule 2: The small square alternates between being in front of or behind the large square.

160.   C

Rule 1: All circles alternate between being shaded and unshaded. Those 'hanging' from the top have a left-right alternation while those connected to the side have a bottom-top alternation.

Rule 2: In each step, two circles are added to the figure. In even steps, they are added to the bottom group on the side and to the left group on the top; in odd steps, they are added to the top group on the side and the right group on the top.

Rule 3: The lines connecting the circles alternate between being visible and invisible.

12. Succeeding in Situational Judgement Tests

> *Although many AD competitions do not include situational judgement tests, they may be used, especially in the annual AD5 graduate competition, where they can be an important element in the scoring (see page 27). Note that situational judgement tests are taken in your language 2.*

Situational judgement tests (or SJTs for short) present candidates with a series of hypothetical but realistic work-based scenarios in which they are required to make a decision. It is important to understand that even though called "tests", they are very different in nature from the verbal, numerical and abstract reasoning tests you will face during the selection process as they measure how you evaluate certain situations instead of testing your harder analytical skills and behaviours.

Situational judgement tests are employed because they can be used to consistently and fairly assess at an early stage behavioural attributes such as decision-making ability and interpersonal skills that are difficult to measure by other techniques.

SJTs are a fast-growing area in the selection and development field. The basic idea of presenting a relevant hypothetical situation has been in use in recruitment since the early 1900s, but SJTs in a format comparable to today's SJTs have been more prevalent since the 1940s, used in particular for predicting supervisory and managerial potential.

More recent research has found that SJTs are strong predictors of real-life job performance. This means that in the development or review of SJTs, those people doing well in the tests were also the people who performed well in role. Not only that, but SJTs seem to measure an additional aspect of performance that is not measured by other assessment tools such as ability tests or personality questionnaires. This suggests that the SJTs are tapping into a different skill, and one that is highly relevant to job performance.

In AD competitions the following competencies are measured by means of situational judgement tests:

- Analysis and Problem Solving
- Delivering Quality and Results
- Prioritising and Organising
- Resilience
- Working with Others

Theory behind Situational Judgement Tests

At the heart of social psychology is the idea that what makes us human is our ability to make sense of social situations. When we evaluate an important or new situation most of us try to understand the intentions of others in the situation, and possible causal explanations, to guide our response (e.g. "How would you react if you discovered that your colleague had leaked some confidential information to the press?").

Social psychology theory also holds that there is a similarity in how people evaluate situations, and that most people will have a shared expectation of what is an *appropriate* response. This theory forms the basis of why situational judgement tests can be used to provide an indicator of our likely behaviour in an EU job-context or elsewhere. By presenting the candidate with relevant hypothetical scenarios and a set of responses which have been previously scored for their level of effectiveness, it is possible to assess how appropriate the candidate's response selection is, and to use this information to predict their likely behavioural response if faced with similar situations in the role.

What They Measure

The name "situational judgement test" suggests that what is being measured is indeed "situational judgement", actually tapping into an aspect of "practical intelligence" or "general intelligence". It is likely that SJTs are indeed multi-dimensional; they measure a number of different constructs including social or behavioural judgement, practical or general intelligence and aspects of personality such as conscientiousness. In the EPSO assessment process the SJT has been specifically developed for the purpose of measuring the candidate's situational judgement in relation to selected EPSO competencies.

How They Are Developed

Robust situational judgement tests are developed in the same way as other psychometric tests. The particular job profiles EPSO is seeking to select for are analysed by experts to understand what type of workplace situations occur that are critical to achieving good performance outcomes. This was done by interviewing current EU officials, heads of unit, directors and subject matter experts to gain a number of perspectives on what is important and what would be effective behaviour.

At the same time, examples of how less effective behaviour could lead to less desirable outcomes are gathered. Once these situations are identified, they are written up as possible test scenarios: a paragraph or two that summarises the situation and a range of four or more response options (from *most effective* or *desirable* to *least effective* or *least desirable*). The scenario and response options are crafted so that there is no "obvious" answer and even the "undesirable" options sound plausible. This is of course necessary to avoid the risk that candidates would be able to identify the "desired" answer too easily.

Careful consideration is given to the design of the test introduction and instructions and the scenario wording, format and content. It is well known that in the case of public opinion surveys, how the question is formulated will significantly influence the answer. As this is certainly true for SJTs as well, even subtle details of presentation must be thought through carefully.

It is important that the SJT design fits within the organisational setting and the assessment process, and that it reflects realistic elements of the job role in question. However, EPSO has said that its situational judgement tests are designed so that they require no specialist knowledge to complete: they are purely behaviourally-based assessments.

How They Work

The theory of planned behaviour states that an individual's behaviour in the past is a good predictor of their likely behaviour in the future. As with a standard competency based interview, this is the basis on which a situational judgement test is used to predict a candidate's job performance or suitability for the given job profile.

For each given situational judgement test, a *scoring key* is developed so that the candidate's response can be compared against this key. Initially, this can be developed by making rational judgements as to which are the most and least preferred responses to each scenario, based on the job analysis data collected in the design process and from additional evaluations made by subject matter experts.

The SJT can then be *validated* by demonstrating a clear relationship between good performance in the test and real-life good performance in the role. In order to validate the test design, and to select which scenarios will be in the final test, groups of existing job holders such as – for example – Administrators in the European Commission or Assistants in the Committee of the Regions will be tested on the sample scenarios and their responses will be compared to their real-life competency-based job performance (as judged by their superior's appraisal ratings).

Those scenarios for which the high performers have consistently selected the most preferred response as their *own* most preferred response will be selected as good ones for the final test. If there are scenarios for which high performers consistently select different responses, these will be brought into question as to their appropriateness and dropped from the test. When used in the organisation's assessment process, the candidate's score in the SJT will be based on their performance across all scenarios within the test and a score will be given to each competency in question.

What They Look Like

When sitting the test, you will be presented with a number of workplace scenarios, or "situations", together with options for how you should respond to the problem in the situation. You will have to choose which of the options in your view represent the most and the least appropriate responses. The scenarios will not be specifically limited to tasks and roles in the EU institutions, but instead will relate to more generic workplace situations of the sort that can arise in many jobs, involving working with colleagues and within hierarchies.

Each of the situations measures one of the key competencies for the job (although you would not be informed which is being measured when answering each question) and also cross-checks the consistency of your answers. Consequently, each competency will need to be measured more than once in order to reliably estimate your ability and therefore more than one scenario will relate to each competency. The test will have been designed especially for EPSO by expert occupational psychologists and it typically might contain 20 questions with 2 points per question though this can vary.

You have been approached by your superior and asked to deliver a project within a very tight deadline. You are pleased that your head of unit has approached you to work on the project but are concerned about delivering it within the timeframe given. What do you do?

A. Review and reprioritise the projects you are currently involved in so you can start work on the new project straight away.

B. Schedule a meeting with your head of unit to discuss options for delivering the project, suggesting colleagues that you would like to involve to ensure the project is delivered within the timeframe given. (**Most Effective**)

C. Develop a plan outlining how you intend approaching the project and use this to emphasise to your head of unit your concern about the deadline and ask if it can be extended.

D. Delegate the task to another person, stressing to them the importance of meeting the deadline. Retain an overview so that you can track progress and keep the ultimate credit for the work. (**Least Effective**)

On the previous page is a sample SJT test scenario, designed to measure a generic "planning"-type competency (which is not itself a specific EPSO competency, but see the next chapter for a comprehensive sample test and explanations based on the EPSO competency framework). It also includes what can be judged to be the most and least effective courses of action (although this could vary according to exact competency definitions):

The Candidate Experience

SJTs contribute to the assessment by being a two-way process for EPSO and the candidate.

EPSO can evaluate the candidate's responses to the scenarios against the structured scoring key and evaluate the extent to which the candidate's behaviour is likely to fit in with the competencies and way of working at the EU institutions.

The candidate is also able to take a view of what it would be like to work with the EU by reflecting after the test on the types of scenarios and response options presented. These may provide a general insight into what situations or behaviours might be expected in the role. Reviewing this chapter and trying out some of the practice questions in the next chapter will prove beneficial for you: those candidates who are familiar with SJTs have been found to view the experience of completing SJTs as part of an assessment process more positively than those without that familiarity.

How to Prepare

It is a bit challenging to prepare in advance of taking an SJT: a response to a situation that may be appropriate in one role may be inappropriate in another (e.g. the way you would react to a critique from your supervisor is very different from your reaction to an issue raised by an EU citizen affected by a policy you are covering). Therefore, your answers should draw from your intuitive, *honest* responses about how you would address such situations.

However, doing some practice questions on the lines of those in the next chapter can help to alleviate stress and allow you to focus on the *content* of the questions once you start the real test, rather than spending time becoming familiar with the *format*. Also, ensure that you are familiar with the EPSO competencies, as each scenario will be based around one of these. By doing this, you will be more aware of what is likely to be looked for across all the questions. Once again, however, it should be reiterated that you must be honest in your responses and not spend time trying to second-guess what is being looked for.

If you wished to, you could look up some reference material on current best practice thinking on areas related to the competencies being assessed. Ideas for research topics on the competencies measured by EPSO through SJTs are as follows:

- **Analysis and Problem Solving** – *Identifies the critical facts in complex issues and develops creative and practical solutions*. Research areas such as troubleshooting techniques, how to approach dealing with large amounts of information, techniques to stimulate creative problem solving, how to gather appropriate information.

- **Delivering Quality and Results** – *Takes personal responsibility and initiative for delivering work to a high standard of quality within set procedures*. Research areas such as how to effectively balance quality and deadlines, how to judge when rules or procedures might be bent or broken.

- **Prioritising and Organising** – *Prioritises the most important tasks, works flexibly and organises own workload efficiently*. Research areas such as project management tools and techniques, how to prioritise effectively, how to distinguish the important from the urgent, how to respond to shifting deadlines and goalposts, when and how to delegate.

- **Resilience** – *Remains effective under a heavy workload, handles organisational frustrations positively and adapts to a changing work environment.* Research areas such as how to stay calm under pressure, how to keep an optimistic outlook, how to respond to criticism, how to balance work and home life, how to cope with ambiguity.

- **Working with Others** – *Works co-operatively with others in teams and across organisational boundaries and respects differences between people.* Research areas such as effective team working, working across organisational boundaries, how to support others.

However, it should be noted that this will be a lot of background work and it would be unrealistic to expect to become an expert in all of these areas prior to the test if you are not already. A better tactic might be to decide which one or two competency areas are your prime areas for development and focus upon these.

Tips for the Assessment itself

Several tips mentioned in the verbal reasoning chapter can be successfully applied for SJTs as well. Review and adapt those hints to match the specialties of SJTs.

- **Read Everything**: Read the scenario and each of the possible answers fully before responding. You may find that the answer that originally seemed to be the best does not turn out to be upon closer inspection. Remember that the options will be carefully worded and watch out for subtle differences in wording that could differentiate a truly exceptional response from an adequate one. If possible, try to judge which EPSO competency is being assessed so you have a good idea about what qualities they will be looking for you to emphasise.

- **Relative Answers**: Bear in mind that you are being asked to make *relative* judgements: you are not asked to say which courses of action are right or wrong. In other words, you may find that *all* of the possible responses are appropriate to some degree. In this case, just rank them in order of appropriateness to help you make the "most effective" and "least effective" decision.

- **Limited Context**: As with verbal reasoning exams, try not to bring in outside knowledge – base your responses solely on the information contained within the scenario itself. This is because your outside experience may colour your response in a way that means it is not relevant to the question being posed. To take a light-hearted example, you may know that in your team at work, they are all huge fans of pizza and therefore this would be a good way of motivating them. However, in the SJT test item, there may be no reference to this and the best way to motivate a team may well be to give a motivational talk. Therefore, your outside experience might negatively impact on your ability to perform well in the test.

- **Outcome Focus**: Take the time to consider what the possible *outcomes* would be, both positive and negative, of each of the courses of action you are considering. This will help you to narrow down the choices.

- **Communication is Key**: When a situation is described where you need to choose between handing responsibility for discussing an issue to your superior or discussing an issue with another party face-to-face, it is likely that the latter option will be preferred.

- **Internal Issues**: In a situation involving a conflict, try to look for options that favour keeping a certain issue in-house and involve only those affected by it; your loyalty to your unit or institution is highly valued.

- **Stay Positive**: When faced with a problem that may be resolved by making someone take the blame, avoid the temptation and try to act as fair as possible even if that means a disadvantage for you in the short term.

Though the primary focus of situational judgement tests is not your factual knowledge of EU procedures or administrative practice, it is advisable to read through the Code of Good Administrative Behaviour of EU officials. This includes fundamental principles such as lawfulness, proportionality, non-discrimination, consistency, objectivity and others which can *indirectly* help in your judgement of the questions. Another valuable source is EPSO's very own statement of the values based on which it aims to conduct its mission : integrity, ambition, professionalism, quality service, diversity and respect. If you bear these in mind when making your "situational judgement", it will surely yield the best result.

In the following chapter, you can find a sample Situational Judgement Test with detailed explanations, based on EPSO's competency framework.

13. Situational Judgement Test

The following practice situational judgement test questions have been developed to test the types of behaviours assessed by EPSO with specific exercises (rather than only by observation of behaviour in other assessment exercises). By completing this test you will gain an insight into the question types you will face and subject matter areas that will be invaluable in your preparation for the real test.

Each of the "situations" below is designed to relate in particular to one of the following EPSO competencies, and the answers at the end of the chapter tell you which one it was:

- Analysis and Problem Solving

- Delivering Quality and Results

- Prioritising and Organising

- Resilience

- Working with Others

Please complete these questions in a quiet place with few distractions. You have a series of scenarios and then four possible ways to approach that scenario. It is your task to decide which of the answers you think would be most effective and which would be the least effective.

There is no time limit in this exercise (at the EPSO exam timings can vary but in the 2018 AD5 graduate competition candidates had 30 minuites for 24 questions). However you should try not to ponder too long on any one question: your first reaction to each of the possible approaches is usually the most honest one. Try to identify which competency you think is being assessed to help focus your response, but aim to give your honest response rather than attempting to "second guess" the examiners.

If you feel that you agree or disagree with ALL of the possible options, then please choose the ones that you think are the most and least effective from those presented in a RELATIVE sense.

Remember: For each of the following situations you should pick the MOST and the LEAST effective of the options listed.

The answers come after Situation 30.

Situation 1

You have spent a lot of time putting together a long and very detailed EU report. A more experienced colleague in your Unit offered to review it for you before submission. Although they were not directly involved in the project it covers, you accepted this offer. Their review has come back to you and is highly critical of the report content and its structure. You believe that the critique is unnecessarily negative, and that many of the criticisms are unjustified. How do you respond to this criticism?

A. Submit the report as it stands. You were the person initially given the task of producing the report and were personally involved in the project.

B. Ask your colleague to explain his criticisms so you can better understand which of them to address.

C. Make all of the changes recommended by your colleague, as his experience is likely to contribute to the validity of his criticisms.

D. Dispassionately analyse the criticisms to determine which of the recommendations are sensible and which should be ignored.

Situation 2

You have been assigned a fairly lengthy project which will require you to work closely with a teammate who you have previously found to be distant and stand-offish. You have also previously overheard him saying negative things about your abilities to another team member. You are concerned about having to now work closely with him. How do you proceed?

A. Try to approach working with the teammate with an open mind.

B. Discuss your concerns with your Superior prior to starting the project.

C. Ask the teammate to explain the negative comments you overheard.

D. Adopt a high degree of caution in your interactions with the teammate.

Situation 3

You are part of a project team that provides data to DIGIT, the Commission's IT Directorate-General, which they then utilize in implementing a complex computer generated report about performance against agreed monthly targets. They are dissatisfied with the format in which your team provides the data and provide details of the alternative format they would prefer instead. This format would require additional analysis from your team and would not be viable within the timescales your team has to turn the data around. How do you proceed?

A. Continue to use the existing format in order to ensure that timescales are appropriately managed.

B. Adopt the elements of the new format that you know can be easily changed and that would not impact on timescales.

C. Adopt the new format in its entirety whilst explaining that timescales for getting the data to them will need to be longer as a result.

D. Ask the IT Unit to explain which elements of their preferred format are of greatest value to them and adopt these if timescales are not dramatically impacted.

Situation 4

You are responsible for preparing key aspects of a presentation for a more senior colleague. These will be inserted into the overall presentation, some aspects of which are already written, some of which are being prepared by other members of your Unit. The senior colleague has provided everyone with a clear overview document and she has promised to inform the relevant individuals if aspects of their part of the presentation require any changes. How do you tackle this task?

A. Frequently telephone your colleagues who are also working on the presentation to understand how the presentation is coming together.

B. Work primarily from the overview document provided by the senior colleague and from any changes that come directly from her.

C. Request that colleagues inform everyone involved in preparing the presentation of any changes affecting their area using e-mail or similar.

D. Arrange regular meetings for everyone involved in preparing aspects of the presentation where changes can be discussed collectively.

Situation 5

You have been finding your work relatively unchallenging recently and asked your Superior for more opportunities to challenge yourself. In response to your request, he put you in charge of a project, the output of which has clear visible benefits to EU policy. However, the work is taking up more time than you initially anticipated and you are finding much of the work even more tedious and mundane than your regular responsibilities. How do you act?

A. Continue to deliver the work without commenting on the fact that you are finding it tedious as the policy benefits are clearly evident.

B. Continue to deliver the work as requested, whilst informing your Superior that it is not actually challenging you as much as you had hoped.

C. Point out to your Supervisor that the work is more time consuming than anticipated and request some assistance from another team member to share the time commitment.

D. Tell your Superior that you would like someone else to take on this work as you are finding it time consuming without being challenging.

Situation 6

There are unconfirmed rumours that the roles within your Directorate are being reviewed and people's responsibilities will be changed. Your Superior has confirmed that a major restructure will take place, and although the final details are not yet clear, from the information provided it seems that your role will be affected. As a result of this uncertainty, morale is low across the Directorate. How do you approach this situation?

A. Spend some time putting together an outline of your skills so you can align them with any new responsibilities that may come your way.

B. Put most of your energy into performing your existing role as effectively as possible, thus demonstrating how much you can achieve and await further clarity.

C. Offer to contribute to tasks that are similar to those that you believe are likely to be required after the restructure has taken place.

D. Request a meeting with your Superior to understand the nature of the restructure more fully and how it will affect you.

Situation 7

One of your colleagues has become very erratic in their time-keeping, which is very out of character. In addition he is apparently trying to avoid another member of your Unit with whom he previously appeared to have a close working relationship. This behaviour is impacting on the performance of the team and the team dynamic on a project that involves all three of you. How do you act in this situation?

A. Ask your colleague in private if there are any issues underlying his time-keeping and the deterioration in both performance and dynamic in the team.

B. Ask the team member that the colleague may have difficulties with if they know of any issues that might be affecting your colleague.

C. Raise your concerns about your colleague with your Superior as you feel they ought to know and may be able to advise on how to proceed.

D. Decide that the matter is none of your business and allow the two individuals concerned to deal with the issue themselves.

Situation 8

You are in a meeting, trying to get your point of view heard, when another person interrupts you saying that you are "talking nonsense" and then puts forward his views instead. The group all agree with the other person's idea even though you did not finish describing yours and you feel it still has merit. Moreover, the other person's plan has some obvious flaws. The group is about to move onto another topic of conversation; what are you most likely to do?

A. State that you, likewise, feel that the other person's idea is "nonsense" and that if he hadn't interrupted so rudely, he might have had a chance to hear your idea as well. Then proceed to give your views.

B. As the group is about to move on, don't hold up the meeting by disagreeing now, but send round an email that outlines your alternative idea afterwards, asking for feedback and whether you could call a subsequent meeting to discuss.

C. Let them proceed with the other person's idea, as it is the group consensus decision. However, do some preparation in advance to manage the fall-out when things go wrong.

D. Despite holding up the meeting, you state clearly and firmly that whilst you appreciate the other person's idea has merit, there are some drawbacks and you would like to suggest an alternative. Then proceed to give your views.

Situation 9

Your Superior has asked you to urgently analyse possible proposed new approaches to managing cases of legal infringements and provide a report on your recommendations by the end of tomorrow. She has provided you with various documents outlining the different proposals. However, when you take these away to read through, you quickly realise that many of them are incomplete or lacking in detail. What do you do?

A. Explain to your Superior that the information she has provided lacks sufficient detail for you to be able to make an informed recommendation and ask where further information can be found.

B. Try to track down the people who put the various proposals together and speak with each of them in order to be able to make a more informed recommendation to your Superior.

C. Summarise the pros and cons of the proposed approaches based on the information provided, acknowledging the limitations of the information and recommending more thorough research.

D. Assume that the information you have been provided with is sufficient to express the key points of its authors and produce a report based on this information being sufficient in itself.

Situation 10

You are working as part of a team to discuss how to resolve a problem that has occurred with a technical system. The conversation seems to be going nowhere, with lots of people suggesting their own solutions but no-one listening. About halfway through you notice that the technical expert who was responsible for the problem has been quiet for most of the meeting, only contributing the occasional fact when asked by others. You know he is shy as you have worked with him for a while, but you definitely feel he could be contributing more. What do you do?

A. Explain that you feel the meeting is not achieving its objectives and you are running out of time. Summarise what has been discussed and then say that you want to make sure that everyone's views are heard. Then ask for the technical expert's views directly in front of the rest of the group.

B. Make a note of the fact that the technical expert not only caused the problem, but was also unhelpful in resolving the issue. Feed this back to him and his superior following the meeting.

C. Ask him for his views immediately and assertively. The meeting is already halfway through and you do not wish to waste any more time on discussions that might be irrelevant.

D. Suggest that the group pause for a moment and refocus on the purpose of the meeting. Then ask if anyone would like to comment on what we have covered so far whilst looking at the technical expert in the hope that they will take the opportunity to speak.

Situation 11

You are new to the role and one of your team members comes to you for an urgent decision. Apparently, they are in a heated debate with someone from another team about the best way to implement a new piece of software. Your team member has presented you with a large amount of information that they say backs up their case and asks you to give them your support at a project meeting tomorrow. What do you do next?

A. Demonstrate your faith in your team member's judgement and promise to give your full support at the meeting.

B. Ask if the meeting can be postponed so that you have a chance to look through the information and analyse it in more detail before arriving at a decision about what to do.

C. Go and see the individual from the other team to get their side of the story before making up your mind about what to do.

D. Start from scratch in analysing the situation for yourself and see if you can suggest something that meets both party's needs.

Situation 12

You have just been given responsibility for overseeing a special project team that has been put together to work on a large piece of translation work over the next 6 months. You have worked with everyone before and you feel you know their strengths and weaknesses. They are all hard workers and you are confident they have the motivation to do an excellent job. However, you do know that the commissioning client is likely to change the specification of the project as time progresses, so you want to keep things flexible. How would you approach the management of the team?

A. Gather the team together at the start and reiterate the faith you have in their ability to deliver. Avoid patronising them by telling them exactly what is expected of them. Ask for regular updates from them and hold ad hoc meetings to check on progress.

B. Identify the key milestones, risks and contingencies facing the project in partnership with the team and pull together a formal project plan that you can all refer to as the project progresses.

C. Instruct the team to begin by working towards the first deadline target, without looking too far into the future so that you can respond flexibly to the client's changing requests.

D. Start with a broad plan, but then arrange one-to-one meetings with every team member on a daily basis in order to check on progress and assign new tasks and responsibilities as they arrive from the client.

Situation 13

You are responsible for compiling the results of an important opinion survey that is running behind schedule and you are due to present the findings in two days' time. The work required is fairly basic data entry with some simple calculations required to get average scores. You already have a full diary and are feeling exhausted, your superior is away on holiday and you have no additional budget to spend. How do you approach the situation?

A. Decide to request an extra temporary member of staff anyway and worry about the budget later: delivering the project on time is the most important issue.

B. Scale back the scope of the project and report on what you have been able to complete in the available time and then give a follow-up presentation at a later date that covers subsequent work.

C. Work additional hours yourself in order to get the data entered, even if you already have a very busy schedule.

D. See if some extra resource is available from another team to help with the data entry.

Situation 14

You have been asked to manage the transition from an old database system to a newer replacement, a task that will require many people's contributions and cooperation. The new system has improved search facilities but data input is more complicated and time-consuming. You have a target date several weeks down the line for when the entire task must be completed, but it is up to you to determine how best to meet this deadline. How do you approach the task?

A. Break the task down into a series of smaller processes, complete with individual deadlines and targets for each task.

B. Concentrate on engaging with those required to input data into the system as these are likely to be the people most resistant to the transition.

C. Heavily publicise the target date to ensure that everyone affected is aware of when it must all be completed.

D. Focus on examining in detail the elements of the task you expect to be most challenging.

Situation 15

You submitted a report making several efficiency recommendations to your Unit and you received a lot of praise for your work. However, you recently reread your report and noticed an error in your analysis of one key process, upon which one of your main recommendations was founded. As a result of this recommendation, which has already been adopted, savings in time and money have been great. Unfortunately a previous stage for checking data has now been omitted and there is an increased risk of errors continuing into later stages. Although this has not happened so far, if it did, bad policy decisions could be made or, if the mistake was spotted, delays could be severe, as much work would need to be redone using the correct data. As your recommendations resulted in a complex process overhaul rather than tackling processes in isolation, the stage cannot easily be reinserted in its previous form. How do you act?

A. Continue with the revised processes without saying anything as they are delivering savings in both time and money.

B. Alert everyone using the process to your oversight to ensure they are especially careful in inputting the data first time round.

C. Say nothing but explore ways to address the omission which, once identified, you can include in a second set of recommendations.

D. Point out your oversight and suggest reverting to the original processes until you can formulate a new set of recommendations.

Situation 16

It is your first week back at work after two weeks of annual leave. You come back to find that a large amount of work has been set for you by different people in your Unit. All of the work is to be completed by the end of the day and you feel overwhelmed. Each of the people who set you work has asked what time you will complete it by and insists that their work is of the utmost importance. Your Superior then reminds you of another important task you have with a non-negotiable deadline of tomorrow morning. What do you do?

A. Arrange to see your Superior, explain that you are feeling overwhelmed due to the unrealistic amount of work you have been set, and discuss together how to move forward.

B. Speak straight away to each person in your Unit who set you work; explain the situation and ask them whether the deadlines can be extended, apologising for the inconvenience.

C. Take 5 minutes to reflect on the situation and take hold of your emotions before persevering with the tasks as they were set. Ask for support from your colleagues if needed.

D. Tell each person that due to a lack of communication, you have an unrealistic workload. Explain that it is not just their work which is important and if they need the work completed by today, they need to see if someone else is available.

Situation 17

You have been tasked with creating a presentation based on a project which you and some colleagues from your Unit recently undertook. Your Superior will give the presentation to the Directorate tomorrow. You want to show your Superior that you are personally capable of producing the necessary content so that your efforts and skills will be recognised. Ultimately, the most important thing is that a high quality presentation is produced. How do you proceed?

A. Create the presentation yourself based upon what you learnt during the project. Run the final version by your colleagues for feedback before sending it to your Superior.

B. Ask the other people you worked with to send you any notes they made about the project when working on it, but decide on the content yourself.

C. Invest some time reflecting on the project and deciding what is the most relevant content. Create the presentation based upon your own experiences and expertise.

D. Call together the colleagues who worked on the project with you and discuss it in order to get their views on the most suitable content for the presentation.

Situation 18

Your Superior has compiled some data for you to analyse and then include in a report. After looking at the data, you start to think that something isn't right. You believe you may have identified an error in the dataset – however you are not certain at this stage. What approach do you adopt?

A. As you are not certain, and to avoid embarrassment, include the original data in the report and send it to your Superior to review.

B. Look at the dataset in more depth before raising the issue. Carry out the appropriate analysis to confirm or deny the suspected error.

C. In order to address the potential issue, notify your Superior of the possible error straight away and explore the dataset together.

D. Ask a colleague to look over the dataset and see if they identify an error. If an error is confirmed, raise the issue with your Superior.

Situation 19

It is a very busy period for your Unit, with everyone working to tight deadlines. You've been given three tasks by three different senior staff members, all of which are to be completed before tomorrow morning. You are finding it difficult to juggle all three tasks. What are you going to do?

A. Contact the people who set the tasks. Enquire about the urgency and importance of each task and ask whether the deadlines can be extended.

B. Complete the most important task to the very best of your abilities by the deadline. Move on to the other tasks later once you have the time.

C. Persevere with all three tasks and aim to get all of them to a fairly good standard by the deadline, despite the lack of time.

D. In order to complete all three tasks, work throughout the night until all of the tasks have been completed to a high standard.

Situation 20

You are about to embark on a new project. You have had a preliminary project briefing and are due to have one final meeting with your Superior before you start, just to confirm arrangements. The project is scheduled to start by the end of the week as the timeframe is quite tight. However, due to unforeseen circumstances, your Superior has been called away and will not be contactable until the middle of next week. How do you act?

A. So as not to begin the project before having had the final meeting with your Superior, postpone the start date until after your Superior returns.

B. Before you start the project, spend however long is needed consulting your colleagues in order to get ideas for how best to approach it.

C. Attempt the parts of the project where everything is confirmed and delay the rest of the project until your Superior is back.

D. Despite no final meeting, make a start on the project based on the information gathered from the initial briefing and your own ideas.

Situation 21

Your Superior asks you to finalise a report on a major new EU initiative because the person who started it has been called into an urgent meeting. When you finish the report, you send it to the Directorate as requested by your Superior. The Directorate complains that the data in the report is inaccurate and not what they originally produced. You are sure that the data is right as you did not change it. When your Superior learns of the Directorate's reaction he is very disappointed and asks you to explain what happened. How do you handle this situation?

A. Approach the person who started the report when you next see him. Ask him to explain his approach when compiling the report and use this to see if he made any errors.

B. Contact the Directorate yourself and apologise for what happened, assuring them that you will investigate to ensure this does not happen again.

C. Inform your Superior that you used the data you were given. Suggest that he asks the person who started the report if he made a mistake or altered the data.

D. Request a meeting with everyone involved in compiling the report and try to understand what happened. Take the necessary actions and apologise where necessary.

Situation 22

You are running a Unit project and hold weekly meetings for your Unit members. One of the members repeatedly arrives late to the meetings and then wastes time and makes disrespectful comments to you whilst you are asking for input from the group on your ideas. The person is appearing increasingly agitated as the weeks go by. How do you act in this situation?

A. In order to resolve the issue, contact the person's manager and ask them to speak to the individual: he may be more likely to listen to a more senior individual.

B. Send an email to the whole project team which stresses how important the meetings are and how everyone needs to arrive on time and be fully committed.

C. Meet with the individual on a 1:2:1 basis and ask him why he is often late. Ask him for feedback on how he thinks the meetings could be improved.

D. The next time the Unit member arrives late or is disruptive, stop the meeting and challenge the person there and then to try and prevent it happening again.

Situation 23

You recently started to think that your Unit would benefit from having someone who is tasked with generating new systems and ways of working, and improving existing ones. You believe that this would benefit everyone in the Unit and the majority of people appear in favour of your suggestion. However the senior Unit managers you approach say that adding the cost of an additional role is not currently feasible. What do you do?

A. Put together a site in the intranet where all Unit members can share new ways of working. This way, all members have easy access to them and can adopt them if useful.

B. Arrange to meet with the most senior person in your Unit and put together a proposal for your ideas which is tailored to her, in order to win her support.

C. Look at other ongoing projects within your Unit that could benefit from new ways of working. Use these examples to support your case and approach the senior managers again in a few months.

D. Due to the seniority and knowledge of the managers you approached, accept their decision for now. Share ideas informally with colleagues as they arise.

Situation 24

You are managing a group of colleagues on a key project. You are eager to prove to your Superior that you are capable of leading the group to success. One way you want to show your ability is to finish the project 3 days ahead of the deadline, which means there will be ample review time for your Superior. You are aware that some of the group members have other fairly demanding tasks to complete within this timeframe, but you believe your aim to be achievable. However, you then receive a request from your Superior for the project to be completed a whole 14 days prior to the deadline. How do you respond?

A. In order to show your Superior what you are capable of, agree to the new deadline and ask the group members to invest additional hours in the project if required in order to complete it on time.

B. Agree to the new timeframe and ask other colleagues from your department not already involved in the project if they have any spare time to assist with the workload.

C. Explain that due to your group members' other commitments, you don't think that the requested deadline is feasible; however, say that you aim to complete the project 3 days ahead of schedule.

D. Inform him you are unsure whether or not you could achieve the new deadline. Work on the project as planned and let him know nearer the deadline if you think it is realistic.

Situation 25

There is a set of internal procedures that you have abided by since working for the EU. When you first started, you were told that it was important that organisational rules and procedures were followed, and any instances where they were breached should be highlighted upwards. When speaking to a Senior Manager from another Unit, he asks you if you can find a way around one of the procedures in order to help him get a report completed before an important deadline. He presents a strong rationale for his argument. How do you proceed?

A. Help the Senior Manager as he put forward a good argument and this will strengthen your working relationship.

B. Inform your Superior of the situation and ask him to respond to the Senior Manager on your behalf.

C. Explain to the Senior Manager that you cannot help him and inform your Superior of the situation that has occurred.

D. Refuse to bypass the procedure and remind the Senior Manager of the importance of following organisational procedures.

Situation 26

You have been asked to take responsibility for writing a complex policy document within the next month. One of your colleagues has offered to support you as he has experience in the subject area. There is a very large amount of available information that you could use to write the document, including a series of documents of different styles such as spreadsheets, slides and reports. A lot of the information is unfamiliar to you and you are concerned about your experience in the overall topic you are looking at. How do you respond?

A. Figure out some of the key documents and focus on understanding them first, as these may give you a good understanding of the area overall.

B. Ask your colleague to put together a plan for how to tackle the information, to ensure your approach is based on his experience.

C. Create a detailed list of all the different documents that could possibly be used so that you have a clear reference for these.

D. Meet with your colleague to propose an approach to tackle the data, stating that he is welcome to contribute insight to your plan.

Situation 27

You have been working closely with a colleague on putting together a review of recent international legislation. There are only a couple of days before the review is due. You have just found out that your colleague is unwell and will not be in the office today. While the review is almost complete, you feel that your colleague could still add value to the process. What do you do?

A. Wait until your colleague returns tomorrow to finalise the review to make sure you don't make incorrect changes to the report.

B. Focus on finishing off the review yourself and try to send it to the relevant people today, a day before the expected deadline.

C. See whether anyone else can help you finalise the review and then run the work past your ill colleague tomorrow if they return.

D. Contact the relevant people in your Unit, explaining the situation and ask for an extension to make sure the review is finalised.

Situation 28

You are responsible for managing an important project which requires input from several of your colleagues. You are reaching an important point in the project's progress and, while it is mostly running well, a few of the team have not delivered everything you expected and needed from them by this stage. While you are still on schedule overall, this may well have a knock-on impact on the rest of the team's work and change their schedules. How do you deal with this?

A. Re-work your timeline for the project and then communicate new goals for the different team members.

B. Immediately look for additional resources to ensure that you can meet your timelines comfortably.

C. Meet with the team members who were not able to meet their targets and ask how you can support them.

D. Write to the whole project team, highlighting the incomplete work and how it will negatively impact the project.

Situation 29

At a weekly meeting you are making a presentation to a large number of members of your Unit, including several senior staff. You prepared well for the presentation, but halfway through you realise you are working from an incomplete version of the slides and you do not have the final few slides that show the conclusion. There are still some slides remaining in your slideshow that you know are not missing. You have about 15 minutes left to talk, and know that it will take about 5-10 minutes to find the updated version of the slides.

A. Apologise and state that you will need to complete the talk next week as you are missing important slides.

B. Apologise and ask a colleague to find the correct slides while you continue to talk on the available slides.

C. Continue the talk but focus mainly on the slides available, discussing the conclusion briefly where possible.

D. Call a break while you find the slides, locate them, then return and talk through what you can in the remaining time.

Situation 30

You are leading a small team putting together a significant risk assessment for a piece of proposed legislation. Two of your team members are constantly getting into disputes and this is distracting other members of the team. In your current meeting you are discussing who will do what work. The two team members quickly get into an argument regarding how you have allocated the work, with one agreeing with the way you have suggested and the other stating he disagrees. They are raising their voices and this is clearly upsetting the other members of the team. How do you deal with this?

A. Assertively tell the whole team that you are leading the project so they need to follow your instructions to ensure that it is a success.

B. Ask both team members to stop raising their voices as it is having a negative impact on the meeting rather than helping with the task.

C. Try to solicit the views of each team member independently and ensure they are presenting their ideas to you rather than arguing with each other.

D. Allow the debate to continue for the meanwhile, but make a note to talk to both team members after the meeting.

Answers with Explanations

Situation 1. EPSO competency: RESILIENCE

The most appropriate answer in this case is **Option D**. A dispassionate approach to criticism demonstrates great resilience, whilst the analysis will ensure that effort expended in amending the report is more likely to be in areas where amendments are genuinely needed.

Option A is probably the least desirable as it simply dismisses the criticisms out of hand, in spite of your colleague's experience, and also means that his review of your work has been a waste of his time.

Option C, in contrast, whilst demonstrating a desire to take criticism on board, assumes that overall experience is everything; your colleague may not have sufficient knowledge of your particular project to be able to advise on all aspects of content.

Option B is arguably the second best option, but requires your colleague to invest more of his time having already done you a favour.

Situation 2. EPSO competency: WORKING WITH OTHERS

The most appropriate answer in this case is **Option A**. An open minded approach is the best way to give the working relationship a decent chance, and for you also to ultimately disprove their negative opinions of you.

Option D, in contrast, risks damaging the relationship.

Option B has some merits, in that your Superior will be aware of the potential issues should anything go wrong; however your teammate has not said anything negative to you directly, so it is difficult to raise this issue.

The least desirable option, however, is probably **Option C**; it means your teammate knows you may have a problem with him, which risks damaging the relationship, and also involves admitting to listening in on other people's conversation.

Situation 3. EPSO competency: ANALYSIS AND PROBLEM SOLVING

The most appropriate answer in this case is **Option D**. This option balances meeting the needs of the end user of the data (i.e. DIGIT) whilst recognising that timescales cannot be greatly affected if the data is used to analyse performance against monthly targets.

Option B also demonstrates a pragmatic approach, but without knowledge of how the data is converted into the final report, it would be difficult for you to make a call as to which elements of the proposed format should be retained and which are less critical.

Option A demonstrates a desire to maintain the status quo and disregard the request.

However, **Option C** is probably the least desirable option; if the reports are produced monthly, a delay in their production will make it difficult for DIGIT to react swiftly enough to the messages they contain.

Situation 4. EPSO competency: PRIORITISING AND ORGANISING

The most appropriate answer in this case is **Option C**. This makes the most effective use of everyone's time whilst ensuring that everyone is kept informed via a clear written record.

Option B is the least desirable option, as it does not keep track of any changes to other people's parts of the presentation that may impact on your own.

Option A involves time-consuming chasing of information and multiple communications of the same information.

Option D includes the benefit that changes can be discussed in a single forum, but may prove a waste of time; it can always be added into the process if changes prove to be very frequent and complex, but as a starting point is less sensible than the e-mail approach of Option C.

Situation 5. EPSO competency: DELIVERING QUALITY AND RESULTS

The most appropriate answer in this case is **Option B**. Your Superior will be made aware that the work is not challenging you, whilst the work continues to be done.

Option A also ensures that the important work is completed, but your Superior may believe that it is challenging you if you do not speak up, and future tasks may be at a similar level.

Option C could be seen as a rather underhand attempt to share the dull duties and could also make you look less capable in the eyes of your Supervisor.

However **Option D** is probably the least desirable option, as it is an attempt to shirk any personal responsibility for delivering output that is important to EU policy.

Situation 6. EPSO competency: RESILIENCE

The most appropriate answer in this case is **Option B**. It demonstrates great resilience to continue to work effectively under difficult circumstances.

Option C is probably the least desirable as everyone will wish to demonstrate their skills on tasks that will be relevant, and not everyone can do them at once. Your Superior will have assigned tasks with people's skills in mind and chasing the ones that will exist after the restructure may not be in alignment with your Superior's wishes and without further information your guesses as to what will be required may be wrong.

Option A contains some good qualities (it is always useful to be aware of your skills and consider how they could be applied), but without further knowledge of what the new responsibilities will look like, this exercise could lack focus at this stage.

Option D is also a reasonable reaction, but your Superior will likely have shared as much as they can already, and will wish to inform others according to a timetable set by the organisation.

Situation 7. EPSO competency: WORKING WITH OTHERS

The most appropriate answer in this case is **Option A**. A private discussion with your colleague where you seek to better understand any potential underlying issues and give the opportunity to talk about them both demonstrates concern for their well-being and potentially enables the issues to be addressed.

Option B is probably the least desirable option; if there are issues between the two teammates, it is not advisable to talk to one about the other as this could appear to be taking sides with the one you have the discussion with rather than the one who is externally exhibiting behaviours that are out of character.

Option C does allow you to get advice about how to proceed, but it also involves you highlighting someone else's potential personal issue to your Superior without their knowledge that you are doing so.

Option D is not an accurate reading of the situation; your project is being affected, and this option does not address it in any way.

Situation 8. EPSO competency: RESILIENCE

The most appropriate answer in this case is **Option D**. It demonstrates great resilience to not only come back against a challenger that everyone else has agreed with, but also to do so in a calm and measured manner. It will be far more efficient to raise the point now, even if it means extending the meeting, as it ensures all subsequent discussions are relevant.

Option A is likely to simply cause antagonism by being equally rude in return. Although your views will be heard by the group, they will also note your emotional reaction and may hesitate about engaging with you or challenging you in the future. Additionally, the person you were originally in conflict with may then feel obliged to argue back just because of the approach you adopted, in order to maintain his pride.

Option B may be acceptable, depending upon the timescales available, but it would show greater resilience to address the issue there and then, face to face. It also runs the risk of the rest of the meeting being unproductive because it will be based on the premise that the alternative idea will be adopted.

However, **Option C** is probably the least desirable as because you failed to speak out, now an entire project's success is at risk: Option C almost feels like you are getting your own back on the other person through spite. It also shows a tendency to shy away from confrontation, which shows a lack of personal confidence.

Situation 9. EPSO Competency: ANALYSIS AND PROBLEM SOLVING

Option C is the most effective answer. Given the urgency of the request and the tight timescale, you should make recommendations on the basis of the information provided, whilst acknowledging the limitations that exist and recommending more thorough research before making a decision.

Option A acknowledges the limitations in the information provided and alerts your Superior to them at the earliest opportunity. However given the tight timescale, if you spend a lot of time researching additional information, you will not be in a position to do justice to analysing it and completing a report within the time available. If you analyse and report on the information you have, you will be in a position to understand which approaches are worth further analysis and focus on those.

Option B is the least effective answer. Given the urgency of the request, you will simply not have time to gain the detail you would like about the various approaches from different people. You would be more productive in conducting a thorough analysis of the information you have and reporting on it, identifying in your report which approaches warrant further analysis.

Option D has a plus side in that it acknowledges the urgency of the request and the timescale and ensures a report is produced to meet those as requested. However, by failing to highlight the limitations in the information provided, you may potentially recommend a risky approach that has not been thoroughly analysed.

Situation 10. EPSO competency: WORKING WITH OTHERS

The most appropriate answer in this case is **Option A**. By pausing the meeting and summarising, this gives the chance to ensure everyone has the same understanding so far and also allows a pause for the technical expert to speak. Choosing Option A not only demonstrates empathy on your part, it also shows a certain drive to help the team achieve its goals.

Option B shows no real attempt to aid the team-working process and is therefore the least desirable option. It also abdicates responsibility for resolving the issue there and then yourself which would have aided the team-working process.

Option C shows a certain lack of appreciation for the technical expert's current mind-set: this action may embarrass him and/or lead to him being unable to contribute by feeling too exposed. Introducing a pause in proceedings and then asking the technical expert to contribute in a non-threatening way shows far greater emotional intelligence.

Option D is unlikely to be successful as it seems from the scenario information that the technical expert is so shy or embarrassed they may not pick up on your cue to speak. More direct action is needed to encourage their contribution.

Situation 11. EPSO competency: ANALYSIS AND PROBLEM SOLVING

The most appropriate answer in this case is **Option B**. It is likely to be unrealistic for you to make a sound judgement before you have reviewed the evidence and it sounds like there is not only complex data to analyse, but also some internal politics to consider before reaching a conclusion. There does not seem to be an urgent deadline for a decision, other than the scheduled meeting, and therefore a delay would probably be acceptable.

The least effective is **Option A**: this shows perhaps a tendency to shy away from detailed analysis and does not take into account the possible biases of your team members in presenting their views to you. Although it may demonstrate unwavering loyalty to your team, it may result in a less than optimum outcome – especially considering you are new to the role and you presumably know little about your team members' trustworthiness to date.

Option C would be a potentially good course of action at some point, as it will help not only give you a balanced view but also build bridges with the other team and help reduce conflict. However, to go and see them before having first reviewed your team member's documentation and doing some preparation may result in you not having all the facts to hand. Therefore it would be better to do Option B first.

Option D is a possibility if you had a lot of time, but it seems an uneconomical way of problem solving if a lot of the research has already been conducted. It would be better to capitalise on the existing information, even if it is biased, and then once you have reviewed all the evidence you can then decide if a full analysis from scratch is required or not.

Situation 12. EPSO competency: PRIORITISING AND ORGANISING

The most appropriate answer in this case is **Option B**. Despite the fact that project scope is likely to change, in order to stand the best chance of successful delivery, an initial project plan with milestones, risks and contingencies is required. By involving the project team, not only will you formulate a better plan but you will gain their buy-in to it and show how you value their expertise. You can always build contingencies into the plan from an early stage to try and pre-empt any difficulties.

Option A reflects too much of a relaxed approach and this lack of planning is likely to lead to difficulties later on due to a lack of clarity over deliverables. Whilst you may expect this to lead to your team feeling empowered, it is actually likely to make them feel a little directionless and therefore possibly demotivated and certainly less productive.

Option C reflects a very "short-termist" approach. It may mean that some time is saved in planning, but it would be more effective to consider all the steps required in the lead up to the ultimate objective rather than dealing with each in isolation. Without a view of the bigger picture, it is impossible to plan effectively for each stage in isolation. Option C is therefore probably the least effective course of action.

Option D reflects a micro-management approach that is likely to make the team members feel a lack of empowerment, as well as taking up a lot of your time. If you are meeting that regularly with your team and issuing frequent changes of direction or new tasks, this may cause frustration: better to meet less frequently and have time to consolidate all the feedback from the commissioning client into coherent, larger pieces of information that could be fed back to all – e.g. at a team meeting.

Situation 13. EPSO competency: DELIVERING QUALITY AND RESULTS

The most appropriate answer in this case is **Option D**. If extra resource is available from another team, this should help to ensure the deadline is met and with no additional cost implications. If the extra resource is not available, you are still free to pursue one of the other options, meaning that this gives you the most possible flexibility.

Despite demonstrating drive and determination, **Option C** runs the risks of errors being made due to fatigue. There is the additional risk that the other work you have on the go will also suffer as a result. Therefore, this answer falls down on the quality focus aspects.

Choosing **Option B** means that you fail to deliver the project objective. There is no indication that this course of action will be acceptable in the scenario and it is likely to be unsatisfactory to the stakeholders. Therefore it is probably the least appropriate answer.

Option A shows initiative, and should get the project delivered on time and with less chance of mistakes than working extra hours yourself (although a temp will still need to be fully briefed). However the extra budget goes beyond the remit of the project and this is therefore not an ideal solution as you will not have worked within the project objectives.

Situation 14. EPSO competency: PRIORITISING AND ORGANISING

The most appropriate answer in this case is **Option A**. This converts the single overall deadline into a practical project plan that everyone involved in the transition can make use of in order to ensure that targets are being met.

Option C is probably the least desirable option, as it focuses on just one key date that will initially seem relatively distant, so will not create any urgency. As a result, the project may drift from a lack of focus in the initial stages and the final deadline may either be missed or else the latter stages may involve working under pressure with a greater risk of mistakes being made as a result of that pressure.

Option B recognises where the resistance to the project may come from, which is always useful, but concentrating too much on this aspect may result in the bigger picture being ignored.

Option D is similarly useful in so far as understanding the most complex elements will be important, but as with Option B, too much focus here could result in ignoring the bigger picture, and indeed in ignoring other elements that may be challenging but which you have not identified as such.

Situation 15. EPSO competency: DELIVERING QUALITY AND RESULTS

The most appropriate answer in this case is **Option D**. The impact of errors creeping into later stages is potentially great, so temporarily reverting to the original processes is safer than continuing with the new ones.

Option A is the least desirable option, as it does not involve any attempt to address the oversight.

Option B at least ensures everyone is aware of the issue but still relies on the data being handled accurately in the first place without a later independent check, and would probably slow down the process anyway.

Option C relies on no errors being made until you find a solution, and once you have found the solution you will need to explain why you are proposing a second set of recommendations anyway, thus demonstrating your recklessness and the fact you were not open about the issue once you had identified it.

Situation 16. EPSO competency: RESILIENCE

The most appropriate answer in this case is **Option B**. Addressing the issue yourself without showing emotion shows an ability to remain calm under pressure and to persevere with a task.

Option D is probably the least desirable as it could be seen as being defensive and shifting the blame onto the people who set the work.

Option C, in contrast, demonstrates an ability to control one's emotions and know when to take some time out. However, persevering with the workload when it is unrealistic may lead to greater pressure in the long run.

Option A is also a plausible option as a solution is being sought, but it involves passing the problem on to someone else to help resolve your issues.

Situation 17. EPSO competency: WORKING WITH OTHERS

The most appropriate answer in this case is **Option D**. Including your colleagues in the decision making process and the creation of the presentation not only allows for a greater breadth of ideas to be generated and therefore a better outcome, but the collaboration could also help to strengthen relationships.

The least desirable option is probably **Option C**: it involves no collaboration with the relevant people, thereby losing the chance of getting help in making the presentation better.

Option A is a plausible answer as feedback is sought on the presentation before it is sent off; however, collaboration during the creation of the presentation could have benefited both the presentation and team relationships further.

Likewise, in **Option B**, the colleagues are consulted but there is no direct collaboration.

Situation 18. EPSO competency: ANALYSIS AND PROBLEM SOLVING

The most appropriate answer in this case is **Option B**. This shows an ability to challenge presented data, analysing it further rather than taking it at face value. Taking responsibility is also evident in investigating whether there is an error or not before consulting others.

Option A is probably the least desirable as the issue is not being addressed but simply being avoided: further analysis/investigation should be carried out.

Option C has its merits in raising the issue, but more analysis should ideally be carried out first in an attempt to see whether or not there is an error.

Option D shows an ability to consult others in order to get a second opinion, but the data still could have been looked at in more depth first.

Situation 19. EPSO competency: PRIORITISING AND ORGANISING

The most appropriate answer in this case is **Option A**. Finding out which task is the most important/urgent, and exploring whether there is a way to reduce the workload, will lead to prioritisation and allow a high standard to be maintained on all three tasks.

Option C is the least desirable option, as although all three tasks may get completed within the timeframe, they are likely to be rushed and not completed to the same standard as if more time had been spent on them.

Option B focuses on the right priority, but without a clear plan for the remaining tasks, this could result in disappointing the other stakeholders.

Option D includes the possibility that all tasks could be completed to a high standard before the deadline. However, working throughout the night may lead to a reduction in performance levels which could lower the standard of work. Time management and task prioritisation would be better options.

Situation 20. EPSO competency: DELIVERING QUALITY AND RESULTS

The most appropriate answer in this case is **Option D**. It shows an ability to act and start the project without receiving complete instructions, using the information already gathered and one's own initiative.

Option A is probably the least desirable option, as it shows a reluctance to take the initiative and start the project despite the tight deadline.

Option B has its merits as there is an element of proactivity shown by consulting others in order to start the project before your Superior returns. However, there is a danger of over-consulting and this delaying the start date.

Option C shows proactivity in starting the project; on the other hand, not progressing past the areas confirmed with your Superior is likely to impact on completion by the deadline and again misses an opportunity to take the initiative.

Situation 21. EPSO competency: RESILIENCE

The most appropriate answer in this case is **Option D**. It demonstrates an ability to assume a degree of responsibility in trying to find out what happened but without being defensive.

Option C is probably the least desirable as it demonstrates an element of defensiveness in reaction to the Superior's disappointment and request for an explanation. Potentially, blame is also passed onto the colleague.

Option B contains some good qualities as it shows the ability to apologise and investigate an issue regardless of fault; however there is less emphasis on taking action on the current report.

Option A is also a reasonable reaction as again some responsibility is taken. But the potential blame is simply passed on to the colleague, rather than a more objective, holistic approach being taken.

Situation 22. EPSO competency: WORKING WITH OTHERS

The most appropriate answer in this case is **Option C**. By trying to find out why they are behaving in that way you are more likely to be able to find a solution. Asking the member for their feedback shows an ability to listen to others and to involve them in reaching a resolution.

Option D is probably the least desirable option – confronting the member in front of the rest of the group is unlikely to resolve the issue. It is possible that the member has some personal issues outside work, or is faced with other pressures at work: therefore trying to address the issue in front of others could be quite insensitive.

Option A does at least ensure that someone speaks to the problematic member and that his behaviour is addressed. But by not speaking to the team member yourself, you are failing to take full responsibility for your group.

Option B may be a good way of avoiding conflict, but it is not getting to the root cause of the issue or allowing the member to explain his actions.

Situation 23. EPSO competency: ANALYSIS AND PROBLEM SOLVING

The most appropriate answer in this case is **Option A**. Coming up with a different way of enabling all members to benefit, despite the rejection of the initial idea, demonstrates an ability to produce creative ideas and effective solutions.

Option B is probably the least desirable: the senior managers have already said the idea would not be feasible on cost grounds, therefore a 1:2:1 meeting is likely to be a waste of time as the resources are simply not available at the moment.

Option C is more practical than option B and budgets may have changed in a few months; however this still does not address the issue in the short term.

Option D shows respect and understanding for the views expressed by the senior managers, but there is no structure to the proposed idea-sharing, and this may well make it less likely to succeed.

Situation 24. EPSO competency: PRIORITISING AND ORGANISING

The most appropriate answer in this case is **Option C**. Being realistic about what can be achieved and by when, allows both your Superior and your colleagues to know where they stand and what the outcome is likely to be.

Option A is probably the least appropriate, as the desire to impress overrides the ability to set a realistic timeframe. You know that the other people involved in the project have other demanding tasks; therefore it is unrealistic to suppose that the project could be completed so far ahead of the original deadline.

With **Option B**, although there is recognition that the suggested deadline is not realistic without additional support, it is risky to agree to the new timeframe without arranging extra support beforehand.

Option D does not commit to the deadline; on the other hand, it fails to confirm a deadline at all, therefore creating ambiguity for both the Superior and rest of the project team.

Situation 25. EPSO competency: DELIVERING QUALITY AND RESULTS

The most appropriate answer in this case is **Option C** as it shows adherence to set procedures and a willingness to escalate situations where there is an attempt to breach procedures.

Option A is the least desirable, as it is clearly involves breaking procedures put in place by the organisation.

Whilst **Option B** demonstrates an ability to raise the issue with your Superior, asking them to deal with the situation abdicates responsibility.

Option D correctly refuses to go against organisational rules; however the issue is not raised with anyone else to prevent this happening in future.

Situation 26. EPSO competency: ANALYSIS AND PROBLEM SOLVING

The most appropriate answer in this case is **Option D**. This shows that you are thinking about how to break down the data into something manageable, but also looks to run your idea past someone who may well have insight into how effective it will be.

Option A is an acceptable response. This does not draw on your colleague's existing expertise at all but is still likely to be a logical way to tackle large amounts of data.

Option C is also an acceptable response. This detailed list could serve as a useful resource; however, it's not clear how much information there is. If there is a manageable number of documents this may well be a good starting point, but if there are a lot and some are less relevant you risk wasting valuable time.

Option B is the least effective response. You are responsible for this project and there are several ways you can tackle the information yourself rather than passing the responsibility on to your colleague. You risk losing control of the project at an early stage by handing over such a major task to your colleague entirely.

Situation 27. EPSO competency: DELIVERING QUALITY AND RESULTS

The most appropriate answer in this case is **Option C**. This ensures that you hit your original deadline and get the input of others wherever possible – while also leaving your colleague with the opportunity to contribute final comments if they are back to work in time.

Option A is the least effective response. You do not know whether your colleague will return tomorrow and you risk falling behind in finishing off the report. You should be prepared to take responsibility for getting this finished in your colleague's absence.

Option B could be seen as an acceptable response as it means you are taking full responsibility for delivering the report. However, while it is admirable that you are striving to deliver ahead of schedule, it may still be worth seeing if your colleague returns tomorrow to add additional value and, if not, seeking input from elsewhere. That way, you may add something to the quality while still delivering on time.

Option D has the merit of being open and clear about the situation. It also gives the relevant people the opportunity to insist on getting the job finished faster, if that is their priority. However, it would be better if you took the initiative yourself for meeting the deadline.

Situation 28. EPSO competency: PRIORITISING AND ORGANISING

The most appropriate answer in this case is **Option A**. This shows that you can adjust plans as needed while still setting clear timelines. By communicating clear goals, you will let your colleagues know exactly what is needed of them. It will be important to think about how to communicate the importance of meeting the new deadlines to everyone involved so as to leave no doubt about the need to stick to the plan.

Option B could help in keeping the project on track. However, you are still on schedule overall, so while this step may help the group to successfully complete the project, it may not actually be necessary. Furthermore, adding extra resources may not be possible without affecting other work, may make the project not stretching enough to get the most out of the team, and does not tackle the fact that some members of the team are not currently pulling their weight – it may even encourage the idea that if the work doesn't get done, someone else will be brought in to do it.

Option C has the merit that you are trying to get the most out of the team and this approach could well help your underperforming colleagues improve if handled well. However, it is important that you ensure that they fully understand the importance of their input to the project as a whole.

Option D is the least effective response. Sharing this information may have a deleterious effect on the team's morale. It is possible that the underperforming team members may not know what you expected of them. This is especially true as you are still on target overall, so the team are likely to feel positive about their output overall and that things are on track. A better approach is to look forward and ensure it is clear what is needed for the rest of the project.

Situation 29. EPSO competency: RESILIENCE

The most appropriate answer in this case is **Option B**. While this involves admitting that a mistake was made with the slides, it should not undermine confidence in what you have to say. By talking off script (if you have to) while the slides are located, you can demonstrate your breadth of knowledge in the topic which could actually add credibility to your talk.

Option A is the least effective response. While it is a difficult situation to find yourself in, you should seek to resolve it now. You risk losing impact and interest if you resume in a week's time. You also risk wasting the time of those who are unable to attend the meeting both weeks.

Option C is a possible response and it may actually help the presentation appear to go the most smoothly to your audience. However, it has the downside that you risk losing impact by not addressing the conclusion in as much depth as you could. You are also potentially wasting important slides that you spent time developing and could illustrate your key conclusions well.

Option D is an appropriate response. This shows a determination to fix the issue despite the difficult situation. However, by breaking off your presentation you may damage the flow of the talk, and you may also need to rush your final slides to keep to time. Thus, it would be better to ask a colleague to locate the slides.

Situation 30. EPSO competency: *WORKING WITH OTHERS*

The most appropriate answer in this case is **Option C**. It shows an interest in their input while managing the situation actively and ensuring the team know that you are leading the project. By getting them to address you rather than argue with each other, you are aiming to keep a focus on the task itself rather than their individual dispute.

Option A is the least effective response. This authoritarian approach may prevent you from getting potentially valuable input from team members – including those who are not involved in the argument. And it does not deal properly with the core ongoing issue of the two disputing team members.

Option B is an appropriate response in the sense that it is likely to help with the immediate issue and highlight the damage that they are doing to the meeting. It does not, however, take account of the possibility that they might both have valid points to make that you can listen to and try to understand.

Option D has the benefit that it may allow you to tackle the issue with the sensitivity it deserves, rather than choosing an inappropriate response in the heat of the moment when tempers are high. However, it does not deal with the immediate situation, which may have a damaging impact on morale and could undermine your credibility in leading the team.